The Oxford Companion to
Architecture

The Oxford Companion to
Architecture

Edited by Patrick Goode

Consultant editors

Stanford Anderson
Sir Colin St John Wilson

Volume 2: K–Z

OXFORD

UNIVERSITY PRESS

OXFORD

UNIVERSITY PRESS

Great Clarendon Street, Oxford ox2 6DP

Oxford University Press is a department of the University of Oxford.
It furthers the University's objective of excellence in research, scholarship,
and education by publishing worldwide in

Oxford New York

Auckland Cape Town Dar es Salaam Hong Kong Karachi
Kuala Lumpur Madrid Melbourne Mexico City Nairobi
New Delhi Shanghai Taipei Toronto

With offices in

Argentina Austria Brazil Chile Czech Republic France Greece
Guatemala Hungary Italy Japan Poland Portugal Singapore
South Korea Switzerland Thailand Turkey Ukraine Vietnam

Oxford is a registered trade mark of Oxford University Press
in the UK and in certain other countries

Published in the United States
by Oxford University Press Inc., New York

British Library Cataloguing in Publication Data

Data available

Library of Congress Cataloging in Publication Data

Data available

Typeset by Graphicraft Limited, Hong Kong
Printed in China
on acid-free paper by
C&C Offset Printing Co. Ltd.

ISBN 978–0–19–860568–3

1 3 5 7 9 10 8 6 4 2

Cover images vol. 2: (main) Rose window, Westminster Abbey; (back panel) (l) Mausoleum of
Habib Bourguiba, Tunisia, (c) Swakopmund, Namibia, (r) Millau Viaduct, France

Contents

Note to the Reader

Entries are arranged in strict alphabetical order of their headword.

For architects, dates have only been given when they are significant, e.g. to indicate the generation the architecture belonged to, or to highlight the architect's position in relation to a general trend. In addition, there was a practical reason for not giving the dates of every architect mentioned in the text: that those articles which mentioned several architects would then become a thicket of dates. The reader wishing to know either the dates not given for a particular architecture or biographical details is referred to J. S. Curl, *A Dictionary of Architecture and Landscape Architecture*, which also has an extensive bibliography in pdf format (2007), and *Oxford Art Online* (www.oxfordartonline.com).

Similarly, the dates given for buildings are those considered to be the most significant, which may mean either the start date, or the date of conception, or the date of completion. As a rule, the point to which the date refers is clear from the context.

Within the text, an asterisk (*) in front of a word denotes a cross-reference and indicates the headword of the entry to which attention is being drawn. Cross-references are given only when reference will provide further information relevant to that subject, and are not given merely to indicate that a separate entry can be found.

The illustrations are generally positioned next to the article to which they refer. In some cases, an illustration will serve more than one article. As there are no cross-references from the text to the illustrations, if there is no illustration adjacent to the text you are reading, there may be an illustration included with one of the cross-referred articles.

PATRICK GOODE
Editor

Kahn, Albert (1867–1942) US architect, the foremost industrial architect of the early 20th century, who founded his firm in Detroit in 1895. His *factory for Buffalo automaker George N. Pierce (1906) pioneered the 1-storey roof-lit plan. His Ford Highland Park Plant in Detroit (1910), using gravity to assist assembly, introduced assembly-line production, and influenced Walter *Gropius' Faguswerk (1911), a cornerstone of European *Modernism.

Kahn's steel-framed buildings of the 1920s for Ford's Rouge Plant near Detroit, the largest factory complex in the world at the time, combined Pierce's 1-storey roof-lit configuration with Ford Highland Park's attention to manufacturing processes. Tailored to assembly-line manufacture, and designed for rapid erection, they placed American industrial architecture in the vanguard. Kahn's efficient and elegant factories of the 1930s pioneered fast-track construction; they also influenced late American Modernism, as evidenced by *Mies van der Rohe's Concert Hall proposal superimposed on a photo of Kahn's Glenn Martin Building (1936).

At the time of his death, Kahn had designed over 2,000 factories in the United States, and many elsewhere, including 531 in Stalin's USSR.   GH

Hildebrand, G., *Designing for Industry—the Architecture of Albert Kahn* (1974)

Kahn, Louis Isadore (1901–74) US architect. He designed some of Modernism's most poetic and meticulously detailed buildings, including, in the United States, the Salk Institute for Biological Studies in

La Jolla, California (1965), the Kimbell Art Museum in Fort Worth, Texas (1972), the Library at Phillips Exeter Academy in Exeter, New Hampshire (1972), and the Yale Centre for British Art in New Haven, Connecticut (1974). Two equally important works are in the Indian subcontinent, the Indian Institute of Management in Ahmedabad, India (1974), and Sher-e-Bangla Nagar, the National Assembly Complex in Dhaka, Bangladesh (1983, completed posthumously).

After a Beaux Arts based education at the University of Pennsylvania under Paul *Cret, Kahn became overtly politicized in the 1930s. With partners George Howe and Oscar Stonorov, Kahn built five workers' communities in Pennsylvania, all recalling modernist social housing projects in Europe.

In the years after World War II, from his own practice Kahn gradually reshaped these early left-wing convictions. This entailed reconceptualizing early Modernism's social agenda, technical principles, and stylistic dispositions to respond to post-war social, political, and economic developments in the United States. Through a succession of buildings and projects from the 1940s to the 1960s, he developed the interest in monumentality that had preoccupied him since at least 1944, increasingly focusing on an 'Architecture of Institutions', by which he meant projects with a civic component, such as buildings for the arts, the academy, or governments. He believed that civic institutions should become symbolic landmarks that could be appropriated, and continually reappropriated, by their communities. 'People-marks', as he called them, would forestall the disintegration of vibrant communities by fostering loyalty to democratic institutions, and thereby nurturing civic participation, the foundation of democratic society.

In fits and starts, he developed a formal language which incorporated some of the traits of *CIAM Modernism, while reconceptualizing or eschewing others. Central to his approach was the view that the design of a building should exhibit its primary structural components and materials, the processes by which the building was actually constructed (such as leaving the shuttering marks left by pouring concrete), and in many cases also its services. Kahn propounded these convictions in the sometimes obscure apothegms for which he became famous in the 1960s, such as asking the brick what it 'wants to be' or insisting that designs be developed around 'servant' spaces—HVAC (heating, ventilation, and *air conditioning), electrical systems, and functionally secondary spaces (see also ENGINEERING SERVICES); and 'served' spaces—the spaces of socially symbolic importance and primary use. Steel and glass-based transparency and lightness gave way to stasis, opacity, and heavier materials, brick and reinforced concrete, because they evoked not fast-paced industrial culture but durability and permanence. Much of this could be seen in the buildings that first brought him prominence: the Yale Art Gallery in New Haven, Connecticut (1954ff.), and the Bath House in Trenton, New Jersey (1955).

By the late 1950s and 1960s, in works such as the Salk Institute and the National Assembly Complex in Dhaka, Bangladesh, Kahn also alluded to historical monuments that project the impression of long-lastingness such as Roman walls, Scottish castles, the fortified towers of Italian hill towns, and Mughal mausoleum-gardens and forts.

Sensitive to a user's phenomenological experience of a building or place, Kahn had by the mid 1950s rejected one of Le Corbusier's premises for a new architecture—the open plan. To Kahn, rooms that were created by and integral to the building's overall form and structure were more psychically satisfying because they anchored a user to a building, and a building to its site and the community it served. After a visit to Angola in 1959, he also became fascinated with the changing qualities of natural light

Richards Medical Research Building, Pennsylvania University, Philadelphia (Louis Kahn, 1965)

as indicators of diurnal rhythms, the passing of time, and the changing of seasons. In all his mature buildings, natural light falls even into internal spaces, and into spaces usually closed to the sun, such as libraries and museum galleries.

In his highly monumental landmarks, Kahn made it a point of pride to go beyond the client's specified demands, the programme, to develop an architectural language suitable to the role the institution should play in society at large. For example, at the National

Assembly Complex in Dhaka, Bangladesh, a parliament building for a new democratic nation, Kahn created an unusual series of spaces and circulation sequence that emphasized less the place of formal democracy, the assembly chamber, and more a 7-storey 'ambulatory' encircling the assembly chamber, through which every user of the building, from janitor to legislator, must democratically pass. Such unusual sequences, combined with the complex layered spaces and disjunctive compositional moments created by his layering of geometries, exemplify how Kahn, in his mature buildings, both relies on and simultaneously dismantles monumental architecture's traditions.   SWG

Goldhagen, S.W., *Louis Kahn's Situated Modernism* (2001)

Kanvinde, Achyut (1916–2002) Indian architect. One of the pioneers of modern architecture in India, Achyut Kanvinde was responsible immediately after the independence of India in 1947 for designing architecture which represented Nehru's vision of a modern, industrial state. His early buildings, like the Azad Bhaban in Delhi (1953), reflected his training under Walter Gropius at Harvard, but later ones like the Indian Institute of Management at Kanpur (1960), the dairy at Mehsana (1970), the Nehru Science Centre in Bombay (1978), and the National Science Centre in New Delhi (1986), demonstrated a newer articulation of functional expressivity and relationship with landscape.   KA

Kauffmann, Richard (1887–1958) German-born Israeli architect. *See* PALESTINE, UNDER THE BRITISH MANDATE 1918–48.

Kazakov, Matvei Feodorovich (1738–1812) Russian architect. Although the leading proponent of neoclassical architecture in Moscow, Kazakov's early work often displayed elements of the Gothic Revival, particularly in the Petrovsky Palace (1775–82) and in his

rebuilding of the palace at Tsaritsyno (1789–93), original designed by his mentor *Bazhenov. His most important state commission was the Senate building (1776–87), a complex triangular structure with Ionic columniation on the exterior and Corinthian for the monumental main rotunda, whose dome rises above the east wall of the Kremlin. He also designed the main building of Moscow University (1784 onwards; rebuilt after the fire of 1812) and the Noblemen's Assembly (1784–7). Of his several neoclassical churches, the most notable is the rotundal Church of Metropolitan Philip (1777–88). He was also a brilliant designer of town and estate mansions, a number of which survived the 1812 fire.   WCB

Kempthorne, Sampson (1809–73) English architect. *See* WORKHOUSES.

Kent, William (1685–1748) English painter and architect. Despite modest origins and a small purse, Kent improved his skills as a painter in Italy where he met several English aristocrats, including Lord *Burlington who became his lifelong patron. From painting historical scenes and grotesques, he turned towards architectural decoration, working at Burlington House, London (before 1727), Chiswick House, London (*c*.1726–9), and Houghton Hall, Norfolk (*c*.1726–9). He excelled at garden buildings, notably at Stowe, Buckinghamshire (*c*.1730 onwards), and Pope's Villa, Twickenham (*c*.1730, demolished). He built Holkham Hall, Norfolk (from 1734), the Gothic Gateway, Hampton Court Palace, London (1732), and Treasury Buildings, Whitehall, Westminster (1733–7), becoming a member of the Board of Works in 1735. This led to his design of the Horse Guards, Westminster, shortly before his death (built 1750–59). Though a committed Palladian, his work has a decorator's lightness of touch, admirably demonstrated in two domestic works, 22 Arlington

Street (1741–50) and 44 Berkeley Square (1742–4), London.   APQ

Wilson, M. J., *William Kent* (1984)

Key, Lieven de (*c*.1560–1627) Dutch architect. In Leiden he contributed to the design for the renovation of the Town Hall (1594); and in Haarlem was probably the principal designer of the weighhouse (1596–9) next to the great church in the central square. These buildings, key structures in the economy of the city, were given quite dissimilar treatments. When closed, the weighhouse, completely clad in sandstone, offers no clue to its function; the red-brick Meat Hall (1602–04) is decorated with sheep- and ox-heads, as well as other stone ornaments reminiscent of the manner of Vredeman de *Vries.   FS

van der Blom, A., *Lieven de Key* (1995)

Keyser, Hendrick de (1565–1621) Dutch architect, who became head of the Amsterdam office of works. During his career the city was enlarged several times, and in that period, together with the city's carpenter Staets and the mason Danckertsz, he built the new exchange (1608–11, inspired by the London exchange, demolished 1836), several new churches, city gates, and private houses. The Zuiderkerk (1603–11) was the first newly built Protestant church in the Netherlands, based on the medieval nave with flanking aisles, also the starting point for the more experimental Westerkerk (1620–31). De Keyser's many spires for church and city towers functioned as the jewels in the cityscape, with their accumulation of 'modern', i.e. classical elements. After his death his key works were engraved and published under the title *Architectura Moderna* (1631), illustrating his preference for sculptural ornament over spatial innovation.   FS

khan Established within city walls, rather than on a trade route, a khan is also less fortified than a *caravanserai but equivalent in its spatial layout of vaulted storage, apartments set back from a gallery overlooking an open courtyard, and stables. Its function was to accommodate market commerce, social activities, lodgings, and warehouses. Khans were important elements of a city, located near the souk and *hammam, the *mosque, and *madrasa.

The scale of khans mirrored the growth of urban centres. In Cairo the Khan of Qansuh al-Ghuri (1504) is a 6-storey stone building, its interior punctuated by pointed arches, covered vaulted walkways, and wooden mashrabiya. Shops and storage areas overlooked the inner courtyard on the first two levels, with the remaining floors reserved for apartments. Bazaars in San'aa, Yemen, and Aleppo (Haleb) host multiple khans reaching heights of 6 and 7 storeys. In the *Ottoman Empire, khans were known as 'hans'.   DM

Michell, G. (ed.), *Architecture of the Islamic World, its History and Social Meaning* (1978)

Kikutake, Kiyonori (1928–) Japanese architect. Kikutake's design of his own home, the Sky House (1958), expressed architecture as a living organism responsive to change and technological advances—a fundamental tenet of the *Metabolist group which he co-founded in 1960. While his futuristic urban schemes such as Marine City (1959) remained unrealized, Kikutake built his own home as a square-plan living space suspended by four concrete piers from which auxiliary living/service units were freely added and subtracted. He also expressed the organic nature of traditional wood-frame construction through reinforced concrete both visually in his Izumo Shrine Administration building (1963) and conceptually in the Hotel Tôkôen (1964). Kikutake influenced his younger associates, including Toyô *Itô and Itsuko Hasegawa, and has continued to pursue the construction of 'Cities in the Air', exemplified by his megastructural Edo/Tokyo Museum (1992).   KTO

kiosk A small summer *pavilion, usually associated with *Ottoman architecture. PG

Klenze, Leo von (1784–1864) German architect. Through his buildings, paintings, and theoretical writings, Klenze developed a Classicism matched in sophistication and influence only by Karl Friedrich *Schinkel. His projects in Munich for Ludwig I were central to the future king's plan to transform the city into an architectural centre comparable to Athens or Rome. Klenze's Renaissance palace-inspired Ministry of War (1826–131), Leuchtenbergpalais (1818–21), and Odeon (1826–8) gave a monumental character to the grand axis of his plans for Ludwigstrasse. In his design for the Glyptothek (1816–30), one of the first free-standing museum buildings of its kind, a synthesis of Greek, Roman, and Renaissance elements complemented the array of antique sculpture housed inside. The museum is set within an urban *ensemble* centred on Königsplatz that includes Klenze's classical Propyläen (1846–60) and his nearby neo-Renaissance Pinakothek (1825–36). Klenze's most famous building is the Walhalla (1830–42), a Doric temple resting on a massive three-stepped base and set within the picturesque Danube landscape near Regensburg. In contrast to his nearby Befreiungshalle (1847–63), a cylindrical monument to the Wars of Liberation against Napoleon that recalls an ancient tumulus, the Walhalla is inspired by both the Parthenon and Friedrich *Gilly's design for a monument to Frederick the Great. AN

Nerdinger, Winfried (ed.), *Leo von Klenze* (2000)

Klerk, Michel de (1884–1923) Dutch architect, the figurehead of the *Amsterdam School. His talent and invention were discovered by Eduard *Cuypers, for whom he worked from 1898 to 1906. With great mental adaptability he took very diverse images from the visual culture of his time to create an architecture that had not been seen before. Scholars have traced sources in the symbolist movement in painting, Art Nouveau, Arts and Crafts, Charles Voysey, Charles R. Mackintosh, Josef Hoffmann, Joseph Olbrich, masques and totems made by North- and South-American Indians, and art objects from India, Indonesia, and China.

He applied his own very personal imagery in the design of unique furniture and elegant façades that transformed a street into a work of art. His refined visions demanded very costly masonry and carpentry; thanks to state funding (Housing Law 1901) it could also be used in social housing (Spaarndammer Plantsoen, Amsterdam, 1913–14, 1917–21, built for the Building Society Eigen Haard; Burgemeester Tellegenstraat, 1918–23, for De Dageraad, both in Amsterdam). The opposite also occurred: for contractors he used one or two economical inventions to create a monumental street front (Vrijheidslaan, Amsterdam, 1921–3). AVDW (trans. CVE)

Bock, M. *et al.*, *Michel de Klerk 1884–1923* (1997)

Knobelsdorff, Georg Wenzeslaus von (1699–1753) German architect. For the Crown Prince Frederick of Prussia, Knobelsdorff remodelled Schloss Rheinsberg, Brandenburg (1737–40). Following his appointment by Frederick (now King) as Director of Royal Palaces and Gardens in 1740, Knobelsdorff designed in rapid succession a new wing to Schloss Monbijou (1740–42) and to Schloss Charlottenburg (1740–43), the Opera House, Berlin (1741–3), and the Sanssouci Palace, Potsdam (1744–51).

For interiors, Knobelsdorff used *Rococo forms; for the exteriors, a restrained use of decoration, aiming instead at simplicity, refinement, and carefully considered proportions. According to the requirements of the commission, Knobelsdorff, with the close involvement of the King, aimed for an impression of regal dignity. His first major building, Schloss

Rheinsberg, established the pattern: coupled orders articulate the main façade; the colossal order marks the projecting wings. At Sanssouci, a pleasure palace, there is a lighter touch, since the divisions of the bays in the single-storey building are marked by pilasters, fronted by statues. But the most striking and original effect, perhaps the only element of originality in all Knobelsdorff's works, are the six curving terraces leading up to the palace. The scenographic possibilities of the design were ignored, as Frederick, who sketched the plan of the palace, overruled Knobelsdorff's request to set the building on a plinth.   PG

Koolhaas, Rem (1944–) Dutch architect. Koolhaas' early career as newspaper reporter and movie scriptwriter stood him in good stead for the media-saturated world of which he would become architecture's greatest critical guru.

Trained at London's Architectural Association, he formed OMA (Office of Metropolitan Architecture) in 1975 and won critical acclaim with the publication of *Delirious New York, A Retroactive Manifesto for Manhattan* (1979) which redescribed the city's history as a conscious architectural project. In 1982 OMA won the judges' prize (not the commission) for the Parc de la Villette, with a striped 'cross-programmed' landscape juxtaposing unlikely activities—tactics students were to emulate for decades.

Koolhaas' early buildings, notably the Kunsthal, Rotterdam (1992), and the Villa dall'Ava, Paris (1991), established his part-ironic revisiting and rethinking of Modernism, teasing, flipping, quoting its formal tropes, remaking them in grandiose or cheap materials—both critical rhetoric and genuine extension of Modernism's possibilities. His fast-track Euralille masterplan (1994), less acclaimed as building than concept, paved the way for huge projects to come.

S,M,L,XL, his much-imitated book of essays, projects, and speculations, was one of architecture's rare bestsellers (1995). He continued to lead the field of fashionable architectural concerns, investigating shopping and the extreme developments of latterday China, setting up OMA's sister research company AMO. *Content* (2003), a cheap, provocative magazine-book, included AMO's half-joking patent for OMA innovations ('condensers'; 'loops'; 'stacks') being mimicked so quickly.

Nevertheless, he confounded critics keen to dismiss him as a clever 'paper' architect with his increasingly varied, serious, and impressive buildings. The House in Bordeaux (1998), with its elevator centrepiece (the client was paralysed) and its massive cantilever tethered to the ground, was followed by the Netherlands Embassy Berlin (2003), which refined earlier Koolhaas work, folding high security and complex circulation into a modest, International Style cube; his irreverent-adulatory extension to the Mies van der Rohe Illinois Institute of Technology (2004); and the Prada Epicentre in Beverly Hills (2004), a deadpan Baroque confection of modern materials. Later work is more formally experimental and physically spectacular, varying from his heroic-utopian Seattle Library (2004), to the Breuer-esque Porto Casa da Musica (2004), and the twisted loop CCTV television headquarters in Shanghai. Koolhaas is sometimes criticized for cynical embrace of commerce, but his work remains essentially modernist—even utopian—attempting to criticize and reformulate real contemporary conditions.   KR

Korea The beginnings of an architectural civilization in the Korean peninsula may be traced to Neolithic times, when a peculiar floor heating system, later developed into the *ondol*, was already in use. Nonetheless, a narrative of Korean architecture properly begins with the Three Kingdoms of Kokuryŏ (37 BC–AD 668), Paekche (18 BC–AD 660), and Silla (57 BC–AD 935), when the principles and techniques of

Chinese timber construction were introduced. The creation of centralized aristocratic states, the introduction of Buddhism, and the widespread use of the Chinese writing system provided the basis of a classical system of planning for walled cities, temples, and palaces. In the case of Buddhist temples, the alignment of gate, pagoda, main hall, and auditorium along a north–south axis was established as a canonic principle. The Korean peninsula was first unified by Silla. Centred in the great capital city of Kyŏngju, Unified Silla created an international yet self-consciously unified cultural tradition. Though none of its original wooden structures remain, its pagodas and building foundations, such as in Pulguksa (528, rebuilt *c*. late 8th century), provide evidence of a refined stereotomy— granite forms based on wooden structures, massive yet delicate in its treatment of iconic forms. The singular cave temple of Sŏkkuram (*c*. late 8th century), which consists of an earth-covered masonry rotunda and a rectangular access chamber, demonstrates the innovative transformation of India's cave temple. The role of Unified Silla and the Three Kingdoms as a mediator of cultural transfer was crucial in the formation of a larger east Asian civilization, and provided the backdrop to the sense of Korean identity formed around the 1st millennium.

After the fall of Unified Silla, the Koryŏ Dynasty (918–1392) continued and developed the classical paradigms toward a more decorative and dynamic sensibility. Like Unified Silla, Koryŏ adopted Buddhism as a state religion, stimulating the widespread growth of temples and numerous innovations in construction and spatial planning. Since the 14th century, the decorative and monumental *tap'o* system of brackets, more mechanical in production compared to the *chusimp'o* system, was widely adopted. Continuing a later tendency of Unified Silla, Buddhist temples in mountainous regions transformed the classical rules of axiality by incorporating geomantic principles and indigenous beliefs. Pusŏksa and its main hall, the Muryangsuchŏn (*c*.1270), mark the culmination of this complex fusion of Buddhist symbolism with principled adaptations to a magnificent mountain site.

A radical shift in politics and culture occurred with the founding of the Chosŏn Dynasty (1392–1910), whose central cultural logic lay in the Confucian ethic of order and self-restraint. In the planning of the capital city of Hanyang and its palaces, an ingenious fusion of classical planning, Confucian ritual, geomantic principles, and political expediency was achieved. Within Hanyang (which continues as the capital city of Seoul) the royal ancestor shrine of Chongmyo (1395, rebuilt and extended since 1608) epitomizes the architectural qualities of a dignified order, an effacement of physical form towards metaphysical value. In the provinces, this ethic finds its most appropriate architectural manifestation in the *sŏwŏn*, a private educational institution established by Confucian scholar-gentlemen. In the *sŏwŏn*, built form is a relaxed and convenient medium through which the learned scholar could attain learning and communion with nature. Residential architecture typically consisted of a careful composition of the *maru*, wooden floor areas open to exterior space, and the *ondol*, which had spread throughout the peninsula since the Koryŏ Dynasty. In the simultaneously rustic and refined houses of the ruling literati class (called *yangban*), the hierarchies of class and gender were constructed along a primarily horizontal yet complex spatial configuration.

The global shifts of power and mercantilism in the late 16th and 17th centuries were marked in Korea by the Japanese and Manchurian invasions. They created a divide after which the cultural and social order of the early Chosŏn period was in continuous crisis, at once dissolved and ossified. Diversity of materials, exaggerated decoration, chromatic exuberance, and picturesque landscaping were characteristics of a dynamic of diversified needs and expanding markets. In the 18th century, the new proponents of *Sirhak* (literally 'real scholarship'), a pragmatism influenced by the growth of commerce and Western science, openly criticized the abstractions of neo-Confucianism and advocated the adoption of rational methods of planning and construction. The advances and limitations of this proto-Enlightenment project are best illustrated in the new walled city of Hwasŏng (1794–6) and its detailed construction report. The ambitious reconstruction of Kyŏngbok Palace (1870, first built 1395, destroyed during the late-16th-century Japanese invasion), while extending the technical achievements of the 19th century, also symbolized the political insecurities of this period.

The forced opening of Korean ports in 1876 introduced Western-style buildings into the urban landscape, most of which were designed and constructed by foreigners. Furthermore, the pressures of colonial domination under Japan (1910–45) did not foster a productive assimilation of Western architectural traditions. After the Korean War (1950–53), which resulted in the division of North and South Korea, the conservative cultural politics of military dictatorships and its dual motives of nationalistic symbolism and technocratic rationality dominated the post-war decades and continued into the 1980s in the guise of a postmodern historicism. The two dominant figures of the 1960s and 1970s were Kim Joong Up (1922–88) and Kim Swoo Geun (1931–86), who self-consciously constructed Korean models of the modern creative architect. The former's French Embassy (1959) and the latter's Space Group Building (1970–71, extended 1977–8), both in Seoul, were the exceptional examples of what was mostly heroic sculptural work. With the democratization and globalization processes of the past two decades (symbolically initiated by the 1988 Seoul Olympics), modern architecture, as with all other areas of cultural activity, has met a new era of freedom and creativity. Whanki Museum (1988–93) by Kyu Sung Woo (1941–) and Sucholtang (1992–3) by Seung Hyo Sang (1952–) marked a shift toward more spatial and typological approaches to both Modernism and the continuing issue of Korean identity. From an abstract spiritualism of material surfaces to a tough realism of high-density, hybrid urban environments, contemporary Korean architecture is characterized by a healthy diversity, at once promoted and threatened by the global condition.   BHJ/HP

Kramer, Pieter L. (1881–1961) Dutch architect. *See* AMSTERDAM SCHOOL.

Kurokawa, Kishô (1934–2007) Japanese architect. A collaborator and student of Kenzô *Tange at Tokyo University, Kurokawa gained international prominence as a founder-member of the *Metabolist group in 1960. In his own urban proposals and futuristic schemes, Kurokawa advocated architecture that accommodated growth and change, epitomized by his design of the Nakagin Capsule Tower (1972) in which replaceable modular living units are suspended from service core frames. Yet such projects were never realized as a cohesive urban scheme, and the capsules proved to be more fixed than flexible. Kurokawa's extensive subsequent built projects, ranging from museums to office buildings, evolved to express a Buddhist and ecologically inspired 'Philosophy of Symbiosis'.   KTO

Kuwait *See* GULF STATES.

529

Labrouste, Pierre-François-Henri (1801–75)
French rationalist architect. He studied at the Ecole
des Beaux-Arts and as a pensioner in Rome (from 1824),
returning to Paris in 1830 after extensive travels which
included the most important Greek sites. As a teacher
independent of the official establishment, he promoted
a structural functionalism derived from the doctrine
preached by Durand at the Ecole Polytechnique
established by Napoleon I. His major commissions
were for the Bibliothèque Ste Geneviève (1838–50)
and the Bibliothèque Nationale (1855–75). In the
former the support of the tunnel-vaulted reading
room on a basement of offices is clearly expressed in
the façade; internally, structure and ornament are fused
in the exposed iron arcading. The Salle de Lecture at
the heart of the latter work draws its effect from the
iron work of domical, rather than tunnel, vaults, but
functionalist sensitivity ceded to Second Empire
opulence on the exterior.   CT

Lady chapel A chapel dedicated to Our Lady, the
Virgin Mary. As the cult of the Virgin developed in the
Middle Ages, emphasizing her contemplative nature,
chapels dedicated to her for prayer were increasingly
built beyond the main altar of a church, as at Salisbury
(begun 1220), or separately, as at Ely (*c.*1335–53) and
Long Melford, Suffolk (1496).   APQ

La Guêpière, Philippe de (1715–73) French-born
architect, who worked mainly in Germany, where he
attempted to introduce the elegant Paris school of
architecture (cf. PIGAGE). As a rule, he only succeeded

in completing the works of other architects, such as the Residenz, Karlsruhe, or the Neues Schloss, Stuttgart (to 1762), or parts of a building, like the central pavilion of the Schloss Solitude (from 1764). These rather frustrating works are compensated for by the Seeschloss, Monrepos (completed 1765), where a façade consisting of two pavilions and a domed centre are perfectly sited overlooking a lake. PG

landscape architecture embraces planning, design, and management of the landscape. It is allied to architecture and town planning, but informed by geography, botany, ecology, and horticulture. The scope ranges from the design of gardens and parks, to environmental assessment, derelict land reclamation and landscape planning.

The term was used first by Gilbert Laing Meason to mean picturesque architecture. His *On the Landscape Architecture of the Great Painters of Italy* (1828) is a collection of views of such buildings in landscape settings taken from 'great painters' such as Raphael and Michelangelo. John Claudius Loudon then used the term in his edition of Repton's works, *The Landscape Gardening and Landscape Architecture of the late Humphry Repton* (1840). The following year the American nurseryman and landscape gardener Andrew Jackson *Downing (1815–52) also used the term in the chapter 'Landscape or Rural Architecture' in his *Treatise on the Theory and Practice of Landscape Gardening adapted to North America* (1841).

The scope of the discipline has since grown from being a visual appreciation of picturesque architecture and landscape (in the style of Gilpin and Uvedale Price) to cover human settlement and people's physical relationship with the land. In a sense, this can be seen as a democratization of ideas, which began with private garden design, applied to a wider constructed environment, for both public and private good.

It was the American architect Calvert Vaux (1824–95) and the journalist Frederick Law Olmsted (1822–1903) who first used the term for their new profession. Vaux was a former partner of Downing; and with Olmsted he won the competition for Central Park, New York, in 1858. Vaux had favoured the title landscape architect more so than Olmsted, but jointly they promoted it and the Board of the Central Park Commission used it officially in 1865. Olmsted, Vaux and Company went on to design parks, campuses, and housing estates in several cities in the 1860s and 1870s. Previously, professional designers of both private landscape gardens and city parks, such as Downing and Humphry Repton, called themselves landscape gardeners.

With the growth of the North American city came the scope for large municipal park systems. For instance, in 1881 Olmsted and his nephew, John Charles Olmsted, began a park system for Boston that was 11 km (7 miles) long, linking Boston Common and the Charles River to Franklin Park on the edge of the city, which became known as the Emerald Necklace.

In Europe municipal park design was equally pursued by the landscape gardeners such as Peter Josef Lenné (1789–1866), who designed the first public park in Germany, Park Klosterberg in Magdeburg (from the 1820s); the horticulturist Joseph Paxton in England (his Birkenhead Park of the 1850s had influenced Downing and Olmsted); and the engineer Jean Charles Adolphe Alphand (1817–91) who designed many Second Empire parks in Paris in the 1860s.

Both in North America and Europe these designers were applying private park and garden ideas to public projects and involving elements of utility in their design, whether concerned with storm water as in the Boston Emerald necklace, or public health ideas of air quality and concern about civil unrest (post the 1848 revolutions) in Berlin, Paris, and London.

On 4 January 1899 eleven landscape architects including Downing Vaux, son of Calvert Vaux, met to form the American Society of Landscape Architects, and in 1900 the university course in landscape architecture at Harvard University began with Olmsted's son, Frederick Law Olmsted Jr, as head. Further courses were established at Cornell (1904) and at the Department of Forestry at Berkeley (1913).

The North American example, of one or two practitioners promoting the idea and practice and then, with like-minded professionals, establishing a professional association and starting education in landscape architecture, has been a model followed elsewhere. The key impetus for the growth of the profession has been legislation requiring landscape plans and the use of landscape architects. Political lobbying has been key to its development (and this was Olmsted's genius).

For example, the establishment of the American National Park Service in 1917 led to a landscape architecture division under Charles P. Punchard Jr. The Tennessee Valley Authority, set up in 1933, employed landscape architects in the design of new towns; while the New Deal policies of the Roosevelt administration included the work of the Farm Security Commission landscape architects, such as Garret Eckbo (1910–2000), who planned new settlements for migrant farm workers from the Dust Bowl states. Eckbo with Daniel Kiley (1912–2004) and James C. Rose (1913–91), were classmates at Harvard in 1937–8, and together formed the 'Harvard Revolution' of the 1930s, which applied Modernism to landscape architecture, and emphasized space, asymmetry, site, functionality and social ideas of public good.

Parkways (landscaped roads for recreational driving) promoted by state and local governments were widely constructed in the US in the 1930s and involved landscape architects. For instance, the Westchester County Park Commission's work began in 1932 with Gilmore D. Clarke as landscape architect. Such work was to influence *Autobahn* design in Germany in the 1930s and elsewhere.

The first European professional association was the German Bund der Deutsche Landschaftarchitekten (BDLA), which began in 1913 as the Bund Deutscher Gartenarchitekten. From this garden design basis the profession expanded in the 1920s and 1930s. *Autobahn* landscape design was under the direction of Alwin Seifert (1890–1972) and by 1936 they extended to 6,000 km (3,728 miles); Seifert later became *Reichlandschaftsanwalter* or state landscape architect.

Ideas such as the value of public parks and gardens, street beautification, garden cities, public access to sunshine and fresh air, and ideal national landscapes, were shared by ideologies of left and right. They were influenced by public health concerns over diseases such as rickets and tuberculosis, and also about providing unemployment relief through public works: concerns common to Berlin, Paris, London, and New York in the 1930s. Ideas of national landscape plant communities with native plants were promoted by the Dutch biologist and ecologist Jac P. Thijsse (1865–1945) with his notion of a *heempark*, which represents native landscape types. These ideas were also current in Germany and North America in the 1930s. Moscow's 1930s *Genplan* celebrated the birch forests of Russia in the form of green wedges. These ideas were expressed in an extreme form by German landscape architects after 1939 in their plans for 'Aryanizing' the conquered Polish landscape.

Erwin Barth (1880–1933) established the first university landscape architecture course in Germany at Charlottenburg Technical University in 1926 and became the first holder of a chair in Garden Design at Friedrich-Wilhelm University, Berlin, where his successor was Heinrich Wiepking (1891–1973), who promoted nature conservation legislation under the Reich Nature Conservation Office. However, the first landscape architecture course in Europe was in Norway at Ås near Olso in 1919, influenced by American example.

In the United Kingdom the practitioner who first established the role of the profession was Thomas Mawson (1861–1933). With Patrick Geddes (1854–1932), he used the term in the competition for Pittencrieff Park in Dunfermline in 1903. However, Mawson described himself as 'garden architect' for much of his career. The Institute of Landscape Architects (now The Landscape Institute) began in 1929 (initially as the British Association of Garden Architects) with Mawson as first president.

By the 1940s the discipline was established in North America and much of north-western Europe, and also in Portugal where Francesco Caldeira Cabral (1908–92) had created both the profession and the first school in Lisbon. In the 1950s, colonial and post-colonial governments used expatriate landscape architects in new town planning and university campus design, such as the work of Portuguese landscape architects in Angola and Mozambique or the work of Michael Lancaster (1929–2004) in Islamabad.

Landscape architecture associations were established in Japan in 1964, in Australia in 1966, and in New Zealand in 1969. More recently the Chinese Society of Landscape Architects began in 1989. By the 21st century landscape architecture was established worldwide with the exceptions of Africa (except for South Africa) and the Middle East (except Israel). The most dynamic growth of the profession has been in China, where the expansion of the economy has led to large-scale environmental problems viewed with an urgency comparable to 19th- and 20th-century Europe and North America.

The International Federation of Landscape Architects was established in 1948, with Sir Geoffrey Jellicoe (1900–96) as first president, while the European Foundation of Landscape Architecture was established in 1989 and represents national associations to the European Union.

Landscape architecture is a discipline nourished by both the applied arts and the natural sciences so the professional education reflects this, based either in architecture schools or in agriculture, horticulture, or forestry universities. The early American courses at Harvard and Cornell were founded on the basis of design and architectural schools, and this is the usual pattern in the United Kingdom. In The Netherlands and France much education is based on land sciences; indeed the oldest French school, the Ecole Nationale Supérieure du Paysage (ENSP), is in Versailles. In central and eastern Europe many schools are in forestry faculties (e.g. Moscow Forestry University). China's leading course is at Beijing College of Forestry.

Development of landscape architecture theory has been slow and much has been historically based. In the English-speaking world, interesting work has been done by Ian McHarg in his *Design with Nature* (1969), the geographer J.B. Jackson on vernacular landscape, and landscape architect Geoffrey Jellicoe on Modernism and allegory since the 1960s; while a late-20th-century flowering of theoretical writing includes John Dixon Hunt's and Marc Treib's work. There have been similar developments in France (centred on the Versailles school), in Holland centred on Wageningen and Delft, and in Germany.

Industrialization and international trade lead to the growth of urban settlements and to changes in the way the countryside is used. Landscape architecture responds initially by focusing on provision of recreation, both public and private, and general 'city beautification', and then with a widening concern to manage the impact of a changing society on the wider landscape. This leads to protection of natural areas (for instance, Olmsted was one of the Commissioners for the proposed Yosemite reservation in 1864–6) and eventually a concern about the whole landscape, including industrial and non-designed or vernacular landscapes.

The design of purpose-built public municipal parks (a 19th-century innovation) is the initial impetus for both the discipline and the profession; and national legislation widens its role. For instance, the 1946 British New Towns Act led to a whole generation of British landscape architects working on new town masterplans. Post-war German *Bundesgartenschauen* were prompted by the need to deal with war damage, and the 1984 Liverpool Garden Festival was a reaction to civil unrest. International legislation such as the European Community Directive on Environmental Assessment (1985) has also benefited landscape architecture. The landscape has received its most emphatic international imprimatur in the Council of Europe's European Landscape Convention (2000). This commits countries to preparing inventories of the landscape of the *whole* territory, good and bad, not just special areas of landscape interest such as national parks.

As the growth of the profession in China reflects, landscape architecture is a discipline well placed to face the problems of industrialization, rapid urbanization and consequent changes in the countryside. Since the 1960s landscape architecture has increasingly addressed society's concerns of ideas of sustainability, ecological health (including derelict and toxic land), and concern about global warming.

In relation to the design of external spaces, architects have a concern for buildings, which are relatively finite and made of dead materials; while landscape architects have a primary concern for site, the *genius loci*, a wish to embrace living process, ecological systems and change, and a basis in an understanding of the natural world. Due to this holistic base landscape architecture is a profession most eminently suited to face the problems of people's paramount settlement of the planet. RH

Chadwick, G. F., *The Park and the Town* (1966)
Diedrich, L., and Holden, R. *et al.* (eds.), *Landscape Architecture in Europe* (2006)
Newton, Norman T., *Design on the Land: the Development of Landscape Architecture* (1971)

Langhans, Carl Gotthard (1733–1808) German architect. Langhans' most influential project was the Brandenburg Gate (1789–94). With its direct, almost archaeological, reference to the form of Greek propylaea, the gate signals the emergence of Prussian Classicism. After a series of largely neo-Palladian buildings in Breslau (now Wrocław), he was summoned in 1788 by King Friedrich Wilhelm II to help make Berlin a cultural capital comparable to London and Paris. By virtue of his theatre in Breslau (1782), the theatre at Schloss Charlottenburg (1790), the State Theatre at Potsdam (1795), and the National Theatre in Berlin (1800–02), Langhans was also renowned for his expertise in theatre layout. He transferred this expertise to the design of numerous churches inspired by the sightlines and acoustics of his theatre plans. These include the churches at Wartenberg (1785), Waldenberg (1785), Oberadelsdorf (1789), Reichenbach (1795), and Rawitsch (1802). AN

Lanyon, Sir Charles (1813–88) One of Northern Ireland's foremost 19-century architects and engineers. Born in England, he moved to Dublin in the early 1830s to work as a civil engineer in the Irish Board of Works. He was appointed County Surveyor for Antrim in 1836, and simultaneously initiated the development of his own prolific private practice, forming partnerships with W. H. Lynn and his son John from 1854 and 1860 respectively. From the early 1860s he abandoned architecture in favour of a career in politics.

As County Surveyor, Lanyon's achievements range from the Larne to Ballycastle coast road (completed 1842), the design of the Glendun viaduct (1837), the

Italianate Crumlin Road Gaol, Belfast (1841–5), to the neoclassical County Court House (1848–50). His practice produced an eclectic, though not always inspired, range of churches, public, commercial, and domestic buildings. Key works include the Palm House (completed 1840 and 1852), Queen's College (1846–9), and Custom House (1854–7), Belfast. Outside the city examples include Ballywalter House, Co. Down (1847) and St Paul's Church, Castlwellan, Co. Down (1847–53), and an early passage in 'Celtic' revivalism at St Patrick's, Jordanstown, Co. Antrim (1866–8).   RM

Lasdun, Sir Denys (1914–2001) British architect, *modernist. Though it may be more evident to the expert than the layman, Denys Lasdun's austere, restrained, uncompromisingly modernist buildings include abstractions of Classicism, landscape and their surrounding context, and are inherently romantic in their spatial sequences, grouping, and massing, and humanist in their relation to their users, based on careful research. They are architects' architecture, and among the most eminent work of their generation.

Arguably, Lasdun is the toughest, most individual, British exponent of an 'alternative tradition', the development of Modernism which rejected 'functionalism' and 'internationalism' to accommodate local context and historical tradition, though he is more usually grouped with the *brutalists, whose buildings he respected but whose polemics he questioned.

While working for Britain's notable modernist practices Wells *Coates and Berthold *Lubetkin, he developed his own practice with 32 Newton Road (1937), influenced by Le Corbusier, but mildly adapted (partly by planning legislation) to the London street context in its height, verticality, and materials. His practice grew with Hallfield School (1951), and the Cluster Blocks in Bethnal Green (1954–9), a reworking and 'critique' of monolithic slab housing blocks, grouping pairs of duplex apartments to catch the sun,

like semi-detached houses in the sky—a complement to, rather than an overthrow of, the traditional urban fabric. In quite a different situation, overlooking St James's Park, and next to a Palladian mansion, his luxuriously detailed and spatially lavish block of flats at 26 St James's Place, London (1958), again showed his sensitivity to context.

His most revered building is the Royal College of Physicians in Regent's Park (1959–64). The building assimilates the rhythm, proportions, line and colour of the neighbouring John *Nash terraces into an indubitably modern form. This includes a white symmetrical façade—described by Lasdun's most eminent critic, William Curtis, as an abstraction of classical forms—facing the park, but sitting on piloti, with deeply shaded areas opening around it. The symmetry is offset by the Corbusian service tower to one side and a blue brick 'hump' lecture theatre pulled out beyond the piloti on the other, its form and colour echoing the slate roofs of surrounding buildings. Yet this powerful composition almost vanishes into its leafy environment. Organized around a loosely spiralling 'ceremonial' route centred on the Censors' room (its 17th-century panelling relocated from an earlier RCP), it combines the paraphernalia of the old institution with the *gravitas* of a new, yet opens it up, cutting views between the heavier, enclosed elements to the park and houses beyond.

After about 1960, Lasdun's characteristic use of horizontals, deep recesses, formal order, and visible building section was joined by expressed terraces. Lasdun always saw himself as designing not a discrete building but part of a town or landscape, but these later buildings were also seen as a geological abstraction in themselves, possibly the most contentious aspect of his work.

The principal examples are the student accommodation buildings at the University of East Anglia (1962–8), with their stepped section 'hills' of

National Theatre, South Bank, London (Denys Lasdun, 1967–76)

student rooms opening onto vast terraces. A similar section was adopted in more restricted and urban sites at Christ's College, Cambridge (1966), and the University of London, where the underside/backside of the terraces form a somewhat hostile, if impressive, streetscape.

Most famous of all these 'terraced' buildings is the National Theatre (1967–76), on London's South Bank. The building, from outside, seems a complex mass of heavy strata, pinned by heavy uprights, open to the river, and almost brutally unadorned (Lasdun said that the people using the balconies were the decoration), a total overthrow of traditional theatre façade/foyer sequence. But this highly sophisticated building works in a range of scales and ways, from the design of the three varied theatres, to the building's internal foyer landscape opening to the river beyond, and the use of materials, especially concrete: raw and forceful from a distance, rich and sensuous close up.

Ironically, the building was finished in the midst of UK reaction against modern architecture, and the romance of its carefully composed, ambitious cityscape as enacted by massive terraces of exposed aggregate concrete is still debated. Later projects (notably the European Investment Bank in Luxembourg, 1974–80) are less well known. But by the time of his death, Lasdun's eminence was again widely recognized and he was a seminal figure for a very different generation of architects experimenting with looser abstractions of context and building type, as well as for modernists.

KR

Curtis, W(illiam) J. R., *Denys Lasdun* (1994)

Latrobe, Benjamin Henry (1764–1820) English-born founder of the architectural profession in the United States. He trained briefly under engineer John Smeaton, and then entered the office of S. P. *Cockerell in London for three years (c.1789–92). He designed two country houses in Sussex in 1792–3, Hammerwood

Lodge and Ashdown House, in the advanced neoclassical style of the day, with Greek detailing. Latrobe left for America in 1796, settling in Richmond, Virginia, where he struggled to find commissions and filled notebooks with social and nature commentary and sketches, an invaluable record. The Virginia State Penitentiary (demolished) was his major project in Richmond, but he soon departed for the more promising destination of Philadelphia, summoned to build his early masterpiece, the marble Bank of Pennsylvania (1798–1801, demolished), which introduced the Greek orders to America and set a high standard. Finding success as an engineer–architect, Latrobe gave the city a steam-powered waterworks focused on Centre Square Engine House (1799–c.1803); like the bank, it showed the influence of *Soane. Latrobe brought the Gothic Revival villa to America with Sedgeley, Philadelphia (c.1799–1802). None of these early buildings survives, but fortunately we still have his splendid Baltimore Cathedral (1806–21). Here and in the United States Capitol (first campaign, 1803–12), likewise in an advanced neoclassical style, Latrobe introduced sophisticated masonry vaulting. His rebuilding of the interiors of the Capitol after a fire (1815–17) forms his most famous legacy, his command of spatial complexity and artistic detail everywhere apparent. Latrobe moved constantly in near-desperate search for work, finally to New Orleans. Many of his buildings have been demolished, but his extraordinary papers survive and have been published in an ambitious scholarly edition.

WBM

Carter, E. C. *et al.*, *Journals of Benjamin Henry Latrobe* (1977–80)

Cohen, J. A., and Brownell, C. E., *Architectural Drawings of Benjamin Henry Latrobe* (1994)

Latvia Shortly after the foundation of Riga in 1201, work began on its cathedral, the largest but not the most architecturally distinguished of the *Baltic brick

churches. The smaller red-brick churches, St Peter's (1491ff.)—which originally had the tallest wooden spire in Europe, at 137m (449 ft)—and St John's, make better use of brick patterns.

Other periods seemed to have left little architectural mark, apart from the appearance of *National Romanticism in Riga, with several apartment buildings (1904–9) and Kenins school building (1905) by Eizens Laube (1880–1967). In its Latvian version, rather monumental façades were adorned with shingled roofs, pointed gables, and irregularly shaped windows, all showing little obvious debt to a previous Latvian vernacular or to any historic precedents.   PG

Laves, Georg Ludwig Friedrich (1788–1864) German architect. As head of building administration in Hanover, Laves remained dedicated in most of his projects to a neoclassicism typical of his time. In addition to innovative bridge designs, private projects, and his important urban planning schemes for Hanover, Laves' most influential buildings are the Royal Palace on the River Leine (1817–51) and his design, in an Italianate mode, for the Hanover Opera House (1843–52). Laves travelled to England several times, and even submitted an ingenious entry for a building to house the 1851 Great Exhibition that, in its modular construction scheme, called for the use of borrowed railway rails for the structure's columns and beams.   AN

law courts Under the Roman Empire, legal proceedings were conducted in the *basilica, a simply planned rectangular building. When a more formal system of justice was re-established from the early medieval period onwards, courts were held in town halls which were used for other purposes. Even the title of Palais de Justice was misleading, in that such buildings (e.g. Rouen, 1499–1526; Rennes 1619ff.) were not exclusively dedicated to the legal process.

From about the end of the 18th century, as the legal process became more complicated and accessible to a greater proportion of the population, a different kind of building was required. Some of the most interesting solutions to the problems of law courts as a modern building type were worked out in Britain, in the half century after 1820.

The first new law courts were at Westminster (1823–6), one of *Soane's few failures. The design did not meet the more complicated requirements of modern law courts, since it lacked important ancillary rooms (law library, consultation rooms, and retiring rooms), and failed to enable different groups of users (judges, barristers, witnesses, the public) to remain separate from each other. Contemporaries also criticized the design for lack of light and space, but both faults were inherent in the site and could not fairly be attributed to Soane.

A solution to these problems was found at *Elmes's Liverpool Assize Courts (designed 1839), though on a small scale, with only four courtrooms. The building included all the ancillary rooms, and, by keeping apart different types of visitors to the court by means of separate entrances and corridors, it solved the problem of circulation. In other respects, Elmes's design did not set a precedent: using Doric columns for the façade meant that the building could too easily be mistaken for another building type, such as a museum.

But as the law reform movement gathered pace, following the enactment of the first substantial law reform legislation in 1846, the complexity of the plan requirements continued to increase. The first building to respond to the continuing discussion about how to plan courthouses was the Manchester Assize Courts (*Waterhouse, 1859). While the planning problem was ingeniously solved, other architectural questions remained, primarily the relationship between plan and façade, and also between building and site. A *Gothic Revival exterior, sufficiently convincing to draw the praise of *Ruskin, concealed a fairly symmetrical plan (shades of the Houses of Parliament!); and little use was made of the slightly irregular urban site.

The competition for the Law Courts, the Strand, London, revealed the complexity of the problem and uncertainty about its solution. The first decision (1867) awarded joint first prizes: Charles Barry for plan and distribution, G. E. *Street for architectural composition. Faulted for planning weaknesses, Street prepared an entirely new layout (completed 1868–82). He succeeded in every respect. The plan not only solves all the technical problems of circulation, but also includes the Great Hall, solemnly expressing the Majesty of the Law (very much in capital letters). Within a restricted site, the Strand façade cleverly creates a series of picturesque viewpoints, by means of an imposing clock tower, turrets corbelled out of the wall, and arched entrances.

Contemporary with the British examples, those in France, Belgium, and Italy should be mentioned for different reasons.

In France, Louis-Joseph Duc began a long programme of restoring and extending the Palais de Justice (1840–79). But he was more interested in contributing to an academic discussion about whether columns should be engaged or free-standing than in ingeniously solving problems of circulation or designing a distinctive façade appropriate to the building type.

For Belgium and Italy, the buildings of the national law courts were made to carry a heavier weight of symbolism, to represent newly emerging nations, only a generation old. In Brussels, the immense dome of the Palais de Justice (Poelaert, 1866–83) towers over the city from all directions; seen close up, it fired the imagination of the poet Verlaine: 'It has elements of the Tower of Babel, of Michelangelo and of Piranesi, and not a little madness...Externally it is a colossus, internally a monster...'

In Rome, the Palazzo di Giustizia (Guglielmo Calderini, 1880–1910) was conceived of as a symbol of the 'third Rome', the administration of justice and peace in a united Italy, rather than as a working building. Consequently, the ceremonial and professional functions are lavishly celebrated by the façade over-laden with architectural details, and the profusion of corridors, courtyards, and grand stairs; while the offices and clerks are meanly provided for, in mezzanines opening onto interior courtyards.   PG

Lebanon, historic The only significant site from the period of Roman rule in Lebanon is Baalbek, high above the Bekaa valley. From a distance, the temples are impressive, because in outline they mirror the perfect relationship between the width of the valley and the height of the mountain. Closer to, the temples are seen to be ungainly or merely curious. The earliest, the Temple of Jupiter (mostly complete by AD 60) is set on a platform of enormous blocks, an appropriate support for the tallest columns (19.9 m, or 65 ft) of any classical temple. Given that the apex of the pediment is 44 m (144 ft) above ground level, while the interior is only 88 by 48 m (289 × 157 ft), it is apparent that the whole building lacks a sense of proportion. In the Temple of Bacchus (largely built in the 2nd century AD), the tendency to gigantism is confined to the interior, the giant engaged columns running along the north and south sides. The Temple of Venus (3rd century AD) does not suffer from these faults, being a circular cella only 10 m (33 ft) in diameter. However, its form, a series of concave curves unprecedented in the classical world, has stimulated much unprofitable speculation about the existence of a supposed '*Baroque' avant la lettre.   PG

Fedden, R., *Syria and Lebanon* (1965)

Lebanon, modern Architecture in Lebanon is intensely dominated by influences from France, as manifested in important buildings by Michel Ecochard, such as the Hospital in Beirut (1961) in collaboration with Henri Edde and Andre Wogenscky, and his Ministry of Defence, Beirut (1962–4), in collaboration with Maurice Hindie. English and US firms received commissions in Lebanon, among them Edward Durrell Stone for the Hotel Phoenix, Beirut (1954), and Paul Rudolph for the Raouche Centre, Beirut (1975). The Swiss architect Alfred Roth designed a commercial centre in Sabbe (1967–70), the Italian architect Paolo Riani and the Danish architect Joern Utzon carried out projects for an SOS International Children's Village in Behrssaf, and—more recently—the firm Webb Zerafa Menkes Housden Partnership designed an office building in the Beirut Trade Centre in 2002.

The few attempts by Arab architects to define the Lebanese identity are the Maison de l'Artisan in Beirut by Pierre Neema and Jacques Aractingi (1963–8), the Aysha Sakkar Mosque by Jafar Tukan (1971), and the Music Hall in Beirut by Bernard Khoury (1999). The most promising developments can be seen in new works by Samir Khairallah, such as the Al-Kafaa Rehabilitation Institute (1969–74), and by Maath al-Alousi and Manfredo Nicoletti in their design for the reconstruction of the Beirut Souks (1994). There are several plans for the reconstruction of the Beirut centre, among them the project by Angus Gavin and the firm Dar al-Handasah (1993), demonstrating a departure into a new direction.   UK

Skeels, Frank and Laura, *Lebanon—Highways and Byways* (2000)

Le Breton, Gilles *See* BRETON, GILLES LE.

Lechner, Ödön (1845–1914) Hungarian architect. His driving ambition was to create a 'Hungarian language of architecture', and in the process he charted unknown heights and antagonized the political establishment of his country. In the Museum of Applied

Arts (1893–96), Lechner fused French Renaissance, Mughal-Indian, and Hungarian folk themes, and also relied on modern technology. The Postal Savings Bank (1899–1901) in Budapest, another of his mature works, displays on its tall roof a wealth of zoomorphic motifs relating to Hungarian mythology, all made of bright ceramics manufactured in the Zsolnay factory. His original art is comparable with Antoní Gaudí's in Europe.   JS

Le Corbusier (Charles-Edouard Jeanneret)
(1887–1965) Swiss-born architect, who may be said to have created almost single-handed the idea of modern architecture that dominated the 20th century. He was a proponent of *Functionalism, and of the machine aesthetic—architecture as if it were a kind of engineering (*see* ENGINEERING AND ARCHITECTURE). On the other hand, he insisted that the architect should aim to go beyond the engineer in search of poetry, in the emotive aim of touching the heart. These two ideas are very different, and in Le Corbusier they are both present in dialectical opposition.

Jeanneret was largely self-educated, as he learned from looking. In 1907 he left on a voyage to Italy, where he made drawings in Florence and Siena. On a later voyage (1910) he was inspired by the white cubic houses on the Mediterranean coast, which may now be seen as the models for his white-walled modern architecture (his sketchbooks were published in English as *Journey to the East*, 1988).

He also spent a formative time (1908–9) in the Paris offices of Auguste *Perret, acquiring a life-long interest in reinforced concrete, and in Germany (1910–11) with *Behrens, where he saw the possibility of a new kind of architecture, influenced by engineering forms.

Returning to Switzerland, he immediately conceived a system for building mass housing, which he called Domino Houses: a concrete frame, which could be extended in any direction. He made many sketches of them, in a 2-storey version, with flat roofs and windows freely disposed. More extraordinary, the examples of layouts were in a free picturesque manner. He also carried out several designs for villas. Of these the Villa Schwob in La Chaux-de-Fonds (1916) is the most significant. Although it shows an innovative conception of space, with a double-height living room overlooked by balconies, it is compromised by a heavy brick cornice.

In 1917 he moved permanently to Paris, and in the following year he began an important collaboration with the painter Amédée Ozenfant. Together they began to paint in a mimimal cubist style that they called Purism, and this was supported by their magazine *L'Esprit Nouveau*, which made a strong polemic for Modernism, in both painting and architecture.

The future is foreshadowed in his design of 1920 for the Maison Citrohan, with its main double-height living room. In1922 he designed a studio for Ozenfant in Paris, effectively the first building in the new style, with white walls and a strip window, as well as a large studio window. His pair of houses for La Roche-Jeanneret (1923) in the Rue du Docteur Blanche consolidated the new approach, and was enormously influential. It is now known as the Fondation Le Corbusier, and houses his archive.

In 1923 he published *Vers une architecture*, which summed up his theory of architecture. It is a polemic in favour of the engineer's aesthetic, supported by photographs of bridges, grain elevators, factories, workshops, hangars, liners, aircraft, automobiles, and machines. But it also praises architecture as a pure creation of the mind; and it includes many historical examples, as well as his own work. Combining two apparently opposing attitudes, the book promised architecture as the alternative to revolution, and had a mesmerizing effect on architects, particularly after it appeared in English in 1927.

In 1925 he designed a pair of houses for the Weissenhof-Siedlung in Stuttgart, a built demonstration of modern architecture, directed by Mies van der Rohe. In the same year he published his five points of a new architecture, which advocated the use of framed construction rather than accepting the constriction of masonry walls. These were:

1 The *piloti*
2 The roof garden
3 The free plan, based on almost invisible point supports
4 The strip window, admitting light continuously
5 The free façade, since a concrete frame could be enclosed in many different ways

The houses at Stuttgart were effectively a built demonstration of the new architecture, showing that his theory was matched by his practice.

During the 1920s his villas, of which the most famous were the Villa Stein at Garches and the Villa Savoye at Poissy, defined a white-walled modernity and came to give the decade the aura of an 'heroic' period. They demonstrated the practicality of the five points, but also maintained a certain interest in pure form, often influenced by classical precedents. In the Villa Savoye, for instance, the front door is one axis, and leads directly to the dog-leg ramp that bisects the building, but this axis is silently crossed on the half landing, and the rest of the plan is completely asymmetrical in layout.

Larger buildings like the Salvation Army hostel (1929–33) and the Pavillon Suisse, Cité Universitaire (1930–33), both in Paris, widened his appeal, and his trip to Moscow gave him a radical image. Although he failed to win international competitions for the League of Nations Building and the Palace of the Soviets, he succeeded with a building for the Central Union of Consumer Co-operatives in Moscow, the Centrosoyus (1929–34), which eventually confirmed his reputation as the leading modern architect of the 20th century.

Despite his enthusiasm for the house as 'a machine for living in', Le Corbusier was advocating a new technology without knowing anything of the physical problems it caused. The Villa Savoye was plagued by water entry through the steel window frames and the flat roof, because no building contractor in France had yet learned how to deal with this technology. The Salvation Army building had problems of heat gain from the entire wall of window, leading him to use the *brise-soleil*, a structure standing in front of the glass.

Modern architecture had now become a matter of public concern, which led to the inauguration (in 1928) of the *CIAM, which Le Corbusier effectively dominated until its demise in 1956. He gave it an increasing emphasis on town planning, a subject in which his ideas were less constricted by the physical problems he encountered in buildings, although they were realized only in theoretical proposals, such as the Ville Contemporaine of 1922, the Plan Voisin for Paris of 1925, and the Ville Radieuse, displayed at the third CIAM in Brussels in 1930. Here, his rational analysis led to a rigid functional division of the city into zones, separated by green belts. It can be asserted that his ideas did more harm to the dynamic art of town planning than they benefited the development of a functional architecture.

The war years restricted his output, and when he built again his architecture had changed: no longer smooth and precise, but massive and sculptural. The block of flats in Marseilles, the Unité d'Habitation (1946–52), was supported by huge legs of rough-finished concrete, retaining the marks of the shuttering. The building was based on a system of proportions (including the Golden Section), following the precepts set out in his book *Le Modulor* (1948). The Unité at Marseilles was rationally conceived as a unit that could be built anywhere, and indeed five others were built, in

Notre Dame du Haut, Ronchamp, Haute-Saône, France (Le Corbusier, 1954)

quite different contexts: four in France (Nantes-Rezé, 1952–7; Meaux, 1957–9; Briey-en-Forêt, 1957–60; Firminy-Vert, 1962–8) and one in Germany (Berlin, 1956–8).

The Maison Jaoul in Neuilly (1956) used concrete vaults supported on brick walls, and the pilgrimage chapel at Ronchamp (1954) and the monastery at La Tourette (1960) were both uncompromizingly sculptural in design and effect, and the least influenced by his obsession with engineering.

In 1950 Le Corbusier was commissioned by the Indian government to design a new capital city for the Punjab, Chandigarh. The city plan, and the buildings for the Government Centre—secretariat, law courts, and parliament—were built. The commercial centre was based on a Le Corbusier type, and a secondary school also bears his mark.

A number of other commissions followed in India: at Chandigarh, the College of Art, a Museum and Art Gallery, and a yacht club; in Ahmedabad, the Mehta Museum of Miniatures, villas for the Sarabhai and Shodhan families, and a headquarters for the Millowners Association: all these kept him going through the 1950s and 1960s, when development in France was recovering from the war. He also built in Japan, the National Museum of Western Art, Tokyo (1959). In Latin America he had collaborated with Lúcio *Costa in a design for the Ministry of Public Health in Brazil (1938, 1943), with the *brise-soleil* adding a certain glamour; and with Amancio Williams he designed a town house for Dr Currutchet in Buenos Aires (1949). In the USA he was consultant for the United Nations Building, and built the Carpenter Centre for the Visual Arts in Harvard (1963).

His last buildings were the Centre Le Corbusier in Zurich (1967) and La Maison des Jeunes at Firminy (1965). The church of Saint-Pierre de Firminy-Vert, begun in 1965, took 43 years to be completed.   RMA

Baker, Geoffrey H., *Le Corbusier: an analysis of form* (1996)
Frampton, K., *Le Corbusier* (2001)
Jencks, C., *Le Corbusier* (1973)
Von Moos, S., *Le Corbusier* (1979)

Ledoux, Claude-Nicholas (1736–1806) French neoclassical architect of radical eclectic tendency. He enjoyed a spectacular private career, working across society for the nobility (Montesquieu and de Livry on chateaux, Montmorency and d'Uzès in Paris, 1765–76), for court officers (d'Hallwyl, 1766), actresses (Guimard, 1771), bankers (Thélusson, 1778), provincial governors (theatre at Besançon, 1775–83, courts and prison at Aix, 1779–86), and housing estate developers (Hosten, 1792), before the onset of the Terror. The patronage of Louis XV's mistress du Barry (Louveciennes, 1771) and of crown tax collectors on works for the royal salt monopoly (the Chaux factory at Arc-et-Senans, 1774–9, the toll-gates in the Paris customs cordon, 1784–9) nearly cost him his head (1794). The last decade of his life, unproductive in practice, was devoted to preparing the publication of his extraordinary treatise *L'Architecture considérée sous le rapport de l'art, des moeurs et de la législation* (1806, 1846) which,

novel in its sociological content and radical in the near-mystical idealism of its attempt to distance aesthetics from taste, is not without indications of mental distraction.

At the outset of his career Ledoux conformed to enlightened neo-Palladian principle in homogeneous massing and the restriction of ornament to structural elements, but he soon revealed a native virtuosity. Ingenious at planning for awkward city sites (e.g. for Montmorency) but increasingly obsessed with elementary geometry and massive forms, by the mid-1770s he was pressing the extensive repertory of classical motifs into an idiosyncratic Mannerism at Chaux and in his later Parisian houses—particularly the Hôtel de Thélusson. Beyond that, the engraved plates of *L'Architecture* took the exercise to the extreme in the imaginative redevelopment of executed work, and above all in the visionary completion of the Chaux project as a completely integrated community linked to its rural environment but distinguished as a rationalist concept by its cosmic perimeter circle. Formed to proclaim their purpose, several of the facilities within and without that circle (most notably the brothel and the house of the Controller of the River) introduced the radical concept of *architecture parlante*.   CT

Gallet, M., *Claude-Nicholas Ledoux* (1980)

Lefuel, Hector-Martin (1810–80) French architect. He was employed mainly on the completion of the wings which join the Louvre to the Tuileries (in succession to L.-T.-J. *Visconti from 1853). Baroque in scale and richness, his style is essentially Mannerist in the late-16th-century French mode: in principle not inappropriate in the context, in practice it presses the virtuoso invention of surface detail to the extreme.   CT

Legeay, Jean-Laurent (c.1710–after 1786) French architect. *See* FRANCE (BAROQUE, ROCOCO, AND ACADEMIC CLASSICISM).

Legorreta, Ricardo (1931–) Mexican architect. His productions are the fruit of his study and appreciation of traditional architecture in combination with his mastery of rationalist architecture. The outstanding works of his early period are the Hotel Camino Real in Mexico City (1968), those at Cancún and Iztapa, as well as factories and residential buildings, for which, as a necessary complement, he also designed furniture. Since 1995 in Legorreta + Legorreta, with Victor Legorreta and Noé Castro, he has worked in several countries, designing, in particular, a number of buildings for cultural purposes: the National Arts Centre in Mexico City; the libraries of San Antonio and Chula Vista, and buildings for the Monterrey Technology College as well as for the Universities of Stanford, Santa Fe, Chicago, and California, in the USA; and the University of Qatar. Recent projects include the Sheraton Hotel in Bilbao and a building in London for the Zandra Rhodes Museum (2001).   LNM (trans. KL)

Leiviskä, Juha (1936–) Finnish architect. His first mature work was the addition (1970) of the Parish Hall of the Church in Nakkila, built by Erkki Huttunen in 1937. Between 1971 and 1975, beginning with the Church and Parish Centre of St Thomas (Oulu), he built the first of an outstanding series of such centres (the others are at Myyrmaki, Kirkonoummi, and Mannisto) in a building language that carried the abstracted elements of De *Stijl to a level of complexity as rich as facet cubism.

He expressed his view that 'my most important building material is light' in a unique configuration of overlapping layers in depth (hence the analogy to facet cubism) or stepped in echelon in which light is filtered with inter-reflections to create a wall of diaphanous light without glare. A roof-system extends the same syntax overhead in layered beams and lattices of sky-light. Artificial light sources in the form of suspended lanterns (to his design) are distributed in rhythmic clusters, but the main source of ambient light is natural. The space appears to be under constant, albeit subtle, change in response to Nature. In the later churches this light is passed through veils of pale colour, resulting in a unique space–light continuum.

The repertoire of his projects extends beyond that of religious buildings—to art galleries, schools, the German Embassy in Helsinki, the Dar Al-Kalima multi-faith Academy in Bethlehem, and some large-scale residential complexes—but his supreme achievement lies in his churches.   CSTJW

Juha Leiviskä (Museum of Finnish Architecture, 1999)

Leliman, Jan H. (1828–1910) Dutch architect. As he was financially independent he built very little, but was very active and prominent as the defender of the architectural profession (education, professional societies, copyright, and standard fees), as a pioneer of social housing, and as a writer. In 1852 he studied in Henri Labrouste's atelier in Paris, and in 1855 he introduced *Eclecticism in the Netherlands (the club and exhibition building Arti et Amicitiae, Amsterdam), through the architecture of artistic freedom that he propagated for 30 years.   AVDW (trans. CVE)

Lemercier, Jacques (c.1585–1654) French classical architect, trained in Rome (c.1604–14) amongst followers of Giacomo *della Porta. Promoting their Academic Classicism, he challenged prevailing Mannerist and Baroque tendencies, notably in his Sorbonne chapel (1626) commissioned by Cardinal Richelieu, for whom he also worked at Rueil (from 1630), on the chateau and town of Richelieu (from 1631), and in Paris on the Palais Cardinale (later Royale, from 1633). He built palaces and chateaux for other grandees (particularly de Liancourt) and replaced F. *Mansart on the Queen's Val de Grâce project (1646). Meanwhile he had worked since 1624 at the Louvre where, as Premier architecte du roi, he extended Lescot's court in a complementary style. CT

Leonardo da Vinci (1452–1519) Italian painter and sculptor. No building can with any degree of certainty be attributed to Leonardo, but his interest in centrally planned domed buildings may well have influenced his contemporary, *Bramante. PG

Leoni, Giacomo (c.1686–1746) Venetian architect. Leoni's fame rests on his career in England. This began, after a brief sojourn in Düsseldorf, with his edition of Palladio's *I Quattro Libri* (1715–20), a principal source of inspiration for the first generation of English Palladians, and he also published a translation of *Alberti's *De re aedificatoria* (1726–9). Presumably first-hand knowledge of Palladio's architecture stood him in good stead for his own buildings, notably Carshalton Park, Surrey (1725, never completed), Lyme Park, Cheshire (c.1725–35), Clandon Park, Surrey (probably c.1730–33), and major additions to other country houses. His Queensbury House, London (1721–3), was a model Palladian town house, and he designed several garden monuments. APQ

Lescaze, William Edmond *See* HOWE AND LESCAZE.

Lescot, Pierre (c.1500–78) French architect. His main work is the Cour Carrée of the Louvre (commissioned 1546), a design which shows the emergence of a distinctively French style. The façade is essentially decorative and sculptural, in the use of the most delicate of the orders, the Corinthian and the Composite, and extensive surface decoration in the attic storey. Both the central and the two end pavilions have niches with sculpture by Jean Goujon.

He also designed the Hôtel Carnavelet, Paris (c.1545, substantially altered), much plainer than his design for the Louvre, but with a similar prominence given to sculpture. PG

lesene A pilaster, lacking a base or capital, and sometimes just a vertical strip of projecting stone that may penetrate a rubble wall to bind it together. Characteristic of Anglo-Saxon and Norman buildings, lesenes may be the vestigial remains of classical decoration designed to articulate a wall, as pilaster strips may articulate an attic. APQ

Lethaby, William Richard (1857–1931) English architect and educator. Lethaby joined Norman *Shaw in 1879, as chief clerk, but came to prefer the work and ideals of Philip Webb. Lethaby's houses (from Avon Tyrrel, Hampshire, 1891–3, to Melsetter House, Hoy, Orkney, 1899) were solid but spiritual, devoid of grand gestures. His only urban design was for the Eagle Insurance Offices at Colmore Row, Birmingham (1900), an awkward amalgam of historic motifs, Tudor and classicizing, and abstract pattern-making.

His building career ended rather disappointingly with the church of All Saints, Brockhampton-by-Ross, Herefordshire (1902), where the vaults of unreinforced concrete supported a thatched roof. The difficulties he experienced in completing such an unusual form of construction caused him to reconsider his view of architecture completely. Moving away from the *Arts and Crafts ideas he had formerly espoused, he now argued that architects needed to understand the basis of modern structures, using machine-produced materials such as steel and concrete. Consequently, he urged fundamental reform of architecture, dispensing with the superficial copying of styles and returning to principles of engineering construction and deep-rooted symbolism. Ever since, he has remained a guiding star for a certain puritanical strand in English architecture. AP

Rubens, G., *William Richard Lethaby* (1986)

lettering and architecture Roman lettering, familiar from stone-cut inscriptions, suits the geometry and order of classical architecture, and the two have marched together through history. The Roman letterforms, most famously (if accidentally) those on Trajan's Column in the Forum (AD 114), were apparently lapidary versions of brush lettering, the end of the brushstroke creating the form of the serif. In Pompeii, loosely if skilfully painted electoral notices survive on walls. The layout of inscriptions over the gates of Imperial towns are spaced in accordance with the unique local variation of the foot and inch measures used in that town, and seem to have been based more on mathematical than visual criteria.

The forms of the Roman alphabet are capable of infinite variation, and their recovery in the Renaissance was also the recovery of architectural lettering, now subjected to proportional analysis. The inscription on the frieze in the courtyard of the Ducal Palace at Urbino, added by Guidobaldo da Montefeltro (1482–1508), is especially harmonious in its letterforms and spacing. In the northern Renaissance, against duller skies, cut-out stone lettering ornamented the parapets of French churches and English country houses, starting with Hardwick Hall, 1597. Only in the late Baroque period did the actual letterforms used on buildings begin to explore alternatives to this pure Classicism, as seen in a frieze of fanciful letters supported by putti at S. Angelo, Lecce, 1663.

Neoclassical lettering lost its connection with the process of brush or chisel, and copied the new style of printing known as 'Modern', with thin straight-line serifs, introduced by the typefounders Didot and Bodoni from the 1780s. English typefounders developed 'Fat Face', a broad letter Egyptian (with slab serifs), and Sans Serif, also known as Grotesque and, confusingly, as Gothic. The last was adopted as an inscriptional letter by Sir John Soane. Lettering of shop fascias and cast-iron street names from the 1830s

onwards show the vitality and variety of these forms, including shadowed versions. Monumental lettering declined in the late 19th century, until rescued by the influence of Edward Johnston and his pupil Eric Gill, who insisted on purity of form, Roman or (in the case of Johnston's 1916 Underground type; *see* HOLDEN) Sans Serif, showing the human touch of the pen or the chisel. By the 1920s British lettering had been transformed, although to many it became a desert of Trajan good taste. Other countries went different ways, Germany to Sans Serif before 1933, and Italy to blocky stone Sans letters during the Fascist period.

Architects spearheaded the revival of Victorian lettering, as seen in the shaded Fat Face of the Finsbury Health Centre (Lubetkin and Tecton, 1938) and the lettering at the Festival of Britain (1951) with a lettering panel to coordinate. Supergraphics (large-size lettering) were a feature of the 1960s, introduced by Edward Wright. A tradition of fine carving of Roman letters survives in Britain, represented by Michael Harvey (Sainsbury Wing, National Gallery, 1991) and the Cardozo Kindersley Workshop (British Library, 1997) among others. Engraved lettering on glass doors became popular in the 1970s. German lettering, influenced by the type designer Rudolf Koch at the beginning of the 20th century, is typically more angular and emotional, as in the work of Sepp and Wolfgang Jacob.

Now that computers appear to perform the letterer's task, few architects show sensitivity to the specific match of letters to buildings, although signage whether humble or monumental continues to be required and can lift an ordinary building to higher levels. AP

Baines, P., and Dixon, C., *Signs: lettering in the environment* (2003)
Gray, N(icolete), *Lettering on Buildings* (1960)

Le Vau, Louis (1612–70) and **François** (1613–76) French architects. Their education is obscure before they emerged with their mason father as speculative house builders in Paris (mid 1630s). Both developed private practices and worked for the French crown under Louis XIV: the older brother, by far the more significant, replacing Lemercier as Premier architecte du roi (1654).

Louis's earliest notable work, the Hôtel Lambert (1639), distinguished him as adept at commodious planning, free of the traditional *enfilade* yet admitting scenographic vistas, though incoherent in his application of varied orders to articulate external form without consistent reference to the nature of the spaces behind them. He was a decorator and garden designer as well as architect. Given to display, Mazarin and his grandees (Bordier, Séguier, Servien, Lamoignon, de Lionne, etc.) were his enthusiastic clients for hotels and chateaux. Of the latter, the most spectacular was built for the Minister of Finance, Fouquet, at Vaux-le-Vicomte (1656) where C. Le Brun was prime decorator and A. Le Nôtre collaborated on the axial garden: masterly in planning, with rooms grouped into apartments to either side of the full-height oval salon which was Le Vau's hallmark, the building was uncertain in the integration of its masses and showed no advance in coherent articulation. These traits were less worrying in Mazarin's legacy (l'Institut de France, 1662), but they did not commend Le Vau's Louvre projects to the king's reforming minister, Colbert, who invited Italian and French competition (1664). Bernini was preferred by the king but not by Colbert, and Le Vau was joined by Le Brun and Claude Perrault in a definitive committee (1667) in which his role is obscure. However, from 1667 François was involved in work on the Louvre project, and Louis was increasingly preoccupied in enveloping the old nucleus at Versailles in an Italianate range responding to the garden under development by Le Nôtre.   CT

Lewerentz, Sigurd (1885–1978) Swedish architect, a contemporary of *Asplund, whose work has not

received comparable acclaim. Lewerentz did what few other architects have been able to do successfully: he mastered one approach to design—modern *Classicism—which he then unequivocally abandoned for another, somewhat misleadingly termed *Brutalism.

Many of his projects were not built, and his major completed work amounts to only three projects. But all his schemes share two preoccupations rare in the 20th century: *sacred* architecture, and the idea of rites of passage, for mourning or for worship. His classicist phase, far removed from the approach of *Piacentini or *Speer (*see*: FASCISM and STILE LITTORIO), is represented by the Chapel of Resurrection in the Woodland Cemetery, Enskede, Stockholm (1922–6). At first sight, its subtle modifications of the language of Classicism, such as the disengaged portico, and the separation between roof and cornice, seem mere mannerisms. In truth, these 'devices' are not only a way of establishing the sequence of 'the rite of passage' during the ceremony of mourning, but also of framing a common experience, the necessary acceptance of death. Unfortunately, his two major projects for the Eastern Cemetery, Malmö (1926), set out in a series of drawings which rival *Schinkel in their austerity of form and metaphor, were not realized.

Like Asplund, Lewerentz was initially attracted by the 'white' architecture of the 1930 Stockholm exhibition. However his most original work, the competition design for the Johanneburg church (1933), was far removed from the usual secular concerns of *Modernism, prefiguring his interest in planning for a new approach to the liturgy, the principle of *circumstantes*, in which the altar was moved into the heart of the congregation.

At St Mark's, Skarpnäck, Stockholm (1956–60), Lewerentz was obliged to adopt a conventional form, the linear basilican plan with the vaults running laterally to the axis, so that he was denied the opportunity of implementing his new approach. But at St Peter's, Klippan, near Helsingborg (1963–6), the square plan-form required by the principle of *circumstantes* called forth his masterpiece. Apparently concerned only with the banal structural necessities, Lewerentz used the steel beams necessary to support the roof members, and for every other element standard-sized, roughly coursed brickwork in which the ratio of mortar to bricks is freely adjusted, to produce forms evoking the Discovery of the True Cross, and a rough shelter for the discovered element. His handling of light deepens the significance of this haunting metaphor. In a rare statement about his design, Lewerentz argued that only by providing subdued light would the nature of space emerge, in response to exploration. A new poetry had been forged out of the endless struggle with apparently outmoded forms.   PG

Libera, Adalberto (1903–63) Italian architect, a key member of the Gruppo 7, which he joined in 1927. During the 1930s his work, like the Post Office on Via Marmorata in Rome (with Mario De Renzi, 1933–4), was a fusion of the principles of *Italian Rationalism with the sculptural qualities of Roman architecture. Libera became the director of INA-Casa following World War II, completing a single-storey housing complex in the Tuscolano housing quarter in Rome (1950–54) that utilized a series of courtyard spaces. BLM

libraries, to 1850 In their earliest forms libraries were often combined with collections of objects and works of art. Before the mass diffusion of texts brought about by printing, they were the domain of the educated and wealthy elite—royalty, princes, popes, monasteries, and colleges. Even when printing arrived, the possession of books, and writing and reading, still remained a means both for the extension of knowledge and for domination. Literacy was a tool for alienating

land from illiterate people—through law courts and bureaucracies. Wills, testimonies, written law, and property deeds, as also works of science and the humanities, which on account of their rarity or cost were only accessible to a privileged class, created asymmetries of power; and the spaces needed for producing, storing, retrieving, and using these texts were therefore spaces of privilege.

Origins Medieval and Renaissance libraries followed a similar ('stall') arrangement: books, often chained, were ordered into classes and placed on one or two high shelves at right angles to the walls, above sloping-top single or double-sided reading ledges, by which readers stood, and later sat. The University of Leyden library (1610) was typical. A contemporary illustration shows the names of the categories on top of the shelf units: mathematics, literature, theology, history etc.; in reality, these would have been written on the ends of the units, and the same categories would have been used in the classified library catalogue. The space in effect was a classifying device.

As books became cheaper and more numerous, and readership wider, additional shelf space was provided around the walls; this included the wall between the units. The centre was left open, for reading tables. The combination of the 'stall' and 'wall' systems led to the widening of the space between the 'stalls' to accommodate reading tables, so that these became miniature reading rooms, as in *Wren's Trinity College Library, Cambridge (1676). Eventually the 'wall' system became dominant, and is still in common use. The change from stall to wall necessitated a change in window design, affecting both the interior and the exterior character of libraries, as it was no longer possible to have large glazed areas, giving a view of the readers from outside, between stalls.

As subject classes became increasingly subdivided, they also needed an author index, and aspects of a given

549

subject which appeared under various classes were collated into an alphabetical subject index. Indexes and catalogues represent the librarian's perennial struggle with the multi-dimensional nature of knowledge. And it was not just a question of how to *record* an individual work, but also of where to *locate* it, in space. When a librarian is also a philosopher, the correspondence between epistemology, book classification, and spatial organization becomes most illuminating. This is exactly the case with Leibniz (1646–1716), who dreamt of a 'demonstrative encyclopaedia' to avoid the disaster of scholarly chaos threatened by the explosion of knowledge.

The fear which seemed to grip his imagination was of 'that horrible mass of books which keeps on growing'. Having entered the service of the Duke of Brunswick in 1676, Leibniz took over the celebrated library at Wolfenbüttel in 1690, for which Herman Korb designed a new building (1706–19). Leibniz superintended this project, which was Europe's first secular library. He inherited an older subject classification system, which he was not allowed to change, so besides compiling a mammoth author catalogue, he set down his ideas for how a subject catalogue *might* be organized. In 1668 he had started work on his encyclopaedia, in which all knowledge would be arranged in an alphabetically classified subject order. The elementary concepts in the works indexed would be represented by symbols which, in combination, formed complex ideas. Eventually the encyclopaedia would obviate the need for books altogether!

Leibniz regarded a library as a 'storehouse of knowledge' whose printed equivalent would be his encyclopaedia. No matter how sophisticated the catalogues and indices, the materiality and hence spatiality of real books (an object has to be *some*where) arranged linearly on shelves was a limitation which was contrary to logic.

It is precisely to overcome this linearity, which ignores the multi-dimensional relations amongst books, and forces a librarian to choose one amongst many possible relations, that made his classified, alphabetic subject index so essential. After three hundred years, and despite the development of sophisticated faceted systems, such as the Dewey and UDC, and modern computer-based multi-dimensional databases, as long as books are on shelves, the librarian's perennial problem of where to locate a single work remains as it was for Leibniz.

Korb's Wolfenbüttel library showed a number of features that became widespread in later library design. Firstly, the building was centric, with an oval dome. The dome form symbolized the universal, cosmic nature of knowledge, as well as the unity of its various branches. Secondly, as shown by a later plan of the arrangement of books on the two floors, the two key classes of the pre-1705 library—jurisprudence and theology—were located in the main ambulatory, centrally. Thirdly, the entire ambulatory surfaces, on both floors, as well those of the pillars and the outer walls, were used for shelving. So on all interior surfaces the texture of the books formed part of the Baroque decorative scheme.

Wolfenbüttel became a model not only for centric 18th-century Baroque libraries, such as *Fischer von Erlach's at Vienna, those in Mannheim and Stuttgart, the great monastic libraries of Melk, St Gall, Altenburg, and Admont, and James *Gibbs's Radcliffe Camera in Oxford, but also for later versions, such as the British Museum's Reading Room (1852). But books as architectural surfaces appeared in other forms—such as Boullée's proposed Royal Library (1784). The long hall is covered by a Roman coffered vaulted ceiling with an immense skylight, and the walls have four tiers of galleried shelving, with the books acting as a kind of rustication, above which rise the severe neoclassical columns.

The reading room,
Bibliothèque Nationale, Paris
(Pierre-François-Henri
Labrouste, 1855–75)

The idea of a centre was achieved in other than domed forms. For instance in the mid-18th-century Ducal Library at Karlsruhe, from a central reading room radiate cruciform galleries, giving access to all the books. In the 17th-century old St Geneviève library, Paris, the plan itself is cruciform.

The spread of reading In all these designs the reader was geometrically central, and spatially deep inside the structure. But the reality of systematic storage, catalogues, secure storage, constant expansion, a reading space open to the public rather than an élite readership, and efficient surveillance made these grand visions unworkable. The centuries-old direct link between shelves, books, staff, and readers was fractured when massive storage in 'stacks', accessible only to staff, became the norm. The revolution is shown in della Santa's ideal 'universal public library' (1816). The

(square) reading room is still central, but in shallow, outer space, just a step or two from the entrance. Book requests are handled at a window, behind which are located the cataloguing and other staff, who have access to shelved storage deep inside the structure. The shallow space shared by prince, librarian, and scholarly reader has disappeared; in its place there is now a professional librarian, invisible and hidden deep in space, but exercising strict surveillance.

In Robert Smirke's 1852 design for a vast, domed, circular reading room to fill the courtyard of the British Museum, many of the recent trends were embodied. Although most of the collection was now in stacks, its walls were lined with 20,000 classified volumes. The division of the interior surface of the cylinder by classification made it into a map of knowledge. The superintendent was located at the centre, from which radiated the readers' tables. In a ring between them were the catalogues. These are also texts—sometimes books, but located in a privileged, central position. They contain entries to other libraries' catalogues, guides, handbooks, and bibliographies. They may even contain an entry to themselves, which gives them a disconcerting, topologically impossible character like the famous Klein bottle: something which is the whole, both outside the system, and also inside it, as a part. So at the centre, under the eye of the dome, is the total seat of power: cosmic origin, total surveillance and control, and embodiment of all knowledge (the catalogue).

Of course much smaller libraries were built everywhere in Europe and North America during the two centuries before the British Museum Reading Room. These were in bookshops, clubs, coffee houses, mechanics' institutes, colleges and universities, Literary, Philosophical and Scientific Societies, and Lyceums. Stylistically, as with the larger libraries, there was virtually no alternative to Classicism. That, after all, was the obvious form for recalling the classical origins of Western learning. This tradition continued with the arrival of the public library after the passing of the permissive Museums Act of 1845 and the Libraries Act of 1850 (1853 in Scotland) which gave local authorities far greater powers. As was the case with other building types, once legislation allowed or compelled provision, and public finance became available, specialist architects emerged and not only built up large and lucrative practices, but also wrote the standard design guides. Such was John and Wyatt Papworth's 1853 *Museums, Libraries and Picture Galleries* which showed model libraries of various sizes, to suit various budgets. Of course censorship by librarians was long established. But in the burgeoning growth from the mid 19th century onwards, where bourgeois, artisan and working-class demand had to be met, it grew more overt and widespread. Architects such as the Papworths realized that this would affect design

provision: they warn that '… to be well supported by the lower classes, the library must contain books that a narrow-minded librarian might consider only amusing' and that the librarian must have the power to deny certain books to '… youths and ladies'. One classical model is recommended because its '… pure Italian style [is] so completely identified with the growth of the intellect.' ™

Markus, Thomas A., *Buildings and Power* (1993)

libraries, since 1850 Until the middle of the 20th century, the library as a building type had as clear a public identity as the church and the town hall.

Reading requires good glare-free light, and the anatomy of the typical library developed around the seemingly conflicting requirements for light and for uninterrupted shelf-lined wall space. Reading rooms were designed around the happy conjunction of heavy lower walls and tall windows above, and this gave their exteriors the pleasing high-shouldered look which so clearly identifies the building type.

The late 19th century was interested in the library as a public gesture which could redress some of the social ills of the industrial society. In America, the Ames family in North Easton Massachusetts employed H. H. *Richardson to create a town library in 1877–9, and Andrew Carnegie financed more than 2,000 small libraries before 1918. The Passmore Edwards libraries at Highbury, Truro, and other towns in England played a similar role. All announced themselves with monolithic stone walls at lower levels, and tall windows or clerestories above.

The model worked equally well for large libraries, but the quantities of books made simple storage around the reading room walls inadequate. One of the purest examples is the Bibliothèque Ste Geneviève in Paris, completed by Henri Labrouste in 1851, where the reading room with its huge high arched windows sits firmly on a full windowless storey of books below. At the Boston (US) Public Library completed by McKim, Mead, and White in 1888 the reading room is similarly raised on a stone plinth. At the largest scale, the British Museum Reading Room, completed by Smirke in 1856, and the Bibliothèque Nationale in Paris, completed by Labrouste in 1868, focused on a reading room surrounded with dense book stacks, with light coming entirely and lucidly from above.

This building type, with its load-bearing stone walls and high reading halls, persisted into the middle of the 20th century, but at that point a number of changes in library science conspired to bring about radical alterations, particularly in academic and research libraries. The rate of book publication increased in a parabolic curve. Compact storage systems helped, but not in older libraries whose floor loading would not permit their installation. Various forms of reproduction and miniaturization also helped, but in turn led to the need for specialist reading machines. And of course the electronic information age introduced onerous cabling requirements.

So a new library type began to emerge, driven by a generation of librarians frustrated by the limitations imposed on them by the inflexible, load-bearing, beautiful libraries inherited from the 19th century. Foremost among these was an American librarian, Keyes Metcalf, who wrote *Planning Academic and Research Libraries* in 1965. He argued that the need for flexibility in libraries was of primary importance, and identified the essential characteristics to achieve it: no bearing walls, a square grid of columns based on stack dimensions, uniform artificial lighting, and ceiling heights to allow for the location of readers or stacks at will, and near square building plans to increase locational options. Such buildings had to be air conditioned to deal with the electric light load and the depths away from the perimeter. The John Crerar library at the Illinois Institute of Technology, completed by Skidmore, Owings, and Merrill in 1962,

was a classic example, and a number of academic and large city libraries in Britain followed suit in the 1960s and 1970s.

This generation of libraries did answer some of Metcalf's criticisms, but some librarians were dismayed at the concomitant losses. Gone were the reading rooms which lifted the spirit, and equally absent was a clarity of organization. A building largely organized around groupings of furniture lost any sense of structure and orientation. And a uniformity of space and light often produced a sameness of environment which some readers found both physically and mentally tiring. (A notable exception was James Stirling's History Faculty Library at Cambridge, completed in 1968. It is sad that its failure in providing controlled environmental conditions has meant that its brave attempt to retain daylight and some spatial differentiation has not been more admired.)

The tyranny of the type (institutionalized by Library Associations and Funding Bodies) became ubiquitous, and it was only seriously tested at the time of the energy crisis in the 1980s when the air conditioning and heavy electrical light loads began to seem environmentally irresponsible. A number of university libraries in England (Queen Mary College in London, the University of Brighton at its Moulsecoomb campus, East Anglia University, and Liverpool), all built in the late 1980s and early 1990s, made use of the funding rules which tend to define the ratio of stacks to students within fairly close limits. Readers were again distributed along window walls, and narrow building sections allowed for good daylight and cross-ventilation. Computers have not notably reduced the number of books in university libraries, but have certainly increased group working and the resulting need for acoustic separation.

Smaller town libraries, especially in Scandinavia, avoided much of the meaningless uniformity of the mid century, and the radical shifts in library typology. Many architects were inspired by the relaxed openness of some of the town libraries of Sweden (Solna, Helsingborg, and Vaxjo, all from the mid 1960s) and especially the group of delightful libraries completed by Alvar Aalto in Finland (Seinajoki and Rovaniemi both completed in 1965, for example). In England, the Hampstead Central Library of 1964, by Sir Basil Spence, was a cool reinterpretation of the Bibliothèque Ste Geneviève: a long day-lit vessel for reading over a base holding stacks. Local libraries have moved from stony closure to glassy openness, but their mission bears out the prediction of Andrew Carnegie that they would serve as social centres for their communities. They continue to evolve to serve all age groups, to include new ingredients like internet cafés, but at their best they also continue to welcome serious readers, and even the old man or woman who wants a warm corner to doze over their newspaper.

At the largest end of the scale, two new national libraries were completed toward the end of the century: the Bibliothèque Nationale in Paris, and the British Library in London. In these libraries of 'last resort', unique and rare books remain at the heart of the pattern of use. Both libraries articulate the relationship between stacks and readers. At the French library, the readers look into a dramatically planted underground courtyard, and the books are elevated in four corner towers. At the British Library, by contrast, Colin St John *Wilson has stayed closer to the typological roots of the 19th century. The book collections are located below ground (like fine wine) and delivered to large day-lit reading rooms that retain some of the spatial quality of a previous generation. MJL

Brawne, Michael, *Libraries* (1970)

Libya, historic This territory became the Roman province of Tripolitania, after the destruction of Carthage in 146 BC. However, it was not until the rule of Augustus (27 BC–AD 14) that the cities of Sabratha (64 km or 40 miles west of the modern capital, Tripoli) and Leptis Magna (120 km or 75 miles to the east) were established, both in striking coastal settings. Most of the buildings in Sabratha were domestic or commercial, but a well-planned theatre survives in a good state of preservation.

Leptis was far more significant architecturally and culturally. During the rule of Augustus several temples were built, but the real development of the city took place in two later periods. Under Hadrian (r.117–38), white and coloured marbles replaced the grey limestone previously used. The new materials were first seen in the Hadrianic baths (AD 127ff). Septimius Severus (r.193–211), a native son, patronized the vast expansion, which largely survives today. He built a new forum and basilica, both notable for their red granite columns; and long colonnaded streets (cf. Antioch and Palmyra under SYRIA, HISTORIC). A grateful citizenry erected a *triumphal arch in honour of the city's patron. Like many of the other buildings, its wealth of graceful ornament betrays an Eastern influence, subtly different from the prototypes of Rome. PG

Libya, modern *See* AFRICA.

lierne A subsidiary rib in a vault, not directly connected with the springing of the vault, nor from the central boss. Characteristic of English Gothic, lierne-vaults were already employed early in the 14th century at Malmesbury Abbey, Wiltshire, and rapidly became characteristic of Perpendicular Gothic, as exemplified by the presbytery of Gloucester (after 1340). APQ

lighting When *Le Corbusier stated that 'Architecture is the masterly, correct and magnificent play of masses brought together in light' (*Towards a New Architecture*, 1927, p.31), he saw the changing patterns of direct sunlight and diffused skylight to be integral to the expression of architecture. Louis *Kahn was even more forceful in stating 'The sun never knew how great it is until it struck the side of a building' (*Light is the Theme*, p.12). These expressions describe how some architects tend to envisage their creations as three-dimensional forms placed in a landscape to interact with light, and this is a recurring image in architectural illustration and photography.

The interior illumination of buildings may arouse less passion, but it has been a strongly influential factor in architecture. As space is enclosed, so barriers are formed that must be pierced for daylight to be admitted. The Roman inventions of the arch and the vault enabled the creation of interior spaces with less intrusion by supporting structure and more opportunities for daylight admission, as exemplified by the oculus of the Pantheon. However, as the empire extended to higher latitudes, the pleasure of day-lit spaces would have been increasingly compromised by the human need to keep warm. There is no evidence that the Romans applied their glass-making skills to the apertures that connected indoor spaces to the outside.

The introduction of window glass in the Middle Ages had a profound influence on the development of architecture. As the pointed Gothic arch broadened into the perpendicular style, fenestration took over so much of the walls that flying buttresses became a necessity to provide structural support. In the temperate climates of the UK and northern Europe, the residences of the wealthy flaunted extensive areas of glazing, enabling the occupants to enjoy abundant daylight while protected from the wind and rain. Hardwick Hall in Derbyshire, built in 1597, inspired the epigram: 'Hardwick Hall / More glass than wall'. High ceilings and tall windows provided for penetration of daylight remote from the walls, and for even more effect, long galleries were sometimes provided with windows on both sides.

The Baroque style of architecture, inspired by the work of *Bernini (1598–1680) and *Borromini (1599–1667) in Italy, is characterized not only by richly ornamented oval openings and curved forms, but also by surfaces that are washed with light from apertures adroitly located to be concealed from direct view. As the style spread through Europe, dramatic lighting effects were achieved by use of lantern lights, high-level windows concealed by cornices, and openings formed some distance inside the perimeter walls. Examples range from St Peter's, Rome, to the white and gilt decorated ecclesiastical buildings of southern Germany, and these influences are reflected in *Wren's London churches, most notably St Paul's Cathedral (1675–1710).

As the Baroque gave way to neoclassicism, some architects carried through these lighting details. The London house (now a museum) of Sir John *Soane, which was built in stages between 1792 and 1824, is a veritable showcase of ingenious devices for admitting overhead daylight.

The notion that artificial lighting could be a source of delight, rather than a mere utilitarian substitute for daylight, developed in France. In the early 17th century, the Sun King Louis XIV would light the Hall of Mirrors in the Palace of Versailles with one thousand beeswax candles, delighting his courtesans and setting a new standard for opulence. While flame sources remained the only means of providing night-time illumination from antiquity right up until the late 19th century, the introduction of gas lighting at the beginning of the 19th century led to substantially increased light levels. High ceilings and ventilation apertures located above hanging gas lights were necessary to reduce the vitiating effect on air quality, but the attraction of reliable and affordable night-time illumination was sufficient to offset some level of discomfort. Theatre audiences were able to experience brightening and dimming of illumination without apparent human intervention.

Lighting technology erupted in the late 19th century. Substantial improvements were made in oil lamps and gas lighting, but these were overshadowed by the development of carbon filament electric lamps in 1879, although it was not until 1909 that electric lamps became reasonably efficient and robust after the introduction of drawn tungsten filaments. Further developments in lamp technology were paralleled in illumination engineering. In 1924, the International Commission on Illumination (CIE) established the basis of photometry, and in the 1950s illuminance standards were issued in many countries based on visual performance, this being the measure of how a person's ability to perform a particular task may be affected by the level of illumination provided.

While many designers saw that the luminaires for electric lighting could provide opportunities for new forms of decorative arts, some of the leading modernists saw the naked light bulb to be a pure expression of the machine aesthetic. Banham has referred to 'the bedazzled inhumanity of lighting in the 1920s' (*The Architecture of the Well-tempered Environment*, p.128). For the living-room of Villa Cook (1926), Le Corbusier provided a single bare lamp in the centre of the ceiling, but by 1930 he had become more concerned for the comfort of occupants, and for Villa Savoye he provided an indirect lighting trough running the length of the room, which totally concealed the lamps and utilized the white ceiling as a diffusely reflecting surface.

Other architects had never doubted that while lamps are to see by, they are not to be seen. For the Robie House (1910), Frank Lloyd Wright provided general illumination by placing frosted globes in square frames in the perimeter of a central ceiling upstand, with dimmer-controlled lamps adding dappled light through oaken grilles. For local lighting, he incorporated decorative glass lampshades into his purpose-designed furniture. His innovative approach to lighting inspired many architects, the indirect ceiling lighting at the

Johnson Wax Company (1936) being particularly notable. Banham has also quoted examples of architects in the 1920s as far apart as Berlin and California, who sought 'to exploit the left spaces and hollows of normal construction to provide light without making its sources visible' (ibid., p.201). They devised architectural features such as luminous beams and laylights, and with the introduction of the suspended ceiling to conceal building services, they added the luminous ceiling. This gained some popularity in the 1940s and 1950s, despite the bland uniformity of the illumination it provided.

Of greater architectural significance was the role of electric lighting within changing forms of building construction. The development of curtain-wall construction originally had the aims of providing for increased daylight admission and expansive outdoor views, but the development of vast retail stores and deep-plan multi-storey office buildings inevitably led to increased reliance on electric lighting. This trend was evident in the early part of the 20th century, and accelerated with the introduction of the fluorescent lamp in 1938. New types of low-transmission window glasses were introduced in the 1960s, and they became common features of curtain-walled buildings. These glasses enabled the extent of the view to the outside to be retained, with the advantages of reduced solar heat gain and glare, but of course with reduced daylight admission. For commercial buildings, daylight had generally ceased to be thought of as a useful source of illumination.

The tubular form of the fluorescent lamp made it eminently suitable for cornices and similar architectural features, but the widespread application of this lamp was in regular geometric layouts of ceiling-mounted luminaires. Extensive floor areas could be uniformly illuminated to prescribed illuminance levels, and in an era when electrical energy had become readily affordable, illuminance levels escalated. Between 1955 and 1977, the recommended illuminance for general office work in the UK increased from 200 lux to 500 lux. Initially the brightness of fluorescent lamps had been considered acceptable for many commercial and industrial applications, but gradually suspended or surface-mounted bare lamps gave way to domino patterns of recessed luminaires set into suspended ceilings.

In spite of these developments, the provision of daylight illumination within buildings was being developed as a scientific discipline. There were two main objectives. The first was that all buildings should have access to daylight, and the second was that certain types of indoor spaces, notably school classrooms and hospital wards, should continue to be designed for sufficiency of daylight illumination.

The city of New York instituted the Zoning Ordinance of 1916 to prevent commercial development reducing the streets to sunless canyons and creating inhuman working conditions. The height that a central city building could rise sheer from the sidewalk depended on the size of the site and the width of the street. Above this, the building had to be pulled back in a series of setbacks, and only then could a tower, with a floor area not exceeding some 25% of the site area, be raised as high as the owner wished. This substantially affected the developing skyline of the city, and led to some outstanding urban development. New York's lead was followed in many other parts of the world, and tables of data and graphical indicators to ensure access to sunlight and daylight found their way into town planning controls in many countries.

In 1955 the UK government published a 'Daylight Code' based on the Daylight Factor, which expresses the illuminance at a point indoors as a percentage of the simultaneous outdoor illuminance. To standardize measurements, the outdoor value is due to an unobstructed hemisphere of a standard overcast sky, and from this concept evolved procedures and

instruments for prediction and measurement. Daylight factor specifications were devised for the design of new school and hospital buildings in several countries, and were particularly influential in the UK during the period of construction that followed World War II. Too often the results were unsatisfactory, usually because of selective attention being given to daylight without concern for thermal consequences. Architects are now conscious of the need to address the overall performance of environmental control systems.

Outdoor floodlighting has often been focused onto architectural features, particularly with landmark buildings and monuments, and architects have responded by designing building façades that incorporate lighting to reveal selected features. Instead of the façades being simply washed with light, elements that characterize the building by day may be seen to glow in the night sky. Many cities have developed lighting master plans to coordinate the effects of floodlighting with the needs to illuminate traffic routes and to provide safe and attractive environments for people on foot. Other controls restrict light pollution of the night sky, and also light trespass, which is a cause of nuisance to neighbouring properties.

Indoor lighting is again in a state of reassessment. As architectural lighting design has become a recognized profession, concerns for visual performance have become less prominent. For many of the activities, the detail that has to be seen has been automated or replaced with digital displays, or it is presented on self-luminous screens. Emphasis has shifted to creating environments that provide for people's health, safety, and welfare, and this concept is set into the context of sustainability. The energy performance of lamps and the optical performance of luminaires have shown dramatic improvements since the early 1980s, and further developments are anticipated in lighting control systems to ensure that electric lighting is provided only where and when needed, and to achieve effective use of daylight. A revival of interest in daylight is gaining impetus from the necessity to meet greenhouse gas emission targets.   CC

Bowers B., *Lengthening the Day: A history of lighting technology* (1998)

Cuttle C., *Lighting by Design* (2003)

limestone a rock geologically defined as being composed of carbonate minerals, calcite or dolomite, or a mixture of the two. It is closely related to *travertine and *tufa. The stone is widely available, since it covers almost a fifth of the earth's land surface. Easily quarried, the stone is also easy to cut into blocks, to form into neat joints, and to carve into sharp mouldings.

Limestone was used to render the Step Pyramid of King Djoser (*c*.2650 BC; *see* EGYPT, ANCIENT (ORIGINS)); the pyramids of Dahshur and Giza (*c*.2550–2450 BC) were cased in limestone used as a masonry form, i.e. not imitating brick. The stone must have given the pyramids a dazzlingly white appearance under the desert sun, an effect difficult to recapture, since the casing was stripped off many centuries ago. A grey limestone was used at Mallia (*c*.1675–*c*.1635 BC; *see* MINOAN ARCHITECTURE), but in classical antiquity more highly coloured stones, such as *marble, were usually preferred.

Among the numerous varieties of limestone, two are conspicuously important: Caen and Portland. A light, cream-yellow stone, Caen was first used for the *Romanesque churches of the Abbaye-aux-Dames (1062–*c*.1130) and the Abbaye-aux-Hommes, Saint-Etienne (*c*.1060–81), and then transported to England for Canterbury Cathedral, the Tower of London, and Norwich Cathedral—very visible signs of the Norman Conquest, as the stone had never previously been used in England.

Portland stone, and in particular the middle layer of its formation, known as Whitbed, is often regarded as the finest English limestone. From about 1670 it was possible to cut large blocks, which could then be transported by sea to London. Attracted by its possibilities for use in monumental architecture, *Wren chose Portland stone for sections of his 52 City churches and the rebuilding of St Paul's (1675–1710). In monumental buildings at least, Portland stone was the defining feature of London for about 250 years from the end of the 17th century, just as the very similar Istrian stone was used for all types of buildings in Venice from the 13th century, particularly the churches by *Palladio.

However, while Portland stone does have an even texture and close grain, its extremely even whiteness, due to the reflection of light from the space between the grains of calcite, can seem rather dead. This defect is remedied when the stone is used in combination with red brick, as at Wren's Fountain Court, Hampton Court Palace.

Its only competitor was Bath stone, first quarried on a large scale from *c*.1730. Most of 18th-century Bath was built from this stone, as were parts of Windsor Castle, and *Nash's designs for Buckingham Palace. However, Bath stone does not reliably resist rain and frost; and its yellow colour can be rather dominant. The related Cotswold stones are bright yellow when first quarried, then turn to a more beige shade of yellow, which like Bath stone can look prominent in its landscape setting.

The most effective 'yellow' (in fact, a golden brown) limestone is Ham Hill, which is widely used in Somerset church towers and at Montacute House. However, before mechanized transport, builders could only use local stone, and Ham Hill, to its great detriment, often has to be combined with another limestone, the dull grey Blue Lias (for example, St Mary, Ile Abbots, Somerset). Some limestones, such as the golden-tinted *pietra leccese*, are almost too easy to carve, encouraging the architect to cover his buildings with rather florid sculpture (*see* ZIMBALO). Limestone is also found in other colours, such as the pale creamy brown of Stamford stone, widely used in the town of the same name.

Though limestones continued to be used mainly for monumental buildings well into the 20th century, the advent of machine cutting, and the demand for more showy materials such as *granite or marble, meant that it was rarely used as a *curtain wall cladding.

But the shelly, highly textured Portland Roach had a brief period of popularity in the 1960s, in buildings such as Staircases 16–18, Brasenose College, Oxford (*Powell and Moya, 1960–61), and the *Economist* building, London (*Smithson, 1962–4).   PG

Lissitzky, El (Eleazar Markevich) (1890–1941) Russian architect and writer. *See* THEORIES OF ARCHITECTURE (1880–2000).

Lithuania   In the capital of ancient and modern Lithuania, Vilnius (Polish Wilno), two good 16th-century Gothic buildings remain, the Bernardines' severe hall church and the chapel of St Anne with its flamboyant front in moulded brick. But the glories of Vilnius are to be found in the range and quality of its Baroque.

The Counter-Reformation brought a surge of Italianate building, led by the Jesuits' St Casimir (1604–18), followed by Tencalla's Carmelites (1634–52) and his Cathedral chapel of St Casimir (1636–41) and by a Cracow architect's church at Antokol (1668–75), both richly decorated. The next century saw lavish rebuilding and refurnishing: the Dominicans' Holy Spirit (1752–70); St Catherine (J. C. Glaubitz, 1741–53); the Uniate Holy Trinity, with a gateway that looks moulded (1761); and St John (1738–49), with a rolling façade made up of 16 Ionic columns and as many pilasters. The tall proportions and pastry-cook elaboration of Vilnius church architecture extend far:

north-east to Hlybokaye (1735) and Beresvec (1750–62), south to the Jesuit college at Pińsk, whose aisles are five times as tall as broad.

Vilnius saw the brief career of one of the strictest neoclassical masters, Gucewicz, who rebuilt the Town Hall (1786–9), planned the Pantheon-domed church at Suderve in 1783, and in 1783–6 designed the encasement of the Cathedral in Doric colonnades.   DBK

lodges   *See* GATE LODGES.

loggia   A roofed open structure which projects from a building. One of the earliest examples of what was to become a common feature of Italian architecture, the Palazzo Piccolomini (1459–64) has three superimposed loggie (the correct plural), to take advantage of the hillside site to view a wide prospect. It forms an interesting contrast with contemporary urban *palazzo design, such as the Palazzo Rucellai (begun *c.*1453) with its flat façade. The Loggia Cornaro, Padua (Falconetto, 1524), was a significant *garden building in its own right. A loggia could also serve as a dedicated space for giving benediction (*see* FUGA; GALILEI).   PG

Lombardo, Pietro Solari (*c.*1435–1515) Italian architect. Like his contemporary and rival, *Coducci, Lombardo drew inspiration from S. Marco, *Venice, but exceeded Coducci in that he was a master not only of spatial effects, but also surface decoration and perspective illusions.

His masterpiece was Santa Maria dei Miracoli (begun 1485). Initially, the building was to be a simple chapel, but as the popularity of the miracle-working image of the Virgin and Child rapidly increased, he was required to build a church rather than a chancel, on a very cramped site. His ingenious solution was to elevate the chancel, to be approached from the lower level by a flight of steps and spiral stair. He then lavishly encrusted all the surfaces, internal and external, with panels of different coloured marbles, porphyry, and verd antique. To make the tiny building (about 10 × 42.7 m or 33 × 140 ft) seem larger, he created various perspective illusions, using the placement of the external pilasters.   PG

long-and-short work This means alternating long stones on end and flat ones forming quoins or jambs, usually in an Anglo-Saxon church. The low stones penetrate the wall horizontally to some depth and therefore both secure it and provide a sound base for the tall stones. First found in County Durham at Benedict Biscop's Monkwearmouth (founded 675), Jarrow (consecrated 685), and the contemporary Escomb, the method may have been imported by masons whom Bede records as being sent from France to build in the Roman manner, probably employing stone robbed from Romano-British buildings. The method was still in use in the mid-11th-century Saxon–Norman overlap, at Earls Barton, Northamptonshire, and St Peter's, Barton-upon-Humber, Lincolnshire.   APQ

Longhena, Baldassare (1596/9–1682) Italian architect. From a prolific career as the architect of the city of Venice for 45 years, three works can be singled out.

Santa Maria della Salute (1631–87) has an ingenious plan, an octagon surrounded by an ambulatory, which allows carefully controlled views of the high altar and of the side chapels (for an exemplary analysis, see Rudolf Wittkower, *Studies in the Italian Baroque*, 1975, pp.125–52). Longhena wrote that he had built the church in the shape of a crown to express its dedication to the Virgin Mary. The exterior is far less successful. The giant scrolls, in pairs at each angle of the octagon, look extremely awkward, and though the dome has a striking profile when seen from a distance, the distinctive plan form is not well integrated with its immediate surroundings.

By contrast, the façades of his two palaces, the Pesaro (begun 1649/52) and the Ca' Rezzonico (begun 1666, but not finished until 1759) are more inventive than their somewhat conventional plans. The ground floor of the Pesaro is strongly rusticated, and in the two upper floors the columns stand well clear of the wall plane, except where the main façade turns the corner. In the Rezzonico, the apertures between the columns are almost entirely filled by glass, making the palazzo seem less monumental.   PG

Longhi family Italian architects.

Martino the Elder (c.1534–c.1591) was involved in the restoration of numerous churches, usually with other architects, so that his personal contribution cannot be securely identified. He was solely responsible for the façade of S. Girolamo degli Schiavoni (finished 1589), which shows a delicate touch in the lightly moulded friezes carved in travertine. By contrast, his design of the longest palazzo front in Rome, that of a wing of the Palazzo Borghese, is plain to the point of monotony, even more so than most Roman *palazzi of the period.

Onorio's (1568–1619) design for the church of SS. Carlo e Ambrogio al Corso (begun 1612) is of negligible importance, following a medieval type of plan, three aisles with side chapels, and a vast nave on a rather inhuman scale.

Martino the Younger (1602–60) had a trial run with S. Antonio dei Portoghesi (begun 1631), after which he designed SS. Vincenzo e Anastasio (1646–50), a building critical for the development of the Roman Baroque.

He worked out a brilliant solution to the problem of giving the building sufficient presence in its awkward location, a narrow site looking onto the junction of six streets near the Piazza Trevi. A number of optical subtleties are employed to increase the apparent width and dominance of the upper storey. The columns of the upper storey are of a smaller diameter, and their intercolumniation is greater, than those of the lower;

and the upper storey at 14.5 m (47½ ft) is 2 m (6½ ft) taller. More obviously, the central front breaks forward slightly; all the columns are detached from the wall; and the very large heraldic device crowning the building is framed by three encased pediments. The terminal columns, set back on a bevelled corner, alert the visitor approaching through the narrow streets on either side of the nave to the presence of an important building. PG

Loos, Adolf (1870–1933) Austrian architect and cultural theorist, whose polemical writings and thoughtful architecture continue to be highly regarded.

Loos's training was diverse and peripatetic: a bricklayer's certificate in his native Brno, crafts schools, military service, and studies at the esteemed Technische Hochschule, Dresden, and the Academy in Vienna. From 1893 to 1896 he travelled widely in the United States. His return to Vienna came in the midst of *Jugendstil enthusiasms and the emergence of the Vienna *Secession. Loos reacted strongly through effective cultural journalism (collected later as *Ins Leere gesprochen*, 1921, and *Trotzdem*, 1931). He deeply mistrusted appeals for a Gesamtkunstwerk as manifested in the dominating will to bring artistic form to the whole of life. His argument was telling against Jugendstil ornament and cultural ambitions, and Loos perceived that the same purportedly modern movements like the Werkbund would find success equally elusive. On the contrary, Loos urged simplicity, but also sought to discriminate and incorporate what was of value in tradition and social convention as well as in the recognizable imperatives of current changes in society and culture. Futurism had no hold on his thought.

Loos's cultural position is evident in two noted works of 1910 in Vienna. The interiors of the Steiner House accept the complexity of family life unfolding

Steiner House, Vienna (Adolf Loos, 1910)

according to diverse needs of various individuals engaged in the changes of day, season, and life span. While there is simplicity to the interiors, allied with Loos's Anglo-American proclivities, they incorporate various styles and standardized production. The human intimacy of the interiors is enveloped in such a decorous skin that the house is often misinterpreted as a forerunner of intentional architectural minimalism of the 1920s. Loos took the opposite strategy for the commercial/residential Haus am Michaelerplatz. Sited on a square opposite the Hofburg, Loos employed a classical order, cornice, and an orderly array of windows. The interior again reveals English sympathies, but the changes of level and robust detailing in simple, elegant materials are remarkably bold.

Thus in two works, interiors and exteriors are not only different by type and location, but even from the interior to the exterior of each building. Design decisions vary according to their position in what might be termed a complex cultural field. Loos and his friend the critic Karl Kraus spoke of accepting and maintaining the proper distinction between a funerary urn and a chamber pot—distinctions they did not trust historicists, Secessionists, or later the modernists, would maintain.

The spatial structure at Michaelerplatz—changes of level within a contained volume—was later developed in Loos's *Raumplan*, spatial development in the section of an otherwise confined volume. Seen as an affirmation of the autonomy of architectural space, this freedom was nonetheless to be employed to allow a building's inhabitants to live the culture of their time. Two brilliant products of this programme are the Moller House (Vienna, 1927–8) and the Müller House (Prague, 1928–30).   SA

Munch, Anders V., *Der stillose Stil—Adolf Loos* (2005)

Lorimer, Sir Robert Stoddart (1864–1929)

Scottish architect. At the beginning of the 20th century, Lorimer was the principal representative of 'Traditionalism', the Edinburgh offshoot of the Arts and Crafts and Domestic Revival movements. Trained chiefly by R. R. *Anderson, he began practice in the 1890s with a series of sensitively crafted houses and churches, notably Earlshall (a Fife castle restored and landscaped in 1890–94), and graduated in the post-1900 imperialistic years to a more bombastic rubble monumentality, exemplified in houses such as Ardkinglas (1905–7) and Formakin (1912–14). Greater scope for collaboration with artists came from ecclesiastical commissions, notably the Thistle Chapel, St Giles's Cathedral, Edinburgh (1909–11), but his crafts Gesamtkunstwerk tendency reached a climax of intensity in the secular setting of the Scottish National War Memorial (1924–7) at the summit of Edinburgh Castle. In the 1920s, alongside J. J. *Burnet, he was widely seen as a leader of Scottish architecture; his partnership, from 1927, with John F. Matthew (1875–1955) spawned, after his death, a new architectural dynasty of Edinburgh modernists led by Matthew's son Robert Hogg *Matthew.   MGl

Savage, P., *Lorimer and the Edinburgh Craft Designers* (1980)

Louis, Victor (1731–1800)

French neoclassical architect, trained at the Royal Academy school and in Rome (1756–9). He developed a private practice in Paris and in the provincial cities where he found his major commissions. Of these the most important is the grand theatre at Bordeaux (1770–78), with its portico of colossal Corinthian columns extended to the full width and continued by the pilasters of the rectangular perimeter, its monumental foyer staircase, square in plan, and its near-semicircular auditorium. Beside the Palais Royale in Paris he built the Comédie Française (from 1787) as part of an extensive development of shops and housing bordering an elongated *place*.   CT

lowside window

A window of uncertain origin and use, usually towards the western end of the south chancel wall of many English churches and a few in Normandy. Set lower than the main windows and so clearly not for lighting, such windows may have allowed those forbidden to enter the church to see the sacrament, and hence were formerly called leper windows. Perhaps they were intended for no more than general communication between the officiating priest and someone outside. Apparently originating in the 13th century, several examples of these windows retain hooks or other evidence of being unglazed and provided with shutters, as at Packwood church, Warwickshire.   APQ

Lubetkin, Berthold (1901–90)

Russian-born architect. A leading figure in the early Modern Movement in Britain, his practice Tecton was arguably the most accomplished exponent of the new style. Such works as the Penguin Pool, London Zoo (1934), Highpoint I (1935), and Finsbury Health Centre (1938) became icons of the period.

Lubetkin's experience of the Russian Revolution gave him a strong belief in architecture as an instrument of social progress, underlaid by a profound understanding of its formal disciplines and emotive power. His ten-year journey of self-education through Europe, culminating in Paris, where he achieved his first significant building (25 avenue de Versailles), gave him a pre-eminence and sophistication in the English context when he arrived in 1932.

His assured use of new building techniques, notably reinforced concrete (in fruitful collaboration with Ove *Arup), lifted his work—especially the virtuoso series of zoo buildings (London Zoo, 1934–8; Whipsnade, 1933–6; Dudley, 1936–7)—above a merely functionalist interpretation, and gave it a poetic quality symbolizing the optimism of the early movement. His dynamic use of geometry may be traced to his direct experience of *Constructivism, while his grounding in the classical tradition (he had studied with *Perret in Paris) also imbued his designs with a sense of order often underpinned by symmetrical planning.

Despite his fastidious and didactic attention to practical detail, Lubetkin's engagement with the formal obligations of architecture soon became controversial. Highpoint II (1936–8), which superseded the white monolithic aesthetic of its predecessor, Highpoint I, by using a richer range of materials, offended contemporary critical opinion in seeming to betray the *Functionalist cause—a judgement reinforced by the incorporation of classical Greek caryatid figures in the entrance porch. This building marked a transition point in the 1930s and anticipated the syntax of the next decade of British architecture.

Yet his most prolific output was still to come. For it was his public sector engagement by the determinedly socialist Finsbury Borough Council that provided Lubetkin with the opportunities he sought for social building, and served as the link between his pre- and post-war careers. Finsbury Health Centre—arguably the most complete synthesis of Modernism's social, technical, and aesthetic ideals to be achieved before the war—led to a series of substantial housing projects in the early period of reconstruction, e.g. Priory Green (1937–51) and Spa Green (1938–46) estates. These schemes further demonstrated Lubetkin's technical and compositional mastery, though his pre-eminence in British Modernism was by then being eclipsed by the oncoming generation.

The new town of Peterlee, to which he was appointed Architect Planner in 1947, should have been the culmination of his career, but the project became mired in technical difficulties and inter-departmental disputes. Having built nothing, he left in 1950, and resumed practice with Skinner and Bailey until the late 1960s. The Royal Gold Medal award in 1982 led to renewed acclaim, yet his unique contribution in demonstrating how the rational ideals of modern architecture could be fused with lyricism, humanity, and humour still remains to be fully appreciated. JAl

Luckhardt, Wassili (1889–1972) and **Hans** (1890–1954) German architects. They founded an architecture practice in 1924 with Alfons Anker (1872–1958). Prime exponents of the 'New Objectivity' (*Neue Sachlichkeit*), their first project was for a housing estate at Berlin-Dahlem, a very early example of the combination of rectangular blocks and bands of horizontal windows typical of this period of the *Modern Movement. All their pre-war work was in housing, but after 1945 they diversified into university and civic buildings. PG

Lurçat, André (1894–1970) French architect, city planner, and writer. Lurçat's work was wide-ranging, from furniture to urbanism. As a founding member of *CIAM, and a militant communist, his commitment to modern architecture as a vehicle for social reform was reflected in his numerous writings. In the mid 1920s he produced artist-studios reflective of the simplified functionalist aesthetic of *Le Corbusier, including those in the Villa Seurat in Paris, the Guggenbühl house

(1924–6), and the Nord-Sud Hotel in Calvi, Corsica (1929–31). His political position was manifested in his Karl Marx School (1931–3) in Villejuif, where his collaboration with specialists produced a progressive model of education. His increasing commitment to the socio-architectural concerns of the working class coincided with travels in the Soviet Union (1934–7). His treatise *Formes, compositions et lois d'harmonie* (1954) stresses the theme of monumentality. Following World War II he devised policies for post-war reconstruction in France, rebuilding Maubeuge (1946–50), and housing in Saint-Denis (1946–60). KMB

Lutyens, Sir Edwin Landseer (1869–1944)

English architect. It is not easy to appreciate Lutyens' great skills as an architect without over-reacting to the exaggerated claims made by his anti-modernist admirers. His *penchant* for architectural witticisms, in plan and detail, may have amused his contemporaries and delighted some later architectural historians, but too often seems merely arch whimsicality.

His early houses, which numbered about 30 (from 1896 to 1906), were inventive exercises in the *Arts and Crafts manner, beginning with Munstead Wood (1896), where he showed his ability to combine steeply pitched roofs, over-sized brick chimneys and leaded casement windows. Of these, the Deanery Garden (1899–1902), red brick and tiles, is the most representative example. During this period, his partnership with the garden designer Gertrude Jekyll (1843–1932) was of great importance, particularly for his understanding of how to set a house in its landscape.

Unfortunately one of their finest works, Hestercombe, Somerset (1906), was almost their last, as Lutyens' architecture took a completely different direction. In the same year, Lutyens now turned to the 'high game' of *Classicism (his own oxymoronic phrase) for a house at Heathcote, Ilkley, Yorkshire (1906), using an idiosyncratic version of the *Doric

order to organize the main façade. Playing this game meant that from this point Lutyens seemed to be less interested in integrating house and landscape.

Although he continued to design houses, including such fine examples as the Salutation, Sandwich, Kent (1911), Lutyens wished to apply his new enthusiasm on a different scale. Surprisingly, he did not obtain any commissions for the large public buildings being constructed in London at the time. Instead, his opportunity arose from two quarters: the planning and building of New Delhi, India; and a series of war memorials.

A diehard imperialist, Lutyens apparently found little to admire in Indian architecture. His bombastic design for the Viceroy's House, New Delhi (1912–30), is the perfect expression of a dying regime: large masses organized on an overpowering scale, with pastiches of 'Indian' elements, such as the small roof-top pavilions; and a symmetrical *Beaux Arts plan.

From 1917, he became one of the principal architects to the Imperial War Graves Commission, designing many of the cemeteries, the Cenotaph, Whitehall, London (1919–20), with its highly suitable use of *entasis, and the Thiepval Memorial (1927–32), in the form of a *triumphal arch. Because Lutyens did not have a literal understanding of Classicism, but valued its underlying geometric principles, his approach was ideally suited to abstract structures.

In the 1920s, Lutyens found a new application for his classicist principles, designing banks and offices, such as Britannic House, Finsbury Circus, London (1920–24), the Midland Bank, Piccadilly (1921–5), and its HQ in Poultry, London (1924–39). His great talent at modelling façades sometimes over-reached itself in resorting to optical subtleties, such as diminishing the width and set-backs of upper floors (the Midland Bank HQ), barely apparent even to the skilled viewer.

His largest project, for the Roman Catholic Cathedral, Liverpool (from 1929), which envisaged a

The main entrance, Viceroy House, Delhi (Sir Edwin Lutyens, 1912–30)

dome larger than St Peter's Rome, was not built, apart from a section of the crypt. PG

Butler, A. S. G., *The Architecture of Sir Edwin Lutyens* (1950)

L'viv *See* UKRAINE, L'VIV.

lyceum A place of study or instruction, named after the garden with covered walks in Athens where Aristotle taught his philosophy. It is practically synonymous with Athenaeum, which derives from the temple of Athene in ancient Athens, where professors taught their students, and orators and poets rehearsed their compositions. The name 'lyceum' was subsequently applied in Italy and Switzerland to certain universities, and by 1778 Germany had its Lyceum Fridericianum at Kassel, housed in a grand classical mansion at 47 Königsstrasse. In 1786 there was a lyceum in Paris where eminent professors lectured on literature and science. When Napoleon abolished ecclesiastical schools he replaced them with public lyceums or academies where secondary education was conducted, hence the term *lycée*. In England, the terms 'lyceum' and 'Athenaeum' were adopted early in the 19th century for both literary and scientific institutions

and the buildings in which they met. These comprised classrooms, lecture rooms and a library, and every town and city that aspired to the advancement of knowledge had one, usually designed in an appropriate neoclassical style. The United States rapidly followed suit: by 1820 there was a Lyceum of Natural History in New York. Another shift in meaning gave London its first Lyceum Theatre in 1816. APQ

Lyle, John (1872–1945) The paradigm of the Canadian architect in the early 20th century, John Lyle sought 'Modernism' within tradition—'look[ing] at the modern movement as a new spirit of design and a release from the historical styles of the past', while avoiding the excesses of 'the extreme modernist of the engineering view-point'. Lyle's solution lay in 'fresh, vital, contemporary decoration'. Trained at the Ecole des Beaux-Arts in Paris and then with several New York classicists, his development is seen in a series of buildings for the Bank of Nova Scotia. The Georgian Revival bank at St Andrews, New Brunswick (1920), and the robust neoclassical bank in Ottawa, Ontario (1923–4), were followed by the flatter and tauter bank in Calgary, Alberta (1929–30), which featured low-relief ornament with western Canadian subjects: prairie flowers, Aboriginal people, mounted police, horses, buffalo, and oil. This search for a regional and national expression peaked in his head office for the bank in Halifax, Nova Scotia (with Andrew Cobb, 1930), whose gracious banking hall is resplendent in decorative symbols and scenes. This was the prototype for modern *Classicism, reducing form to essentials and expressing volume rather than mass. HK

Hunt, G(eoffrey), *John M. Lyle* (1982)

Mackintosh, Charles Rennie (1868–1928)
Scottish architect. The work of Mackintosh, chiefly
carried out in partnership with John Honeyman
(1831–1914) and John Keppie (1863–1945), and in
collaboration with Mackintosh's wife, Margaret
Macdonald (1865–1913), formed a Glasgow branch
of the international *Art Nouveau, Jugendstil and
*Secession movements. He intensified the Aesthetic
Movement's rejection of public monumentality and
the worship of the home into a highly charged, total
artistic vision. Rejecting conventional historicist
façade ornament, Mackintosh proclaimed in 1902 that
his 'modern individual art', with its 'hallucinating
character', was 'like an escape into the mountain air
from the stagnant vapours of a morass'. His new,
personal style was made up of natural and symbolist
elements; initially, in the 1880s and early 1890s, they
were curved or sinuous in character, but later, in the
late 1900s, they changed to a more geometrical,
rectangular character. His work with Honeyman and
Keppie included various interior schemes for houses
and tearooms; several complete villas; and a small
number of public, religious, and commercial buildings,
including his chief work, Glasgow School of Art (from
1896).

Mackintosh insisted on a sharp contrast between the
architecture of his exteriors and interiors. The former
were relatively conventional, late offspring of Scottish
Baronial, with Arts and Crafts touches. It was halfway
in character between the Scottish work of *Lorimer
and the more English Arts and Crafts work of *Lethaby
and *Voysey—or James McLaren (1853–90). His first

works for Honeyman and Keppie combined classical regularity with *Arts and Crafts or *Art Nouveau features—for example, the sinuously ornamented corner tower of the 1893–4 *Glasgow Herald* building. At Glasgow School of Art's original block (1896–9), Mackintosh exploited the steeply sloping site with Baronial drama, with dramatic projecting rear wings, and an asymmetrical Arts and Crafts entrance porch between big, asymmetrical studio windows on the north façade. At Queen's Cross Church, 1897, Mackintosh combined Arts and Crafts and Art Nouveau details. His domestic work, externally, combined a geometrical 'simplicity' (based on harling or roughcasting) with elements of Baronial drama, in houses like Windyhill, Kilmacolm (1899), and Hill House, Helensburgh (1902–4). His influential 'Art Lover's House' ideal-home design of 1901 was more symmetrical, like a 17th-century laird's house.

In Mackintosh's interiors, the traditional stylistic contrasts between spaces, especially dark 'masculine' and light 'feminine' ones, became more abstract and formal, including carefully positioned pieces by himself and Macdonald. The main series of interiors started in the late 1890s, including the Kate Cranston Tearooms. Pre-eminent among these was the Willow Tearooms of 1903: its Secession-style asymmetrical rendered frontage gave access to spaces dramatically contrasted by shape and lighting, including the jewel-like upper-floor 'Salon de Luxe', with symbolist gesso panel by Macdonald. The 'Art Lover's House' drawings took to a climax the polarization of dark and light rooms, with its panelled, sombre dining room and its airy, swirling music room.

Mackintosh's last works, from 1905 onwards, echoed idiosyncratically the 'return to order' unleashed by *Burnet and the later Edwardian classicists. The west wing which completed the Glasgow School of Art (1905–9) was built in a more formal, linear manner, by

The library block, Glasgow School of Art, Renfrew Street, Glasgow (Charles Rennie Mackintosh, from 1896)

comparison with the earlier parts of the school, its dramatic west façade featuring a line of tall, gridded oriels. Behind these oriels, the new college library was a complex space, defined by a grid of gables, projecting columns, and geometrical, boxy light fittings, decorated with incised panels of almost *Art Deco character.

He adopted a more geometrical, grid-like way of subdividing space in his later interiors of 1910–11 at

Ingram Street tearooms, and presaged the complexities of Cubism in his remodelling of 78 Derngate, Northampton (1916). All in all, while Mackintosh's work anticipated some key aspects of the Modern Movement—notably its more 'poetic' elements—it remained still firmly bedded in the bold individualism of the late 19th century. Thereafter his architectural practice ceased, and he concentrated on his drawings and watercolours.　　　　MGl

Howarth, T., *Charles Rennie Mackintosh and the Modern Movement* (1952)

Maclure, Samuel (1860–1929) Canadian architect. *See* CANADA.

Madeira was colonized by the Portuguese following its discovery at the beginning of the 15th century. Funchal, founded as a small village soon after the discovery, was granted the title of *vila* in 1451, then *cidade* in 1508 because of its rapid expansion, the most important settlement on the island. It is the largest city and has a distorted grid pattern dating from the period of transition to the Renaissance. This is now the historical centre of the city with a typical main street (*rua Direita*, *rua da Alfandega*) connecting the small squares (*Largos*) and the municipal square (*Pelourinho*). Its special feature is the observation towers, erected over the manor houses, sometimes with several floors, and oriented towards the sea, due to the needs of the maritime trade.

Both urban and rural architecture used only volcanic stone (grey and brown basalt), plastered and whitewashed when used for walls. This practice, which dates from the earliest period, is certainly due to the persistence of the stone-building tradition, brought over from the Iberian peninsula. Wood (*madeira*, in Portuguese) was used only for floors and roofs (covered with tiles).

Vernacular rural houses once used straw-covered roofs, but today they survive only in the Santana area, on the north coast. In the 1980s there still existed some houses (in the village of Caniçal) with the old system of a separate kitchen.　　　　JMF

Maderno, Carlo (*c*.1556–1629) Italian architect and engineer. His was a bright talent in a very dull period for Roman architecture (roughly 1570–1620), though he often worked under considerable constraints.

The façade of S. Susanna (1597–1603) appears at first sight to be a conventional Counter-Reformation façade of the type initiated by *della Porta a generation earlier, at Il Gesù. But closer inspection shows that the façade appears to have a more vertical orientation. The effect is achieved by the narrowing of the S-shaped scrolls on the much abbreviated outer bay, and the forward thrust of the pilasters and engaged columns, which project further from the wall than those of the earlier church. However, the differences are not decisive, and have perhaps been exaggerated by historians anxiously looking for precursors of the *Baroque.

In 1604, Maderno was appointed Architect of St Peter's, a timely appointment as the newly elected pope, Paul V (1605–21), was determined to complete the rebuilding of the cathedral. In September 1607 it was decided to accept the principles of the *Counter-Reformation and transform the centralized plan of *Bramante and *Michelangelo into a Latin cross by adding a nave. Maderno's design for a three-bay nave was approved in 1608, and built 1609–15. Although in itself the nave is rather squat (about 76 m or 250 ft wide and 85 m or 280 ft long), and is poorly scaled, the barrel-vaulted roof, with the piers faced by pilasters, blends most harmoniously with the earlier building.

For the façade, Maderno faithfully replicated the *order, scale, and many of the elements of Michelangelo's design. He made one felicitous addition: low columns set into the three main doorways, which humanized the scale of the adjacent giant orders. Unfortunately, in 1613–15, Maderno had to add outer bays to support campanili, which in the end were never built. As a result the proportions of the façade were disastrously changed, over-emphasizing its width.

Maderno's most important secular work was the Palazzo Mattei di Giove, Rome (begun 1598). The façade is exceedingly humdrum, but the plan is inventive. Set on a corner site, the place had two entrances, one on the axis of the court, the other leading to an ingenious arrangement of staircases, creating surprising vistas. Shortly before his death, he planned the layout of the Palazzo Barberini (begun 1628), exceptional among Roman palaces in that it consisted of a single block with projecting wings, rather than the usual courtyard layout. However, his contribution to the detailing of the façades cannot be securely established. PG

madrasa Literally 'place of study', or an institutional residence for students, teachers, and visiting scholars. Typically the plan consists of a series of collegiate rooms arranged in 2 storeys around an open rectangular or square courtyard. In some instances, an enclosed teaching hall and library located on the ground level form one side of the building.

The popularity of the madrasa as a significant institutional development in the 11th century signifies a period of intellectual and religious achievement which reoriented Islamic scholarship across the Islamic world. Studies in Islamic law, Hadith, and Qur'an reading would occur in the side niches which accommodated circular groupings of students and teachers seated on raised carpeted platforms. Teaching niches were emphasized by the *iwan, a highly decorated and architecturally distinguished frame centred on the interior side of the building façade, raising the height of

the façade to extend above the roof. The *qibla iwan typically was given more prominence than the other three *iwans*. The madrasa became integrated with mosques, funerary monuments, sabils, and hospitals such as the Sultan al-Mu'ayyad Shaykh Complex, Cairo (1415–122).

Saljuq vizier Nizam-al-Mulk is recognized for the founding of the madrasa in 1055 as a means of revitalizing Orthodox Islam, which had become diluted during the Fatimid and Bybid reign. Originating in Iran and Khorasan, the first madrasa was endowed as a private residential institution dedicated to Islamic legal scholarship. The Khorasan madrasa became a model for similar religious educational endowments in other cities, symbolizing the importance of religious scholarship. The first madrasa arrived in Cairo in 1175, and by the 15th century 73 were to be found in the city. The first madrasa in Mecca was founded in 1175, and in 1200 Baghdad contained 20 madrasas. DM

Bulliet, Richard W., *Islam: the view from the edge* (1994)

Maekawa, Kunio (1905–86) Japanese architect. After an apprenticeship with *Le Corbusier (1928–30) and Antonin *Raymond (1930–35), Maekawa rose to prominence as an advocate of modern architecture within a regressive nationalist and traditionalist climate during the 1930s and 1940s. In the post-war period, Maekawa extended Le Corbusier's model of the Unité d'Habitation (1945–52), Marseilles, to integrate Japanese domestic living successfully within his monumental housing block at Harumi, Tokyo (1956–8). He further designed extensions to Le Corbusier's Museum of Western Art (1957–9) and designed his own adjacent monumental concrete Metropolitan Festival Hall (1958–61). Throughout his designs of residential, commercial, and governmental buildings, Maekawa sought to address regional context through a 'technical approach' embodied in his use of *in situ* concrete faced with domestically produced ceramic-tile-set precast panels that could resist rain and earthquakes and imbue local colour.   KTO

Maiano, Giuliano da (1432–90) Italian architect. His first large-scale architectural work was the Chapel of Santa Fina, San Gimignano (1466); his design of Faenza Cathedral (1474–86) reflects *Brunelleschi's Florentine churches in its modular plan and use of sail vaulting. His Palazzo Spanocchi in Siena (1473–5) recalls the Florentine Palazzo Rucellai by *Alberti in its façade rustication, 3-storey façade and *all'antica* cornice. From 1485 to 1490 Giuliano worked in Naples for Alfonso II, completing the imposing, classicizing gateway of the Porta Capuana (1485), and the villa of Poggioreale (begun 1487, destroyed) whose form, a rectangular plan, with interior courtyard, corner towers, and loggias opening onto the extensive gardens, was widely influential.   ACH

Maillart, Robert (1872–1940) Swiss engineer, who invented flat slab construction. By designing the location and size of reinforcement in concrete slabs to respond to specific loading conditions, he eliminated the need for beams. Working on the design of multi-storey industrial buildings, he introduced a two-axis system where loads flowed continuously from column to floor slab. In 1910 Maillart used this system in his design for a warehouse in Zurich where each of the columns had a mushroom head connected to a flat slab. He also developed a series of monolithic reinforced concrete frames for single-storey factories that allowed the introduction of generous roof lights and good daylighting at the Pirelli Factory in Villanueva and the Benet spinning mill in Barcelona.

However it was Maillart's design of elegant long spanning bridges, where the integration of horizontal and vertical slabs created a series of slender and elegant structures, which established an impressive and widely recognized new aesthetic for concrete. Early designs like the Tavanasa Bridge over the Rhine at Grisons (1905) spanned 51 m (167 ft), and subsequent examples include the bridge at Schwandbach (1922) and the bridge at Lachen (1940) which spanned 40 m (131 ft) over the railway line from Zurich to Arlberg.   BC

Billington, D., *Robert Maillart* (1990)

maintenance, design for Buildings of every kind require maintenance. However well constructed, they will gradually show the effects of weathering, pollution, insect and fungus attack, and general wear and tear. The way they are designed can help limit the onset of such effects; it can also anticipate the need for future maintenance by making all parts of a building easy to access, inspect, and repair.

When maintenance is talked about, what is generally referred to is the exterior skin of a building—walls, roof, and windows. But maintenance also includes the renewal of decoration and furnishings, and the replacement of building services—the pipes, ducts, and wires which help create a livable interior environment. In some cases the building structure itself requires maintenance, especially if the exterior skin has failed to protect it from the weather and other forms of attack.

The maintenance of these different facets of a building takes place over different time cycles. Generally a building is redecorated more often than it has its services renewed. Similarly, exterior maintenance seldom takes place all at once: window-cleaning may occur frequently, while other tasks, such as the replacement of a roof covering, may only happen once in fifty years. The major overhaul of a building's structure, which may occur at any time after about twenty-five years, is more an admission that the design hasn't worked than a part of the regular maintenance cycle that could have been anticipated. Generally buildings are designed on the assumption that the structure will never change, even if everything else in the building is renewed.

571

Most forms of traditional construction throughout the world have taken account of how a building will be maintained. This is evident in three ways: the overall design, which aims to minimize the effects of weathering and thus the need for maintenance; the selection of materials; and the forms of construction and exterior coating. In design the most obvious techniques are those used to reduce the effects of rain and snow on a building, by the use of eaves and moulded entablatures which throw water away from the wall. Also the design of the wall is not just to provide enclosure, but to help protect the building structure from deterioration. In regions where the effects of wind or vermin attack are major anxieties, traditional design similarly aims to anticipate such problems.

In the selection of materials, in most places throughout history it has been customary to use whatever comes most readily to hand. That makes future maintenance easier, because the original source of timber, stone or brick is often still available if parts of a building have to be renewed. This continuity between the original form of construction and the subsequent maintenance makes it difficult to detect the phases of renewal in historic buildings.

Most significantly, traditional construction takes account of the quality of available materials by giving them where necessary a protective coating. Thus stonework, plaster, and timber have often been limewashed, a form of coating which protects the wall while allowing it to breathe. The rendering of brick or stonework, and the painting of exterior paintwork, are other examples of sacrificial finishes which can be renewed. In constructing brick walls, the use of lime mortar provides another form of sacrificial layer. As well as allowing water to evaporate through it, the lime mortar can easily be renewed by repointing without damaging or replacing the bricks.

The virtue of many of these forms of construction is that they are visible and accessible (e.g. the Great Mosque at Jenne, Mali). However there are aspects of traditional construction which have proved more problematic in the long run, generally the result of an attempt to achieve certain aims of architectural form and proportion. Thus in the typical English terraced house, the use of hipped roofs running at right angles to the frontage, hidden behind a parapet, creates the problem of a gutter which is hidden from view.

The onset of industrialization in the 18th century created new issues for building maintenance. First, industrial pollution accelerated the decay of certain materials, especially more porous kinds of stone, and thus encouraged the search for more resistant materials. The increasing use of terracotta and faience in the second half of the 19th century in England, America, and elsewhere was one result. Secondly, industrialization enabled traditional materials to be produced more efficiently and transported over large distances, as well as transforming the use of materials such as iron, steel, and glass. The effect was to permit the design of buildings of unprecedented scale, often without consideration for their future maintenance. As with traditional construction, where materials are visible and can be coated or repaired they have given less trouble than when they are hidden within the structure. Thus iron and steel perform well while properly treated—hence the cyclical painting of the Forth Railway Bridge (1882–90)—but when used with concrete in fireproof floor construction they are vulnerable to damp or chemical attack from the concrete. The growing use of reinforced concrete at the end of the 19th century also took place before its long-term performance was fully understood.

The third impact of industrialization was on building services. The location of chimneys and open fires had been fundamental to building layout, but now there were other services to be threaded through a building—plumbing for baths and lavatories, gas (for lighting from the 1840s and for cooking from the 1890s), electricity (from the 1880s, but most commonly in the 1920s and 1930s), and hot water central heating. A typical house in Britain, Europe, or North America had the capacity to absorb these changes without a fundamental redesign, but large industrial and institutional buildings were increasingly designed with building services and their maintenance in mind. This was especially true of forced air ventilation systems, as at the Houses of Parliament (1835–60), and the subsequent development of fully air-conditioned office structures in North America in the 1920s.

While the advance of steel and reinforced concrete continued throughout the 20th century, scarcity of labour and materials, plus a commitment to new technologies born of war-time experience, led to the adoption of other innovations in building; for instance, in concrete the use of pre-stressing and shell construction, and in glass the development of the curtain wall and the structural use of glass, both of them merging the distinction between wall and window. These have taken construction far beyond the normal realms of building maintenance, since the long-term durability of pre-stressing cables or silicone joints for glass walls is still not fully understood. Above all, through Europe and North America after World War II there was a commitment to the factory-based production of standardized building components, without a comparable commitment to how they were assembled and connected on site. The partial collapse in 1968 of a housing block in East London of concrete panel construction showed just how vulnerable such systems were.

At the same time, more purely aesthetic considerations have generated modern architectural forms which disregard the lessons of traditional construction. The classics of the early Modern Movement, such as the villas of Le Corbusier, abandoned the principle of projections to throw off rainwater and other weathering details in favour of the pure flat wall, rational and undefiled. But one strand of the Modern Movement, the high tech group of British architects which first came to notice in the 1960s, has sought to develop an aesthetic which instead of turning its back on the needs of maintenance and adaptability expresses their primacy. In the Pompidou Centre, Paris (Piano and Rogers, 1970–77), and in its later progeny, the traditional building hierarchy is inverted by the prominence given to building services and flexible interior spaces.

The considerations which influenced such high tech designs have also led, amongst the developers of commercial buildings and their advisers, to a more sophisticated understanding of building maintenance. What is known as life-cycle costing involves a calculation of the time-span of each part of a building—furnishings, services, communications, and structure—to arrive at a summary of its long-term value. Similarly, but for different reasons, exponents of sustainable design seek to calculate the energy costs involved in construction, and in the replacement of buildings, to justify designs which make low demands on maintenance and repair. These incentives coincide with the interest of building conservationists in minimizing the loss of historic fabric and erosion of the building's character. Thus maintenance, which once was a natural consideration in how buildings were designed and put together, has been brought to the forefront again in the world of construction.   RT

Brand, S., *How Buildings Learn. What Happens After They're Built* (1994)

Maki, Fumihiko (1928–) Japanese architect, educator, urban planner, and writer. While resolutely modernist, Maki's architecture seeks to stage 'unforgettable scenes' to construct spaces for human activity rather than monumental forms. Maki was educated at the University of Tokyo under Kenzô

*Tange, Cranbrook, and Harvard University, then worked with José Lluis Sert and SOM before establishing his own office. As a member of the *Metabolist group, Maki pursued the notion of 'group' or 'collective' form, rather than the megastructural schemes of his co-members (see his *Investigations in Collective Form*, 1964), as embodied in his design for Hillside Terrace, Tokyo (1969, 1973, 1976, 1992), built as a complex of commercial and residential buildings over three decades.

Maki's designs are primarily urban and public, spanning the typologies of museums, universities, libraries, gymnasiums, and exhibition halls. Since the 1980s, Maki pursued the effect of lightness in his designs through the manipulation of light and meticulous attention to detailing evident in his stainless steel shell roof gymnasiums at Fujisawa and Makuhari. His masterworks include the Spiral Building, Tokyo (1985), a multi-use cultural complex whose façade and spatial organization are a heterogeneous collage of elements reflecting its urban context, and the Kaze-no-Oka Crematorium (1997), integrated into a park-like setting.   KTO

Taylor, J., *The Architecture of Fumihiko Maki* (2003)

Makiya, Mohamed Saleh (1914–) The

dominating force for the renewal of architecture in Iraq and in the Arab World. His early buildings, such as the Khulafa Mosque in Baghdad (1960–65), demonstrate a programmatic attempt to unite tradition and contemporary requirements, which has been continued in his bank buildings in Kerbala and Al-Kufa (both 1968). The most significant, still unbuilt project by Makiya is the Headquarters for the Arab League, first designed for Baghdad and later for Tunis. The architectural excellence and political relevance of the design have been seen as a symbol of the aspirations of the Arab countries, inherent in the integration of administration offices, a congress hall, lounges,

reception halls, and housing for the ministers and ambassadors.   UK

Makovecz, Imre (1935–) Hungarian architect.

Opposing Communist Hungary's regimented architectural profession and expression, he gradually developed an individual form of organic architecture. His art and philosophy owes much to Rudolf Steiner's idea of anthroposophy, many of his buildings assuming zoomorphic and even antropomorphic features. He designed ski shelters and other small-scale structures for a forestry in his early career, and wood has remained his favourite material ever since. He prefers to design buildings for small towns and villages, such as communitiy centres and churches, even if the latter do not lack certain references to Hungary's pagan past. The mortuary chapel of Farkasrét Cemetery in Budapest (1975–7), with its evocation of a rib-cage, exerts a striking, even haunting effect. Makovecz achieved international acclaim with the Hungarian pavilion he built for Seville's 1992 World Fair. The huge bulbous, wooden structure, surmounted by seven spire-like towers, accommodating even a barren tree with its roots exposed under a glass floor, was a metaphor of Hungary's history. In 1992 his office lauched in Piliscsaba the reconstruction and enlargement of former military barracks into the campus of Pázmány Péter Catholic University, whose impressive main building, called Stephaneum, is composed of natural as well as historically evocative forms.   JS

Malaysia The earliest buildings of the indigenous

people were strongly influenced by Austronesian sea migrations; by the kingdom of Patani in Thailand; and by the Minangkerbau from Sumatra. Hindu–Buddhist beliefs were conveyed to the peninsula in the period 500–1300, and Islam was introduced by Arab and Indian merchants in the 14th century. European influences arrived with the Portuguese who conquered Melaka in 1511. St Paul's Church (1521) was erected with stones from the demolished Melaka Sultanate palace. The Portuguese were ousted by the Dutch in 1641, who occupied Melaka until the end of the Napoleonic Wars in 1824, when the British set up the Straits Settlements of Penang, Melaka, and Singapore. The ubiquitous shophouse was introduced in the early 19th century by immigrants from southern China.

The British brought with them European Classicism together with Indian and Mughal influences. Two significant buildings in Kuala Lumpur were the Secretariat Building, now known as Bangunan Sultan Abdul (Spooner and Bidwell, 1894–7), and the Railway Station (Hubback, 1911).

The Anglo-Oriental Building (1936–40) signalled the arrival of Art Deco, followed by the International Style (Iverson, 1951). Malaysia gained independence in 1957 and several buildings expressed its new status: the Stadium Merdaka (1957); the Parliament House (1963); and the National Mosque (1965), a mixture of Islamic and modernist principles.

The skyline of the capital changed dramatically in the 1980s. The 45-storey Menara Maybank (1987) designed by Hijjas Kasturi took as its precedent a Malay dagger or *keris*. The Dayabumi Complex (1984) by MAA and BEP Architects also used Islamic references in a modern form. Other Malaysian cities also saw significant changes. The 65-storey Komtar project (1976–87), designed by Jurubena Bertiga, transformed the centre of Penang, while the Sabah Foundation Building (1977) by James Ferrie and Partners dominated the skyline of Kota Kinabalu.

Reaction to rapid change came in the form of vernacular revivalism, when a Malaysian identity in architecture was sought. This was evident in the design of the Sabah Museum (1984) in Kota Kinabalu. The destruction of Malaysia's built heritage led, in 1983, to the formation of Badan Warisan Malaysia, a non-government organization that has had some success in raising the level of appreciation of historic buildings. The conservation of Cheong Fatt Tze Mansion (1989–2000) in Penang by Lawrence Low is a brilliant example of this raised consciousness.

Houses are frequently the most powerful indicators of cultural change. Significant examples are the Salinger House (1993) in Bangi by Jimmy C. S. Lim and the Sek San House (2000) at Serendah by Ng Sek San. Tourism plays an important role in the Malaysian economy, and pre-eminent amongst the impressive resort architecture is The Datai (1993) in Langkawi by Kerry Hill Architects.

In the late 1990s mega projects were driven by spectacular economic growth. Kuala Lumpur International Airport (1998) was conceptualized by Kisho Kurokawa and is carved out of the jungle 50 km (31 miles) south of the capital. The gigantic Petronas Twin Towers (*Pelli, 1997–9) has a form derived from an Islamic pattern, with two interlocking squares modified by eight semicircles in the corners. Ken Yeang is the principal advocate of bio-climatic architecture. His seminal projects are the Menara Mesiniaga (1992) in Kuala Lumpur and Menara Umno (1998) in Penang.

RP

Chen Voon Fee, *The Encylopedia of Malaysia: Architecture* (1998)

Mali *See* AFRICA (THE TRIPLE HERITAGE CONCEPT).

Mallet-Stevens, Robert (1886–1945) French architect and designer. Mallet-Stevens, a representative of avant-gardist design in France in the 1920s and 30s, designed a wide range of work, from film sets and furniture to private homes and apartment buildings. Employing a variety of materials (especially steel and other metals) within a diverse array of cultural and artistic influences, such as painting and contemporary music, he was especially adept at uniting architecture with the decorative arts. He is particularly recognized for the *ensemble* of five houses on the road that bears his name in the 16th *arrondissement* of Paris (1926–27). This *ensemble* was influenced by the Cubist vanguard, with open living spaces, accessible terraces, and a play of cubic volumes, yet with an aesthetic uniformity on the street façade, and it was intended as a prototype of the modern street. Mallet-Stevens was a founder of the Union des Artistes Modernes in Paris (1929). His collaboration with artists is reflected in works such as the De Noailles villa in Hyères (1923), where he worked with Frantz Jourdain and Pierre Chareau; and the Art Deco tourism pavilion for the1925 Exposition Internationale des Arts Décoratifs in Paris. He exhibited internationally and wrote numerous books and articles.   KMB

   Pinchon, Jean-François, *Robert Mallet-Stevens* (2000)

Malta Colonized from Sicily *c.*5000 BC, the inhabitants of Malta were building some of the most extraordinary monuments of the Mediterranean by 3500 BC. For a thousand years these so-called 'temples' exploited a basic apsidal form created in cyclopic masonry, probably with corbelled-in roofs, long before either the Egyptian pyramids or Britain's Stonehenge, and indeed they go beyond both in architectural sophistication. The 'temple', built *c.*3500 BC at Ggantija near Xaghra, Gozo, comprises a central passage with a well-formed doorway, off which open a pair of flanking apses, and, after a short interval, three terminal apses, like a cloverleaf, the whole apparently being roofed. Before it is a curved wall flanking the entrance, this and a second similar 'temple' being enclosed by a megalithic wall up to 7 m (23 ft) high. Solar alignments between the entrances and various inner features, though perhaps coincidental, may be evidence of cult use, as are furnishings including possible altars. Clearly related to Ggantija and temple groups at Hagar Qim, Mnajdra, Bor-in-Nadur, and nearby at Tarxien, among many others, is the remarkable Hypogeum at Hal

Saflieni. This is an underground system of chambers, used as an ossuary, cut out to resemble the apses of the 'temples'. Its continuing development, like the construction of the temples, was interrupted suddenly *c.*2500 BC, and Malta's unique prehistory fades from sight.

   What came later is a reflection of the history of an island that grew in strategic importance. Roman villas, Roman Melita, and Christian catacombs have their place in Mediterranean history, as do the Venetian Gothic palaces at Mdina and Victoria. The Knights of St John and their heroic defence of the island against the Turks in the Great Siege of 1565 led to the immediate construction of the immense fortifications around Grand Harbour. Francesco Laparelli assisted with the fortified city of Valletta, its characteristic bastions and a rebuilt Fort St Elmo facing the sea. Only at the end of the 17th century was the promontory of Vittorioso similarly fortified, and Fort St Angelo rebuilt. The Order of St John built what is now Valletta Cathedral to a domed Italian Baroque design by Girolamo Cassar in 1572–7. Meanwhile the Grand Master and the various nations of the Order built themselves Italianate palaces around cool courtyards. Interestingly, the Manoel Theatre is one of only four in Europe to survive intact from the 18th century. Every parish has a church of Jesuit pattern with a crossing dome and western towers—Xewkija church is a replica of the Salute in Venice—and in such number that no view of Malta lacks a handful of them. Because of Malta's tempting strategic importance, the Order built square forts around the island too, the first six of them *c.*1609–20. In 1878–86 the British built immense gun emplacements, but the second siege, of 1940–43, is marked by another underground system of chambers, one that provided command posts, shelters, hospitals, and indeed the homes of the Maltese who survived the intense bombardment of World War II.   APQ

   Hughes, Q(uentin), *Malta* (1978)
   Trump, D. H., *Malta: Prehistory and Temples* (2002)

Mannerism Together with '*Baroque' and '*Gothic', 'Mannerism' is one of the most carelessly applied terms used to characterize architectural movements, buildings, or details of buildings. It is a product of the formalist approach adopted by German historians, such as Wölfflin, at the end of the 19th century. More carefully defined, it does not mean simply 'distorted', 'disproportional' or 'abnormal', but the *conscious* distortion of elements of *Classicism to achieve a bizarre effect or to make a learned witticism. On this strict definition, the term only applies to the architecture of *Giulio Romano, and possibly to some elements of *Michelangelo's architecture. *Artisan Mannerism is quite different, as it is based on a *lack* of knowledge of the principles of *Classicism.   PG

Mansart, François (1598–1666) is generally recognized as the greatest 17th-century French architect, who laid the foundations for the hybrid Baroque–classical style evolved for the mature Louis XIV. Trained in the building craft traditions, he is not known to have travelled abroad.

The mantle of the early classical masters, inherited from de *Brosse, had passed to Mansart by the 1630s (Feuillants church façade, 1623; the chateaux of Berny and Balleroy, 1623, 1626). He continued de Brosse's experiments with the logical and coherent approach to articulation promoted by *Lescot and *De l'Orme. He was clearly impressed with the conception of de Brosse's late secular works as discrete entities, but, constrained by existing work at Berny, his roofs assert the autonomy of the parts in the manner of *Du Cerceau. At Balleroy, however, there are no wings and a clear hierarchy in the massing of the main block is entirely untrammelled with ornament. On the other hand, his early Parisian altar designs (St-Martin-des-Champs, 1624; Notre Dame, 1628) suggest that he was familiar with the books of G. B. Montano (such as *Scielta di varii tempietti antichi*, 1624). By 1632, in a

centralized scheme inspired by De l'Orme, he was experimenting with ovoid spaces and vertical perspectives for the Parisian church of the Visitation.

In his additions to the chateau of Blois (1635–8) and his unconstrained work at Maisons (1642–51), as in his later Parisian churches (Val-de-Grâce, 1645–6; Minimes, 1657), he gave the fullest expression to the qualities generally associated with the French classical spirit of the 17th century—concentration by the elimination of inessentials, clarity combined with subtlety, restraint in ornament with richness in planar variation, obedience to a strict code of rules but flexibility within them. Nowhere is balance between delight in variety (characteristic of the French tradition) and the classical will to unify more triumphantly effected than at Maisons, his masterpiece—though some observers find the disparity in roofing more awkward than at Blois where the type traditionally associated with 'Mansard' predominates. Though the planning is conservative in retaining the traditional enfilade, in a way utterly characteristic of his individualism, much of the work there and at Blois reveals a command of Baroque techniques concurrently being evolved in Rome: vigorous contrast in the contours of walls and the profiles of masses, colossal scale, alignment of varied space shapes to provide rich vistas both horizontally and vertically, and dramatic lighting. Then, as at Balleroy, landscaping on a monumental scale anticipated the later achievements of A. Le Nôtre.

Mansart's fortunes suffered a sharp reversal when in 1646 he was dismissed by the crown (on behalf of the Queen Mother, Anne of Austria) from the Val-de-Grâce commission, for which he was evolving a variation on Palladio's scenographic Redentore associated with an extensive convent-palace: his project arrested, he was given the opportunity to realize it in miniature at Fresnes, where the vertical perspective and the extension through it of the movement of figures represented in painting and sculpture

Main façade, Château Balleroy, Calvados, France (François Mansart, 1623, 1626)

anticipated Bernini. The problem for the crown commissioners was Mansart's inability to draw the creative process to a practical conclusion. Likewise, a controlled flood of astonishing invention led to his exclusion from the major project of his late years, the completion of the square court of the Louvre, and his failure to realize the funerary chapel at Saint-Denis commissioned by Louis XIV for the Bourbon dynasty.

Mansart had an extensive private practice, largely involving work on existing courtyard houses (Hôtel de la Vrillière, 1635; St-Paul, 1642; Tubeuf, 1644; Nevers, 1648, etc.). Adhering to the enfilade tradition here too (until the unconstrained Hôtel de Jars, 1648), he proved himself particularly adept at dramatizing staircases, siting them to avoid interference with ground-floor communication, and at conjuring symmetry from disparate axes. Judicious sleight-of-hand set an important precedent at the Hôtel Guénégaud des Brosses (c.1653)—one of his few unconstrained exercises. *Pavillons* and *corps de logis* subsist, but the elements are assimilated by the roof line (in the form traditionally identified as 'Mansard'), and articulation is

confined to rustication and plain rectangular window frames: the rustication appears as quoins on the side pavilions, but on the central frontispieces (as at the Hôtel Carnavalet 1660–61) it is masked by shallow panels punctuated by the fenestration, the implied continuity suggesting greater strength than is actually revealed. Not lost on Jules *Hardouin-Mansart, in all essentials this anticipated the 18th-century concept of *noble simplicité*. CT

Braham, A., and Smith, P., *François Mansart* (1973)

Mansart, Jules Hardouin *See* HARDOUIN-MANSART, JULES.

Mansfeld, Al (1912–2003) Israeli architect. Born in Leningrad, he studied in Berlin 1931–3 and Paris 1933–5, where he was a student of August *Perret. Mansfeld moved to Palestine in 1935, and from 1937 to 1959 he worked in partnership with Munio Weinraub-Gitai, who had studied with *Mies van der Rohe in the Bauhaus. Their projects include the dining hall at Kibbutz Hazorea (1950), a memorial to the fallen of Israel's War of Independence at Kiryat Haim (1948–53), the Administration and Library Building at Yad Vashem—the National Holocaust Memorial in Jerusalem (1953)—and the Mazer Building at the Hebrew University of Jerusalem (1959). That year he entered a planning competition for the Israel Museum with Dora Gad, and they won first prize. The building was dedicated in 1965—and construction continued until 1994. Mansfeld and Gad achieved international fame for the way the construction blended into the landscape and made provision for expansion by means of modular units. Mansfeld considered the Israel Museum, the Carmel Auditorium, and the Jerusalem Municipality unbuilt compound as concrete examples of his ideas on Structuralism: designing for growth, change, and uncertainty.   ML

Anna Teut (ed.), *Al Mansfeld, An architect in Israel* (1999)

Manueline   A style named after King Manuel I of Portugal (r.1495–1521). It has been variously interpreted as: a mixture of late Gothic and Renaissance forms, together with unorthodox decorative elements; a 'Lusitanian-Moorish' style (South Portugal); and an 'Atlantic Baroque' (the Azores). But in the author's view, the essence of Manueline was its experimental aspect, looking for new and rational rules of building, using clear and elementary geometric forms, the Portuguese return to the pure and luminous cubes and spheres of southern European and Mediterranean architectural traditions. The style expanded from the early example of the church of Jesus in Setúbal (Boytac, 1490), to the masterpiece of Jerónimos monastery in Belém, Lisbon (Boytac, 1501–17), and the late Priorado do Rosário church in Goa, India (1540).   JMF

marble   Geologically speaking, marble is a limestone composed of calcite and or dolomite, which has completely recrystallized under heat or pressure. In a looser definition, 'marble' is any decorative limestone which will take a polish, a definition which is etymologically justified since the original Greek word means 'shining stone'. True marble occurs in a great range of colours, the white of the basic material being veined with grey, blue, rose, red, yellow, and many combinations. The veins register the presence of various mineral impurities such as silica or iron oxides (the reds) or serpentine (usually red, but sometimes green).

Marble is very unevenly distributed throughout the world, and is usually found only in mountainous regions. There are no true marbles in the United Kingdom, though there is a pale green marble in Ireland—Connemara marble. Purbeck 'marble', in fact a Jurassic limestone, was widely used in the 11th–13th centuries, mainly for thin shafts and colonettes, and had a rather unfortunate second life in the *Gothic Revival, when it was sometimes used to excess.

True marble from the nearby Mt Pentilikon was used extensively in the Parthenon (447–432 BC), though it is possible, however incredible it may seem to today's taste, that it was painted over in rather bright colours (*see* POLYCHROMY). But classical and Hellenistic Greece made relatively little use of marble, and it was left to the Romans to use the full range of colours. During the 1st and 2nd centuries AD, marble was brought to Rome from all provinces of the Empire, to such an extent that by the end of this period the imperial quarries were quite exhausted. Even in the provinces marble was transported a great distance, as shown by the example of an Anatolian marble being used in Colchester. One of the most productive Roman quarries was on the island of Proconnesus in the Sea of Marmara, which continued to be used during the Byzantine era. The panels of this green marble are found in the lower storeys of Hagia Sophia, and it must have been widely used in other buildings, as is evident from the panels looted by the Venetians in 1204.

Although there are large quantities of the white-ish Carrara marble quite near to Rome, it was used relatively little in the Renaissance and Baroque eras, possibly because architects preferred the clear forms of *limestone, or, if they required a more textured effect, *travertine was easily available. By contrast, in India, a very white marble, sculpted very delicately in scrolls and mouldings, rather than simply used as panels, seems to have replaced sandstone after the period of Humayun (*see* INDIAN SUBCONTINENT (THE MUGHALS)).

In the modern period, marble was first used for exterior cladding on London buildings from about 1905, its opulent character being ideally suited to the Edwardian era. For the same reason it was out of favour with modernists, but surprisingly *Mies used marble walls in the Barcelona Pavilion (1929). It made a return as a cladding material in the 1960s, particularly for prestige buildings such as bank headquarters.　PG

Markelius, Sven Gottfrid (1889–1972) Swedish
architect. The club house for the Royal Institute of Technology (1928–30) is abstractly geometric, one of the earliest examples in Sweden of International Modern, but his first important design was the Helsingborg Concert Hall (1925–32), a rather basic exercise in the same manner, consisting of a taller, flat-roofed auditorium block, and a lower building with semicircular extensions for entrance and lobbies, in the conventional white rendering over a steel frame.

Markelius showed his commitment to the social goals of Modernism in his collective house at John Ericssonsgatan 6, Stockholm (1935). It consisted of 57 mostly small apartments served by a central kitchen and restaurant with elevators for food deliveries to the kitchenettes of the flats. A laundry and a nursery for children were also provided. The front of the building shows four vertical sections placed at an angle to the street, with recessed, rounded balconies between them.

As City Planning Director for Stockholm (1944–54), he was responsible for the planning of Vällingby, outside Stockholm: a self-contained township with an urban centre, a pedestrian zone, and workplaces.　TF

Marot, Daniel (1661–1752) is regarded as the
principal Dutch architect of the first half of the 18th century, based on his work as *dessinateur*, leaving the execution entirely to architects and surveyors. He arrived at Prince William III's court after 1685, and worked both in the Netherlands and in England. After 1702 he worked for clients in Amsterdam and The Hague, and also at their country seats. His work is the subject of frequently rather speculative attributions. His engraved designs include everything from upholstery to garden layouts in a Dutch Louis XIV style.　FS

Martin, Professor Sir (John) Leslie (1908–2000)
English architect. Martin was the most influential figure in architecture in the UK from 1950 to 1975; his influence continues. His vision of architecture as an intellectual activity, integrating arts and sciences, had its roots in his interest in the constructive arts, jointly editing *Circle* (1937), and led to a rationally and aesthetically motivated lifelong quest for underlying principles and patterns in building types and form. Through this vision and quest he brought about profound and lasting changes in architectural education, research, and practice.

An early life in the *Arts and Crafts, a *Beaux Arts education, and an immediate affinity for *Le Corbusier and *Aalto, all played obvious parts in the formation of his architecture. He first came to prominence when appointed the LCC's Deputy Architect, as principal architect of the Royal Festival Hall (1951), the UK's first major post-war work of modern architecture.

On appointment as Professor at Cambridge (1956–72), with Colin St J. *Wilson, he established the school of architecture as one of the most influential in the world, producing numerous eminent academics and practitioners. In 1958 he organized the seminal 'Oxford Conference', and presented a paper which led to a massive expansion of architectural education and research in universities, initiating the shift from architecture as a subjective, craft-based activity to an intellectually rigorous social and aesthetic discipline.

At Cambridge there was a mutually informing interplay of teaching, practice, and research. The Centre for Land Use and Built Form Studies initiated research into patterns and principles of the form and organization of various building types. Work on the geometrical potential of form in *The grid as generator* (1972) with Lionel March demonstrated how cities could be developed with medium-rise buildings at the same densities as high-rise but with more open space.

Based on this research with Wilson, he built a student residence, Harvey Court (1962), Cambridge; the Law, Economics, and Statistics Libraries (1964), Oxford; presented proposals for the British Museum Library (1964); and, with March, designed the redevelopment of Whitehall (1965), a demonstration of his belief in the indivisibility of architecture and planning. Much in demand but maintaining only a small studio, where each building, such as the Gulbenkian Gallery of Contemporary Art, Lisbon (1983), was an exemplar, he was unique in the breadth and authority of his support in commissioning many young, later distinguished, practices.　　　　RJS

Carolin, P., and Dannatt, T., *Architecture, Education and Research: The work of Leslie Martin* (1996)

Martin, J. L., *Buildings and Ideas 1933–83* (1983)

Martinelli, Domenico (1650–1718) Italian-born architect, active in central Europe, who played an important role in introducing a version of the Roman Baroque into Vienna. Unfortunately, it was a rather block-like variety, which also paid little respect to

context. His three main designs—the Harrach Palace (1690), the Liechtenstein Town Palace (1692–1705), and the Liechtenstein Garden Palace (1698–1711)—deploy an emphatic centre, and side bays articulated by giant pilasters. Despite being in very different settings, the latter two buildings are almost identical. However, the triumphal staircase of the Town Palace was a successful innovation.　　　　PG

mashrabiya Grille made of turned woods, covering windows or enclosing balconies on houses in the Middle East. The term derives from the word *shariba* (drinking), relating to the practice of storing water near the window. This feature is an indigenous screening device that veils the domestic realm in the house from the public world while providing a visual access to the social life outside the house. This screen accommodates provisions in Islam that demand a clear distinction between public, semi-public, and private spaces. The mashrabiya also allows air and light to penetrate and circulate into the house.　　　　ABS

master masons Of all the medieval craftsmen, two types stand out for their inventive skill, and might on occasion be called *architectores*. These were master masons and master carpenters, of whom the masons were generally considered the greater by virtue of the superior status of stone over timber. Like other craftsmen, masons entered their craft as apprentices, and would learn at work how to choose stone for specific use, how to cut it, how to carve it, and how to lay it. Having successfully completed their apprenticeship, they would then take on part of a job under the control of a master, whose role they might aspire to but would reach only rarely through talent, energy, ambition, and luck.

The master's job was part managerial, being responsible for the execution of work to a proper standard of quality within a specific time and to a set

581

price, and part artistic, being responsible for producing a design and ensuring that this was worked out in detail, often on the tracing floor of the lodge attached to the site of the works, and then executed. The artistic side, apparently more important, was certainly more significant in the development of styles, particularly innovating styles as Gothic was between the 12th and 16th centuries, and this has led to master masons being seen as architects in the modern sense, despite their craft training and intimate knowledge of building. Yet the management side remained just as important, not only throughout the Middle Ages but also long afterwards, even when the term architect was current—the tasks of clerk of the works, quantity surveyor, and building surveyor being integral to the job. Master masons would be contracted by ecclesiastical and royal dignitaries, usually for specific works, such as to design or oversee works or often both of these, at a cathedral or palace. Often these contracts or the accounts rendered as a consequence of them name the masters, and offer clues to their role and the work in hand, usually in frustratingly imprecise terms. Patron and master sometimes worked together in determining a design, the mason being treated as a valuable and even equal partner in bringing a work to fulfilment. Most building works, however, are shrouded in obscurity. Although some masons had characteristic skills by which their work may be identified, this is an uncertain route in an age that was unconcerned with personality, and pupils began by following their master. APQ

Matcham, Frank (1854–1920) English theatre architect. By the 1880s Matcham led this specialized field, combining an understanding of the emotional quality required in the theatre with the ability to improve the technology of unobstructed vision, ventilation, and means of escape. He was innovative in the use of steel for supporting serpentine galleries,

creating an intimate feeling even in larger houses. A riotous adaptation of Baroque decoration was applied inside and on the streets. In 1892 the impresario H. E. Moss commissioned Matcham to design the Edinburgh Empire, the first of a succession of large variety theatres, merged in 1900 with the similar enterprise of Oswald Stoll, for whom Matcham also designed. This produced theatres still serving the public a hundred years on, such as the Hackney Empire (1901), and, the greatest of them all, the London Coliseum (1904). Other theatres from the more than 100 built or adapted by Matcham include the Gaiety, Douglas, Isle of Man (1900), and Buxton Opera House (1903). AP

Walker, B. (ed.), *Frank Matcham, Theatre Architect* (1980)

Matthew, Sir Robert Hogg (1906–75) Scottish architect. As Architect to the London County Council (1946–53), with Leslie *Martin as his Deputy, he oversaw the LCC's lasting contributions to the 1951 Festival of Britain, the Royal Festival Hall, and the Lansbury neighbourhood. He also transformed the LCC's approach to housing. Under his leadership, the LCC, with a pragmatic rather doctrinaire approach to modern architecture, gained worldwide renown.

In 1953 he established a practice (later known as RMJM) with Stirrat Johnson-Marshall (1912–81). From their extensive practice, three schemes may be singled out: one of the best campuses for an English *university, at York (1963); and two rather contrasting buildings in London, New Zealand House (1960–63) and the Commonwealth Institute (1960–62). The former, a 15-storey tower on a 4-storey podium, clearly expresses its structure of columns and projecting floor slabs; in the latter, a hyperbolic-paraboloid roof and the externally visible structure bear little relation to the series of galleries within. PG

mausoleum and tomb A mausoleum is a free-standing monumental structure for a tomb or tombs, sometimes with spaces for rituals and gatherings, or whole complexes with gardens as in Mughal India. The name is derived from the tomb of Mausoleus at Halicarnassus (*c*.350 BC), which combined a pyramidal roof with elements of temple-like and circular colonnaded tomb buildings. *Vitruvius classed it as one of the Seven Wonders of the World. Copied for centuries, it was still being used in 1934, as the model for Melbourne's Shrine of Remembrance.

As a symbol of both dynastic power and deification, the mausoleum suited the beliefs and hierarchies of Imperial Rome, from the complex structures for Augustus (28 BC) and Hadrian (AD *c*.120), to more modest ones for the nobility on their own estates, and the communal mausoleums or columbaria for those who could not afford even a wayside stela. In consolidating this building type, the Romans also produced an eloquent design vocabulary of obelisks, domes, pyramids, porticoed enclosures and entrances, raised plinths for burial chambers, niches for urns or busts, open canopied sarcophagi, exedras and tempiettos, affecting reliefs, and altar-shaped tombs, which have fascinated Western antiquarians and architects, artists, and romantics ever since.

Under the Empire, Christians and Jews eschewed cremation and tended to bury their dead in catacombs or hypogea. The tombs of martyrs sometimes took the form of altars as they became shrines. Later relaxation of prohibitions on intra-mural burial, and the desire to be close to the sacred, resulted in medieval churches across Europe becoming, in effect, mausoleums and repositories of funerary art. Piety and prestige were realized in fine materials and often exquisite craftsmanship. Pre-Christian forms often prevailed: tomb-chests in niches or enclosed in grilles or screens; tabernacled sarcophagi; canopied effigies; chantries within and mortuary chapels without demonstrating some of the most refined Gothic and Renaissance workmanship.

Beginning in Italy from the 15th century, there was a cultural shift celebrating the individual: in Rimini the Tempio Malatestiano, by *Alberti (*c*.1450); in Florence new mausoleums for the Medici by *Michelangelo (1520–224) and Nigetti (1604–40). During the 16th century the Pantheon evolved to become a prototype for the commemoration of the illustrious as their remains were transferred there, just as happened for more dynastic and nationalistic reasons at St Denis in Paris, Westminster Abbey, and St Paul's Cathedral. Philip II of Spain built a royal pantheon at El Escorial (Juan de Herrera) and Emperor Maximilian the Hofkirche at Innsbruck (consecrated 1563). If the iconography used was potent, so was the language, as with the Panthéon in Paris (1764–90) by *Soufflot and the Walhalla (1830–42) at Regensburg, modelled on the Parthenon.

With the Reformation and the abolition of chantries, mausoleum building flourished in Protestant countries. By the 18th century individual mausoleums were being built separately from churches and even outside churchyards. More modest and secular, the tomb of Rousseau on the Ile des Peupliers, Ermenonville, by Hubert Robert (1779) is the first example of a public burial in a garden. The largest structures since Roman times were in Britain, where the unconsecrated landscaped park provided an Arcadian setting for 'scholarly' antique, gloomy romantic, or inventive neoclassical buildings: Castle Howard (*Hawksmoor, 1731–42), Cobham and Brocklesby Parks (James *Wyatt, 1783 and 1787–94), and Trentham Park (Tatham, 1808). Greek, Etruscan, and Egyptian influences are evident at this time, but also Mughal as those returning from India sometimes favoured typical mandala-based tombs with their kiosks and canopied domes, verandahs, and pierced screens. Many Enlightenment architects were fascinated by the classical iconography of death and sepulchral architecture. None more so than *Soane, who, influenced by Piranesi and his own collections, experimented with form, mood, and pre-Christian symbolism to engender notions of civic virtue. Of Soane's many illustrations and designs, the most celebrated are those realized for the Dulwich Picture Gallery's benefactor (1811–13) and for himself and his wife at St Giles' churchyard, London (1816).

Sublime proposals for heroic monuments, cenotaphs, and vast mausoleum-like solutions to the burial crises, though never built, extended neoclassical, ante-clerical funerary language to a new level of invention and scale. But it was the more practical solution of the Garden Cemetery in Europe and the USA which gave an impetus to mausoleum and tomb building for the middle classes. Monuments at Père-Lachaise and the Staglieno are chiefly 'pagan' neoclassical. Ecclesiologically correct *Gothic Revival examples are to be found at Norwood, London (by *Barry, *Street, *Godwin, J. O. *Scott, *Burges, and Tite), and in other metropolitan cemeteries of the same era. Many of the older examples in the USA are exquisitely constructed facsimiles of ancient Greek, Egyptian, French Gothic examples demonstrating hubris, taste, and fashion. Despite much of the mass-produced, the vulgar, the bizarre and the mawkish tombs, mausoleums have continued as a staple of celebrated designers in Catholic Europe and the Americas, either family-sized or communal provision.

The best 20th-century examples are notable for their ingenuity in the miniature, exploiting threshold and enclosure, light and dark, ritual chapel and symbol, display or privacy, and thereby a record of the design idiom of the day. Fine examples include: Philip *Webb for William *Morris at Kelmscott; *Plečnik at Ljubljana (1925–40); Gio *Ponti at Milan (1931); Aldo *Rossi at Modena (1987); *Saarinen at Joensuu (1910); *Sant'Elia at Monza (1913); *Sullivan at Chicago's Graceland (1887 and 1890); *Wagner in Vienna (1894); Max *Taut at Stahnsdorf, Berlin (1923); Carlo *Scarpa in Venice (1943–4), Udine (1951 and 1960), and most famously his Brion Vega sequence near Treviso, Italy (1967–78). The year 2004 saw the building in Buffalo of Frank Lloyd *Wright's 1928 design of stepped, terraced vaults known as Blue-Sky, and a gentle essay in light and materials in Murcia, Spain, by Manuel Rojo.

The potent device of the Tomb of the Unknown Warrior as the focus of public grief and nationhood has become widespread from British and French examples (Westminster Abbey, 1920; Arc de Triomphe, 1921) to New Zealand (Wellington, 2004). More overtly political are the mausoleums of leaders as varied as Lenin, Atatürk, Ho Chi Minh, General Franco, and Primo de Rivera. The latter two lie in a vast chamber cut into a mountain near Escorial (El Valle de los Caidos, c.1940–59). Nothing sublime here, just awesome, from the overscaled entrance colonnades to the funerary hall with its torches and heightened false perspective.   HB

Colvin, H., *Architecture and the After-life* (1991)
Gili, M. (ed.), *The Last House* (1999)
Waterfield, G. (ed.), *Soane and Death* (1996)

Maya architecture married mass and void to landscape, using a small inventory of forms: the massive platform, and its opposite, the open plaza; a volume based on the house form; and the line that gives direction, expressed in either the step, path, or road. Less attention was paid to the design of interior spaces. Although best known for towering pyramids and ranging palaces, Maya architecture also required less visible feats of engineering, from the aqueduct system that kept Palenque's torrents in check to the reservoir system at Tikal that made year-round habitation possible.

Characteristic of Maya architecture is the corbel vault, a replication in stone of the thatched hip roof, which is formed by courses of stone approaching one another until they can be spanned by a single capstone.

View of the Avenue of the Dead, from the Pyramid of the Moon, Teotihuacán, Mexico (AD ?500)

Unstable as a stone form, it requires sturdy massing of walls. The Arch at Kabah is a rare free-standing example; it seems to have functioned as a city entryway. Roofcombs, which are both decorative and bearers of complex iconography, also contribute to instability of interior space. A roofcomb aligned over the corbel required internal buttresses (Yaxchilan) or heavy massing and reduced interior space (Tikal); the roofcomb over the front load-bearing wall (the 'flying façade' of Puuc sites), or the parallel alignment of corbels with the roofcomb over the central load-bearing wall (Palenque) enhanced stability and allowed for larger interior spaces. The occasional vast corbel, attempted in Structures 19 and 21 at Palenque, must have collapsed as soon as roof maintenance ceased. At Chichen Itza, engineers executed a trabeated roof for many buildings.

Maya architects took advantage of natural elevations, massing structures directly on bedrock, where early clusters of ceremonial architecture were built. Although the grid is absent and the street unknown, massive raised causeways connected sections of cities to one another, often across swampy areas (Tikal, Uaxactun, Coba; from AD 378); in some cases, causeways linked one city to another (Kabah to Uxmal). In Yucatán, causeways directed movement to cenotes, natural sinkholes, most notably at Chichen Itza (the main city of the Itza, AD 750–1000).

Free-standing pyramids with single stairways often house tombs: deaths of members of the royal family initiated construction or called for the rebuilding of pyramids in order to enshrine an additional ancestor for veneration. Some rebuildings carefully interred earlier structures, such as Rosalila at Copan, while others were ritually 'killed' or partly recycled as building fill. Radial pyramids, with staircases on all four sides, are rare, but usually refer to cycles of time and their completion, from the solar year (E-7, Uaxactun; Castillo, Chichen Itza) to the katun, a period of 20 years (Twin-Pyramid Group, Tikal).

Ranging galleries with multiple entryways that frame smaller courtyards and patios characterize palace

585

El Castillo, Pyramid of Kukulcan, Chichen Itza, Mexico

architecture, centres of royal and noble dwelling, as well as court ritual and administration. Many may have originally been made of perishable materials; rebuilt through time, ranging palaces sometimes incorporated some early funerary monuments (Uaxactun); most became closed and private over time. At least two such compounds (Palenque, Copan) featured towers. Built-in stone thrones in many palaces provide evidence of royal receiving rooms; carved depictions and texts on palace steps suggest celebrations of victory. The so-called Mercado ('Market') at Chichen Itza probably functioned as a royal palace, arranged around a single central atrium framed by towering columns.

Almost every Maya city included a ball court, a specialized architectural form consisting of two parallel buildings that frame the playing alley between them, either with sloping or perpendicular walls. Some ball courts terminate in I-shaped end zones; some provide spectator seating; no two courts are identical. Markers run down the alley floor of some courts; others have rings or other scoring devices along the playing walls. Although Palenque had only a single court, Copan had three. Chichen Itza is home to the largest ball court known, but featured several others as well; adjacent to its Great Ball court is a rare example of a Maya skull rack.

Sweat baths for ritual purification often form part of palace complexes. The Piedras Negras examples are the largest and best preserved, with ample fireboxes and dressing rooms. Round buildings are rare; the most elaborate example, the Caracol at Chichen Itza, features tiny windows on its uppermost storey for observation of Venus.

From the earliest expressions c.500 BC, Maya architects used stucco cement, made by burning limestone or seashells, both to decorate architectural surfaces and to pave plazas, whether to keep the forest at bay or to direct water to reservoirs. Abundant forest fuel supported huge projects to adorn building exteriors with massive images of gods, but even in regions of scarcer resources, as at Ek Balam, complex stucco ornament continued through AD 800. Particularly in southern and western Yucatán, but also at Copan, stucco and stone was used to form doorways into vast deity mouths, usually personified mountains. Heavy block masonry with stucco mortar before AD 550 yielded to smaller and more finely cut stones 600–900. At Comalcalco, builders made bricks; at Tonina and elsewhere, builders used adobes, which only rarely survive. A rubble core finished with finely cut ashlars and veneer stones characterizes 8th- and 9th-century Puuc buildings. Rough and imprecise block stonework at Mayapan and Tulum, after AD 1100, required thick stucco cement for finishing. Columns first appeared in the 7th or 8th century, along with squared piers. Holes adjacent to doorways and in cornices made it possible to hang curtains, divide rooms, or attach awnings. Windows—often in the shape of the glyph for wind, or what we see as a T-shape—most commonly appear at Palenque.

Many architectural surfaces once featured polychrome or monochrome painting, often including writing. Interior mural painting is known principally at Bonampak and in the Puuc region; smooth white interior walls at Tikal and elsewhere often retain casual drawings, or graffiti, many of which reveal skilled craftsmanship. Many exteriors were painted red: exceptions, like House E of Palenque's Palace, with its polychrome flowers on a white ground, stood out at the centre of the complex.

During the 1st millennium BC a moat protected Becan; a wall 10 km (6 miles) from its centre defined Tikal a few hundred years later. At Dos Pilas, desperate residents ripped down buildings to build palisades to protect a small zone in the 8th century. Both Mayapan and Tulum were designed to be walled cities from the outset, with little stone construction outside the walls. Tulum's unwalled side faced the sea, but watchtowers were designed so that coastal travellers and traders would approach under observation.   MEM

Miller, Mary Ellen, *Maya Art and Architecture* (1999)

Maybeck, Bernard Ralph (1862–1957) US
architect. Bernard Maybeck ranks among the most original and eccentric architects practising in the US in the early 20th century. He drew from a wide variety of historical precedents as well as contemporary theoretical tracts to create an architecture unusually multi-faceted in its complexion. While embracing the monumental, classical tradition advanced by the Ecole des Beaux-Arts, which he had attended, Maybeck also utilized a spectrum of rustic, vernacular sources. In many instances—most adroitly in the First Church of Christ Scientist in Berkeley, California (1910–11)—facets of these dissimilar spheres were brought together in unorthodox, personal, and compelling ways. Such designs possess a strong, underlying compositional rigour in the development of form and space, yet often seem arrestingly new, even whimsical, in character.

Maybeck employed both fine, costly materials and cheap ones associated with utilitarian functions with equal vigour and freshness. He was a champion of the Arts and Crafts commitment to expressing materials' intrinsic qualities and to handwork.

No less enthralled by the possibilities of theatrical expression, he was inspired by precedents as disparate as imperial Roman baths and great medieval halls. Irrespective, landscape design played a major, integral role in his architectural conceptions. Maybeck proved adept at working in a grand scale. His Palace of Fine Arts in San Francisco (1913–15, reconstructed 1962–7) is among the few realized of many such schemes. But he also relished designing small, intimate, inexpensive buildings, frequently experimenting with materials and construction techniques in the process. Maybeck's practice remained modest in size, catering primarily to clients in the San Francisco Bay area, where he moved in 1890 and remained throughout his long life. RWL

Cardwell, K. H., *Bernard Maybeck: Artisan, Architect, Artist* (1977)

May, Ernst (1886–1970) German architect and urban designer. He is best known for his housing and city planning in Frankfurt am Main (1925–30), where he built 15,000 units of housing, located in *Siedlungen* (settlements) set in a green ring of parks that circled the existing city. Their layout responded to and articulated their surroundings, and the buildings were open, varied, and employed bright colours. The rationally planned compact interiors, a paradigm of *Existenzminimum* housing, offered agreeable living conditions at less cost than was otherwise available in Frankfurt. The units were built in assembly-line manner, using prefabricated concrete panels. May published his housing and urban design initiatives in a monthly magazine, *Das neue Frankfurt*, which promoted a new metropolitan culture of citizens with equal rights and unified ideals. Internationally he played a prominent role in *CIAM. In 1929 its second congress was held in Frankfurt to address *Existenzminimum* housing. From 1930 on, May worked in the USSR and Africa, returning to practise in Germany from the early 1950s until his death. CO

Mohr, C., and Muller, M., *Funktionalität und Moderne* (1984)

May, Hugh (1621–84) English architect. Thanks to his royal connections, May entered the Office of Works (1660) and worked on restoring palaces, particularly Windsor Castle, after the Restoration. He designed the east front of Cornbury House, Oxfordshire (1663–8), and Eltham Lodge, London (1664), which, although not fully exemplifying the mature Baroque style of his demolished interiors, set a pattern of domestic design. This was confirmed by Wren, whom he assisted in the rebuilding of London after the Great Fire. APQ

McIntire, Samuel (1757–1811) US architect. He began as a carpenter for ships and houses, and was soon designing dwellings himself, following London pattern books and the example of *Bulfinch. He also undertook cabinet making and wood carving, and his surviving houses in the McIntire Historic District of Salem, Massachusetts (only a few are in other towns), show elegant proportions and richly carved detailing, making his name synonymous with the New England Adamesque, or Federal. The Gardner-Pingree House (1804) today forms part of Peabody Essex Museum in Salem. WBM

McKim, Charles Follen (1847–1909), **Mead, William Rutherford** (1846–1928), and **White, Stanford** (1853–1906) US architects, who constituted one of the largest and most influential architectural firms active in North America between the years 1879 and 1914.

They were responsible for some of the most esteemed buildings of their epoch. After pioneering the

'Shingle Style' for summer houses, they developed a chaste Renaissance-based Classicism that was employed for residences, public buildings, and commercial buildings, beginning with the complex of six town houses commissioned by Henry Villard, New York City (1882–5).

The partners established their leading position through the design of the Boston Public Library, Boston, Mass. (1887–95), which set the standard for the rest of their careers, as well as for public architecture throughout the United States. Their close relationship with major sculptors, such as Augustus Saint Gaudens, resulted in many public monuments and memorials which also established a new US standard (for example, the Washington Memorial Arch in Washington Square, New York City, 1889–92). One of their best large public buildings is the Rhode Island State Capitol Building, Providence, Rhode Island (1891–1903), a paradigm for subsequent state capitols.

The firm was particularly successful in the design of building *ensembles*, such as collegiate campuses, including Columbia University, New York City, and New York University, New York City, done concurrently from 1892 through 1910 and later. At the turn of the century they designed the campus of Radcliffe College for women, as an adjunct programme of Harvard University.

In the 1890s the firm also designed several industrial facilities, including the first major electrical generating plant at Niagara Falls, New York. In New York City and Boston they designed most of the most prestigious men's clubs as well as several women's clubs, including the Century Club, the Metropolitan Club, the University Club, and the Harvard Club. In the new concert hall for the Boston Symphony Orchestra, Boston (1899–1901), they worked closely with Wallace Sabine to demonstrate for the first time the practical application of acoustical planning (*see* ACOUSTICS).

Perhaps their crowning achievement was the enormously complex Pennsylvania Railroad Station, New York (1902–10, demolished). The firm exerted phenomenal influence, as a result of its training scores of young architects who established their own offices across the country, from Boston to Portland, Oregon, and San Francisco, California.   LMR

Roth, L. M., *McKim, Mead & White, Architects* (1983)

McMorran, Donald Hanks (1904–65) British

architect. Though omitted from mainstream accounts of 20th-century architecture, British post-war rebuilding continued largely in the hands of traditionalists such as McMorran with his pared-down but inventive neo-Georgian style including: social housing (Holloway Estate, 1960–65; Lammas Green, Sydenham, 1962); educational buildings (Phoenix school, Poplar, 1951; the education faculty and two halls of residence, Nottingham University (1954–60); offices (Exeter CC, 1954–64); police stations (Wood Street, 1962–6); and extensions (Old Bailey, 1966–72).

Today his buildings are being re-evaluated and protected for they have lasted well. McMorran worried about the separation of architectural education from practice and the neglect of the craft of reliable building in favour of the pursuit of novelty. Yet his open-minded choice of the unknown firm of *Chamberlin, Powell, and Bon as winners of the Golden Lane competition began the end of this tradition and its patronage.   HB

megaron The house of a Mycenaean tribal chief:
literally a large room, usually with a central hearth and, embraced by an extension of its side walls, a porch and anteroom before it. This provided the model for the temples of ancient Greece. Early megarons had earthen walls and timber posts to support their porches and overhanging roofs, but they are known with walls of stone, for example one of the 6th century BC on the

acropolis at Selinunte in Sicily. The megaron temple
developed into the temples of classical Greece,
following a process of formalization and conversion
from timber and earth to stone.   APQ

Meier, Richard Alan (1934–) US architect. From
1963 to 1973 Meier designed a series of private houses,
which seemed to replicate *Le Corbusier's 1920s villas.
As in his predecessor's work, structure contrasts
strongly with the natural setting, but with a more
marked emphasis on the vertical and some disregard
for the context. For instance, Douglas House, Harbor
Springs, MI (1971–6), on a steep wooded hillside, has a
similar form to the Smith House, Dorien, Connecticut
(1965–7), on a flat site.

Beginning with the New Harmony Atheneum,
Indiana (1975–9), Meier undertook much larger public
commissions, for which he paid more attention to the
sites' existing shapes, routes, and contexts (e.g. the
Museum of Contemporary Art, Barcelona, 1987–95),
and to creating a sense of approach and arrival (the
Museum für Kunsthandwerk, Frankfurt-am-Main,
1979–84). The different characters of the internal spaces
are defined both by forms and by lighting. Externally,
Meier now makes much greater use of curves and pure
geometric forms, such as cylinders, though arguably
some of the clarity of form is diminished by the use of
large panels rather than completely smooth surfaces.
Apart from his almost unvarying use of white, Meier
has developed a very flexible modernist approach to
projects at a very large scale (the Gerry Centre, Los
Angeles, 1984–97) or a small scale (the Jubilee Church,
Rome, 1996–2003).   PG

Meij, Johan M. van der (1878–1949) Dutch
architect. *See* AMSTERDAM SCHOOL.

Melnikov, Konstantin Stepanovich (1890–
1974) Russian architect. At first, in his pavilions for the

Moscow Agricultural and Cottage Industry Exhibition
(1923) and the Paris Exposition (1925), Melnikov used
abstract forms based on traditional woodworking skills.
In a country with an abundance of wood, and a
shortage of modern materials, this was an interesting
approach, but of limited relevance for a society
committed to mass construction.

His intuitive, almost mystical, approach to
architecture was far removed from the *Constructivists'
commitment to modern technology, but he shared
their interest in primary forms, particularly cylinders
and circles. His first major commission, a large *bus
garage in Moscow (1926), had both an ingenious plan,
enabling the buses to circulate, and a striking façade of
circular windows and angled entrance and exit portals.
He then designed five *workers' clubs in Moscow—the
Frunze (1927–8), Kauchuk (1927–9), Svoboda (1928),
Pravda (1928), and Burevestnik (1929)—which followed
Melnikov's usual practice of gathering the elements of
the building into one striking, if irrational, form. The
exception, the Rusakov (1927–9), consists of three
cantilevered wedges accommodating the different
functions of the club.

His own house in Moscow (1927–9) consists of two
intersecting cylinders. The entrance, consisting of a 5 m
(17 ft) glass wall topped with the architect's name, is
fairly conventional, but the second cylinder, cut by five
rows of vertically oriented rhomboids, is a unique
form. The interior is suffused with an uneven, rather
eerie light.

The design showed that Melnikov was as inventive
as he was self-indulgent, and consequently ill-suited to
the stern collective realities of Soviet life, which now
required mass production of housing and triumphalist
monuments. His career was at an end, apart from two
works, the car garages for Intourist (1934) and Gosplan
(1936), both in Moscow. Their façades were organized
around a very large circle, a striking form, but with no
functional rationale.   PG

Rusakov Workers' Club, Stromynskaia Square, Moscow (Konstantin Melnikov, 1927–9)

Mendelsohn, Erich (1887–1953) German architect. By around 1930 he was the best known and most successful German modernist, but as a Jewish architect with Jewish clients he had to flee the Nazis, and never regained his position. Prejudice against *Expressionism by leading historians further diminished his reputation.

Mendelsohn studied in Munich under Theodor *Fischer and enjoyed contacts with avant-garde art and theatre, but his reputation exploded in 1919 with an exhibition of visionary architectural sketches produced during World War I. Mainly corner views of soaring buildings in a few lines, they included occasional plans and some had designated functions. Their promise brought the commission for the Einstein Tower, Potsdam (1920), the best-known built work of the Expressionist period. Mendelsohn was disappointed not to have built it in concrete as intended, but his Hat Factory at Luckenwalde (1920–23) soon demonstrated a mastery of material expression. The *Berliner Tageblatt* conversion of 1921–3 suggested a new approach to urban planning inspired by the flow of traffic, and the Sternefeld Villa of 1923 was revolutionary in its asymmetrical massing, with some influence from Frank Lloyd Wright. Mendelsohn met him on a visit to the United States in 1924, but he also admired Manhattan, producing the photo-book *Amerika* on his return. That same year he completed his Herpich shop, with a fully glazed façade and ingenious artificial lighting, and this led to many further commissions, including the department stores for Salman Schocken: Nuremberg 1925–6, Stuttgart 1926–8, and Chemnitz 1928–30. These pioneered the type and provided an international model, as did Mendelsohn's Universum Cinema, part of Berlin's Woga Complex, a new kind of urban development.

When Hitler took over, Mendelsohn had to leave. He divided his time for several years between Britain and Palestine. His main British work was the Bexhill Pavilion of 1934–5, a competition entry in collaboration with Serge *Chermayeff. Buildings in Palestine included the University and Hospital at Mount Scopus, the hospital at Haifa, the Anglo-Palestine Bank, and the Schocken and Weizmann houses. War induced further flight to the United States in 1941, where Mendelsohn began a third career. He built a hospital in San Francisco and a number of synagogues before his comparatively early death from cancer in 1953, but he failed to attract the following enjoyed by his compatriots *Mies and *Gropius.   PBJ

> James, K(athleen), *Erich Mendelsohn and the Architecture of German Modernism* (1997)

Mengoni, Giuseppe (1829–77) Italian architect.
His most well-known project, the Galleria Vittorio Emanuele II (1861–77), was the centrepiece of a competition for restructuring the Piazza del Duomo in Milan. The project was the first example of a monumentally scaled iron and steel arcade in Italy, and was executed in a neo-Renaissance style that has become synonymous with the modern identity of post-unification Italy. Mengoni was also responsible for the construction of three iron and glass covered markets in Florence, including one in the San Lorenzo neighbourhood (1869–74).   BLM

Mesopotamia In the ancient Near East, the
southern region of Mesopotamia was the land of Sumer, the home of the earliest cities and the first public buildings. Building materials, normally obtained locally, were limited in a land lacking good timber or stone. The rivers Euphrates and Tigris, however, provided natural routes for heavy cargoes. Bitumen was available from natural springs, and was used for drains, pavements, and kiln-fired brickwork. Mud,

straw, reeds, and date palm trunks were the basic building materials, with alabaster and gypsum employed in the Late Assyrian palaces. Mud-brick, with chopped straw, had mud mortar bonding often reinforced by reed matting.

The construction of public buildings required a large labour force. This appears from the 6th millennium BC in successive temples, each with its sanctuary and altar, expanded to include side aisles. These temples were frequently rebuilt; but a practical necessity probably became a ritual obligation, with structures demolished while still intact. With their distinctive façades with niches and buttresses at regular intervals, these temples conferred sanctity on their very site. The temples of Mesopotamia diversified, with rectangular and square plans and a distinctive form of mud-brick termed plano-convex during the Early Dynastic period (c.3000–2370 BC).

Meanwhile the temple tower, or *ziggurat, reaching maturity at Ur in the south (c.2100 BC), here had successive rectangular stages, in this case rising to a height of 19.6 m (64 ft), the façades very slightly convex and relieved by shallow buttresses. The ascent of the ziggurat was by three staircases on the north-east side, one at right angles to the façade and two running up it. No trace remains of the shrine on top of the ziggurat, functioning as a high place or sacred mountain. The casing of this ziggurat, not bonded into the largely earlier mud-brick core, was of burnt bricks with bitumen mortar, with weeper-holes through to the core for drying the interior.

Builders from southern Mesopotamia were in demand in the north, their skills demonstrated at Tell al Rimah, west of Mosul, in the techniques of 'pitched-brick' and radial vaulting. A staircase with two flights shows the original height of a temple as at least 11 m (36 ft) above floor level; and 277 engaged columns on the façades display the skill of the Babylonian bricklayers, with their spiraliform and palm trunk designs. The most imposing known palace is that of the city of Mari on the middle Euphrates. Its hold on the lucrative upstream trade provoked its destruction by Hammurabi, king of Babylon (1757 BC). This palace displays the typically Mesopotamian tradition, found also further afield, of rooms looking inward onto a court and showing blank walls to the outside world. Privacy and security were thus ensured, the latter also by the indirect access through the main entrance. This was a single-storey building, with screens acting as doors and with flat roofing. The palace of Mari served many functions, as a governmental centre and royal residence.

It was Assurnasirpal II of Assyria (884–859 BC) who inaugurated the flourishing Late Assyrian period in architecture, and whose North-West Palace stood at Nimrud, 32 km (20 miles) down the Tigris from present-day Mosul. The palace complex stretched 200 m (656 ft) north to south and 120 m (393 ft) east to west, with a ziggurat to the north. A great public square gave access to the palace proper, comprising public and domestic wings. A long throne room was entered at one end, with exit near the king on his throne. The Assyrian king recorded the wealth of materials employed in building and decorating the palace, impressing on every beholder his military skill and equipment and the cruel fate of those who would not submit, this message conveyed through long series of reliefs. The effect of terror was accentuated by the gloom within the palace, also giving a cool feeling in the summer. The rooms were long and narrow, allowing the span possible with the imported roof beams, coated in white plaster and painted in vivid blue, red, black, and white, as were the walls above the reliefs. The palace walls, over 5 m (16 ft) thick and probably 15 m (49 ft) high, could have supported an upper storey in parts. The courtyard was paved with alabaster slabs, sealing intact brick-vaulted tombs, yielding an impressive weight of gold jewellery and ornaments from royal burials.

The great city of Babylon had walls, public buildings, and a 12.9 km (8 mile) outer perimeter of kiln-fired bricks, whose general use was an innovation of the neo-Babylonian period (626–539 BC). Eight entrances included the Ishtar Gate, with rows of lions, bulls, and dragons in relief on glazed bricks, a technique originating in Assyria. The most imposing landmark was the great ziggurat, about 90 m (295 ft) high, probably having eight stages, the height of the first two corresponding exactly with the horizontal measurement of the main staircase.   CAB

Roaf, M., *Cultural Atlas of Mesopotamia and the Ancient Near East* (1990)

Metabolism is a Japanese architectural movement, active from 1960 to the early 1970s. It was launched at the World Design Conference in Tokyo (1960), and its initial members were the architects Takashi Asada, Kiyonori *Kikutake (see Kawazoe, *Metabolism 1960*, 1960) and Kishô *Kurokawa, journalist and critic Noboru Kawazoe, industrial designer Kenji Ekuan, and graphic designer Kiyoshi Awazu; the architects Fumihiko *Maki and Masato Ôtaka soon joined them. Metabolism was critical of orthodox Modernism as represented by *CIAM, advocating instead a more dynamic, organic approach in which urban and architectural infrastructure could embrace short-term replaceable elements. While conceived during Japan's phenomenal growth of the 1960s, the movement was effectively ended by the ensuing social and environmental problems of the early 1970s. Metabolist architects did build extensively, especially compared with *Archigram, but not on the grand urban scale of their visionary schemes.   KTO

Métezeau, Jacques-Clément (1581–1652)
French architect. He is known to have laid out the imposing Place Ducale, Charleville (1610), a conventional grid plan within bastion fortifications, and

a number of architecturally undistinguished chateaux and houses. But the extent and nature of his involvement with de *Brosse at the Luxembourg Palace, Paris (1615), and the west façade of St-Gervais, Paris (1616–23), is unclear: he may have acted more as a building contractor than as a designer.   PG

metope The square space between two triglyphs in a frieze of the *Doric order, usually plain, but sometimes decorated with trophies or other carving (e.g. sculptures of ox-skulls). The metopes of the Parthenon, Athens, which Phidias and his assistants famously carved before 438 BC, depict scenes of combat between Centaurs and Lapithae, and Greeks and Amazons.   APQ

metro stations The first underground railway in the world was the London Metropolitan Railway, which opened in 1863. The earliest station to have an imposing entrance is Blackfriars, with a 4-storey main section flanked by two towers and intricately ornamented façades. Later buildings, such as the City and South London Railway stations at Kennington (1890) and Moorgate (1900), were more modest affairs of red brick, with limestone dressings. *Terracotta and glazed red tiles were also used extensively, as at South Kensington (1906–7).

In Europe, there were two interesting developments. For the Stadtbahn, Vienna (from 1894), Otto *Wagner designed a functional and practical series of 36 stations, of two types. Stations where the lines run at street level were conceived as gateway buildings, and correspondingly designed in a conventionally classical manner. When the train lines are below street level, Wagner opted for decorative pavilions in metal and marble, of which the best-preserved example is Karlplatz. *Guimard's involvement in the design of the entrances to Paris Métro stations (1898–1913) is limited to decorative details—writhing flower stalks

carry the letter 'M', sometimes associated with a glass canopy.

London Underground design took a turn to a muted Modernism, with the new stations on the Piccadilly Line by Charles *Holden, working in partnership with the administrator of the Underground Electric Railways, Frank Pick. The inspiration of *Dudok and *Asplund, whose work Pick and Holden had seen in 1930, is very apparent in the booking halls of Sudbury Town (1931) and Arnos Grove (1932–3), rectangular and cylindrical brick and glass blocks respectively. The architecture is an integral part of a complete redesign, involving fittings, wall coverings, and *lettering.

All previous metro station designs are eclipsed by the almost impossibly extravagant designs for the Moscow Metro (from 1935). Not only are the circulation spaces and entrance halls very generous, they are decorated with columns, chandeliers, and opulent murals. The finest of this type is the Mayakovskaya (Dushkin, opened 1938), which used different shades of granite and marble.

The rapid worldwide increase in metro transport in the 1960s offered more opportunities to artists than to architects, but the London Jubilee Line extension has some very distinguished architecture. Two stations in particular, Canary Wharf (*Foster, completed 1999) and North Greenwich (Alsop, 1999), create vast spaces, not only for circulation but to bring light as far down underground as possible. In England these are perhaps the finest modernist buildings of the decade, admittedly rather a tawdry one for architecture.   PG

Mewès, Charles (1860–1914), French architect, and **Davis, Arthur Joseph** (1878–1951) English architect. Davis, whose youth was spent in Brussels, studied at the Ecole des Beaux-Arts, Paris, and joined Charles Mewès in professional partnership in 1900. The Ritz Hotel, London (1903–6) struck the contemporary mood of the *Entente Cordiale*, described

Canary Wharf Underground Station, Jubilee Line Extension, London (Norman Foster, 1999)

by Goodhart-Rendel as 'the American section of Heaven'. In 1907, Inveresk House, Aldwych (altered), put the crudity of Edwardian Baroque and neo-Grec to shame, while the Royal Automobile Club, Pall Mall (1908–11), with its marble swimming bath, was quietly opulent. Davis's Westminster Bank at 51 Threadneedle Street, London (1922), is a cool adaptation of Italian Renaissance.   AP

Mexico This country's vast territory offers a wealth of wide-ranging artistic expressions, resulting from its diversity both geographical and cultural. During the pre-Columbian era it was part of the area known as Mesoamerica, and the most distinctive features of building during this period are produced by the play of volume and open space, with little emphasis on the inner space. Thanks to a careful and original use of stone, the meticulously located structures were planned in accordance with astrological movements.

In the pre-classical period, between 1200 BC and AD 200, the most noteworthy constructions were those found at the Olmec city of La Venta. During the classical period, the great ceremonial centres featured pyramid-like constructions built using the *talud y tablero* (slope-and-panel system) and crowned by temples that were accessed via sloping stairways. These are found at Teotihuacán, the most influential urban complex of Mesoamerica, in Mayan cities like Palenque, and Zapotec settlements, especially Monte Alban. During the post-classical period, after 900, architecture was characterized by the juxtaposition of religious buildings and those representing secular power in the Toltec settlements such as Tula, and numerous Mayan settlements in Yucatán. Finally, the Aztecs who settled on the island of Tenochtitlán extended their influence over a broad area.

The Spanish occupation, begun in 1521, brought a radical change in both the cultural and religious sphere, blending local customs with the spirit of the Conquistadores. The most representative buildings of the 16th century were the monasteries with their splendid churches and attached cloister, preceded by a spacious atrium with open chapels and closed shrines—known as *capillas posas*. The religious orders who evangelized the territory—Franciscans, Dominicans, and Augustinians—built complexes like Huejotzingo in Puebla, Santo Domingo, and Yanhuitlán in Oaxaca, and Actopan and Ixmiquilpan in Hidalgo. The quality of the structures and their decoration varies depending on the materials available and the skills of the local artisans, as well as on the origin of the missionaries. The new cities were built on the grid pattern established by Philip II's 'Ordinances of the Indies' (1573), with the main government and church buildings constructed around a central square.

The capital of the viceroyalty of New Spain was established at Tenochtitlán, where Renaissance architecture was superimposed upon that of the Aztecs. The end of the 16th and the 17th centuries saw the rise of other cities where secular architecture was surrounded by large numbers of religious buildings. Baroque became the predominant style, based on European influence and on the skill and imagination of *criollos* and *mestizos*. The mining and agricultural boom during the 18th century generated a wave of grandeur, coinciding with the excesses of Baroque style, after which the imposition of the neoclassical style by the Royal Academy of Noble Arts of Saint Charles was external evidence of a change of attitude in the run-up to independence.

In religious architecture, cathedral building is of particular note. Mexico Cathedral was begun in 1573, according to a plan drawn up by Claudio de *Arciniega, and completed three centuries later by Manuel *Tolsá. Puebla cathedral was designed by Francisco *Becerra, while that of Mérida was completed by Juan Miguel de Agüero. In addition to the monasteries, convents also began to appear. These were built to a special design with two side entrances and a choir separated off by grilles and latticework, as at San Jerónimo and Santa Teresa la Antigua in the capital, or Santa Rosa and Santa Clara in Queretaro.

There was widespread building of schools built within impressive cloisters, some of the most important being the Santa Cruz College in Tlatelolco and the Jesuit College of San Martín at Tepozotlán, or the Hospital de Jesús, founded by Hernán Cortés.

In the realm of secular architecture, the most important building was the Viceroy's Palace, now the National Palace. Others of note were the Holy Inquisition, the Casa de Moneda (Mint), and, during the later period, the Royal Mining School. Domestic architecture also flourished, producing mansions that justified the description of the capital of the viceroyalty as the 'City of Palaces', with warehouses and commercial offices at street level surrounding a courtyard from which a magnificent stairway led up to the noble first floor, as in the work of Francisco Antonio de Guerrero y Torres.

In 1821 Mexico gained its independence, but was faced with economic and political instability that forced it to close the Academy. The country's development was gradually set in motion, a modern approach to architecture being adopted with regard to both the choice of building systems and the conception of new forms of design. The period of peace—known as *la paz porfiriano*—under Porfirio Diaz (1877–1911) saw the production of works that were academic in inspiration and French in influence. Cities were keen to appear progressive in the run-up to the Centenary of Independence in 1910, so built theatres, markets, and railway stations. This flurry of building activity prompted the arrival of a wave of foreign architects, like Adamo Boari, who built the National Theatre, or Silvio Contri and Emile Benard, who lived and worked alongside the locals such as Antonio Rivas Mercado, Carlos Herrera, and Emilo Dondé. In commercial

buildings, new effects could be achieved by the use of new structures (iron) and materials (cement).

From 1910 the Mexican Revolution put a stop to building activity for some years. However, this situation occasioned a break with the authority imposed by academic models, encouraging the espousal of Modernism. By 1925 the country had emerged from this critical phase, and José *Villagrán García put forward an avant-garde approach when he built the Hygiene Institute at Popotla, in accordance with the tenets of the 'theory of architecture' expounded from his Chair at the National School of Architecture. Early pupils included Enrique del Moral, Juan O'Gorman, Juan Legarreta, and Enrique Yáñez, who, together with their professor, waged the first battles of Functionalism in an effort to tackle the country's main shortages, namely housing, education, and health.

Simultaneously, much building was taking place to meet the demands of government departments and the growing bourgeoisie, providing work for large numbers of talented architects such as Carlos Obregón Santacilia, Mario *Pani, Enrique de la Mora, Augusto H. Álvarez, Juan Sordo Madaleno, Francisco J. Serrano, and Juan Segura. Their work was characterized by great enthusiasm and a distinct sense of social responsibility.

This was also the period of the *Integración Plástica*, one of the most significant examples of which was the University Campus, a collaborative effort by a large number of architects and artists who, in spite of the diversity of their individual styles and expression, achieved an overall unity, constituting a landmark in Mexican architecture.

Around the same time there arose a concern for affirmation of values specifically Mexican, as typified in the country's traditional architecture. This approach was initiated by Luis *Barragán, together with a few of his contemporaries, such as Del Moral and Alberto T. Arai. They sought to establish a new architectural language that would constitute a refinement of popular feeling and give rise to an atmosphere of great simplicity. In parallel, there developed a third generation of architects who sought new solutions in terms of both design and technique, including among others Pedro Ramirez Vázquez, Alejandro Prieto, Jorge González Reyna, Francisco Artigas, and Reynaldo Pérez Rayón. A highly important contribution here was that of Félix *Candela Outeriño who, in collaboration with various designers, designed and constructed a series of innovative thin *shell coverings.

At the present time these architects and their work have acquired international repute as a result of their creativity and the quality of their buildings, which while impressive as cultural solutions are also constructed in a manner that takes due account of local geographical conditions. Three distinct trends may be identified, their common denominator being the search for results that simultaneously give pride of place to the specific location while catering for the building's users. These three trends exist alongside a fourth that is well able to hold its own within the international avant-garde movements.

The products of the first trend, known as Integral Functionalism, are solid constructions, horizontal in profile and with heavy protective walls of exposed concrete, while also rehabilitating traditional local features such as the courtyard and the portico. Teodoro González de Léon and Abraham Zabludovsky are two of the most important designers, responsible for numerous public buildings, alongside Alejandro Zhon, David Muñoz, and J. Francisco Serrano. The second, 'sculptural', trend has recourse to bold structures, Agustín Hernandez being the most audaciously creative and innovative architect, alongside Manuel González Rul. The third trend, 'Emotional Architecture', derives from the ideas of Barragán and is an offshoot of Regionalism. Constructions are dense and of low height with thick walls and internal areas designed to produce an emotional impact by their use of rich textures and

traditional colours, with careful attention to lighting and the constant presence of water. There are numerous proponents of this style, the most famous being Ricardo *Legorreta, as well as Antonio Attolini, Carlos Mijares, Fernando González Gortázar, and Diego Villaseñor; and, in landscape architecture, Mario Schjetnan. Finally, within the international trend, a wealth of new ideas flowed from younger designers such as Luis and Félix Sánchez, Nuno-Macgregor-De-Buen, Enrique Norten, Alberto Kalach, and Issac Broid, who suggested a number of thought-provoking approaches. LNM (trans. KL)

Sanford, T. E., *The Story of Architecture in Mexico* (1947)

Meyer, Hannes (1889–1954) German architect. Notorious for his uncompromising Functionalism and absolute rejection of aesthetic considerations in his projects, Meyer promoted a rational Modernism through his participation in the left-wing organization ABC and his stormy directorship of the *Bauhaus, to which he was appointed by *Gropius in 1928. As a member of ABC, he advocated a progressive collectivism, and joined forces with another member, Hans Wittwer. Their projects for the Petersschule in Basel and the League of Nations in Geneva were starkly dramatic designs, even though Meyer developed them according to his famous dictum, 'Building is only organization: social, technical, economic, psychological organization.' At the Bauhaus, Meyer emphasized a scientific architectural training and product design. He also realized his major built work during these years, the austere General German Trade Unions Federation in Bernau. Sympathetic toward Communism, Meyer was dismissed from the Bauhaus as the Nazi party gained power. He moved to the Soviet Union until 1936, when Stalin replaced all radical cultural activities with Socialist Realism. After two years in Switzerland, he emigrated to Mexico, only to languish in various public agencies until his return to Switzerland in 1949. CO

Winkler, K.-J., *Der Architekt Hannes Meyer* (1989)

Michelangelo Buonarroti (1475–1564) Italian architect. He was apprenticed to the painter Domenico Ghirlandaio and practised painting, mostly in fresco, throughout his career, but he considered himself primarily a sculptor. He claimed not to be an architect, and wrote in his only theoretical statement about architecture: 'Surely the architectural members derive from human members. Whoever has not been or is not a good master of the figure and most of all, of anatomy, cannot understand anything of it.' A sculptural disposition infused his architectural design, starting with his winning—but unexecuted—competition project for the façade of San Lorenzo, Florence (1515–20). The façade project was abandoned in 1520 in favour of a memorial chapel.

Michelangelo adopted the basic articulation (dark *pietra serena* pilasters and entablatures) of *Brunelleschi's Sacristy on the opposite side of the chancel. Within it, he introduced an entrance level faced entirely with veined marble, the articulation of which launched his career as a daring innovator, introducing fantastic variations of classical elements, most strikingly in the doors and tabernacles flanking the two Ducal tombs that occupy opposite sides of the chapel. The coffered dome was completed by 1524, but the carving of the sculptures dragged on into the mid 1530s.

Work on the Library of the monastery of San Lorenzo, which the Medici supported as a public resource, began in 1523. Monastic libraries were normally on the upper storey to escape water damage; in this case Michelangelo raised the reading room half a floor above the second level of the cloister arcade in order to permit illumination from windows placed above the arcade roof. This required a stairway in the contiguous entrance *ricetto* to access the higher reading room. He also had to support the whole structure on the thin pre-existing walls of the monastic quarters, and to avoid the traditional employment of columnar aisles.

The vestibule is a shocking space to enter, as the stairway seems to pour down from the entrance (the curvilinear forms of the steps recall the flow of lava), and the columns are mysteriously recessed into niches. The reading room desks were placed along the walls, and each bay was a coordinated design binding floors, desks, walls, and ceiling. A triangular reading room planned for Greek books was never built.

When the Pope and his allies attacked the Florentine Republic in 1529, Michelangelo was put in charge of fortifications to supplement the obsolete medieval walls. Many inventive and vigorous drawings survive, some resembling crustaceans and other biomorphic forms; the bastions explode outward from the walls and gates as if to attack the enemy. The proposals were impractical, being conceived—at a crucial moment when the only hope was to make ditches and earthworks—for masonry structures that would have taken years to build. But they foresaw forms that became standard in later centuries.

Michelangelo moved to Rome in 1534, and was soon involved with the scheme of Paul III Farnese to modernize the civic piazza on the Capitoline Hill—which already had a medieval palace of the Senators (judges) at the rear and a 15th-century one for the Conservators (counsellors) on the west. During the Renaissance and after, the papacy controlled most of the city's functions. Michelangelo began by setting the ancient equestrian statue of Marcus Aurelius on a high base at the centre of an oval pavement that served to coordinate the unrelated buildings and the ramp leading up the hill. He gave the two existing buildings new faces, giving the Senators a climactic double-ramped staircase, and adding a third palace for theatrical effect (it had no function) to the east, mirroring the Conservators'. The lateral palaces, which had ground-floor loggias with rectangular bays topped by flat arches and separated by colossal Corinthian pilasters, expressed a dynamic tension between

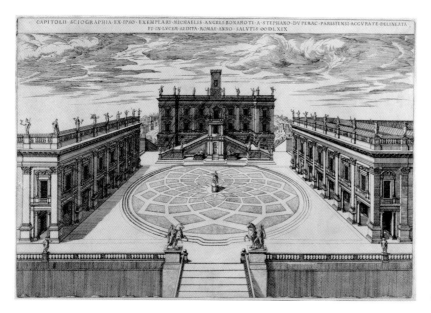

CAPITOLII·SCIOGRAPHIA·EX·IPSO·EXEMPLARI·MICHAELIS·ANGELI·BONAROTI·A·STEPHANO·DV PERAC·PARISIENSI·ACCVRATE·DELINEATA
ET·IN·LVCEM·AEDITA·ROMAE·ANNO·SALVTIS·∞·DLXIX

The Campidoglio, Rome
(Michelangelo, from c.1535)

weighing-down and pushing-up. The result was one of the most impressive public spaces in modern history. Construction was delayed until the 1560s, when Michelangelo could no longer supervise it. We know his intentions only from a posthumous engraving, which may or may not represent his final intentions.

In 1546 Michelangelo was summoned to work on the Basilica of St Peter. The central core of the structure—the vast central crossing and the four arms extending from it to form a Greek cross within a cube—was largely fixed, but he was still able to determine the design of the exterior (except for the façade). To realize his majestic and fluid perimeter he demolished the outer shell, just initiated by his predecessor and adversary Antonio da Sangallo the Younger. He created a compact outer elevation employing a colossal Corinthian order, the vertical accents of which were echoed by paired columns around the drum of the central dome. He gave the

dome itself an inner and outer shell, the latter being articulated by 16 external ribs rising to a prominent lantern, recalling the Cathedral of Florence. His final intention seems to have been to make the dome hemispherical. Subsequently the dome was heightened, following the more Gothic elevated curve which Michelangelo had considered in some of his early sketches (*see* DELLA PORTA, GIACOMO), the nave lengthened, and a different façade added (*see* MADERNO).

In 1559 the Florentine community in Rome turned to Michelangelo to design its church San Giovanni de' Fiorentini, so he produced a suite of innovative drawings for a central-plan structure of which one was chosen as the basis for a model (destroyed, but reproduced in engravings) of uncharacteristic sobriety.

In 1561 Pope Pius IV commissioned the Porta Pia, a city gate at the terminus of the Via Pia, which linked the piazza on the Quirinal Hill to the city walls. Michelangelo faced his structure toward the city rather than toward the incoming visitor as in earlier city portals, emphasizing the theatrical character of the commission. The façade is a flat wall upon which Michelangelo applied pseudo-classical ornament particularly bizarre in its inventiveness. At the same time Pius asked Michelangelo to transform the nearby ruins of the Baths of Diocletian into a church and monastery, Santa Maria degli Angeli. Michelangelo adapted the huge laterally disposed *frigidarium* space as the transept, and extended a chancel and choir perpendicular to it and opposite the entrance, which faced the outdoor semicircular exedra. The transformation, since then completely erased by a late Baroque reconstruction, rescued the baths from decay.

Michelangelo oversaw few of his projects, and many were never realized. Fortunately his drawings, those of contemporaries, and prints preserve the record of his inspired architectural imagination.   JA

Ackerman, James S., *The Architecture of Michelangelo* (2 vols., 1961)

Argan, G. C., *Michelangelo* (1993)

de Tolnay, Charles, *Corpus dei disegni di Michelangelo* (4 vols., 1975–80)

Michelozzo de Bartolommeo (1396–1472)

Italian architect and sculptor. After working in the studios of Ghiberti and Donatello, Michelozzo turned to architecture.

In the countryside outside Florence, Michelozzo attempted to moderate the fortress-like appearance of existing buildings such as the villas Il Trebbio (1420s) and Cafaggiolo (1420s) with their towers, machicolations, and closed plans, by inserting courtyards wherever possible, and opening up the building to the landscape. At Villa Careggi (1433), he was able to add a courtyard and a *loggia.

Turning to Florence, he designed a circular plan with 9 radiating chapels, Santa Annunziata (1444–55), a clumsy addition tacked on to the existing basilica, a design fault recognized by his contemporaries, such as Brunelleschi. Paradoxically, in the more secure environment of the town, his major work, the Palazzo Medici-Riccardi (1444–59), showed all the characteristics of a fortress.

Since the building is the first example of what was to become a familiar Italian type, the *palazzo, it is worth examining in some detail. The tremendous bulk of the palazzo (68 m or 223 ft by 57 m or 187 ft) is emphasized by the heavy rustication of the base, the 3 m (10 ft) tall oversailing cornice, and the preponderance of wall over round-headed window. The effect is lightened somewhat by the ashlar masonry of the two upper storeys. The entrance is set at one-third of the way on the longer side, and leads to an arcaded courtyard, which itself has an entrance to a plain courtyard. Apart from the ornamental detail of the cornice, and the arcading of the courtyard, the building owes more to medieval precedents than to *Renaissance principles.

PG

Michelucci, Giovanni (1891–1991) Italian

architect, whose first major built work, the Santa Maria Novella railway station in Florence (with N. Baroni, P. N. Berardi, I. Gamberini, S. Guarnieri, and L. Lusanna, 1932–5), was an important victory for Italian Rationalism in a state-sponsored competition. Following World War II, his projects, like the Chiesa di San Giovanni Battista on the Autostrada del Sole near Florence (1960–64), explored the idiosyncratic and expressive dimensions of space and materials.   BLM

Mies van der Rohe, Ludwig (1886–1969)

German architect. Mies was among the most influential of 20th-century architects, whose pursuit of universals and reducing design to its bare essentials produced work central to the ideal of an *International Style, and helped his transition from Europe to North America. His philosophy of 'less is more' also later made him the patron saint of minimalists, but he was too easy to imitate badly, and there were paradoxes at the heart of his work.

Mies's education was predominantly technical, and he gained early experience of building with his father, a monumental mason. In 1905 he moved to Berlin to work in the office of Bruno Paul, then undertook a longer stint with Peter Behrens, where he worked on the AEG Turbine Factory and was job architect for the St Petersburg Embassy. His first independent commission, the Riehl house of 1907, already shows sober simplicity and mastery of detail. His second, the Perls house of 1911, adds the influence of Karl Friedrich Schinkel, a study advocated by Behrens. Marriage to Ada Bruhn in 1913 improved his finances and sustained a small practice of private houses until the mid 1920s, but it was contact with the Berlin avant-garde in 1921–2 that launched Mies, for he joined the Novembergruppe and wrote for the magazine *Gestaltung*, started by Hans Richter, El Lissitzky, and Theo van Doesburg.

His debut was a series of speculative projects for exhibition and publication which proved extraordinarily prophetic: the glass skyscrapers of 1922, a concrete office building of 1923, and the concrete and brick country houses of 1923 and 1924. The latter, with walls of glass and brick treated as free-standing planes, brilliantly mixed the influence of Frank Lloyd *Wright with compositional ideas from Lissitzky and De *Stijl. Mies shared his office with Hugo *Häring, and together in 1925 they set up the Ring, an association which brought modernists together and paved the way for *CIAM.

The following year, as vice-president of the Deutsche Werkbund, Mies gained leadership of the Weissenhof housing exhibition at Stuttgart (1927), the first great demonstration of modernist solidarity. He crowned it with a beautifully proportioned 3-storey block of flats whose generalized form maximized variation in partitioning, announcing a lifelong

obsession with flexibility. It was justified on the basis that we cannot predict how buildings will be used, but it permitted Mies an easy abdication from functionally specific and place-specific design. The virtue of reduction was shown again in the almost functionless Barcelona Pavilion of 1929, populated only by a single sculpture and his own elegant chairs. Drawing on the brick country house project, it was spatially fluid and fastidiously executed, standing out among its traditional neighbours like a modernist pearl. Though demolished after the exhibition, its mythical life in print prompted its resurrection on the same site in 1986. Mies's other pre-war masterpiece, the luxurious Tugendhat house in Brno of 1929–30, was similar in style and conception.

The economic downturn following the Wall Street crash left him without work, so he took the headship of the Dessau Bauhaus in 1930, developing the architectural course. After the Bauhaus was finally suppressed by the Nazis in 1933, Mies attempted to ingratiate himself with the regime, competing for the Reichsbank in 1933 and taking part in other state projects, but by 1937 it was clear that modernists would be ousted from every field.

Reluctantly he accepted the Headship of the Armour Institute's school in Chicago (IIT from 1940), beginning an American career which brought work of a different scale. It began with the planning of the IIT campus in the late 1940s, and the construction of a modest, elegant, and fastidiously detailed series of buildings whose virtues were immediately evident, even enhanced in their simplicity and perfection in the black and white illustrations. There followed prototypes for high-rise steel buildings that became international models: Lake Shore Drive apartments in Chicago of 1948–51, and Seagram Building, New York, of 1954–7. It mattered not to Mies that an apartment block and an office be treated the same way, nor whether it was intended for New York, Chicago, Toronto (Dominion

Main entrance, Crown Hall, Illinois Institute of Technology, Chicago (Mies van der Rohe, 1956)

1963–9), Montreal (Westmount 1965–8), or London (the ill-fated Palumbo project). A design for a great open hall under an exposed trussed roof submitted for the National Theatre Mannheim competition of 1953 was equally unspecific to place and purpose.

Mies's most extreme statement of universality was a late masterpiece, the New National Gallery in Berlin of 1962–8. It had been proposed ten years earlier as the headquarters of Bacardi in Cuba. The perfect square black steel temple on eight columns serves merely as the temporary exhibition gallery, the permanent collection being relegated to the basement under artificial light. But loss as a gallery is countered by gain as a monument, marking a return to native soil and a more overt Classicism saluting *Schinkel. The building is unique and would be devalued by repetition, particularly use for another purpose. This is the Miesian

paradox, for he proclaimed that serial production was the 'spirit of the age', and the great prototypes could supposedly run on automatically. But it never worked: through restriction of the field and tireless devotion to detail, Mies created a haunting mirage of calm and ease which his countless followers were unable to emulate.   PBJ

Neumeyer, Fritz, *Das kunstlose Wort* (1986, translated 1991)
Schulze, Frank, *Mies van der Rohe* (1985)

mihrab A recess in a *mosque, often adorned with a pair of columns and an arch, articulating the *qibla* wall. This recess, a concave niche on the wall, was often elaborately decorated with vegetal motifs and verses from the Qur'an. However, a concave mihrab was not a sacred element, serving only as the indication of the *qibla*.

The mihrab emerged long after the time of the Prophet, when the direction of prayers was indicated by a stone. The mihrab was first incorporated in a mosque in the reconstruction of the prophet's mosque in Medina by the caliph al-Walid (AD *c*.709), in which the Muslims employed Coptic and Syrian artists and masons. Most likely, these masons and artists introduced the use of classical niches to articulate the direction of the *qibla*. This niche then became an essential feature in the architecture of mosques, in which its significance was indicated by intricate decorations. In its evolution, variants of mihrab appeared, such as the flat mihrab and the recessed mihrab that formed a particular room. In *Sinan's mature works, the space inside a mosque was turned into a single, unobstructed space in which the narrow, elongated mihrab became a visual focus inside the mosque.   ABS

military architecture Fortresses and fortifications are military architecture, and so are such details as embrasures and battlements; but the original and ultimate purposes of military features are seldom the same. A town wall designed to deter intruders readily becomes a symbol of power, and hence a necessary indication of civic dignity long after any military threat has receded. Military features are so accepted in architecture that even their symbolic meaning may be passed over without a thought. When archery was the most effective means of attack, a high embattled parapet that could protect archers at the same time as providing narrow gaps through which they shot their arrows was a sensible means of finishing the wall of a powerful fortification. Yet already in the early 13th century Bishop Puiset began his new palace at Wells, Somerset, within a proud, moated, and embattled site, in a more chivalrous than defensive mood. But even that was forgotten by the numberless church builders who scattered embattled parapets atop their naves and chancels as though they were expecting mortal combat

with the devil on a daily basis. The route from serious purpose to sensible symbol and then to forgetful decoration is indeed quick and easy.

Military architecture is essentially about walls. They impede attackers and elevate defenders, a demonstrable purpose from the time of the Great Wall of China to the present West Bank wall of Israel. Their history is not entirely illustrious because history likes events, but it is worth remembering that it was not the walls of ancient Troy that were breached. So long as walls are complete, unlike the Maginot Line, they have an encouragingly fair chance of success when their purpose is put to the test. The hill-forts of Iron Age Britain had embanked walls that were doubled in height by making use of the earth thrown up from the ditches dug out below them, and these, formed like Maiden Castle, Dorset, in triplicate with palisaded parapets, were an even more terrible obstacle to attackers who, having breached the outer line, found themselves confined within the ditch of the next line. This was a lesson that the Crusaders relearned in the Levant, not from the infidel Moors but from the Christians of the East. Just as many British hill-forts had double or even triple walls, so it became common practice in the 12th century to surround castle keeps with enclosing walls of stone, and then to double them so that an enemy who penetrated the outer wall would be trapped between it and the inner wall. Nowhere is this better exemplified than in the great Crusader castle of Krak des Chevaliers, which the Knights of the Order of St John of Jerusalem began in 1142. The lesson was heeded in Europe, spectacularly at Dover Castle, where the outer curtain wall, completed in 1214, though breached in 1216, so successfully impeded any development of the attack that it quickly failed.

Unfortunately walls have to have their breaches simply to allow those who need their defence to go in and out. Maiden Castle forced those seeking entry to take a contorted route through its triple walls, each angle being overlooked by a powerful salient. The stone walls of early European citadels did likewise. The narrow entrance to Mycenae (c.1450 BC) was confined by high walls that formed a dromos, thus making attackers advancing by this route vulnerable to defensive fire long before they reached the gate. The route to the Acropolis of Athens is similarly tortuous, but its lack of defensive buildings suggests that the intervening millennium had transformed it into a traditional processional way up the sleep slopes of the hill. Even the apparently highly conscious provision of confined and angled approaches to the main entrances of some medieval castles seem on analysis to be designed as much for the formalities of welcome as for the repulse of enemies. The steep staircase by which a visitor gains access to Castle Rising (begun c.1138) in Norfolk is more attuned to friendly processions of dignitaries than to repulsing belligerent foes, for all the evident *meurtrières* (loopholes) along the way. Nor is this an exception to the rule, since that most magnificent of all English castles, Dover (largely 1180s), was similarly provided with a staircase rising up to its first-floor entry and the provision of a chapel along the way. Gateways themselves took on an undoubted defensive guise, often with massive flanking towers, overhanging machicolations, and embattled parapets, and with such purposeful intent that an attacker would prefer to attempt a breach elsewhere along a fortified *enceinte*. But a gate still provided a route through which a victorious army would progress, and hence played a symbolic role in the celebrations, and descended into the formalities of a chivalrous introduction to a stately mansion or college. For the Romans it was the point of departure for the *triumphal arch, the purpose of which was entirely ceremonial and commemorative.

While strong gateways deterred attackers, walls were readily breached by scaling, battering, or mining. Projecting towers gave the defenders a better means of bringing concentrated fire on to the attackers. Roman

military engineers consequently built towers at intervals along their walls, just as the Chinese had done along the Great Wall. Hadrian's Wall, which from the late 1st to the start of the 5th century divided Caledonia from Roman Britain, was similarly punctuated by mile castles, with smaller turrets between them, and, at greater intervals, forts that comprised buildings to serve all the domestic and logistic needs of the local garrison.

The walls of Roman towns were similarly provided with towers and gateways, as the remains of London's Roman walls still show. This enhancement of a wall's defensive capability passed from Rome to Byzantium and thence to medieval towns generally. The 5th-century Theodosian walls of Constantinople, as Byzantium was renamed, together with their polygonal and round towers built of tile-laced stone, became a model for any town aspiring to the power of imperial Rome, notably Edward I's Caernarfon (begun 1283) in north Wales. The greater efficacy of round rather than square towers was quickly understood, since they presented no corners or dead ground to aid miners, a fact graphically demonstrated at Rochester Castle, where a square corner tower was mined in 1215 and so replaced with a round one.

A later age, which understood the efficacy of towers, but, as a result of greater military mobility and the advent of guns, was disenchanted with long walls, relied on chains of towers, usually to defend steep valleys and strategic roads running through them or to defend the coast. Hence the Knights of St John defended the Maltese coastline with a line of six forts c.1609–20, each one in the form of rectangular towers carrying artillery pieces, and later on added another two dozen similar smaller ones. The Napoleonic wars produced similar chains of towers, notably the hundred and more Martello Towers (1805–12) of south-eastern England, whose efficacy, never tested, was already proved by their prototype, the tower on Mortella

Point, Corsica, which successfully repulsed an attack by two British warships in 1794. Although not strictly military, the most notorious defensive towers were the domestic strongholds of the internecine families of medieval Italy, whose utility was quickly copied elsewhere for symbolic purposes as a means of establishing the potency of a family's patrician standing.

The effects of gunnery on military architecture were slow at first, largely because early cannons were as dangerous to the gunners as to their targets. The main evidence of the new weaponry lies in the loopholes that appear in fortified walls from the 1370s, for example on Canterbury's West Gate. By the 16th century the effect on architecture was becoming established. Guns did not particularly need elevation, so their mounting could be low. This was an advantage since a low tower offered a lesser target than a high one. Moreover, although often rectangular, towers were more usually rounded so as to deflect shot, and had battered walls, sloping inward as they rose. The parapet rounded off the battering, once again to deflect shot. Cannon either fired from splayed embrasures set into the walls or from splays in the parapet itself so that they might be traversed. Apart from its lack of height, this form was already ancient, and, suitably adapted for advances in the ordnance it mounted, continued in use until the age of the guided missile. It was nevertheless augmented, mainly by the addition of an outer ring accommodating further gun platforms, or of round lobes, so as to present all-round fire against any direction of attack. These practicalities produced several plans that suggest the triumph of ideal geometry over military efficiency. Thus Henry VIII countered a Continental threat to the English coast in 1539 with a series of artillery forts that include: Camber Castle, Sussex, a circular tower surrounded by an octagonal outer curtain with four projecting semicircular bastions and a fifth one for an entrance; Sandown and Walmer Castles, Kent, circular centres with circular outer curtains with four projecting lobes; Deal, Kent, a circular centre with six projecting lobes and an outer curtain of a further six, syncopated lobes; Hurst Castle, Hampshire, with inner and outer dodecagons and three projecting lobes; and Sandgate Castle, Kent, based on a central circular tower and a spherical triangle for the inner curtain with corner turrets.

The generally attractive plans of these forts had long been superseded by a far more threatening plan that could combine all-round fire with raking fire along the walls to cut down any attacker who reached them. The plan was based on the arrow-shaped bastion, which pointed outwards from every angle of a curtain wall and mounted artillery which could traverse in an outward direction. The great innovation of the form, however, lay in the embrasures hidden in the neck of the arrow behind its triangular head, because the fire from the cannon behind these was trained to sweep the outer face of the adjacent arrowheads. This covered all eventualities, as had been already found in Italy c.1450, and is wonderfully exemplified by the town walls of Lucca. The English already utilized arrow bastions to defend Calais in 1532, and they were taken up rapidly across Europe for defensible town walls from Antwerp to Vienna. Less common in Britain, Portsmouth has some, and Berwick was defended against the Scots with five bastions (planned 1558). The Knights of St John defended their new city of Valletta on Malta after the siege of 1556 with massive walls, four great bastions to defend the landward side, and a reconstructed Fort St Elmo utilizing yet more still. The outer defences of Paris incorporated twelve such bastions, a form which the great French military engineer Vauban adopted for the extensive works he inaugurated as commissary general of fortifications (1678–1707). The arrow bastion plan remained in use for forts too, notably Fort George (planned 1747) in Scotland, which housed a garrison and all its impedimenta to defend the north against Jacobite uprising. The forts planned in the 1850s to protect Portsmouth from French invasion on its vulnerable landward side, as exemplified by Fort Brockhurst (c.1860), still employ elements of the arrow-shaped bastion, albeit of modified form.

The increasing calibre of ordnance in the later 19th century, combined with breech loading and rifled barrels, so increased the power of artillery that fortifications made ever greater use of underground chambers that would resist bombardment. Much of the Rinella and Cambridge Batteries on Malta, built by the British in 1878–86 to accommodate 100-ton cannons, were built within a pentagonal earth embankment which housed magazines and the steam-powered hydraulic equipment to charge and load them, as well as barracks for a permanent garrison. It was not such a long step to the complex arrangement of gun emplacements and underground chambers for magazines and garrisons that formed the Maginot Line and the Atlantic Wall, nor, for that matter, to the hardened silos that thankfully kept intercontinental ballistic missiles well below ground.

See also JAPAN, TO 1912 (GENERAL CHARACTERISTICS). APQ
Hughes, Q(uentin), *Military Architecture* (1991)

Mills, Robert (1781–1855) US architect. He trained in Washington around 1800 under James Hoban (c.1762–1831), with guidance from Thomas *Jefferson (1743–1826). During his apprenticeship with Benjamin Henry *Latrobe (1764–1820), from 1803 to 1808, he designed Charleston's Circular Church (1804–6, demolished). In his thirties he created the Monumental Church, Richmond (1812–17), and the Washington Monument, Baltimore (1813–42)—the latter city his home for five productive years. The 1820s were spent in South Carolina, where he designed a canal, many courthouses and jails, and the noted Fireproof Building, Charleston (1822–7). As later in Washington, fireproofing by heavy masonry construction, vaulting, and use of iron provided the unifying theme to a series

of rather stolid *Greek Revival productions. As Architect of Public Buildings, Mills gave Washington many landmarks, including the Patent Office, Treasury, and Post Office, all begun in 1836–9, and, although interpreted as uniquely American, in fact echoing British examples. Most prominent was the Washington Monument (designed 1845), an immense obelisk that never received its planned embellishments. As was typical of many of his peers, Mills struggled to find commissions and by the time of his death he was virtually forgotten. He left behind a dozen publications on architecture and a built legacy of solidity and permanence. WBM
Bryan, J. M., *Robert Mills* (2001)

minaret A tower attached to a mosque, an English term derived from Turkish. Various terms in Arabic reflected varieties of purposes of minaret. The most common term, *manara,* related to ancient signal towers, while the common term used in North Africa, *sawma,* reflected its evolution from ascetic cells on top of a mosque. A rarer term, *madhana,* referred to its use as a platform for muezzins to call for prayer. However, in central Asia, the origin of minaret also relates to commemorative structures for a victory or for a death. The first minaret appeared on the Amr Mosque in Fustat (near modern Cairo), Egypt (AD c.673). In general, minarets served as a marker for a mosque, expressing a mosque as a centre in Islamic communities or even announcing the presence of Islam in a particular place.

The minaret appeared in various forms, indicating the geographical and cultural regions in which they were used. Minarets in Arabia and North Africa were square-based, echoing the influence from the Great Mosque of Damascus. In Persia, Turkey, central Asia, and India, minarets took a cylindrical form. The Ottomans produced a rather distinctive minaret, a slender cylindrical tower with two or three circular balconies, topped with an elongated conical roof, resembling a pencil. ABS

minbar A pulpit from which a preacher delivered his sermons, located to the right of the *mihrab. The minbar originated from the small steps that the Prophet used to address his followers in his mosque in Medina. It assumed a definitive form during the Umayyad era (AD 660–750). In this early Islamic period, mosques became the centre of social and political life, in which the caliphs or local rulers delivered their religious and political messages from the minbar. Thus, the minbar acquired its secondary role as a symbol of prestige and authority, so that it was reserved for the congregational mosque only. Over time, however, caliphs withdrew from daily affairs and sermons were delegated to professional preachers.

A minbar commonly took the shape of a wooden pulpit, intricately decorated, with a series of steps terminating on a platform, often topped with a cupola. A preacher would stand on the last step, because the platform was symbolically reserved for the Prophet. Other materials were also employed, such as stone in India and marble in Ottoman Turkey. ABS

Minoan architecture The Minoan civilization flourished for almost 600 years, but the character of its architecture is rather difficult to judge. Most is known about palace architecture, which falls into two distinct periods: the Old Palace (1900–*c.*1625 BC) and New Palace periods (*c.*1625–*c.*1375 BC). All the palaces were destroyed, either by earthquakes, or, in the later period, possibly by the *Mycenaeans.

Extensive remains of palaces (Knossos, Phaistos, Mallia, and Kato Zakros) have been excavated, but because the purposes of many of the rooms are unknown, it is difficult to make sense of the layout. This uncertainty applies particularly to the largest palace, Knossos, imaginatively restored by Sir Arthur

Evans from the beginning of the 20th century. In his own words, what we see today is a 'reconstitution', but at this distance of time the reconstructed entrances look uncannily like 1920s stripped Classicism, and some of the colours applied to the architecture resemble a fashionable interior of the same period. The other palaces are more truthfully if less entertainingly restored, but still present many enigmas.

However, the following characteristics do seem to be beyond dispute. All the palaces have a courtyard of about 50 m by 20 m (164 ft by 66 ft), but the rooms are not arranged symmetrically or, to the modern eye, very intelligibly around this open space. The walls consist of gypsum faced with plaster, enclosing a rubble core, and are tied together by wooden crossbeams, a firm but elastic structure well suited to an earthquake zone. At Mallia a wider variety of materials was used: sandstone, grey limestone, red mud-bricks, and red plaster. PG

Mique, Richard (1728–94) French architect and garden designer, who worked for Queen Marie-Antoinette from 1770, and was appointed Court architect five years later. Perhaps for financial reasons, Louis XVI was immune to the *bâtomanie* which possessed his predecessors, so Mique's opportunities were at first limited mainly to the elegant decoration of the Queen's apartments, and to garden buildings such as the graceful Temple d'Amour (1778). At the Petit Trianon, Versailles, he designed the Hameau (1778–82), a model village consisting of a farm and a small group of thatched-roof cottages of quite substantial size, to accommodate the Queen's fantasies of peasant life. PG

Mithraeum A temple dedicated to the Persian demigod Mithras. The cult's rites, like those of its deadly Christian rivals, included a sacred banquet, taken before a statue or fresco of Mithras and his associates Helios, Selene, and Serapis. As well as a banqueting room, Mithraic temples included a grotto, since Mithras was born of a rock, and initiation rooms. They are common in the provinces, notably at Dura Europos. The Mithraeum at S. Clemente, Rome, was founded in an apartment built after the fire of AD 64, the grotto being in its courtyard; and the Mithraeum at S. Prisca incorporates restored statues and frescoes. The remains of a possible Mithraic temple were discovered during excavations in the 1950s when Bucklersbury House, City of London, was under construction, and they are now displayed in its forecourt.   APQ

models, architectural The definition that models are three-dimensional structures at varying scales may seem unnecessary, but the original Italian word *modello* often refers to a drawing, and Inigo Jones called some of his plan drawings 'models'.

Models may help non-designers to visualize an architect's proposals more easily than do *drawings or plans. This purpose may have been what *Alberti had in mind, in one of the earliest references (1452) to the use of models: 'All these Particulars [embellishment which continues to delight upon repeated viewings] you must provide for by means of your Model' (*De re aedificatoria* Book IX chapter 9). Palladio submitted models (1576) for a longitudinal and a central plan for his church of Il Redentore, to assist the Venetian Senate in their choice.

Historians have occasionally benefited by being able to examine a model of a proposal which was not accepted or not completed, such as Antonio da Sangallo the Younger's 1:24 scale model for St Peter's (1538–43) and Lutyens' model for the Catholic Cathedral, Liverpool (1931–4), respectively. The latter is at a scale of 1:40 (approximately), so that the model itself is 5 m (17 ft) long and 3.8 m (12 ft 6 inches) high, giving an overwhelming sense of the massiveness of the project.

But the most interesting type is the model which shows something of an architect's thought process, although a model is inevitably less informative than a series of drawings. The role or the form of models in the pre-Renaissance period is not well documented, but when we reach the era of *Brunelleschi, the situation is much clearer. In searching for the appropriate visual and structural form for the dome of Florence Cathedral (from 1417), Brunelleschi used several models in a variety of materials (apparently, even vegetables).

From this point, Italian architects seem to have used models as a matter of course, for almost the next three centuries. In particular *Michelangelo, who said of his buildings that 'I had prepared an exact model, *as I do of everything*' (Vasari, *Lives*, Book IV), relied heavily on the use of models for composition. His model of the façade of St Peter's was realistically coloured, so as to illustrate the difference between brick and stone. For the cornice of Palazzo Farnese, a full-scale wooden model was placed in position to judge its effect *in situ* (1546).

The oldest definitively authenticated English model was made by *Wren for the chapel of Pembroke College, Cambridge, in 1663. Thereafter, Wren made frequent use of models, including several for St Paul's Cathedral at different stages of design. His example was followed by *Vanbrugh and *Hawksmoor, but from the mid-century onwards these seem to have been superseded by drawings. *Chambers and *Holland rarely employed models; *Adam and Holland appear to have used only drawings. *Soane was a significant exception, as he made far more use of models in the design process than any other previous architect. His splendid collection of 150 models, in a variety of materials, and to explore different aspects of design (plan/façade/ornament/volume) is to be found in the Sir John Soane Museum, London.   PG

Wilton-Ely, J., 'Architectural model', *Grove Dictionary of Art* (1996)

modern Classicism *See* CLASSICISM, MODERN.

Modernism, to 1975

The question In what ways does the Modern Movement claim to have produced an architecture that did not exist before?

In the first place we have to draw a clear distinction between the two terms 'Modern Architecture' and 'The Modern Movement'. The term 'modern architecture' has purely chronological connotations, meaning 'of the moment', and that is a property enjoyed, in its day, by every building of whatever nature. On the other hand, the term 'The Modern Movement' is grounded in specificity and intentionality and all its attributes are defined in the language of the revolutionary. These are the grounds upon which it will claim to have a basis of principle that differs from that of any other architecture.

Relationship to power As its very title indicates it was born in the Age of Revolution, and it was the child of much heated polemic between rival 'movements'. It raised challenging questions about the relationship of architecture to power, to stylistic order, to technology, to time.

It was born at the moment when William *Morris asked the question 'what is the use of art if it is not art for all?' In doing so, he had challenged once and for all the terms on which architecture might enhance the quality of life for all rather than the privileged few; and this in turn came to provoke recognition of the fact that what was needed was a profound change of ethos and working method in order to respond to a whole new

range of activities. The new element to be introduced was a desire for the engagement, assent (even collaboration) of those who would occupy the buildings rather than the privileged agents of 'power' who had commissioned them. It was a desire that changed everything. The architect was to assume something like the Hippocratic oath of the doctor—to listen, to explain, to advise, to heal, almost to redeem.

In a book about William Morris published in 1947, Giancarlo de *Carlo makes a number of striking claims. Firstly: 'The fundamental premises of the whole Modern Movement lie in the work and theory of Morris.' Secondly: 'the part of his teaching that remains today the most lively and of the hour is that which deals with the status of the architect. Morris, in teaching that architecture cannot be dissociated from the social and moral conditions of the day, restored an awareness to the architect of a mission towards men. It is necessary for those who wish to build for man to live close to man, to participate in his problems and his ventures to fight at his side for the satisfactory resolution of his moral and material priorities. For the architect to act authentically he cannot limit his contributions to that of taste and style but to expand his concerns to become a principal activating force in all the activities of his fellow men.' He goes on to say: 'It is this element in the teaching of Morris that constitutes the fundamental ethos of the Modern Movement, that inserts modern architecture into the story of the battle for human liberty.'

And he quotes from Morris as follows: 'To create a living art it is necessary above all to engage the public with the arts. It is essential that art should become an integral part of his life, as important as water and light . . . I cannot conceive of art as the privilege of the few, in the same way that I cannot conceive an education for the few or a liberty for the few.'

For the first time in history power was perceived to lie with every member of society (or at the very least

Fagus factory, Alfeld an der Leine, Germany (Walter Gropius, 1911)

their proclaimed representatives) and not just with the privileged few. This was the first plea for what in our time Alvar *Aalto was to call 'the democratization of architecture', and which he summed up in the phrase, 'architecture is only authentic when man is at the centre'. At the very beginning of his career he declared his belief that what was needed was a change in the values and ethos rather than the formal language of architecture. 'What is the use of a change in form if it is not a change in content?' (1927). Giancarlo de Carlo in his own practice was to press for the participation of the workers (who were to occupy his housing project in Terni in the formulation of the programme of requirements).

The question of style Inevitably, the democratization of architecture in political terms, and in the all-inclusiveness of tasks, entailed a comparable democratization in the language of form by sweeping aside the traditional hierarchy of style—a hierarchy

most eloquently illustrated in the map of the centre of Rome by Nolli (1748). It is based upon a convention that makes a hierarchical distinction between those structures that are deemed to be of a superior order ('architecture') and those of 'mere building'. In this convention only the monuments are credited with the status of 'architecture' by representing their interior floor plans, whereas everything else is submerged into an inarticulate quagmire. Everything else—one might say the whole of the day-to-day life of the city—is conceived of as formless.

The very strength of hieratic form lies in a heightening of the formal language through symbolism, prescriptive rules, symmetry and proportional systems, and ritual patterns of performance. All of these bestow poetic force and vividness in presentation: we are enjoying the spell-binding of high style. But, this trance-like spell demands a certain sacrifice because the immediacy and lucidity of impact rely as much upon what it leaves out, as what it celebrates: the very eloquence is

compounded of a courtly disdain which will not bend
to accommodate inconvenience and contradiction. The
goal of style is pure form.

Now this exclusiveness, this prerogative of 'Fine
Art', whose objective is, in Aristotle's definition, 'to
serve only itself' is a denial of the nature of a 'practical
art' whose very definition is 'to serve an end other than
itself'; and, as we will shortly see, the ends entailed by
serving the Everyman of William Morris are of a
different order, and now become multifarious in
responding to all sorts of demands, whose nature and
priorities may well conflict with the disciplines of
formal order. And so, another form of order is called
for, non-hierarchic and resourceful in accommodating
the unpredictable occasions of life. The attempt in
1932 by the tourists to Europe, Hitchcock and Philip
Johnson, who sought to encapsulate the essence of the
Modern Movement into an aesthetic formula entitled
'International Style' (*see* INTERNATIONAL MODERN) were
deeply resented by the true innovators, particularly in
Holland and Germany, who had gone so far in the
opposite direction as even to renounce the word
'architecture' itself in favour of the phrase 'the new
building'.

A new mandate By the middle of the 19th century, a
radical shift in both the diversity and scale of tasks to be
carried out came into being, and this brought with it
the responsibility to invent an ever widening range of
building types (many of them without precedent)
summoned to fulfil the appetite of a new society
grounded in massively growing industrialized enterprise.

The practical impact was itself twofold: for not only
was the traditional remit of architecture exploded out
of all proportion in comparison with the portfolio of
the 18th-century practitioner in qualitative terms, but
also the level of quantitative demand expanded almost
out of control to a scale at which sheer number became
an issue in itself.

The panoply of building types to be evolved
inevitably broke the mould of 18th-century precedent.
It embraced museums, theatres, hospitals, libraries,
railway stations, exhibition halls, town halls, asylums,
shopping malls, factories, schools, concert halls,
abattoirs, sporting arenas, prisons, ministries, hotels,
banks, exchanges, conservatories, department stores,
galleries and arcades, warehouses and office buildings,
and, most problematic of all, the growing demand
for dwellings for the workers. The proliferation
became endless. And within all these broad types,
diversification into yet further sub-types (a children's
hospital, an eye hospital, a chest hospital) deepened the
game into ramifying cycles of development,
obsolescence, and novelty.

This explosive diversity of requirements demanded a
freedom in formal invention that could not be satisfied
by the rules and conventions of a pre-established 'style'.
In his *Stones of Venice* (1851–3) Ruskin adumbrated a
design strategy that clearly anticipated later analogies
to organic form. He wrote: 'Gothic is not only the best
but the only rational architecture, as being that which
can fit itself most easily to all services, vulgar or noble.
Undefined in its slope of roof, height of shaft, breadth
of arch, or disposition of ground plan, it can shrink into
a turret, expand into a hall, coil into a staircase or spring
into a spire, with undegraded grace and unexhausted
energy, and whenever it finds occasion for change in its
form or purpose, it submits to it without the slightest
sense of loss either to its unity or majesty—subtle and
flexible like a fiery serpent, but ever attentive to the
voice of its charmer. And it is one of the virtues of the
Gothic builders, that they never suffered ideas of
outside symmetries and consistencies to interfere with
the real use and value of what they did. If they wanted
a window they opened one, a room they added one, a
buttress they built one.'

This is the great incantation celebrating the birth of
the English Free School.

The organizational complexity of many of these tasks has to be matched by an equally complex analytical and rational response. I illustrate this point by an astonishing project by Alfred *Waterhouse for the Law Courts in London in 1866–7. The bound volume presenting his competition submission contained 100 large pages, comprising 21 pages of closely argued text, 30 plates of drawings, 9 of which were elaborately detailed perspectives, and 50 pages of accommodation schedules, with a cost breakdown and further detailed descriptions.

In the design, the levels of access or segregation weave in strands with the delicacy of Swiss watchwork: isolation of the judges; segregation of the witnesses; jurors' consultation rooms, three separate types of public gallery ('general', 'respectable', and 'ladies')— and all of these in turn with separate access from a huge Galleria acting as a 'place of rendezvous for all who have business to transact in the courts as opposed to the public who come only to see and hear and who would have no access to it'. And this whole structure itself is held aloft over a pedestrian route at the level of the Strand and running north at right angles to the Galleria above. The intricacy of the parts and the grandeur of the urban concept constitute a new order of functional organization; and in his text Waterhouse even entertains consideration for factors of growth and change that anticipate by a hundred years concepts of morphological complexity in forms.

By definition the form of built order that can match the unpredictable demands of such participation will not conform to the tradition of literate vision controlled by central perspective, symmetry, proportional rigour, and canonic elements. A very different experience of space is introduced which offers simultaneously different viewpoints within the space rather than looking in from outside—total immersion. By definition therefore there are no rules, albeit that *Le Corbusier's set of 'Five Points' (or tactics) do

prepare a venue for play with five forms of freedom: independent structure; free plan; free façade; free ground; and free roof. In his later work he did deploy these freedoms with less subjection to *l'angle droite*, but it is above all in the exemplary work of *Scharoun and *Aalto that we are offered a hugely wide and richly diverse application of these tactics to concrete occasions.

Technical innovation   This demand for an ever widening range of building types, together with an ever increasing scale of demand, provoked in turn a prodigious surge of technological innovation, both in engineering design and in the invention of new materials. Above all, the possibility of erecting frame structures out of iron and steel components manufactured through industrialized mass production methods made possible the erection of the Crystal Palace in eight months: and in so doing, it tore up whatever visual order still arose from the limitations of the masonry arch (round or pointed). The invention of the elevator and associated mechanical systems broke the last limitations imposed by gravity.

All has changed   And so we have arrived at a position in which every aspect of architecture has been challenged in its traditional mould—its relationship to power, rejection of the concept of style, a complete transformation in the methods and scale of its technical base, a quantum leap in the range and diversity of its mandate and demand. All, it seems, has changed.

But how did it fare in practice after its proclaimed establishment at the first meeting of *CIAM in 1928?

In brief, the element of revolutionary polemic out of which this movement was born has never come fully to rest: the claims of the 'establishment' have never been acknowledged by many of the innovators who kept their distance from CIAM. That situation was epitomized when, at the very moment at which 'the victory of the Modern Movement' was all the cry, Alvar Aalto opened an important public lecture with the following words: 'Our time is full of enthusiasm for architecture because of the architectural revolution that has been taking place during these last decades. But it is like all revolutions: it starts with enthusiasm and it stops with some sort of Dictatorship. It runs off the track . . .' Aalto went on to invoke the engagement of a 'garde d'honneur, the hard-fighting squadron for humanizing technique in our time' of those who had remained true to the original aspirations of the Movement as opposed to those who settled for the compromises of establishment. Certainly it can be argued that Aalto's garde d'honneur can be likened to a running 'resistance movement' to certain tendencies, that have always lain entwined in the very heart of the revolutionary ethos itself. They stem essentially from the philosophy of Positivism and were stated in the late 1920s with deadly succinctness by the one-time Director of the *Bauhaus, Hannes *Meyer: 'All life is a striving after oxygen + carbon + sugar + starch + protein.' The place of art in the design process was confined to 'a system of organizing principles' directed to 'the sole reality that can be mastered—the measurable, visible and ponderable'. Science was to take the place of art. 'All things in this world are a product of the formula function times economics.'

This definition of 'functionalism' as a formula for avid instrumentality utterly failed to respect the traditional role of art as the imponderable factor of play that raises necessity to the level of a celebration of life; and it certainly has nothing to do with the joyous *functionalism of Aalto, Scharoun, Duiker, Häring, and other members of the resistance for whom the Play of Use and the Use of Play are interchangeable in the Practical Arts.

This rejection of 'play', which is the alchemy that transforms mere existence into a society of culture, was paralleled by a further undermining of cultural depth

by overt rejection of any continuity with past tradition. Time was to be celebrated but only as 'the time for change'. Gropius, who founded the avant-garde platform of the day, the Bauhaus, declared that 'Modern architecture is not built from some branch of an old tree, but is a new plant growing directly from roots'; Hannes Meyer wrote in 1926 that 'the unqualified affirmative of the present age presupposes the ruthless denial of the past'. Only the future mattered—the dream of a 'Brave New World'. This constituted a 'scorched earth' policy applied to the remembrance of things past and created a vacuum into which, as we all know too well, the Nazi and the Fascist quickly marched under the banners of a faked tradition.

But this rejection of true-tradition was not the attitude to the past held by contemporary Masters of the other arts. We have only to mention the names of Stravinsky, Picasso, Joyce, and Proust to be aware of an intense exchange of recall and allusion such that, in the phrase of T. S. Eliot, 'the past is altered by the present as much as the present is directed by the past'. Even within the Bauhaus itself, a very different voice (that of Paul Klee) warned that 'The people are not with us': this is the point at which we must face the fact that it was this assertion more than anything else that drained public approval from the Movement. The concept of a 'Brave New World' was itself bracing and was driven by a redemptive vision bustling with promises of a better life for the survivors of the slums. What was not acceptable was the denial of roots of personal identity as inheritor of a past, pride in family history and of birthplace, reassurance of some anchor against the indifferent tide.

Virtually all of those whom I have identified as the champions of the Resistance happily retained almost as a defining feature this positive relation to the past. Scharoun's approach to each new project was to initiate a deep excavation of the history of the site in order to reveal ancestral features of grain, orientation, or historic memory to inform the spirit of the new construction: Aalto's Villa Mairea is a love-song between the ancient chant of Karelia and the challenging voice of the truly new; Giancarlo de Carlo's rejuvenation of Urbino was inspired by findings in a recovered manuscript by Francesco di Giorgio.

Brave New World And so we have arrived at a position in which every aspect of architecture has been challenged in its traditional mould: its relationship to power; rejection of its models of form; upheaval in the scope of its technical base; and a quantum leap in the scale and diversity of its mandate.

Therein lies its claim to have produced an architecture that is radically new, profoundly other than all that preceded it.

How has it fared?

As a child of the Age of Revolution, it has not escaped a number of the internal conflicts and betrayals that are part of the revolutionary condition. In 1956, Alvar Aalto, the youngest of the Masters of the Heroic period between the two World Wars, announced that it had 'like all revolutions, begun with enthusiasm and ended in some form of dictatorship'. He had always been sceptical of every attempt to institutionalize its goals, establish standards, prescribe rules, and prioritize technological innovation, which became the ambition of the self-appointed establishment of the International Congress of Modern Architects.

And it is interesting to find that Giancarlo de Carlo, whose views about the birth of the movement in the ideas of William Morris we have described, should in his term, as a member of the third generation of the movement, announce that 'the modern movement has died many times'. And I believe it to be the case that the true original goals of the movement have only survived as the result of a kind of 'resistance movement' resolutely pursued pre-eminently by such architects as Aalto, Scharoun, and Asplund of the first generation of the movement and Giancarlo de Carlo and Aldo van Eyck of the later.

It is a continuous open-ended revolution that always resists the temptation to become a dictatorship.   cstjw

Wilson, C. St J., *The other tradition of modern architecture* (1995)

Modernism, 1975–2000 Modernism is often seen as a single orthodox ideology and style, although the movement split into different schools of thinking already at its outset. In fact, the very essence of Modernism is the continuous questioning and challenging of the convention and the accepted understanding of reality. In that fundamental sense, Modernism is centrifugal in its essence rather than centripetal, and consequently bound towards diversification rather than uniformity. During the 1960s, however, standard architecture in the industrialized Western world began to stifle into a shallow and unambitious technocratic practice, a banalized version of the International Style. The negative developments were particularly evident in the violent shattering of city centres and the repetitiousness and alienation of large housing areas. Due to its initial utopian aspirations, Modernism projected a universalizing tendency, which was reinforced by the inherent universality of technological and scientific rationality. Modernist architecture degraded into a visual aesthetic manner instead of its original social, cultural, and technological motifs.

On the individually creative front, however, the modern idiom kept branching into novel and more responsive approaches. Alongside the revival of the modernist language, as exemplified by the New York Five Group, the search for a culturally and geographically rooted architecture became a growing concern during the 1970s, but even these regional tendencies had their origins in early modernity. The concepts of place and *genius loci*, as well as cultural and geographic specificity, gained ground both in theory and practice. At the same time, Modernism became increasingly rooted in countries outside the Western economic sphere, and numerous culturally and regionally adapted architectures began to emerge in Africa, Asia, Australia, Mexico, and South America. On the other hand, since the late 1950s, European architecture had been inspired by non-Western architecture and vernacular traditions, as well as structuralist anthropological views of the interrelations of space, place, myth, and behaviour.

Criticism of modernist planning and architecture grew increasingly vocal. This violently critical attitude was exemplified by *Form, Function and Fiasco* (1974) by Peter Blake, who had earlier written the enthusiastic and widely read book *The Master Builders* (1960) on Frank Lloyd Wright, Le Corbusier, and Mies van der Rohe, and *Farväl till Funktionalismen* (Farewell to Functionalism) (1980) by Hans Asplund, son of the Nordic modern master Erik Gunnar Asplund.

Towards the end of the 1970s the criticism turned into a revisionist and historicist position, which was quickly named as *postmodernism. This movement had its beginnings in Robert Venturi's writings, such as *Complexity and Contradiction* (1966), and early buildings, whereas Leon and Rob Krier were among its early European proponents. Aldo *Rossi's writings and projects reintroduced the interest in traditional urban qualities and architectural typologies. Charles Jencks became the influential and diligent spokesman of this arrogant and nostalgic movement. The first influential presentation in Europe of the style was the Presence of the Past exhibition in 1980 at the Venice Biennale. An American equivalent was the mock competition for Late Entries to the Chicago Tribune Tower Competition (1922), organized the same year. Modernism was criticized for the abstractness and meaninglessness of its language, which made it unable to communicate with common people. The philosophical ground of postmodernism was shallow and the movement reverted to propagandist rhetoric.

Yet the attack made a number of established modernists, such as James Stirling, convert to historicism with such works as the Neue Staatsgalerie in Stuttgart (1977–84). Historicist appropriation and stylistic collage became fashionable also in architecture schools, which tend to reflect the shifts in architectural values.

Postmodernism was rather quickly replaced by the deconstructivist imagery of juxtaposed grids and forms and excessive verbalization and theorizing. The style was deliberately launched by the Deconstructivist Architecture exhibition in 1988 at the Museum of Modern Art in New York, curated by Phillip Johnson and Mark Wigley. The exhibition connected the trend with the Russian Constructivism of the 1920s, but Deconstruction turned into a highly intellectualized and theory-oriented approach, which drew its inspiration from the French deconstructivist philosophy of Jacques Derrida. The architectural movement lost its philosophical roots and turned into an aesthetic mannerism of fragmentation, distortion, and collage. As professional journals around the world were still presenting projects echoing deconstructivist aesthetics, a minimalist aspiration gained strength. The new Minimalism drew inspiration from similar ideas in painting and sculpture, but it also returned back to early modernist ideas of striking image and formal reduction. Minimalism was represented early on by Tadao Andô and a host of young Japanese designers, and the style had supporters also in England, France, Holland, Spain, and the Nordic countries, for instance.

Since the mid-1970s, high tech architecture has been one of the dominant lines of architectural thinking, as exemplified by the celebrated works of Norman *Foster, Richard *Rogers, Renzo *Piano and Jean Nouvel. During the prevailing stylistic profusion and confusion, this architecture seems to have obtained an authority among both clients and critics through the apparent unarguability of technological logic. In fact, high tech architecture has become symbolic of progress and technical sophistication. Even ecological architecture, which initially used low technology and rather primitive formal expression, has increasingly developed towards the use of advanced technologies. One of the most important current lines of modernist thinking combines the use of advanced technology with regional specificity and ecological objectives as exemplified by Renzo Piano, Glenn *Murcutt, and Thomas Hertzog.

During the past decades, Spain has continuously produced significant architectural projects, which demonstrate the social and cultural possibilities of architecture in creating a democratic, stimulating, and optimistic environment. The example of Spain provides assurance that Modernism can become fused with a cultural continuum.

Modern architecture has been accused of its bias to visual qualities and its failure to mediate emotional experiences. At the turn of the millennium, architecture has become increasingly interested in materiality, sensory richness, and emotive contents. During the last decades of the 20th century, Modernism has convincingly demonstrated its continued capacity for transformation, renewal, and adaptation, as well as for projecting cultural meaning and sensuous experiential qualities. Forceful globalization of values and the dominance of consumerist ideology, however, pose serious challenges to architecture, which is increasingly seen merely as a commodity and investment instead of being a genuine cultural expression.   JUP

modillion A small scrolled bracket in the shape of a console, usually placed regularly along the underside of a Corinthian or Composite cornice so as to support its upper member or corona. Being ornate, modillion cornices became fashionable decoration beneath the eaves of late-17th- and early-18th-century houses, often being exuberantly carved in wood.   APQ

module In *Classicism, a unit of measure based on the diameter of a column at its base, which is used to determine the proportions of other elements of a building; alternatively, a unit of measure for standard components which can be used for *prefabrication. The Modulor (*proportion) was *Le Corbusier's distinctive version of the concept (explained in *Le Modulor*, 1948).   PG

Moffatt, William Bonython (1812–87) English architect. *See* WORKHOUSES.

Moghul *See* INDIAN SUBCONTINENT (THE MUGHALS).

monasteries A monastery is a group of buildings devoted to accommodating monks, usually comprising a church, a cloister, and, laid out around it, a refectory, a dormitory, a chapter house, a house for the superior, a hostel for guests, and a sick house. Apart from these, there would be a kitchen and service rooms of various sorts, and, either within the precinct or in separate granges, there would be the agricultural and even industrial buildings that helped to provide economic support. Similar buildings known as nunneries or convents accommodated nuns.

Monasticism, which developed from the desire of hermits devoted to the faith to live together in communities, was formalized by St Benedict of Nursia (c.480–543), whose rule devised (c.529) for his own monastery at Monte Cassino became the basis of monastic life once Charlemagne had imposed it on all communities within the empire in 789. In a world rent by political turmoil and barbarian turbulence, monasteries became centres of civilization through their economic development of extensive estates as well as their devotion to religion, learning, and the arts. Despite vows of poverty, chastity, and obedience, monasteries became extremely rich through their skills as well as gifts, and ultimately transferred many benefits of Roman civilization to the Middle Ages.

The reform and revival of monasticism under St Benedict of Aniane (d. 822) coincides with an ideal layout for a monastery, now in the monastic library at St Gall in Switzerland. It is remarkable for depicting the standardized arrangements of future monasteries, particularly a square cloister on the south side of the abbey church with its adjacent rooms, a warming room or calefactory; above it, the monks' dormitory in the upper storey, placed on the east side of the cloister; the refectory with an adjacent kitchen on the south; and the cellar on the west. Rather more diagrammatically represented are the remaining buildings: animal shelters and a hostel on the public, west side of the precinct; service rooms and stores on the south; and novitiates' accommodation, an infirmary, and a monks' cemetery on the private east side.

Such arrangements were far from being simply an ideal, being put into effect at the island monastery of Mittelzell at Reichenau on Lake Constance. Founded in 724, dedicated in 819, and enlarged in the 10th century, its cloister layout was much the same as that of St Gall. The great Burgundian monastery at Cluny, from which Benedictine rule was directed throughout Western Christendom, again took this basic layout and augmented it (c.1010–50) on a par with the wealth that this most successful of establishments had garnered. The dormitory, refectory, and cellar follow the standard arrangement; significantly, though, a large chapter house, designed to accommodate the abbey's governing body, lies beneath the dormitory, with a Lady chapel leading off it, and there is a second, more southerly cloister, designed for novitiates. While this was partly rebuilt on a yet grander scale a century later, the basic layout was retained, and indeed, such was the influence of the St Gall prototype and its fulfilment at Cluny that it reappears in practically every Benedictine monastery built thereafter.

There are nevertheless variations between monasteries, some being caused by the individual preferences of specific orders of monks, others by the lie of the land. This may, for example, cause the north–south axis to be reversed, since practicality required the church to lie uphill and the arrangement of domestic rooms to be such that the channelled flow of water through them would allow fresh water to be supplied where it was needed, for example to the lavatorium for washing, and waste water, lower down, to be directed toward flushing out latrines.

There are other variations introduced by specific monastic orders. The late 11th and early 12th centuries saw a sudden diffusion of monasticism into several new orders which had particular characteristics of their own. The Cistercians (founded 1098) gradually turned against the worldly aspects of Benedictine Cluny in favour of an ascetic, withdrawn life. Apart from the resulting severity of their architecture, they favoured an arrangement which set their refectories end-on to the south side of the cloister instead of parallel to it. Their most characteristic surviving Burgundian monastery was laid out at Fontenay (c.1118–1260) in just this way, although the monks' lavatorium is placed within the cloister garth exactly as it is at Cluny. No order differed more radically from Benedictine rule than St Bruno's Carthusians (founded 1084), whose monks followed the hermitic life of the desert father and enjoyed confined lives devoted to silent prayer and contemplation in solitary cells. They reached England in the 13th century, their priory at Hinton, Somerset, being founded in 1232. It follows the standard Carthusian pattern for a Charterhouse with a plain, small church, lacking aisles and transepts, and an adjacent cloister to the south around which are placed fourteen individual cells, each comprising a living room and closet, with a small attached private garden. Between the church and cloister lay a small yard with a chapter house and upper library to its east, and refectory to its west.

A view of monastic life can be restored from its despoliation through amalgamating its many fragments. For example, the cloister of the former abbey, now Gloucester Cathedral, has a lavatorium attached to its northern range (i.e. that furthest from the church), which has a stone trough, once lead-lined, with spigots to supply water, and a drainage system that also flushed the abbot's lodging. Opposite the lavatorium, within the cloister, is a recess or manutergia where towels were hung. A stone bench and graffiti indicate that here novices whiled away spare time with such games as Nine Men's Morris and Fox and Geese. It was also a place of work: the south range was apparently screened off and the lower section of the windows opening on to the garth were replaced by recessed carrels where up to twenty monks could study at a time, together but each in seclusion, just as modern students do in a library.   APQ

Braunfels, W., *Monasteries of Western Europe* (1972)

Moneo Vallés, José Rafael (1937–) Spanish architect and educator, practising architecture in Madrid since 1965. He rose in the profession from local practitioner to designer of international acclaim in the mid 1980s with his Museum of Roman Art in Mérida (1980–85), its gigantic exposed brick arches being reminiscent of Roman construction. Among the architect's best known works are the Kursaal Auditorium and Congress Centre in San Sebastián (1999) and our Lady of the Angels Cathedral in Los Angeles (2002), again demonstrating his ability to organize massive, dramatically lit concrete forms.

His teaching and writing have imbued his built projects with a programmatic character derived from his critique of modern architecture, investigations in architectural theory, and deep understanding of the role of the site, construction, and materials in architecture. Moneo's architecture, detached from any stylistic references, could certainly be appreciated for its subtle references to old architectures and its urge for experimentation. Often described as introverted, his buildings find their way into the city fabric as contemporary versions of classical Modernism, balancing contemporary values with the past.   VM

Montenegro became independent from the Ottomans in 1837. The religious, cultural, and architectural distinctions are striking between mountainous Montenegro, with its small, aisleless Byzantine / Mediterranean Orthodox churches and vernacular houses in stone, timber, and shingle, and the coastal region, which was part of Dalmatia until incorporation into Montenegro by Yugoslavia.

The coast has significant 'Venetian' towns (Herceg-Novi, Kotor); Roman Catholic Romanesque churches of St Tryphon, St Paul, St Mary (Collegiata), St Luke, and the island church Gospa od Škrpjela with Baroque elements (9th century); and Renaissance palaces in Kotor and Perast.

Communist extravagance in construction (1945–90) resulted in little of architectural value.   PT

Montferrand, Auguste de (1786–1858) French architect active in St Petersburg. His primary commission was the building of a fourth version of the Cathedral of Saint Isaac of Dalmatia (1818–58), next to the Admiralty and one of St Petersburg's defining landmarks. Although responsible for the general design of this massive neoclassical structure, Montferrand was assisted by other architects and artists, particularly in the lavish decoration of the interior. His other major project was the Alexander Column on Palace Square (1830–34).   WCB

Moore, Charles Willard (1925–) US architect. The design team of MLTW (Moore, Lyndon, Turnbull,

Whitaker) created two unusual schemes. With its mono-pitch roofs, supported by redwood sidings, the ten-condominium development, Sea Ranch, Sonoma County, California (1949–65), suggested local vernacular structures such as barns—or a stage set. The latter type was more in evidence at Kresge College, University of California, Santa Cruz (1973–4), looking like a village in a forest clearing. Staginess without any other qualities is the note struck by his Piazza d'Italia, New Orleans (1977–8), a facetious essay in postmodernism.   PG

Moosbrugger, Caspar Andreas (1665–1723) German architect. He collaborated in the design of about ten abbey and parish churches between 1684 and 1712, although the precise extent of his involvement is difficult to establish. The only major work which can be definitely attributed to Moosbrugger is Einsiedeln abbey church (from 1719), where, as in most of his work, he was faced with complex problems of remodelling an earlier structure and adapting it for a new purpose. Into the existing complex of abbey buildings had to be inserted an abbey church, with, at its centre, a chapel for pilgrims worshipping at the shrine of St Meinrad.

To give the shrine sufficient prominence, Moosbrugger placed a large octagonal rotunda at the western end, one side abutting the convex façade of the exterior. The rotunda is an impressive structure, but its junction with the rest of the church is rather awkward, and out of scale with the long nave leading to the high altar. The exterior is surprisingly coherent, with the two flanking towers of the western façade well proportioned both in relationship to the convex centre and to the long nave.   PG

Moretti, Luigi Walter (1907–73) Italian architect. His work in Rome during the 1930s, like his Casa della Armi at the Foro Italico (1933–6), explores the fusion of rationalism with Roman imperial architecture. After World War II he founded the magazine *Spazio*, where he argued for an architecture of space and surface. This approach is best found in his Casa del Girasole in Rome (1947–50)—a work that has since been linked to the architecture of *postmodernism.   BLM

Morgan, Julia (1872–1957) US architect and designer of exceptional ability. Inspired by her mentor, Bernard *Maybeck, she was adept at working in a broad range of scales and expressive modes. Unlike him and a number of other San Francisco area colleagues, her work is more conspicuously rationalist, a characteristic achieved through composition and exposed structure. A major shift occurred after World War I, when much of her time was spent on extravagant retreats (such as San Simeon, 1919–38) for newspaper tycoon William Randolph Hearst.   RWL

Boutelle, S. H., *Julia Morgan, Architect* (1988)

Morocco *See* AFRICA (NORTH AFRICA).

Morris, Roger (1695–1749) English architect. A bricklayer turned successful building speculator, Morris was associated with Colen Campbell and Henry Herbert, 9th Earl of Pembroke, and thus English Palladianism. With their assistance he designed Marble Hill, Twickenham (1724–9), and White Lodge, Richmond Park (1727–8), two highly fashionable but somewhat standardized Palladian villas. Later works exhibit greater individuality, such as the developed pyramidal roof and *œil-de-bœuf* windows of Combe Bank, Kent (*c*.1725, altered); Whitton Park, west London (*c*.1732–9, demolished); the arcaded wings of Adderbury House, Oxfordshire (1731), which come from Palladio via Vanbrugh; and the Jonesian Tuscan portico of the Althorp stables, Northamptonshire (*c*.1732–3).   APQ

The Red House, Bexleyheath, London (Philip Webb, 1859)

Morris, William (1834–96) English designer, poet, and writer. Unlike his influential predecessors Pugin and Ruskin, Morris influenced architecture and design not just in Britain, but ultimately abroad as well. His hostile attitude to the establishment and his romantic solution to the anguish of industrialized society, expressed in his utopian socialism, embraced fundamental values in art generally. His study of divinity, followed by a stint in the office of the church-architect G. E. *Street and an attempt to learn to paint under his friend Rossetti, set him on a moral crusade to reform the decorative arts. Together with like-minded artists and architects he founded the Arts and Crafts movement. This had a remarkable homely, softening effect on design, including architecture, by simplifying it to suit the materials in which it was to be executed. To put his beliefs into effect, he set up a firm of manufacturers in 1861—Morris, Marshall, and Faulkner—for which he and his fellows designed wallpaper, furnishing fabrics, carpets, tapestries, and stained glass. Morris also designed books and their

typeface, now famous, which he published through his Kelmscott Press.

While his immediate effect on architecture, through his commissioning from his friend Philip Webb of Red House, Bexleyheath, London (1859), was slight in his time—its 'vernacular' style being widespread among other architects, such as *Devey, *Butterfield, and Norman *Shaw—Hermann Muthesius promoted it in his influential *Das englische Haus* (1904–5) as an icon of modern domestic design that mixed stylistic details rather than displayed an allegiance to just one style, and was supposedly planned to serve practical needs, despite its rambling form and many other practical failings which caused Morris to leave it. More immediately effective was his founding in 1877 of the Society for the Protection of Ancient Buildings (*see* CONSERVATION), whose liberal attitude to architecture of all styles was matched by an illiberal attitude to dissent characteristic of Morris. If he could not reconcile himself to the machine, if he would 'dream of London, small and white and clean', his utopian vision of an egalitarian society devoted to individual endeavour still appeals, and, paradoxically, he inspired a later generation to liberate itself from the tyranny of the past.   APQ

Thompson, P. R. *The Work of William Morris* (1993)

mortar A mixture of sand and lime which, when wetted, undergoes a chemical change to become a relatively hard binding material. With affinities to concrete and plaster, its main use is to bind stone and brick, particularly by making good gaps caused by irregularities, and by making a rubble core solid enough to be faced in good stone or brick. It came into widespread use after the collapse of Rome, together with its building skills. While mortar was sensibly used to join stones, it caused problems when medieval walls became ever thicker in order to support greater weights or to gain the strength needed by castles and defensive walls. It proved itself to be far less efficacious than cement-based concrete, because it readily wore away when penetrated by water, and over an extended period of time the binding quality would deteriorate causing failure. Many collapses of cathedrals, such as Ely (1322) and Chichester (1861), seem to have been caused by a failure of the mortar core.

While mortar lacks the durability of concrete, it is far more flexible. This is advantageous when it is used to bind relatively soft or brittle stone and brick. Gaps caused by differences in size are readily made up in mortar so as to ensure a flush face, and it is used to finish or point joints as well. Changes in temperature and the slight movement inherent in buildings are both taken up by the soft, flexible nature of the mortar without ill effect. When such buildings are repaired with cement-based concrete, these movements cause the deterioration of the brick or stone which, being less strong than the concrete, are the first to give way by chipping, cracking, and generally deteriorating. Mortar used for pointing can be coloured and its constituency

modified by the addition of linseed oil for special effect or to improve its waterproofing quality.   APQ

mosaic A surface decoration using small pieces of glass, marble, or stone, most effectively integrated into architecture when used on the curved surfaces of vaults or domes, particularly in *Byzantine architecture. In Hagia Sophia, Istanbul, and St Mark's, Venice, there are early mosaics representing the original form of the building.   PG

Moser, Karl (1860–1936) Switzerland's most important early-20th-century architect, who made the transition from historicism to modern. With his partner, Robert Curjel, Moser's practice built churches, luxurious Arts and Crafts-influenced villas, and important public buildings, including the Kunsthaus, Zurich (1910), and the University building (1914). The Antoniuskirche (1927) in Basle is Switzerland's first exposed-concrete church. Moser was founding president of CIAM in 1928 and professor at the Eidgenössische Technische Hochschule, Zurich. His radical project for the restructuring of Zurich's old town (1933) betrays the influence of Le Corbusier.
                                      CB

mosques, to 1900

BETWEEN THE SACRED AND THE SOCIAL

ACTIVITIES AND ASSEMBLY PATTERNS

SPATIAL FORM

Evolving through several European languages, 'mosque' stems from the Arabic *masjid*, which generically denotes any clean space—whether permanent or a temporary convenience—in which a Muslim individual or community performs prayers. However, it is the association of a permanent structure, the regular performance of congregational prayer, and some form of community organization which have

Mosque of Ibn Tulun, Cairo (AD c.880)

come to characterize the mosque as a building type and an institution.

Between the sacred and the social Literally, *masjid* is 'a place of prostration'—a Muslim prayer-position in which the subject presses forehead, nose, palms, and knees to the ground, in a fused spiritual–corporeal act of utmost submission to God. Thus, the name of Islam's central institution is derived from a moment of heightened devotion, rather than from the image of a sacred space exclusively dedicated to spiritual activities. Historically, however, the mosque has played a role deeply involved in its social milieu, conjoining the sacred with the social. Variant Muslim prayer-rituals generate hierarchies of social assembly throughout the Muslim calendar; each level has its own type of *masjid*. Five mandatory daily prayers, preferably conducted in congregation, generate heavy social encounter within, but also on the way to and from, street-level *masjids*. Friday prayers convene in larger neighbourhood or town mosques: the *jami* which, connoting 'assembly',

better approximates the institution's social functions by also accommodating organized social activities. Finally two annual rituals, *Eid* (feast) prayers to celebrate fulfilling Ramadan's fast and the pilgrimage to Mecca, assemble larger masses from a whole city and its environs. These were commonly executed in *Eid musallas* (places-for-prayer): natural clearings or walled-in enclosures defined against a *qibla wall, as in Khorasan's Turbat-i Jam (late 15th century).

Mosque architecture straddles an uncomfortable position between the sacred and the social. Islamic jurisprudence considers Islam's early decades (especially 622–62) a reference whose values and praxis are to be emulated. To deviate from this normative model in the sphere of ritual amounts to *bid'aa* (transgression); the cultural and technological domains are open to innovation (*ijtihad*). Being the mould wherein ritual occurs, but also inseparable from material culture's incessant developments, mosque architecture witnessed bitter jurisprudential arguments over spatial layouts and novel components.

To what extent were the spatial form and the physical form (materials, shape, and proportion) of the architecture of the pre-modern mosque architecture determined by and shaped by the mosque's social activities as well as its ritual practice? Attempting to explain mosque architecture along the sacred–social divide, this article employs the Prophet's archetypal mosque (al-Medina, 623) as the basis for comparison against later variations implemented in Islam's vast lands.

Activities and assembly patterns As an institution and a building type, the mosque is the true offspring of the Medinan period, which lasted from the Prophet's migration from Mecca to al-Medina (622) to his death in 632. Little is known about Meccan or early Medinan mosques, except during times of religious persecution, since places of prostration were mostly hidden or makeshift enclosures adapted from, or added onto, private dwellings.

Among activities shaping the mosque's institutional programme, congregational prayer furnishes the essential framework. Heeding the call to prayer conventionally relayed from a *minaret's tall structure adjoining the mosque, the faithful perform ritual ablution, then line up in straight uninterrupted rows, unanimously facing towards the Ka'aba in Mecca— shoulder to shoulder, foot to foot. As the *imam* recites Qur'anic verses aloud, congregants listen attentively, following his prayer movements, being careful not to overtake him. Standing, kneeling, prostrating, then sitting is a full unit of ritual (*rak'aaI*) (ritual-unit), repeated five times per day and night. During Friday congregation, the *imam* delivers the sermon (*khutba*), to which the faithful, seated aground, listen reflectively.

Throughout communal prayer, close-knit prayer-lines generate a dense, contiguous form; the congregation moves in unison, sustaining a common focus of attention. As Friday address and/or communal prayer conclude, this strongly felt collective presence, with its concerted form and geometry, dissipates into dispersed arrangements and divided attentions. Individuals pray non-mandatory prayers (*nafilah*), read the Qur'an, or assemble in various-sized groups for education or socialization.

Besides ritual, the Prophet also guided and exemplified various social activities: some of which were later maintained, others consolidated into specialized institutional buildings. While collective co-presence dominates congregational-prayer, distributions of social activities alternate between focused and diffused patterns.

Foremost among these were educational activities, conducted from the *minbar (pulpit), or informally at designated columns, thereby alternating between collective and decentralized patterns (as in Cairo's al-Azhar, 970–72). Madrasas (collegiate-mosques) emerged from specializing religious instruction, yielding the 4-*iwans* arrangement: decentralized yet converging onto a courtyard (e.g. Mir-i-Arab Madrasa, Bukhara, 1536). Medieval *bimaristans* (hospital-mosque complexes; e.g. Divrigi's Great Mosque and Hospital, 1229) emerged out of an association between spirituality and hospitality, which potentially commenced in the Prophet's mosque as it sheltered the wounded and homeless travellers in its rear portico (*riwaq*).

Political activities included announcing important dictums from the minbar, and rallying troops for battle. Resting against a certain column, the Prophet habitually received delegations in the shaded mosque space. Interestingly, political debate occurred within the confines of the mosque; before the battle of Uhud (625), community deliberations over the military threat unfolded there in some form. As the Caliph's seat relocated from the mosque's public arena into rulers' palaces soon after the Prophet's death, political practice within mosque confines disintegrated into irregular events and incoherent processes, whose impact on the mosque's spatial arrangement remains unexplored.

Spatial form Given the Prophet's pronouncement on the rewarded piety for occupying the front prayer-rows, his mosque's prayer-hall and later ones tended to be rectangles in plan, with longer sides facing the *qibla wall towards Mecca. The Great Mosque at Damascus (709–15) exemplifies such proportions, as the row-like column arrangement further emphasized parallel prayer-lines. Lateral proportions, with their parallel rows of arrangement, signal a departure from previous ritual spaces: deep rectangular church *basilicas, centralized church martyria, and concentrically configured *synagogues. Simultaneously, the prayer-hall's proportions were constrained by the need for clear visual and auditory communication between the *imam* and all congregants during sermons and prayers. Exceptionally, deep rectangular prayer-halls did emerge due to expansion demands amid site restrictions, as in Cordoba's Great Mosque (begun 942).

Within a walled-in square, the Prophet's mosque included a courtyard separating a back *riwaq* from a hypostyle prayer-hall roofed using palm-tree branches on supporting palm-tree trunks. Until the 11th century, this threefold arrangement prevailed (the *riwaq* encircling the courtyard), thereafter evolving into regional types throughout the Muslim world, as the Abbasids' central authority waned. Variations occurred mainly in the physical form, especially in prayer-hall roof designs, and were influenced by local building techniques and inherited cultural tastes—particularly Byzantine and Persian precedents. Flat roofs dominated in Africa, and—punctuated by small domes—also in Andalusia, North Africa, and the central Arab lands. Multiple domes were arrayed against the *qibla* wall in India; domes along bi-axial arrangements in Persia; while a massive central dome flanked by smaller ones flourished in Anatolia. Indonesia saw centralized

pyramidal roofs; China's mosques employed traditional hip roofing. From the mid 15th century, mosque architecture of regional imperial powers (*see* INDIAN SUBCONTINENT (THE MUGHALS); IRAN (THE SAFAVIDS); and OTTOMAN EMPIRE) acquired qualities of monumentality: immense scale, axiality, and verticality.

What persisted among such various physical forms was a tendency towards shaping the prayer-hall as a continuous field, uninterrupted by liturgical artefacts or furniture—whether visually, in terms of physical accessibility, or symbolically. Unlike the Bima or Ark in synagogues, the chancel or altar in churches, no object may be introduced within the mosque's prayer-hall, except temporarily, then promptly cleared away to guarantee prayer-lines' continuity; and for instrumental use without sanctified associations. Since prayer occurs through moving the body in relation to the ground, stalls were never required. Unlike the Bible and the Torah, the Qur'an—as a physical volume—was assigned no liturgical location within the *masjid*. Although men and women prayed in separate clusters of lines (to avert mutual distraction), walls were not erected between them—despite precedents of prohibited visual contact in the Prophet's own mosque.

Mosque components evolved as articulations within this field-like space. Initially developed by the Prophet for better auditory delivery, the minbar was thrust against the *qibla* wall, disrupting the open field minimally. The *mihrab (qibla-wall apse) was more controversial. Early objections by the prominent jurist Malik centred on its distracting ornamentation and unjustified costliness. Later protestation centred on its emulation of other religious traditions, besides effecting an undue spatial centrality in a ritual of parallel arrangement. Significantly, ablution fountains—frequently accommodated in courtyards—remained outside the prayer-hall from the mosque's early days.

Components more 'intrusive' upon the field included the seat of the *muballigh*, introduced in pre-modern mosques to relay calls during prayer as the congregation became too large for the *imam's* voice to reach. However, while raised above the mosque floor, the seat remained open and aligned to prayer lines. Occasionally, as in Cairo's Sultan Hassan Mosque (1356–61), it is thrust back towards the courtyard to avoid unwarranted importance. Furthermore, the *maqsura*: a small enclosure within the prayer-hall, it was first constructed to protect the early Caliphs from assassination, amid considerable controversy. To mitigate the status effect they unavoidably evoked, *maqsuras* had openings permitting visual connection, and some—in North African mosques—folded upwards to clear the prayer-floor when unoccupied by dignitaries. Tensions betrayed by such arrangements underscore a core characteristic: social hierarchies operating outside the mosque are to be subjugated to the uncompromising parity of prayer-rows.

The prayer-hall's enclosing planes and different components explored the limits of its uniform continuity. Variant construction systems introduced subtle distinctions within the continuous spatial form. Two distinct spatial types may be hypothesized: hypostyle halls and 'columnless' volumes. Simpler in construction technique, hypostyle halls appeared earlier and prevailed more widely in Islamic lands. In Cairo's al-Azhar Mosque, columned porticoes ran parallel to the *qibla* wall, emphasizing linear array. In Isfahan's Friday Mosque (*c.*771 onwards), two-way columned grids, carrying small domes and cross-vaults, diffuse the perception of spatial orientation, while oversized piers limit the field of vision, allowing but a few actually to see the *imam*—a characteristic of several Shi'ite mosques. While not disrupting physical or visual accessibility, wider and higher aisles—occasionally punctuated by domes—provided emphasis: axially towards the mihrab for royal ceremony (first introduced by the Umayyads [a dynasty] in the Great Mosque at Damascus), and/or in T-shaped plans (e.g. Samarra's

Abu-Dulaf Mosque, also known as the Great Mosque, 847–61), emphasizing a central approach and the front row(s) along the *qibla* wall.

More sophisticated building techniques yielded complex dome structures in Ottoman Turkey, under which prayer-halls enjoyed even more continuity unobstructed by piers (always irksome in prayer-rows alignment). Among the more magnificent spatial compositions are the architect *Sinan's Süleimaniye (Istanbul, 1550–57) and Selimiye (Edirne, 1569–75) mosques. Piers supporting the central dome of the Süleimaniye mosque generate smaller-scale side-aisles distinct from, but still contiguous with, the vast central prayer-hall. Implied intersecting volumes, organized around local axes, cohere into one unified composition. Contrastingly, bearing Selimiye's central dome onto stalactites and shallower double-piers, Sinan defines its vast, single-spaced interior as if bound by a light, folding 'skin'. With most entries unaligned to the mosque's axes, circulation affords oblique views of interior and courtyard.

Articulated with implied volumes, the prayer-hall's spatial form remains essentially unaltered by such variations: uniform extensions delimited only by the *qibla* wall expand around utilitarian objects. Exemplifying an emphasized interruption of this extension, Jerusalem's Dome of the Rock (691) exhibits an exceptional centralized configuration with a large central dome and four main portals. Emulating Christian martyria, its aspect as a memorial overshadows its character as mosque; two octagonal ambulatories encircle the rock commemorating the Prophet's heavenly voyage, while decorations and inscribed Qur'anic verses celebrate Islam's succession of Christianity and Judaism.

Routinely adjoining the prayer-hall, the courtyard maintained a flexible role, adjusting its logic to the prayer-hall's needs. While accommodating spill-over prayer-lines as congregations grew larger—thereby acquiring some of the prayer-hall's spiritual aura and behavioural codes—the bustle alien to the prayer-hall is tolerated in the courtyard. Omar, the second Caliph (d. 644), confined loud conversation and poetry-chanting to the courtyard. Additionally, artefacts (both ritualistic and 'secular' in nature, such as ablution fountains and state treasuries) are unhesitatingly juxtaposed in central locations within the courtyard's open space, as in the great Mosque at Damascus. Compared to the prayer-hall, this signals a significantly different spatial logic.

Interesting variations coloured the prayer-hall to courtyard relationship. Immense courtyards in the Indian subcontinent dwarfed prayer-halls, creating a sharp difference in scale, as in Lahore's Badshahi Mosque (1673–4). Detachment also prevailed in Ottoman mosques, where a windowed wall insulated the courtyard from the geometrically self-contained prayer-hall. Contrastingly, hypostyle-halls of the central Arab lands usually met the courtyard with porous arcades. Kashan's Masjid-i Agha Bozorg (19th century) displays another distinction, where the courtyard drops full-height to introduce air and light into student accommodations below. Khirki Mosque's (Delhi, c.1375) prayer-hall completely encircles the courtyard, producing a bi-axial, four-courtyard arrangement. Strong centrality evoked by the square plan and axes is diffused by alternating roofing, effecting a sense of continuous pattern instead of centralized arrangement. Similarly, Anatolia generated the small, central courtyard (e.g. Khuand Khatun Mosque, Kayseri, 1237–8), which became nearly engulfed by the hypostyle prayer-hall, and roofed in other cases (see SALJUQS).

Concern with social relations influenced the mosque's contextual presence. The Prophet's general directive to build mosques within the fabric of dwellings served to immerse mosques in their communities' everyday lives: to be a short walk away from dwellings and street activity. Unsurprisingly,

grand mosques like al-Qarawiyyin (Fez, 859)—monumental in scale and initially free-standing—soon attracted unplanned physical attachments of domestic and retail structures. Ottoman architects advanced such popular 'neighbouring' into more formalized programmatic and spatial formulations. *Külliye* complexes—centred on the mosque, but also comprising madrasas, hospitals, shops, guesthouses, and mausoleums—emerged as an urban type; later *kulliyes* (e.g. Sinan's Selimiye, Edirne) exhibit robust spatial compositions. Additionally, minarets, mosque tower structures from which the prayer-call was raised, also developed as urban landmarks structuring cities' visual identity.

While forging close physical 'attachment' to secular surroundings, appendages to the mosque, such as student dwellings, or *ziyadas* (extensions) to accommodate more congregants, or a *majaz* (bent entrance)—all served to 'thicken' the interface between mosque and street. Not only were momentary inside–outside glances eliminated, but also the prolonged exterior-to-interior journey effected a gradual dissociation of activities and experiences, as it generated a spiritual preparation for prayer. Manipulating scale, light, colour, and sensitive acoustic properties, designers further detached the faithful from street bustle—as Cairo's Sultan Hassan Mosque masterfully demonstrates. To what extent such devices sever the mosque from surrounding social life awaits exploration. Notably, some mosques generate this transitional experience without offering a façade to the city; unassuming walls mask rich subtleties behind Cairo's al-Mu'ayyad Mosque (1415–22). Others, such as Yazd's Friday Mosque (1324–1470) and Samarkand's Bibi-Khanum Mosque (1398–1405), mark an aesthetic threshold using massive *iwans* ornamented with calligraphy and coloured tiles.   HZ

Creswell, K. A. C., *A Short Account of Early Muslim Architecture* (1958)

Ettinghausen, R., and Grabar, O., *The Art and Architecture of Islam: 650–1250* (1987)

Frishman, M., and Hassan-Uddin, K. (eds.), *The Mosque: History, Architectural Development and Regional Diversity* (1994)

Ibn-Saleh, M., and al-Kokani, A. (eds.), *Proceedings of the Symposium on Mosque Architecture* (1999)

Michell, G. (ed.), *Architecture of the Islamic World: Its History and Social Meaning* (1978)

mosques, since 1900 The mosque, the quintessential Muslim building, was built in unprecedented numbers from 1950 to 2000. Within the Islamic world, post-colonial movements, demographic growth, and massive urbanization influenced its appearance. In countries previously not settled by Muslims, the mosque mirrored patterns of migration and conversion. Socialist regimes, Iraq, Algeria, Syria, the former Yugoslavia, or even secularist Turkey also witnessed the construction of mosques as extensions of social networks, if not of outright political control. By the early 1990s, groups vying for power utilized the mosque as a marker in the expanding metropolis, and, in many cases, as ideological space for traditionalist and Islamist thinking. These buildings acted as magnets for community life, but also for sectarian or political strife. The processes of the creation of state image, the dynamics of regional politics, and global Muslim identity can be tracked by studying the building programmes and designs of mosques.

The styles have ranged from vernacular (Great Mosque, Niono, Mali, builder Lassine' Mint'a, 1950s–1973), vernacularist (New Gourna, Egypt, architect Hassan *Fathy, 1945–8), modernist (Sherefuddin White Mosque, Visoko, Bosnia, architect Zlatko Ulgen, 1970–80), historicist (Mosque and Islamic Centre, Rome, architect Paolo Portoghesi, 1994), to postmodern (al-Ghadir Mosque, Tehran, 1987). While modernist expressions continued to be built, by the last part of the century clients increasingly pressed for an 'Islamic' image, requiring the minaret and dome as markers for mosques within a cityscape. This insistence forced architects to undertake the design of a vaulted form, no longer at the centre of design achievement, either formally or technically. Populist taste challenged architects and exerted pressure to conform. Expressed through the small metal pre-fabricated domical covers or finials that were fast becoming the markers for mosques, this taste could be understood as a desire to belong to a non-regional, pan-Islamic visual world.

The immediate post-colonial period (1960–70) was marked by large-scale modernist examples, all with reinforced concrete shells or folded plates, mostly in newly independent countries, such as Indonesia, Malaysia, and Pakistan (Istiqlal Mosque, Jakarta, architect F. Silaban, 1955–84; Masjid Negara, Kuala Lumpur, Malayasia, architect Baharuddin Abu Qasim, 1960; King Faisal Masjid, the state mosque, Islamabad, Pakistan, architect Vedat Dalokay, 1968–82). These were reinterpretations of monumental historical architectural forms in contemporary concrete technology. The 20th-century nation state extended its role as client for mosques through its local representatives as well as through specialized educational, social, and other institutions constituted as semi-autonomous bodies. For example, the Capital Development Authority for the new capital Islamabad, Pakistan, supported the modernist image, commissioning Anwar Saeed in 1969–73 as architect for neighbourhood mosques of varying sizes. Likewise, the individual Malay states followed a modernist image for the state mosque, as in the1967 Negeri Sembilan State Mosque in Seremban (Malayan Architect Co-Partnership and Baharuddin). The Salman Mosque at Institut Technologi Bandung, Indonesia (1959–72, architect Achmad Noeman) was also uncompromisingly modernist and demonstrated an implicit criticism both of the 'folkloric' design of the

Hassan II mosque, Casablanca, Morocco (completed 1993)

Institut as well as of the imported Middle Eastern forms. Identity rested in completely modern images, without reference to earlier local vernacular forms.

The 1970s–90s building programmes of the oil-rich states, such as Kuwait, Saudi Arabia, and to some extent Iran, called for mosques of every scale and location, from ones in recreational areas to those attached to airports and universities. Often the historic monuments were the bases for design inspiration. Thus, the Dome of the Rock on its platform is shadowed in the hybrid design and space-age technology of the 1,500 sq m (1,794 sq yard) mosque with a geodesic dome (span 33.5 m or 110 ft, height 40 m or 131 ft) for the Riyadh Airport (architect Gyo Obata of HOK, 1983). The Kuwait State Mosque (1984, architect Mohamed Makiya) with its 43 m (141 ft) high dome echoed in profile those in the shrines of Karbal, Najaf, Samarra, and al-Gailani. Robert Venturi's design for the Iraq State Mosque competition (1982) also utilized the historic record, establishing the Mosque of Ibn Tulun and the idea of the *muqarnas* as touchstones for the

design but, typically, recasting the hypostyle plan into a series of hanging screens and expanding the *muqarnas* into a parasol over the courtyard while still providing the mosque with a small dome over the mihrab and a minaret.

In a vernacularist style following Hassan Fathy, Abdel Wahed al-Wakil designed three small (*zawiya*-like) mosques in 1983–9 as part of the waterfront development of Jeddah. Based specifically on local Najd vernacular expression but on a monumental scale is the Imam Turki Jami of the Qasr al-Hokm in Riyadh designed by Rasem Badran in 1992. Seeking a formal vocabulary within Iranian brick-building traditions, but avoiding the obvious dome and minaret, Kamran Diba reinterpreted the wind-tower (*badgir*) into a half-cylinder mihrab in the Jondishapur University Mosque in 1975. In Turkey, where Modernism was fully integral to architectural practice, mosque design has had a mixed history because of secularist ideology and the religionist reaction against it. Nonetheless, the Grand National Assembly Mosque, Ankara (architects

Cinici, Cinici and Cinici, 1985), eschewed all formal conventions for roof cover, niche and tower, featuring a glass mihrab overlooking a closed garden. In contrast, the globalized new mosque allows little variation from the formulaic dome and minaret, viz. Islamic Centre, New York (Skidmore Ownings, and Merill, 1995). RHd

Holod, Renata, and Khan, Hasan-Uddin, *The Mosque and the Modern World* (1997)

Serageldin, Ismaïl (ed.), with James Steele, *Architecture of the Contemporary Mosque* (1996)

moulding An ornament of continuous section, or formed by a pattern. Mouldings serve to enliven flat surfaces, decorate angles, define areas, and protect openings from the weather, when they are known as hoodmoulds or dripmoulds. A moulding of semicircular section is a scotia if concave, a torus if convex. A projecting moulding of more than semicircular section is a roll moulding, and if of only a quarter of a circle an ovolo. A roll moulding projecting from a chamfered edge is a bowtell moulding. A wave moulding combines concave and convex mouldings. When two convex mouldings meet at an angle to produce an edge, it is said to be keeled. When a combination of a convex and a concave moulding meets its mirror image at a point, an ogee moulding results. All of these mouldings are of continuous section and cut in stone or timber by using a shaped wooden former as a guide. When made in plaster the former is run from one end to the other so as to shape the moulding.

The mouldings which decorate classical entablatures were usually enriched by various forms of carved decoration that break up their otherwise uninterrupted lines. An ovolo might be continuously carved with braided decoration, known as *guilloche*, or with a twisting pattern to resemble the strands of a rope to form a cable moulding. An ovolo can be carved to resemble a run of hemispheres known as a bead moulding. When the beads are regularly interrupted by cylindrical reels they form bead and reel, more usually called an astragal. More complex still is egg and dart. A billet moulding at its simplest comprises two adjacent but discontinuous roll mouldings, appearing like a string of cylinders, broken so that a gap in one lies beside a cylinder in the other; and other more complex forms substitute raised cubes or pyramids. While many of these classical forms descended into the medieval Romanesque style, others of a more fantastic form made their appearance. Nailhead is a line of pyramids decorating a chamfer, and when carved to represent a four-pointed star set diagonally along a hollow moulding this is called dogtooth. A roll moulding set in a zigzag pattern is called chevron, and a chamfer and roll moulding may be interrupted by grotesque heads to form beakhead. Rather like tracery, complex mouldings became the characteristic trademark of many individual medieval masons. APQ

Moura, Eduardo Souto de (1952–) Portuguese architect. After practice with Álvaro *Siza Vieira in the 1970s, he started as an independent professional in 1980. His work pays special attention to geometry, spatial simplicity, and material detailing. His language may be considered 'rationalist', and he admires the use of glass, steel, and stone by *Mies. His main works are the Braga market (1980–81), the Ministry of Culture offices and auditorium in Oporto (1981–90), the Geo-Sciences Faculty in Aveiro University (1989–94), the Santa Maria do Bouro Pousada, and the innovative Braga Football Stadium (2000–04). JMF

Mozarabic Literally, 'Arabized' (from the Arabic *musta'rib*). After reconquering Muslim areas of northern Spain, the Asturian kings (r. 718–1037) adopted the Visigothic form of Christian liturgy, which meant separating the nave from the sanctuary by means of an iconostasis, but otherwise used the architectural

Mosque, Djenne, Mali (Ismaili Traore, 1906)

forms of their Muslim predecessors: the arches, windows, and plan of the apse are all horseshoe-shaped. The best surviving example is San Miguel de Escalada (near Léon, 912–13), quite a small church (about 25 m or 82 ft long), with a 5-bay nave. There are some regional variations. The western churches (such as San Miguel de Celanova, near Orsense) are structurally ingenious and lack aisles. The churches in Catalonia are the least typical examples of Mozarabic design, poor in sculpture and basilican in plan. In liturgy and architecture, the Mozarabic gave way to the *Romanesque.   PG

mud apparently an unpromising material, but with a long and honourable history in *vernacular architecture, not only for simple structures but also for monumental public buildings, such as the Mosque, Dienne, Mali (*see* AFGHANISTAN).

There are three main methods of using mud: as unfired bricks (*see* ADOBE); rammed earth or shuttering (*terre pisé*); and lifts, i.e. clay is placed in layers about 300–500 mm (12–20 inches) high, the most infrequently used method, as it is slow and laborious (*see* COB).   PG

Mudéjar from the Arabic *mudejjan*, 'permitted to remain', or perhaps *mudijalat*, meaning 'a vassal', is a style of Spanish architecture characterized by the use of glazed tiles, interlaced blind arcarding, and horseshoe or lobed arches. It was mainly confined to small churches and synagogues, in nearly all the areas reconquered from Muslim territory, beginning with Toledo (1085). Only the patrons of the great abbeys and cathedrals could afford to use stone, for which brick and plaster was substituted in lesser commissions.

The most distinctive Mudéjar building in Castile is the Hieronymite monastery of Guadelupe, which includes a 2-storey cloister (1402–12) with arcades of horseshoe arches. Aragon displays a regional variation, with tall, detached belfries clearly derived from Almohad minarets (such as the Giralda at Seville), i.e. square and without buttresses. The decorative elements of Mudéjar later re-appeared in the *Plateresque and the *Isabelline.   PG

Muet, Pierre Le (1591–1669) French architect working primarily for private clients (Hôtels l'Aigle, d'Astrée, Daveaux, and Duret de Chevry in Paris and the Château de Tanlay) whose style ranged from the decorative Mannerism of Du Cerceau to the stricter Classicism of de *Brosse. Inspired by the publications of J.-A. Du Cerceau the elder, he produced his *Manière de bien bastir* (1623, 1647) and *Augmentations des nouveaux batiments faits en France* (1663).   CT

Mughal architecture *See* INDIAN SUBCONTINENT (THE MUGHALS).

muqarna A stalactite-like ornament on parts of a building, usually made of plaster, wood, or marble, and a three-dimensional replication of geometric patterns, exemplifying the intricate use of mathematics and geometry. Muqarnas evolved from a technical solution of resting a series of squinches on top of other squinches. They first appeared in the 10th century in Egypt and Iran almost simultaneously and had spread widely in the Islamic world by the 12th century. In the eastern part of the Islamic world, muqarnas served both structural and decorative functions, while the western version, mocarrabes, served the decorative function only. ABS

Murano, Tôgo (1891–1984) Japanese architect. Murano was a prolific Osaka-based architect distinguished by the expressive diversity and range of his humanistic architecture before and after World War II. Noted for his personal articulation of materials, textures, colours, and forms, Murano's pre-war work is highlighted by the Ube Public Hall (1937) with its curved monumental dark tile façade contrasted by a decorative interior of mushroom-shaped marble columns and checqered-pattern terrazzo floor. His World Peace Memorial Cathedral (1953) in Hiroshima is a unique composition of a reinforced concrete frame with bricks mixed with the ashes of the burned city. While sometimes seen as a commercial or eclectic designer of hotels, department stores, office buildings, and traditional teahouses, Murano is noted for his skill in satisfying both his buildings' clients and public visitors. KTO

Murcutt, Glenn Marcus (1936–) born in England, Australia's most well-known architect. Winning the Pritzker Prize as a sole practitioner made Australia's

Marie Short House, Kempsey, New South Wales, Australia (Glenn Murcutt, 1974–5)

'ideal' villas internationally known. His romantic quest for an architecture based on Australian experience, materials, and landscape led to a series of extraordinary individual houses in harmonious relationship with their sites but at the same time using glass and metal. Some critics have suggested that the Local History Museum in South Kempsey (1981–2) could be the first truly Australian building. His houses in Kempsey, Mount Irvine, and Kangaroo Valley refine this language. One of his largest projects with Wendy Lewin and Reg Lark was the Arthur and Yvonne Boyd Education Centre (1999) at Bundanon, south of Sydney, which is both a celebration and a resource centre for the great Australian painter Arthur Boyd. LN

Murray, Sir James (d. 1634) Scottish architect. Most important of a series of Scottish royal masters of work (serving from 1607 until his death), Murray was responsible for a range of pioneering projects in a hybrid classico–castellated style, including palace lodgings at Edinburgh (1615–17) and Linlithgow (from 1618), and country houses such as his own mansion, Kilbaberton, 1623. His chief works formed part of the Stuart monarchs' early-17th-century improvement programme in Edinburgh: the palatially scaled,

The mausoleum, Dulwich Picture Gallery, Dulwich, London
(Sir John Soane, 1811–14)

towered George Heriot's Hospital (from 1628) and the
flat-roofed Parliament House (1632–8), with its arched
timber ceiling.   MGl

museums and art galleries, to 1945 Galleries
within buildings for private collections of paintings
and sculptures date back to the late 16th century (e.g.
Buontalenti's east range of the Uffizi, Florence 1574),
and separate buildings to the mid 18th century (Kassel,
the Museum Fridericianum 1769–77, by S. L. du Ry),
but the art gallery/museum designed for the public
dates from the beginning of the 19th century.

The first architecturally significant gallery open to
the public, *Soane's Dulwich Picture Gallery, London
(1811–14), is in most respects not typical of later
developments. It was set in suburban fields, rather
than occupying an important urban site; the gallery
formed only part of the building, which also included
almshouses and a mausoleum; and it was quite small,
consisting of five galleries only, 45 m (149 ft) long.
Soane exercised all his ingenuity to counter the
meanness of the materials, the cheapest brick and
the exiguous stone dressings, to give the building a
relatively dignified appearance. He also took great care
to light the pictures, by means of roof lights. Similarly
he remodelled the interior of his own house (now
Sir John Soane's Museum, London) using mirrors
and top lighting to his collection, which was to be
left to the public after his death.

The development of the civic museum began in
earnest with the Altes Museum, Berlin (*Schinkel,
1823–30), the Royal Institution of Fine Arts,
Manchester (Sir Charles *Barry, 1824), and the British
Museum, London (Sir Robert *Smirke, 1823–46). The
model for the Altes Museum's colonnade of 18 fluted
Ionic columns was not a temple front, but the stoa
bordering the agora of Athens. Behind the colonnade,
an open staircase led to a platform from which the city
was seen to be a clearly separate realm: Schinkel
believed that art could be a means for civic
improvement, only if distanced from the secular
world. The plan created lighting problems, not
entirely solved by the provision of two internal
courtyards and by locating the picture galleries
on the second floor.

By contrast, the English galleries emphasized the
'sacred' character of a gallery by employing a temple
portico at the centre. Such an arrangement can cause
problems in a long façade, especially when the bays are
weakly articulated and the skyline is too indecisive, as
at the National Gallery, London (*Wilkins, 1832–8). At

633

the British Museum, Smirke avoided the problem by using an open courtyard layout. The other English galleries of this period, the architecturally distinguished Fitzwilliam, Cambridge (Basevi, 1837ff.), and the Ashmolean, Oxford (C. P. *Cockerell, 1839–45), being much smaller, neither face the same difficulties nor offer any solutions to the problem of designing large-scale public museums.

It was the Alte Pinakothek, Munich (von Klenze, 1825–36), which established the pattern for the next 50 years of museum design, the main period in the 19th century. Klenze made lighting and clarity of form, rather than an architectural statement, his main objective. Small pictures were lit from the side only; larger ones from the top, by means of roof lights. Fortunately, he could choose the orientation of the building (east–west), so as to maximize the incidence of northern light. The façade corresponded to the organization of the interior spaces, perhaps so as to prepare the visitor for what to expect. It was followed by the Neue Pinakothek, Munich (1846–52); the Dresden Gemäldegalerie (Semper, 1847–55), and the Kunsthistorisches Hofmuseum, Vienna (*Semper and Carl von Hasenauer, 1872–89). Other European capitals followed suit (e.g. P. J. H. *Cuypers' Rijksmuseum, Amsterdam, 1876–85), with the notable exception of Paris, where the Louvre was extended (by *Visconti and *Lefuel, from 1852), instead of a new building being commissioned.

Following the established formula could lead to monotonous and predictable results. The decorative solution was adopted at the University Museum, Oxford (Deane and Woodward, 1855–60), where stone and wrought iron were used sculpturally, with leaf mouldings in the arches and spandrels; the blue, grey, and cream *terracotta façades of the Natural History Museum (*Waterhouse) clad a fairly conventional plan.

By the end of the 19th century, in Europe at any rate, the provision of large museum buildings was virtually complete. A fleeting alternative to their often ponderous historicism now appeared in three, much smaller buildings. C. H. *Townsend's Whitechapel Gallery, London (1896–1901), and the Horniman Museum, London (1901–12), favoured by a more picturesque hillside site than most museums enjoyed, carried naturalistic decoration on the façades while retaining the 19th-century virtues of careful planning and lighting. *Olbrich's Secession Gallery, Vienna (1897–8), was designed as an exhibition building, but offered three new points of departure for galleries and museums housing permanent collections. The entrance front was under a dome composed of laurel leaves, for which there was no historical precedent; a new combination of side- and top-lighting improved the quality of light; and, by using partitions, the spaces were designed to be highly adaptable.

In the USA, the era of museum building occurs some 50 years later, from 1890 to the 1940s. Here a rather different formula was established. The façades and the plans followed conventional *Beaux Arts models (e.g. the Museum of Fine Arts, Boston, 1907–15; the Cleveland Museum of Art, 1916ff.). The final example of this kind, the National Gallery of Art, Washington DC (by John Russell Pope, 1937–41), is perhaps the most successful, because of its lavish spaces. It is unfortunate that really inspired architects of this school, such as *McKim, Mead, and White and Paul *Cret, were not given the opportunity of designing museums or galleries.

With the exception of the Museum of Modern Art, New York (1937–8), designed by Goodwin and Edward Durrell *Stone, the application of Modernism to museum design did not occur until after World War II.   PG

museums and art galleries, since 1945 After more than two centuries of consistent generic solutions, the building type underwent dramatic architectural transformations after 1945 to keep pace with changing institutional demands.

A veritable explosion in museum construction commenced in the 1960s, continuing unabated up to the present day. Museums of all kinds became paramount public edifices, supported by cities seeking to revitalize their economic base. Initially a Western invention, after World War II they appeared around the globe; Japan especially became noted for the genius of its museum architects, such as Tadao Andô, Arata Isosaki, and Fumihiko Maki, whose work spanned the continents. Once elitist bastions, museums became popular venues offering entertainment and consumer goods as well as education. In the competition for audiences, the architectural envelope and internal plan of a once fairly static building type underwent metamorphosis, while additions needed to accommodate expansion frequently overshadowed original structures.

Two celebrated 20th-century architects dissolved the traditional image of the museum and provided inspiration for future projects. Ludwig *Mies van der Rohe in the new National Gallery, Berlin (1962–68), posited the concept of the universal space—no fixed partitions or rooms, no masonry envelope, and reliance on artificial rather than natural illumination. His concept would be tremendously influential despite its shortcomings—amorphous space that often left the viewer confused as to route, and glass walls that were unsuitable for displaying pictures. The other iconoclastic model was by Frank Lloyd Wright, whose Guggenheim Museum (1943–59) established the trend for the autonomous sculptural artefact, calling attention to itself more than serving the art objects, although some exhibitions in the spiral-girt volume have succeeded beautifully. The large addition of 1990–92 by Gwathmey Siegel Associates gave the Guggenheim more orthodox galleries to accommodate the permanent collection.

The architect who first succeeded in bridging the gap between tradition and modernity was Louis I. *Kahn, who satisfied not only long-standing concerns—the need for natural light to impart vitality as well as visibility, and for a clear structure to guide the visitor—but also more recent demands for flexible spaces and technological advances serving conservation. Many consider Kahn's Kimbell Museum in Fort Worth (1966–72) to be the most successful museum design of the second half of the 20th century: it restores the top-lighted vaults of the conventional museum but tames natural light, using it for ambient illumination supplemented by benign electricity for task lighting. Dazzling in the structural daring of enormous spans made possible by the concrete structure, the Kimbell boasts travertine walls that link it with historic structures. Between the vaults are servant spaces that allow reconfiguration of display and circulation areas while supplying the necessary mechanical services.

Much more startling, recalling 19th-century exhibition buildings that were alternative sites for art displays, was the competition design for the Centre Pompidou, Paris, which won for Richard *Rogers and Renzo *Piano the opportunity to construct their first major building (1971–7). The programme was revolutionary in its democratic intention, comprising a place of information and leisure as well as the viewing of fine art, accessible via escalators until late in the evening, transparent conceptually as well as visually, made not of customary masonry but of the high tech materials of metal and glass, looking more like an oil refinery than a cultural institution. The Pompidou Centre's public success made innovation the byword in museum design, although one should note that the galleries proved inhospitable to painting and sculpture and a more conventional interior was devised for the museum of art within its open frame. Nevertheless the Pompidou's flexibility was ratified when in 1999 it was renovated to keep pace with new institutional priorities.

Some architects were troubled by the new dispensation and sought to restore *gravitas* and a measure of organizational order. In the postmodern mood, they resuscitated traditional verities in a novel guise. Chief among them were James Stirling/ Michael Wilford Associates, and Robert Venturi Denise Scott Brown Associates (VSB). The former's Neue Staatsgalerie in Stuttgart (1977–84) ingeniously merges the archetypal image of *Schinkel's Altes Museum (Berlin, 1823–30) with late-20th-century requirements for greater freedom and new constructional methods. It also serves as a dramatic link between parts of the dismembered city. The footprint with a central rotunda surrounded by an enfilade of galleries refers to Enlightenment ideals, but these are challenged by references to contemporary insecurities. The perfection of the hypaethral rotunda, providing a ramp between upper and lower city that can be navigated without visiting the museum, is eroded by vegetation and exposure to the elements, so that the museum appears both sublime and contingent. In the Sainsbury wing (1992–5) of the venerable National Gallery, London, VSB have reconstituted traditional vaulted rooms and cabinets, but the vocabulary of attenuated pilasters and functionless vaults proclaims this a late-20th-century addition.

Architects like Frank *Gehry (e.g. Guggenheim Museum, Bilbao, 1993–7) jettison all connections with the history of museum architecture to mint unique solutions that tend to overshadow contents. Such buildings succeed best when exclusively housing contemporary art rather than encyclopaedic holdings. They frequently serve new foundations without extensive collections so that the structure itself becomes the chief aesthetic attraction. Perhaps a more promising trend for museums of contemporary art has been the recycling of existing industrial structures. Since the 1980s many examples abound, most notably Tate Modern, London (1997–2000), by Jacques Herzog

and Pierre de Meuron. The former power station at Bankside (1947–59) by Sir Giles Gilbert *Scott provided a formidable enclosure for an imposing entrance hall, shops, cafes, and three levels of vast but logically subdivided galleries.

The variety manifest in museum buildings accommodates conflicting demands. Some designers maintain still-vital traditions, others forge new templates for display and conservation. Architects coveting this most prestigious commission exercise ingenuity to astonish and defy expectations; the more scrupulous continue to serve the age-old purposes of felicitous and meaningful display.　　HSe

Davis, D(ouglas), *The Museum Transformed: Design and Culture in the post-Pompidou Age* (1990)
Newhouse, V., *Towards a New Museum* (1998)

mutule A square block above a *triglyph projecting from the soffit of the corona of the cornice of a Roman Doric entablature. While mutules are not always present, they appear near Rome at Albano carrying guttae, as though pegged beneath the corona, and Vignola's *La Regola delli Cinque Ordini d'Architettura* (1562) shows the same.　　APQ

Muzio, Giovanni (1893–1982) Italian architect. Following World War I, Muzio set up his practice in Milan where he became the most well-known polemicist and practitioner of the *Novecento movement. As early as 1921 he set out his theoretical position, extolling the virtues of 19th-century neoclassical architecture in Milan. His most well-known project from this period, the Ca' Brutta (the ugly house), an apartment building in Via Moscova in Milan (1922), established him as an eccentric interpreter of Lombard neoclassicism. His position was further articulated in the 1930s through a series of projects constructed for the Jesuit Università Cattolica del Sacro Cuore in Milan (1929–38). After World War II, Muzio continued his practice with projects that avoided any overt references to modern architecture, like the Basilica of the Annunciation in Nazareth (1959–69).

BLM

Myanmar *See* BURMA.

Mycenaean architecture The heyday of Mycenaean civilization between the 15th and 12th centuries BC produced some of the earliest monuments of mainland Europe, whose significance is the greater for their influence on classical Greece. The Mycenaeans took much from the *Minoan civilization of Crete, the first in Europe, which had established cities with complex stone palaces exemplified by the ruins of Knossos, Phaestos, and Gournia.

The Mycenaeans, who emerged *c*.1450 BC from the Minoan civilization after either the conquest of Crete or its devastation by natural causes, developed the Minoan form of city by setting it around a fortified hilltop enclosure or acropolis, which served as a civic and religious centre. The enclosure, exemplified by the walls of Mycenae itself, comprises cyclopean stone blocks, at once practical for defence and symbolic of political power. Unlike Crete, an island defended by the sea, Mycenae had to protect itself from mainland marauders. So entrances were guarded by confined approaches in the form of a dromos, and had a formal quality, well expressed by the Lion Gate at Mycenae. This is in the form of a trilithon bearing a large triangular stone, like a pediment, carved with a pair of lions supporting an architecturally decorated column. This is an early case, for Europe, of architectural carving, and it was apparently accompanied by brightly coloured paintwork as well.

Within the gates the Mycenaeans imposed order on the haphazard labyrinthine arrangements that they had seen in Minoan palaces and cities, by setting out a series of courtyards, staircases, and rooms along a single axis. Important houses, now known as megarons, literally a large room, usually had a central hearth within their main room and, embraced by an extension of its side walls, an entrance porch and anteroom at the front. These probably had timber roofs of low pitch, and, slightly modified, were taken up by the later inhabitants of classical Greece for their temples. The Mycenaeans also exploited the corbelled-in roof, already known in the Mediterranean, for the circular chamber, or *tholos, which probably served as an important tomb. The finely preserved example, the so-called Treasury of Atreus at Mycenae, is simply a circular beehive structure comprising increasingly corbelled-in squared stones forming a tall curved cone. The entrance, reached by an open embanked passage or dromos, has a carved architrave-surround to its doorway enriched with attached half-columns, and carries further attached columns and a notional pediment. (*See also* NURAGHE.)

APQ

Mylne, Robert (1733–1811) Scottish architect. Descended from a line of Scottish masons and architects, Mylne undertook the Grand Tour, gaining Piranesi's friendship and a silver medal in Rome. Returning to Britain he won the competition for Blackfriars Bridge (1760–69, demolished) with nine graceful elliptical spans between piers adorned with paired Ionic columns. Bridges and waterworks filled much of his career, culminating in his surveyorship of the New River Company (1767). His country houses, notably those in Shropshire, such as Woodhouse, Whittington (1773–4), which has a striking portico, and also Addington Lodge (1773–9) and Bickley Place (*c*.1780, demolished) in south London, already show Dance's and Soane's restraint.

APQ

n

naos The sanctuary of a classical temple, housing an effigy of a deity. It is the principal chamber, entered through a doorway at the further end from the statue, windowless and either simply rectangular or aisled, as was the Parthenon. It may also be the sanctuary of a centrally planned Byzantine church.   APQ

narthex A space extending transversely across the full width of a church at the opposite end to the altar, for those who were not yet admitted to the faith. It is found in most *Early Christian and *Byzantine churches, and also in some *Romanesque churches in southern France.   PG

Nash, John (1752–1835) English architect. A pupil of Sir Robert *Taylor, Nash became involved in speculative building, and after going bankrupt gave up architecture for some years. His fellow pupil S. P. Cockerell persuaded him to start again, and thus he became the leading architect of late-Georgian picturesque. He first found success building attractive houses in Wales, notably Castle House, Aberystwyth (c.1795), a triangular lodge for Uvedale Price, who, with his friend Richard Payne Knight, apparently introduced Nash to the picturesque and a more natural approach to landscape and architecture. This Nash perfectly expressed by the Italianate Cronkhill, near Shrewsbury (1802), whose asymmetrical form is characterized by a round tower and attached loggia. He was nevertheless quite competent in orthodox neoclassicism, as Southgate Grove, London (1797), shows. Returning to London, Nash produced many

Cumberland Terrace, Regent's Park, London (John Nash, 1828)

picturesque designs, including the cottages of Blaise
Hamlet, Bristol (1810–11), where thatched roofs,
peek-a-boo dormers, and crazy chimney stacks
became a symbol thereafter of the quaintly rustic.

An official appointment (1806) to the Department
of Woods and Forests led to his major work, the
development of Regent's Park, London (1811–27),
together with palatial terraces around it, all fronted in
stucco and opulently if haphazardly detailed with
entablatures and pediments. He laid out Regent Street,
linking the park to St James's Park and Carlton House,
the Regent's residence, which he rebuilt as the twin
blocks of Carlton House Terrace. Regent Street
cleverly follows a line of least resistance, dividing
seedy Soho from snobbish Mayfair, turning around
such eye-catchers as the tholos-spire of the church of
All Souls, Langham Place, and the Quadrant leading
into Piccadilly Circus. This finest of all London's
metropolitan improvements continued with the West
Strand improvements which joined up the Strand and
another picturesque building, now Coutts Bank, with

Trafalgar Square, Lower Regent Street, and Pall Mall.
Finally, he enlarged Buckingham Palace (1825–30) for
the Regent (since 1820 King George IV), as he had also
enlarged the Royal Pavilion, Brighton (1815–22), in a
unique concoction of oriental styles with ogee domes
and minarets that exactly catch the raffish atmosphere
of the London-by-the-sea resort.

Criticized in his lifetime for extravagance, Nash fell
from grace at the death of George IV in 1830, and the
works at Buckingham Palace were put into the safer
but more mundane hands of Edward Blore. Nash's
career was effectively over, and he retired to East
Cowes Castle, Isle of Wight (which he had designed for
himself *c*.1798), for the last five years of his life. He was
soon criticized for his architectural style too. Despite
his limitless versatility, his entrepreneurial and urbane
talent seemed to have got the better of his architectural
quality. Certainly his detailing is slapdash, but he was a
master of scenic effect. The Regent's Park metropolitan
improvement is touched with genius, and has never
been matched. Its architecture, however patrician in

concept, was meretricious in execution, but that exactly suited the London of the times, and perhaps London at any time—if only later planners had shown his wit!   APQ

Summerson, John, *The Life and Work of John Nash* (1980)

Nasoni, Niccolò (1691–1773) Italian-born architect, working in Portugal. He arrived at Oporto in 1725, where he settled and mainly worked on churches (chancel and lateral galilee of Oporto Cathedral, 1731–6). Gradually identifying himself with the northern and Portuguese traditions of construction, he modernized and innovated them with works of a refined Baroque style and profound originality—mostly erected in Oporto and its surroundings: the church and tower of Clérigos (1732–63), the church of Misericórdia (1749), and several palaces like Freixo (on the banks of the Douro river, *c.*1750, designed with a composite 'Rocaille' freedom), and the Solar de Mateus (Vila Real, 1749), as well as manor houses in Prelada and Ramalde.   JMF

National Romanticism A movement in art, literature, music, architecture, and interior design that occurred primarily in northern, central, and eastern Europe from the late 1880s to about 1920. In countries such as Germany, Finland, Sweden, Denmark, Norway, Poland, Hungary, Estonia, and Latvia, where national feeling was particularly strong at the end of the 19th century, architects turned to medieval and peasant models in search of new forms, materials, and modes of expression, which they put to use in new building types. They found in primitive medieval buildings—especially castles and early churches—symbols of national identity that permitted the introduction of radically simplified building masses and the use of rough, 'natural'-looking materials (stone and brick). And in each place, ordinary farmers' dwellings, with their simple furnishings, were believed to offer patterns for a new way of life, closer to nature and to long-standing local tradition.

In the Scandinavian countries and in Germany, National Romantic architects and designers believed in ancient myths as the embodiment of national identity (the Eddas and Sagas in Germany, Norway, Denmark, and Sweden; the Kalevala in Finland). And in each country, national origins seemed to be located in a particular region (Karelia in Finland, Dalarna in Sweden, for example). Thus, National Romantic architecture tended to be strongly regional in its inspiration.

National Romantic architecture paralleled some of the formal expression of Art Nouveau, Jugendstil, and Expressionism, while interior design was related to Arts and Crafts movements in Britain and the United States. But it was above all the native medieval and peasant traditions in each place that served as the inspiration for architects and designers. Thus National Romantic buildings differed in appearance from place to place: Martin *Nyrop's Copenhagen City Hall; *Gesellius, Lindgren, and Saarinen's National Museum in Helsinki; Hans *Poelzig's Löwenburg Town Hall; Ragnar *Östberg's Stockholm City Hall—all used different materials and referred to different prototypes, but shared a striking originality and an appearance of archaism.

As a movement, National Romanticism lost coherence during World War I, when nationalism came to be suspect among most progressive artists and intellectuals. But the legacy of the movement can be traced, especially in the architecture and interior design of the Scandinavian countries, in a concern with regional tradition, a fondness for brick, stone, and wood, and a modest, almost domestic, scale. Alvar *Aalto's Town Hall at Säynätsalo exemplifies these qualities, as do the late works of Kay *Fisker and Ivar *Tengbom. In Germany, the Nazi espousal of peasant motifs and neo-Romanesque traditions under the rubric of *Blut und Boden* ideology resulted after World War II in a more far-reaching repudiation of National Romantic ideas than anywhere else. BML

> Lane, Barbara Miller, *National Romanticism and Modern Architecture in Germany and the Scandinavian Countries* (2000)

nature, inspiration from Whether architecture derives its forms, meaning, and validity from nature, or should attempt to do so, remains one of the unanswered questions. The idea of 'Natural Law' makes nature into a moral principle, yet never one on which agreement can be reached in a field as peculiar as architecture. It is often assumed that the human mind is formed to read and recognize certain patterns of form, often those involving complex figure and ground relationships and repeating patterns, with or without hierarchies. The earliest art forms from different civilizations indicate the possibility of abstracting from natural form, usually with magical and cosmological meanings rather than simply pictorial representation.

Aristotle defined imitation in the arts following the nature in its operations (*mimesis*), rather than a literal reproduction of forms, while his analysis of nature stressed the purposive aspect of form, suggesting the idea of related form and function as natural and desirable. By contrast, Plato suggested abstract geometric forms without pictorial connotation. Did the Greek orders originate as *Vitruvius states, or from the formalization of natural objects? Were his explanations post-rationalizations of other origins? The form of the column, regardless of cultural origin, carries much of the symbolic weight of nature in architecture, and the temple form was readily extrapolated back to its origins in a 'primitive hut' by enlightenment thinkers in the 18th century. The separation of nature and culture, probably derived from Aristotle's separation of spirit and matter and embodied in Christian doctrine, has given Western civilizations a unique ability to

misunderstand nature and to treat as primitive the other cultures of the world in which nature was understood more readily as a universal principle, whose reflection in architecture, as in other forms of art, was never problematic.

One route to nature is to open the door or window onto the landscape, and create a relationship between a building and its surroundings. Gardens can be a form of architecture made partly with growing material, when formal or 'naturalistic', like the Arcadian landscape garden. The *picturesque movement challenged the Classicism of the English landscape garden, replacing its generalized forms with a greater sensitivity to location and vernacular building styles. Throughout the 18th century, garden buildings were a fertile source of experiment, sometimes evoking imagined primitive origins for architecture in timber construction.

While the obsession with architectural precedent in the 19th century seemed increasingly remote from nature, theorists tried to find ways of returning to first principles. In *Semper's case, these were derived from concepts of materials and making; in Ruskin's from a moral idea of making combined with the deeper vision of form that Aristotle called *theoria*. *Viollet-le-Duc interpreted Gothic architecture as engineering, and saw it as a primary route for returning to a logical and therefore natural relationship between construction and form. Nature therefore became allied to the principles both of function and decoration, and much of the novelty of the 19th century derived from the attempt to separate and then recombine these two, with increasing assistance from other cultures, above all Japan, which represented 'unspoilt' civilization. Art Nouveau was an attempt to find a new style with a natural but non-historical basis, but it passed out of fashion with much of its business unfinished.

In Modernism, no single image or style can capture a simple truth about how to achieve a relationship with nature. Modernism might offer a neutral frame through which nature could be viewed, as in Mies, or it might mimic nature in its operations, as Wright hoped to do in his organic architecture. If mechanical form is unnatural, then it appears as a rejection of nature in favour of Cartesian abstract reason in its forms and favourite materials—instance the grid as a plan form and elevational system. If nature is equated with instrumental and purposive form, then the culturally neutral art of the engineer, as instanced by the bridge designs of Robert *Maillart, approaches nature most closely, and ornament and representation are redundant. Both these options may fail to recognize the need for a human response to places and their distinctive organic growth, which require that rigid forms must be set free and materials show their telluric origins. Ralph Waldo Emerson's philosophy of the omnipresence and spiritual significance of nature influenced Frank Lloyd *Wright to continue themes from Art Nouveau and Arts and Crafts into the Modern Movement. Japanese architecture was a corrective to Western rationalism. *Le Corbusier made nature a leading principle in his work, although the results were diverse. A softer understanding of nature characterized the 'second generation' of modern architects, born between the late 1890s and late 1920s, such as Alvar *Aalto. There was a wave of 'biomorphic' form in architecture, graphics, and other fields during the 1940s, found in the TWA terminal, New York, by Eero *Saarinen, or the curves of the Sydney Opera House by Jørn *Utzon.

In the history of post-war architecture, a variety of positions have been taken in relation to nature. The general trend of construction was towards highly processed materials and a loss of individual and regional character, although Wright's tradition of resistance to complete mechanization was continued as a minority trend in many countries. Awareness of the physically damaging effect of buildings on their location, and the impact of the energy inputs and waste outputs from them, was evident in the 1940s to a few thinkers, including Buckminster *Fuller, and also to a few practitioners, but despite a brief upsurge of 'green' activity in the 1970s, there was not enough demand from clients and society before the 1990s to make these part of the mainstream (*sustainable architecture). The situation has developed rapidly in recent years, producing a variety of architectural interpretations ranging from neo-vernacular traditionalism to the colourful but rather crude design solutions that have long characterized 'ecological' or 'green' architecture. Glen *Murcutt is admired for the clarity of his climatically and culturally adjusted buildings in Australia, which incorporate concerns about the use of resources with many of the earlier ideas about representing nature through architecture.

Regulation has encouraged new building forms for adaptation to the seasonal cycle through passive cooling and improved retention of heat, reshaping the form of the typical office or institutional building. Germany leads in Europe on efficiency of individual buildings, but urban and regional planning may be equally significant. In 1961, Jane Jacobs cited developments in cybernetic and systems thinking as a model for understanding the complex human ecology of existing cities, but in the USA the car-dependent low-density suburban housing development has remained the only legally available form, producing a reaction from the Congress for New Urbanism in favour of denser settlements that enable public transport to be developed.

Seemingly detached from these practical concerns, the architectural avant-garde continues to play with the idea of nature, favouring 'zoomorphic' shapes, like those from science fiction cartoon books (such as the Kunsthaus, Graz, by Peter Cook) partly because computers have made them almost as easy to construct as straight lines. Engineers such as Cecil Balmond of Ove Arup and Partners have developed algorithms that

643

generate apparently complex forms from simple operations, as used by Daniel Libeskind, but only simplistically related to natural form or process. Around 2005, computers were still seen as an exciting way of mimicking naturalistic form, with some promise of translation into efficient or elegant structure. Veteran modernist John Johanssen expounded a belief that nano-bots could generate plant-like buildings without human invention.

In 2004, Christopher Alexander completed publication of *The Nature of Order*, an ambitious hypothesis about the relationship of mind, nature, and building that suggested a post-Cartesian synthesis in which human agency, newly attuned to natural process and form, is crucial to a sustainable future in construction. Other authors express belief in the possibility of a new convergence between sustainable construction and appropriate, delightful architectural form that avoids sentimentality, or literalism, but while not unimaginable, the results seem elusive, owing perhaps to advanced industrialization, budget constraints, and division of labour enshrined in the way that buildings are made. The widespread confusion between working by analogy with nature and the more literal homology, or copying of nature, compounds the difficulty.   AP

Buchanan, P., *Ten Shades of Green: Architecture and the Natural World* (2005)

Hagan, S., *Taking Shape: A New Contract between Architecture and Nature* (2001)

Powers, A., *Nature in Design* (1999)

nave A long internal space, usually the central *aisle of a *basilica or a church to the west of the chancel, choir, or sanctuary, and hence any analogous space. In a basilica it is usually divided from the side aisles by arcades and lit by clerestory windows, these making it suitable for public transactions. Similarly, in a Christian church it is usually devoted to the main congregation, lay or, in the case of a monastic church, clerical, as opposed to the officiating priests. In smaller two-cell churches it stands alone without aisles, divided from the chancel by an arch or screen.   APQ

necking A narrow concave moulding, usually part of a capital, immediately above the shaft of the column, such as the echinus of a Doric capital, and the ring that separates the shaft from Ionic and Corinthian capitals, and the various types of *Romanesque capital.   APQ

neoclassicism The revival of the classical styles of Greece and Rome inaugurated in the second half of the 18th century. This resulted from detailed study of antique remains, and introduced a style which aimed to reproduce accurate representations of classical detailing, albeit within the context of current architectural and artistic requirements. As a consequence of a contemporary interest in primitive styles, it also sometimes aimed at an extreme simplicity of form and detailing, in which classical ornament is implied rather than fully applied. A sense of history, and the growing understanding in the Age of Reason that humanity might control its destiny, led to a romantic belief, nevertheless based on reasoning, that the ills of the world might be erased by a re-appraisal of human endeavour and a radical approach that implied a fresh start from basic principles. In architecture that meant a return to the earliest styles known, namely the classical styles of the noble Greek and virtuous Roman, and, even more radical, the very foundation of these styles in the so-called primitive hut—'the model upon which all the magnificences of architecture have been imagined', as the Abbé Laugier put it in his *Essai sur l'Architecture* (1753).

Already Giovanni Battista Piranesi (1720–78) had illustrated romantic views of ruined Greek and Roman temples that promoted their noble virtue, and in about 1743–4 published the first of his *Carceri*, extraordinary views of the insides of prisons whose massive, primitive forms and rough-hewn masonry overwhelm their inhabitants. More a reflection of Laugier than Piranesi, J.-G. *Soufflot (1713–80) began the church of Ste Geneviève or the Panthéon, Paris (1757–90), as the first great monument of neoclassicism so far as its walls were strictly trabeated, and its details followed classical Roman precedent as far upwards as its saucer domes (though not its drum and dome, inspired by Wren's St Paul's).

More readily, Etienne-Louis *Boullée (1728–99) designed several projects (1782) for ideal buildings of abstract use—a metropole, a museum for the statues of great men, a cenotaph for Isaac Newton—which were of megalomaniac size. They were either Roman or Greek in detail, or dependent on plain geometrical forms—the Newton cenotaph was a vast hollow sphere, punctured to give the effect of a planisphere, set in an equally vast egg-cup. Slightly more practical were Claude-Nicolas *Ledoux's (1736–1806) projects so far as they served real needs and were smaller—a house for the directors of the river Loue in the shape of a water pipe, an inn with a plan based on a circle and triangle—but were still wildly impractical. Nevertheless he built half of his project for the ideal circular town of Chaux at Arc-et-Senans, near Besançon (1774–9), in which geometrical form took the place of classical detail. Similar characteristics imbue the three remaining *barrières* or toll-houses he built around Paris (1784–9).

This radical approach had no place in Britain. Instead it extended the Grand Tour into the Turkish lands of ancient Greece and rediscovered Periclean Doric and Ionic. Among the first were James 'Athenian' Stuart (1713–88) and Nicholas Revett (1720–1804), whose *Antiquities of Athens* was published in 1762, four years after they had built a Doric temple at Hagley, Worcestershire. Robert *Adam (1728–92) likewise travelled east, publishing the *Ruins of Spalato*

in 1764 and incorporating finely observed and reproduced classical detail into his houses, including the less formal detail of classical houses and villas, which he believed were Etruscan, as can be found at his Osterley Park, Hounslow (1762). His contemporary and co-patriot Charles Cameron (c.1714–1812) achieved similar artistic advances in St Petersburg, notably at Tsarskoye Selo (1782–5).

By the time of the French Revolution and Napoleonic wars (1789–1815), France had shown a radical approach to neoclassicism, Britain a decorative approach, based on archaeology. This changed in the hands of John *Soane (1753–1837), who reduced classical detail to allusive mouldings, resulting in a stripped-down Classicism that suited an age when industrialization was bringing mass production to architectural detailing. His Bank of England interiors (1778 onwards) made wonderful use of plain spaces minimally articulated by groovings and flutings representing orders and entablatures, with saucer domes overhead. In his own home in Lincoln's Inn Fields he added mirrors to the walls and domes, giving them an enhanced feeling of weightlessness, with space rather than mass as the controlling factor.

After the Napoleonic wars, neoclassicism made greater strides in Germany than France, its greatest exponent being Karl Friedrich *Schinkel (1781–1841), whose Altes Museum in Berlin (1822–30) has far greater nobility, as of a Greek temple, than any contemporary work in France. In St Petersburg, Thomas de Thomon (1754–1813) found inspiration in Paestum's Greek temples for the Bourse (1804–16), as did A. D. Voronikhin (1760–1814) for the Academy of Mines (1806–11), but the greatest of Russian works was A. D. *Zakharov's (1761–1811) Admiralty (1806–15), which gave French megalomania permanent form in his magnificently scaled façade, which is a third of a kilometre (quarter of a mile) long.　　APQ

Neo-Liberty The term used by Italian and foreign critics—and sometimes in a derogatory manner—to refer to a renewed interest on the part of Italian architects of the 1950s in references to past historical movements, and in particular to the architecture of the Italian Art Nouveau, which was called Stile Liberty.

BLM

Nepal is a rather large, landlocked kingdom, surrounded by many of the highest Himalayan peaks. However, its artistic achievements are limited to the immediate Kathmandu area, which includes the nearby ancient cities of Patan and Bhaktapur. Its culture derived from India, although the Nepalese people are closer to their ethnic neighbours, the Tibetans, and the development of Tibetan art reveals a debt to those Nepalese sources. Buddhism enjoyed its greatest success between the 8th and 13th centuries—a period that coincides with many of the Buddhist achievements in Sri Lanka and South East Asia—although legendary belief claims Buddhism arrived through the Indian King Ashoka in the 3rd century BC. It remains likely that the historical Buddha was born in south-western Nepal. As in India and South East Asia, during this period of Buddhist success, it coexisted with Hinduism, and artistic styles remain similar, for the same artists and builders worked for patrons of both religions. Nepalese architecture, perhaps even more than its sculpture and painting, emerged from its Indian sources not only with distinction and a local character but interestingly with stylistic similarity to aspects of wooden architecture of east Asia.

The continuous use of wood is well established in Nepal, an area rich in timber. On one level this enables one to view the extension of early Indian styles, where wooden construction was once dominant. However, a distinct Nepalese style of building evolved in ways unique to Nepal, albeit building upon the Indian sources. One remarkable aspect of Nepalese wooden architecture is the buildings with multiple extended roofs, each supported by elaborately carved wooden struts, readily seen in the central area of Bhaktapur. The *chaitya halls, typically accommodating numerous images, are placed atop stone foundations, and their design, often with multiple roofs, suggests the better known wooden pagodas of Japan, leading some to speculate that a reverse course of influence may have occurred.

It is with the use of a particular wood and brick wall treatment that Nepalese architecture formed yet more of a distinct style, again best seen in older remains, such as Bhaktapur or Patan. These buildings feature elaborately carved window frames and pediments over the main doors, framed by the brick walls. These richly carved elements extend well beyond the geometric shape of the windows and doors, pushing out into the brick walls, providing patterns of their own and yet more areas for surface carving. When joined with the elaborate bronze castings on doorways, the façade of a Nepalese brick building reveals an enriched surface of varied materials: wood, brick, and metal, often surmounted by a series of pagoda roofs, whose supports are themselves richly carved and painted, thus creating a unique blend of materials and decoration.

The Nepalese stupa, the best known being the dramatically sited Swayambanath, essentially continued the Indian and Sri Lankan prototype. Visible from Kathmandu below, the large hemispherical dome sits on top of a stone base, surmounted by a series of thirteen diminishing circles, symbols of the thirteen stages of Buddhahood. The most remarkable, indeed startling, feature is the painting of eyes on each of the four sides of the harmika, the square element atop the large dome. They are partly closed, as if following the worshipper circumambulating the monument, perhaps expressing the omniscience of the deity Vairochana—a feature not found outside the Kathmandu valley. RF

Palazzetto dello Sport, Rome (Pier Luigi Nervi, 1956–7)

Nering, Johann Arnold (1659–95) German architect and military engineer, who exercised a dominant influence over architecture in Berlin for the two decades preceding his death. In Berlin, his main works were: the Stadtschloss (from 1679); the Alabastersaal (1681–5), and the Orangery (1684) in the adjoining pleasure garden; the plan and 300 small houses for the newly established district of Friedrichstadt, as well as a number of noblemen's palaces; and the Zeughaus (1695ff.). Outside Berlin, he designed a chapel for Schloss Köpenick (1684–5) and extended Schloss Oranienburg, Brandenburg (1689–95). All his works bear the imprint of the military engineer, capably planned but rather severe in form.   PG

Nervi, Pier Luigi (1891–1979) Italy's most well-known engineer. Throughout his life he explored the potential of a single material—reinforced concrete, and succeeded in bringing delicacy and lightness to a material customarily associated with raw mass and weight. Working as both designer and builder he was intimately involved with the development of ideas, forms, and techniques that advanced the use of concrete

and constructed a body of work that included many large, innovative, and elegant structures—not only innovative projects for industrial clients but also major civic buildings planned for sport, exhibitions, and public assembly.

His first large-scale work was the Florence Municipal Stadium (1930–32), but the first to show a distinctive mastery of his chosen material were a group of airport hangars at Orvieto (completed 1940). These elegant concrete structures attracted widespread interest in his work, and after the war Nervi went on to design numerous large column-free spaces that became the basis for radical experimentation. The Grand Salon of the Turin Exhibition Hall, completed in 1950, and the Palazzetto dello Sport (1956–7) explored the use of 'ferro-cemento'—a technique that utilizes fine steel mesh sprayed with cement mortar, while he was to develop elegant large-scale structures and refined prefabricated building systems for other schemes. He sought to integrate architecture and engineering, and worked closely with architects—most notably with Gio Ponti on the design of the Pirelli Building (Milan, 1955–8) and Marcel Breuer on UNESCO's Headquarters

647

(Paris, 1953–70). He also designed three stadia in Rome for the 1960 Olympic Games and the Port Authority Bus Terminal in New York (completed 1963). BC

Nesfield, William Eden (1835–88) English architect and furniture designer. After his training under William *Burn, Anthony *Salvin, and also *Viollet-le-Duc, Nesfield sketched buildings in France and Italy for his *Medieval Architecture* (1862). Starting his own practice in 1858, he and Norman *Shaw often travelled together, notably in the Weald, where they were impressed by the vernacular architecture of the region. This came to be expressed in the Old English style of his smaller buildings, and the 'Queen Anne' style of others such as North Lodge, Kew Gardens, London (1866), Kinmel Park, Denbighshire (1866–8), and Loughton Hall, Loughton, Essex (1878). APQ

Netherlands, medieval Although the country turned to Christianity from about AD 695 with the inauguration of the diocese of Frisia, there is no significant architecture until the beginning of the millennium. In the south, Romanesque architecture appears in Maastricht, with the westwork of Onze-Lieve-Vrouwekerk (*c*.1000), of a similar character to that found in other parts of the German empire, as there is no regional style. St Servatius, Maastricht, rebuilt several times between *c*.1000 and *c*.1150, had a basilican plan, and an impressive westwork. In the north, a new cathedral, which formed the centre of a group of similar churches, all of a conventional Romanesque type, though partly built of brick, was built in Utrecht from *c*.1010.

The vertical emphasis and other characteristics of the true *Gothic are only to be found in the choir and the south aisle of Utrecht Cathedral (*c*.1288–*c*.1320). The distinctively shaped tower, an octagon set over a rectangular base, was much imitated elsewhere in the Netherlands. From *c*.1350, the example of Utrecht may have encouraged other large towns, such as Amsterdam, Delft, and The Hague, to rebuild their churches during the succeeding century. But none followed Utrecht's Gothic, and it was Brabant Gothic, with its elaborate decoration and well-articulated rib-vaulting, which was to have more influence in the northern Netherlands (for example, the Onze-Lieve-Vrouwekerk, Dordrecht; St Gertrudis, Bergen-op-Zoom) until the close of the medieval period. PG

Netherlands, 16th–18th century Early in the 16th century, several Italian court artists like Tommaso Vincidor (1493–1536) and Alessandro Pasqualini (1493–1559) introduced Italian Renaissance architecture in the Netherlands. Soon the fashion for the new architectural ornaments spread among native artists and craftsmen like Pieter Coecke van Aelst, Hans Vredeman de *Vries, and Lieven de *Key, who applied them to traditional and Gothic structures.

Dutch architecture entered a Golden Age with the independence of the United Provinces from Spanish rule. The rapid urbanization of the Netherlands—by 1650 half of the Republic's population lived in cities—stimulated the architectural expression of the city as a political, legal, and economic unity. City gates, town halls, charitable institutions such as almshouses, poorhouses, and old people's homes, trade buildings (especially weighhouses), were the centres of civic pride, and therefore were treated with special care. Catholic buildings were confiscated and transformed, and the new Protestant churches in the new neighbourhoods, of which several in Amsterdam were designed by Hendrick de *Keyser, demanded a new, centralized space around the pulpit.

After 1585, the small late-medieval pilgrimage town of Amsterdam became the centre of world trade, and as it expanded, was surrounded with a girdle of canals. As in most other Dutch cities, water was the central artery, regulating traffic, transport, and the depth and width of the individual building lots. The need for daylight dictated the gable patterns of the houses as decorated, semi-transparent screens, with side walls bearing the wooden beam construction and floors. Wealthy patrons, assisted by craftsmen-builders, created individual petite canal-side palaces, shoulder to shoulder with smaller houses on the side-streets, forming blocks enclosing deep and narrow gardens. Brick was the most widely used building material; stone was imported from the Ardennes and Germany.

In the court circle of Prince-Stadholder Frederik Hendrik of Orange (1625–47) and his secretary and *uomo universale*, Constantijn Huygens, French models of planning were combined with the Dutch need for intimacy and a growing interest in the architecture of *Palladio and Scamozzi. The result was a specifically Dutch form of Classicism. Jacob van *Campen, Pieter *Post, Philips *Vingboons and their generation established a sophisticated architectural language based on Vitruvian rules of harmony and proportion, resulting in plans, façades, and interior spaces of increasing geometrical simplicity.

During the reign of William III (1672–1702) the court regained its leading position, with the architect Jacob Roman and the French-trained designer Daniel *Marot playing a central role. Marot also followed the King to England after the Glorious Revolution (1688). The age without stadholders (1702–47) was also an age without architects, in which the building industry was dominated by craftsmen-builders, who fulfilled most architectural demands, contracting sculptors to apply ornaments or design interior decorations for the expanding and luxurious apartments of the rich.

Under William IV (1747–51) and his architect Pieter de *Swart, the court stimulated the renewal of architectural fashion (Rococo), followed in the early 1770s by a renewal with traces of nostalgia for the—lost—Golden Age. The largest new buildings, such as old people's homes and workhouses, were erected by

municipalities. The craftsmen-builders Jacob Otten *Husly and Abraham van der *Hart received the most important commissions. The most innovative structures, apart from the steam pumping stations, were museums and community centres, commissioned by learned and cultural societies and built for the public.   FS

Netherlands, 19th–20th century Dutch

architecture in the 19th century was as internationally oriented as in the 20th, but Dutch architects and their work would participate actively in international architectural debates only after World War I. The 19th century brought roughly the same fundamental social, ideological, and technical changes to the Netherlands as to other parts of Europe. The architects, their patrons, the education, and their work changed more or less in the same way.

At the start of the 19th century, until *c*.1835, French architecture and international Classicism were the main points of reference. Next the German Rundbogenstil (Romanesque Revival) became the guide to Dutch modern architecture for architects such as Willem *Rose. In the 1850s a variety of the *Gothic Revival was developed, using examples and theories from Belgium, Germany, England, and France, among others by Pierre *Cuypers. At the same time Jan *Leliman introduced Eclecticism from Paris. In the 1860s the emulation of the Renaissance became an important issue. In these years the Netherlands discovered their own national style, continuing the architecture of the early 17th century: façades of red brick accentuated by white sandstone. This ancient architecture, with its accompanying colourful and intimate Dutch cityscape, became a favourite sight for tourists.

Compared with British, German, French, or Belgian 19th-century building, Dutch architecture looks a bit pallid. Possibly the cause lies in the image the Dutch

The Mauritshuis, The Hague, Netherlands (Jacob van Campen, 1633–7)

had of themselves in the 19th century: a small, democratic people who cherished their liberty. Because of the absence of a prominent aristocracy, architecture was not opulent or monumental but 'picturesque'; in this middle-class society the aim was not impressive and costly ostentation, but a cultivation of simplicity.

In 1891 a new generation of architects arrived whose spokesman was Willem Kromhout. They had had enough of tradition and wanted to make a new start, with an empty agenda. Images from the *Deutsche Bauzeitung* and in particular the British journal *The Studio*, as well as Eclecticism's liberal attitude and method, showed the way towards an architectural design that said goodbye to styles from the past. Indeed, *images*: the modernization of architecture was prepared not through theory but by architects, clients, and the public with their appreciation of a new visual expression of the new century. Architecture without

ornament and without style irresistibly became the new fashion. The articles of Hendrik P. *Berlage about style were less important than the flat façades of his Stock Exchange.

Style became an old-fashioned concept anyhow after 1900, except for the few artists and architects who wanted 'The Style'—with capitals. Their ideals were hardly central to daily practice, because architecture faced tasks that were not primarily artistic, but social, economical, and technical. Between 1900 and 2000 the Dutch population grew on a relatively small territory from 5 to over 15 million souls. As a result housing remained a dominant factor, its central issue the rationalization of building and dwelling. Dutch architects had become trained in the 19th century to work within tight budgets and honour simplicity as a virtue. In the 20th century they vied with each other to design housing of maximum quality at minimum cost, and with a hint of culture. This ambition was lost after c.1980 when mass housing became a matter of property development conglomerates.

A second legacy from the 19th century was the idea that architecture was not the embodiment of an aristocratic culture, but the citizen's picturesque, small-scale, and often also egalitarian expression. There is some connection with the first legacy, the egalitarian trends to identify with mass production rather than the unique. The best Dutch architects, including J. J. P. *Oud and Willem M. *Dudok, Aldo van Eyck and Herman *Hertzberger, have defended the potential of a grand but small-scale architecture.

A third legacy of the late 19th century is a dislike of traditionalism. The solid brick edifices of architects such as A. J. Kropholler and M. J. Granpré Molière, who were full of respect for the Dutch past and the timeless laws of the art of building, have only been admitted with great reluctance to the canon of the Dutch 20th century. The audacity to oppose the laws of tradition quickly led to canonization, whether in the fragile experiments of Johannes *Duiker, the stubborn attempts of Theo van *Doesburg to destroy architecture, or the pitiless psychological experiments of MVRDV.

The fourth legacy is the only tradition that is deeply rooted: the cult of construction. Eugen Gugel, the first professor of architecture in the Netherlands, stated for many generations of young architects in his handbook (1869) that construction in itself is not architecture—that only comes into being when art 'ennobles' uncouth construction. This view with its Semperian (and even older) origins has been reaffirmed in many guises in education; under the names 'rationalism', Nieuwe Zakelijkheid, 'Dutch structuralism' and even in many cases of Dutch postmodernism it remained one of the most important principles.

Because of the strong modernist tradition, postmodernism reached the Netherlands at a late stage, and did not fundamentally change Dutch architecture. Aldo Rossi's urgent appeal to architects to become responsible, as designers, for the continuity of centuries of history and culture was received respectfully in the Netherlands, but could not be put into practice because the appropriate mentality does not exist there. The opposite, Koolhaas's visions in which the traditional idea of a building is reinvented radically or disappears, also gained much respect but even more distrust. There is an old, strongly internalized norm which in Dutch 'rationalism' has determined the direction for a long time: craftsmanship from the pre-industral age. An architect in the Netherlands is applauded most not when he or she is a philosopher, or an industrialist, or a successful entrepreneur; and a reputation as an artist is quite disastrous. A good Dutch architect is ingenious like a constructor of mills; ideal Dutch architecture is slim and strong like a sailing ship, and every centimetre is useful.   AVDW (trans. CVE)

Groenendijk, P. et al., Guide to Modern Architecture in the Netherlands (1987)

Van der Woud, A., The Art of Building. From Classicism to Modernity: The Dutch Architectural Debate 1840–1900 (2001)

Neumann, Johann Balthasar (1687–1753)

German architect. Creator of some of the most complex and commanding architecture in western Europe, Neumann conceived of his buildings as compositions of architectural space, articulated by curved frameworks and vaults. Both his sacred and secular interiors were transparent, dynamic, deluged with daylight, and integrated with painting, statuary, stucco, gilding, metalwork, crystal, and carving by other artists whose work was directed by Neumann. Fully active from 1719 to 1753, he built numerous churches, two dozen palaces, an array of other buildings, utilitarian structures, and urban constructions.

Neumann's early training included hydraulics and architectural study with the military, which he completed in 1715 with an orthographic map of Würzburg. He began work with architect Josef Greising, which exposed him to the architectural legacy of the region. Following a 1717 military campaign in Belgrade, he journeyed within Austria, Bohemia, and north Italy. Shortly after his return to Würzburg in 1718, he was appointed architect to the newly elected prince bishop Johann Philipp Franz Graf Schönborn, beginning his life-long association with the powerful Schönborn family, major figures in the politics and economy of the Holy Roman Empire, and enthusiastic, generous patrons of art and architecture. With their support, Neumann also became legally established as final architectural authority in the Würzburg and Bamberg bishoprics.

Under Johann Philipp Franz, Neumann initiated work on his largest commission, the Residenz in Würzburg (the structure was built from 1719 to 1744), which occupied him until his death. The entrance courts, stables, and gardens of this imposing building are brilliantly integrated within both fortifications and urban fabric. For the building exterior, differently shaped pavilions mark entrances and corners; surfaces, architectural elements, and sculpture were originally painted yellow, white, and silver. Inside, Neumann designed an astonishing sequence of public spaces which served purposes of ritual and prestige; these included a magnificently vaulted stair hall and spectacular imperial hall, both with Tiepolo paintings, still overwhelming to visitors. None of Neumann's other palaces, whether new designs or remodellings, built or projected, matched the scale, grandeur, and completeness of the Residenz. Yet many are stunning in their own right, among them Werneck, Schönbornlust, Bruchsal, and projects for Stuttgart and the Vienna Hofburg.

Neumann's churches were greater in number and variety of design than his palaces. In these commissions, where patron demands and programmatic considerations were less demanding, the epic power of his architectural language was boldest, clearest, and richest. Within lucidly transparent interiors, he choreographed movement in the architecture and for the user, orchestrated a plentitude of natural light, and saw to the elaboration of these works by means of aesthetic media such as painting, sculpture, stucco, and gilding.

Several churches stand out within the collection of extraordinary ecclesiastic buildings: the court church for the Würzburg Residenz (1732–43), the parish church at Kitzingen (1740–45), the pilgrimage church of Vierzehnheiligen (1743–72), and the monastery church at Neresheim (1745–92). For them, Neumann employed thin, planar outer walls extensively opened by swathes of substantial windows. Set within and separate from the walls, he arranged curved openwork forms consisting of columns, pilasters, balconies, and deep vaults opened by broad lunettes. He balanced the vaults (which structurally were primitive versions of reinforced concrete shells, using iron bars) upon the point supports of the elevations, so that the horizontal plane of the plan and the vertical surfaces of the elevations were drawn into voluminous vaults, three-dimensional developments of two-dimensional geometries, in which space swells into light.

Related to his church architecture are Neumann's many designs for altars, conceived as open, framework structures designed to reiterate and synthesize the interiors as a focus for prayer and contemplation. He also designed and built houses, monasteries, hospitals, a hotel and city hall and courthouse, and a miscellany of religious structures. He undertook various urban design projects for Würzburg, including streets and squares, a water system and fountains. He built fortifications and barracks, bridges and gardens. He ran a glass factory and mirror-polishing workshop, and consulted on restorations. And he taught architecture, first within the context of his practice, than as a course of instruction at the university.

Vierzehnheiligen pilgrimage church, near Bamberg, Franconia, Germany (Balthasar Neumann, 1743–72)

Neumann's architecture is both traditional and unique. A lineage extending back to the 15th century informs the basic arrangements of his palaces, churches, and façades, as well as the integration of other artistic media with his buildings. An architecture as space composition had evolved since the mid–17th century. But Neumann accepted all of this merely as a point of departure. With consummate authority he combined clarity with complexity in plan and section, charged interiors with light and dematerialized mass, and thrust both into powerful encounters with space. He orchestrated the experience of space in ways that are striking, lucid, and imposing, gradually revealed, demanding, and humane, bold and unique. CO

Otto, Christian F., *Space into Light: the Churches of Balthasar Neumann* (1979)

Neutra, Richard (1892–1970) Austrian-born US architect. He introduced International Style Modernism to southern California in the mid 1920s. Known largely for his residential designs, Neutra's work evolved from European-influenced lightweight white and silver volumes to later works that spread into the landscape, employing more natural materials and exemplifying Californian indoor/outdoor living.

Educated in Vienna, Neutra found work after World War I in Berlin with Erich Mendelsohn, where he was influenced by the European work represented by *Mies van der Rohe and Le Corbusier. However, eager to move to the United States, Neutra arrived there in 1923, moving west from New York to Chicago to Wright's Taliesin in Wisconsin, to Los Angeles, where he moved into his friend R. M. *Schindler's Kings Road house and studio (1921–2) early in 1925.

By 1930 Neutra had published two books, *Wie Baut Amerika?* (1927) and *Amerika: Neues Bauen in der Welt* (1930), both emphasizing American technological innovations, and completed the project that made his international reputation, the Lovell Health house, Los Angeles (1927–9), the first documented steel-framed house in America, lightly covered in an abstract composition of bands of windows and stucco. This led to Neutra's inclusion in the Modern Architecture exhibition at MoMA, New York (1932), which sealed his reputation as one of the most significant *International Style architects in the United States.

Despite his fascination with American technology, Neutra's works were seldom technologically advanced. The Lovell Health house was a notable exception, with its H-columns and open-web joists, as well as the steel house designed for film director Josef von Sternberg, Los Angeles (1935). Largely due to the expense of steel construction, other works of this period were made of conventional materials, wood frame and stucco, including Neutra's own compact studio and residence, Los Angeles (1932). Many were covered in silver-grey metallic paint, to give the appearance of steel, such as the expansive Brown house, Fisher's Island, New York (1938).

Around 1939, Neutra began to design single-storey pavilions featuring large sheets of glass and significant overhangs. These later houses made use of brick, stone, and wood, and employed a variety of construction systems. They opened to the landscape in L-shapes and pinwheel configurations, recalling Schindler's Kings Road house and Wright's Usonian houses (1933–59). Notable examples were the Kaufman house, Palm Springs (1946), which combined stone and wood with a minimal steel frame, and the modest wood-framed Bailey house, Los Angeles (1947), the only built project among those Neutra designed for John Entenza's Case Study House Program.

Neutra had some larger commissions, including the 600-unit Channel Heights Housing (1942) in San Pedro, one of the few built demonstrations of his ideas on social housing. From 1949 to 1961 he worked with architect-planner Robert Alexander on larger projects; these were generally uninspired, lacking the programmatic and contextual imperative to merge with the landscape that was a strength of the house designs. The most successful were school projects, such as Palos Verdes High School (1961), single-storey buildings integrating indoor and outdoor spaces; Neutra's school designs established a widely influential Californian model.

An architect of refinement rather than invention, Neutra made efficient plans, but the designs showed little sectional variation. Details were often repeated. Living rooms were sometimes more like hallways, despite Neutra's stated interest in the sensory and psychological aspects of architecture, expressed in his book *Survival Through Design* (1954). He was, however, an accomplished designer of built-in and free-standing furniture. He innovated in small ways, introducing fire-resistant materials and sun-tracking louvres in his post-war work. JES

Hines, T. S., *Richard Neutra and the Search for Modern Architecture* (1982)

Lamprecht, B., *Richard Neutra—Complete Works* (2000)

Newton, Ernest (1856–1922) English architect. *See* ARTS AND CRAFTS.

New Zealand

Polynesian voyagers Maori civilization and building in New Zealand dates from AD 1200. Maori *whare* (tribal meeting houses) were gabled timber constructions of *raupo* (reeds) and timber framing in village (*kainga*) ensembles or fortified villages (*pa*). Barge boards were elaborately carved in the wonderful softwoods of New Zealand such as *totara*. The timbers of New Zealand were fundamental, both for the Maori and for the *pakeha* (European) architectural tradition. *Kauri* is a superb wood for almost all carpentry, joinery, and especially boat building. *Rimu* similarly can be used structurally for flooring and commonly for carving.

Pakeha missionaries from Sydney settled at Kerikeri in 1814. The stone store at Kerikeri is New Zealand's oldest *pakeha* building based on a similar building in Parramatta. Busby House (1832) by John Verge was prefabricated in Sydney in the colonial Georgian style and became the place of the signing of the Treaty of Waitangi (1840) setting out indigenous rights and grand goals.

Sophisticated carpentry Timber framing resisted earthquakes. Bishop Selwyn, a follower of the Ecclesiologists, ensured that the timber tradition continued in churches in the Gothic style with steeply sloping roofs. St John's College Chapel (1847) was Frederick Thatcher's first work in the timber 'Selwyn' style. This style was to echo through much New Zealand architecture.

In Christchurch, the tradition of wooden Gothic buildings continued in the provincial council buildings (1859) by Mountfort and Luck. These combined timber buildings with masonry towers. Inside the buildings were extraordinary spaces, particularly the almost 200 m (656 ft) passage that runs continuously around the inner courtyard. The council chamber designed by Mountfort in 1861 is in a highly decorated neo-Gothic style.

In the Presbyterian establishment of Dunedin, the First Church (1873) by R. A. Lawson used native stone to make an extraordinarily virtuoso geometric-style church. But elaborate timber vernacular buildings, often in the picturesque Gothic style, continued in cottages, villas, and country houses. The Government Buildings, Wellington (1876), by W. H. Clayton, a timber 4-storey Italianate palazzo, is one of the biggest timber buildings in the world.

Concrete and style Reinforced concrete gave new strength, particularly to monumental building. By the time of World War I, styles from the movies, Spanish

Mission, and Art Deco became popular. The Spanish Mission's Auckland Grammar School (1913) by R. Atkinson Abbott was conspicuous as a non-Gothic educational building. The neo-Gothic St Mary's of the Angels, Wellington (1919), by F. D. J. Clere used slender concrete and brick.

An earthquake and fire in Napier destroyed the Victorian seaside town in 1931, forcing the introduction of a national code for earthquakes, which has now become the most advanced in the world. Napier was rebuilt as an almost complete Art Deco city whose clean lines suited the reinforced concrete structure. The Masonic and the Criterion Hotel (1932) by W. J. Prouse had rhythmical massing. Before World War II, the Department of Housing Construction produced some sophisticated European modern buildings with the assistance of Ernst Plische, an Austrian refugee, such as the Berhampore Flats (1937). Particularly successful by the same architects were the Grey Flats (1940) in Auckland. In Christchurch, Peter Beaven's Road Tunnel Building (1963) and Warren and Mahoney's Christchurch College (1968) were successful and influential pieces in concrete.

Pitched roofs In the 1950s some young Auckland architects formed 'the Group' to provide good environments in the simplest form. Their shallow pitched roofs were labelled 'woolsheds' by the public. Steeply pitched roofs of Selwyn made a return in the Dillworth School Chapel in Auckland (1969) by Abbott Hole and Annabell. Ian Athfield and Roger Walker used the steeply pitched roofs as a basis of architectural language.

In Christchurch, Peter Bevin's Commodore Hotel (1980) referred to his predecessor Mountford. The most sophisticated of the steeply pitched roof language is John Scott's Fortuna Chapel (1961) in Wellington using shingles, stucco, and concrete block in subtle combination.

Public gestures The 1990s in Wellington produced some grand gestures. Athfield and associated architects carved a Civic Square behind the waterfront, complete with metal Nicau palms. The Museum of New Zealand's *Te Papa* (2000) by Jasmax, on the waterfront, tried to bring a narrative architecture of bi-culturalism around a massive 4 m (13 ft) wide ordering wall. The Westpac Trust Stadium (Bligh Voller Nield / Lobb Partnership / Warren and Mahoney, 2000) on the waterfront provided a large stadium for cricket and rugby (almost a religion in New Zealand), enclosed in a circular corrugated metal container to keep out the Cook Strait's notorious winds.   LN

Shaw, P(eter), *A History of New Zealand Architecture* (1998)

Niccolini, Antonio (1772–1850) Italian architect. His enlargement of the Villa Floridiana, near Naples (1817–19), is a rather derivative combination of the villas of Palladio and the English picturesque landscape, but his most idiosyncratic work is the façade of the Teatro San Carlo, Naples (1810–12).

The façade is a confused combination of a lower storey divided into two parts, marked by heavy, then lighter rustication; and an upper storey consisting of a long screen of columns and a rather flat pediment. Viewed separately, each storey is an interesting version of *neoclassicism, but together they lack integration.   PG

Niemeyer, Oscar (1907–) Brazilian, one of the great modern architects, possessing a formidably expressive personal language rooted in the traditional architecture of Brazil. He was a member of the Ministry of Education and Health team (1937–43), with Lúcio *Costa, Affonso Eduardo *Reidy, Jorge Machado Moreira (1910–), and Le Corbusier as a consultant. With Costa he designed the Brazil Pavilion at the New York World Fair, 1939. When invited by the mayor of Bello Horizonte, Juscelino Kubitshek, to

Brasilia Cathedral, Brazil (Oscar Niemeyer, 1957–64)

work in Pampulha (1942–4), his personal and deeply sensual style found powerful expression in a series of buildings that won him international fame. These were the church of Saint Francis of Assisi, the Yacht Club, the Casino and the Dance Pavilion, along with a number of houses. During the same period he constructed the Grand Hotel at Ouro Preto (1938–40), a building remarkable for the extent to which it incorporates respect for the colonial heritage and environment. In 1947 he took part, with Le Corbusier and Sven Markelius, in the design of the United Nations complex in New York. In Rio de Janeiro he built several houses, in particular his own in Canoas (1953), as well as commercial buildings and the South American hospital (1952). In São Paulo he designed the Parque Ibirapuera complex (1951), with gardens by Roberto Burle Marx (1909–94). It came as no surprise that, for construction of the first government buildings, Kubitschek invited him to Brasilia in 1956–64, where he again collaborated with Burle Marx on the landscape architecture; in addition to the regular blocks of the various ministries, he designed some particularly attractive buildings including the National Congress, the Palacio de Planalto—the Government headquarters—and the

High Court around the Plaza de los Tres Poderes (Square of the Three Powers), as well as the Palacio Itamaratí and the Ministry of Justice, the Palacio Alvorada, the Cathedral, the National Theatre, the stadium, the airport and the University of Brasilia. In around 1965 he began to undertake work in Europe and Africa: in Paris the Communist Party Headquarters (1966); in Le Havre, the Cultural Centre (1972); in Milan, with Luciano Pozzo, the Mondadori publishing headquarters (1968); in Algeria the Algiers city plan and the University of Constantine (1968–9). Returning to Brazil, he constructed numerous buildings, for residential and office use, as well as the controversial Memorial de América Latina complex in São Paulo (1988–98), and, recently, the interesting Niteroi Museum (2000–01).   LNM (trans. KL)

Nigeria *See* AFRICA (WEST AFRICA).

Nobbs, Percy Erskine (1875–1964) Scottish-born architect. Nobbs was an influential teacher, author, and practising architect, who inspired two generations of Canadian architects to respect traditional building, high standards of design, and skilled craftsmanship as the

way to prepare the ground for a contemporary
Canadian architecture. He served as a jurist on several
important competitions, providing another platform
for his ideas. After training in Scotland, Nobbs went to
Montreal in 1903 as Professor of Architecture at McGill
University, Canada's first university architectural
department. He entered into partnership with George
Taylor Hyde in 1910. In the firm's many residences,
such as his own modest brick house in Montreal
(1913–15) and the manorial stone Todd House in
Senneville, Quebec (1911–13), he emulated vernacular
building, following the lessons of the Arts and Crafts
movement. His buildings for McGill University, such as
the Scottish baronial Pathological Institute (1922–4),
were excellent contextual designs. Nobbs never
adjusted to the profound technological and economic
changes of the 20th century. He dismissed European
Modernism as an 'adverse influence', writing that
Canadians should 'accept (only) so much of their
doctrine as will help us, and solve our own problems
in our own way'.   HK

Wagg, S., *Percy Erskine Nobbs* (1982)

Noiers, Geoffrey de (*fl*.1189–1200) English mason.
Possibly a Norman settled in Lincoln, Noiers or Noyer
was the 'builder of the noble fabric' of St Hugh's choir
of Lincoln Cathedral (1192–1200). This was part of a
scheme for the whole cathedral, but his design of this is
doubted, and his role beyond that of executive mason
uncertain. However, the choir broke fresh ground in
the layout of its chapels, and even more so in its
vaulting, which introduced a ridge-rib and
asymmetrically arranged tiercerons.   APQ

Nonconformist architecture *See* CHAPELS,
DISSENTERS'.

Norman Of the period of the Norman kings, from
William the Conqueror to Stephen, 1066–1154, and
before the accession of the Angevins, hence the British
form of Romanesque architecture current at that time
and for a short while afterwards. Norman architecture
is characterized by thick walls, sometimes with wall
passages, and round-headed openings, as in several
cathedrals such as Ely, Norwich, and Peterborough;
and in castle keeps such as those of the Tower of
London; and in castles at Colchester, Norwich again,
and Rochester. A few small houses of the period
survive, notably Boothby Pagnell Manor House,
Lincolnshire, and Jew's House and Norman House,
Lincoln.   APQ

Norway, medieval Norway was converted to
Christianity at the end of the 10th century. The first
churches are of timber, either log-built as commonly
found in northern Europe, or stave-built. The oldest
of the latter, Holtålen church (*c*.1050–1100, now in
Trondheim Museum), has round, mast-like posts at the
corners of its nave and chancel, and rebated sills to
accommodate tongue-and-groove stave walls, with
much carving of interlaced animals and human figures.
The first church at Urnes (*c*.1060) had this form,
perhaps following the plan of earlier heathen temples,
but its successor (1125) is more elaborate, its tall
rectangular nave being surrounded by tall aisles, from
each of which it is divided by arcades of four posts with
double beams and bracing to make them stiff enough
to carry steeply pitched roofs. Royal halls, such as
Eysten's palace at Bergen (1117), may have been
similar, though more horizontal in emphasis. Stone-
built churches are more conventional. English practice
influenced Stavanger Cathedral, whose nave (*c*.1130) is
typically Norman with arcades of short, round piers;
and its Gothic choir (1272) could be English too.
Similarly, Trondheim Cathedral has a typically English
square east end, which gives on to an octagonal chapel,
housing the shrine of St Olav, evidently dependent on
Becket's corona at Canterbury Cathedral.   APQ

Lund Cathedral, Sweden (c.1150)

Norway, modern Following the economic depression in the late medieval period, building and architecture did not revive until the reign of Kristian IV (1588–1648). He turned the stronghold Akershus near Oslo into a Renaissance palace. Continuing prosperity funded the building of the nobleman's house at Austeråt (Trøndelag, 1654–6) with sculptural decorations in stone and wood, and the Church of the Saviour, Christiania (1694–9).

During the 18th century, fishery and a flourishing economy promoted intensified building. Wood remained the dominant building material, also used for more ambitious works like the mansion Damsgård,

Bergen (rebuilt in the 1770s), and the grand-scale Stiftsgård, Trondheim (1774–8), a vast private palace. Lantern-crowned Damsgård has an ornate, scrolled front gable, elaborately carved dormers and window frames, translating masonry decorative forms into skilful carpentry. Stiftsgård is a somewhat more strict, elongated 2-storey pedimented block, its height augmented by leaving an empty space between the ceilings of the ground storey and the floor of the upper one—perhaps to strengthen the tall construction and to make the building even more impressive. Both buildings were adaptations of Danish influence to Norwegian conditions.

By contrast, Norwegian farm buildings, built in wood, still had rather a medieval character. Monumental building in wood continued during the 19th century, as exemplified by the private house at Arendal (P. K. B. Jessen, 1812ff.) with its timber construction of 3 storeys above a bottom masonry one. Its very tall, neoclassical façade with a stylized pediment, like Damsgård, shows the vocabulary of masonry architecture. Of the Norwegian mostly wood-built towns, Røros is one of the best preserved with houses of the 18th and 19th centuries.

After Norway became part of a union with Sweden (1814), a new royal palace (H. D. F. Linstow, 1823–48) and a university complex (C. H. Grosch, 1838–54) were built on prominent sites in Christiania. Linstow was inspired by the work of C. F. *Hansen, although his palace front is also akin to C. L. *Engel's almost identical though more ornate façades on the Senate and University buildings in Helsingfors. Grosch's university is more original and strongly influenced by *Schinkel. Its central building has a Greek Ionic temple front, opening onto the central staircase.

Medieval forms are represented by the hunting lodge, Oscarshall (J. H. Nebelong, 1852), built for King Oscar I, and by the hospital at Gaustad (H. E. Schirmer, 1849–55). Brick-faced and medieval-inspired is also the

659

Christiania (Oslo) Parliament Building (E. Langlet, 1861–6), with a semicircular central block.

During the second half of the 19th century architecture was dominated by German or German-trained Norwegian architects, working in the international historical styles of their time. Architects could not be trained in Norway until a technological institute opened in Trondheim (1910). Wooden buildings, still very widespread, followed the Swiss chalet style, mainly applied to hotels. An alternative national trend, the Norwegian Dragestil ('dragon style'), inspired by the ornate medieval stave-churches, shows in the Frognerseteren restaurant near Oslo (H. Munthe, 1891).

Traditional Norwegian countryside farm buildings with their decorative carvings inspired the shape of new wooden houses both in Norway and Sweden, and also the pavilions of these countries for international exhibitions. At the time, Norway was regarded as the most romantic of the northern countries, with many memories of the past (*see* NATIONAL ROMANTICISM). In the beginning of the 20th century international Jugendstil was combined with Norwegian animal motifs in the Government Building, Oslo (H. Bull, 1906). Also in Oslo, the Classicism of the 1920s is represented by the Vigeland Museum (L. Ree, C. E. Buch, 1924); Functionalism or Modernism by the House of Artists (H. Munthe-Kaas, G. Blakstad, 1930), and the business complex by R. E. Jacobsen (1933). The former is brick-faced and still classically symmetrical; the latter has a curved façade, with the top 3 storeys recessed.

During this period, Oslo Town Hall developed from a National Romantic to a modernist project (A. Arneberg, M. Poulsson, first plans 1917–18, modernized and executed 1931–50). It consists of two towers for offices, and a lower block for representation. The massive brick-faced complex was adorned with rich sculptural and pictorial decorations. At the same

time, A. Korsmo and K. Knutsen adapted their small wooden modernist houses to their environments. Korsmo's villas are elegant and varied examples of Functionalism.

Of later works may be mentioned the Bank of Norway, Oslo (the firm of Lund and Slaatto, 1973–86). Postmodernism was introduced by J. Digerud (1938–) and J. Lundberg (1933–), known as the firm of Jan and Jon. Among their projects is the rebuilding of a small wooden 19th-century house Akersveien 12–14, Oslo (1981–2).   TF

Guthorm, K., *Norwegian Architecture, Past and Present* (1958)
Norberg-Schulz, C., *Modern Norwegian Architecture* (1986)

Notman, John (1810–165) British-born architect. He trained with William Henry *Playfair (1790–1857) before emigrating to Philadelphia in 1831, where he designed Laurel Hill Cemetery (1836–9) in emulation of Kensal Green Cemetery, London. British precedents are obvious throughout his career, as in the Athenaeum, Philadelphia (1845–7), copying London clubs, and his various Gothic and Romanesque churches. Notman brought to America the fashionable Tuscan villa, first at the Bishop Doane House, Burlington, New Jersey (1839, demolished), and later at Prospect, Princeton, New Jersey (1851–2). He gave Nassau Hall, Princeton University, its Italianate cupola after a fire (1855–9).

WBM

Nouvel, Jean (1945–) French architect, noted for his inventive if not always practical designs. The south façade of the Institut du Monde Arabe, Paris (1981–7), is covered with small steel prisms which respond electronically to the changing light, a mechanized version of the *mashrabiya, or wooden screen, found in Arabic architecture. A similar concern with mediating between the inside and outside space is found at the Hotel St James, Bordeaux (1987–8), which employs steel sun screens; the social housing scheme, Namausus

1, Nîmes (1985–7), is clad with prefabricated aluminium panels which can easily be replaced and recycled.

Nouvel showed that he could manipulate space with similar inventiveness, by tripling the area of the Opera House, Lyon (1987–93), while retaining the existing façade—he added eleven new levels, five underground, and six under a glass dome in the shape of a barrel vault. Denied permission to build his Concert Hall, Lucerne, Switzerland (1998), out over the lake, he brought the lake into the building, in shallow channels.　　PG

Novecento Italian artistic and architectural movement of the 1920s and 1930s that echoed the broader 'call to order' that was felt in European artistic culture after World War I. The term was initially applied more narrowly to a group of seven artists who were associated with the Galleria Pesaro in Milan, beginning in 1922. With the support of art critic Margherita Sarfatti, who wrote for Mussolini's *Popolo d'Italia*, these artists sought to renew Italian art through a new classical tradition. The architecture of the Italian Novecento, though inspired by neoclassical architecture, also derived some of its power from its association with the metaphysical painting of Giorgio de Chirico. This is particularly true of the Milanese circle of Novecento architects like Emilio Lancia, Giovanni Muzio, and Gio Ponti, whose projects emphasize the surface qualities of the external walls. An equally compelling set of developments are found in Rome in the work of architects like Pietro Aschieri, Enrico Del Debbio, and Innocenzo Sabbatini. Due to the interest of Novecento architects in a return to Italian classical traditions, this movement has sometimes been erroneously regarded by historians and critics as the *Stile Littorio or official style of the Fascist regime of Mussolini.　　BLM

nuraghe Literally a 'heap' or 'hollow'. A conical tower used as a fortress and a house, found in Sardinia,

possibly influenced by *Mycenaean architecture. About 7,000 are still visible, found all over the island, but mainly concentrated on the upland plateaux north of the river Tirso, in the Nurra region around Sassari, and the Trexenta (the central southern region). They consist of two main types: the simpler form from the Archaic period (1400–950 BC), a 1-storey-high truncated cone; and the more complex type, in which a number of towers form part of a defensive system, dating from the Middle Nuragic period (c.950–500 BC).
　　PG

nymphaeum A shrine dedicated to the nymphs, the female deities of ancient Greece and Rome, who were devoted to nature and especially water. Remains of such shrines, usually in the form of a grotto, are known at Domitian's 1st-century palace at Rome, and also perhaps in England at Lullingstone villa, Kent. Descriptions inspired several Renaissance architects to design them. Vignola's nymphaeum at the Villa Giulia, Rome (1551–5) is an integral part of the house and its ravishing garden, and comprises terraced viewing points opening on to *Ammanati's 3-storeyed 'scene', set with triumphal arches, alcoves containing reclining statues, and at the lowest level a grotto, flanked by herms, sheltering ferns, fountains, and lilies, the mysterious centrepiece of a garden of delights, all for the entertainment of the worldly Pope Julius III and his guests. Palladio's nymphaeum at the Villa Barbaro, Maser (1560s), is in the form of a pedimented arc, backing a semicircular lake immediately behind the villa itself. To each side are niches sporting languid nymphs and fawns, flanked by similar caryatid-like figures, from which water sensuously fountains into a semicircular lake. Although a regular feature of landscaped gardens thereafter, grottoes with nymphs never matched these for sheer voluptuous beauty—the one at Stourhead, Wiltshire (1740), being but nature 'improved'.　　APQ

Nyrop, Martin (1840–1921) Danish architect, craftsman, furniture and textile-designer, the 'father' of Scandinavian *National Romanticism. Having begun his career as a carpenter and builder, Nyrop rose to become professor, and later director, at the Royal Academy of Art in Copenhagen. Here he introduced a new and lasting curriculum on the history of Danish architecture and building methods. Through his buildings and teaching, he exercised great influence on successive generations of architects and interior designers.

Nyrop's Vallekilde Folk High School (1884) and the buildings for the Nordic Exhibition of Industry, Agriculture, and Art (Copenhagen, 1888), executed in brightly painted wood, with many references to folk art and older traditions of wooden buildings, established his reputation in Denmark. His most important work was the new City Hall in Copenhagen (competition 1887; execution 1892–1905). In his choice of materials for the dramatically turreted building, Nyrop was influenced by current ideas about the national importance of medieval brick architecture. He also sought to celebrate the common people of his own times. The great glazed lobby and assembly area (one of two courtyards on the ground floor) offered an easy yet festive approach to city offices. Through furniture, textiles, paintings, and decorative elements, Nyrop created a new kind of symbolic language that he hoped everyone would understand. References to Norse mythology and Danish prehistory intermingled with images of farming, seafaring, and modern citizenship in colourful profusion. Nyrop's influence outside Denmark is clearest in the Netherlands (Berlage, De Klerk) and Sweden (Östberg, Tengbom, Grut), but he also exerted leadership by serving on a number of juries, including that for the Finnish National Museum in Helsinki. BML

Lane, Barbara Miller, *National Romanticism and Modern Architecture in Germany and the Scandinavian Countries* (2000)

obelisks To the ancient Egyptians obelisks were sacred to the sun god. The earliest were erected in the time of the Fifth Dynasty (2494–2345 BC) in Heliopolis. They were often used in pairs to frame the façades of temples. Sometimes the pyramidion (the pitched topmost section) was covered in gold or other metal to reflect the sun's rays. Pliny the Elder (AD 23–79) wrote that obelisks were meant to resemble the rays of the sun. At Piramesse, the capital of Egypt under Ramesses II (1304–1237 BC) there were more than twenty obelisks, though most of these were smaller than those of Thebes and Heliopolis.

Since the Roman period obelisks have been prized objects of plunder, and more than 50 were relocated from Egypt to Rome from 10 BC onwards where they were used to decorate both public and private places, such as the Circus Maximus and the Gardens of Sallust. It was these plundered obelisks, rediscovered largely by excavation in Renaissance Rome, that informed a revival of interest in them, rather than a knowledge of their Egyptian origin.

In Renaissance and Baroque Rome they were relocated as the centrepieces of newly created piazzas. Sixtus V placed one at the centre of the Piazza del Popolo in 1589 where it terminates the view along the Via del Corso and the flanking radial streets (*see* FONTANA, DOMENICO). Another was placed on a stone elephant by Bernini in the Piazza della Minerva (1666–7).

Their needle-like form was much used to embellish the skyline of Baroque and Palladian buildings where the form is used to disguise chimneys (particularly in the Veneto) and as finials on parapets. This idea became popular in Elizabethan England where obelisks were much used to decorate rooflines, and clustered above gateways and doorcases.

Their use in gardens is common particularly in the 17th and early 18th centuries. They are used to theatrical effect on the stage-like exedra of the Garden at Isola Bella, and were much favoured by the English neo-Palladians. A large obelisk was the first structure built (1719) by Kent for his vast scheme at Holkham, Norfolk. Obelisks also figure strongly in Lord Burlington's own house and garden at Chiswick.

A re-awakening of interest in all things Egyptian in the late 18th/early 19th centuries, further stimulated by the battle of the Nile, led to more plunder, and to ancient obelisks being re-erected in Paris and London as focal points to streets and next to riverscapes.   GRC

O'Donnell, James (1774–1830) Irish-born architect. *See* CANADA.

œil-de-bœuf (bull's-eye) a small round or more usually oval window, set horizontally, and so called from *Hardouin-Mansart's (1646–1708) use of one in the Salon de l'Œil-de-Bœuf at Versailles (1701). Already appearing in Renaissance Italy, in spandrels and lighting attic rooms behind pediments, they were common in France in the 17th century.   APQ

office buildings

THE ORIGINS

CHICAGO

'FORM FOLLOWS FINANCE'

INTERWAR LONDON

US HEGEMONY

EUROPEAN INNOVATION

THE FUTURE

The origins The office as a building type is an essentially late-19th- and 20th-century phenomenon created by two related but different movements: the growth of bureaucracy and the rise of the equally mechanical but industrially based notion of 'scientific management' or Taylorism. The growth in its importance can be gauged by the massive rise in the absolute size of the office population.

The urbanistic and architectural consequences of this explosive growth have been compounded, until very recently, by the rigidity of the conventional timetable of office work, which required very large numbers of office workers to commute daily into city centres. Rapid growth and the necessity of co-location explain why a profile of densely packed, high-rise office buildings became the quintessential symbol of the 20th-century city.

By the middle of the 19th century three very different stylistic tendencies were evident in British office design: modest, functional entities often attached to industrial premises; more architecturally ambitious speculative offices, often called 'chambers' to cloak commercial realities by referring to the genteel traditions of the Inns of Court; and finally much grander, commercial palazzi built specifically for richer corporate clients.

The earliest survivor in London of Victorian office chambers is I'Anson's no. 22 Finch Lane (1845–6) characterized by exceptionally large windows. Oriel Chambers in Liverpool (Peter *Ellis, 1864) is another early example, a series of small, undifferentiated, professional chambers, neatly arranged behind a framed and highly glazed façade. The exactly contemporary City office at 59–61 Mark Lane is also an iron-framed building behind a highly fenestrated Ruskinian stone front (George Aitchison Jnr, 1864). Providing enough natural light was a vitally important feature of these early office buildings. One of the major challenges that faced architects working for speculative developers in Victorian cities was to maximize rentable space in small, self-contained units arranged on

Willis Faber and Dumas building, Princes Street, Ipswich, Suffolk (Norman Foster, 1975)

multiple floors, all to be achieved on tight, complicated sites. Hence extra storeys, highly glazed façades, light wells lined with reflective ceramic tiles, all strong inducements to abandon the discipline of the *piano nobile* and the orders. Even C. R. Cockerell, when designing the purpose-built Sun Insurance building on a prime site in the City of London, contrived to slip in extra, classically unwarranted floors.

Chicago Office building in the United States, after the end of the Civil War, followed quite a different pattern. New communications devices (the typewriter, the telegraph, and later the telephone) were matched by revolutions in building technology—the iron and later the steel frame (for rapid construction), the elevator (to conquer height), artificial lighting (to extend working hours), and eventually artificial environments (to make deep spaces habitable).

Though some of these technical developments had already been in extensive use before the Civil War, it was Chicago, especially after the great fire in 1871, which took maximum advantage of technology to push forward the development of the commercial office building. The rebuilding of the city gave exceptional opportunities to a remarkable group of planners, architects, and engineers—William Le Baron *Jenney (1832–1907), Dankmar Adler (1844–1900), Daniel *Burnham (1846–1912), Louis *Sullivan (1856–1924), and the greatest of them all, Frank Lloyd *Wright (1867–1959).

The modest 5-storey (later 7) Leiter warehouse building by William Le Baron Jenney (1879), characterized by standard floor heights and huge, triple-light windows, is generally held to be the first building of what became known as the *Chicago School. It exhibits in miniature many features of subsequent office buildings, demonstrating that the technical means for indefinite vertical expansion was available and that centuries of aesthetic constraint on the proportioning of elevations could be abandoned.

A decade later the first wave of really high office buildings had been completed. William Le Baron Jenney designed the Manhattan building, 16 storeys, the first building with a steel frame (1890). There followed in quick succession Burnham and Root's bold but anachronistically load-bearing brick, 16-storey Monadnock Building (1889–91); the same architects' (with D. H. Burnham and Co.) delicate, faceted, 15-storey Reliance Building (1890, 1894); and D. H. Burnham and Co.'s 18-storey Fischer Building (1896). Two other great contemporary buildings, by the Chicago architects Adler and Sullivan, although not in the city itself, complete this assured debut of the skyscraper office—the Wainwright Building, St Louis, Missouri (10 storeys, 1891), and the Guaranty Building, Buffalo, NY (12 storeys, 1894–5). Both are magnificent reconciliations on an unprecedented scale of building high with the use of a residually classical but fundamentally revolutionary formula of base, shaft, and capital—the last being the confident sweep of huge cornices.

These buildings, despite the historical significance of their bold leap in scale, are not so dissimilar in terms of office use to the earlier London offices described above. Relatively small, naturally lit and ventilated floor plates were designed predominantly to accommodate small businesses in small suites. The Guaranty Building, for example, despite its impressively complete palazzo-like appearance did not have deep square floor plates but relatively shallow U-shaped floors, in order to provide as many as possible naturally lit and ventilated small office rooms. Although huge department stores with very deep floor plates were already common in Chicago and elsewhere, big office floor plates with central cores were not the norm, not least because environmental systems were still primitive—early high-rise offices sported external blinds.

'Form follows finance' Early deviations from Chicago's generally bulky, site-filling office building stock were Graham, Anderson, Probst, and White's classically inspired Wrigley Building (1919–21) with its mounted tower and twin floor plan geometry,

necessitated by an unusually shaped riverside site and Howells and Hood's adjacent Gothic *Chicago Tribune* Tower (1925). The latter was the result of an important architectural competition which attracted many European entries, some by Modern Movement architects fascinated by what must have seemed to them the entirely exotic potential of building high. An important New York precedent for the eclecticism and the spikiness of these Chicago buildings was Cass Gilbert's brilliantly planned Woolworth Building (1911–13). In New York, suavity and architectural sophistication had quickly overtaken the constructional directness of the Chicago pioneers. The novel characteristics of this new generation of high-rise buildings were the exploitation of buildings as a brand, confidence in building high, bigger floor plates, and much more cleverly located and more compact cores. Most of these buildings, both in Chicago and New York, were financial speculations, built to generate income for developers.

The three greatest New York skyscrapers commissioned immediately before the Depression are the climax of the complex balance between entrepreneurialism, civic regulatory control, burgeoning architectural ambition, and increasing technical accomplishment—Raymond Hood's chunky *Daily News* Building (1929–30), Van Alen's highly decorative Chrysler Building (1930), and Shreve, Lamb, and Harmon's vast Empire State Building (1930–32), for four decades the tallest building in the world. A greater urbanistic achievement, largely office space but creating a city within a city, is the Rockefeller Centre on which three firms of architects collaborated—Reinhold and Hofmeister, Corbett, Harrison, and MacMurray, Hood and Fouilhoux (1932–40). Given the magnificence of both the urban context and the scale of architectural ambition, it is a shock to be reminded that, when first occupied in the late 1930s and the early 1940s, office rooms even within the prestigious Rockefellre Centre were still not air conditioned.

The way forward for the American office had already been indicated in the early 1930s by two much more radical high-rise buildings, influenced by the more adventurous European entries to the 1922 *Chicago Tribune* Competition (e.g. the influential modernist entry by Walter Gropius and Adolf Meyer). Raymond Hood's offices for McGraw Hill in New York (1930) and Howe and Lescaze's boldly minimalist Philadelphia Savings Fund Society Building, Philadelphia (1932), anticipate the magnificent achievements of the great post World War II wave of American office design.

Interwar London Office buildings constructed in London in the early decades of the 20th century were technically dependent on American precedents, but smaller and more conservative. While North American innovations such as the steel frame and the elevator had been quickly adopted, the exteriors, and indeed the interiors, of this generation of British office buildings were designed to disguise technical proficiency. However, office buildings erected in London between 1900 and the beginning of World War II had become much larger. The change in scale is less obvious in the narrow and irregular streets of the City of London than in newly opened thoroughfares or on big sites by the Thames.

Lutyens obviously did not want the Midland Bank, Poultry (1924–5), to look as big as it really is. Set-backs and carefully wrought fenestration play down its very modest (by American standards) 10 storeys. The same architect's Britannic House in Finsbury Circus (1920–24) is an example of a relatively new phenomenon in London, a corporate office designed to house a large number of clerical staff in central London. Such operational demands could only be satisfied by deploying electric light, lifts, and the steel frame. Lutyens deployed all his considerable skills not only to

fit his building into the curve of the circus but also to use the array of columns above the cornice to express his oil company client's mixed imperial and mercantile pride.

Similar in scale are the largely speculatively built offices (many by Trehearne and Norman, 1903–22) that line Kingsway, a new street trying very hard to be a Parisian boulevard. Prominent riverside offices were built to house imperial enterprises such as the ICI headquarters by Sir Frank Baines of the Office of Works (1927–9) and J. Lomax Simpson's Unilever Building with Burnet, Tait, and Partners (1930–32). These buildings share a more or less common height (approximately 10 storeys), reliance on light wells, Roman façades with gigantic orders to broadcast grandeur, while enlivening regular fenestration. Unambiguously hierarchical interiors emphasized order—directorial splendour united with clerical thrift by infinite corridors.

Very different to these timidly schizophrenic interwar British office buildings is Frank Lloyd Wright's Administration Building for S. C. Johnson and Son, Racine, Wisconsin (1936–9)—a transparently original building housing a transparently modern business. In the Taylorist system, process mattered more than hierarchy. Wright was, after all, Sullivan's pupil, and Sullivan was an exact contemporary of Frederick Taylor. Wright's much earlier purpose-built office for the Larkin Company in Buffalo, NY (1904), was the most seminal office of the century, not least because it was such a brilliant and consistent application of Taylorism to office work.

US hegemony The strength of the US economy immediately after World War II was not just military and political but economic, the reward of applying scientific managerial techniques on a very large scale. US self-confidence is nowhere better manifested than in this unparalleled sequence of splendidly

667

accomplished and technically highly advanced office buildings.

The modernist approach to high-rise office design had been kept alive in the war years in Latin America. Le Corbusier, who was a consultant on both projects, provides a link between Lúcio Costa and Oscar Niemeyer's curtain-walled offices for the Ministry of Education and Health in Rio de Janeiro (1936–43) and the startlingly crisp United Nations Secretariat Building in New York (W. R. Harrison, 1950). The victory of Modernism in North American office design was soon complete. Lever House in New York was one of the first offices to take advantage of the newly permitted form of a slab above a podium—*Skidmore, Owings, and Merrill (1952). *Mies van der Rohe and Philip *Johnson's incomparable Seagram Building (1958) soon followed. The Inland Steel Headquarters in Chicago, SOM (1958) is innovative in that its core stands proud of the column-free floor plate. The Union Carbide Building, New York, SOM (1960), with its curtain wall and central core established the classical form of the North American high-rise office building which continues to be replicated worldwide.

During the same period a parallel genre of huge, low-rise commercial palaces emerged: the Connecticut General Headquarters, Bloomfield, Connecticut (SOM, 1957); the John Deere Headquarters, Moline, Illinois (Eero Saarinen and Associates, 1964); and Weyerhauser's Headquarters in Tacoma, Washington (SOM, 1971). Corporate architectural patronage on such a splendid, Versailles-rivalling scale had no precedent.

These buildings would not have been achieved without a division of labour between architects and new professions—environmental engineering, interior design, and space planning. Also critically important were furniture manufacturers and suppliers, such as Herman Miller, for whom Ray and Charles Eames designed Knoll and Steelcase furniture. Comparable sophistication in the management of the supply chain, as well as in design services, did not emerge in Europe until two decades later.

The last great achievement of this golden age of office design was the Ford Foundation Headquarters, New York (*Roche, Dinkeloo, and Associates (1967), which re-introduced the internal atrium on a huge scale. In America the scene was now set on the one hand for postmodernism and on the other for corporate rationalization and cost cutting. The initiative for innovation in office design had shifted to Europe.

European innovation The exquisite *Economist* Building in London (1964) owed less to contemporary North American office design than to the Smithsons' homage to a much earlier masterpiece of the Chicago School—Burnham and Co.'s Reliance Building (1895). This reverence contrasts with the cheerful and architecturally relaxed novelty of the low-rise Nino Administration Building in Nordhorn, Germany (Werner Zobel with the Schnelle brothers, 1962), an early example of the first original European contribution to office design for many decades. This completely open-plan office building illustrates the principal proposition of office landscaping: that floor plates should be shaped by internal business communications, not by developers' norms.

An ambitious attempt to reconcile community with individuality is Herman *Hertzberger's highly programmatic Centraal Beheer building in Apeldoorn, the Netherlands (1970–72), the last of the great European open-plan offices. A robust spatial structure imposes a Platonic order in the interstices of which office workers are free to organize their own workspaces as they wish.

Office landscaping was completely superseded in Europe in the 1970s by a stronger imperative, social democratic and anti-Taylorist in origin: that the shape of the office building should be primarily determined by the well-being of office workers, all of whom have an equal right to daylight, views, privacy, and enclosure. These requirements, supported by statutory Workers' Councils, quickly found their way into Building Regulations. The architectural consequence was a proliferation in northern Europe of low, linear, narrow, and highly cellular office buildings.

The next step was an inevitable reaction to excessive insistence upon individual needs: the countervailing idea, also post-Taylorist, that offices should be designed as communities, either in the form of interlinked pavilions—Thomas Beucker's Colonia complex, Cologne (1987)—or as streets—Niels Torp's urbane offices for SAS in Stockholm (1987) and for BA, Heathrow (1995), Ton Albert's offices for NMB in Amsterdam (1987).

In the UK in the early 1980s the impact of the computer on office work, allied to global competition, led to the deregulation of the all-important financial services industry. The architectural consequences were concentrated in the City of London, notorious for the poor quality of its office stock, and led to a series of urgent innovations in office design. An important precedent was Norman *Foster's site-filling, curvilinear, open-plan Willis Faber and Dumas building in Ipswich (1975). Richard Rogers' great building for Lloyd's of London (1984) reversed the conventional American model by stripping out the central core, replacing it with a great atrium, and distributing vertical services to the perimeter. Huge developments such as Broadgate and Canary Wharf quickly taught the British the defects as well as the virtues of American office design. The European offices of American architectural practices began to do more original work than their colleagues in the US. Norman Foster's Hongkong and Shanghai Bank, Hong Kong (1986), had already shown the benefits of applying first-class architectural imagination to office design. Subsequent Foster projects, including

Commerzbank in Frankfurt (1996) and St Mary Axe, London (2004), demonstrate a pattern of continuing innovation, now spreading to the US. It is significant that after the 9/11 disaster in New York two high-rise offices are being constructed by European architects— the Hearst Tower by Foster and the *New York Times* building by Renzo Piano.

The future While office design has become more diverse and inventive in Europe in the last two decades, the influence of conventional North American real estate practice continues to be powerful. In the Asian Pacific region an enormous amount of office building is underway, only a fraction of which is currently influenced by the social and technological innovations that have been so important in Europe. However, two new factors are likely to influence the design of office buildings everywhere: the need for sustainability and the mobility made possible by ubiquitous information technology. The first will change the nature of the building envelope. The latter is more far-reaching in that new ways of working will bring into question the very stability of this fascinating building type.   FD

Albrecht, Donald, and Broikos, Chrysanthe, *On the Job: Design and the American Office* (2000)
Duffy, F., *The New Office* (1997)
Willis, C(arol), *Form Follows Finance* (1995)

ogee arch A double-curved arch in which the lower arcs are centred within the arch and curve inwards, while the upper arcs are centred outside and curve outwards, each side forming a drawn-out S. Although drawn in *Villard de Honnecourt's sketchbook, *c.*1230, ogee arches first appear *c.*1300, rapidly becoming common, particularly in England.   APQ

ogive arch from the French term for a pointed arch, such as a lancet, hence *ogival*, the style of architecture characterized by such arches, namely Gothic. But, like the terms 'first', 'second', and 'third pointed' for the three phases of English Gothic, it is no longer in current usage.   APQ

O'Gorman, Juan (1905–82) Mexican architect. He proposed radical approaches to building, inspired by the teachings of José *Villagrán and based on his socialist beliefs as well as his study of Le Corbusier. Most noteworthy in this respect are the houses for Diego Rivera and Frida Kahlo (1932), and for Julio Castellanos, the highly austere Technical and Training College (1934), as well as some twenty other schools which reformed the building system through the design of prototypes. He made a decisive contribution to the creation of the Engineering and Architecture School of the National Polytechnic Institute (1936), propounding an anti-academic ideology in the *Pláticas sobre Arquitectura* (1933), with Juan Legarreta (1902–34) and Alvaro Aburto (1905–76), and coming out firmly in favour of rationalism and in opposition to purely artistic concerns. He gave up architecture in 1936 to devote himself to painting, making a comeback with the famous University Campus Library (1952), a simple rational structure covered by 4,000 sq m (4,784 sq yards) of mosaic in natural stone, and his own house in San Jéronimo, 1953–6 (destroyed 1970), innovatory on account of its organic and surrealist design, produced by using the existing natural caves and covering them in stones set in relief, influenced by Frank Lloyd Wright, Max Cetto (1903–80), Diego Rivera, and the fantastic images encountered in his own paintings.
                                        LNM (trans. KL)

Olbrich, Joseph Maria (1867–1908) Austrian architect. He worked in Otto *Wagner's office from 1893 to 1898, and is credited with introducing the older architect to Jugendstil tendencies. In 1897–8 he executed his only significant Viennese project, the exhibition building for the Vienna Secession. It was praised for its innovative, flexible, and light-filled exhibition spaces, and criticized for its exterior eclecticism. The front, with its laurel-leaf dome, was inspired by late romantic symbolism and subjectivism, while the exposed skylights at the rear spoke to the influence of Wagner's realism.

In 1899 Olbrich moved to Darmstadt, Germany, where he took part in the creation of the artists' colony there, designing most of its buildings. The Ernst Ludwig Haus (1899–1901), containing the artists' studios, was a more successful attempt at creating a synthesis of symbolist monumental drama and attention to purpose. In seven artists' villas, Olbrich combined Arts and Crafts influences with references to the vernacular of southern Italy, and Jugendstil formal gestures. The Hochzeitsturm and exhibition buildings of 1905–6 introduced a darker palette, more rugged textures, and contrasting volumes to the colony.   LET

Latham, I., *Joseph Maria Olbrich* (1980)

Olmsted, Frederick Law (1822–1903) US landscape architect. *See* LANDSCAPE ARCHITECTURE.

opera houses Opera, defined as drama set to music where the music is an essential, not an incidental, element, originated in the spectacular entertainments of singing and dancing held at the houses of the wealthy in 16th-century Florence and Rome. Early operas were regarded by their aristocratic patrons as a re-creation of classical drama, and appropriately contemporary theatres were based on the semicircular Roman amphitheatre plan, as at Andrea *Palladio's Teatro Olimpico, Vicenza (1580–84). Giovanni Battista Aleotti's Teatro Farnese, Parma (1618–28), was derived from the Teatro Olimpico, but the amphitheatre was extended into a U-shape. The spectacular opening performance, a *torneo* ('music for a tournament'), *Mercurio e Marte* (Mercury and Mars) had *intermedii* by

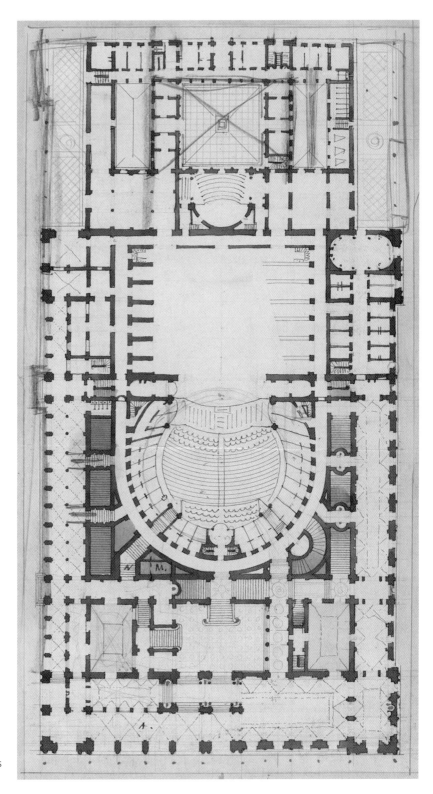

Plan of the Opera House, Paris
(Charles Garnier, 1861–75)

Monteverdi, and concluded with a sea battle where the central arena was flooded.

It was only when opera was exported from Rome to Venice that it became truly accessible to the public, and it was there that the first theatre specifically for opera was built, the Teatro San Cassiano of 1637, with galleries around the walls instead of the amphitheatre, stage facilities necessary for opera's spectacular effects, and the orchestra (for the first time) placed in front of the stage. About a dozen further opera houses along similar lines were built in 17th-century Venice, but the most notable was the Teatro SS. Giovanni e Paolo, built in 1638 for drama, but remodelled for opera in 1654 by Carlo Fontana. Its significance was that it was the first fully developed horseshoe-shaped Italian Baroque opera house, the walls lined with multiple tiers of boxes, an architectural form that remained little changed over two hundred years, except in size and the sophistication of stage machinery.

Besides the U and the horseshoe, the other common plan shape for opera houses was the truncated ellipse; the first to be built was the (remodelled) Teatro Tordinona, Rome (1695), again by Carlo Fontana. Another notable elliptical Roman opera house was the Teatro Argentina (1732), designed by the Marchese Teodoli, which remained a centre of *opera seria* for nearly a hundred years. One of the finest elliptical opera houses was the Teatro Regio, Turin (1738–40, destroyed), by the Conte di Castellamonte and Benedetto Innocente Alfieri, with its good acoustics and scholarly, restrained decoration and spacious foyer. Among its admirers was Diderot in his *Encyclopédie* and Pierre Patte in his *Essai sur l'architecture théâtrale* of 1774. Contemporary architects and theorists favoured the elliptical plan on acoustical grounds. Patte recommended concave surfaces in general, especially the double-focus ellipse, for 'concentrating' the sound, while he considered convex shapes to be worst.

(In reality the exact opposite is true, and convex, diffusing surfaces are desirable, although the relief surface decoration used in Baroque-style theatres and concert halls did help to achieve a diffuse, or evenly scattered, sound field.)

Another plan shape was the bell- or trumpet-shaped plan, the hallmark of theatres by the extraordinary Galli da *Bibiena family, specialist opera house architects and designers of brilliant and fantastic theatrical sets. This was also traditionally supposed to have been adopted for acoustic reasons, but unfortunately there is no surviving statement by the Galli da Bibienas on acoustics. A supremely delightful example of their work that stands to this day is Giuseppe Galli da Bibiena's Markgräfliches Opernhaus, Bayreuth (1744–8).

Many 18th-century Italian opera houses were designed with curious acoustic devices to help amplify and project the orchestra's sound. An airspace was often incorporated below the orchestra pit to help the wooden floor resonate, while at the Teatro Nuovo in Parma the entire parterre was built over a great semi-elliptical masonry saucer connected with passages from the orchestra pit.

In reality the effect of these devices must have been slight, and it is the dimensions and construction materials that make these early opera houses suited to the music of contemporary composers. Their most important attribute is acoustic clarity, enabling the listener to hear the words and highly articulated musical detail of rapidly sung passages, especially at the tongue-twisting tempi of Mozart and Rossini arias. Seating was more closely spaced in 18th-century theatres than would be acceptable today, so for a given size of audience the auditorium was much smaller. An important acoustical advantage was the projecting forestage, so that the relationship of singer and audience was acoustically intimate. (It was only in the 19th century with advances in theatre lighting that the performers retreated behind the proscenium arch and the stage was cut back, which placed them, acoustically speaking, in a different space from the audience.)

Sound clarity was further enhanced by the large amount of sound-absorptive material that an audience in full costume provided, crowded into boxes and on the parterre, so that there was very little reverberance to obscure musical detail, while the thin wood panelling of the box fronts reflected higher-frequency sound, giving bright acoustics for the music.

As opera-going in Italy became an institution, opera houses became larger and grander. Among these was La Fenice, Venice, designed by Giannantonio *Selva, opened in 1792, rebuilt after a fire in 1836 and again in 1996–2004. But the highpoint was Milan's Teatro alla Scala (1778, restored 2001–4) by Giuseppe *Piermarini, enormous by previous standards, with 2,800 seats, including 7 tiers of boxes, 260 in all, which subscribers could buy, decorate and furnish, and in which they could receive visitors, play cards, and have supper.

Opera house boxes, except for listeners at the front, had poor acoustics, and they provide an interesting example of the interrelationship between acoustics and social needs; when the partitions between boxes were removed in Rome for the sake of morality, the acoustics improved. French society, on the other hand, required less privacy and intimacy, and Victor Louis' Grand Théâtre, Bordeaux (1777–80), has galleries instead of boxes, and this, combined with small size—it has a truncated circular plan—provides outstanding acoustics.

Elsewhere, the conventional Italian opera house model continued to be adopted, as at Berlin's national theatre, the Schauspielhaus am Gendarmenmarkt (1818–21) by Karl Friedrich *Schinkel; Edward Middleton Barry's Theatre Royal (now Royal Opera House), Covent Garden, London (1856–8); and Gottfried Semper's Opernhaus, Dresden (1871–8, destroyed 1945, rebuilt 1977–85). Then there is the magnificent Théâtre National de l'Opéra (1861–75), designed to reflect the power and splendour of the Second Empire in France; every detail of the operatic event was considered by its architect, Charles *Garnier, from the ceremony of arrival from the street to the progression through the building via the grand staircase. Among the specialist theatre architects who worked at this time, the most prolific was the Viennese firm of Fellner and Helmer, who designed about 70 opera houses and theatres from New York to Odessa, of which about 50 were built.

In direct reaction to the Italian Baroque theatre based around rigid social requirements, Richard Wagner, through his architect Otto Brückwald, built his ideal theatre for performing the *Ring*, and in doing so transformed German theatre design. His Festspielhaus, Bayreuth (1872–6), is based on a segment of the classical amphitheatre—where the sightlines are excellent and everybody is equal before his music, and where the drama is seen as though in the distance. Wagner further distanced his performers by creating a sunken and hooded orchestra pit. Although the location of the pit was determined by visual rather than acoustic reasons, the sound reaching the audience is entirely reflected. The rural setting compels the visitor to undertake a journey into countryside as a preparation for Wagner's music—as much a deliberate part of the entry progression as Garnier provided at the Paris Opera in a building of very different social intentions.

Wagner's theatre was imitated in several theatres by Max Littmann, such as the Prinzregenten Theater, Munich (1900–01), including the sunken orchestra pit. In 1919 the Expressionist architect Hans Poelzig developed Wagner's idea of fusing the arts at his Grosses Schauspielhaus, Berlin, a remodelled circus with a thrust stage and a fantastic interior with stalactites coloured blood red.

Most 20th-century opera houses retained the tradition of galleries and a proscenium stage, as at the

Metropolitan Opera House, New York (1966), by Wallace K. Harrison, and the Opera House at Glyndebourne, East Sussex (1992–4), by Michael Hopkins and Partners. The Opernhaus in Essen (1988) has an asymmetric plan with free-flowing forms, based on Alvar Aalto's competition entry of 1959. The Opéra de la Bastille, Paris (1989), by Carlos Ott is notable for its high technology stage equipment. Finally, mention should be made of the iconic role of opera house architecture as embodied in the monumental stage tower of Aldo Rossi's Teatro Carlo Felice in Genoa (1991), and most powerfully realized at the Sydney Opera House (which is an opera house in name only as the main auditorium is a concert hall), which stands as a cultural emblem for its country.　MF

Beranek, L., *Music, Acoustics and Architecture* (2004)

Forsyth, M(ichael), *Auditoria: Designing for the Performing Arts* (1987)

Forsyth, M(ichael), *Buildings for Music* (1985)

opus Alexandrinum, incertum, listatum, quadratum, reticulatum, sectile

Opus, literally meaning 'work', applies to various ancient Roman methods of laying walls and pavements. *Opus quadratum* is walling composed of squared stones, the equivalent of ashlar. *Opus incertum* is concrete walling faced in (inserted with) irregular stones, or rubble. *Opus reticulatum* is concrete walling faced in square stones, laid diagonally, their joints thus appearing like a net. *Opus listatum* is walling comprising alternate courses of brick and similar-sized stone. *Opus sectile* is ornamental paving made from marble slabs of various, generally geometrical shapes, unlike the haphazardness of crazy paving. *Opus Alexandrinum* is ornamental paving combining *opus sectile* with mosaic to form a guilloche pattern.　APQ

Orchard, William

(d.1504) English mason, responsible for numerous building works in Oxford,

probably as designer as well as executor. Orchard worked at Magdalen College from 1468, including its prominent tower (1479 onwards), and on the vault of the Divinity Schools (1480–83). He was associated with Oxford Cathedral, perhaps being responsible for the choir vault (*c*.1478–1503) and cloisters (*c*.1489–99), and also St John's College (from 1502). He worked at Eton College (from 1479), including the antechapel, and on several churches.　APQ

orders

Classical architecture is founded on the three determinants of symmetry, order, and proportion. This was recognized by *Vitruvius, who went to great lengths to define what these meant, though not with complete clarity where symmetry is concerned. By order he meant shape—the placing of the various parts in a way proper to their function and as determined by an already ancient usage with due regard to symmetry and proportion. So, in classical architecture the orders have come to mean the formalized systems of post and lintel or column and entablature, each with its own particular forms of decoration and proportion, comprising base, column, capital, architrave, frieze, and cornice.

Vitruvius described four orders, together with the proportions that govern their relative sizes, and used an explanation of the origin of each one as a reason for prescribing its appropriate uses. While some of these explanations are far-fetched, the notion that their proportions relate to those of human bodies, that is proportion in relation to the whole, for example, of heads and feet determining the proportion of capitals and bases, struck a particular chord among Renaissance humanists, and this resonates just as clearly today. The orders he described omit the oldest of the classical Greek orders, namely the *Doric, which originated in mainland Greece, and is characterized by a stout column, the lack of a base, a plain mushroom-shaped capital with an abacus, and an entablature with a frieze

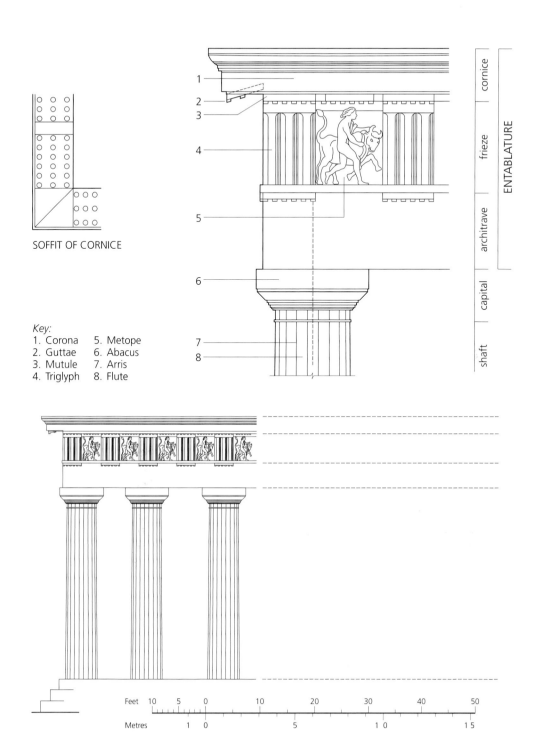

SOFFIT OF CORNICE

Key:
1. Corona   5. Metope
2. Guttae   6. Abacus
3. Mutule   7. Arris
4. Triglyph 8. Flute

cornice

frieze

ENTABLATURE

architrave

capital

shaft

THE GREEK DORIC ORDER, 447–438 BC (The Parthenon, Athens)

675

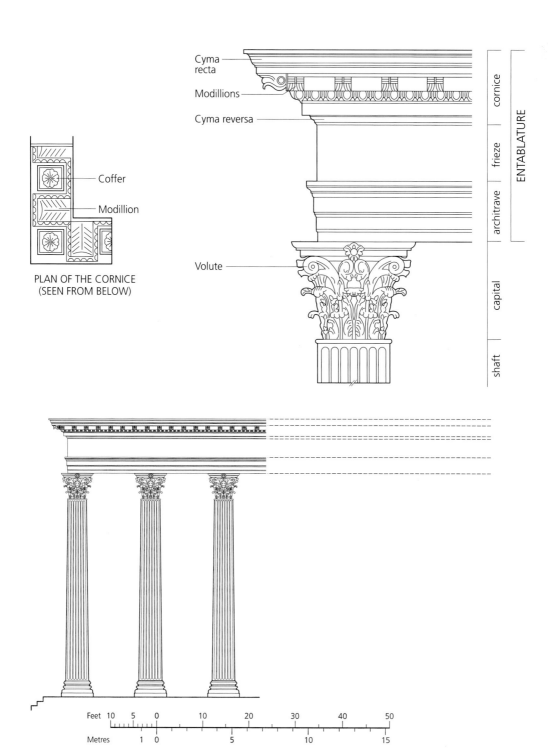

Cyma recta

Modillions

Cyma reversa

Volute

Coffer

Modillion

PLAN OF THE CORNICE
(SEEN FROM BELOW)

cornice

frieze

architrave

ENTABLATURE

capital

shaft

Feet 10 5 0   10   20   30   40   50

Metres   1 0   5   10   15

THE ROMAN CORINTHIAN ORDER

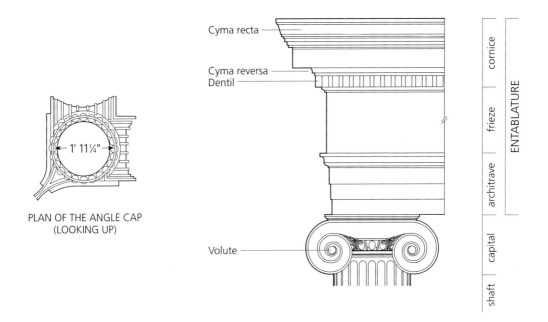

Cyma recta

Cyma reversa
Dentil

Volute

PLAN OF THE ANGLE CAP
(LOOKING UP)

1' 11¼"

cornice

frieze

architrave

ENTABLATURE

capital

shaft

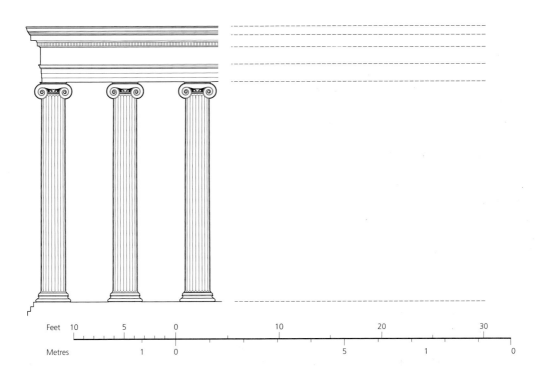

Feet 10 5 0 10 20 30

Metres 1 0 5 1 0

THE GREEK IONIC ORDER

677

of alternating *triglyphs and *metopes. The Vitruvian orders begin with the Roman Doric order, a slender and more ornate version of Greek Doric, but with a base to the column and a more pronounced capital (these representing the proportions of a man).

Then comes the *Ionic order, a classical Greek order, originating on the Aegean islands, characterized by more slender proportions than the Doric (representing a woman), a moulded base, a capital decorated with volutes, and a continuously decorated frieze as opposed to alternating triglyphs and metopes. The *Corinthian order is a major variant of the Ionic order, in which the capital is decorated with stylized acanthus leaves rather than with volutes, and whose proportions he said were based on those of a virgin, and its entablature is more ornate, a consequence of an apocryphal origin in which an acanthus plant grew under the tombstone of a virgin, when in fact this order was first used in the late-5th-century Temple of Apollo Epicurius at Bassae in a position where its greater ornament was particularly valued. Vitruvius then described the *Tuscan order, a primitive version of the Roman Doric in which the column lacks fluting, the base and capital have plain mouldings, and the frieze lacks either triglyphs or metopes.

The later Composite order is a Corinthian order whose capital combines Ionic volutes with Corinthian foliage. Other orders include the Aeolic order, a primitive form of Ionic, the Ammonite order, a 19th-century invention in which Ammonite fossils replace the volutes of the Ionic, and other novelties that briefly marked an enduring tradition.   APQ

organic architecture The word 'organic' can be applied retrospectively to aspects of architecture that seek or recognize a relationship to nature, especially in the form of geological formations, plants, and animals. The scientific knowledge in the Enlightenment and the 19th century led architects and theorists dissatisfied

with the classical tradition or the eclectic application of historical styles to seek alternatives by analogy with the forms and processes of nature. In this, it reflected the Romantic movement's engagement with the natural world, but although organicism is usually seen as opposed to the Vitruvian classical tradition, Caroline van Eck (*Organicism in Nineteenth-Century Architecture*, 1994) finds it integral to the classical continuum from antiquity to the Renaissance. Indeed, there is no clearly identifiable organic style or movement, but rather a great variety of theories and applications of related ideas during the 19th and 20th centuries, including *National Romanticism.

After 1900 the theory of organicism lost its spell, but in altered and theoretically simplified form the idea remained potent. The term was returned to circulation by Frank Lloyd *Wright, who used it to counterpoint the mechanistic development of Modernism, as he saw it. He declared that 'Organic ideals of integral building reject rules imposed by exterior aestheticism of mere taste' (*An Organic Architecture*, 1939). However, a fellow practitioner, William Lescaze, complained that the definition meant no more than this: 'Organic is the word which Frank Lloyd Wright uses to describe his own architecture.'

Wright's idea of the organic as a corrective to Modernism was developed by Zevi who wrote, 'We have to decide whether there is a difference... in the mentality and the psychological outlook of architecture on their work—between Greek and Gothic, between Le Corbusier and Aalto' (*Towards an Organic Architecture*, 1951). Arguably, the division of the whole history of architecture into opposing strands served to perpetuate misunderstandings, since more recent studies of Le Corbusier have emphasized the importance of nature for his work. Curved forms and exaggeratedly natural materials that usually attract the term organic have been typical of a sequence of designs by architects such as Imre *Makovecz of Hungary (a throwback to the

National Romanticism of Karoly Kos) and Bart Prince in the USA, a third-generation follower of Wright.   AP

Östberg, Ragnar (1866–1945) Swedish architect. Although he designed several other distinguished buildings, all in Stockholm (the Östermalms Läroverk School, 1906–10; the National Patent Office, 1911–21; and the National Maritime Museum, 1936), his undoubted masterpiece is the Stockholm Town Hall (1911–23). It realized his ambition to create a national style (see NATIONAL ROMANTICISM), partly based on the precepts of *Arts and Crafts.

Östberg took full advantage of the stunning waterside site. The building's main tower and an open arcade, rising dramatically over the water, are placed in one corner of a vast complex grouped around two courtyards, the smaller one covered—a plan to some extent inspired by *Nyrop's equivalent building in Copenhagen (1892–1905). The three crowns on the rather slender lantern of the tower are similar to those on the great tower of the old Stockholm castle. The façade, dark red brickwork, carefully crafted in its details, has a massive presence. It is a modern continuation of the great northern European tradition of imposing brick buildings (see BALTIC BRICK; BERLAGE).

Östberg could not readily accept the developments towards a more radical Modernism (see MARKELIUS). Nevertheless, his Minor Industries Centre (1930) is a valiant attempt at a compromise with flat roofing and streamlined bands of windows. But the wall was faced with brick, not plaster.   TF

Otto, Frei (1925–) German architect and writer, a pioneer in the development of tented structures. His first works, the pavilions for the Bundesgarten exhibitions at Cologne (1957) and Hamburg (1963), use standard materials and structural forms, but create beautifully sculptural shapes. For Expo '67, Montreal,

he designed asymmetrical forms, with high and low points, made possible by pre-stressed materials. Next, Otto designed at a larger scale (Olympiapark, Munich, 1967–72, with Günter *Behnisch), more flexibly (the retractable canopy for an open-air theatre, Bad Hersfeld, Hessen, 1967–8), and to fit in with a context of traditional nomad tents (several projects in *Saudi Arabia).   PG

Ottoman Empire The breakdown of *Saljuq power meant that all over Anatolia leaders of small communities set about forming petty lordships (or Beyliks), some of which were to trouble the Ottomans into the reign of Mehmet II (r.1444–5; 1451–81), called Fatih or Victorious after his conquest of Constantinople (1453). There were many nomadic tribes, often hostile, some of whom were exiled to Albania in particular. Villages were poor and neighbours were often hostile to each other, in some cases into the 20th century. Poor soil and taxes made for total poverty in central Anatolia and the Taurus Mountains. Under the decaying rule of Byzantium, priests hated the Anatolian plateau and were hard to keep: even if they ever reached their churches.

The Islamic invaders had the dervish orders to help them. After a victory, they took over villages only too glad to have a local governmental system again. It meant that a *masjid*, or small mosque, was a centre where local problems could be discussed. Later, mosques would have rooms for travelling dervishes. A bey of an area, like Ertuğrul, who founded the Ottoman dynasty, was always on the move to keep in touch with his folk, holding meetings in meadows or under tall trees, which had a religious significance. Yet he also made friends with Byzantine landowners and won rapid support until he captured the small town of Iznik. Then his grandson Orhan (r.1324?–62) finally took the prosperous town of Bursa, where he first saw a tiled roof.

Villages were built of mud-brick unless stone could be found in ruined buildings or fortress walls. But even then they would have only one or two rooms under flat roofs on which crops could mature. Animals still shared a room in humbler hamlets as late as the 20th century. But two rooms or even three were normal. By the 15th century some small towns had houses with a second floor for use as a harem, from which through lattices women could watch life go by. If wood was available, balconies grew into second upper floor rooms to rival the front door step. Tall trees had religious significance and were (and are) hung with rags to draw the attention of a saint in heaven to those in need.

Ottoman architecture began with the small mosque of a hamlet. That of Söğüt, now rebuilt, had space for some sixteen men and a portico with a well. Such *masjids* spread all over Anatolia from Seljuk times. Ertuğrul later occupied a fertile area, and his heirs captured Iznik where an Ottoman style developed. The first mosque, some 8 m (26 ft) square, had a dome supported on shoulders at each corner. Built of stone encased in brick, the Hacı Özbek mosque still stands. Then wealthy Bursa capitulated in 1333, and now stone mosques and dervish tekkes, monasteries, became centres of government. They were also centres of religious education and Islamic law.

Orhan took the city, but the largest early foundation was the Hudavendigâr built by his son Murat I (r.1366–85). The ground-level mosque supported a dervish college above with a balcony above the portico. This marriage was never repeated. Murat's son Yıldırım ('lightning') Bayazit (r.1389–1402) built his complex in a suburb with a grand stone portico, to match the interior, damaged by earthquake. He also built the Ulu Cami (Great Mosque) which has nineteen domes and one open above a larger ablutions pool. Inscriptions cover columns and walls, and a master craftsman created a grand mihrab. It is a skyscape of carved

planets. Once inset tessarae in the crannies of the carving set it gleaming.

The mosque presides over a vast market. Great hans (*see* KHAN), like the Koza Han (Cocoon Han— a reference to silk that made Bursa rich) had large courtyards for pack animals and wagons. On each side there were storerooms with a *masjid* raised above the turmoil. Rooms for merchants on the first floor opened off open terraces on all four sides. There were also market halls, closed *bedesten* (covered markets) for valuables, and spaces for food barrows besides two hammams over hot springs to wash away dust.

The Koza Han still stands after 600 years. It belonged to a state organization which supplied loans and technical advice to private enterprise as well: hence the similarity of hans everywhere. Grandees like Davut Pasha might build 116 shops and houses in Istanbul, farms and a melon garden as well as hans.

Timur defeated Yıldırım, and his sons fought each other. Edirne became a temporary capital where the architect Hacı Alaettin built a new Ulu Cami with only nine although larger domes. But by 1412 Mehmet I (r.1413–21) triumphed in Bursa and his Vizier Hacı İvaz built the greatest Bursa-type mosque: the Green Mosque (Yeşil Cami). In 1912, *Le Corbusier acclaimed it for the interplay of spaces and the mysterious quality of light. The Sultan's gallery, including the unequalled golden ceiling, was clad in tiles by Tabriz potters working on the spot. The great *mihrab is rivalled by that of the huge mausoleum which dominates the complex.

On the outskirts of Bursa, Murat II (r.1421–44; 1445–51) founded the family burial ground with his own tomb designed to be a garden: the open dome welcomes the rain. It was appropriate because he was a mystic besides being a military genius. Indeed, he moved his capital back to Edirne in order to control the Balkans. Then he went into retreat. His son Mehmet II (r.1444–5; 1451–81), aged twelve, was at the mercy of

Selimiye Mosque, Edirne, Turkey (Sinan, 1569ff.)

crooked courtiers, and the army was defeated. Murat returned, and, disposing of the enemy and frightened ministers, took over power again.

His mystical spirit between 1435 and 1457 built the Üç Şerefeli Mosque, named after the three balconies of the minaret, each with its own stair, a minaret 67 m (220 ft) high, and the first of the truly Ottoman courtyards followed. The 24.4 m (80 ft) wide dome was the greatest triumph. It is supported by two massive piers in opposite walls and two exposed midway between them in the central prayer hall.

At the age of 19 Mehmet II welcomed power, and within two years he had embarked on the conquest of Constantinople. He built Rumeli Hisar, the massive fortress that controlled the Bosphorus. It kept his troops busy and out of trouble. He also protected the conquered city and built a university of eight colleges, with preparatory departments behind, facing each other across a vast space. But his mosque, apart from its beautiful courtyard, disappointed Fatih—the Conqueror—so much that the architect was executed. In 1766 the earthquake destroyed it. Its successor is worse.

Fatih built a harem with sloping gardens at Beyazit, and Topkapısarı as seat of government and the college of janissary cadets. His own apartments formed a suite of grand chambers ending at a gazebo overlooking Marmara, Bosphorus, and the Golden Horn. Fatih could also escape to Çinili Kiosk in the park overlooking his polo ground and the snowfights of his cadets in winter.

By his reign, the Ottoman camp was established to be the wonder of Europe and other enemy countries. It was indeed two camps. Until reaching the enemy, before moving on, the second set of tents would be pitched c.12 km (7–8 miles) ahead. The army could then march on to the forward camp. The abandoned tents would in turn go forward. Fans of tents would form neat rows, while wooden fences would be used to bridle horses or mules. Areas were reserved for cooking, and there were pickets for the mounted watch beside an exact place for each cannon. In the Sultan's enclosure were grand tents, his hammams, and the wooden tower that surveyed all.

Before he was Sultan, Beyazit II (r.1481–1512) governed Amasya and had his grandees build as lavishly as he did himself, all in the late Bursa style but with variations in form. Beyazit Pasha mosque, for example, has a powerful stone portico, while that of Mehmet Pasha had re-used antique marble columns that give a spring to the arches, as did the future Sultan with his own riverside complex. A more radical monument is the Pir İlyas Tekke, or monastery, of the Halveti dervishes. Another was the octagonal madrasa built by Kemalettin, who could have been architect of Beyazit II's monumental asylum at Edirne. The hexagonal principal dormitory has a grand central fountain and an apsidal platform for musicians, who helped the vegetarian regime cure the disturbed. Violent patients were chained in cells behind a long 'columned' portico. There is a large medical college and mosque with wings for dervish nurses. These are uncomfortably joined to the minarets, suggesting that two teams were at work. There were two kitchens, refectories, bakeries, and a vast hall for storage beside grounds remarkable for their wild flowers.

Beyazit's Istanbul complex is widespread because it is built over a vast Byzantine cistern. The courtyard is beautifully proportioned. The mosque with dome and half domes would have pleased Fatih. The architect was Yakup Shah bin Sultan Shah, whose plan reflects the structural logic of Hagia Sophia.

His son Süleyman I (r.1520–66), in 1553 awarded *Sinan his first major commission, that of the memorial complex to his loved son Şehzade. The square mosque (1543–8) is filled with light under a lofty central dome supported by four semi-domes. The arcades along the flanks keep the mosque cool in summer and warm in

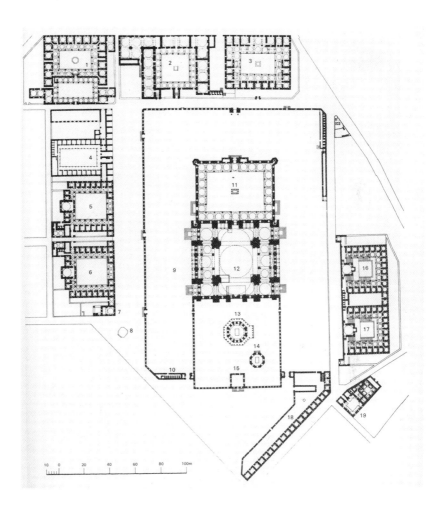

Plan of the Süleymaniye
Mosque, Istanbul, Turkey
(Sinan, 1550–57)

winter. The large complex includes the prince's türbe, rich with cuerda seca tiles. Now Sinan was ready to build Süleyman's own complex.

The seven hilltops were built on, so Sinan cut away the hillside below the harem and created a 3 ha (7 acre) plateau. Great drains were dug, and huge buttresses built. Meanwhile materials needed were estimated and ordered correctly. Complete accounts exist. Craftsmen

from specialist villages were summoned to camps and the organized commissariat. An army of janissary recruits was mustered as unskilled labourers.

The 26.2 m (86 ft) dome of the great mosque (1550–57) is central to a complex of a school, colleges, a medical college, and an immense hospital with two courtyards and an asylum below patients' rooms, and the foundations let out as metal workshops. Down the opposite side are the *imaret* (soup kitchens) with a beautiful court and equally grand hostel. The mosque gardens were the caravan camp with grazing for mules, camels, and horses.

The mosque courtyard is entered by a triumphal gate, covered with marbles and porphyry. There are four minarets at the corners. All washing facilities are down the double-storey flanking arcades, leaving the court free; once, its columns and metalwork were polished. Inside, each window formed a study room. The magnificent floor is now hidden under a carpet. But the mihrab wall has Venetian glass windows refitted in plaster, panels of Iznik tiles, and great circular glazed inscriptions designed by Ahmet Karahisari. The teacher's throne, shutters, and the inlaid great doors were the work of master craftsmen. Paintwork from the 19th century by the Fossati brothers and others has desecrated the dome, although the colours of the original design are accounted for. Fortunately the inner dome of Süleyman's türbe survives restored: a red and black dominated skyscape in which carved crystal buds gleam as if stars.

The original plans executed, it was decided to add three more madrasas, a hammam below the plateau, and the graduate college set back from the graveyard wall to leave space for a wrestling ground, sacred because no one is injured, which is now a lorry park.

Monument upon monument followed, which included many that Sinan never saw. The rebuilding of the great mosque courtyard at Mecca, and the repair of the central *masjid* carrying the Ka'aba stone, may have demanded his presence, but he had major works in Istanbul at the time, nor is he ever mentioned as *haji* or pilgrim. But he certainly did create his masterpiece between 1568 and 1574. This was built for Selim II (1566–74), the surviving son of Süleyman, after endless conflict between brothers.

There was no commanding site in Istanbul, but there was right in the heart of Edirne, now very

much patronized by sultans as an escape from the ever-expanding prison that was Topkapısarı where Süleyman had moved the 25 elite members of his harem under the unique Haseki Hürrem, who was his only wife. He called her the springtime of his life, and her türbe next to his is panelled with spring blossom in Iznik tiles.

Selim II when sober was an aesthete and a poet, and his mosque reflects his qualities. So it was on the only hill in Edirne that Ottoman architecture reached its climax with the great dome 31.4 m (103 ft) in diameter, and the four minarets 70.89 m (232.5 ft) high, two with independent stairs to each of the three balconies. Minarets need such deep foundations that they must be completed before those of the mosque can be started.

The dome is supported on eight piers which eliminate the need for half-domes. They also create narrow passages under the galleries and a shadowed region, before the great upper windows flood the prayer hall and dome with light. The dome commands acoustics better than most opera houses. In the centre is a large platform where the muezzins make the final call to prayer. Under this is the fountain of life. Great tile panels each side of the windows of the mihrab apse are of the finest period of Iznik. They are used sparsely elsewhere except in the incomparable royal gallery.

The most beautiful of Sinan's smaller mosques, that of Sokollu Mehmet Pasha (1571–2), was built in the same period in Istanbul. Cut off by a slope, a stairway ascends to pass under the hall of the madrasas. The lofty interior of the mosque is clad in brilliant tiles which even cover the hood of the minber. Significantly, pieces of the Ka'aba stone are displayed.

Sinan died when 100 Islamic years old, to be buried beside the Süleymaniye complex. Only his military career and his bridge at Büyükçekmece appear on his memorial plaque. The bridge presented the most difficult of all the structural problems that he had to solve among so many.

His student, Mehmet Ağa, built the Sultan Ahmet complex (1606–17), with six minarets, a large if repetitive court, and a dome only 23.5 m (77 ft) wide, supported on four huge elephant feet. Destroyed by the earthquake of 1894, the coloured windows of the mihrab were replaced with poor quality panes and cheap blue paint all over the place. But from a distance, the six minarets and spacious complex make a deservedly famous monument. Another student began the Yeni Valide complex beside the Horn. But it was flooded—like Winchester Cathedral. The problem was solved, and the most gifted student, Davut Ağa, took over, but the Valide—or Queen Mother—lost her income when Davut was executed in 1599 because of his too free intellectual ideas. Work was abandoned until 1620 when the mother of Mehmet IV completed the complex, including the famous Egyptian Bazaar and the fine pavilion from which she watched work in progress.

Baroque was at hand to be crowned by the Nuruosmaniye complex in 1755. A glazed-in ramp carried the mounted Sultan to his loggia, and a romantic horseshoe-plan court overlooks the Grand Bazaar. The ponderous interior lacks light. But the Haleli Mosque was built for Mustafa III by Mehmet Tahir over a thronged bazaar, and is lighter hearted. Rococo was an ideal period for fountains from the Ahmediye at the gate of Topkapısarı, giving the terrace a soft-spoken pool of spray, across which Süleyman could sit and survey the city, as could the grand Revan and Bagdat kiosks, built by Murat IV. Little garden fountains with water making a tune by dripping down from cup to cup were the most romantic; so the life-giving fountains of the neighbourhoods were rebuilt with style during this period in particular.

By the 19th century, towns had houses of two floors with yards, while the grander mansions reached 3 storeys with stalls, kitchens, storerooms, and even hammams opening onto a court and garden. Stairways led to deep verandahs with summer and winter chambers. The greater houses, and those called *yalis* on the Bosphorus, had gardens stretching back up the hillside, while the harem quarters could be separate. The first part of a salon had cupboards for bedding, washing facilities, and space for a servant. A few steps up led to the rest of the chamber with windows and sofas on three sides. A grand example is the Ċakir Ağa Konak, Birgi. Karaman houses have nostalgic frescoes of Istanbul. The best example of a country town is Sagmanbace, which is a conservation site.

The 19th century saw the arrival of foreign architects such as the Fossatis or Jasmond, who built the romantic mainline railway station of Istanbul. Some of them trained students, such as Kemalettin who built the giant Vakuf Han and romantic apartments at Beyazit, now a luxury hotel, besides small mosques.

The Balyan family built Dolmabahçe, the enormous romantic palace on the Bosphorus with grand staircases, vast landings, and romantic halls for Abdul Mecit. Others followed: the old saray became a department of Istanbul University, while Topkapısarı was, until 1911, a refuge for abandoned ladies. Wood remained the common building material for humble folk, so frequent fires were nightmares. Modern apartment blocks were to be welcomed along with giant hotels and an underground railway.   GG

Goodwin, G., *A History of Ottoman Architecture* (1971)

Ottonian architecture The architecture of the Saxon Ottonian dynasty (919–1024), named after Otto I (936–73), who rebuilt its German lands following the collapse of the Carolingian Empire. Defence against Magyars, Slavs, and Vikings raised fortifications that developed into the towns of Merseburg, Goslar, and Quedlinburg, as well as thousands of castles. The Ottonians rebuilt the imperial palaces at Paderborn and Ingelheim, with great halls set defensively over undercrofts. Otto's support of the church, ultimately as Holy Roman Emperor (962), initiated a campaign of church building, including a Benedictine abbey at Merseburg, and cathedrals at Mainz, Augsburg, and Worms, all now lost. A second cathedral at Mainz (978–1009) took the form of a basilica with transepts and crossing tower, and a westwork (actually oriented to the east) of transepts, attached stair turrets, and crossing tower, all in a style founded on the Carolingian and its Italian sources. St Michael, Hildesheim (1001–33), was an enlarged version of Mainz, with apses and crossings at both ends of its basilican nave, and incorporates arcades reusing Roman material. This early Romanesque basilican form was taken further at Strasbourg (begun 1015), where the west front comprised a triple-arched entrance and twin towers, these being the forerunner of what became a widespread arrangement in Europe.   APQ

Grodecki, L., *L'architecture ottonienne* (1958)

Oud, Jacobus Johannes Pieter (1890–1963)

Dutch architect. Theo van *Doesburg awakened the ideal of a new architecture in Oud's mind. In the very first issue of the journal *De *Stijl* (1917) van Doesburg considered Oud's 'perspective sketch' for a row of houses along the beach as the sign of the recovery of 'absolute architecture', in which the square was not simply a form but 'the expression of a concept'. Like *Mies van der Rohe and *Le Corbusier, Oud felt easy wearing the prophet's mantle to lead architecture back to her essence and guarantee her a new future. Precisely for this reason he ended the collaboration with van Doesburg in 1922, because the latter wanted to 'dissolve' architecture through his art.

Unlike Mies and Le Corbusier, Oud had a modest practice. From 1918 to 1933 he worked as a civil servant for Rotterdam Public Works; his task was housing. From then on he worked independently, in a one-man studio; for commissions he often hired temporary personnel. Although he kept in touch internationally through a stream of letters and publications, he refused to take part in CIAM, and the five small model houses in the Weissenhof Siedlung, Stuttgart (1926–7), remained his only executed commission outside the Netherlands.

His housing projects in and around Rotterdam (Hoek van Holland, 1924–7; De Kiefhoek, 1925–30) are dwarfed by the production of, for instance, Bruno *Taut in Berlin and Ernst *May in Frankfurt, but they are part of the paradigm of the modernist house produced in series. Just like Mies and Le Corbusier, Oud cherished the technology of mass production as an image rather than as a reality that could be put into practice, and he executed his designs with careful craftsmanship. In this as well he kept to an old tradition: unlike Rietveld's and Duiker's, his buildings did not leak.

His Shell Headquarters building in The Hague (1937–42) was a courageous criticism of the claim of Modernism, by then almost twenty years old, that it was the unique and universal solution to all problems. His use of 'classical' aids such as ornaments and symmetry caused misunderstanding and enormous damage to his reputation. After World War II he acted, like *Berlage before him, as the conscience of Dutch architecture, but in fact his role was marginal. The Biomedical Centre in Arnhem (1952–60) and the Congresgebouw (1956–63, completed by Hans Oud) are the masterworks within his *oeuvre* for which he prepared himself during the interwar years.

AVDW (trans. CVE)

Taverne, E. *et al.* (eds.), *J. J. P. Oud* (2001)

Pagano, Giuseppe (1886–1945) Italian architect.
See ALBINI, FRANCO.

pagoda A sacred building, usually in the form of
a tower; derived from, and in some cases identical
with the *stupa of *Buddhist architecture, found
mainly in India, *Sri Lanka, and China (*see* CHINA
(ARCHITECTURE OF FOUR CENTURIES OF DISUNION)).
For European examples bearing rather a remote
resemblance to the original, *see* CHINOISERIE.   PG

Paine, James (1717–89) English architect. One
of the second generation of Palladians, Paine 'nearly
divided the practice of the profession' with Sir Robert
*Taylor by designing or altering nearly thirty country
houses in the north of England as well as many others
elsewhere. He exploited early connections with
Palladians by superintending works at Nostell Priory,
Yorkshire (*c*.1737–50), and proved himself as a designer
at Alnwick Castle, Northumberland (*c*.1754–8),
Kedleston Hall, Derbyshire (1759–60), Worksop
Manor, Nottinghamshire (1763–7), and Sandbeck Park,
Yorkshire (*c*.1763–8). His ready facility as a classicist
on smaller works, such as Heath House, Yorkshire
(1744–5), and Gibside Chapel, Derbyshire (*c*.1756–60),
is a clue to his deserved success.   APQ

Pakistan The traditional link between the
professional architect and the building craftsman
became a casualty of the British Raj. While the state
recognized only professionals trained in the European
system, the hereditary craftsmen, relegated to the

Timber pagoda, Hingxian, Shanxi, China (1056)

service of country squires, religious institutions and unauthorized developments on the urban fringe, became the last repository of the indigenous architectural tradition.

More than any other Pakistani architect of his generation, Mehdi Ali Mirza absorbed and understood the philosophy of the Modern Movement. In his residences in Karachi and Lahore the influence of Frank Lloyd Wright is easily recognized.

The first regular courses in architecture became available within the country at the National College of Arts in 1958, and the West Pakistan University of Engineering and Technology in 1962. Among the early graduates was Nayyar Ali Dada, who gained recognition for his eclectic Modernism. Yet in later buildings such as the Alhambra Arts Council and the Open Air Theatre in Lahore he displays a concern for indigenous materials and forms.

A number of the most talented students of the National College of Arts were employed by the government-owned firm PEPAC (Pakistan Environmental Planning and Architectural Consultants), established in the late 1960s. As a result, this office sustained a relatively high standard of design, and has been responsible for some of the largest commissions undertaken by Pakistani architects, including the Frontier House, NAFDEC (National Film Development Corporation) Cinemas and the HBFC (Housing and House Building Finance Corporation) buildings in Islamabad.

Where the criterion of excellence is the assimilation of 'Western' values, the foreign-educated architect has an edge over his purely home-grown colleague. Thus, adhering to the idiom of the International Style, Habib Fida Ali attains a degree of sophistication and maturity in the Burmah-Shell Headquarters building in Karachi, while the slick commercialism of Yasmeen Lari's Trade Centre in Karachi is in sharp contrast to her earlier quest for a regional idiom in the Angoori Bagh Housing in Lahore. Similarly, while Fuad Ali Butt in Lahore exploits the structural logic of brick arches and shell concrete vaults, Anwar Saeed in Islamabad explores the permutations of elementary architectonic forms.

With less than one architect per million persons during the first two decades since Independence, Pakistan relied heavily on the services of foreign architects for the largest and most prestigious projects, including the grid-iron plan for the new capital, Islamabad, by Doxiades. The less remarkable amongst these have been Edward Durrell *Stone's

WAPDA (Water And Power Development Authority) House in Lahore and PINSTECH (Pakistan Institute for Nuclear Science and Technology), the Presidency, National Assembly, and the University in Islamabad; Gio *Ponti's Secretariat and Sherazad Hotel; Vedet Dalokay's Faisal Mosque; and Kenzô *Tange's Supreme Court in Islamabad.

By comparison, the following are more thoughtful and responsive to the local climate, materials, and culture: Doxiades' new campus of the Punjab University in Lahore; William Perry's IBA (Institute of Business Administration) and the American School in Karachi; Echochard's Karachi University and the Museum at Moenjodaro; Denis Brigden's Government Hostel in Islamabad; Tom Payette's Aga Khan Hospital in Karachi; and Ramesh Khosla's Serena Hotels in Faisalabad and Quetta.   KKM

Mumtaz, K. K., *Architecture in Pakistan* (1985)

palaces

DEFINITION

ANCIENT EGYPT

CLASSICAL ANTIQUITY

MESOPOTAMIA AND IRAN

EUROPE

CHINA

JAPAN

INDIA

AFRICA

Definition The strict dictionary definition of 'palace' is: 'The official residence of an emperor, king, pope, or other sovereign ruler' (*OED*), but for the purposes of this entry, a palace is defined as a building used for the staging of court ceremonial, or for the demonstration of political power, which receives some form of architectural expression.

A ruler may live in a 'palace' which fulfils neither of these functions, and so cannot be distinguished from a large or even medium-sized house (e.g. Buckingham Palace, London, or the Amalienborg palace, Copenhagen). The less stringent definition, 'a palatial dwelling-place', may apply to private houses in town (*see* PALAZZO) or country (*see* COUNTRY HOUSES, ENGLAND; COUNTRY HOUSES, IRELAND) which are loosely or even nominally called 'palaces' (e.g. *Vanbrugh's Blenheim Palace). In line with our definition, this entry only deals with those buildings where the functions of the spaces have definitely been identified. For this reason, the palaces of pre-Columbian civilizations (*see* INCAS; MAYA ARCHITECTURE) and the *Minoan palaces of Crete have not been considered.

It is instructive to illustrate the divergence of the definition used here from the dictionary definitions. Ironically, it should be noted that the word derives from 'Palatium', the residence of the Roman Emperor, which in this definition does not qualify as a palace. In some societies, the connection between secular and religious power is so intimate that buildings for both types of power are to be found within the confines of the palace area; and in at least one case (Persepolis; see subheading below, Mesopotamia and Iran) the palace represents both temporal and spiritual power.

Ancient Egypt Since palaces were far less important than temples and tombs in ancient Egypt, they were built of timber and brick, so that few remains have survived. Palaces of the early dynasties served many functions, including workshops, military quarters, the royal apartments, and audience halls. Although the palace complex could cover over 32 hectares (79 acres) (as at Thebes), much of this space was occupied by temples, since the Pharaoh was also the high priest. Two distinctive characteristics were established in this period: the audience hall; and the 'window of appearance', at which the Pharaoh showed himself to certain chosen subjects waiting in a reception courtyard. It is possible that in the earlier period the hall was used for other purposes, but in the palace at Thebes (for Amenhotep III, *c*.1391–*c*.1351 BC), its use as a ceremonial space, shown by the throne dais set on the entrance axis, is more clearly demarcated from the private rooms.

Classical antiquity The political systems of archaic and classical Greece, Etruscan Italy, and Republican Rome did not require palaces. In the Roman Empire, the Augustan compromise (31 BC) by which 'The image of a free constitution was preserved with decent reverence' (Gibbon, *The Decline and Fall*, chapter I) extended to architecture, in that the emperors' extravagant official and private residences did not function as palaces in the sense used in this entry. Even when Diocletian (r.AD 284–305) decided '... to introduce the stately magnificence of the court of Persia...' (Gibbon, chapter XIII), the regime was confined to dress and court ceremonial, and did not affect architecture, since existing palaces were not re-modelled, and no palaces were built to serve the new purpose of ostentation.

Mesopotamia and Iran These are the sites of the most truly regal palaces, in which the architecture and decoration serve to emphasize the might of the ruler and the lowliness of the subject. As the most militarized nation in the ancient world, the Assyrians built palaces like barracks, to impress by sheer size, or by a representation of power. The palace of Assurnasirpal II (r.884–859 BC) included a courtyard of 200 × 120 m (656 × 394 ft); emissaries to the palace of Sargon II (742–705 BC) at Khorsabad had to follow a lengthy processional route, lined with carvings and paintings reminding them of the dangers of defying Assyrian power. Within the palace precinct there is a *ziggurat. Similarly, the palace of the Babylonian king Nebuchadnezzar II (r.604–562 BC) impressed by five large courtyards, which gave access to a throne room on the south side

and residential quarters on the north. The arched gateway to the Grand Entrance Court was flanked by tall towers, decorated with polychrome glazed bricks.

In Iran, the Achaemenid palaces at Pasargadae, Persepolis, and Susa featured *apadāna*, *hypostyle audience halls with fluted stone columns. The palace at Susa, built by Darius I (by 521 BC), was set on a large foundation platform (254 m × 152 m, 833 ft × 499 ft), the basis for a large courtyard and an audience hall, with very tall columns. It was eclipsed in size, complexity, and grandeur by Persepolis (mostly built by Xerxes, 486–465 BC), with its square audience halls, laid out on a terrace of 460 × 270 m (503 × 295 yards), and rose 15 m (49 ft) above the plain. By means of its imposing architecture, and its sculpted friezes which showed the offering of imperial tribute, the palace represented its role not so much as a political capital as a dynastic shrine dedicated to the staging of the spring festival (Noo Ruz). It is probable that in the main audience hall, which was large enough to hold 10,000 people, processions moved concentrically towards the king seated at the centre, concealed by sumptuous draperies.

The Sasanians built several palaces, of which the most outstanding is the Taq-i Kisra, Ctesiphon, Iraq (AD 250). Four *iwans* surrounded an immense audience hall, 23 × 46 m (75 × 151 ft) and 27 m (88½ ft) high, where, concealed by a gold-embroidered curtain, Shapur I, the king of kings, sat on a raised dais. Just above his head, suspended by golden chains, was a jewelled crown weighing 272 kg (600 pounds); at his feet was the fabled Spring in Paradise carpet, 'encrusted with thousands of precious jewels' (Pope, A. U., *Persian Architecture*, 1965, p.56).

Europe After the fall of the Roman Empire and the rise of feudalism, rulers were mainly concerned with building fortified residences—secular authority was embodied in the castle, rather than the palace (*see* MILITARY ARCHITECTURE). The only 'palatial' or non-military element was the great hall, first introduced by Charlemagne (*see* CAROLINGIAN ARCHITECTURE), and seen as late as the end of the 14th century in the Great Hall of the Palace of Westminster, begun 1394.

From the mid 13th century, feudalism was displaced by the growing power of the cities, which expressed itself in civic 'palaces', the *town halls of Flanders, and the *palazzo pubblico* of Italy. Feudalism partially reasserted itself in the absolute monarchies, which began their struggle for power from the middle of the 16th century, at first in Spain. The Escorial established the pattern for Spanish palaces: a monotonous façade pierced by ordinary windows, looking more like a monastery or a barracks than a palace. It was well suited to Philip II's purpose of administering his crusade against heretics in his distant dominions, rather than to impressing the fractious nobility at home, over whom he had limited authority. During the period of Spain's drastic economic decline, Philip IV could not afford to impress his nobles by the architecture of the Buen Retiro (begun 1630), so for architecture he substituted the political imagery displayed on his paintings, in the Hall of the Realms.

The most successful ruler to enlist palace architecture in his absolutist purpose was Louis XIV (r.1660–1715). Although building the Louvre palace continued during his reign (*see* PERRAULT), it was unsuited to his purpose of keeping the nobility away from their country estates and corralling them into one place under his supervision. The Louvre was vulnerably located on the edge of a rebellious city (Paris), and its layout of courtyards made surveillance difficult.

The palace of Versailles was one enormous block, in which the main façade was 402 m (1320 ft) long (fittingly, over twice as long as the new façade for the Louvre, by Perrault). The unprecedented dimensions posed too great a challenge to designers; the first sections, designed by Le Vau, were relatively coherent, but the task of finishing the remaining block was ideally suited to *Hardouin-Mansart, a designer quite lacking in finesse. More surprisingly, for a building meant to impress, the entrance on the Cour Royale side is mean and insignificant; there is no grand entrance hall, and the Grand Gallery (97.5 m or 320 ft long), though sumptuously decorated, is entered quite abruptly, without a preparatory vestibule or staircase—and it leads nowhere. Rather than Versailles' architecture, it is the landscape design centred on the palace which is its most impressive feature.

Versailles set the model for absolute monarchs, but the only two monarchs with sufficient resources to emulate Louis XIV were the Habsburgs and the Romanovs. Neither improved upon the architecture of Versailles: the Schönbrunn Palace, Vienna (*Fischer von Erlach, 1696) is a rather basic exercise in symmetry on too large a scale; and the Romanovs' Winter Palace (*Rastrelli, completed as late as 1754–64) is very clumsy in its fenestration.

The myriad palaces of the lesser European monarchs and minor German principalities emulate Versailles at a lesser scale, but several of the latter exceed Versailles in one respect: their lavish staircases in a central, dramatic position. At the Episcopal Palace, Bruchsal (Balthasar *Neumann, from 1728), the oval staircase which dominates the palace rises from a dark grotto to a dome flooded with light; at the Residenz, Würzburg (Neumann, 1732–43), the broad staircase provides a vantage point for Tiepolo's magnificent ceiling fresco.

China The imperial palace type was established in the Qin and Han dynasties (221 BCE–AD 200). The Emperor had a palace or palaces in his capital city, and also outside the city for use on his tours of inspection or for pleasure. The two main features of both types of palace were the north–south axis and the courtyard layout. Following the Analects of Confucius (c.551–479 BC), the ideal ruler should be located to the north, and face the south looking at building complexes in which state rituals were performed. The principal buildings were set out in straight lines around a series of courtyards, a layout which can be seen on a large scale in the Forbidden City, Beijing, as late as AD 1417–20.

Japan Our knowledge of Japanese imperial palaces appears to be rather limited. Temples and shrines are much more fully documented, perhaps because temples and shrines were considered to be more important. Up until the construction of the Heian capital, Kyoto (794), Japanese imperial palaces followed the Chinese pattern, usually standing in the middle of the north side of the city, but other details are lacking. The Shishinden Imperial Palace, Kyoto, as rebuilt in 1855, consists of a central block 3 bays wide and 9 bays long, enclosing the imperial throne and surrounded by galleries. However, it is not clear whether this layout replicates earlier versions.

India There are few remains of ancient Indian palaces, perhaps because they were built of fragile materials such as wood, but more probably because, unlike temples, they were not considered worth preserving.

In the period before British rule, and independently of a ruler's religion, palaces had a number of common characteristics. They were nearly all forts, as shown not only by their massive walls, but also in the plan, which often included narrow and confusing passageways to frustrate invaders. The interiors were divided by high walls into separate courtyards, sometimes for audience, arranged in a hierarchy leading from the public zones nearest the outer walls to the private areas (including separate areas for women) in the centre. Usually a religious building (mosque or temple), often as splendid

as the palace itself, if not more so, was located in a central position.

The earliest reasonably complete works to survive are the (Hindu) palaces of Chitor, in particular the palace of Rana Kumbha (1433–68), which consists of a series of courtyards, surrounded by accommodation for the ruler and his family, and an audience hall. The Chitor palaces form part of a similar group, the Rajput fortresses of Rajasthan, the four largest of which (Chitor, Gwalior, Jodhpur, and Jaiselmer) are each built on an outcrop rising sharply from the surrounding plain. Of these, Gwalior (1486–1517) is the most striking, with its massive walls and cylindrical tower-buttresses enlivened by a frieze of polychrome tiles representing birds and beasts. The most interesting Rajput palaces of those of Orchha (Ramji Mandir, 1531–4; Raj Mandir, 1554–91; Jangir Mandir, c.1605) and Datia (Govind Mandir, Datia, 1620), in that they are symmetrical in their planning and massing. In the centre of the courtyard at Datia rises a square, 5-storey tower connected by bridges to the enclosing buildings.

Outside Rajasthan, the greatest Hindu palace was Vijayanagar (1406–1565). In the account (1520–22) of the Portuguese traveller Domingos Paes, it was decorated with great extravagance, with structures of fragrant woods and precious stones, ivory, silver, and gold, on the roofs and the pillars. The King's Audience court was a hypostyle hall with 100 timber columns.

Vijayanagar is, however, the exception. Mughal palaces, in particular the Red Forts of Agra and Delhi, and Fatehpur Sikri (1571–86), are much more splendid in their use of materials (white marble with red sandstone) and the truly palatial use of audience halls, both private (known as the *diwan-i-khass)* and public (the *diwan-i-am*). Unlike the Rajasthan fort-palaces, those of the Mughals tended to be on level sites, allowing for a more open layout. Within the palace complex is often the mosque, which is the most carefully detailed building, rather than the palace, as for example in the Moti Masjid or Pearl Mosque at Agra and Delhi.

Following the end of the Mughal era, palaces continued to be built by local rulers, but few are of any architectural distinction.

Africa A common pattern—one or two large interior courtyards and several smaller ones—occurs in diverse countries and periods (Ta'akha Mariam, Axum, Ethiopia; the palace of Husuni Kubwa, Tanzania, c.1245; the Swahili palace, Gedi, Kenya, 15th century). The palaces of west Africa, of the Ashanti, the Yoruba, and at Benin city seem to have consisted of complexes of ordinary houses, built of mud, and apart from size, in no way architecturally distinguished.

The palace of Gidan Rumfa, Nigeria, housed 1,000 people. In order to enforce Islamic law, the ruler Emir Mohammad Rumfa (r.1463–99) built a mosque on the edge of the large open public space surrounding the palace. The juxtaposition was designed so that the Emir could lead a procession from the palace to the mosque for Friday prayer.

In other cases, one must distinguish between the ruler's house and a palace. In some African societies, political decisions were taken in special meeting halls or in the open air, so that palaces were unnecessary.   PG

palaestra In classical Greek and Roman times, an exercise ground or a public building, smaller than a gymnasium, for athletes. Often this was no more than an enclosed rectangular field with some sort of shelter, rather like a modern sports field and pavilion. It might be surrounded by an arcaded pentice, rather like a cloister, as excavated at Pompeii. A palaestra was often incorporated within a public swimming bath, such as the baths of Caracalla and Diocletian in Rome, and was intended as a place where bathers could loosen up before entering the bath rooms.   APQ

palazzo Italian for 'palace', a building type socially distinct from the *palace, in that it is the residence of a private individual; it is also visually distinct from the *hôtel particulier (with which it shares some of its social characteristics), in that as a rule the palazzo is distinguished by the magnificence of its façades or its courtyards, rather than by ingenious planning.

Initially, the palazzo served a dual purpose. It was both the private and the official residence of the governor of a city, because by law the governor had to be a resident of another city, and to live in, or in some cities was even confined to, the civic palazzo during the term of his rule. As a consequence, three characteristics of the palazzo endured for most of its history: all the main rooms have similar shapes and sizes, so that they can be used for a variety of purposes (cf. the *hôtel particulier*, which disposed of a multitude of specialized spaces, of different shapes and sizes); the best rooms, on the upper floors, were reserved for living areas; and it enjoyed dual purpose, which survived into a change of use, from private/political to private/commercial.

The medieval civic type, such as the Palazzo del Podestà (in Florence, the Palazzo Bargello, 1255), had massive, rather unarticulated exteriors, with a scattering of small windows, surmounted by tall watch towers. In the following century, this type was adapted by merchants, particularly in Florence, to use the ground floor for business, as a shop or warehouse was reached through an arched doorway.

In the post-medieval period, although the civic function of the palazzo no longer applied, Florentine patrons faced a different set of conflicting objectives, summed up *post facto* by Giovanni Rucellai (in 1473), that his architectural projects served to honour God, the city, and himself. This problem was solved by *Michelozzo in his design for the Palazzo Medici-Riccardi, Florence (1444–59), as the palazzo is large (occupying a block of 68.5 m (225 ft) by 58 m

(190 ft) and 24.4 m (80 ft) tall), impressive, with its heavily rusticated base and giant oversailing cornice, but quite plain, in terms of the articulation of the main wall surface.

A more refined version of this type, *Alberti's Palazzo Rucellai, Florence (begun c.1453), is the first *Renaissance palazzo, because of its relatively knowledgeable use of the *orders. The façade is a grid articulated by superimposed pilasters, Doric on the first floor, two versions of Corinthian on the upper storeys. As an indication of Alberti's rather abstract approach, the design of the façade is difficult to see because the palazzo is set on such a narrow street. Alberti's classicizing approach was not generally adopted in Florence, but is seen to better advantage at Pienza, in *Rossellino's Palazzo Piccolomini (1459–64), which stands in an open space. Later Florentine palazzi show an unusual combination of non-classical façades fronting a symmetrical plan around a centrally located courtyard—the Palazzo Strozzi (1489ff.); or a much more subtly graduated use of stonework than the abrupt transition in the Palazzo Rucellai from the very rough ground-floor rustication to the ashlar of the upper storeys—the Palazzo Gondi (Giuliano da *Sangallo, 1489–1504). But the basic design, of an unarticulated façade, dominated by its rustication, persisted even a century later, in *Ammanati's addition to the Palazzo Pitti (1560–77).

In Rome, the few surviving medieval palazzi, such as the Palazzo della Cancelleria (c.1485–c.1511), follow the Florentine pattern. But with the Renaissance, a new monumentality appeared, pioneered by quite a small palazzo of only five bays, the so-called House of Raphael (*Bramante, c.1510). The effect of monumentality was produced by the massive rustication on the ground floor, and the engaged Doric columns, supported on pedestals, framing the piano nobile. By contrast with the Florentine palazzo type, the façade articulation expressed the different purposes of each storey (shops at street level, and living accommodation on the floor above), and the orders were only used for the piano nobile and above.

Unfortunately, in the hands of less gifted architects, monumentality led to monotony. The Palazzo Farnese (Antonio *Sangallo the Younger, 1534–46) is imposing by virtue of its sheer bulk, but there is little else to be said in its favour. The façade is rigidly symmetrical around the central, rather insignificant doorway, and there are no variations in the alternating segmental and triangular pediments above the windows. Even Michelangelo's design for the cornice cannot redeem its sheer banality. The plan equally lacks variety, as do nearly all Roman palazzi, with one splendid exception: the Palazzo Massimi alle Colonne, by *Peruzzi (begun 1532). Most Roman palazzi occupy a rectangular block facing a regular piazza, but in this case Peruzzi had to fit his design onto the curve of an ancient street. Peruzzi integrates the street façade by means of the ground-floor vestibule, and behind the regular façade integrates four courtyards all set at angles to each other (the design is brilliantly analysed in J. Lees-Milne, Roman Mornings, 1955). Otherwise the dullness of Roman palazzo design during this period is highlighted by signs of inventiveness elsewhere. Thus Palladio's Palazzo Chiericati, Vicenza (begun c.1547), turns the urban palazzo inside out by emphasizing the street façade, by means of an open loggia on the piano nobile, rather than the inner courtyard.

The possibilities of Bramante's model palazzo were ignored in Rome, but inventively explored elsewhere by *Sanmicheli, in three palaces in Verona and two in Venice. The Palazzo Pompei (c.1530) and the Palazzo Canossa (c.1530) introduce a number of subtleties, particularly the widening of the central bay, but Sanmicheli's crowning achievement in Verona is the Palazzo Bevilacqua (c.1530–35). Here Sanmicheli creates a very complex rhythm by alternating the widths of the bays, by using varied groups of fenestration, and by employing every sculptural detail to highlight the articulation of the façade.

The Verona palazzi were located on regular sites overlooking open spaces, but in Venice Sanmicheli faced quite a different problem: irregular sites facing onto a gently curving canal. The Venetian palazzo tradition was also quite different: the palazzo accommodated several different households on the upper floors and sometimes a variety of businesses on the ground floor; and in order to bring more light into long narrow buildings, the *salone* on the first floor extended the depth of the building. Sanmicheli's solution (the Palazzo Grimani, 1559–70) was to give the building great height in relation to its width (roughly 7:6, as compared to 4:6 for the Palazzo Farnese, or 2:6 for the Palazzo Riccardi) and by making the window frames occupy almost the entire bay. The majestic façade was coupled with an ingenious plan, which appears to be symmetrical even though the building is set an angle to the canal front. The continuing applicability of his solutions is shown a century later in *Longhena's Palazzo Pesaro (begun 1649/52) and Ca' Rezzonico (begun 1666).

After Peruzzi, Roman palazzo design languished for almost a century, with only two interesting exceptions. In the façade of the Palazzo Serlupi Crescenzi (?1585), *della Porta spaced the windows unevenly, so as to counteract the effect of foreshortening when regularly spaced windows are seen along a narrow street. For the corner site of the Palazzo Mattei di Giove (begun 1598), *Maderno devised an inventive plan: two entrances leading to a group of staircases which together establish surprising vistas.

Between 1620 and 1670 about a dozen large palaces were designed. The first, the Palazzo Barberini (begun 1628), to which Maderno, *Bernini and *Borromini all made a contribution, is an exception in terms of its site, being located in a large *vigna*, rather than facing an urban piazza. Consequently it is a solid mass with projecting wings, rather than a block planned round a central court. Streets and piazze were widened to form large open spaces in front of palazzi, not only to display their grandeur, but to allow wide enough turning circles for visitors' carriages. Unfortunately, a large unvaried façade seems to have been sufficiently impressive to contemporaries, and the view *from* the palazzo is undoubtedly imposing, but to today's spectator these palazzi do seem rather bleak. The problem of animating a long flat façade looking onto a large open space is almost insoluble. Even Bernini's solution for the Palazzo Chigi-Odescalchi (1664)—a giant order on the upper two floors of a central 7-bay block, which breaks forward slightly—is not very convincing.

Although the art collections and the decor of Roman Baroque palazzi were magnificent, the architecture of their interiors is by comparison very unrewarding. The plans are fairly predictable; there is only one grand staircase, in the Palazzo Ruspoli (Martin *Longhi the Younger, 1640); and only one really outstanding room, the Sala Grande in the Palazzo Colonna (Antonio del Grande, after 1654).

With the exception of the example mentioned above, staircases are not an important feature of Roman palazzi in the 17th and 18th centuries (even during the period 1700–40, when they were an important feature in the cityscape); whereas it can virtually be said of this period that in Naples almost the only important feature is the staircase. As the city became more and more overcrowded from the end of the 17th century, palaces became taller, and the staircases ran through 5 storeys. The staircase rather than the façade or the plan is the main feature in a Neapolitan palazzo, particularly in the designs of *Sanfelice, to the extent of occupying the whole side of the courtyard and rising the full height of the building, in his own Palazzo Sanfelice (1723–28).

The displacement of the *piano nobile* from the first to the second floor allowed the introduction of vast *portes cochères*, another distinctive feature found only in Naples, if not designed with such éclat.

Finally, two outstanding examples from Turin show the great diversity of this building type. *Juvarra's Palazzo Madama (1718–21) presents the palazzo as a stage set. The staircase occupies the entire length of the building; the vault above is twice as high as the ascent to the central landing, and the windows below the vault create a zone full of light. But the most perfect palazzo design of all is *Guarini's Palazzo Carignano (1683–93). The plan consists of a carefully considered sequence of light/dark, open/closed spaces which lead to the main salon, with the staircases fully integrated into the plan; the main façade is a series of curves, cleverly adapted from Borromini.   PG

Palestine, historic The city of Jerusalem has three significant buildings built on two of the most sacred sites in Christianity and Islam. It must be admitted that the buildings' religious and political importance markedly outweighs their architectural quality.

The Church of the Holy Sepulchre is built over the site of the Crucifixion and of the Tomb of Christ. The outlines of the first scheme, begun in AD 326, consisting of a linked basilica, colonnaded atrium and rotunda, all under one roof, have been retained through all subsequent alterations. The most important change was that carried out by the *Crusaders following their capture of the city in 1099. A new, roofed structure was created for the atrium, the Sepulchre itself enclosed in a magnificent aedicule, and the basilica reorganized as a conventional *Romanesque plan, of apse, ambulatory, and three radiating chapels.

The area of the Noble Sanctuary contains the Dome of the Rock and the Aqsa mosque. Begun in AD 692, it is the earliest *mosque to have an imposing presence,

typical of Umayyad patronage (*see* SYRIA, HISTORIC). The similarity of the dimensions of the dome (20.2 m or 66 ft high and 20.48 m or 67 ft diameter) to those of the Church of the Holy Sepulchre suggests that it was built to rival its Christian counterpart. The plan, of two octagons, is unusual, but the building is more memorable for its lavish decoration and the golden dome.

The Aqsa mosque, the third holiest after Mecca and Medina, was built as the congregational mosque for Jerusalem. The first structure was raised in 685–705 and enlarged in 709–15, consisting of a *hypostyle hall, the arcades supported by marble columns. It has been damaged by earthquakes and reconstructed several times. The most striking feature made during the reconstructions is the imposing dome, completed 1035.   PG

Palestine, under the British Mandate 1918–48 The British architects in Palestine chiefly built public buildings characterized by Romantic Eclecticism, which incorporates oriental and Christian details. The most noteworthy British architects who created an impressive synthesis of East and West were Austin St Barbe Harrison (Government House and Palestine Archaeological Museum) and Clifford Holiday (St Andrew's Scottish Church and City Hall). The regulation requiring buildings in the city of Jerusalem to have stone facing, still in force today, was issued in 1918. Aside from the differences deriving from a diversity of style, the regulation ensures unity for the city. The British master plans for Jerusalem sought to ensure that the city's development would be planned. All of them emphasize preservation, particularly in the areas near to the Old City.

The concept of the garden city was a highly important source of inspiration in the planning of cities, neighbourhoods, *kibbutzim* (kibbutz—collective agricultural settlement), and *moshavim* (moshav—

cooperative agricultural settlement) in Palestine in the first half of the 20th century.

The idea of a garden city was initiated in England towards the end of the 19th century by Ebenezer Howard, largely in response to the maladies of the Industrial Revolution. One of the guiding principles was that garden cities should be limited in size. In Palestine, these two factors were not particularly relevant at that stage, because the towns and settlements were newly founded and their founders wished to see them expand rapidly and were as yet unaware of the problem of their dimensions. The idea can be seen as a sort of pre-emptive cure for the evils of industry—which did not yet exist. Being close to the land, to nature and plants, the importance of green 'lungs' and the cooperative principles guiding the designers of the idea of garden cities captivated the Zionist movement. The concept of garden cities was first applied by the planners of new *moshavim*, garden neighbourhoods, and garden cities, and was only later followed at *kibbutzim*. Moshav Nahalal (1920) was the first example. Richard Kauffmann presented an ideal plan with a clear shape—a round, slightly elliptical settlement surrounded by arable fields divided into equal-sized triangles. Nahalal is similar in form to Ebenezer Howard's general scheme—but he stressed that it was just a diagram, as he could not draw up detailed plans until the location had been chosen. One could of course argue that Kauffmann took the diagram in its simple form and adopted its schematic nature. However, as can be seen in the planning of more than a hundred localities in the country, what distinguishes his work is the way it has been adapted to suit the topography, climate, and the special needs of each settlement, which compensated for the dogmatism. The problem that ensued at Nahalal was due to the fact that it was planned as a complete entity and did not allow for the possibility of expansion. The idealistic nature of the residents and the idea of a workers'

cooperative settlement led to an attempt to see a connection between the plan of Nahalal and the ideal city in all its incarnations.

The concept of a garden city also guided Richard Kauffmann in his plans for neighbourhoods in Jerusalem and most of the new neighbourhoods in Haifa. City planning was also influenced by the idea of the garden city. The first Hebrew city, Tel Aviv, was also based on that idea, originally according to ideas put forward by Kauffmann. He was replaced by Patrick Geddes, who drafted the master plan in 1926. In 2003, UNESCO declared Tel Aviv a World Heritage City, one of the only two 20th-century cities to be included on the list. It was awarded the title because of the special blend of garden city and the highest concentration in the world of the early Modern style.

Students from the avant-garde schools of Europe came to Palestine, including *Bauhaus graduates and architects who had worked with *Le Corbusier, Erich *Mendelsohn (who worked in Palestine between 1934 and 1942), Hannes *Meyer, Bruno *Taut, and Auguste *Perret. Dizengoff Circle, as planned by Genia Averbouch (1934), which prescribes a unified façade regardless of function and architect, testifies to the influence of Modernism on urban planning. Within a few years, a synthesis of the various sources of Modernism had been created.

In contrast to garden neighbourhoods and concentrations of modernist architecture in Europe, the spirit of the garden city and the high concentration of modernist buildings were planned for the inner city and were not confined to the outskirts. The radicalism of Tel Aviv is expressed in the choice of the idea of garden city and adoption of the Modern Movement of architecture, planned for the entire city starting from the centre and not just in the suburbs—an idea that was maintained for years.   ML

Levin, M(ichael), *White City* (1984)

Palladianism is the style of *Palladio, as first revived in Britain by Inigo *Jones, and particularly in the 18th century by Colen Campbell (1676–1729), Lord *Burlington, and their followers. Campbell's *Vitruvius Britannicus* (1715) advocated the 'Antique Simplicity' of Vitruvius, which had passed to Palladio and thence to Jones, decrying the 'affected and licentious' Baroque of *Wren and his associates. His exemplar, Wanstead House, Redbridge, London (*c*.1714–20, demolished), attracted Burlington (1694–1753), for whom Campbell remodelled Burlington House, London (1718–19), and established Campbell as the founder of British Palladianism. Even licentious *Vanbrugh (1664–1726), whose Castle Howard (1700–26) was at least based on a Palladian plan, reinterpreted Palladio's Rotonda for his Temple of the Four Winds (1724–6). Burlington's influential villa, Chiswick House, London (*c*.1725–9), became a doctrinaire model of Palladian taste, and his Assembly Rooms, York (1731–2), a remarkable interpretation of Palladio's Egyptian Hall. His cooperation with William *Kent (1685–1748) at Holkham Hall, Norfolk (*c*.1734), produced the classic English country house, rather cold, consistently detailed, and magnificently massed.

The second Palladian generation, notably James *Paine (1717–89), softened the doctrinaire aspects of the style, adding porticoes and antique simplicity to their country houses for a touch of grandeur. Grandeur could though become flaccid, as in *Flitcroft's (1697–1769) Wentworth Woodhouse, Yorkshire (*c*.1735–70), whose façade comprises fifteen separate sections, with three porticoes and terminal pavilions. This is redeemed by the magnificence of its marble saloon hall (1750–75), in essence Jones's Queen's House, Greenwich, done opulently. Smaller houses and villas were more successful. Campbell's Stourhead, Wiltshire (*c*.1720–24), a porticoed four-square plan with well-proportioned rooms as anything in Palladio, is a successful entrée to a romantic landscape, adorned

with such classical stereotypes as the Pantheon (1753, possibly Flitcroft's), the Temple of the Sun or Apollo (based on the original at Baalbec, certainly Flitcroft's) and the Temple of Flora (1755, Tuscan). There was no finer designer of Palladian villas than Robert *Taylor (1714–88), whose Asgill House, Richmond, London (1761–4), Danson Hill, Bexleyheath, London (*c*.1762–5), and Sharpham House, Devon (*c*.1770), rely more on Palladio's plain massing than porticoes. Taylor cleverly adapted Palladio's ability to embrace nave and aisles with interlocking pediments, as at the Redentore, by giving his wings sloping roofs, continuing the line of the pedimented centrepieces, and adding characteristic canted bays to complete the effect of simplicity. By 1770, however, architects looked further back than Palladio, and, in a fresh response to the antique, heralded the neoclassical style. APQ

See also COUNTRY HOUSES, ENGLAND; COUNTRY HOUSES, IRELAND.

Palladio, Andrea (1508–80) Italian architect. Andrea was apprenticed to a stonecarver, but at age 16 fled the constraints of his contract to the nearby Venetian satellite city of Vicenza to join a flourishing firm of carvers. His progress toward recognition as an architect was furthered by the patronage of the local elite, and his career centred upon their eagerness to build palaces and villas in the surrounding countryside and to sponsor public buildings. He was first discovered by a humanist poet and playwright, Giangiorgio Trissino, perhaps when employed as a craftsman for the construction of his villa, Cricoli, on the outskirts of the city.

Trissino introduced him to ancient architecture and literature, took him on the first of his several trips to Rome (1541) to see and to record in drawings the remains of antiquity and major modern buildings by *Bramante, *Raphael and their followers, and probably gave him the classical name, Palladio. His progress in

learning and social stature culminated in his induction
into the Accademia Olimpica, a society of nobles and
intellectuals, for which he designed one of his last
works, the Teatro Olimpico, an indoor version of the
Roman theatre.

Palladio's earliest designs, of the early 1540s, perhaps
conceived before his visit to Rome (Villa Godi at
Lonedo, Villa Gazotti at Bertesina, and the Casa Civena
in Vicenza), employ, as at Cricoli and model woodcuts
in the treatise of Sebastiano Serlio, a restrained style
still reflecting the local traditions of the Veneto,
avoiding bold relief and even, as in the villa, leaving the
façade almost without ornament. But by the mid-1540s
the lessons of his Roman sojourn emerge as he
gathered commissions for villas and palaces. Palazzo
Thiene was initially designed by *Giulio Romano in the
early 1540s, but Palladio took over on the author's
death in 1546 and claimed authorship in his *I Quattro
Libri*. Although he adopted its rusticated style in the
Villa Pisani at Bagnolo (1542), the commission for
which was the first of many from the higher nobility in
Venice itself, he shifted to a purer Classicism focused
on bold reinterpretations of the classical columnar
orders in projects for the palaces of Iseppo Porto and
Girolamo Chiericati (both late 1540s). The façade of the
former is a homage to *Bramante's Palazzo Caprini in
Rome (before 1510) in the use of a ground floor of
drafted masonry supporting robust Ionic half-columns
and a strongly projecting entablature on the *piano
nobile*. A 2-storey court, which remained unbuilt, was
to have had a colossal order of columns, and an open
gallery attached at the upper-storey level. The
Chiericati palace has an innovative plan, shallow in
depth and extended in width to conform with the
piazza before it, with loggie on the ground and upper
storeys.

The architect gained steadily in stature, starting
in the late 1540s with his project for rebuilding the
Basilica in Vicenza, a late medieval market hall and

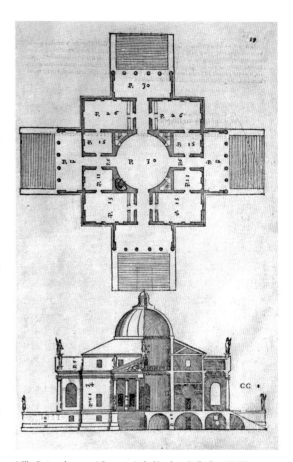

Villa Rotonda, near Vicenza, Italy (Andrea Palladio, 1569)

assembly-place, the exterior of which had been
destroyed. Because the interior and external corridors
and the clerestory walls of the assembly hall in the
centre had to be preserved in the new programme,
Palladio's challenge was to design a more classical
exterior sheaf that could cope with the irregularities of
the medieval core. His key to the solution was to adopt,
on both the ground and upper level, bays of what
became known as the 'Palladian Motif' (although it had

been initiated by Bramante and employed in many of the buildings of *Serlio's treatise), an arch on free-standing columns flanked by rectangular openings which could be imperceptibly expanded and contracted as required by the spacing of the medieval vaults behind. The intensely white Istrian marble brilliantly reflects the sunlight, as it does in the Venetian church façades. For reasons of economy, private palace and villa patrons (most of whom could not afford to complete their residences) had to be satisfied with plaster-covered brick, but, in Palladio's hands, that material also permitted a subtle modulation of light, especially in the villas. The later Vicenza palaces, of the Valmanarana and the Loggia del Capitaniato (both 1565), represent idiosyncratic departures from the classical canon.

The Veneto spawned an unparalleled development of villas after vast drainage projects from the 15th century onwards opened new agricultural ground and encouraged affluent Venetians and citizens of satellite cities to combine an investment in crops with the pleasures of elegant country living extolled in Roman literature. Palladio gave the villa a variety of new forms, most of which featured a central cubic mass with a temple-like entrance and lateral arcaded or colonnaded wings destined for the storage of agricultural produce and equipment (sometimes terminated in towers with dovecotes) derived from the traditional rustic *barchese* of the Veneto. The type is most elegantly realized in Villa Barbaro in Maser (1554/5), for Daniele Barbaro, a scholar and churchman (whose translation of and commentary on Vitruvius was the best in the Renaissance, and was illustrated in part by Palladio), and the contemporary Villa Emo in Fanzolo. Villa Foscari in Malcontenta (1564), which is accessible by water from nearby Venice, seems to have been primarily a leisure retreat, the best known example of which is the Villa Almerico 'La Rotonda' built for a retired cleric on the outskirts of Vicenza (1566–7). The villa was placed on the crown of a hill overlooking the hills and fields from extending stepped Roman porticoes on all four sides. In his treatise, Palladio illustrated it among the palaces, with an elevated dome rather than the existing low saucer dome. Major contemporary Venetian painters, including Paolo Veronese, executed frescoes in the interiors of many of the villas.

Though Palladio's work in Vicenza did not include churches, the support of his patron Daniele Barbaro brought him commissions in Venice. The first was his purest classical work, the cloister of the Convent of the Carità (1560), conceived as a reconstruction in brick of Vitruvius' description of the Roman house. The façade of the Franciscan monastery church, San Francesco della Vigna (c.1564; the church itself had been designed by Jacopo *Sansovino in the 1530s), was an early solution to a dilemma—posed by applying the elements of the Roman temple to the Christian church form that required a high nave and low lateral aisles—which was to be masterfully resolved in the Redentore.

The Benedictine monastery of San Giorgio Maggiore commissioned Palladio to design its church, one of its cloisters, and its refectory. The church project followed the order's mother-church, San Giustina in Padua, with its large choir hidden behind the altar, and an airy, light-filled interior. The façade, surely Palladio's best-known work because of its privileged position directly across the lagoon from the Piazza San Marco, was completed after the architect's death. It does not entirely reflect his intentions: he apparently wanted a large oculus over the portal (it is preserved on the interior) and perhaps a free-standing portico.

The Church of the Redentore is perhaps the architect's most harmonious achievement. Commissioned in 1576 by the Venetian Senate to honour a vow made at the time of a devastating plague, it features a space under the cupola large enough to accommodate all the senators, who established an annual commemorative visit (a pontoon bridge is regularly constructed for one day to gain access to the church, on the island of the Giudecca). Palladio initially projected a central-plan church reminiscent of the Roman Pantheon (a similar design was realized in small scale for the private chapel of Villa Barbaro, 1580), but his sponsors were outvoted by a more conservative majority favouring the traditional longitudinal form. He enriched that heritage with a light-filled and integrated interior inspired by the Roman baths.

Palladio left a large corpus of drawings, most of which are preserved in the library of the Royal Institute of British Architects in London, which help us to define his career. His treatise, *I Quattro Libri dell'Architettura*, published ten years before his death, is richly illustrated with woodcuts. While it treats ancient buildings, orders, and decoration in great detail, it is unique in the Renaissance for its focus on his own secular designs, which he discusses with emphasis on their function and on the special requirements of the clients. Plans and elevations in many of the illustrations differ from the existing buildings, in most cases because the author sought to improve on his original project. Though he discussed ancient temples, he omitted his own churches, perhaps because he had completed only one façade prior to the publication.

Palladio may have been the most imitated architect of all time. His mature classical style, typically known more from editions of his treatise and books illustrating his work than from the originals, exerted a powerful influence on European and American architecture of later centuries, and was even briefly revived by so-called postmodern architects at the end of the 20th century.   JA

Ackerman, James S., *Palladio* (1977, revised edition)
Burns, Howard *et al.*, *The Portico and the Farmhouse* (1975)
Palladio, *I Quattro Libri dell'Architettura* (1570; English translation by Robert Tavernor and Richard Schofield, 1997)
Puppi, Lionello, *Andrea Palladio* (edition revised by Donata Battilotti,1999; English edition, 1975)

Pani, Mario (1911–193) Mexican architect who studied in Paris at the Ecole des Beaux-Arts. His contribution consisted in his innovative approach to problem-solving, rather than in the use of new materials or forms. He sought maximum benefit for users, designing the first housing complex of more than a thousand dwellings, the Centro Urbano Presidente Alemán (1949), followed by the Benito Juárez (1952) and Nonoalco Tlatelolco (1964) complexes. He made a foray into hospital building with the Perote tuberculosis hospital, also designing the National Teacher Training College and the National Conservatory for Music. In his urban planning workshop he drew up a large number of regional plans, and, as a means of rationalizing the growth of cities, designed the first *supermanzanas*—or super blocks. Foremost among these was the University of Mexico Campus (1949–52), designed in collaboration with Enrique del Moral (1906–87).

He founded and edited the magazine *Arquitectura/Mexico*, 1948–76.

LNM (trans. KL)

Papworth, John Buonarotti (1775–1847) English architect. A prolific architect with a large country-house practice, much of it as a skilful decorator, landscape gardener and illustrator, Papworth also specialized in shop fronts. He laid out the Brockwell estate, Dulwich (1825–30), and worked extensively elsewhere in London, notably in Clapham. In Cheltenham, he worked on the Montpellier estate, laid out Lansdowne Place and Crescent (1825–9), and built houses and churches as well. Papworth's sons were the architects John Woody Papworth (1820–70) and Wyatt Papworth (1822–94) who founded the Architectural Publication Society and edited its

Dictionary. His brothers Thomas (1773–1814) and George (1781–1855) Papworth were also architects, the latter working successfully in Ireland.　APQ

pargeting Plastering, more commonly patterning in plasterwork. Patterned pargeting is characteristic of England's eastern counties and much practised on framed buildings from the late Middle Ages until the present. Regular patterns were applied by scraping a comb over the freshly laid surface to produce incised herringbones or shells. More ingeniously the plaster was modelled to make overall patterns of tendrils, foliage, figures, symbols, and achievements of arms. Nowhere better illustrates these possibilities than the Sun Inn, Saffron Walden, Essex. While much pargeting is modern, this is often a consequence of renewal, and old work may be found hidden under layers of limewash.　APQ

parish churches In England these number at least 16,000, more than half of which date from 1700 onwards. They are unsurpassed in quantity and diversity, but not always in quality, by any European country.

The earliest churches (see ENGLAND (ANGLO-SAXON)) are of two types. The south-eastern group, exemplified by Bradwell-Juxta-Mare (c.654), have apsidal *chancels, separated from the nave by a set of arches. The northern type, such as Monkwearmouth (completed c.678), has straight-ended chancels. These tall, narrow churches, forlorn today, can never have been splendid architecture, but their interiors must have been dazzling, the walls covered with purple hangings, the altars carrying gold and silver ornaments inset with precious stones. On the exterior, the full development of *long-and-short work is not seen until the 10th century, at Earl's Barton and Barton-upon-Humber.

Following the Norman Conquest there was a very significant increase in church building, in the English version of the *Romanesque (initially using the thick wall form of construction). The west façade now became an elaborate feature, particularly the highly sculptured doorways, which by the end of the period could be extremely lavish, as at Iffley, or Tutbury (both c.1170). In general, parish churches follow, although usually with a time lag, the sequence of *Gothic cathedral architecture—*Early English, *Decorated, and *Perpendicular. The grandest churches date from the Perpendicular period, notable for their imposing towers (particularly in Somerset), their extensive use of glass, and the variety of timber roofs (such as the *hammerbeam roof of St Wendreda, March, Cambridgeshire).

Church building came almost to a halt with the Reformation (1530ff.), but when it revived it did so with the finest examples of parish churches ever built. From about 1672, *Wren rebuilt over fifty churches for the City of London. Most were built on restricted sites, offering little scope for impressive elevations, and requiring fairly straightforward plans. Wren therefore concentrated on the steeples, using a great variety of forms: convex (St Magnus the Martyr, 1671–6), concave (St Martin, Ludgate, 1677–84), telescopic (St Bride, 1671–8), or highly elaborate (St Mary-le-Bow, 1670–80). London was further favoured by the 'Queen Anne' Act (1711) for building fifty new churches in London, which resulted in some of the finest works by *Archer, *Gibbs, and *Hawksmoor.

There followed another relatively quiet period for church building until the *Commissioners' churches initiated by the Church Building Act of 1818. All that was required was an economically constructed preaching box, so that only the portico and the spire offered an architectural opportunity. Consequently, although nearly every famous architect of the period (*Soane, *Nash, *Barry, *Smirke) built one of these churches, the results are far from inspiring.

By the 1830s, many medieval parish churches were mouldering into ruin. Their rescue by restorers such as

Sir Giles Gilbert *Scott turned out to be problematic, but an eventual stimulus to the movement for *conservation. But for a generation, from about 1840, the new churches of the *Gothic Revival attracted the most eminent architects of the period, such as *Pugin, *Butterfield, *Street, and *Pearson. However, perhaps the most sensitive works occur in the next period: *Bodley's Hoar Cross (1876) and *Comper's St Mary, Wellingborough (1908).

The 20th century has seen a surprising continuation of church building, particularly after 1945. Some churches, such as St Paul's, Bow Common (Maguire and Murray, 1958–60), were planned for the new liturgy, involving a central altar; others followed the traditional liturgy, while being architecturally inventive, such as the work of *Goodhart-Rendel or *Spence.   PG

  Bond, F(rancis), *An Introduction to English Church Architecture* (1913)

Parkin, John B., Associates Canadian architects.
International Style Modernism in Canada is best represented by the work of the Toronto firm of John B. Parkin Associates. Business partner John B. Parkin (1911–75) and design partner John C. Parkin (1922–8, unrelated), who studied with Gropius at Harvard, developed Canada's largest (with 180 staff) and most successful firm in the 1950s and 1960s. Their Headquarters of the Ontario Association of Architects, Toronto (1953–4), and the Ortho Pharmaceutical Plant and Office, Don Mills, Ontario (1955–6), are uncompromisingly rectilinear, exquisitely detailed, transparent, and clearly expressive of their structure. The Toronto-Dominion Centre, Toronto (with Ludwig Mies van der Rohe and Bregmann and Hamann, 1963–9), clustered two tall towers (subsequently expanded to five) and a low banking pavilion in perhaps the most classic statement of the International Style skyscraper aesthetic built anywhere.

The crisp and spartan black (bronzed) glass curtain walls and steel structures, enhanced with exposed I-beams painted black, feature an asymmetrical but balanced composition that is proportioned on a 1.5 metre square (5 foot square) module. This fundamental solution is a thing of great beauty. Sadly it led to countless inferior imitations—boxy and boring steel-and-glass towers that ultimately proved the undoing of international Modernism.   HK

Parler family The name of Parler first appeared in the mid 14th century, probably from Cologne, to exert a decisive influence on the transition to 'late' Gothic in European architecture.

The first Parler we hear of is **Heinrich** (b.c.1300), at work on the church at Schwäbisch Gmünd, perhaps on the nave in the 1330s, certainly on the new chancel in 1351. He set out a spacious hall, supported by internal buttresses and great smooth cylindrical columns, and filled with light.

Of Heinrich's three sons, it was the youngest, **Peter** (c.1333–99), who in 1356 took charge of the cathedral at Prague. He was to complete and ornament the apsed chancel and to start on the transept and a huge south tower set to dominate the city. The chancel is a turning-point in the shift to the emphasis on the diagonal, with the elegantly undulating arcade of the triforium, the diagonally set blank arches above, and the parallel diagonal ribs on the continuous vault of 1385. He vaulted St Wenceslaus' chapel with a star of ribs forming a dome, and he used hanging skeleton ribs in the sacristy and the south porch. If any of this was learnt, it must have been from English churches such as Bristol and Wells.

Peter can be seen at work elsewhere in Prague, above all in the engineering of the Charles Bridge (1357–66) with another elegant vault in its eastern gate tower. Between 1360 and 1378 he built the chancel of the church at Kolín, a basilican addition to a classic hall nave of about 1280, with a four-sided apse linked by an ingeniously vaulted ambulatory to a ring of five chapels. Peter died in 1399, and is commemorated among kings and bishops by a portrait bust in his cathedral triforium. His influence, and that of his family, was to extend all over central Europe.   DBK

Líbal, D., entries in Legner, A. (ed.), *Die Parler und der schöne Stil* (1978/80)

Passalacqua, Pietro (active 1706–48) Italian architect. For one of the seven ancient pilgrimage churches, S. Croce in Gerusalemme, Passalacqua was probably the designer of the impressive, sharply convex porch, articulated by giant pilasters (1741–4) and clad in a light-coloured, sharply modelled travertine. Unusually the porch, possibly used as a Benediction loggia, is an oval with its long axis at right angles to the main body of the church. S. Croce marks the end of an era, as it is the last Baroque façade in Rome.   PG

patera A round or occasionally oval ornament in shallow relief, often decorated with acanthus leaves or rose petals. Pateras decorate the metopes of some Greek and Roman Doric friezes, and also the capitals. Similarly they decorate the space between the modillions under Corinthian cornices, and thus came into wide use for plaster cornices generally.   APQ

pattern books These were originally intended to provide builders and craftsmen with copies of architectural elements, such as the orders, rather than to advance new ideas about architecture, as in the works of *Serlio or de *Vries. Among the first and the most successful was *Practical Architecture* (William Halfpenny, *c*.1724). However, in later books both the Halfpenny family and Batty Langley (1696–1751), an equally prolific author of pattern books, popularized new ideas in the vanguard of taste, by publishing designs for *Gothick and *Chinoiserie.   PG

Pautre, Antoine Le (1621–81) French architect. After various minor works in Paris, Le Pautre published *Desseins de plusieurs palais* (1652–3), engravings of his own designs and some ideal projects showing a talent for spatial complexity and unusual combinations of space, a talent he was soon able to employ in a scheme which is a masterpiece by any standard.

His design for the Hôtel de Beauvais (1660) is a brilliant solution to the problem of dealing with a very irregular site. On the ground floor a long *porte cochère* leads through the deep main block (used as shops) to a staircase. On the first floor, the visitor encounters Le Pautre's masterstroke: a gallery, a salon, and a regularly shaped garden, all on a layout quite different from that of the lower floor. This spatial tour de force more than compensates for the ordinariness of the detailing of the façades.   PG

pavilion A term with a wide meaning, embracing many architectural forms and styles. A pavilion may be a tent, a temporary building, an ornamental building, one of light construction for occasional use in a garden, park or sports ground, or a projecting part of a building, distinguished by its height or unusual relationship to the whole, such as terminating a wing. As a temporary building, pavilions house exhibitions or their specific exhibits, such as *Mies van der Rohe's ideological Modern Movement German Pavilion at the Barcelona Exhibition (1929); similarly Richard Rogers' Millennium Dome, London (1999–2000), is a pavilion, despite being a tent larger than ever a tent was before. These buildings were exhibits in their own right, but modesty is more typical. Garden pavilions are an essential part of a formalized landscape, and, however modest in size, are meant to attract. Like a banqueting house, they are designed for pleasure, both to be looked at and looked from, their style a topic of comment. A sports pavilion, meanwhile, must serve the needs of changing rooms, club house, and viewing platform. Thomas Verity's Pavilion at Lord's Cricket Ground, London (1889–90), accommodates a committee room and members' writing room as well as two viewing balconies within a stately building of multicoloured terracotta, but a traditional sports pavilion is much simpler, typically with white-painted weatherboarding and a prominent verandah beneath an overall pitched roof surmounted by a clock that does not work. In a public park, this form is varied and also embraces the needs for refreshment and lavatory.

As a projecting part of an architectural *ensemble*, it may take the form of a high centrepiece, as do the facing Pavillon du Roi and Pavillon de la Reine in the former Place Royale, now Place des Vosges, Paris (begun 1605), but more usually serve as terminal blocks to a long range of building, as do the two-bay projecting domed pavilions of *Flitcroft's Wentworth Woodhouse, Yorkshire (c.1735–70). François *Mansart cleverly completed his Château de Balleroy, Normandy (c.1626), by flanking the *corps de logis* with a pair of detached pavilions, intended for servants, in the place of attached projecting wings. His nephew *Hardouin-Mansart went one better at the Château de Marly (begun 1679), where Louis XIV's *corps de logis* faces on to formal lake and gardens graced by two very separate rows of six pavilions, designed for courtiers so as to maintain royal privacy.   APQ

Paxton, Sir Joseph (1801–65) English gardener and architect. In 1826 Paxton became the Duke of Devonshire's garden superintendent at Chatsworth, Derbyshire. Here he built the Great Stove (1836–40, demolished), a large greenhouse using small flat panes of glass set into a ridge and furrow pattern so as to produce curved sides. His giant lily house was a prototype for some of the details of the Crystal Palace. In about 1839–41 he laid out Edensor near Chatsworth, followed by Birkenhead Park, Cheshire (1843–7).

Prompted by the impossibility of manufacturing enough bricks required for a building of its great size in time, Paxton's design for the Great Exhibition of 1851 used prefabricated cast-iron trusses and framing, incorporating guiding rails to enable its speedy erection, and mass-produced sheets of glass of hitherto unachieved dimensions. Crystal Palace, re-assembled at Sydenham (burnt down 1936), was later heralded as the world's first modern building, because of its materials, and the mass-production and prefabrication of its parts.   APQ

Chadwick, G. F., *The Works of Sir Joseph Paxton 1803–65* (1961)

Pearce, Sir Edward Lovett (c.1699–1733) Ireland's earliest exponent of Palladian architecture. An Englishman, Pearce arrived in Dublin c.1726 after extensive travel in Europe, and in 1730 became Surveyor General.

His earliest known Irish work was his collaboration with Italian architect Alessandro Galilei in the design of Castletown House, Co. Kildare. In 1728, despite his relative inexperience, he was commissioned to design the new Parliament House for Dublin (now the Bank of Ireland). He quickly established a significant private practice, and among the domestic buildings attributed to him are the south façade of Drumcondra House, Co. Dublin (1727), Cashel Palace, Co. Tipperary (begun 1729), and Bellamont Forest, Co. Cavan (c.1730), as well as a number of town houses in Dublin. Following his sudden, untimely death, his practice passed to his assistant, Richard *Castle.   RM

Pearson, John Loughborough (1817–97) English architect. More varied than Butterfield, Scott, and Street, Pearson's churches are distinguished by faultless massing, effortless vaulting, mysterious interiors, and proportions owing much to Classicism, despite close adherence to Gothic precedent. He founded his style on the great northern churches, and later those of

Normandy. His practice quickly expanded from 1843, notably at Llangasty Talyllyn, Brecknockshire, where he built a church and Treberfydd House (1849–51). *Ruskin and foreign travel influenced vigorous church designs (begun 1857) at Daylesford, Gloucestershire, and Scorborough and Dalton Holme, East Yorkshire. His second London church, St Peter, Vauxhall (1860–64), exploited brick vaulting. His masterpiece, St Augustine, Kilburn (1870–97), a wonderful amalgam of Gothic forms woven into a rational plan, was followed by the equally magnificent St John's, Red Lion Square, Holborn (1875–8, demolished), St Michael's, Croydon (1880–81), St Stephen's, Bournemouth (1883–1908), and Truro Cathedral, Cornwall (1880–1910). His prolific career kept abreast of the developing *Gothic Revival during its period of greatest influence, setting him among its most distinguished architects.   APQ

Quiney, A., *John Loughborough Pearson* (1979)

pedestal A tall block in classical architecture which carries a column, pilaster, statue, or vase. While each order had a specific form of pedestal, and this was governed by proportion, in practice pedestals had the great advantage of raising an order that was applied to a storey so that it would fit.   APQ

pediment A formalized classical gable. A broken pediment is one whose crowning cornice is omitted at the apex; an open pediment is one the centre of whose base is omitted; a segmental pediment is one whose crowning cornice forms a segment of a circle; and a swan-neck pediment is one whose crowning cornice is not only broken but also in the form of two ogee curves terminating in volutes.   APQ

Pei, Ieoh Ming (1917–) Chinese-born architect. After teaching at Harvard under *Gropius, Pei left in 1948 to work as the in-house architect for Webb and Knapp, a real estate corporation in New York. For

almost two decades, he not only designed many large-scale architectural and planning projects across the United States, but also mastered his marketing skills with high-profile clients. Both skills proved catalytic when in 1966 Pei converted the Webb and Knapp architectural division to I. M. Pei and Partners in partnership with Henry Cobb, Araldo Cossutta, and Eason Leonard, to become one of the most successful architectural practices of the second half of the 20th century.

As a visionary and an effective salesman, Pei's strategy was to attract both institutional and corporate clients internationally by being attentive to high quality design buildings and developing an expertise on the efficiency and engineering of the tall building. With regards to the design, Pei's architecture has been characterized by clarity of form, attention to natural light and materials. Since the 1960s he explored the formal possibilities of poured concrete and masonry, focusing on the effects of light and space. These studies were consolidated to a theory of form in the design for the East Building of the National Gallery of Art in Washington (1968–78). Consequently the firm's expertise in museum design culminated in the commission for the Louvre extension (1983–9). To substantiate their expertise in the tall office building, the firm has been supported by a full in-house team of structural engineers, who have made several contributions in the field of curtain-wall design using innovative materials and techniques. One of Pei's most celebrated tall buildings is the Bank of China in Hong Kong (1982–9).

In 1989 he changed the name of the firm to Pei, Cobb, Freed and Partners and retired to concentrate on choice projects, such as the Four Seasons Hotel in New York (1989–93), the Rock and Roll Hall of Fame in Cleveland, Ohio, and various international museums. At the dusk of his career, it would be fair to assess that Pei's approach to buildings being the result of the architect's artistic creation in the city places him among the late masters of International Modernism. VM

Pelli, Cesar (1926–) Argentinian-born architect. His work exemplifies a particularly US vision for late-20th-century architecture—bold and formal volumes defined by the ubiquitous frame of modern structures and sheathed in richly textured skins of contemporary materials. Free from ideological responsibilities, they serve a great diversity of corporate and institutional clients, while reaffirming the positivism of judicious urban design and functional planning.

His first major design was the well-received Pacific Design Centre, Los Angeles (1972). In 1977, he founded Cesar Pelli and Associates, a staggeringly prolific design practice responsible for the design of dozens of high profile and many enormous buildings, including: the expansion of the Museum of Modern Art (1977–84) and the World Financial Centre (1981–7), both New York City; the highly regarded Herring Hall at Rice University in Houston (1982–4) and several other university buildings; the North Terminal of Reagan Washington National Airport (1989–97); the Performing Arts Centre of Miami, Florida (1995–2005); and many prominent office towers, including the ponderous Canary Wharf Building in London (1986), the International Finance Centre in Hong Kong (1996–2004), culminating in the gigantic Petronas Towers in Kuala Lumpur, Malaysia (1992–7, 994,062 sq m or 10,700,364 sq ft). JF

pendant A hanging decorative feature. In timber roofs, it may be the lower part of a timber that separates barge-boards, the upper part rising over the roof as a finial. In a stone-vaulted roof, a pendant boss may hang well below the level of a vault or from whatever it is suspended, as in the Divinity School, Oxford University (c.1450–87), and Henry VII's Chapel,

Westminster Abbey (1503–52). Common in late Gothic, especially in France, pendants are an integral part of the prolix decoration of the porch of Notre-Dame, Alençon (c.1510). Tudor and Jacobean plaster ceilings commonly sport them in a more mundane context. APQ

pendentive The triangular section of a vault, with the apex resting on a pier, and the base supporting the drum of a *dome, which enables a dome to be built over a square, effecting a smoother transition than is achieved by the *squinch. Typical of *Byzantine architecture (at Hagia Sophia, the pendentives are on a gigantic scale, rising 18 m (60 ft) vertically), it is occasionally used in the *Romanesque, as in the Cathedral of Saint-Front, Périgueux, and frequently in the Baroque. Unusual versions of the pendentive are the superimposed pendentives founded in many 15th-century churches in Moldavia; and *Vittone's gouged-out pendentives, in the chapel of the Albergo di Carita at Carignano (1744) and the church of S. Maria in Piazza in Turin (1751–4). PG

Percier, Charles (1764–1838) and **Fontaine, Pierre-François-Léonard** (1762–1854) French neoclassical architects and decorators. They trained at the Royal Academy school and in Rome (1786) and published their *Palais, maisons et autres édifices modernes dessinés à Rome* in 1798. Under Napoleon I they evolved the *style Empire*, serving the First Consul from 1799. By 1801 Percier and Fontaine were executing their repetitive design for the façades along the Rue de Rivoli, parallel to the wings of the Louvre, which they were extending to join the Tuileries. Having published their influential *Recueil de décorations intérieures* in 1801, they exercised their particular talent in that medium at Malmaison and several former royal palaces, most notably inside and outside the Tuileries where their refined variation on the Roman triumphal arch (Arc du

Carrousel, 1806) alone survives. Fontaine also worked extensively for the restored Bourbons, notably on the *Chapelle Expiatoire* dedicated to Louis XVI, the restoration of Versailles, the Elysée palace, and the Palais Royale, to which he added the glazed Galérie d'Orléans (1829). CT

peristyle In classical architecture a range of columns surrounding a building. The *tholos at Delphi (*c*.390 BC) has the remains of a peristyle around a circular building, but it may equally surround a rectangular building, such as the slightly later tomb of Mausolus at Helicarnassus, or an open space such as a garden. APQ

Perpendicular The last style of English *Gothic, flourishing from the middle of the 14th century, and characterized by the repetition of vertical traceried panels, large windows, wide light interiors, and vaults decorated with *liernes and *tiercerons. Nowhere better exemplifies the effectiveness of this essentially repetitive form than the choir of Gloucester Cathedral (*c*.1337–57), whose *Norman structure hides behind a grid of tall rectangles with foiled tracery that rise up to a new vault, webbed with liernes and tiercerons, punctuated by carved bosses, that equally obscure the bay-by-bay divisions. This terminates in a huge east window that continues the traceried forms practically to the ground. The airiness of its effect is repeated in such prosperous town churches as St Nicholas, King's Lynn (complete by 1419), which, as well as a large area of glass, has extremely thin piers dividing its nave and aisles, all depending on a desire to preach to a large congregation, with little space reserved for ritual. Extremely tall church towers, such as those of Boston (begun *c*.1425–30) and Louth (*c*.1440–1515), Lincolnshire, elaborate the decorative possibilities of Perpendicular in a show of civic pride. An outstanding series of towers, exquisite in composition and detail, is to be found in Somerset, numbering about sixty in all.

The fan vault, as initiated in the cloisters at Gloucester (*c*.1351–71), rises from each wall shaft as a concave traceried cone that spreads out fan-wise to meet its neighbours. The fan vault had a long life, appearing at the end of the Middle Ages at King's College Chapel, Cambridge (1446–1515), and being convincingly revived for the hall staircase at Christ Church, Oxford (*c*.1640). At the Divinity School, Oxford (*c*.1450–87), and Henry VII's Chapel, Westminster Abbey (1503–52), two further vaults marry the decorative effect of the fan vault with an idea taken from timber roofs in which pendants hang down from its surface, defying gravity, and further break up the sense of bay-by-bay division. PG / APQ

Perrault, Claude (1613–88) French architect and theorist, leader of the 'Moderns' as distinct from the 'Ancients' who promoted traditional precepts. Commissioned with the official translation of Vitruvius, he was appointed in 1667 with L. *Le Vau and C. Le Brun to devise the definitive plan for the completion of the Louvre. There is considerable evidence that Perrault was primarily responsible for the executed project—not least for the considerations of practicality and modern usage, which were at least as important as received precept in its conception. His pronouncements in *L'Ordonnance des Cinq Espèces de Colonnes* (1683) challenged the idea of an absolute standard of beauty manifest in proportions. CT

Perret, Auguste (1874–1954) A leading French architect and building contractor in the first half of the 20th century, and an early advocate of reinforced concrete construction. He contributed a distinct aesthetic vision and model of professional practice to the architectural discipline, rooted in a conviction of the importance of a modern classicist project and its socio-political implications for cultural continuity. His intellectual impulses were allied to a generation of artists and writers who shared an allegiance to a classicist ideal—notably Paul Valéry—seeking to resolve the conflict between the more stable aspirations of French culture and the transitory processes of change and innovation.

Perret was both heir to the 19th-century structural rationalist theories of *Viollet-le-Duc, de Baudot, Guadet, and Choisy, and precursor of the progressive explorations of the Modern Movement, especially through his mentoring relationship with the young *Le Corbusier. Sometimes grouped with *Behrens, *Wright, and Otto *Wagner as part of a great generation of architectural innovators, Perret made a significant contribution to the technological advancement and architectural explorations of the 20th century.

Working with his brothers Gustave and Claude in Perret Frères, a family construction business inherited from their father, Perret extended the potential of reinforced concrete, elevating a coarse material primarily used in engineering projects to a highly refined medium. With a keen sense of building typology, he designed over 350 projects, mainly in Paris and North Africa, including churches, theatres, artists' studios, museums, industrial projects, and large-scale urban development. Especially between the two world wars, his stature as a major influence on French modern architecture was broadly recognized in such journals as *L'Architecture d'aujourd'hui*, *L'Architecture vivant*, and *Techniques et Architecture*, where he helped shape contemporary debates on volume, structure, and material.

The Perrets' first concrete frame building was the apartment block at 25 bis rue Franklin in Paris (1904), in which the skeletal frame was clearly revealed on the façade, emphasized by a ceramic tile covering in patterns. In the parking garage on the rue de Ponthieu (1906), Perret demonstrated his ability to achieve the maximum architectural value in even a modest

Notre Dame du Raincy, Paris (Auguste Perret, 1922–4)

structure through his use of proportion, spatial composition, and the regulating discipline of the structural frame.

In the Théatre des Champs Elysées (1911–13) Perret produced a work that embodied the modernist Classicism of Parisian artistic culture. In the highly acclaimed church of Notre Dame du Raincy (1922–4), Perret used concrete to reinterpret the typology of the French Greco-Gothic church, leaving the material unclad while exploiting its tensile strength in slender columns, surrounding the whole with curtain walls containing stained glass. Here Perret gave radical demonstration of his pioneering intentions to continue the French building tradition with a new material.

In another apartment block at 51–5 rue Raynouard (1929–32), Perret exhibited his attachment to the humanistic form of the traditional French window (in contrast to Le Corbusier's *fenêtre en longueur*), celebrating the understated urban domesticity of the Parisian 16th *arrondissement* in his own penthouse apartment. The Musée des Travaux Publics on the Trocadéro hill in Paris (1936–48) is representative of his search for a new French architectural order appropriate to concrete. Perret's craft precision in handling concrete is evident throughout in the elegant detailing, colouring, and texture. The Mobilier National (1946), a national furniture warehouse and restoration studio, is yet another expression of Perret's search for a formal architectural vocabulary, where he elevates the basic conservational programme to the form of a *hôtel particulier*.

Perret's later works were an extension of his early urban explorations. Most significantly, he was responsible for the post-war reconstruction of Le Havre (1949–56), working with a team of devoted students intent on carrying out his theories on a large scale. Perret himself was responsible for the town square and the centrally planned church of St Joseph (1952), which rises like a beacon on the Normandy coastline.

Perret's work is enigmatic and cerebral, balanced between the principles of constructional economy and a modernist pursuit of the classical project. He is therefore an architect whose clarity of form may be said to disguise the subtlety of his intent. He approached the composition of a building as analogous to writing poetry: it is a highly disciplined process of repetition and syntactical distillation, controlled by the constraints of rhythm and cultural habit. This cultural and formal intention is outlined in Perret's laconic aphorisms, many of them published in 1952 as a *Contribution à une théorie de l'architecture*.   KMB

Britton, K., *Auguste Perret* (2001)
Collins, P(eter), *Concrete: The Vision of a New Architecture* (1959)

Perronet, Jean-Rodolphe (1708–94) French civil engineer and writer, and a master of bridge design. He used masonry to create very slender piers, to minimize resistance to water flowing under a bridge, and the piers supported extremely flat arches to ease the movement of people over the bridge. These were the principles of design for his bridge at Neuilly-sur-Seine (1774), which is widely recognized as one of the most graceful stone bridges ever built. In 1788 he began work on the Pont Louis XVI in Paris, completed in 1791, and now known as the Pont de la Concorde. It is acknowledged as his most outstanding work.   BC

Persius, Friedrich Ludwig (1803–45) German architect, *Schinkel's most accomplished and influential student. In addition to his important contributions to Schinkel's Schloss Glienicke (1824–6) and Schloss Babelsberg, Persius' villa designs as court architect at Potsdam include Villa Jacobs (1836), Villa Persius (1837–8), Villa Illaire (1843–6), and a house for the court gardener Sello (1841–2). Inspired by Schinkel's interest in the rural vernacular architecture of Italy, these projects are characterized by asymmetrical cubic massing, crisp stucco exterior treatment, planar surfaces, and an intimate interplay between architecture and landscape. Persius' designs for the Heilandskirche in Sakrow (1841–4) and Friedenskirche in Potsdam (begun 1843), both evoking early Christian basilicas, were important elements in the deliberate transformation of the Potsdam area into a picturesque architectural landscape centred on the Havel river.   AN

Peru has remains of important pre-Hispanic cultures such as the Chavin, Paracas, Moche, Nazca, and above all the Inca sites at Cuzco and Machu Pichu. The viceroyalty of Peru set up its capital in Lima, constructing civic buildings such as the Viceroy's Palace and the Callao fort (1584), both by Francisco *Becerra, who also began the Cathedral, which includes the earliest vault in Peru, while the Cathedral of Cuzco was supervised by Juan Miguel de Veramendi. Other buildings were the Royal Hospitals of San Andrés (1556) and of Santa Ana, the latter with a cruciform ground plan, and the colleges of Santo Tomas, with a circular cloister, and San Bernardo (17th century).

The robust aspect of the buildings, and the construction methods, were influenced by the need to resist earthquakes. In Cuzco, Diego Martínez de Oviedo built the famous Claustro de la Merced (1669), and Juan Bautista Egidiano the Iglesia de la Compañia (1651–68), with towers built into the façade. In Lima, the Baroque church of San Francisco (1657–74), by Constantino de Vasconcelos, inaugurated the 'quincha' (a cane-and-plaster fabric) system designed to allow the creation of wide indoor spaces simulating vaults and cupolas but without danger of collapse.

The sculpted portals of the churches of La Merced (1697–1704) and San Agustín (1720) have ornate Baroque carvings, a style which also spread to the high plateau region where the highly ornate decorations acquired a flattened or 'mestizo' character, as in the Cathedral of Puno (1757) by Simón de Astola, and the portals of the Iglesia de la Compañia, Arequipa (1698). The nuns' convents have lateral twin portals and a latticed choir, as at Santa Catalina, Cuzco (c.1651), and Santa Rosa de las Monjas, Lima (1704–8). The 18th-century Palacio de Torre Tagle, an example of the Lima style of residential building, has rooms on two levels around a courtyard and protruding box-shaped

Cuzco Cathedral, Peru (Juan Miguel de Veramendi, 1560ff.)

latticed balconies in the Andalusian style. Similar features are found in the houses of Almirante and los Marqueses de Casa Concha in Cuzco, and in others in Arequipa, Trujillo, and Ayacucho. Buildings constructed in the neoclassical style during the period of independence include the Cathedral of Arequipa (1834–47) by Lucas Poblete, and official buildings in Lima such as the Dos de Mayo hospital by Mateo Graziani (1869–75), and the Post Office (1895) by Nicolás de Piérola. Railway stations were built in the eclectic style, and there are a number of structures attributed to Gustave Eiffel. Noteworthy developments in the 20th century include the social architecture of Fernando Belaunde Terry and the houses built by Juvenal Baraco.   LNM (trans. KL)

Peruzzi, Baldassare (1481–1536) Italian painter and architect. The Villa Chigi (now Farnesina) in Rome (1505/6) marks his emergence as an independent designer displaying a mastery of spatial organization.

Designing the new basilica of St Peter's in the Vatican occupied much of his career and brought him into contact with *Bramante. A large corpus of surviving drawings provides evidence for this and other unrealized projects; these demonstrate Peruzzi's inventiveness and profound knowledge of antiquity, and proved highly influential during and after his lifetime. Peruzzi realized two churches in Carpi and several projects in Bologna, including the Ghisilardi Chapel, San Domenico (1525).

He returned to his native Siena following the Sack of Rome in 1527, where he became architect to the Republic and *capomaestro* of the Duomo. Siena's refortified walls and bastions are the most visible reminders of his work there. During the 1530s Peruzzi resumed work as co-architect of St Peter's with Antonio da *Sangallo the Younger. His dynamic masterwork, the Palazzo Massimo alle Colonne in Rome (begun 1532), synthesizes his earlier design explorations. A centred Doric portico punctuates the distinctive curving façade. Internally, the axial progression leading to one edge of the main courtyard proved an ingenious method for treating the irregular site. ACH

Peyre, Marie-Joseph (1730–85) French architect. From his studies in Rome (1753), he drew from ancient Roman architecture, particularly the *baths, the ideas of immense scale, and the co-relation of top-lighting and plan, ingeniously combined with disengaged columns forming a screen in front of rather low façades. Returning to Paris, he had only three significant commissions for the rest of his career. His first, the Hôtel Leprêtre de Neubourg (1762, destroyed), was an extremely modest house, only seven bays wide, whose only sign of originality was the six-column screen in front of the central three bays. However, it is the first, if somewhat tentative, appearance of *neoclassicism in France. If his projected palace (1763) for the Prince de Condé, which was much closer to his Roman studies than the Hôtel Leprêtre, had been built, it would have been much easier to assess how effective his schemes would have been in practice. His only other realized scheme, the Théâtre de France, Paris (now the Théâtre de l'Odéon, completed 1782), was designed with de *Wailly, their respective contributions being difficult to identify. Innovative in other respects, the only apparent link with the visionary schemes of his Roman years was the screen of eight plain Tuscan columns which covered almost the entire façade.

As a compensation for this rather disappointing outcome, the publication of his *Oeuvres d'architecture* (in 1765), including twelve of his projects, brought him great renown among neoclassical architects. PG

photography, architectural Ever since the announcement of the first viable photographic process in 1839, photography has profoundly influenced architectural practice and study. The camera was soon used to record endangered monuments, an early instance being the French Mission Héliographique established in 1851, partly as an aid to faithful restoration. No longer restricted to laborious and often inaccurate sketching, architects could now readily acquire 'truthful' images of 'almost every style under the sun' supplied in their thousands by large topographical view-making firms such as the Florentine Fratelli Alinari who concentrated overwhelmingly on the great architecture of the past. The ubiquity of such imagery not only fuelled the historical revivalism and *Eclecticism that characterized late-19th-century architecture but also facilitated the new form of comparative architectural history seen in works by James Fergusson, who made use of original photographs tipped into his publications as well as engravings drawn from photographs, and in Banister Fletcher.

During the 1860s specialist firms sprang up to record the contemporary building boom, one of the most prolific being Bedford Lemere and Co. of London. Taken on large glass plates, its photographs were typical in being sharply defined, matter-of-fact records that, due to the long exposures required, were devoid of people. Two creative exceptions to this norm at the turn of the century were Eugène Atget's haunting documentation of the everyday details of pre-Haussmann Parisian architecture and Frederick Evans' impressionistic renderings of English cathedrals.

From the late 1880s onwards the production and dissemination of architectural photographs were revolutionized by the introduction of half-tone printing, which for the first time allowed photographs to be readily reproduced in books and journals, thus paving the way for the camera to become the pre-eminent means of architectural communication. Commissioned by magazines such as the *Architectural Review* that had been founded to exploit this new technology, architectural photographers enjoyed a greater demand for their work, which was henceforth seen by a larger audience not in its original form but in printed reproduction. It was only in the 1920s, however, with the advent of Modernism, which brought architecture and photography into closer alliance than ever before, that architectural photography was aesthetically transformed. Architectural photographers such as America's Fay Sturtevant Lincoln and Hedrich-Blessing, Holland's Jan Kamman, and Hungary's Zoltan Seidner soon adopted the techniques of what was dubbed the 'New Photography'—worm's and bird's eye views; changes in scale; geometrical abstraction; and strong contrasts of light and dark—to photograph buildings more dynamically, and particularly to proselytize for modernist architecture. Highly influential in this respect were the dramatic images of the white, virginal forms of modernist buildings bathed in perennial sunlight composed by Dell and Wainwright, the *Architectural Review*'s official photographers from 1929 to 1946. These drew criticism for fabricating a utopian dream and engendering monochromatic architecture, even though many modernist buildings were in fact coloured.

After World War II, photographers such as America's Ezra Stoller helped to establish Modernism as the new architectural orthodoxy. At the same time architectural photography became a more protean genre metamorphosing into lifestyle at one extreme—Julius Shulman's evocative coverage of California's Case Study houses between 1945 and 1967 is a significant example—and a wider concern with the built environment on the other, as evidenced by Gabriele Basilico's urban studies. In England, Edwin Smith's photographs of historical architecture were part of a wider revival of interest in the picturesque, while Eric de Maré lauded the *functional tradition of early industrial buildings. In Germany, Bernd and Hilla Becher similarly photographed industrial structures, but in a dispassionate, typological manner that brought architectural photography within the ambit of the art gallery.

For a short period, principally during the 1960s, there was a reaction against mainstream architectural photography's preference for formal abstraction at the expense of showing how people actually experienced buildings. Taking their cue from photojournalism and contemporary street photography and employing new smaller-format cameras and faster films, photographers like Violette Cornelius in Holland and John Donat in Britain sought to portray buildings in use rather than attempting to recapture the purity of the architect's original intention, as photographers such as Stoller were concerned to do. In the 1970s the widespread adoption of colour photography, which had hitherto been little used, abruptly ended this reportage

713

movement, since colour film's slow speeds militated against the inclusion of people and placed renewed emphasis on architecture's more formal qualities. Arguably this explosion of colour imagery contributed to the emergence of postmodernism. Certainly it hastened the commissioning of photography by architects themselves rather than magazines, thus provoking allegations that the pictures represent eye-catching advertising, not independent analysis. The role of the photographer, and the fear that architecture is overly concerned with being photogenic, are not new issues but ones being debated more intensely today in the wake of a digital revolution that is radically reshaping the genre. Not only has it afforded the photographer increased manipulative possibilities and greater freedom to explore buildings in context and use, but it has also allowed unparalleled access to imagery of the world's architecture via the web.   RE

Elwall, R., *Building with Light: the international history of architectural photography* (2004)

Piacentini, Marcello (1881–1960) Italian

architect, urban planner, and critic who became the most powerful figure in Italian architectural culture during the Fascist period (1922–43). In 1921 he founded *Architettura e Arti Decorative* with Gustavo Giovannoni, abandoning an earlier eclecticism for the urban planning principles of Camillo Sitte and an interest in vernacular buildings. In the following years he was a critic of rationalist architects, whom he rebuked for ignoring the Italian identity of modern architecture. Although he executed many fine urban projects, like the Piazza della Vittoria in Brescia (1928–32), his most decisive contribution was as a competition juror and through overseeing large-scale state-sponsored developments, like the Città Universitaria in Rome (1932–5) and the Esposizione Universale di Roma (1937–42, with Giuseppe Pagano, Luigi Piccinato, Ettore Rossi, and Luigi Vietti).   BLM

Piano, Renzo (1937–) Italian architect. Renzo

Piano first became famous as the designer, with Richard *Rogers, of the Centre Pompidou in Paris, that extraordinary urban machine which gave such a boost to the emerging *high tech style in the 1970s. Piano however is not, and perhaps never was, a high tech architect in the stylistic sense. Technology, in the sense of simple making, lies at the heart of his architecture, but image and style are relatively unimportant. His buildings display certain common features, but these are conceptual and practical rather than visual—the result of a development process that takes place not in an office or a studio but in a 'workshop'. The building for the Menil art collection in Houston, Texas, for example (1981–6), is as 'technological' as the Centre Pompidou, but could hardly be more different in character. It makes use of innovative forms of construction, such as curved ferro-cement, daylight-filtering 'leaves' and ductile iron trusses to support them, yet presents them in a modest way, as if they were as normal and traditional as the timber-framed panels that infill the steel frame.

To say that nature is an inspiration to Piano is perhaps misleading. His buildings do not necessarily look 'organic' but they often seem to ask the question 'how would nature have solved this problem?' The wave-like form of the long roof of Kansai Airport in Japan (1988–94) is a rational resolution of structural and aerodynamic forces, like the waves that surround it on its artificial island. The high technology of computers sometimes seems closer to nature than the clumsy forms of the machine age. Piano was one of the first architects to see the potential of computer-aided design to revolutionize building form. His shopping centre at Bercy in France (1987–90) is wrapped in a curvaceous silvery metal envelope that could only have been designed on a computer. 'Blobs' of this kind have since become commonplace, but in 1990 Bercy seemed utterly strange and rather shocking.

Entrance to the Palazzo del Rettorato, Città Universitaria, Rome (Marcello Piacentini, 1937–42)

Participation and collaboration are less tangible but equally important aspects of Piano's architecture. Traditional ideas of architectural authorship seem irrelevant when every major project is developed by a team rather than designed by an individual. Piano is always quick to acknowledge his collaborators. And sometimes those collaborators are clients and users. Lessons learnt in an early UNESCO-sponsored project to repair the ancient town of Otranto by mobilizing the local craftsmen were applied much later on the other side of the world in the design of Tjibaou cultural centre on the Pacific island of New Caledonia (1991–8).

The strange basket-like forms that accommodate the main gathering spaces in the building are reminiscent of local vernacular houses, but this is more than just a superficial resemblance. The design was developed in close consultation with representatives of the local Kanak people.

Piano has not, until quite recently, been thought of as an urban architect. Non-urban, if not anti-urban, buildings such as the exquisite flower-like concrete bowl of the San Nicola stadium at Bari (1987–90) are more typical. Blocks, façades, walls, windows, doors, rooms—the defining features of the traditional city street—seem to belong to a different architectural language. But in 1992 Piano won the commission to master plan the Potsdamer Platz district in the centre of reunified Berlin, and to design about half of the buildings on the site. The plan emphasizes urban spaces—streets, squares, and atriums—rather than the buildings that define them, though these are handsome enough, dressed in the terracotta cladding that has become something of a Piano trademark.   KR

picturesque A way of seeing the world as a picture. Guided by the inspiration of landscape painters, many designers of landscape and buildings in England between 1730 and 1830 consciously sought to make their work read as a succession of unfolding scenes, rather than making it conform to dictates of classical geometry. The taste for artificially contrived 'natural' landscape, in which buildings suggestive of different epochs and national characters were placed for visual effect, spread from England to the rest of Europe in the later 18th century, and is found in the parks of Ermenonville, Tsarskoe Selo, and Schloss Wörlitz. In all these cases, Englishness was presented as a token of political freedom, a reading of nature and history that was one of the driving forces behind the landscape gardening movement in England.

The theorists of the picturesque, Sir Richard Payne Knight and Sir Uvedale Price, writing in the 1790s, were landowners in the Welsh border country. They positioned the already established term between Edmund Burke's categories of the Sublime and the Beautiful. The picturesque was based on ideas of variety and contrast, as opposed to the uniformity of mood required for these classical aesthetic modes, including the landscape practice of Lancelot 'Capability' Brown, which they condemned. By extension, it encompassed historical styles of architecture, vernacular and regional building traditions, illusion and theatrical exaggeration. The experiments in mock ruins,

Chinoiserie, and Gothick found in the ornamental landscape buildings of William Kent and his contemporaries were extended to influence the design of country houses, which, owing to their setting in landscape, lent themselves most readily to application of the picturesque. Coloured perspective drawings of architecture, in England and France, conveyed the emotional excitement of urban and rural projects with realistic atmosphere.

Payne Knight's own house, Downton Castle, was castellated externally but neoclassical within, a disjunction permitted by the style and often found in Robert *Adam's Scottish work. Significantly, it was deliberately asymmetrical in plan, a trait soon copied even in classical buildings, especially the villas of John *Nash. The architectural patronage of George IV was castellated at Windsor, classical at Carlton House and Buckingham Palace, and oriental at Brighton Pavilion, the last two being Nash's work. Nash was associated with Humphry Repton, whose self-promotion as a landscape designer accelerated the spread of the new mode, especially among the middle classes.

By the 1820s, Karl Friedrich *Schinkel developed exquisite variations on picturesque themes, both classical and Gothic, in residences for the Prussian royal family in and around Potsdam.

A picturesque approach added to the range of possibilities in Classicism, but the stylistic relativism that it entailed was also a major factor in the decline of Classical hegemony in the 1820s. The reaction against it could take the form of singular stylistic preference, as in the case of Pugin, who combined this with an insistence on constructional and material truth, both of which were victims of picturesque scenography. The idea never disappeared, and played a major part among the influences that formed Modernism.

See also TOWNSCAPE.   AP

Watkin, D., *The English Vision: The Picturesque in Architecture, Landscape and Garden Design* (1982)

Piermarini, Giuseppe (1734–1808) Italian architect, the leading architect in Lombardy during the last quarter of the 18th century. His Palazzo Belgioioso, Milan (1772–81), was the model for several other palaces he designed in Milan and also in Monza: long, rather monotonous façades, with ornament reduced to a minimum, a northern counterpart to the work of *Vanvitelli. The Teatro alla Scala, Milan (completed 1778), followed the traditional horseshoe plan, but was much larger than any previous *opera houses. Piermarini also designed several theatres, in Novara (1777), Monza (1778), and Mantua (1782–3).

PG

Pietilä, Reima (1923–93) Finnish architect; his wife, Raili Paatelainen (1925–), was also his architectural partner. He first came to prominence with his Finnish Pavilion for the 1958 Brussels World Fair, claiming it to be 'both intellectual and natural'. In the 1960s he designed the Kaleva Church, Tampere (1959–66); Dipoli Student Centre, Otaniemi (1961–6); Suvikumpu Housing, Tapiola (1962–9); and the Finnish Embassy, New Delhi. His design of Malmi Church (1967) conforms to his theory of literal morphology (whereas metaphors 'stand for' something else, the literal method requires interpretations to 'look as if' they were some other thing): but professional jealousies meant it was not built.

His later works include: the Sief Palace / Ministries Complex (SPAB) in Kuwait City (completed 1982), which allowed him to explore his theories of modern Islamic architecture; and the Tampere Central Library (1983–6). His final project was the Finnish President's Official Residence (1985–92): it derives from the metaphor of a mermaid washed up on the Mantyniemi shore; it hints at the organic, but the mermaid's form is too emphatic to accommodate Pietilä's ultimate concept of '*land-shape* architecture'.

MQ

Quantrill, M., *Reima Pietilae* (1988)

Pigage, Nicolas de (Nicolas von) (1723–96) French architect, active in Germany. His masterpiece, the Schloss Benrath (1755–69) near Düsseldorf, reflects his academic education in France, since it is a far more subtle building than it appears at first glance. The private rooms, disposed around the internal courtyards, are separate from the main reception rooms, which face outwards. The façades, apparently a single storey with a mansard roof pierced by decorative lucarnes, are also rather deceptive, since the building is quite substantial, with over eighty rooms occupying four floors. The colours—yellow stone, white woodwork, and pink-coloured stucco—are almost too delicate for an exterior.

Schloss Benrath makes an interesting comparison with *Knobelsdorff's Sanssouci Palace, which it resembles in broad outline. The architectural weakness of Sanssouci is compensated for by its landscape setting, whereas here architecture is the perfect foil to the canal and the *bassin* between which the Schloss is located. PG

Pikionis, Dimitrios (1887–1968) Greek architect. His early small projects (two Experimental Schools, one in Athens and one in Thessalonica, 1933) combined modernist purism with Greek vernacular elements. While the Athens school has flat roofs and set back pure volumes, the Thessalonica school recruits precedents from regionalist folk architecture— courtyard, verandahs, and sloped roof with long eaves—functionally and climatically superior to modernist alternatives in the given context. Pikionis employed the same approach to an apartment house in Athens (1936, with N. Mitsakis as collaborator), a prototype for Athenian architecture after World War II.

Pikionis' best work is a complex of small structures and paths to the Acropolis and to the Summit of Philopappos Hill, Athens (1950–57), constructed mostly without execution plans, relying on verbal instructions and improvisation inspired by site constraints and available local materials, and fragments from building demolitions. More than a solitary promenade, the scheme captures the spatial experience of human interaction, tranquillity, and community. The Philothei playground (1961–5), his last project, reconciles regionalist elements from diverse cultures and historical epochs into a synthesis to demonstrate human universality. Pikionis was not anti-modern and not against modernization; but he opposed architectural globalism and supported regionalist alternatives. AT

pilaster A flat projection with the form of a column in relief, used to decorate and articulate a wall or pier, and, when lacking a base and capital, called a pilaster strip or lesene. Essentially non-structural, a pilaster has a small buttressing and supporting effect, particularly when acting as a respond opposite a column whose entablature carries over to it.

In classical architecture a pilaster is subject to the same rules as govern a column. The Greeks did not use pilasters, seeing columns as structural and so instead attaching half or three-quarter columns to walls when appropriate; but the Romans happily used them, realizing their potential for articulation. Consequently, rising above the attached half columns, Doric, Ionic, and Corinthian, of the Colosseum's (AD c.70–80) three main storeys, is a further storey articulated by a Composite order of pilasters. In the Temple of Rome and Augustus Caesar, which Palladio recorded at Pola, Istria, the Corinthian order of the portico continues as corner pilasters outside its cell, and the Pantheon's Corinthian portico is continued as pilasters along the sides of the building, and also in the interior.

What was good enough for the Romans, the *Renaissance gladly accepted. *Alberti notably exploited the triumphal arch motif, using attached columns for his Tempio Malatestiana, Rimini (begun

1450), but pilasters for the façade and interior of S. Andrea, Mantua (1472). These are like a *giant order in all but name, and the first undisputed giant order. Michelangelo's giant order on the Capitoline also takes the form of Corinthian pilasters.

From the start, Baroque architects had a special use for pilasters when they came to model complex façades. This began when Carlo Maderno refronted S. Susanna, Rome (1597–1603), by employing detached *Corinthian columns on each side of the central entrance for emphasis, and attaching three-quarter columns for the flanking bays and pilasters for the remaining bays, left and right. His façade for St Peter's (1607–12) is similarly, but more grandly, arranged, continuing the giant Corinthian order of pilasters that Michelangelo had already used there. The idea then went from strength to strength, for example in *Borromini's façade for S. Agnese in Piazza Navona (1653–5). It became common practice to use columns for the ground storey and pilasters for the upper in church façades, and similarly in classical mansions, pilasters would articulate the wings using the same order of columns as was applied to the central portico—a common practice of Palladian architects in England. Mixing pilasters and columns of different orders and sizes, starting with Michelangelo's precedent on the Capitoline, again became stock in trade, and a blessing to those architects whose skills were more meretricious than thorough-going classical. In freeing architects from classical usage, Michelangelo designed many variations on classical pilasters, for example the panelled strips that frame the tabernacles in the Medici Chapel, Florence (1521–4). That kind of freedom re-emerged in the stripped-down Classicism of some of Soane's designs, notably the Dulwich Picture Gallery, London (1811), where pilasters with notional capitals and bases articulate the main storey, and others with grooved shafts articulate the lantern above the mausoleum. APQ

pilgrimage churches Many early Christian churches were founded as shrines. St Peter's, Rome, thus embodies the punning notion of building the church, meaning the whole body of Christians, on this rock (in Latin, *petra*), i.e. Peter's tomb. The future of lesser churches was assured through a gift or timely acquisition of a relic—a steady flow of pilgrims brought pence as well as penance. The relic would normally be set up in a chapel, protected by a screen, and worshipping pilgrims reached it by way of a passage, if given the security of a crypt. Romanesque churches, which had chapels dedicated to several saints, whether they contained relics or not, formed a continuous route from the west end by way of the aisles and an ambulatory running around the presbytery off which the chapels opened.

This pattern was established at St Philibert, Tournus (*c*.979–1019), and adopted for the churches of the pilgrimage road. Firstly at St Martin, Tours (after 997), several so-called pilgrimage churches were built for travellers making their way to the shrine of St James (S. Iago) at Compostela in north-west Spain. This had attracted a festival in the 9th century, for some obscure reason, which developed into Europe's greatest pilgrimage site. The routes converged from assembly points into four main streams running across France to the western Pyrenees, thence across northern Spain to their destination, with some forty main stations along the way and several more secondary ones. Here the pilgrims stopped overnight and attended mass. As well as the churches at Tours and Santiago de Compostela (*c*.1075–1211), those at St Martial, Limoges (*c*.1063–95), Ste Foi, Conques (*c*.1050–1132), and St Sernin, Toulouse (begun *c*.1077–83), also responded to the pilgrims' need to take mass by adopting a basilican cruciform plan with an apse, ambulatory and radiating chapels. This enabled the pilgrims to process down fireproof, tunnel-vaulted aisles to reach a chapel, and hear mass

wherever there was room. Both Tours and Limoges have double aisles, and all have five radiating chapels around their ambulatories, save Conques which has three, and all have a further two on each side of their transeptal arms, except Limoges which has one. Later ages served their pilgrims differently. In Bavaria, Balthasar *Neumann designed a shrine to the Fourteen Helpers in Need or Vierzehnheiligen (1747) as a domed, stuccoed and frescoed casket with plenty of space for pilgrims to circulate around a dramatic tableau of the Helpers in the most refined Baroque of the age. By contrast, to accommodate the 22,000 pilgrims to Our Lady of Lourdes, Pierre Vaga designed the reinforced concrete St Pius X Basilica (1958), which resembles a vast underground car park.   APQ

piloti A pier or column carrying a building, so as to leave an open space underneath. For *Le Corbusier, the use of a piloti was one of the five theoretical points of a new architecture. In practice, he used the piloti to great effect at the Unité d'Habitation, Marseille (1947–52).   PG

Pinseau, Michel (1924–99) French architect. *See* AFRICA (NORTH AFRICA).

Piranesi, Giovanni Battista (1720–78) Italian architect and engraver. His highly imaginative, indeed rather overpowering visions of architecture, cities, and interior design, as revealed in *Carceri* (*c*.1745, re-issued *c*.1760 with new plates), *Vedute di Roma* (*c*.1749), *Antichità* (4 vols., 1756), and *Diverse Maniere d'adornare i cammini* (1769), were undoubtedly a source of inspiration to visionary architects such as *Boullée, *Gilly, *Ledoux, and *Soane. His only significant executed work was a church for the Knights of Malta, Rome (1764), a rather modest affair, which, however, displayed a highly erudite knowledge of classical symbolism.   PG

Pite, Arthur Beresford (1861–1934) English architect. Trained at the Royal College of Art, South Kensington (where he was Professor of Architecture 1900–23), Pite's interest in education was expressed as Architectural Director of the London County Council School of Building, as President of the Architectural Association (1896), and as a member of the Board of Architectural Education and the Board of Architectural Studies at Cambridge University. His work in London includes 32 Old Bond Street (1898); the neo-Byzantine Christ Church, Brixton (1899–1902); All Souls School, New Cavendish Street (1906–8); London, Edinburgh and Glasgow Assurance Offices, Euston Road (1907); and the Piccadilly entrance to Burlington Arcade (1929–31). His architectural fantasies expressed a highly vivid imagination. APQ

Plain Style This translation of the Portuguese phrase *Estilo Chão* was defined by George Kubler (*Portuguese Plain Architecture*, 1972) as '…like a vernacular architecture, related to living dialect traditions more than to the great authors of the remote past'. He aimed to characterize Portuguese architecture during the late 16th and the 17th centuries as a simplified version of Classicism, standardized to meet the widespread demand in Portugal, Brazil, Africa, and Indian possessions. Although based on classical orders from Italian Renaissance and Mannerism, churches and manor houses used those motives in a highly simplified fashion, allowing easy repetition. JMF

plan In many building types (e.g. temples, whether Greek, Roman or Hindu, and mosques), the building is either used by one clearly defined category of user, or the functional and/or ritual requirements are so simple that plans are neither complex nor problematic, nor, indeed, very interesting in a formal sense. Even the *Romanesque or *Gothic cathedral has a fairly simple plan, which can easily be adapted to new purposes.

Enlarging the transepts creates the *pilgrimage church; adding an *ambulatory, *chevet or *Lady chapel creates new spaces for the worship of saints, or the provision of additional altars.

In certain types of architecture, the plan has rather a low priority, being completely subordinate to the *façade (as in many *palazzo plans or in much 19th-century architecture influenced by *Eclecticism). But since the history of the plan is virtually co-extensive with the history of architecture itself, the reader is referred to some representative examples, which illustrate different approaches to and requirements of the plan.

Probably the earliest building type accommodating a range of functions for which a complex plan had to be devised was the Roman *baths. The best example is the Baths of Caracalla, Rome (AD 206–17). Because of their newly found mastery of domes and vaults, the Romans were able to construct a series of varied spaces, so that each room is carefully considered in relationship to its place in the building, its access to light, its fitness for purpose, and its decorous shape. Unlike the paper plans of many *Beaux Arts designers, which were supposedly inspired by the Baths of Caracalla, the plan solves architectural problems based on reality.

Sometimes, the problem was not so much complex as insoluble. Following the edicts of the *Counter-Reformation, architects were set the task of designing churches which had to unite two diverse spatial elements: the longitudinal axis (for processions/a dramatic view of the high altar) and the centralized space, uniting the community of worshippers near the altar. Architects such as *Bernini and *Borromini in Italy, J. M. *Fischer and J. B. *Neumann in south Germany, used a variety of plans—ovals, octagons, circles—to try to reconcile the irreconcilable.

When designing for private individuals, rather than the church, the architect faced much simpler problems, so that the shapes of rooms and sequences of spaces could be designed as much for aesthetic pleasure as for functional or liturgical requirements. The most exemplary cases are the plans for villas of *Palladio, and the *hôtel particulier, by a series of architects (see e.g. BOFFRAND; LEDOUX) from 1700 onwards.

But the most important historical change in the development of the plan occurred from the middle of the 19th century, when architects had to design a whole new series of building types for the general public (*town halls, *law courts, *railway stations, and so on). Even traditional building types, such as the English *country house, acquired a new level of complexity, as patrons wished to pursue a much greater range of activities. The ingenuity of architects such as *Burn, *Waterhouse, and *Street reached the limits of what was possible given contemporary technology.

The Industrial Revolution had not yet created the materials and structures that would enable these problems to be solved more easily, but when it did so, architects at first were more engaged in applying technology to solving structural problems, rather than utilizing the new freedom given by construction using steel or concrete frame. For instance, undoubtedly because of financial pressures, the plans of the office buildings designed by the *Chicago School created repetitive and dull, though carefully costed and highly profitable spaces. However, given the opportunity, as in *Sullivan's Auditorium building, architects could use the new technology to devise plans which were both ingenious and which generated a great variety of spaces.

In the first quarter of the 20th century, three architects formulated approaches to planning which were to be of decisive importance in the development of *Modernism, and set the parameters for the rest of the century in terms of plan development. While not using modern structural technology (though indebted to developments in *engineering services), Frank Lloyd Wright devised the 'open-plan' house of free-flowing spaces, which opened the house out to the exterior (see, among many others, NEUTRA, SCHINDLER). In his designs for villas and artists' studios, *Le Corbusier, created the plan libre, in which the new technology made it possible to plan any kind of space one wished. The result was a promenade architecturale through a series of interrelated, free-flowing planned spaces. *Rietveld's Schröder House (1924) showed that instead of being fixed by structural consideration, plans could be extremely flexible, and spaces dedicated to different purposes, changing over time.

PG

plan representation Like elevations and sections, plans are two-dimensional, made by projection on a flat surface. The elevation and section are built up from the plan, for it is the key to a design, showing the organization of space and its elements (such as walls, piers, door and window openings, stairs and lifts) that respond to the client's requirements. A full set of plans might include the plans for the site, foundations, for each floor, roof plan (as seen from above), ceiling plans (as seen from below), and landscape. Plan forms can be described, for example: the Elizabethan H-plan and E-plan, Palladian axial plan, Pugin's additive plan, Arts and Crafts butterfly plan, and the modern free-plan.

The earliest plans, from the Egyptian period through Greek and Roman times to the Middle Ages, were incised into the wall and floor surfaces of their buildings in the course of construction. Designs on parchment survive from the 13th century and show that medieval architects superimposed all the floor plans for a building or part of a building so that the design and structural implications could be more easily visualized and controlled. JL

721

plaster A finishing and decorative material applied since prehistoric times to walls, ceilings, and floors. Common plaster is a combination of lime and sand, but special plasters have added cement, gypsum, powdered marble or other stone, and a binding material such as animal hair, straw or other vegetable fibre, depending on the quality of finish required. Used externally, plaster provides a reasonably waterproof cladding. In 13th-century and later timber-framed buildings, it was applied to laths or wattles as a means of filling the framed panels, and coated in limewash, which might be coloured. It might also be cut or moulded into patterns, when it is known in Britain as *pargeting. From Roman times plaster was used as a cheap substitute for carved stone by being moulded to form architectural details, as can be seen, for example, at Ostia Antica, Pompeii, and other sites in Italy, where it is generally known as *stucco. In Tudor and Stuart Britain plaster was used in the same way, the term stucco being reserved for the harder varieties of cement-based plasters that came into common use in the late 18th century. Hard gypsum plaster was often used as flooring material, for example in Norfolk, where it is laid on tightly packed reeds over the joists. Plaster was used on thatched roofs in London and other towns as a means of reducing the risk of fire. In the 16th century open timber roofs went out of fashion to be replaced by plastered ceilings, and these and also walls were decorated with increasing elaboration. The cornice was often finished with a plaster moulding produced by running a shaped template along the angle between wall and ceiling. The ceiling itself could be decorated with standard pre-moulded patterns or classical features, as well as those specially moulded on site.   APQ

Plateresque from the Spanish *platero*, meaning 'silversmith'. It refers to a completely superficial form of ornament applied without regard to underlying structure, or its effect on the proportions of the façade as a whole. Representative examples are the portal and window frames of the College of San Ildefonso, Alcalá de Henares, near Madrid (1537–53), by *Hontañon, and the Royal Hospital, Santiago de Compostela (1501–13), by *Egas.   PG

Playfair, William Henry (1789–1857) Scottish architect. The most refined and intellectual of Edinburgh's early-19th-century architects, and a pupil of the influential neoclassicist William Stark, Playfair began his career as University architect, and assistant in C. R. *Cockerell's ambitious but uncompleted National Monument project (1821–9). He contributed numerous classical punctuations to Edinburgh's streets in the 1820s and 1830s, including Surgeon's Hall (1827–9), the Royal Institution (1822–6 and 1832–5), and the square-towered St Stephen's Church (1827–8), and he coordinated the façades of the Calton Hill New Town extension. In the 1840s and 1850s, his work culminated in a more eclectic succession of stately institutions, notably the neo-Elizabethan Donaldson's Hospital of 1842–50. He skilfully completed the romantic–classical Mound *ensemble*, through the eclectic juxtaposition of his neo-Gothic Free Church College (1846–50) and chastely Grecian National Gallery (1850–58).   MGl

Plečnik, Jože (1872–1957) Slovenian architect, who worked in Otto *Wagner's atelier in Vienna. His inclination towards the philosophies of high cultural values (*Ruskin), an idealistic view of the world in the tradition of the great masters of Gothic, Renaissance, and Baroque, and the rejection of the machine age, added to his inner conflicts, those between deeply felt social preoccupations and escapism.

Unable to rid himself of the superabundance of representational elements in his architecture, he used the classical cannon, Byzantine decoration, as well as modern techniques (Church of the Holy Ghost, Vienna, 1910–13).

His architecture appeared to be both in harmony with, and to reveal bewildering contrasts in relation to its milieu. For example, the Zaherl House, Vienna (1903–5), is designed in the modern spirit, but has the disconcerting feature of a frieze with caryatids.

His penchant for the archaic remains the *leitmotif* in all his numerous later works: the restoration of Hradcani Castle (1911) in Prague; the National Library (1936–41); the cemetery at Zale (1938–40); the Chamber of Commerce (1925–7); and the Insurance Building (1928–30), all in Ljubljana.

Neither modern nor postmodern, Plečnik remains an enigma. PT

Prelovšek, D., *Jože Plečnik (1872–1957)* (1997)

Poelaert, Joseph (1817–79) Belgian architect. *See* BELGIUM, 19TH CENTURY; LAW COURTS.

Poelzig, Hans (1869–1936) German architect; a great architect, thinker, and teacher at the dawn of Modernism, somewhat eclipsed by the next generation, whose varied work is hard to categorize.

After studying architecture at the Technische Hochschule in Berlin, Poelzig worked for the Prussian Ministry of Works until appointed in 1900 Professor of Architecture at the Breslau Kunstakademie, an Arts and Crafts school that was to rival the Bauhaus. He rose to Director in 1903, remaining there until 1916, when he became City Architect in Dresden. In 1920 he returned to Berlin as Professor at the Technische Hochschule where his teaching was legendary. All this time he never ceased to practise, even his small early buildings in the Jugendstil manner showing shrewd intelligence and originality (town hall at Löwenberg, 1903–6). His international reputation was sealed with daringly plain industrial buildings seen with hindsight as proto-modernist (Chemical Factory, Luban, 1911;

Water Tower, Posen, 1913). He also built a horizontally glazed office in Breslau (now Wrocław) in 1911 that seemed to anticipate the 1920s. Then in 1919 he produced one of the key works of Expressionism: the ingenious conversion of an old Berlin circus into Max Reinhardt's Grosses Schauspielhaus, with a stalactite auditorium ceiling and green cave-like foyers. His sense of drama and illusion carried on in grandiose unbuilt projects like the Salzburg Festspielhaus of 1920 and in the creation of elaborate filmsets, notably for Paul Wegener's *Der Golem*. International functionalism brought a new sobriety, and Poelzig contributed a modest if subtle house to the Weissenhofsiedlung of 1927. His work thereafter returned to a sober and efficient monumentality, with large projects like the offices for IG Farben, Frankfurt (1928–30), and Broadcasting House, Berlin (1929–30). PG

Posener, J., *Hans Poelzig: Reflections on his Life and Work* (1992)

Poland, historic Poland's historical vicissitudes make it simpler to study within its present boundaries; the architecture of its former cities L'viv and Vilnius, relinquished in 1989–93 to Ukraine and Lithuania, is discussed elsewhere (*see* LITHUANIA; UKRAINE, L'VIV).

Little remains of the stone buildings, such as the fragment of an apsed rotunda at Cracow, which began to replace timber in the 10th century; the Romanesque is represented by a dozen buildings of substance, culminating in the *Ottonian-style church at Tum (1136–61) and four late-12th-century Cistercian abbeys.

The Cistercians were to lead the introduction both of *Gothic and of *brick. The flowering of brick on the Baltic is described elsewhere (*see* BALTIC BRICK); its parallel advance in Silesia led to spectacular churches in 14th-century Wrocław, the 2-storeyed Holy Cross with apsed transepts, the great halls of St Mary on the Sand and St Dorothy, and two distinctive asymmetrical 'Piast' vaults. The province had filled up with colonial towns on chessboard plans, and the same emulation as on the Baltic led them to build higher, although with a cold parsimony of detail, until at Brzeg the nave (1370–1416) was three and a half times as high as it was wide.

To north and east new ideas were taken up in stone, with a conventional seven-sided apse of about 1350 in the new cathedral of Gniezno, more opportunistically and with zigzag aisle vaults in the cathedral and great churches of Corpus Christi and St Catherine in Cracow. Most attractive are country churches like Wisilica, which used the Czech idea of a hall star-vaulted from a single row of columns without capitals; the same elegance informs the old synagogue of about 1500 at Cracow. Of secular buildings, a few bare castles remain, like Czersk and Czerwińsk, and at Wrocław one of Europe's showiest medieval town halls.

The appearance of a distinctive architecture followed from the Italian masons summoned, the first in 1502, to make Cracow a Renaissance capital to rival Buda.

They brought mostly Florentine skills, and also, in Bartolomeo Berecci, an innovator who probably devised the double-height upper colonnade of the castle courtyard (1507–35) and certainly the Sigismund Chapel (1517–33), whose dome on tall drum on cube and forceful effigies inspired Poland's successors to build some two hundred imitations.

In the 16th century Polish exports of grain boomed, making the fortunes of the merchants of Gdańsk and the landowners of southern Poland and the Ukraine. The magnates put up huge castle-like palaces, Baranów (1591–1606), Krasiczyn (1592–1614), the megalomaniac pentagon of Krzyżtopór (1627–44), and Wiżnicz (1615–21) with fortifications too elegant to be defended. In 1579 one of the greatest dignitaries began from scratch an ideal town at Zamość. Meanwhile Gdańsk called on Netherlanders to build showpieces like city gates and the brick and stone Arsenal (1602–5), and their influence was to spread up the trade route until it reached L'viv. Poznań employed an Italian on its fine

town hall, too correct to attract imitators; what caught on was the 'Polish Parapet' of Cracow's cloth hall (1556–60), a hybrid of medieval fantasy and Renaissance detail, and we find its relatives on Lublin churches, synagogues like that at Szydłów, and the fairytale merchants' houses of Kazimierz Dolny.

Meanwhile the Counter-Reformation came too. The Jesuits' first brand new church north of the Alps went up at Nyasvizh in Belarus (1582–93) in a severe Roman style; in its final form (1609–30) their Cracow church is a worthy descendant of S. Andrea della Valle. These religious garrisons marched across the land, generally handsome, but, apart from the imitation of the Salute at Gostyń (plan, 1679), seldom original until they reached the east. Baroque palace building reached the new capital of Warsaw with Sobieski's luscious suburban palace of Wilanów (1677–96). But the finest architect was Dutch, Tylman van Gameren, with the first design for St Anne, Cracow (1689), the Warsaw churches of the Sacramentines (1688–92) and at Czerniaków, and palaces for the Krasińskis (1689–95) and others, all possessed of Palladian proportion and severity.

When Augustus the Strong became king in 1696 architecture stagnated while he built Dresden. Great houses still went up, Frenchified at Radzyń Podlaski (1750–60), vast and dreary at Białystok (1728–58); a Cracow architect built the delightful little cross-plan house at Grabki Duże (1742). The best Rococo was built in the east, some of it near Lublin, like the oval-dome churches of Włodawa (1741–80) and Chełm (1753–63); much of it lies beyond today's borders.

It took the election of a Polish king, Stanislaw August, in 1764 to let in new ideas, at the moment when neoclassicism was on the move. He remodelled Warsaw Castle, laid out a new street system, and in the 1780s and 1790s reshaped the Łazienki park and equipped it with buildings in an almost edible style

St Mary on the Sand,
Wrocław, Poland (c.1350)

close to that of Gabriel. His court embraced the *jardin anglais* in gardens like Arkadia (begun 1778), and some seriously severe buildings were designed like Warsaw's Evangelical Church (1777–9). This taste filtered out onto the country, shaping the Polish manor house at its most familiar, the white Tuscan portico among great trees.

The traumas of backing Napoleon and falling under the boot of Russia did little to change Polish taste. Warsaw gained fine neoclassical monuments, like St Alexander (1818–20), the concave arcade of the Pac Palace (1824–8), and the Bank of Poland (1828–30) with its dome set within a great curved corner; Krakowskie Przedmieście filled up to become one of the most attractive main streets in Europe. There followed a flood of 19th-century Eclecticism, elegant in Schinkel's Gothic at Kamieniec and Kórnik and intellectual in his bizarre cross-plan hunting lodge at Antonin, at its most vulgarly exciting in the new textile boom town of Łodz. Poznań was treated to the Prussian version of National Romanticism with the massive 'Imperial Castle' (1905–11), but the movement developed best under Austrian rule in the south, with the lively Art Nouveau (or 'Secesja') of Cracow, where the Stary Teatr was rebuilt in 1903–6, and the elaborate timber villas of the 'Zakopane Style'. DBK

Poland, 20th century Poland's contribution to 19th-century architecture had been less prominent than that of many other central European countries, or at least it was held to be so; this was partly due to the way in which Poland lacked effective architectural publications, which was in turn caused by the fact that none of its centres could act as proper cultural capitals, and because of a lack of architectural institutions; for instance, until World War I Polish architects had to go to neighbouring countries even to study architecture.

Of the architectural innovations around 1900 three must be noted: probably the most successful was the 'Zakopane Style', a type of wooden domestic architecture whose jagged forms and fanciful roofs, first revived by the artistic and intellectual elite (e.g. Stanisław Witkiewicz) when they resided in the southern resort of Zakopane, which are still popular as houses in the countryside, speaking an unmistakable language of Polishness. Secondly, there was the Cracow version of International Art Nouveau ('Secesja'); and thirdly another 'national' style, this time in heavy, plain, even coarse brickwork, in the early work of Oskar Sosnowski (St Jacob, Warsaw-Grochów, 1908–14).

During the interwar years Poland shared with most Western countries a double kind of output: massive, geometrically neoclassical buildings serving mainly the government; and daring innovations in an extreme version of International Modernism, chiefly for housing (Bohdan Lachert). Even after World War II impressive neoclassical buildings arose (Bohdan Pniewski), while for a few years in the early 1950s Soviet Socialist Realist architecture dominated. But Poland rejected that style earlier than most of the other Warsaw Pact countries and embarked again on a course of International Modernism, especially in state-sponsored mass housing, making large new towns (Nowe Tychy, Upper Silesia), but also in many kinds of public buildings, notably railway stations in inventive reinforced concrete (Warsaw-Centralna, Katowice).

The post-International Style phase of Polish architecture began with the new wave of church building in the 1970s. In the climate of distrust of the Communist regime and Soviet domination, the Roman Catholic church fuelled a protest movement which resulted in a seemingly desperate need for places for worshippers. All monies were collected privately. As a result perhaps no other country demonstrates such a diversity of church designs, often very large, of the most daring reinforced concrete structures (Kalisz, by Andrzej Fajans, 1975–90) or using deliberately heavy brickwork (Warsaw-Ursynów, 1984–9) suggesting 'raw Polishness' once more, by Poland's star architect, Marek Budzyński. He went on to make his mark most prominently with the new intensely postmodern Warsaw Law Courts and the Warsaw University Library, contrasting in their complex originality with Warsaw's smart international office blocks.   SM

Atlas Zabytków Architektury w Polsce (Architectural Atlas of Poland), PWN Warsaw (2001)

Białostocki, J., *The Art of the Renaissance in Eastern Europe* (1976)

Lorentz, S., and Rottermund, A., *Neoclassicism in Poland* (1986)

Knox, B., *The Architecture of Poland* (1971)

Miłobędzki, A., *Architecture of Poland* (2000)

Muthesius, S., *An Introduction to Polish Art, Architecture and Design 966–1990* (1994)

Polk, Willis Jefferson (1867–1924) US architect. Early in his career he became a leader in developing a fresh, multi-faceted approach to design, embracing informal, rustic modes of expression tailored to small-scale buildings on rugged, sloping sites and to grand classical visions that were likewise fresh in interpretation. Though this work proved of enduring influence locally, after 1900 Polk began to pursue a more conservative course, inspired by the example of Daniel *Burnham, designing a number of distinguished, if generally conventional, commercial buildings and palatial residences.   RWL

Longstreth, R., *On the Edge of the World: Four Architects in San Francisco at the Turn of the Century* (1983)

polychromy In 1811 C. R. *Cockerell and others detected colour on the mouldings of a cornice in a temple on the island of Aegina. His cautiously evaluated findings were published in 1819, but did not attract much attention. But based upon a very superficial examination of the temples at Selinus, *Hittorff brashly claimed (in *Architecture antique de la Sicile*, 1826–30) that a wide range of colours had been applied to the exterior of Greek temples. Hittorff was not a very rigorous archaeologist, but even the idea that classical buildings were anything but white or monochrome was, at the time, quite sensational. But, with the notable exception of Gottlieb *Bindesbøll, polychromy had little impact on the contemporary *Greek Revival, perhaps because the archaeological evidence was so dubious.

However, there was no doubt that external colour, using materials rather than pigment, had been used in Italian Romanesque architecture. In *The Stones of Venice* (1851), *Ruskin argued for a polychromatic architecture, the 'style of incrustation', in which coloured marble or other materials was used as a veil over ordinary brick construction. By contrast, the proponents of constructional or structural polychromy, particularly the *Gothic Revival architects *Butterfield and *Street, used different-coloured materials as the direct expression of the underlying structure.   PG

Pombaline An urban and architectural practice (and style), named after the Marquis of Pombal, Prime Minister during the reign of King Jose I (r.1750–77). It sought simplicity of form, standardized materials, and geometric rules within a precocious neoclassical spirit. It received a strong impetus after the terrible earthquake of 1755 which devastated Lisbon. The new plan for the city centre was a clearly defined grid (the Baixa), with a spectacular square facing the river Tagus, the Praça do Comércio.   JMF

Ponti, Gio (1891–1979) Italian architect, writer, and designer. In the 1920s, Ponti was involved in the *Novecento movement, sharing the general approach of *Muzio. In 1928 he founded the review *Domus*, which for over half a century was to be very influential on interior design and furnishing. His design approach took a turn towards Modernism in the 1930s, with his designs for the Faculty of Mathematics, University of Rome (1935), and the Montecatini company headquarters, Milan (1936).

After 1945 Ponti became Italy's best-known architect. His 32-storey Pirelli Tower, Milan (1956–8), with its acutely angled sides, was one of the first tall buildings not set out on a rectangular plan. From the 1960s he had an extensive international practice, in Iraq, Iran, Pakistan, and Hong Kong. PG

Pöppelmann, Matthäus Daniel (1662–1736) German architect. In 1704 Pöppelmann was commissioned to rebuild the Dresden palace of the Elector of Saxony. His ambitious scheme for the Zwinger, a combination of garden designs (cascades, grottoes, and fountains) and a large palace / courtyard was not completed, but the existing section is impressive enough. It consists of a long rectangular courtyard, about 106 m (350 ft) long, with two exedrae on the short sides; the framing architecture consists of single-storey galleries, linking 7 pavilions of 2 storeys. Much of the success of the design is due to the sculpture on the skylines and the façades, by Balthasar Permoser (1651–1732), particularly on the southern gate, the Kronentor, an open structure surmounted by a massive onion dome (1713).

At Schloss Pillnitz, further north along the Elbe, Pöppelmann used the same combination of courtyard-pavilion as at the Zwinger in his design for two buildings: the Wasserpalais (1720–23) which has pagoda-shaped roofs and, under the eaves, 'Chinese' figures; and the Bergpalais (1724), in which the courtyard was used for pageantry and tournaments. Both buildings, and Pöppelmann's other minor works, rather lack the exuberance of the Zwinger, perhaps because Permoser's sculpture was not involved. PG

porphyry A geologically not very exact term for a highly coloured igneous rock, containing crystals of feldspar and quartz (cf. GRANITE). In imperial Rome porphyry was often used for monolithic columns or revetments (for example, in the Pantheon). The stone was supplied from one quarry in the eastern desert of Egypt, the Mons Porpyritis (now the Gebel Abu Dokhan). Its final use for this purpose in the ancient world was for eight monolithic columns in the cathedral of Hagia Sophia (see BYZANTINE EMPIRE), of which an astonished contemporary, Procopius, recounted that: 'One might imagine that one had come upon a meadow with its flowers in full bloom...the purple of some...others on which the crimson glows' (*Buildings* 1.59). PG

Porta, Giacomo della See DELLA PORTA, GIACOMO.

porte cochère A porch large enough to admit coaches, ideally from the side, so that they can set down their passengers under cover. So practical an innovation seems to have been devised only in the late 18th century: the Hôtel de Salm, Paris (early 1780s), having a giant portico deep enough to serve this purpose. APQ

portico A porch, in classical architecture, formalized by the application of one or more of the orders. It is normally enclosed, at least across the front, by a row of columns in one, two, or occasionally more storeys, and carries an entablature, sometimes with a pediment. As further definition, it is described as *in antis* when the front is in the same plane as the front of the building; it is also defined by the number of columns it contains, e.g. hexastyle when six; and it is described as 'blind' when its features are applied to a wall without openings. At Paestum, Italy, the Basilica (late 6th century BC) has nine columns in its portico, but, since a central column interferes with a central entrance, it became standard practice to have an even number of columns instead.

A portico might extend so far outwards that it needed more than one row of columns for its support, e.g. the Pantheon, Rome (AD *c*.120–25), which has three rows. *Renaissance porticoes are often 2 storeys high: the portico may be raised over a basement, with steps leading up to it, as at *Palladio's Villa Foscari, Malcontenta (before 1560); it may employ a giant order, as Michelangelo proposed for St Peter's, Rome (1546); or it may have two orders, as on Palladio's Villa Pisani, Montagnana (1553–5). These carry pediments, but Inigo *Jones's giant portico at St Paul's Cathedral, London (1633–40), carried a simple *entablature. Palladio articulated and integrated the nave and aisles of San Giorgio Maggiore, Venice (1565), with two overlapping blind porticoes, and later Baroque architects wove porticoes into columniated and pilastered façades of the utmost complexity. While Pietro da *Cortona gave S. Maria della Pace, Rome (1656–7), a semicircular portico, and Baldassare *Longhena designed S. Maria della Salute, Venice (1631), with a portico in the form of a Roman triumphal arch, many Italian Baroque porticoes defy such simple analysis.   APQ

Portman, John (1924–) US architect. *See* HOTELS.

Portugal Though only part of the Iberian peninsula, Portugal has succeeded in creating, developing, and defending a specific and original architecture and urban culture, both in its European territory, and in the large Lusitanian overseas colonization.

From its independence in the 12th century, medieval Portugal occupied part of the former Roman province controlled by the cities of Guimarães and Braga (north of the Douro). During the 13th and 14th centuries, the *Reconquista*, directed against the Muslims of the southern areas (as far as the Algarve, on the south coast), defined the oldest European national territory, unchanged to the present day. At the beginning of the 15th century, the overseas expansion started, a process contemporary with the creation of new urban settlements along the Portuguese coast, replacing the importance of many of the oldest Roman cities: it was the 'Atlanticization' of Portugal, turning it to the unknown ocean.

Characteristics As a country on the periphery of Europe, Portuguese architecture evolved through a series of imported artistic movements, which over the centuries have generated original responses through a process which reveals and emphasizes the integrative and traditionalist aspects of the existing national context.

This explains the capacity for transforming the Gothic into *Manueline, classical and Mannerist themes into the *Plain Style, the Baroque into the more simple and standardized Pombaline, and, finally, explains the poetic interpretation of modern architecture made in the Oporto school, and later on in Lisbon, during the late 20th century. Being—in a creative contradiction—both conservative and open to experimentation and adaptation, Portuguese architecture managed to transform foreign models, so that they were soon remodelled with originality and such power that their adaptation created very special scales, spaces, and forms.

In a long-term view, Portuguese architecture can best be characterized both by simplicity of form and structural clarity. The façade assumed a vital importance as an 'introduction' to the building (as if the surface aimed to become three-dimensional space and structure). This aspect connects with the Lusitanian tendency to conceive everything as surfaces, thus somehow disdaining the importance of volumes and their play of light and dark.

Selected themes Given the small size of the country, the variety of Portuguese vernacular architecture is tremendous, for it includes: the granite and wooden architecture typical of the northern provinces of Minho and Tras-os-Montes (houses formerly covered with straw); a brick and earth architecture in the coastal region of Beiras; a stone architecture in the central areas (from the interior Beiras to Estremadura); and in the southern sector (Alentejo), a bright white-washed rural architecture of the *montes*. The Algarve again presents different architecture—a kind of cubic-volume brick and wood, traditional way of building. The vernacular tradition in the *Azores and *Madeira is also different, for it works with the volcanic black, brown or grey stone, contrasting with the white-washed façades.

Domestic rural architecture presents a rich variety of examples: 'stone villages' such as Pitoes das Junias (Tras-os-Montes), Piodao and Monsanto (Beira), white-washed villages such as Evoramonte and Montalvao (Alentejo), and the 'marble villages' of Borboa and Vila Viçosa, north-east of Evora; gracious small-scale cities, like Castelo Mendo (a granite *ensemble* in Beira), Obidos (a walled medieval place, in Estremadura), Estemov (a *praca forte* (stronghold) in Alentejo), or Silves (an old Muslim fortified place in the Algarve).

Chronology The historic evolution of architecture in Portugal includes the Roman remains of Conimbriga (Coimbra), Santiago do Cacem (the Alentejo), and Estoi (the Algarve), the Romanesque small rural churches in the northern region (for example Bravaes, in Ponte da Barca, with its beautifully decorated 13th-century porticoes), the 12th-century cathedrals in Coimbra and Lisbon, and the circular Templar chapel (Tomar, from the 12–13th centuries).

Good examples of the Gothic style can be found in the southern regions (corresponding to the military *Reconquista*, south of the rivers Douro and Tagus): Evora Cathedral (the Alentejo, Cistercian influenced,

1267–1325), the Convent of St Francis (in Santarem, the Portuguese 'Gothic capital', 1242–1315), the Abbey of Alcobaca (a gigantic *ensemble*, 1308–11), and Santa Clara a Velha (Coimbra, 1316–31), both by Domingos Domingues. The Batalha monastery (in Estremadura, by Afonso Domingues, 1388–1402) and the beautiful 'fortress church' in Flor da Rosa (Alentejo) are a setting for 15th-century Gothic monuments, as are the Graca Church (Santarem), the Guarda Cathedral (finished in 1426), and the parish church of Silves (1443–99).

Manueline, the national and most original style, was expressed in the precious Belem Fortified Tower (by Francisco de Arruda, 1515–20), and in the Jeronimos Cathedral, also in Belem, Lisbon (church and cloister from 1502–16, by Diogo Boitac and Joao de Castilho, 1517–30), and continued overseas at Funchal Cathedral (*Madeira, 1493–1517) and at Priorado do Rosario church in Goa, India (1540).

The Italian *Renaissance began with the Manga Cloister in Coimbra (1533) or the Santo Amaro chapel (1549) and continued to the Mannerist masterpiece, the Cloister in Tomar (by Diogo de Torralva, 1554–62) and the new series of classic cathedrals in the cities of Leiria, Portalegre, Miranda do Douro, and Goa. Plain Style tendencies started with the depurated Jesuit church of Sao Roque, in Lisbon (1565–72), and with Sao Vicente church (Lisbon, by Filipe Terzi, 1582–90), and proceeded with the Jesuit College at Coimbra (now the 'New Cathedral', 1598–1640, by Baltazar Alvares).

Vast Benedictine buildings were erected in Lisbon (the present Legislative Assembly), Oporto and Coimbra, during the 17th century, together with the renovation of the order's former seats at Santo Tirso (Minho, 1679) and Tibaes (Braga, 1628–61), two most impressive rural monuments. The extremely important role of the decorative arts in the promotion of this austere architecture, which stubbornly resisted the Baroque, is evident in the application of yellow, blue, and white painted and glazed tiles on vast interior surfaces, as well as in the use of gilt woodwork in church altars (Church of Marvila, Santarem, 1635–9), or in luxurious gardens (Marquis de Fronteira Palace, Lisbon, 1670).

Late Baroque finally arrived with the unfinished church of Santa Engracia, scenically placed overlooking the river Tagus (Lisbon, 1681–1713, by Joao Antunes, now the National Pantheon). Opulent and grandiose, the Court Baroque of King Joao V, funded by Brazilian gold and diamonds, was expressed by the giant Convent of Mafra (1715–50, by Ludovice) and in the Aqueduct of Aguas Livres (an engineering marvel, 1729–48, by Manuel da Maia, Custodio Vieira, Carlos Mardel), also in the royal palaces of Queluz (from 1758) and Necessidades (Alcantara, from 1742). *Nasoni was the most talented architect of the Oporto region, with the original Clerigos Tower (1732–48 and 1763) and the Freixo Palace (1750).

After the Lisbon earthquake of 1755, the austere *Pombaline style became the general urban and architectural tendency, especially with the rebuilding of Lisbon (the Baixa and the beautiful Praca do Comércio facing the Tagus). Neoclassicism was expressed in a few significant works—its highlights being the Sao Carlos Opera house in Lisbon (by Costa e Silva, 1792–3), the English Factory in Oporto (by Whitehead, 1785–90), and the D. Maria II Theatre in central Rossio square (Lisbon, by Fortunato Lodi, 1842–6).

Romanticism reached Portugal with the imaginative Pena Palace at Sintra (1839–85) for King Fernando II, while industrial buildings were represented by the Oporto Maria Pia bridge (Eiffel, 1876). The golden age of Revival began in the late 19th century, with works such as the neo-Arab bullring in Campo Pequeno (by Dias da Silva, 1892) or the neo-Manueline Rossio railway station (Jose Luis Monteiro, 1886–7), both in Lisbon. Monteiro also designed the 'Portugal Salon' in the Geographic Society building (Lisbon, 1898), a graceful iron structure.

After the 'Casa Portuguesa' cultural nationalistic movement, led by Raul Lino (Montsalvat house, 1902, at Monte Estorial, and Cipreste house in Sintra, 1914), a brief glimpse of Art Nouveau in the delicate 'Arte Nova' residence in Alexandre Herculano Street (Ventura Terra, 1903), and the ephemeral international Modernism of the 1920s and 1930s, there followed a neo-traditional tendency. This neo-rural and monumental architecture lasted from the early 1940s to the mid 1950s, supported by the traditionalist vision of the 'official taste' dictated by the political regime, the Estado Novo (1926–74), as in Cidade Universitaria de Coimbra, planned by Cottinelli Telmo and Cristino da Silva (1938–74).

In Oporto, Modern Movement architecture managed to survive, after the 1950s, and to win international recognition during the 1970s and 1980s, with architects such as Ramos, Tavora, *Siza, and de *Moura. The Faculty of Architecture in Oporto is a good example of Siza's avant-garde and inventive genius.   JMF

Fernandes, Jose Manuel, *Arquitectura modernista em Portugal, 1890–1940* (1993)

Kubler, G., and Soria, M., *Art and Architecture in Spain and Portugal and their American dominions, 1500 to 1800* (1959)

Watson, W. C., *Portugal* (1908)

Post, George Browne (1837–1913) US architect who contributed significantly to the creation of a new building type, the *skyscraper. As consulting architect for the 8-storey Equitable Building, New York City (1868–70, demolished), he was responsible for the first office building with an elevator. He designed the first 10-storey skyscraper, the Western Union Building, New York City (1872–5, demolished). The iron-framed interior walls of his monumental terracotta-ornamented New York Produce Exchange (1881–4, demolished) forecast the skeleton framing later adopted for skyscraper construction. Highly productive and versed in many styles, Post also designed houses; college buildings, including the picturesquely Gothic-styled City College campus, New York City (1897–1907); the temple-fronted New York Stock Exchange (1901–4); and the domed Wisconsin State Capitol, Madison (1906–17).   SBL

Landau, Sarah Bradford, *George B. Post* (1998)

Post, Pieter (1608–169) Dutch architect, who started as an assistant to van *Campen. He worked as an adviser and architect for the central government and the provinces, for several cities in and outside Holland, and wealthy patrons. Some of his works, such as the new town hall of Maastricht (1659–67), show a special interest in the strict application of the rules of proportion, or examples of building types described in the treatises of the Italian Renaissance, especially *Palladio and *Scamozzi. In Leiden (1657–58) and Gouda (1666), Post designed the weighhouses as regular boxes with a regulated use of sculpture and classicist ornament.

Post published series of engravings of his most important projects (reprinted in 1715). His reputation as the champion of Dutch Classicism leans heavily on his refined drawings.   FS

postmodernism The main ideas of postmodernism were foreshadowed in *Venturi's criticism of Modernism in *Complexity and Contradiction in Architecture* (1966) and *Learning from Las Vegas* (1972). In *The Language of Postmodern Architecture* (1977) Jencks broadened the critique by arguing for the inclusion of style and symbolism in architecture, and focusing on the supposed failure of the social goals of Modernism.

Undoubtedly, there were weaknesses in nearly all tendencies of Modernism: the lack of sensitivity to context; and the failure to work out an adequate visual language. Postmodernism did not offer a solution to these weaknesses, and in practice, the results were disappointing (*see* GRAVES; STIRLING).

Although the immediate architectural results of postmodernism were few and trivial, in the longer term the postmodernist approach has informed the contemporary trend of 'starchitecture' (in the work of Alsop, *Gehry, Hadid, Libeskind).   PG

See MODERNISM, 1975–2000; MOORE, CHARLES WILLARD.

Powell, Sir Arnold Joseph Philip (1921–2003) and **Moya, John Hidalgo** (1920–94) respectively English/US-born architects, in partnership from 1946. They were among the most sensitive modernists of the Welfare State era, paying special attention to the context of each site. Their work ranged across health, education, and housing.

The partnership's competition-winning design for the Pimlico housing estate, London, consisted of slab blocks mixed with terraced houses and lower ranges, built in three stages (1946–62). The main layout, of slabs built in staggered lines, is better handled than in most contemporary social housing estates in London, because of the more careful and varied detailing of the façades. There are minor differences between the stages—the size of the balconies, the emphasis given to expressing the structure—but the estate works well as an *ensemble*, even though rather dominated by roads. A counterpoint to the rather severe lines of the blocks is the glazed tower of the boiler house. At the same time, they were engaged on a much smaller scheme, the Gospel Oak estate, London (1953–4), which consisted of one tall slab and three 2-storey terraces. The slab is placed on a low mound, and highlighted in white brickwork, with each string course marked by a darker colour.

Their work then diversified into buildings for education and for hospitals, of which a number of representative examples may be given. They were particularly adept at fitting buildings onto restricted sites, as at Mayfield School, Wandsworth, London

(1955), or inserting new buildings, such as Staircases 16–18, Brasenose College, Oxford (1960–61) (*see* COLLEGES, OXFORD AND CAMBRIDGE). Equally, in more impersonal institutions such as hospitals, Powell and Moya designed low blocks to try to create a sense of community (e.g. Wexham Park Hospital, Slough, 1958–66).

As the welfare state declined in importance as a client, the partnership continued in the same vein but without the social and political commitment, in buildings such as the London and Manchester Assurance HQ, Exeter (1978), and the National Westminster Bank, Shaftesbury Avenue, London (1982), and, with a last gesture at a more rounded form of Modernism, the Queen Elizabeth II Conference Centre, London (1986).   PG

power stations The first large-scale power station, at Deptford (1888–90), set the form of the building type for almost 70 years: a large block with two chimneys at either end, set on a riverside site (to receive coal from the barges). The scenographic possibilities of the setting were first realized at Lots Road, London (1905), at the time the largest power station in the world. In the earliest examples, architects resorted to familiar classical solutions, first seen at Grove Road, Marylebone, London (1902, by C. S. Peach, an architect with a pioneer interest in the subject, and Charles Reilly), with its huge brick pilasters. The most full-blown of this type was the Interborough Rapid Transit Company, New York (1904, *McKim, Mead, and White), where five chimneys sprout incongruously out of a long brick façade, with round-headed arches framing the windows.

In Britain, the next round of building followed the establishment of a national 'grid' for distributing electricity. The pylons had an innovative form designed by engineers, a design surprisingly approved by *Blomfield, but the power stations themselves generally adopted conventional solutions. The only

modernist example, Dunston 'B', which set the chimneys back from a glass and steel turbine hall, was designed by engineers (Merz and McLellan, 1933, demolished). Sir Giles Gilbert *Scott's Battersea Power Station was designed in the same years (1930–34) as he indifferently applied exactly the same brick vocabulary of large-scale massing and careful detailing to the University Library, Cambridge. However, Battersea had the advantage of a sublime setting on the river, which Scott used to the full. He also designed Bankside (1947–60), and one of the few merits of its subsequent conversion to an art gallery is that the viewer can see the quality of the brickwork at a great height.

Scott's buildings, brick cladding over a steel frame, were understandably anathema to modernists, and the next generation of power station showed exposed structures, and clearly articulated plans, in a series by Farmer and Dark (Marchwood, Southampton, 1951–5; Belvedere, Erith Marshes, 1954–62; and the enormous Isle of Grain, 1970–77). The most striking feature of a modern power station is the cooling tower, a concrete structure usually about 122 m (400 ft) high, carried by an open network of rather spindly struts. When set in groups, and seen across a flat landscape (for example, Drax, North Yorkshire), the towers embody the cliché 'cathedrals of power' far more dramatically than their brick predecessors.

By contrast, nuclear power stations, in Britain at any rate, usually consist of two massive sheds, impressive in size and unintentionally scenographic in their remote, coastal locations (e.g. Bradwell, Essex, 1957).   PG

Stamp, G., *Temples of Power* (1979)

Prandtauer, Jakob (1660–1726) Austrian architect, who designed the church and Benedictine Abbey of Melk set high on a cliff-top 61 m (200 ft) above the confluence of the Danube and the Melk. Perhaps because the Abbot dictated the plan form combining church and abbey, Prandtauer set the church back behind a lower group of three arches, thus not quite achieving the most dramatic effect offered by an ideal site. Prandtauer's brilliance in handling large masses is seen on the long sides, which could have been extremely monotonous.

Compared to Melk, his numerous other designs, such as the pilgrimage church at Sonntagberg, near Waidhofen (1706–32), and the Kremsmünster Hof, near Linz (1719), are somewhat conventional.   PG

Pratt, Sir Roger (1620–85) English architect. A country gentleman who went on the Grand Tour to avoid the Civil War, Pratt turned to architecture and designed four large houses: Coleshill, Berkshire (1662, demolished); Kingston Lacy, Dorset (1663–5); Horseheath Hall, Cambridgeshire (1663–5); and Clarendon House, Piccadilly (1664–7), all now demolished or greatly altered. *Double piles, with central entrances and formal flanking rooms at the front, staircases and service rooms to the rear, they became models for the typical astylar Queen Anne house, the latter particularly so. Pratt also remodelled Ryston Hall, Norfolk (1669–72), for himself, and, with Wren, advised on the repair of old St Paul's.   APQ

prefabrication Building components have been mass produced in factories for at least 200 years. Machine-made bricks, ceramic tiles, sawn timber, sheet glass, sash windows, cast iron columns, and beams—all were familiar industrial products in 19th-century Europe and America. Complete prefabricated buildings were quite common. The most famous example is Crystal Palace, the gigantic greenhouse designed by Joseph *Paxton and erected in Hyde Park to house the Great Exhibition of 1851. Assembled at astonishing speed from a multi-layered hierarchy of standardized, factory-made components in iron, wood, and glass, this temporary building was what would these days be called a 'logistics exercise' of heroic proportions. But it

was not an isolated case. Houses, barracks, hospitals, railway stations, even churches were made in kit form in British factories and shipped all over the world. The great engineer Isambard Kingdom *Brunel designed a prefabricated hospital at Renkioi in the Dardanelles to accommodate British casualties of the Crimean War. The first boatload of components arrived on site on 7 May 1855. Within two months the hospital was ready to receive its first 300 patients and by March of the following year its capacity had risen to 2,200 patients.

But did these prefabricated buildings really count as architecture? In the 19th century the word architecture applied only to solid, monumental buildings like churches, town halls, and art galleries. The idea that architects might design, for example, workers' housing would have seemed eccentric. In the early 20th century, however, a group of progressive architects in Europe, later to be called 'modernists', aimed to bring architecture to the masses and to reconcile art and industry. Suddenly the ordinary house, especially the factory-made house, was at the top of the architectural agenda. Henry Ford's Highland Park plant in Detroit had begun to spew out Model Ts by the thousand and the cry went up, 'why can't houses be mass-produced like cars?'

That cry was to echo down the 20th century, and is still audible in the 21st. As early as 1910, Walter Gropius submitted to the AEG electrical company in Germany an impressively detailed and prescient proposal for the mass production of houses. In 1923 the greatest modernist of all, Le Corbusier, included a chapter on mass-produced houses in his famous book *Vers une architecture*. In it we find the Domino house, represented by a now iconic perspective drawing showing a naked reinforced concrete structure of thin flat slabs and slender columns, and the Maison Citrohan, conceived as a standardized product like its near-namesake car. These were early examples of a building type that is more common in architectural

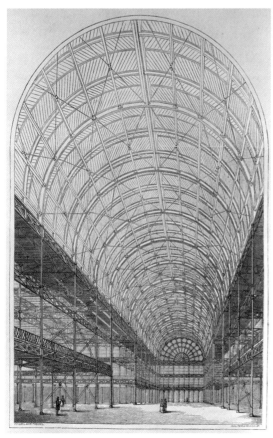

Interior, from the south entrance, Crystal Palace, Hyde Park, London (Joseph Paxton, 1851)

construction, were being produced in considerable volume. In the 1920s the Sears Roebuck Company sold houses by mail order. Customers chose the designs from pattern books, and the bundles of pre-cut timber were delivered by rail. In the years after World War II, companies like National Homes of Lafayette, Indiana, produced thousands of factory-made traditional wooden houses every year. In Britain, the post-war housing shortage was eased by the production of 150,000 temporary single-storey prefabricated dwellings. There were several types, the most advanced of which was the AIROH (Aircraft Industries Research Organization on Housing), designed to take up spare capacity in aircraft factories. AIROHs were made in four sections at a rate of one every twelve minutes. The factory-fitted kitchen included a refrigerator, a rare luxury at the time. 'Prefabs', as they were known, were designed for a ten-year life span, but many lasted much longer.

In 1950s Britain, earnest young architects working in public sector offices saw ever increasing industrialization as the only possible future for building. The process would be accelerated, they thought, by 'modular coordination', an idea first proposed in the 1930s by an American, Alfred Farwell Bemis, in his 3-volume book *The Evolving House*. Bemis saw that if buildings were to be mass-produced like cars, then they would have to be assembled from interchangeable components sized in multiples of a standard dimension or 'module'. His proposed module was a 10 cm (4 inch) cube. Post-war British architects tried to put this theory into practice in 'closed' systems made by single manufacturers or consortia, but all the time aspiring to an 'open' system to which the whole building industry would conform. It was an impractical idea based on a fundamental misunderstanding of the realities of industrial production, but it had a surprisingly long life and gave rise to some modestly successful building programmes. For example, between

history books than it is in actuality: the architect-designed prefabricated house. Later American examples include the plywood Packaged House, designed by Konrad Wachsmann with Walter Gropius, and the aluminium Wichita House, designed by Buckminster Fuller. They were supposed to solve the post-World War II housing crisis, but neither went into full-scale production.

Meanwhile, non-architectural prefabricated houses, based on standard American 'balloon frame'

1945 and 1955 the county of Hertfordshire erected 91 system-built schools, which have since been much admired as examples of a humane and practical post-war Modernism. Other local authorities followed Hertfordshire's lead, cooperating to develop systems with acronymic names like SCOLA and CLASP, but the resulting architecture tended to settle into dull monotony.

It was in mass housing that prefabrication was to have the biggest impact. The combination of a new housing form, the *tower block, and a new building technology, the pre-cast concrete load-bearing panel, inaugurated a heroic but ultimately disastrous episode in modern architectural history. In 1960s Britain, system-built high-rise council estates were favoured by the government, because they were visible proof that the housing shortage was being tackled. Estates like Thamesmead, built on marshland by the Thames estuary, were big enough to be called new towns and were designed with some flexibility and imagination. Others simply applied proprietary systems, often imported from France or Scandinavia, in the most economical way possible. Once completed, many of these estates quickly sank into rubbish-strewn, graffiti-smeared, crime-ridden squalor. Historians still disagree about the reasons for this rapid decline. Was high-rise living intrinsically problematic, or was it simply a matter of bad maintenance and thoughtless letting policies? In the end, it was technical, not social problems that killed the pre-cast concrete tower block. On 16 May 1968 a gas explosion caused a corner of Ronan Point in east London to collapse like a pack of cards, killing three people. Within twenty years, tower blocks all over the country were being deliberately blown up by their local authority owners, to be replaced by ordinary 2-storey houses with gardens.

In Communist eastern Europe, however, pre-cast concrete housing continued to flourish. It was the perfect building technology for a centrally controlled economy where political and media pressure were irrelevant and square miles of city could be cleared without resistance. Typically, a factory large enough to supply about 500 dwellings a year would set up as near to the site as possible, and a light railway would be constructed to link the two. While the foundations of the apartment blocks were being dug, the all-important travelling crane would be assembled on site and set to work laying its own tracks. The site was therefore as much of a production line as the factory. Load-bearing panel systems were the most common, but there were also 'volumetric' systems such as the Soviet Lagutenko method, which combined concrete floors and columns with moulded asbestos-cement walls and ceilings to produce room-size boxes. Whatever the system, outwardly the apartment blocks looked the same: plain and box-like, 4–8 storeys high, making no concessions either to their urban context or to the dreams of the people who lived in them. They were, however, produced very efficiently at a rate of about ten dwellings per construction worker per annum.

In the post-Communist era, the demand for large-scale, heavyweight building systems has evaporated. But there are still housing shortages to be met, and architects are once again becoming interested in prefabrication. There is much talk of 'avoiding the mistakes of the past' and of new concepts such as 'mass customization'. The realization has dawned that in the age of computer-controlled machinery, mass production does not necessarily mean standardization. In Japan, a high proportion of new suburban houses are made on fully robot-equipped production lines, and every house is different. Lightweight materials such as timber and pressed steel are more common than concrete, and panels are sometimes assembled into fully equipped room-size boxes in the factory, reducing the on-site construction time to a minimum. One manufacturer offers a special deal for house replacement—a maximum of 50 days (including weekends) from moving out of an old house to moving into a new one on the same site. But the industrialization of building does not necessarily involve the building of big factories, any more than it necessarily involves the development of a 'system'. In the US, the mobile home industry long ago adapted itself to volume house production. Its products, which are these days called 'manufactured homes', are made using relatively primitive technology in small factories local to their markets. They are cheap, efficient, and popular. Whether they should be described as 'architecture', however, is doubtful.   CD

> See also JAPAN; PREFABRICATION.
>
> Davies, C., *The Prefabricated Home* (2005)
>
> Russell, B(arry), *Building systems, industrialization and architecture* (1981)

preservation *See* CONSERVATION.

Prichard, John (1817–86) Welsh architect. *See* WALES.

Prior, Edward Schroder (1852–1932) English architect. His diverse practice included schools (music schools at Harrow, 1890–91, Winchester 1901–4), university buildings (the Medical School, Cambridge 1899–1902), and churches (the oustanding example being St Andrew's Roker, Tyne and Wear, 1905–7). Prior showed a typical *Arts and Crafts respect for local crafts and *vernacular architecture, but his attempt to combine this approach with innovative planning was something of a failure. For Home Place, Holt, Norfolk (1903–5), following an earlier experiment at The Barn, Exmouth, Devon (1895–7), he used the 'butterfly plan', in which two wings are splayed out symmetrically at 45 degrees from a central block. His intention was to create both a varied silhouette and a sun-trapped terrace overlooking the garden side.

Unfortunately, the design created dark spaces in the centre, and the first-floor galleries overlooking the terrace were so draughty that they had to be glassed in.   PG

prisons

Introduction Prisons had unspecific origins; for in them were incarcerated not only people thought or proven to have committed crimes, but debtors, the mentally ill, unemployed or vagrant, impoverished, and (usually) the mentally handicapped. From the 18th century onwards, and vastly increasing in the 19th, these categories were teased out and provided with separate institutions: asylums, *workhouses, poor houses, debtors', felons', petty criminals', military, and young persons' prisons, and Bridewells.

Early custodial institutions, like hospitals and plague or pest houses, were placed outside town walls, or built into town gates, as in the case of Newgate and other London gates. This was a practical means for the control of infection and contagion, and the exclusion of disturbers of the peace, and also a symbolic device signifying the purity of the city's moral condition. There was a degree of chaos in these early prisons: lack of segregation between the sexes and between young and old, squalor, disease, and paradox. Wealthier prisoners could pay for food and drink, and even to have their servants. Once the threshold of the boundary was crossed, inside there was 'classless liberty' (Bender, J., *Imagining the Penitentiary*, Chicago, 1987). Gay's *The Beggar's Opera* uses these contradictions as its central theme. A fundamental change in attitudes, both with regard to punishment and chaos, became the objective of 18th-century reformers. Beccaria (1764) brought Enlightenment ideas to the issue. He saw discipline and punitive labour as essential components of the contractual proportionality between a crime and its punishment. His aim was to bring to an end idle chaos and unmeasured punishment, for which two fundamental changes were necessary.

Reform The first aim was to get rid of the scourge of gaol fever, as widespread in prisons as in ships, hospitals, and barracks. It was generally assumed to be caused by 'putrid' or vitiated air; hence the continuous attempts to halt it by removing dirt, avoiding overcrowding, introducing plenty of ventilation, selecting high 'airy' sites, and concentrating in sanitary blocks the latrines, washing places, and laundries. It was much later that the louse was recognized as the transmitting agent in typhus (which 'gaol fever' in fact was).

The second change was related—to get rid of *moral* contagion. The solution lay in the classification and segregation of prisoners. One kind of segregation was already common—that based on economic class, for those who could pay were separated from those who could not, and enjoyed less squalid conditions. But segregation by sex, age, or type of crime became a key objective of reformers, foremost of whom was John Howard, who in the last three decades of the 18th century travelled widely in Europe and Russia, and published a series of beautifully illustrated influential volumes. Amongst the prisons he described was the young male offenders' house of correction at San Michele (1701–4), designed by Carlo Fontana for Pope Clement XI as an addition to Pope Innocent XI's Ospizio Generale (1686), which had an orphanage, a women's shelter, an almshouse, together with workshops and training facilities. San Michele housed sixty carefully selected prisoners aged under twenty years on three galleried floors, with an open, full-height central hall. At ground level there were spinning

wheels. The basement contained vats for washing and drying, and weaving looms. Each individual cell had its own latrine, and, beside the door, each had an opening into the hall, so slanted that the celebration of Mass at the altar at one end could be observed. Silence was the rule (emphasized by the large sign *Silentium*). The open hall, with galleried cells, and the attention to ventilation, survived well into the early 20th century. The regime, too, became a model for much carceral management later—silence, segregation, discipline, surveillance, work, and penance.

Howard's recommendations and his model County Gaol (1777) incorporated central surveillance and many of the San Michele features, but stopped short of a fully radial plan, which he regarded as 'Catholic' and Absolutist. Prisoners were in individual cells whose '. . . solitude and silence are favourable to reflection; and may possibly lead to repentance.'

During the War of Independence transportation to the USA ended and precipitated a crisis, which was not resolved till the first convicts landed in Botany Bay in 1787. For a while floating prisons ('hulks')—utterly condemned by Howard—were used. The Penitentiary Act of 1779 was a recognition that prisons for long-term confinement with labour were going to be needed. A competition for penitentiaries for 600 male and 300 female inmates elicited 63 entries in 1782, the winner being William Blackburn. Though his submission has disappeared, and the penitentiaries were never built, he became, for the remainder of his short life, Britain's leading prison designer, and Howard's most faithful interpreter, with an influence stretching well beyond his death in 1790. His and his followers' designs used orderly, segregated wings, sometimes around courtyards, with various points of surveillance. His first (four-armed) radial prison was for Ipswich (1786), followed by Liverpool (1795), with six free-standing radial blocks with central surveillance.

The cruciform or radial layout had arrived in Scotland before Blackburn. James Wardrop had already proposed it for Calton Gaol in Edinburgh (1781), and in the same year (1782) as the English competition results were announced, Lord Provost David Steuart and Sheriff Deputy of the County published their design for a three-armed Bridewell for Edinburgh. It had a central keeper's house, detached from the three cell blocks but with complete visual surveillance of them. They claimed that 'The central situation of the Governor's house, the precautions already described [swivel guns on the outer turrets which could fire both inwards and outwards, and which, they claimed, would have prevented the Gordon Riots in London in 1780]... for strength and security will render the number of officers and servants much smaller than would otherwise have been necessary.' This uncannily anticipated Jeremy Bentham's ideas on central surveillance and economy of staff by nine years.

At the end of the century, there were three types of prison: haphazardly assembled courtyards and wings, such as George *Dance junior's rebuilt Newgate (1769); formal, axially laid out assemblies of courts, wings, and turrets, such as *Soane's proposals for the 1782 competition and Leroux and Middleton's Cold Bath Fields House of Correction (1788–94); and cruciform or radial plans, such as Baxter's proposed Edinburgh Bridewell (1791) and the Blackburn designs already mentioned. Newgate, and the others, expressed their function by means of severe monumental exteriors, often heavily rusticated.

Regimes were rapidly changing—with segregation, surveillance, solitary confinement and silence, sanitary improvements, and organized work put into practice in this heterogeneous mixture of buildings. It was into this scene that Jeremy Bentham's Panopticon or Inspection House and its regime burst forth—with immense consequences for subsequent developments.

Bentham and after Jeremy's brother Samuel was working as a naval engineer at Kritchev in Russia; he found a scarcity of skilled workmen to supervise his canon arsenal, so he devised a circular 'inspection house' where the supervisor at the centre, in an inspection tower, oversaw the unskilled workers arranged in a ring around him. It was whilst Jeremy was visiting Samuel in 1787 that he wrote letters to England proposing to adapt this idea for a national penitentiary. Four years later, in 1791, the Panopticon was published, complete with detailed drawings. The first version was 4 storeys high, the second 6.

The Panopticon was worked out in every detail—the glazed, central inspection tower with viewing slits, muslin veils, and lighting so arranged that the governor could see into every cell around the circular periphery without being seen; an 'annular gallery' around the central tower, on which the turnkeys would move and observe the prisoners, noting infractions of the code of discipline, whilst they themselves, as well as the prisoners, were under observation by the unseen governor; ingenious solutions to drainage, ventilation and water services; communication between the centre and each cell by means of a bell, as a means of instruction or reprimand; and a proposal for opening and closing each cell door from the centre by means of wires and pulleys.

In line with Bentham's Utilitarian principles, the Panopticon was to be run under contract to the government, and it was intended that the prisoners would be engaged in productive, profitable labour. Apart from his twenty-year-long battle to have a Panopticon built in Britain, Bentham tried to promote it in Ireland and France. But finally no Panopticon was built in England, and the London site, now occupied by Tate Britain, was eventually used for building the huge Millbank Penitentiary (1812–21) designed by Hervey (or Harvey). Here there was a central hexagonal court, formed by offices and inspection rooms, in the middle of which was the prison chapel, and attached to its sides were six pentagonal cell courts for the 1,100 prisoners, each court with its own central inspection tower.

Only one prison reasonably true to Bentham's principles was built—and that in Scotland, in 1791, the year when the idea was first published. This was the Bridewell on Edinburgh's Calton Hill, designed by Robert Adam. Here, however, there was a half circle for the peripheral cells; and the exterior was castellated and solid, expressive in the accepted 18th-century Scottish manner. Many designs have had Panopticon claims made for them; but in truth they resembled the original idea only in the sense that their plans were centric, and visual surveillance of every court and cell—or at least cell corridor—was possible. The most famous, and persistent embodiment of this idea was in the great radial prisons built in the latter half of the 19th and the early 20th centuries in Britain, Continental Europe, and in North America. But these were preceded by important early versions.

Amongst these predecessors was the seven-armed prison at Bury Saint Edmunds (1803), designed by the Governor, John Orridge; a larger, six-armed version (1821), also by Orridge, designed for the Russian Emperor; the series of model designs promoted by the Society for the Improvement of Prison Discipline (1820 and 1826); and John Haviland's seven-armed plan for the Eastern Penitentiary, Philadelphia (1821–9). This last was originally a single-storey building, each cell next to its own private, walled garden, as in the medieval Carthusian monastery. Here the regime was the 'separate' system—perpetual, cell-bound, silent solitude, broken only by the visit of warders and the chaplain. Some saw in this a humane, morally efficacious order; others a pathological one, leading to insanity and an incurable, zombie-like state. The alternative was the 'silent' or 'Auburn' system (named after its introduction in the New York prison of Auburn in 1823) where there were separate cells but shared daytime workrooms and

chapel, and where silence was rigorously enforced by an army of guards. American policy veered towards the 'silent', whereas Britain and much of Continental Europe favoured the 'separate' system.

The outstanding 'separate' prison in Britain, which survives and is in use, was the Pentonville Model Prison (1840–42), designed by Joshua Jebb, Surveyor General of Prisons. Here there was a central chapel, a central spacious observatory from which every one of the 520 cell doors was visible, and from which radiated the four 3-storeyed, galleried cell blocks. The design of these was hardly distinguishable from the almost 150-year-old block at San Michele in Rome.

By this time all ideas of profitable, productive work had been abandoned. Instead labour (and exercise) was carried out on the treadwheel, or the cell crank. Each cell had a fresh water supply, a flushing privy, and a hand-turned crank, whose resistance to turning could be adjusted, and whose turns were counted and recorded. Food was supplied through a hatch; the interior of the cell could be seen through an inspection aperture; and night-time gas lighting was provided. Jebb designed a complex system of warm air heating, combined with ventilation, with inlet and extract grilles in each cell.

Corresponding to the physical devices was a regime which enforced absolute silence and segregation. Prisoners wore hoods with eye slits to go to chapel or exercise; the chapel had individual partitioned boxes, from which only the minister was visible, and even the guards wore felt overshoes so as not to make a noise during their rounds.

By 1847 there were 51 prisons built, or under construction, based on the Pentonville Model and under Jebb's supervision. In Continental Europe 'separate' prisons were being widely built. By 1846 there were 30 in France; others were built or under construction in Holland, Sweden, and Prussia.

The 'Model' and its regime brought together two centuries of reformatory ideas: segregation, discipline, physical labour, surveillance, hygiene, and hierarchical systems of control. ᴛᴍ

From 1850 From the middle of the 19th century, prison design seems to have been confined to utilitarian planning. Seemingly the only prison façade designed by a noted architect, or of any marked character, is the Allegheny County Jail, Pittsburgh, Pennsylvania (1883–8), by H. H. *Richardson, with its forbidding cyclopean granite exterior.

The only new plan was the 'telephone pole' layout, first used at the Fresnes prison colony, Val de Marne, France (1898–1901), devised by the architect F. H. Poussin. It has formed the basis for most maximum-security prisons: a long, easily supervised corridor, from which the parallel individual prison units branch off. ᴘɢ

Evans, R(obin), *The Fabrication of Virtue: English Prison Architecture, 1750–1840* (1982)

Markus, Thomas A., *Buildings and Power* (1993)

profession, the architectural

Buildings can arise from amateur knowledge, as well as from the efforts of building workmen, and for most of history, the architectural profession was permeable in both directions. The Greek word *architekton*, used by Plato in the early 4th century ʙᴄ, implies both designer and supervisor of workmen, possessor of theoretical knowledge rather than merely of practical knowledge. Documented instances of Greek architectural practice from Plato's time include what we would now consider as mechanical, civil, and military engineering. Buildings followed established typologies, and architects were paid little more than workmen, although the prestige and expense of temple buildings indicates a higher status based on specialized education, probably based on written texts. In the Hellenistic period, it seems that salaried architects were retained by cities.

Despite the existence of *Vitruvius' text, less is known of Roman architects than their Greek forerunners. Many Roman architects were of Greek origin and so was their culture, as Vitruvius indicates. Apollodorus alone in the whole Roman period can be identified with actual buildings in the time of Trajan. Anthemius of Tralles (d.535 / 40) comes into focus as the architect of Hagia Sophia, after which individuals temporarily disappear.

Monks probably took on many architectural functions in the Christian world, and whoever drew the St Gall plan of *c*.820 (possibly an ecclesiastic or an educated courtier with the training of a Byzantine *mechanicus*) has transmitted evidence of sophisticated architectural thought in the time of Charlemagne. The architect re-emerged in name and practice in the 12th century, associated chiefly with churches, but also involved with palaces, castles, the grander domestic buildings and their gardens, military works, and city planning. The clergy were still crucial both as patrons and participants in the building process. Subsequent research has dispelled the Romantic 19th-century images of teams of anonymous craftsmen building cathedrals (*see* ᴍᴀsᴛᴇʀ ᴍᴀsᴏɴs). The architects seem to have originated in a specific craft discipline, to which they added knowledge of geometry. They operated internationally in Europe, so that William of *Sens was chosen to design the post-fire reconstruction of Canterbury Cathedral in 1174, introducing the Gothic style to England. In 1261, a sermon by Nicolas de Biard complains of the architect, with stick and gloves, 'who directs by word alone and never dirties his hands' yet receives more pay than other workmen.

In the Renaissance, many of the best known architects, including *Brunelleschi and *Bramante, were concerned with other arts, or in Alberti's case with writing. Patrons such as Federigo da Montefeltro, Duke of Urbino, played a major role in design. The revived classical style architecture gave new prominence to drawing skills for design and recording antiquity, while models explained concepts to patrons and construction teams. Direct links with construction mattered less, and were a barrier to achieving status.

The presumption of artistic versatility continued down through *Michelangelo to *Bernini, as a specifically Roman feature when a more specialized profession was emerging in northern Italy. *Palladio rose from his background in masonry as a mature student of classical humanities, representing a new professionalism. Philibert *De l'Orme's text of 1567 shows the transmission to France of the idea of architect as artist and professional, standing defensively between patron and master mason, each of whom evidently might consider him intrusive or superfluous. The publication of illustrated books, including Vitruvius (from 1511), *Serlio (1537), and Palladio's *I Quattro Libri* (1570), helped to establish a universal body of architectural knowledge not available simply from experience of the job, although changing styles made the architect's particular design task lengthier and more complex in the Baroque period.

In England, the mason working according to tradition gave way to the designer with knowledge of Classicism, notably with Robert *Smythson (1534/5–1614) and his son John, who consolidated the tentative beginnings of the Tudor Renaissance. Inigo *Jones came to architecture from a background of general artistic talent, and buildings formed only part of his endeavour, although John *Webb transmitted a more professional approach to the Restoration. Even so, informed amateurs of genius such as *Wren and *Vanbrugh continued to work, with help from another genius, *Hawksmoor, and a strong supporting cast of craftsmen and artisans.

Artistic academies in Italy, seen as gatherings of learned men rather than as teaching institutions, included architects. The Royal Academy of Architecture, founded in Paris in 1671, established a comprehensive and hugely influential teaching programme. Through the Academy, French architects kept in close contact with the state under changing regimes, and contributed to the high reputation of French architecture, but the Royal Academy of Arts in London founded nearly a hundred years later did little to challenge the existing apprenticeship system.

The formation in 1834 of the Royal Institute of British Architects helped architects to assert their special status as gentlemen rather than business or tradesmen, although it was nearly 100 years before the actual title of architect was protected by Act of Parliament (Architects' Registration Act, 1931), and formal educational provision was sufficiently widespread to act as a primary means of entry. The Institute combines the roles of learned society and protectionist trade union. Fee percentages were regulated, and eventually the conduct of competitions, but British governments had little use for architects and their work. Many of the most 'artistic' architects of the later 19th century either refused to join the Institute, or resigned during the 'Profession or Art' controversy of 1891, in protest against the proposal for registration, driven by a rival body, the Society of Architects, formed in 1884. The legacy of these quarrels remains unhappily institutionalized in the distinction between the RIBA (a voluntary membership body) and the Architects' Registration Board (with whose regulations all those wishing to be called architect must comply). The title 'architect' is strictly protected, but only in name, and in most countries of the world it is normal for the proportion of buildings designed by qualified architects to be less than 10%. In the post-1945 period, many architects in Britain worked as salaried employees for local or national government, with a strong ethic of public service. In private practice, many offices expanded in numbers, in some cases forming alliances with other building professionals to offer a 'one stop shop'. The concept of the architect as artist was revived in the postmodernist period and has remained dominant.

The relationship between design and construction varies from one country to another. In France, construction drawings are not prepared by the design architect, but by intermediaries. In the USA, architects do not expect to exercise detailed site supervision in the manner still common in Britain.

The ideal of the British architect was to be a professional gentleman first, and an artist second. Even so, many architects saw themselves as businessmen, although prohibited from having business associations with construction, from advertising, fee-bargaining or acting as developers until 1984. During the 'boom' years of the 1980s, a number of practices were floated on the Stock Exchange, seldom with long-term benefit. The architect's professional position was eroded in the 1990s by the growth of construction management as a separate profession, and the procurement of buildings by 'Design and Build'. From the mid 1990s, the governmental Private Finance Initiative (PFI) for funding major investment has added a further layer of misery to the lives of architects trying to work in what remains of the public sector. Rising levels of mandatory professional practice insurance are a further burden, and architectural practice remains vulnerable to downturns in the economy. At the same time, some of the most famous architects have devised systems of subcontracting with consultants to shield themselves from claims of liability in the event of legal action from clients.

The American Institute of Architects was founded in New York in 1857, and the first architectural registration law in the USA was in 1897, in Illinois. It is organized by state chapters. At most times, it has represented business interests of architects rather than taking a role of social responsibility.

In most countries, a large number of architects are involved with the conservation of historic buildings, a specialized field which remains excluded from the majority of architectural training.

The regard in which the architectural profession is held by non-architects bears little relation to its structures of association. In Britain, the trial of the architect John Poulson in 1973 for bribing local and national government officials (even the Home Secretary, Reginald Maudling, was forced to resign) in order to obtain architectural commissions came at a time of disenchantment with the modernist environment. When HRH The Prince of Wales condemned the failings of the whole profession in their service to the public in 1984, he was widely applauded and his intervention led to an increase in newspaper coverage of architecture. The RIBA worked hard to recover the status of architects, instituting public awards such as the Stirling Prize (1995), that elevated the status of architects as 'stars'. The funding of glamorous new arts buildings through the National Lottery around the turn of the millennium gave architects new opportunities to display their talent. It is uncertain whether this media attention has contributed depth to the general understanding of architecture, or shifted the preference of the British public for old buildings.   AP

Saint, A., *The Image of the Architect* (1983)

pronaos An anteroom before the *naos or main chamber of a Greek or Roman temple. It was usually enclosed at the front by a row of columns separating it from the portico, at the side by a continuation forward of the main chamber's side walls, and by a further wall with a central doorway dividing it from the naos.   APQ

proportion Theories of, and an interest in, proportion are usually identified with the classical tradition. The views of *Vitruvius, the earliest theorist in this tradition, are as usual difficult to interpret. Thus, in stating the rules for the design of temples, he argued that 'Symmetry arises from proportion...Proportion is a due adjustment of the size of the different parts to each other and to the whole; on this proper adjustment symmetry depends. Hence no building can be said to be well designed which wants symmetry and proportion.' (*De Architectura*, Book III, Chapter 1, paragraph 1.)

The proportions of a temple should follow those of a well-formed human body, which he describes in some detail: the length of the foot is a sixth of the height, the fore-arm a fourth, and so on. In another section (Book VI, Chapter 2 *passim*), he states that these proportions may be adjusted, according to '...the nature of the place, the purpose of the building.'

*Renaissance architects and theorists accepted Vitruvius with the addition in *Alberti's *De re aedificatoria* of another set of rules, not found in Vitruvius: 'We shall therefore borrow all our Rules for the finishing our Proportions, from the Musicians, who are the greatest Masters of this Sort of Numbers...' (Book IX, chapter V.) Alberti's purpose in making the analogy with music was to raise architecture from the level of a mechanical art to the loftier sphere of the liberal arts.

The architect most closely associated with the theoretical rules of proportion to architectural practice is *Palladio. In general, he followed Alberti and Serlio, but also employing harmonic ratios (b-a/c=c-b/c, i.e. for a room 1.8 m × 3.6 m (6 ft × 12 ft), the height is 2.4 m (8 ft)) not only in individual rooms, but also in the relation of the rooms to each other.

From about the middle of the 18th century, the 'objective' and mathematical aspects of classical proportion were strongly contested. Rejecting both the musical analogy and the human figure as a source of proportion, William Hogarth (*Analysis of Beauty*, 1753) regarded proportion as a matter of subjective choice. Similarly, the theorist of the *picturesque, Sir Richard Payne Knight, argued that proportion '...depends entirely upon the association of ideas, and not at all upon abstract reason or organic sensation...' (*Analytical Inquiry into the Principles of Taste*, 1805, p.169.)

As the theory of proportion ceased to inspire practising architects, historians began to search for the use of proportions in classical architecture, particularly Greek and Roman temples (e.g. Penrose, *Principles of Athenian Architecture*, 1851; John Pennethorne's *The Geometry and Optics of Ancient Architecture*, 1878). In some cases, the search led to fantastic, barely credible results (Jay Hambidge, *The Parthenon and other Greek Temples: their Dynamic Symmetry*, 1924), in particular the interest in the use of the *Golden Section (1.618 to 1). There is little real evidence that it was used in design, although it is very probable that it was used as a means of setting out.

This point suggests a series of questions about projecting onto historic buildings a proportional analysis heavily reliant on mathematically precise ratios. Have the buildings been measured carefully enough? Do the geometric figures overlaid onto the buildings fit precisely enough to justify suggesting that buildings are designed following a particular set of proportions? Could the architect have used the dimensions purely as a way of setting out his scheme, so that their proportional qualities are merely coincidental? These questions cannot always be answered unambiguously, even when the intentions of the architect have been clearly stated. And such questions have not always been examined thoroughly enough, even by the most careful of architectural historians, such as Wittkower (*Architectural Principles in the Age of Humanism*, 1949).

The long history of the theory of proportion had a surprising finale. In his book *The Modulor* (1954), Le Corbusier suggested that the Modulor, which was based on a series of dimensions taken from the figure of a man 6 feet (1.8 m) tall, was not only an instrument of architecture, but could serve as the unit for standardizing the sizes of mass-produced building components. PG

Neumann, Eva-Marie, 'Architectural Proportion in Britain 1945–1957', *Architectural History* (UK) 1996, pp.197–221

Scholfield, P. H., *The Theory of Proportion in Architecture* (1958)

propylaeon An entrance way to an enclosure, usually a sacred site devoted to temples, associated with a classical acropolis. Originating as a fortified gateway, it became formalized, and assumed a symbolic role, as can be seen at the Acropolis, Athens, where the propylaeon still dominates an access route hard to breach. APQ

prostyle A free-standing row of columns set before a building, for instance to carry an extension of the roof, thus forming a porch or *portico, as opposed to columns set in antis (see ANTA) between extensions of the side walls forward to the front. (*See also* PERISTYLE.) APQ

Prouvé, Jean (1901–84) French designer and innovator in prefabricated structures. As a leader in architectural prefabrication, Prouvé extended the French tradition of construction through his pioneering work in new building techniques and materials such as bent steel, aluminium, and plastic. Prouvé was trained in the craft of iron-working. The collective ideals represented by the industrial guilds were fundamental to his commitment to industrialized housing as a social goal. He participated in a number of experiments with mass and mobile housing. In 1937–39, for example, in response to the Popular Front's efforts to give paid vacation to workers, Prouvé participated with the architects Eugène Beaudoin and Marcel Lods (and in partnership with the Strasbourg steelworks) to develop the prefabricated, demountable steel vacation house. This project prefigured the lightweight, portable sheet steel and aluminium Tropical House (1949), composed with an economy of means and an intention to create an original response to the tropical climate. From 1939 on, his firm built and designed schools, factories, hospitals, barracks, and emergency dwellings as quickly assembled, economical, and easily transported parts. He worked on significant commissions with Robert

*Mallet-Stevens, later cooperated with *Le Corbusier on aspects of the Unité d'Habitation, the chapel in Ronchamp, the Chandigarh parliament houses, and made significant contributions to canonical 20th-century buildings such as La Maison du Peuple by Lods and Beaudoin (1939) and Joseph Belmont's Le Pavillon d'Aluminium (1954). KMB

Sulzer, P., *Jean Prouvé, Complete Works* (2005)

pteron An external colonnade surrounding many classical Greek temples, such as the Parthenon. Its origin appears to have been as a support for an overhanging roof, which was required when the walls beneath it were made of earth or some other material prone to rapid weathering. APQ

public houses Pubs developed as distinctive British buildings during the 19th century. Earlier centuries were no strangers to public drinking, and the Middle Ages enjoyed alehouses, better-class taverns serving wine, and inns for travellers.

Only inns were architecturally distinctive, either set around a courtyard, or with a major block facing the street. The earliest survivors are the George, Norton St Philip, Somerset (late 14th century, refronted 1475–1500), the Angel and Royal, Grantham, King's Head, Aylesbury, and New Inn, Gloucester (all mid 15th century).

Inns survived until the coming of the railways, by which time a new institution had arrived to seduce urban drinkers—gin palaces. They developed in the 1820s and 1830s as brightly lit, gaudily decorated establishments, providing a different, glittering world from the humdrum homes of their customers. There was also an explosion of down-to-earth beerhouses after the 1830 Beer Act allowed anyone to open one on payment of a 2 guinea annual fee.

The rest of the century was characterized by efforts to rein in what were seen as excessive numbers of drinking houses and the perceived immorality and criminality they engendered. Pressure from the temperance movement was crucial, and the eventual effect on pub architecture and arrangements profound as licensing magistrates sought reduced licence numbers and better premises. The 1880s to early 1900s were the Golden Age of the pub, and many were built with great lavishness. Brewers bought up many premises and upgraded them as counter-attractions to the burgeoning competition from sports, clubs, music hall, and other entertainments.

Late-19th-century urban pubs were rarely architecturally distinguished (few were by well-known architects) but were prominent and stylistically very varied. Gothic—associated with the Church—was least popular while the safe, secular world of the Italianate was widely used. The greatest achievement was internal decoration and furnishing schemes, relying on glasswork, ceramics, and woodwork to create striking effects which owed something to the gin palace. Notable London examples are the Argyll, Argyll Street, W1 (c.1895), Princess Louise, High Holborn, WC1 (refitted 1890s), Salisbury, St Martin's Lane, WC2 (c.1898), and Salisbury, Green Lanes, N4 (1898–9). Spectacular provincial examples are the Bartons Arms, Aston, Birmingham (1900–01), Garden Gate, Hunslet, Leeds (1903), Philharmonic (1898–1900) and Vines (1907), both in Liverpool. A key characteristic was separate rooms and small drinking areas, reflecting differences in social and economic status.

A reaction against elaborate decoration set in before World War I. The trend was towards large premises using Tudor, vernacular, and Georgian architectural dress, offering, ideally, a range of facilities apart from alcohol. Post-World War II pubs are generally utilitarian and smaller than their immediate predecessors. Multi-room layouts remained usual until the 1960s: the trend has since been towards opened-out premises. With notable exceptions (e.g.

Oliver *Hill's The Prospect Inn, Minster-in-Thanet, Kent) few modern pubs have achieved architectural distinction. GBr

Brandwood, G., Davison, A., and Slaughter, M., *Licensed to Sell: The History and Heritage of the Public House* (2004)
Girouard, M., *Victorian Pubs* (1975)

Pugin, Augustus Welby Northmore (1812–52)

English architect, designer, and writer. The only child of Auguste Charles Pugin (1769–1832), who established a school of architectural drawing and published accurate drawings of medieval architecture to which the son contributed, Pugin developed a precocious facility for draughtsmanship. He built St Marie's Grange, Salisbury, for himself in 1835, the year he began to assist Charles *Barry with the *Gothic detail for the new Houses of Parliament, and subsequently the design and execution of carved ornament, furniture, fittings, and stained glass.

A passionate medievalist with a preference for Early English and Decorated Gothic, which he saw as indissolubly linked with Christianity, he published polemical tracts promoting these styles, and *Contrasts* (1836) in which he illustrated adverse comparisons between modern society and its architecture and that of medieval England. He elaborated his views in a series of influential publications, especially *The True Principles of Pointed or Christian Architecture* (1841), disdaining the term 'Gothic' as pejorative, in which he stated that ornament should enrich the essential construction of a building, and implying that this was unique to Gothic; that even the smallest architectural details should have a meaning or serve a purpose; and that construction and design should vary according to the material used. The idea of 'truth to materials' became a fundamental tenet of William *Morris (1834–96) and the *Arts and Crafts movement (c.1880–1914). Pugin's writings were quickly taken up by High Church ecclesiologists, who demanded a return to medieval liturgy and architecture.

Pugin designed almost exclusively for Roman Catholics, but, frustrated by shortness of funds, much of his work left him believing he had achieved few of his dreams. St Giles's, Cheadle, Staffordshire (1840–46), did however fully exemplify his idea of a rich Decorated town church, just as The Grange, Ramsgate, Kent, his own residence and church (1843–52), exemplified his idea of a medieval community.   APQ

Pugin, Edward Welby (1834–75) English architect. Trained under his father A. W. N. Pugin, E. W. Pugin took over the practice, completing many of his father's works and building up an extensive practice, devoted to Roman Catholic churches such as St Mary, Warwick (1859–60), St Francis, Gorton, Manchester (1863), St Colman's Cathedral, Cobh, Ireland (begun 1868), and St Gregory, Stratford-upon-Avon, Warwickshire (1866); colleges such as Mayfield and Mark Cross, Sussex (1868–9); and convents, such as Our Lady, Bartestree, Herefordshire (1863); and also houses such as The Towers, Parklands, Leeds (1867). These followed his father's true Gothic principles, but have a nervous intensity that reflects the vigour of High Victorian Gothic as it appeared after 1850.   APQ

pulvin, pulvino A cushion *capital, impost block, or *dosseret, particularly used in Early Christian and Byzantine architecture to enable a thick wall or springing of an arch to be carried on a comparatively slender cylindrical column. Usually of convex section, like a cushion, it may be carved with a cross or other device.   APQ

pylon 1. a tower at the entrance to an Egyptian temple. See EGYPT, ANCIENT (TEMPLES AS SPATIAL AND PROCESSIONAL FORMS). 2. a structure for carrying electricity lines. See POWER STATIONS.   PG

pyramids, ancient Egyptian Pyramids are the most distinctive of all ancient Egyptian buildings, and originated as actual, and in some cases symbolic, tombs of kings. It is possible to trace the form's development in the oldest known example, the Step Pyramid of Djoser (c.2650 BC), and in its successors from the following century, resulting in the definitive shape of a smooth triangular profile with a slope of just over 50 degrees. Kings continued to be buried in pyramids until about 1600 BC, after which they had rock-cut tombs in the Valley of the Kings at Thebes. Pyramidal form was then taken over by non-royal tomb-owners, some of whom built small, steep-sided mud-brick pyramids over their rock tombs (c.1450–1100 BC).

A pyramid was the focus of a complex of buildings, sited on the western edge of the Nile Valley, that typically included a 'valley temple', a causeway leading up to the low plateau, a mortuary temple, and, immediately to its west, the pyramid itself. Most complexes had one or more small subsidiary pyramids in addition to the main one; some of these seem to have been symbolic second tombs of their owners, while queens were buried in others.

The shape of a pyramid complex implies arrival from the Nile Valley, ideally by water. The valley temple and mortuary temple were the locations for continuing cults of the deceased king; they seem not to have been used for funerals. The temples had complex plans with central, colonnaded courts leading to sets of chapels, generally five, that may have housed cult statues of the king. In the 5th–6th dynasties (c.2450–2150 BC) they were lavishly decorated with reliefs of royal activities and of the king receiving gifts from the gods.

Interiors formed a tiny proportion of the volume of pyramids. They were entered from the north and were set within the superstructure in the 4th dynasty pyramids of Snofru at Dahshur and those of Khufu, Khephren, and Menkaure at Giza (c.2550–2450 BC);

later interiors were excavated beneath pyramids. The interiors consisted of a sloping entrance passage, a statue chamber, an antechamber, and a sarcophagus chamber for the burial. Some pyramids had small chapels on their north sides, next to the entrance, which was sealed after burial and remained in principle inaccessible.

The symbolism of pyramids seems to be solar and cosmological. The structure was a primeval mound on which the sun-god emerged as creator. Some images suggest that the sun was also thought of as alighting on the pyramid tip, which was a separate monolith, late examples of which bore imagery of the sun's journey through the night sky.

Pyramidal structures of varying form and function are known in much of the world. Most of these forms arose independently, but those of Napatan and Meroitic royalty in northern Sudan looked to Egyptian models in two phases, first in forms comparable with Egyptian royal pyramids (c.720–500 BC) and from then until AD 300 in smaller, steeper-sided structures comparable with Egyptian non-royal pyramids. A few pyramid tombs influenced by Egypt were also built in the Graeco–Roman world. JB

Edwards, I. E. S., *The Pyramids of Egypt* (revised edn, 1993)
Lehner, M. E., *The Complete Pyramids* (1997)

Pythius (*fl*.353–334 BC) Greek architect and writer. Designer of the Mausoleum at Helicarnassus (c.353–350), and the temple of Athena Polias, Priene (dedicated 334), Pythius described these buildings, and recommended a wide training for architects. APQ

Qatar *See* GULF STATES.

qibla indicates the direction in which Muslims face during prayers, the Ka'aba in Mecca. The direction of prayers is essential in Islam, symbolizing the unity of all Muslims.

Architecturally, the *qibla* is manifested as a wall lying perpendicular to the horizontal axis to Mecca. In the Prophet's mosque in Medina, the *qibla* was only a blank wall. In the evolution of *Islamic architecture, the *qibla* wall was then articulated with the mihrab and the *minbar, both of which signified the importance of the *qibla* wall. The configuration of a wall and a mihrab at the centre became an accepted convention for the *qibla* wall. In its essential form, a mosque consisted of a free-standing *qibla* wall only, evidenced in open-air areas on the fringe of cities for celebrations of the Islamic holidays, called idgah or *musalla*.   ABS

Quarenghi, Giacomo Antonio
Domenico (1744–1817) Italian architect active in Russia. Following architectural studies in Rome during the 1760s, Quarenghi became a devoted follower of Palladio. In 1779, he accepted a contract for work in Russia, where he launched a highly successful career of almost four decades. His first major design was the English Palace at Peterhof (1781–94, destroyed 1942), an understated, yet monumental structure based on Palladian principles. Quarenghi also worked at the imperial estates of Pavlovsk and Tsarskoe Selo, where he built the Alexander Palace (1792–1800), with its heroic double colonnade. In St Petersburg, his

numerous state commissions include the Academy of Sciences (1783–5), the Hermitage Theatre (1783–7), the Assignation (State) Bank (1783–90), the Horse Guards Manège (1804–7), and the Smolny Institute (1806–8).

The key to Quarenghi's style lies in its precisely calculated relationship of the central portico and pediment to the structure's main façade. With their clarity of proportions and simplicity of fenestration, his buildings epitomize the graceful elegance of neoclassical architecture in imperial St Petersburg.   WCB

Quaroni, Ludovico (1911–87) Italian architect, urban planner, and educator who had a profound influence on Italian architecture after World War II. During the 1930s he was primarily involved in competitions, his major built work being the Piazza Imperiale at the Esposizione Universale di Roma (1938; with Francesco Fariello, Luigi Moretti, and Saverio Muratori). After the war he espoused both a comprehensive approach to urban planning and an interest in vernacular building practices in projects like the INA-Casa housing on Via Tiburtino in Rome (1949–54; with Mario Ridolfi), the Borgo La Martella in Matera (1951), and the Chiesa della Sacra Famiglia in Genoa (1956).   BLM

Queen Anne (1707–14) A short reign of an English queen, notable for plain, four-square

domestic architecture, and an extraordinary set of churches, mostly in London and resulting from the Act for building Fifty New Churches (1711). Basically, preaching boxes adorned with porticoes and steeples, they are a singular jewel of English Baroque, ranging from the opulently Roman of *Gibbs's St Mary-le-Strand (1714–17) and *Archer's St Paul, Deptford (1712–30), to the uniquely English interpretation of the antique in *Hawksmoor's St Anne, Limehouse (1714–24), one of eight of his churches. Hawksmoor had a hand in All Saints' Church, Oxford (1706–10), ostensibly designed by Henry *Aldrich, and South Quad, Queen's College, Oxford (1709–34).   APQ

Queen Anne revival An informal style of architecture introduced in the 1870s, owing much to Philip *Webb, J. J. Stevenson, and Norman *Shaw, which revived the features of the domestic Baroque style current in the reigns of William and Mary and Queen Anne, sometimes, and when later applied in an imposing way for large buildings, archly called Wrenaissance. It was especially appropriate in suburbs, such as Bedford Park, London (begun 1875), which includes shops, a hall, and church, as well as houses, a place to lead a 'chaste correct Aesthetical existence', virtues embraced at Hampstead Garden Suburb (begun 1906), and every other suburb that followed.   APQ

r

Rabirius (*fl.*AD 81–96) Roman architect. Said to be the builder of the imperial residence on the Palatine Hill, Rome, from which is derived the word 'palace'. Set on two levels of the hill, this vast complex of buildings incorporated state and private apartments and a library, under several domes, which were associated with the celestial sphere. All around were pleasure gardens, marble-paved courtyards with playing fountains, and even a hippodrome. Here imperial ceremonies unfolded amid the opulence appropriate to a luxurious court.   APQ

Raguzzini, Filippo (*c.*1680–1771) Italian architect. He designed two churches, both in Rome, S. Maria della Quercia (1729–34) and the Ospedale di S. Gallicano (1725–6), which make an interesting use of concave and convex curves. However, both are relatively minor works, and an unlikely prelude to the Piazza S. Ignazio, Rome (1727–35), which is a masterpiece of urban design. Before Raguzzini's intervention, a small piazza was overwhelmed by the uninspired bulk of the church. He transformed the space by redirecting the access streets so that they entered the piazza obliquely rather than axially, thus reducing the visual impact of the church. The nondescript buildings facing the church were given delicately modelled concave façades, drawing attention away from the church, and emphasizing the complex space formed on the segments of three ovals. The scheme offers a fascinating contrast to *Cortona's piazza for S. Maria della Pace.   PG

railway stations A simple *building type as compared to other new building types of the 19th century—*law courts or *town halls. Although even quite small stations were originally provided with an array of waiting rooms (one for each of the three classes of passengers), offices, and refreshment rooms, their arrangement was a relatively straightforward matter. Planning and circulation did not tax the ingenuity of the architect.

But two other features of the new building type did pose difficult problems for architects. Because of their size, railway stations had the greatest impact upon European cities since cathedrals, four hundred years earlier. No immediate precedents could easily be pressed into service, since neither of the two methods of transport superseded by railways—the canal and the turnpike system—had developed new buildings for their passengers.

The first station, Crown Street, Liverpool (1830), was a featureless building next to uncovered tracks; Edge Hill, also Liverpool (1836), was the first to provide a roof to cover platform and tracks. For inter-city services and termini, a different approach was needed. Two experimental types were tried and not repeated.

The façade of the Derby Trijunct Station (Francis Thompson, 1839–41) was 320 m (1,050 ft) long, but only 12 m (40 ft) wide: impractical for the passengers, and lacking in presence. The latter objection could hardly be levelled against Euston, London. In front of the station building, as a gateway to the city, stood the Euston 'arch' (Philip *Hardwick, 1835–9), an oversized version of the propylaeon on the Athenian acropolis, flanked by offices for mail, coach, and parcel offices. The waiting hall, by P. C. Hardwick (1846–90), was almost as grand, especially the Directors' meeting room, but thoroughly inconvenient for the passengers.

The first decade of station building also saw a simplification of railway operations (at first even major stations handled both passenger and freight traffic) and

experiments with the only possible relations between the buildings and the tracks: either the through station (with the buildings parallel to the tracks); or the terminus (a 'head' building connected to a shed); and the island station (the buildings lie between the tracks). It was not until much later that the possibilities of the building being placed over or under the tracks were explored, at the Hauptbahnhof, Hanover (Hubert Stier, 1888–1907) and the Alexanderplatz Bahnhof, Berlin (J. E. Jacobsthal, 1880–85), respectively.

During this experimental period, *Ruskin querulously asked: 'Will a single traveller be willing to pay an increased fare . . . because the columns of the terminus are covered with patterns from Nineveh . . . or because there are old English-looking spandrels on the roof . . .'? (*Stones of Venice* I). The question was never answered, because in the next two decades railway travellers were not given the option of cheap plain stations.

The most logical architectural solution was found not in Britain, but in Paris. The Gare de l'Est (François Duquesney, 1847–52) and the Gare Montparnasse (Victor Lenoir, 1850–52) included an extensive concourse, enabling passengers to wait in greater comfort, and to move from one platform to another. The façade expresses the shape of the great train-shed by means of two very large semicircular glass openings surmounted by a great pediment. A monumental clock in the centre had a particular significance: the railways were the most important force in establishing a standardized national time. The second Gare du Nord (*Hittorff, 1859–66) was a more sophisticated version of the same approach.

The Parisian model was followed in only one major British station, King's Cross (Lewis *Cubitt, 1851–2), and in a cruder form (by dispensing with the pediment). As if anticipating its modernist admirers, Cubitt wrote about his façade: 'The building will depend for its effect on the largeness of some of the features, its fitness for

Gare du Nord, Paris (Jacques
Ignace Hittorff, 1863)

its purpose and its characteristic expression of that
purpose' (1851). At the time, only one attempt was made
to follow this approach and to evade the grip of the
inappropriate historical prototype: the iron-and-glass
Rewley Road station, Oxford (1851; now re-erected in
the Buckinghamshire Railway Centre, Quainton), was
a miniature version of the Crystal Palace *exhibition
building, by the same engineering firm, Fox and
Henderson.

Other London termini included hotel/office
buildings, usually of rather an undistinguished
character, as a screen for the train-shed: at Paddington
(*Brunel and M. D. *Wyatt, 1850–52); Victoria (the
Grosvenor Hotel, J. T. Knowles, 1860–61), Charing
Cross (1863–4), and Cannon Street (1863–6), both by
E. M. Barry. It is often forgotten that Sir Giles Gilbert
*Scott's Midland Grand Hotel at St Pancras was not just
an extravagant *Gothic Revival screen for the train-

shed, but was completely integrated into the workings
of the station, providing entrances and exits directly
onto the platform, and its ground floor was the railway
refreshment rooms.

But if the architects' work is generally
undistinguished, the engineers designed a series of
audacious structures for the train-sheds. The sheds
gradually extended in size, from the three spans at
Paddington (Brunel and M. D. Wyatt, 1852–4) which
covered 72.5 m (238 ft), to culminate in the wrought-
iron single span covering 74 m (243 ft) at St Pancras
(W. H. Barlow, 1864–8) and rising 30 m (100 ft). These
were increasingly impressive feats of engineering, but
far less attractive visually than the curving train-sheds
at Newcastle (1848–65), York (1874), and Brighton
(1882).

The greatest variety in small to medium stations
is to be found in Britain, with every historicist style,

sometimes looking impressively like a small *palazzo (Hull Paragon, G. T. Andrews, 1846) or a *town hall (Huddersfield, James Pritchett the Elder, 1847–50). Space precludes giving further details, and the reader is referred to G. Biddle, *Britain's Historic Railway Buildings* (2003).

Despite its vast railway network, the United States had no architecturally significant stations until the 1880s, when H. H. *Richardson designed a series of stations for the Boston area. With wide overhanging roofs, and massive masonry more suitable to a fortress, they were far too dramatic for their suburban setting. Just as car production was getting into gear (*see* FACTORIES, SINCE 1850), the first decade of the 20th century saw a trio of grandiose Beaux Arts stations. With the tracks and the platforms hidden underground or covered by minimal sheds, the new focus of station design, the concourse, followed an unlikely precedent—Roman *baths, as at Pennsylvania Station, New York (McKim, Mead, and White, 1902–10), Washington Union (1903–7), and Grand Central, New York (Warren and Wetmore, Stem, 1903–13).

At least the façades onto the street were relatively restrained, and the passenger circulation was well planned, which could not be said for the main European station to follow this trend, Ulisse Stacchini's highly bombastic Milan Central (1913–30). The *Beaux Arts skills so wastefully used here were much better employed in France, by Victor Laloux. Following a smaller station, at Tours (1895–8), he made good use of the new possibilities provided by electrification, at the Gare d'Orsay, Paris (1897–1900), by placing the concourse above but at the side of the tracks. The alternative approach adopted by Eliel *Saarinen at Helsinki (1910–14; *see* NATIONAL ROMANTICISM), and Paul *Bonatz at Stuttgart (1911–28) accepted the traditional 'head' arrangement of termini. The granite façade and giant figures of the former, and the rather

primeval-looking stone front of the latter, express a primitivism at odds with modern technology: perhaps, fittingly, the train-shed at Helsinki was a miserably stunted affair, and rather dark at Stuttgart.

In all these examples, it is somewhat paradoxical that just when the technology of roofing large spaces, in *exhibition halls and aircraft hangars, made a sudden leap (for example, the 110 m or 362 ft span of the Galeries des Machines, Paris exhibition 1889), railway stations abandoned the audacious over-all sheds of the previous generation for separate roofs covering only a few platforms each.

During the interwar period, with the railway network complete in the most advanced countries, the most interesting stations were in Italy, Turkey, and Finland. Michelucci's design for Florence (1934–6) was modernist in perhaps the negative sense, of avoiding the use of historic details; more positively, and less well known outside Italy, were the series of stations by Angiolo Mazzoni, of which Spoleto (1939) may be singled out as representative. A country's modernization did not necessarily lead to the adoption of architectural Modernism, as was shown by the application of *modern Classicism to a series of railway stations in Turkey, the most impressive being at Ankara (*Holzmeister, 1935–7), a monumental building flanked by tall colonnades, the primary point of entry to the new capital. Several new stations were built in Finland, the most outstanding being at Tampere (O Flodin and Sepälä, 1933–8), with its tall, pylon-like clock tower.

In the immediate post-war period there were few opportunities for modernists to build complete railway stations, rather than booking halls or entrances (e.g. in Britain, Harlow Town, 1959–60; Oxford Road station, Manchester, 1959–60; Barking, 1961—all by British Railways architects). Even the most impressive of its kind, the Stazione Centrale, Rome, formed only part of the station. Here the lithic monumentality of Mazzoni's pre-war design (begun 1937) for the offices flanking the platform, the kind of railway station which might have been built in Imperial Rome, was superseded by a light, airy, glass and concrete concourse (Eugenio Montuori, completed 1951). Unfortunately, like most stations which depend for their architectural effect on the spaciousness of the concourse, the effect has been greatly diminished by the encroachment of tawdry shops.

Electrification offered new opportunities, and no drawbacks, for the design of railway stations, but the architectural results of the electrification programmes beginning in the late 1950s are rather disappointing. There may be exceptions in the vast numbers of new stations in the Communist bloc, but this is a completely unresearched field.

In Britain, the west coast (London–Glasgow) electrification programme (1957ff.) produced rather mixed results. Euston exchanged the grandeur of the waiting hall and the 'arch' (demolished in 1962, a cause célèbre of the *conservation movement) for a much more practical concourse, of no visual merit; Birmingham New Street benefited from a new *signal box (Bicknell and Hamilton, 1964–6), but with its low roof it is one of the most troglodytic stations in the world; Stafford, with its exposed concrete finishes, is inoffensively *Brutalist; whilst Coventry, with its white-tile and timber surfaces and its clear modern *lettering (by Jock Kinneir), is perhaps the most successful.

A new era of European railway travel opened in the 1980s with the advent of the high speed train. The engineering aesthetic was revived in a modern form at Lille-Europe (Jean-Marie Duthilleul with RFR and Ove Arup) and also at Chur, Switzerland (Richard Brosi and Robert Obrist, 1985–92). Continuing the alternative tradition of applying a façade idea with little intrinsic relation to railways, *Calatrava's Satolas station at Lyon airport (1990–94) has been regarded as the image of a huge bird with elegant wings. As at the beginning of the railway era, Pugin's verdict (*An Apology for the Revival of Christian Architecture in England*, 1843, p.11) on the Euston 'arch' is equally apposite: 'The architects have evidently considered it an opportunity for *showing off what they could do* instead of *carrying out what was required.*'

Today, like *airports, railway stations are particularly vulnerable to the pressures of retail commerce, to the extent that what would appear to be their primary purposes, of circulating and distributing passengers and celebrating the glamour of travel, are universally subverted by the distraction of excessive shopping space.   PG

See also METRO STATIONS.

Meeks, C. L. V., *The Railroad Station* (1964)

Rainaldi, Carlo (1611–91) Italian architect. Rainaldi's first major project was rather unsuccessful. His plan for rebuilding the old church of S. Agnese in Piazza Navona, a Greek cross with the ends culminating in apses, was accepted (1652), but following severe criticism, he was dismissed once the façade had reached about 3 m (10 ft). Unfortunately, he was employed again in 1657 after *Borromini's resignation. Rainaldi reduced the height of the lantern, and replaced Borromini's intricate towers with the insignificant structures we see today. His role in designing the façade of S. Andrea della Valle (1661–5) is difficult to separate from that of Carlo Fontana.

S. Maria in Campitelli, Rome (1663), was the first building for which he was solely responsible. The plan is rather unusual, a sequence of spaces consisting of a cross with nearly equal arms, a square choir and an apse, but not entirely successful, as the spaces are ill-defined and do not flow easily into each other. On the façade the classical order is used 32 times, more than on any other Roman church, to create a jagged profile, lurching forward well clear of the wall. One possible reason for such an exaggerated profile is that the façade is rarely well-lit, since it is oriented to the north-east (compare the similar façade of the Cathedral of Syracuse, Sicily, 1728–54, which faces west).

While the façade of S. Maria in Campitelli has rather an abrupt relationship to its piazza, Rainaldi's churches of S. Maria di Monte Santo and S. Maria dei Miracoli (1661–77) are one of the cleverest examples of using architecture for purely scenographic purposes (cf. RAGUZZINI). Where three streets enter the Piazza del Popolo, the churches occupy wedge-shaped sites of different sizes. Rainaldi solved the problem of making the churches seem identical by giving the church of S. Maria di Monte Santo an elongated oval plan, and S. Maria dei Miracoli a circular plan. Consequently, the diameter of the dome over the oval is actually set further back, but seen from the piazza both domes appear to be the same shape and size. Rainaldi countered the disparities in the width of the façades by a subtle extension of the wall beyond the outer orders. PG

Rainer, Roland (1910–2004) Austrian architect. *See* AUSTRIA, 1900–2000.

rammed earth *See* TERRE PISE.

ramps *See* STAIRS, STAIRCASES, AND RAMPS.

Ramsey, William de (d.1349) English mason, the greatest of a family of perhaps seven masons working in London and Norwich. William III de Ramsey was a key protagonist of the Perpendicular style, working at Westminster Palace (1325), and perhaps in Norwich, before he started the new octagonal chapter house and cloister at St Paul's Cathedral (1332), recorded by Hollar before destruction in the Great Fire. He worked at the Tower of London (1335) and Lichfield Cathedral (1337), and may have designed the cloister at Windsor Castle (from 1337). A fresh campaign at St Stephen's Chapel, Westminster (begun 1346), which included his influential traceried clerestory and wooden vault, ended with his death, probably of plague. APQ

Raphael (Raffaello Sanzio) (1473–1520) Italian architect and painter. Raphael's interest in the architecture of ancient Rome is shown by his painting 'The School of Athens', in the Stanza della Segnatura overlooking *Bramante's Cortile de Belevedere, the Vatican. After Bramante's death in 1514, Pope Leo X promoted Raphael to take Bramante's place as architect of St Peter's, though none of his proposals were realized. His subsequent achievement as an architect is difficult to evaluate, as he relied heavily on Antonio da Sangallo the Younger for practical advice. Three buildings— S. Eligio degli Orefici, Rome (begun 1514), the Palazzo Bresciano-Costa, Rome (*c*.1515), and the Palazzo Pandolfini, Florence—were either partly completed by other architects (*Peruzzi, *Sangallo) or have been demolished, so that we do not have a clear picture of Raphael's contribution, except that the palazzi may have borne some passing resemblance to Raphael's own house, designed by Bramante.

The Villa Madama, near Rome (planned 1518) was intended to be a reconstruction of a classical Roman villa, of the type described in the letters of Pliny the Younger. The design shows that Raphael could solve practical problems of adapting to the site and accommodating the user's needs, as well as designing interiors of great elegance, such as the tripartite north loggia. PG

Rastrelli, Count Bartolomeo Francesco (1700– 71) who defined the late Baroque style in Russia, was born in France. In 1716 he arrived in St Petersburg, where his father worked as court sculptor. The younger Rastrelli's ascent to imperial favour occurred during the reign of Empress Anne (r.1730–40), who commissioned him to build palaces in both Moscow and St Petersburg.

Rastrelli was granted still greater power by Elizabeth Petrovna (r.1741–61), for whom he built some of the most lavish palaces in Europe. His major projects included a new Summer Palace for Elizabeth (1741–3, destroyed), the Stroganov Palace (1752–4), and the final version of the Winter Palace (1754–64). In addition, Rastrelli greatly enlarged the existing imperial palaces at Peterhof (1746–52) and Tsarskoe Selo (1748–56). All of these projects are distinguished by their heroic scale and richly decorated façades.   WCB

Raymond, Antonin (1888–1976) Czech-born US architect active in Japan. Raymond was educated in Prague, worked for Cass Gilbert and Frank Lloyd *Wright, and then established his own office in 1920 after working on the Imperial Hotel, Tokyo. Raymond was a pioneer of the Modern Movement in Japan, where he practised for more than four decades before and after World War II. He was a direct conduit between European avant-garde movements, advanced American building technology, and Japan. Raymond gained international prominence through the design of his own exposed reinforced concrete home at Reinanzaka, Tokyo (1924–26). Working for an international clientele primarily in Tokyo, Raymond built over 400 buildings including houses, offices, factories, schools, churches, auditoriums, and golf clubs. While his work has been criticized for directly quoting from Wright, Le Corbusier, and Perret, Raymond synthesized lessons from his masters and traditional Japanese construction in post-war masterpieces such as the *Reader's Digest* Building in Tokyo (1951), with its daring exposed concrete structural frame and curtain-wall system and 'maruta' log-frame residences and churches.   KTO

Raymond du Temple (*fl.*1360–1405) French mason. Royal mason to Charles V and Charles VI, Raymond worked at Notre Dame, Paris, building the Célestins chapel (1367–70), notable for its sculpture.

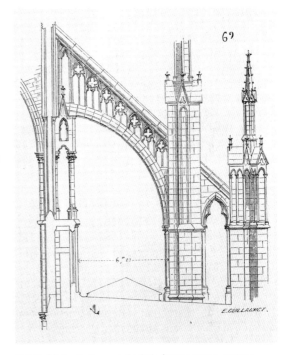

Detail of flying buttress: cathedral of Notre-Dame, Amiens, France (13th century)

When Charles V converted the Louvre from fortress to palace, he added his famed Vis du Louvre (1370s), an external open spiral staircase of a type particularly favoured in France with ornate arcading and central shaft. As well as works outside Paris, he designed the Collège de Beauvais (begun 1387) for Paris University.   APQ

Rayonnant literally 'radiating' or 'shining forth', a late phase of French Gothic, when the programme of large, tall buildings came to a halt in the 1230s. Its pioneering example is the remodelled nave of Saint-Denis, Paris (1231ff.), in which the glazed triforium is linked with the clerestory, to form in effect a wall of glass. At the Sainte-Chapelle, Paris (1242–8), the same principle is applied to the whole building, so that stained-glass windows occupy three-quarters of the total height. The next development applied to façades, as a veil of masonry was draped around the cornice level and in front of the windows and portals. Typified by St Urbain, Troyes (c.1262–70), the development is seen at a larger scale in the cathedrals of Clermont-Ferrand (1262ff.), Carcassonne (1269ff.), and Limoges (1275ff.).

PG

Reed, Thomas (1810–78) Danish architect. *See* ECUADOR.

refinements, Greek As a means of preventing the straight lines inherent in their trabeated architecture from appearing weak or to sag, the Greeks introduced numerous refinements. The most visible of these is *entasis, the slight convexity in the taper of a column counteracting an illusion of concavity resulting from a straight taper. The space between columns, or intercolumniation, normally identical, is slightly reduced between corner and penultimate columns, to strengthen the corner, which might otherwise seem weak. Uniquely at the Parthenon, Athens, the refinements extend much further. It seems that, in their search for perfection, the Parthenon's designers, Ictinus and Callicrates, wished to counteract the distortion the eye introduces when viewing the Parthenon obliquely. The platform slopes slightly downwards towards the edges; this at first was thought to be simply utilitarian, facilitating the drainage of rainwater, but the columns it supports tilt increasingly inwards away from the centre, and the intercolumniation decreases, column by column, by a fraction of 1%. Finally the terminal pediments tip forward by a minute amount. The dimensions of these refinements are so small that only an accurate survey published in 1851 (F. C. Penrose, *Principles of Athenian Architecture*) uncovered them, and

at a stroke increased the Parthenon's reputation for almost superhuman perfection.

APQ

Régence The French style associated with the regency of the Duc d'Orléans in the early minority of Louis XV, which had been evolving for at least a decade before the death of Louis XIV in 1715, and continued to do so for at least a decade after the death of the Regent in 1722. The predominant thread is the decreasingly weighty elaboration of Rococo ornament in the increasingly commodious interiors of the private houses which proliferated when court and courtiers retreated from the strictures of Versailles to relaxation in Paris—though, in contrast, exteriors usually maintained academic classical restraint.

CT

Regency The late Georgian style of art and architecture, current during the regency of the future George IV in 1810–20, and characterized by refined delicate ornament, or its sparing use and plain clearly defined shapes, sometimes contrasting with bold neoclassical elements. Unlike its French equivalent, the Empire style, it is essentially decorative. This is characterized by *Nash's development of Regent's Park (begun 1811) and the metropolitan improvements associated with Regent Street in which stucco terraces are the focus of a picturesque landscape whose scenic qualities triumph over strictly architectural ones. Typically English, the same genius imbues Brighton, where open squares and similarly grandiose but rather slapdash terraces face the seafront. Like wings, these set the stage for a long meandering picturesque green, The Steyne, with at its centre Nash's extraordinary Pavilion (1815–22), a unique concoction of oriental styles with ogee domes and minarets that exactly catches the raffish atmosphere of this London-by-the-sea resort.

APQ

Regionalism A contemporary architectural movement promoting use of local materials, respect for local natural, social, and cultural idiosyncrasies, and preservation of community ties. As a movement Regionalism became significant during the 18th century, linked with the emergence of the picturesque and romantic movements. In the19th century and early 20th, Regionalism was associated with rationalist design methodologies adapting buildings to local climatic and site conditions, drawing knowledge from local successful cases, re-employing tested local materials (Norman *Shaw, E. S. *Prior, Philip *Webb, Eliel *Saarinen) while experimenting in design and construction (Antonio *Gaudí, H. H. *Richardson, *Greene and Greene, Bernard *Maybeck), often linked with anti-centralist, anti-dogmatist, and anti-imperialist emancipation campaigns (Josep Puig I Cadafalch, and Lluis Domenech I Montaner), and can be seen as a pioneering expression of the Modern Movement promoting values of innovation and freedom, to become later a branch of Modern architecture focusing on the particular and contextual rather than the universal (Alvar *Aalto, Erich *Mendelsohn in Palestine, 1930s *Le Corbusier).

But Regionalist architecture often used regional precedents in a freewheeling eclectic manner, applying them to achieve emotion and theatricality for commercial ends (Port Sunlight, Liverpool, for the employees of Lever's, Parker and Unwin, 1910) or for forging group or ethnic identity (Ragnar *Östberg, Peder Vilhelm Jensen-Klint). In such cases, despite the high quality of its production, Regionalist design did not contribute to the evolution of modern architecture. This is most clearly demonstrated in the buildings of international expositions which proliferated from the second part of the 19th century onwards up to World War II, devoted to nationalist propaganda and tourist consumerism (Paris 1900, Palace of the Arts; Exposición Iberoamericana de Sevilla, architect Anibal González, 1929; Exposición International de Barcelona,

1929; Exposition Coloniale Internationale, Paris, 1931). During the 1930s chauvinist Regionalism became overtly anti-modernist, serving emerging totalitarian regimes in Europe. 'Heimat' and 'Völkisch' architecture of the Third Reich applied mainly to houses and municipal buildings (see the work of Paul Schultze-Naumburg). During the 1940s Regionalism was applied in Franco's Spain, for the 'Regiones Devastadas' of the civil war and for regime and ecclesiastical buildings (Luis Moya, Luis Guitiérrez Soto). The Vichy regime in France supported Regionalist architecture in opposition to Modern (exponent Louis Hautecoeur).

The most important critic of the propaganda and commercial abuses of Regionalism was Lewis Mumford, who in a series of scholarly and polemic writings tried to redefine it, giving it a deeper, social, cultural, and ecological meaning, and suggesting it as a means of renewal of modern architecture. AT

regula A short band or fillet, particularly that between the taenia and *guttae beneath each of the *triglyphs in the frieze of a *Doric order, and perhaps representing the ends of the beams of the Greek order's timber prototypes. APQ

Reidy, Affonso Eduardo (1909–64) French-born Brazilian architect. He was a professor at the School of Architecture alongside Lúcio Costa, with whom he collaborated in building the famous Ministry of Education and Health (1937–43). He devised modern architectural forms, developing a personal language which reached maturity with the Pedregulho housing estate in Rio de Janeiro (1947–52); this undulating and multi-level 260 m (853 ft) long construction is adapted to the sloping terrain, offering a full range of services including school, clinic, and gymnasium. He was involved in several urban plans, including the Gavea housing development project (1952), although he produced many plans and few buildings. His most noteworthy creations in Rio de Janeiro are the Marechal Hermes Community Theatre and the Modern Art Museum (1954) in the Aterro de Gloria, by Roberto Burle Marx, with whom he also collaborated in the overall design of the Flamengo Park (1956).

LNM (trans. KL)

Reilly, Sir Charles Herbert (1874–1948) English architect, author, and teacher. *See* BANKS, CONSOLIDATION.

Renaissance architecture The architectural Renaissance occurred first in Italy in the third decade of the 15th century and filtered out first to France (partly resulting from Charles VIII's invasion of Italy in 1498; *see* FRANCE (THE RENAISSANCE)) and then to Spain (*see* SPAIN, POST-MEDIEVAL (1490–1600)), Germany (*see* GERMANY (1500–1780)), and later to England (*see* ENGLAND, FROM PRE-ROMAN TO 1900 (THE REFORMATION)).

It was one manifestation of a widespread cultural shift characterized by the adoption by the intelligentsia and urban patrons of ancient Roman models. Greek architecture did not figure in the classical revival, primarily because Greece was under Ottoman control. Just as the revival and emulation of ancient literature was shaped by the rediscovery, editing, and publishing (printing became widespread by the end of the 15th century) of ancient texts of philosophy, science, rhetoric, poetry, and historical writing, so the revival of classical architecture was founded on study of the remains of antique buildings and the rediscovery of the one surviving ancient architectural treatise, *Vitruvius' 1st-century *De architectura*. The text was difficult, especially since the illustrations had been lost, and the terminology was often opaque (most architects were ill at ease with Latin); the first printed edition became available only at the end of the 15th century and an Italian translation not until 1521.

Architects in the early Renaissance were not trained as such. Their careers began in the workshops of painters and sculptors. Renaissance theory placed the foundation of all the arts in *disegno*, essentially the craft of composition, which was to be acquired primarily through experience in drawing the human figure. This was one aspect of the effort of artists to shake off the stigma which medieval society placed on manual labour and to redefine themselves as gentlemen.

Because the climate of the Italian peninsula is temperate and because the topography of the areas where most new building occurred was even, there was no environmental need for marked differences in design from north to south. But Italy was a patchwork of autonomous entities with dominant capital cities. Duchies, republics, monarchies, and the Papal States, each with its distinctive culture and tradition, promoted distinct architectural expressions. The character of local stone also influenced the conception and appearance of buildings. In Florence, the dense grey-green *pietra serena* combined with the off-white stucco used for wall surfaces accentuated the articulation but also gave buildings a particular sobriety. Rome's travertine, a warm creamy pitted volcanic stone, gave a rich and vigorous texture well suited to large-scale structures; the *pietra d'Ischia* employed in Venice and its territories became brilliant white where exposed to the elements, collecting dark residues beneath projections, so that the major lines were emphasized. Finally, local economic, political, and social structures imposed divergent objectives on architects.

To assert that Renaissance architecture was not grounded in the introduction of significant new building techniques, as Roman and Gothic architecture had been, is not to say that many architects of the Renaissance were not creative in solving difficult structural problems as they arose. The construction of the Basilica of St Peter in the Vatican, with its huge

Pazzi Chapel, S. Croce, Florence (Brunelleschi, 1423)

dome, or of Florence's graceful Ponte Santa Trinità, alone would absolve them from that accusation. To a limited extent they succeeded in rediscovering the chemistry and application of concrete (though not on the scale of the Roman baths or the Pantheon). But structural technique was not at the core of their concerns; no important writing on the subject was published in the period.

Just as the Tuscan dialect became the standard for Italian linguistic usage, so the architecture of Tuscany, Florence in particular—a mercantile centre initially free of the constraints of aristocratic rule—was the seedbed of the new architecture, which remained relatively small in scale, emphasizing planar surfaces. The transition from the Gothic (which the Italians scornfully called 'German') style was initiated by the Florentine goldsmith and sculptor Filippo *Brunelleschi (1377–1436) with a brilliant solution to the construction of the dome of the cathedral, preserving the concept of late Gothic designers who lacked the capacity to span such a vast space. Brunelleschi went on to build several churches and civic structures in a unique personal adaptation of the ancient orders—tall and thin dark stone columns supporting delicate round arches and white stucco walls framed by pilasters (Florence, Foundling Hospital, church of Santo Spirito). An equally influential Florentine, his friend Leone Battista *Alberti, was the author of treatises on architecture (c.1450), painting, and sculpture, and utilized a long experience in Rome to experiment with more robust articulation (Rimini, San Francesco) and grander interior spaces (Mantua, Sant'Andrea).

Early modern Rome, recovering slowly from the absence of the popes prior to the 1440s, burst into prominence in the arts after the election of Pope Julius II in 1502. Julius attracted to the Vatican the greatest figures of the second Renaissance generation, Donato *Bramante, *Raphael Sanzio, *Michelangelo Buonarroti and Leonardo da *Vinci, charging them to give form and symbol to his ambition to make the Holy See one of the great powers of Europe. They were given the means to realize a monumental style, inappropriately called the 'High' Renaissance, which challenged the ancient monuments of the city in scale and grandeur.

The outstanding enterprise was the building of the new Basilica of St Peter, initiated by Bramante (1504), which brazenly replaced the most revered church of early Christendom with the grandest edifice of the Renaissance, fusing elements of the ancient baths with the vast interior spaces of Byzantine church architecture; construction lasted, with many changes, for over 110 years, employing the gifts of Raphael, Michelangelo, Antonio da *Sangallo the Younger (the first Renaissance architect to be trained as such), Baldassare *Peruzzi, Giacomo *della Porta, Carlo *Maderno, and many other major designers. Rome, a city of several hundred churches, set the model for the church design of the Counter-Reformation; the vexing issue of accommodating the medieval high central nave with lower side-aisles to façades and interiors adopting the proportions of the classical orders was resolved by Antonio Sangallo the Younger in Santo Spirito in Sassia (1536) and refined by Giacomo Barozzi da *Vignola and Giacomo della Porta in the Church of Il Gesù. Raphael proposed a monumental vision—only partly realized—of villa design for Villa Madama (1518), inspired by the younger Pliny's description of his villas in the second century, and major new palace concepts were initiated by Bramante for Palazzo Caprini (before 1510, destroyed) and Sangallo and Michelangelo for the monumental Palazzo Farnese (1541). Michelangelo's most imposing project was the monumental square framed by public buildings on the Capitoline Hill.

Elements of the Gothic style, dominant in the Republic of *Venice before the end of the fifteenth century—as attested by the array of grand palaces along the Grand Canal—were incorporated into the first

Renaissance buildings by Mauro *Coducci (Palazzo Vendramin, S. Michele all'Isola) and Pietro Lombardo (S. Maria dei Miracoli). A debilitating war at the start of the 16th century against the combined powers of Europe suppressed architectural enterprise until the 1520s, when Venice, profiting from the flight of artists from the Sack of Rome (1527), called Jacopo *Sansovino to design the Library and Loggetta in the Piazza San Marco and the nearby Zecca. Jacopo, a distinguished sculptor, combined in these buildings and in private palaces the grandeur of the new Roman monuments with a richness of decorative relief and a capacity to capitalize on the brilliant light of the city. Michele *Sanmicheli, having fled Rome for his native Verona, a satellite of Venice, designed palaces, two city gates, and fortifications throughout the Venetian territories. Andrea *Palladio, a generation younger, who rose from working-class origins as a stone carver to become the most imitated architect of all time, was showered with commissions from the nobility of Vicenza (another Venetian satellite) and later of Venice; he is best known for his many villas in the countryside of the Veneto and his Venetian churches, especially San Giorgio Maggiore and Il Redentore.

Mantua, the seat of the Gonzaga Dukes, called *Giulio Romano from Rome in 1524 to design and decorate their suburban retreat, the Palazzo del Tè, a pioneering example of rusticated architecture, and numerous other ducal projects, including plans for the expansion of the city. In Milan, Duke Lodovico Sforza brought the Florentine Filarete to work on the defences of the Castello and to build the Ospedale Maggiore, and called the Painter Donato Bramante from Perugia, where he began an extraordinary career as an architect (church of Santa Maria delle Grazie, Santa Maria Sopra San Satiro), continued in Rome after Lodovico's defeat by the French.

Spanish (Aragonese) and French (Angevin) royalty fought for possession of Naples until a treaty of 1505

awarded the territory to Spain. But starting in 1452 Alfonso I of Aragon called distinguished architects from Florence and elsewhere: Francesco da Laurana, author of the triumphal arch of Castelnuovo; from 1485 on, Giuliano da Sangallo, whose plan for a huge palace, perhaps a judicial centre, still survives; Giuliano da Maiano, designer of Poggioreale, a royal palace on the heights above the town, whose unique form we know of only from drawings and prints; Fra. Giocondo, a major scholar of Vitruvius; and Francesco di Giorgio, a specialist in military as well as civic architecture. In the early 16th century, however, more progress was made in city planning than in architectural schemes.

The increasing political/economic pressure of the French crown and the Holy Roman Empire (now centred in Spain), in the second half of the 16th century, fortified autocracy and the suppression of local identity, particularly in Florence, where the Medici crushed republican government and were elevated to Grand-Ducal rank. This, and the increased mobility of architects in search of commissions, led eventually to a less localized architecture. The Medici glorified their rule in the Uffizi palace and the fortress of the Belvedere.

Genoa, dominated alternately by France and Spain in the early Renaissance, gained partial independence and, aided by Admiral Andrea Doria, formed an oligarchy like that of its enemy Venice. An architectural renaissance began in mid-century, led by Galeazzo *Alessi, who had been apprenticed in Rome; his design of Santa Maria di Carignano on one of the hills embracing the city was based on the early Greek-cross plans of St Peter in the Vatican; he also designed the innovative palatial villas for the Cambiaso, Giustiniani, and other aristocrats. The powerful families collaborated in creating the Strada Nuova, and lining it with grand palaces accommodating the slope of the hill with elaborate staircases.

Alessi moved on to Milan, where he built the Palazzo Marino, the court of which, rich with densely compacted figural and floral high reliefs, signalled the end of strict Classicism. Pellegrino *Tibaldi, the favoured architect of the chief prelate, Cardinal Carlo Borromeo, received the bulk of ecclesiastical commissions in the last decades of the century, most notably for the Jesuit church of San Fedele.

Architectural theory flourished in the mid and late 16th century. Sebastiano *Serlio's *Tutte le opere dell 'architettura* (1537–75) introduced a type of treatise richly illustrated with woodcuts illustrating a canon of the orders (which Vitruvius had left virtually incomprehensible), model palaces and houses, churches and villas, and articulating the need for equilibrating *licenza* (freedom to improvise on the classical heritage) and *decor* (a Vitruvian term understood in the early Renaissance primarily as decoration, which now took on a modern meaning—decorum—requiring reference to the social position of the patron of private dwellings or the teachings of the Counter-Reformation in churches). Giacomo Barozzi da Vignola published an engraved volume (to increase precision) in 1562, *La Regola delli cinque ordini d'architettura*, which succeeded in establishing the most influential canon of the orders, reprinted and pirated innumerable times up to the present. Andrea Palladio, in *I Quattro Libri dell'Architettura* (1570), was innovative in publishing and explaining his own buildings, and warned against the excess of license, a fault frequently attributed to Michelangelo. At the end of the century, Carlo Borromeo published *Instructiones fabricae et suppellectilis ecclesiasticae*, a commentary on church design that set a standard for the accommodation of Counter-Reformation liturgy.

Garden art flourished in Renaissance Italy, celebrated examples being at Villa d'Este in Tivoli, Villa Lante at Bagnaia, Pratolino outside Florence, and the woods at Bomarzo, a fantastic assemblage of aberrant buildings and oversized figural works.

The 16th century was also a time of bold innovation in urban planning, especially in Rome, from the development of the Vatican Borgo to the trident at Piazza del Popolo, Via Giulia, and Sixtus V's overall network of avenues instituted in the 1580s, with hubs marked by the erection of Egyptian obelisks. *Military architecture, which required knowledge of artillery, tactics, and ballistics, broke away from civil design and generated a distinct profession and a rich technical literature.   JA

Heydenreich, L., *Renaissance from Brunelleschi to Michelangelo: the Representation of Architecture* (1994)

Hopkins, A(ndrew), *Italian Architecture from Michelangelo to Borromini* (2002)

Lotz, W., *Architecture in Italy, 1400–1600* (revised Deborah Howard, 1995)

Storia dell'architettura italiana vols. 2–4 (1998–2002)

Rennie, John (1761–1821) British architect and engineer. He began work as a millwright and engineer, then turned from working on milling machinery to planning docks and building bridges of admirable architectural quality. His bridge carrying the Lancaster canal over the river Lune (1794–8), with its level aqueduct, and his bridge at Kelso, Borders (1800–03), with its elliptical arches separated by piers carrying paired Doric columns over the cutwaters, established a characteristic pattern, which would reappear in London. Here, opposite Somerset House, his Waterloo Bridge (1810–17, replaced) spanned the river with nine graceful elliptical arches executed in meticulously cut granite. But his second, Southwark Bridge (1815–19, replaced), employed only three arches and these were of cast iron springing from granite piers. The last, London Bridge (1824–31, removed), replaced its famous medieval predecessor with five elliptical stone arches, and was executed after Rennie's death by his younger son, the engineer Sir John Rennie (1794–1874).   APQ

Renwick, James (1818–95) US architect. Trained as an engineer, his first commission was Grace Church in his native New York. It was *Gothic Revival, but he won the contest for the Smithsonian Institution, Washington, with *Romanesque (1847–55). Renwick pioneered yet another style in America with mansarded Second Empire at his Corcoran Gallery, Washington (1859–71). His most famous church is St Patrick's Cathedral, New York (1858–79), where cost overruns forced many deviations from his wishes. During a long and successful career, Renwick designed public buildings of many types, but a disproportionate number of his churches survive.   WBM

Repton, Humphry (1752–1818) English landscape architect. Having failed in business, and with Lancelot Brown dead, Repton turned his hobby into a profession and at the age of 36 became a 'landscape gardener'. His ideal was through contrivance to marry nature and the picturesque. This he achieved, as none had before, with an elaborately illustrated report in a Red Book, of which over seventy are known as well as nearly two hundred commissions. In these he set out his proposals by means of watercolour perspectives with his improvements shown on flaps for comparison. He rapidly became famous, being mentioned by name in Jane Austen's *Mansfield Park*. His plans sometimes involved making alterations to the mansion, these being turned over to Nash, who was briefly his somewhat dishonourable partner, and then to his eldest son.

This was John Adey Repton (1775–1860), who became Nash's assistant for the Gothic alterations at Corsham Court, Wiltshire (1797–8, demolished), and elsewhere, before assisting his father. Later, on his own account, he specialized in restoration and enlarging

country houses in the Elizabethan style. Repton's youngest son, George Stanley Repton (1796–1858), also worked with Nash, and briefly assisted his father. From about 1820 he practised independently, designing country houses in the West Country in both classical and picturesque Tudor Gothic styles.   APQ

> Carter, G., Goode, P., and Laurie, K., *Humphry Repton* (1983)

respond A half-pier or half-column projecting from a wall so as to carry the end of an arch or architrave, often so as to terminate an arcade, or opposite the corresponding column or pier on the opposite of an aisle or gallery.   APQ

restoration *See* CONSERVATION.

retrochoir A rectangular space beyond the eastern end of the choir and presbyter of a large church, and before a projecting east chapel (often dedicated to the Virgin Mary), that serves as an ambulatory. A particularly English form, it depended on the abandonment of the typically French apse and a round or polygonal ambulatory in favour of a rectangular presbytery. Winchester Cathedral's retrochoir was begun c.1189–1204, as one of the earliest, comprising three bays by three, in the finest Early English. This was taken up early in the 13th century at Southwark Cathedral, which extends three bays, and four bays across, and again at Salisbury Cathedral.   APQ

Revell, Viljo Gabriel (1910–64) Finnish architect, who gained a national reputation as a leading representative of the functionalist school with his Glass Palace building, Helsinki (1935). After 1949, he played a leading role in Finland's reconstruction, beginning with designs for the Meilahti Primary School (1949–53) and the Teollisuuskeskus Building (1949–52), Helsinki, followed by many other projects. His international reputation depends on his design for the City Hall, Toronto (1958–64).   PG

Revett, Nicholas (1720–1804) English architect. Meeting James Stuart in Rome, the pair travelled to Athens recording their observations for three years. The resulting *Antiquities of Athens* (1762) was the first major record of Athens and the Greek *Doric order, and an immediate success. Parting from Stuart, Revett's subsequent travels in the Levant resulted in *The Antiquities of Ionia* (1769–97). His few designs include the portico and internal features at Trafalgar House, Wiltshire (after 1766), and Ayot St Lawrence church, Hertfordshire (1778–9).   APQ

Rewal, Raj (1934–) Indian architect. Based in northern India, Rewal has developed a compelling vocabulary for an architecture of the hot-dry milieu that is at once a striking translation of traditional Mughal and Rajasthani architecture and also eminently modern. Rewal's work demonstrated the viability of a contemporary translation of traditional architectural principles. The deployment of distinctive interlocking cubic forms, creating a rich matrix of volumes and spaces within a clear structural expression, carried out in concrete along with the use of sandstone, marks many of his works including in New Delhi the National Institute of Immunology (1983–90) and Central Institute of Educational Technology (1986–9). Rewal has employed the matrix of interlocking spaces in creating successful housing complexes that resonate with a modernist tectonic clarity and traditional spatial format. The system was adopted at a larger scale in the well regarded Asian Games Village, also in New Delhi (1980–82), that provided a new paradigm not only of a cellular housing matrix but also a revised urban morphology for the hot-dry milieu.   KA

rib A brick or stone *arch (usually pointed in profile) which supports a *vault. Invaluable in setting out a vaulted ceiling, it is structurally independent of the other element which forms the ceiling, the *web. Visually it is distinguished from the web by its unbroken line and is rarely marked out by colour, texture, or a markedly different material. In more complex *Gothic buildings, the rib springs from the *tas-de-charge; in some instances, the point where ribs meet is covered by a *boss.

In the work of *Guarini and *Vittone, the ribs were left as open latticework, to create a subtle lighting effect.   PG

Ribera, Pedro de (1681–1742) Spanish architect, most of whose works are in Madrid, including the most well-known, the Hospice of San Fernando (c.1722–6, now a museum). Over the central door on the main façade tumbles a riot of *estípites, carved drapery, festoons, and volutes, capped by a rather vestigial broken pediment. In effect, it is the extrusion from a façade of the kind of decoration usually applied to an altarpiece. Hardly surprising that when *neoclassicism prevailed, his work was thoroughly reviled.   PG

Ricardo, Halsey (1854–1928) English architect. *See* ARTS AND CRAFTS; COLOUR.

Ricchino (Ricchini), Francesco Maria (1584–1658) Italian architect, who designed many buildings in the Milan area, of which two may be singled out. S. Giuseppe (1607–30) solved the typical *Counter-Reformation problem of combining centralized spaces with a longitudinal axis, by setting two Greek crosses in line, the smaller one at the altar end. Where a Roman architect such as *della Porta or *Maderno would have used pilasters, Ricchino used columns to emphasize the piers supporting the dome. But the exterior is less well assured, as the façade details of columns, half-columns, and encased pediment seem rather confused, an impression heightened by the octagonal drum supporting the dome. By contrast, the much simpler street façade of the Colegio Elvetico (begun 1608) is set out on a graceful concave curve.   PG

Rice, Peter Roman (1935–92) Born in Ireland, he was one of the most influential structural engineers of the 20th century, who worked closely with many architects to design major buildings around the world. Rice joined *Arup in 1956 and was closely involved with *Utzon in the competition for and construction of Sydney Opera House.

He become an influential collaborator on other competitions, and was central to the design of the winning scheme for Centre Pompidou—a project that was the foundation for lifelong associations with Renzo *Piano and Richard *Rogers. Peter Rice's playful curiosity led him to consider different materials and work with a wide range of people. Reinforced concrete in Sydney and the cast-steel that was used for the Centre Pompidou became parts of a bigger palette that was to include ferro-cement and ductile iron for the light-diffusing roof of the Menil Collection in Houston, glass and polycarbonate fabric to provide shelter and shade at the Nuages in Paris and the Mound Stand at Lord's in London, collaborations with the artist Frank Stella and the zoologist Fritz Vollrath, and the use of digitally cut stone for the sweeping arches at Padre Pio Chiesa in Italy and Seville's Pavilion of the Future.   BC

Richardson, Henry Hobson (1838–86) US architect. Richardson's reputation as the country's first celebrity architect has stretched undiminished from his day to ours. He lent his name to the 'Richardsonian Romanesque', a style that swept the country in the 1880s and 1890s, and scarcely a year has since gone by in which a book or one or more articles have not been published about his work. This is an astonishing fact

about a 19th-century designer in the age of *Modernism. He joins Louis *Sullivan and Frank Lloyd *Wright, both of whose work he greatly influenced, in the 'Holy Trinity' of American architecture.

Educated at the Ecole des Beaux-Arts in Paris (1860–62), Richardson began his career after the Civil War in loose partnership with Charles D. Gambrill in New York but later moved his office to Brookline, a suburb of Boston. His winning design for the Episcopal Trinity Church on Copley Square in Boston (1872–7) launched his national and ultimately international reputation. From a cruciform auditorium plan, laid out in response to the charismatic preaching of the rector, the round-arch articulated walls of rusticated granite ashlar and sandstone trim rise to form the base of a central tower. The style is, in the words of the architect, 'free Romanesque', with details derived from works of that era in the Auvergne and the tower adapted from one on the Cathedral at Salamanca. The vast centralized interior beneath the tower is encased with walls painted deep red, decorated with images of the great saints and shot with colour from stained glass windows. It is a church conceived as a 'mighty fortress', one that famously departed from the tall fragile Gothic prescribed by the Ecclesiologists, and it inspired variations across the country, in Europe, and in Australia.

In the short time between the dedication of Trinity and his death, Richardson, now on his own, designed in various building types that established architectural forms for an American society that was shaping itself into urban commercial cores surrounded by leafy domestic suburbs, the two connected by commuter rail lines. His massive granite Allegheny County Courthouse and Jail in Pittsburgh (1883–8) is an unforgettable symbol of 'the majesty of the law'. For the centre of Chicago he designed a wholesale store (1885–7, demolished) for Marshall Field, one of the city's most important merchants. Shaped like a

Florentine palazzo, it was a blockbuster of horizontal granite ashlar, articulated with tiers of semicircular arcades whose size and spacing shifted as they rose, that gave a new scale to downtown America. Rudolf *Schindler wrote that Richardson's urban works looked 'like meteors from another planet'.

The architect stated repeatedly that he sought to achieve a 'quiet and massive treatment of wall surfaces'. His was a conservative approach to design, more akin to the Arts and Crafts ideals of William Morris, whom he visited in 1882, than the industrialized engineering aesthetic of his American contemporary, Frank *Furness, or the subsequent *Chicago School. Where he was forced to use structural iron he buried it out of sight behind superbly wrought stonework to suggest time-honoured load-bearing architecture.

Beyond the commercial core, in the suburbs and small towns ringing Boston, Richardson designed a type of commuter railway station of long and low proportions beneath a sheltering hip roof. These were gateways to both the rail system and the villages it served. He also designed a series of local libraries that marked the rise of literacy and private philanthropy, and provided monumental architecture to these outlying areas. In these buildings Romanesque detail all but disappeared as Richardson sought in the play of materials, colours, and geometry the 'living architecture' he had announced as his aim at the beginning of his career.

Richardson also provided domestic designs for these bedroom suburbs, some in the woody 'Shingle Style' of which he was a major exponent, others in the form of geological analogies. The New England landscape was shaped in the Ice Age, and Richardson seems to have wanted to create buildings that echoed the glacial moraines and granitic coastline of the area. In the Gate Lodge (1880) of the F. L. Ames estate in North Easton, Massachusetts, he used glacial boulders picked up locally and piled into the semblance of something that might have been left by receding ice, except for its orange tile hip roof. Romanesque does not enter the vocabulary here; this is an American building at one with the American land.

Richardson's contemporaries saw in him an eclectic designer who embraced formal historicism as he eschewed structural showmanship. His reputation has lasted because his work is rooted in time and place, while it is also timeless and universal in its expression of architectural vigour.   JFO'G

O'Gorman, J(ames) F., *H. H. Richardson: Architectural Forms for an American Society* (1987)

O'Gorman, J(ames) F., *Living Architecture: a Biography of H. H. Richardson* (1997)

Rickman, Thomas (1776–1841) English architect. In 1807 Rickman began closely observing medieval churches and particularly their tracery. Classifying this under the terms 'Norman', 'Early English', 'Decorated', and 'Perpendicular', he published his findings as *An Attempt to Discriminate the Styles of English Architecture* (1817), and they have been accepted ever since. As a self-taught architect he was very successful, adding Gothic dress to Georgian preaching boxes with conviction at Hampton Lucy, Warwickshire (1822–6), Ombersley, Worcestershire (1825–9), Oulton, Yorkshire (1827–9), and Stretton-on-Dunsmore, Warwickshire (1835–7), and spectacularly for New Court, St John's College, Cambridge (1827–31).   APQ

riding houses Substantial, covered, barn-like structures initially designed to provide shelter for those involved in *haute école*, the ritualized schooling of the horse, these were among the largest sporting buildings of the early modern period. As *haute école* spread to northern Europe, the harder climate made the convenience of a covered riding house popular. The earliest recorded example is the timber winter riding house built at the Hofburg in Vienna in 1572.

Schröder House, Utrecht, Netherlands (Gerrit Thomas Rietveld, 1924)

In England, riding houses were introduced in the circle of enthusiasts round Henry, Prince of Wales in the first decades of the 17th century. After English interest in *haute école* waned following the Civil War, few were built until a revival of interest in *haute école* in the 1750s brought a new wave of riding houses. By the time this interest faded in the 1780s, the convenience of riding houses for those wishing to practise riding or to exercise horses had become clear and numerous riding houses could be found in late-18th- and 19th-centuries towns, cavalry barracks, and greater country houses.

See also STABLES. GW

Worsley, G., *The British Stable* (2004)

Riemerschmid, Richard (1868–1957) German architect, painter, interior and furniture designer, theatre designer, founder of the Munich Vereinigten Werkstätten für Kunst im Handwerk (1898), and planner of the garden city of Dresden-Hellerau (begun in 1909). Riemerschmid began his career as a leader of the Jugendstil movement but soon turned to simplified peasant models for the design of his influential machine-made furniture, thereby exerting great influence on later German design institutions, including the *Bauhaus. Together with other leading members of the *Deutscher Werkbund, he created at Hellerau a famous model community for artists and workers, a centre for 'reform in life, society, and culture'. BML

Rietveld, Gerrit Thomas (1888–1964) Dutch architect who began his career making furniture. He became a member of the small group which founded De *Stijl in 1917; in his furniture, treating it as if it were sculpture, he explored the basic visual qualities of pure planes, proportions, and primary colours (Red-Blue Chair, 1918; Berlin Chair, 1923). His Schröder House, Utrecht (1924, together with Truus Schröder-Schräder), became the revolutionary manifesto of his elementary space-sculptures, executed as architecture. The first floor, with the living-room and bedrooms, had walls made of sliding panels that could be removed so that the space of this small house became open and a composition consisting only of planes and colour. If the windows in the corner were opened the plane of the ceiling seemed to float. Through such experimental creations of space and light Rietveld's buildings sometimes required upkeep by the builder and owner because of technical defects. In the 1950s and 1960s he became a leader in the field through his innovative designs for small houses, exhibition spaces, shops, and interiors. In these years of scarcity he managed to create the greatest possible expression of modern life with a minimum of ordinary, simple materials.

AVDW (trans. CVE)

Küper, M., and van Zijl, I., *Gerrit Tomas Rietveld 1888–1964* (1992)

Rinaldi, Antonio (*c*.1710–94) Italian architect active in Russia. After working with *Vanvitelli on the royal palace at Caserta, by 1752 Rinaldi had moved to St Petersburg, where he become one of the earliest architects to effect a transition from Baroque to neoclassicism. During the 1760s he worked extensively at the Oranienbaum imperial estate. In addition to a small palace for Peter III (1758–62), Rinaldi created for Catherine II an exquisite jewel known as the Chinese Palace (1762–8), after the luxurious *Chinoiserie of its interiors. In St Petersburg he designed the severe Marble Palace (1768–85), one of the rare St Petersburg monuments to be clad in natural stone, marble, and granite. Still more severe is the palace at Gatchina (1766–81). WCB

RMJM *See* MATTHEW, SIR ROBERT.

Roberts, Henry (1803–76) English architect and author. Following work for Smirke and Continental

travel, Roberts set up in London, building Fishmongers' Hall, City (1831–4), and London Bridge Station (1844–6, demolished). His main interest was working-class housing: he thus designed Model Dwellings, Streatham Street, Holborn (1849), Thanksgiving Model Buildings, Theobalds Road, Holborn (1850–57), and Model Cottages for the Great Exhibition (1851, re-erected at Kennington Park). He wrote *The Dwellings of the Labouring Classes* (1850) and much else on this subject. APQ

Robson, Edward Robert (1836–1917) English architect. *See* SCHOOLS, FROM 1870.

Roca, Miguel Ángel (1940–) Argentine architect who began his career by designing houses and residential complexes, as well as a large number of branches of the Banco de la Provincia de Córdoba. He contributed to the planning and design of Córdoba city centre, the Plaza de Armas and pedestrianized streets (1980), including pavement designs representing the façades of colonial buildings, as well as landscape architecture in several parks. In the context of an urban design plan for La Paz (1988) he also worked in Bolivia, employing a postmodernist vocabulary of sharp geometrical forms as seen in five parks and three District Centres as well as the Municipal Administrative Centre, or Alcaldía (1988–90). These constructions with their well-defined shapes and bright colours were continued in the five Centros de Partipación Comunal in Córdoba (1992–4). His works for the University of Cordóba (1993–2004) include the restoration of colonial buildings and creation of a whole new campus, with clear-cut designs in exposed concrete and richly decorated interiors. LNM (trans. KL)

Roche, Eamonn Kevin (1922–) Irish-born, and **Dinkeloo, John Gerard** (1918–81) US-born, architects who set up in practice in 1961. Successful corporate modernists, they favoured the uncompromising expression of modern materials, careful planning for function, and sleek, rather minimal detailing (the Oakland Museum, California, 1961–8; the Cummins Engine Plant, Darlington, Durham, 1963–5). Their most inventive work was the Ford Foundation Headquarters, New York (1963–8), renowned for its 12-storey garden atrium, a much-copied feature. The firm continued its distinctive interest in incorporating landscape spaces into buildings for large business organizations, such as the General Foods Corporation Headquarters, Rye, NY (1977–82). PG

Rococo A term fancifully derived from *rocaille*, meaning 'pebble-work', referring to a form of frivolous and superficial decoration, probably first seen in the Grand Salon, Marly (Le *Pautre, 1699). Decorative features which had marked the edges of woodwork, coving, fireplaces, or mirrors now spread across the surface, in patterns usually based upon shells or scroll-work. This type of Rococo, which is confined mainly to France and Germany, culminates in the two oval salons by *Boffrand at the Hôtel Soubise, Paris (1735–39), and the Amalienburg, a pavilion in the grounds of the Schloss Nymphenburg, Munich (Cuvilliés, 1734–9). In this version, Rococo is non-architectural, in that the whimsical decoration and usually conventional room plans are unrelated to each other.

In the second version, to be found in a series of churches in southern Germany (*see* GERMANY (1500–1780)) the spreading decoration is integrated with architectural form. The extended debate among art historians, agonizing whether the style label 'Baroque' or 'Rococo' should be applied in this case, seems rather pointless, since it is far more important to *see* the highly original relationships between architecture and decoration.

The finest example of such relationships, regardless of the label, is the church of Die Wies, Steingaden, southern Germany (*Zimmermann, 1745–57). The role played by the structural and framing elements of architecture (in this case, columns and vaults), the transition between wall and ceiling, appears to be taken over by ornament, frescoes, and sculpture. Only the lesser architectural elements (volutes, pilaster strips, and pediments) appear unadorned. What could be seem to be merely a set of decorator's tricks is in fact a brilliant *ensemble*, in which all elements (sculpture, painting, and architecture) are integrated to create a particular visual effect: the earthly realm of the structure dissolving uninterruptedly into the scene of the Last Judgement above. PG

Rodríguez Tizón, Ventura (1717–85) Spanish architect, a key figure in the development of *neoclassicism in Spain. First, however, he designed two buildings which show a real, if uninventive, familiarity with the Italian Baroque. San Marcos, Madrid (1749–53), has a complicated plan of five ellipses, and a concave façade; the richly decorated chapel of Nuestra Señora del Pilar, Saragossa (1750), has an elliptical dome with open fretwork creating rather a theatrical effect *à la* *Vittone. He then rather abruptly adopted the neoclassical convention of severe unornamented façades, as in the Colegio di Cirurgía, Barcelona (1760ff.), and a series of churches in Andalusia (1766–84). From 1764 he held several official positions, and was Director of Architecture in the Royal Academy of Fine Arts (1766–77), giving him considerable influence over numerous architectural commissions, which he used to promote neoclassicism as the regally sanctioned style. PG

Rogers, Isaiah (1800–69) US architect. He worked in Boston for a time with Solomon Willard, who later supplied him with the grey Quincy granite he favoured for his fireproof public buildings. These included, most famously, the Tremont House hotel, Boston (1828–9, demolished), and Astor House hotel, New York (1834–6, demolished). The latter was immediately followed by the huge Merchants' Exchange a few blocks away (1836–42). All were *Greek Revival, and the Merchants' Exchange featured a grand Ionic colonnade *in antis*. Rogers contributed designs for hotels and public edifices in many states and concluded his successful career with the west wing of the United States Treasury Building, Washington DC (1862–5).   WBM

Rogers of Riverside, Richard George, The Lord

(1933–) Italian-born architect, based in London. His real work began in 1966 when he designed a family house at Creek Vean in Cornwall, with white walls and large windows, a house of impeccable modernity, still fresh after nearly half a century. Then in 1967 he designed a factory with Su Rogers and Norman and Wendy Foster, a double husband-and-wife group that set up under the name of Team 4. This work, the Reliance Controls Ltd Factory at Swindon (1967), became famous among architects as an example of industrial architecture that makes its impact from the visual quality of its structural system.

Rogers has become increasingly devoted to the kind of architecture that works by exposing its essentials: in the first place the structure, then increasingly the services. The Pompidou Centre in Paris (with Renzo Piano, 1971–7) made this approach an example that was followed by many. The main elevation is marked by a clear succession of rectangular bays overlaid by diagonal tension cables. The services, lifts, pipes, escalators, are all treated in a systematic way, and are colour-coded as well, which adds to the liveliness. The designs for Lloyds in the City of London (1978) and for Inmos at Newport, South Wales (1982), both display structure and service elements on the exterior.

Rogers has thus become a proponent of true functionalist architecture. Through this development, Modernism was pushed closer to the machine, but also to sculpture: Rogers' work emerges from this conjunction. He was influenced by *Archigram, for whom expression was just as important as technology. It was disciples of the Archigram group who, as employees of Piano and Rogers, made the development drawings for the Centre Pompidou. But this building most completely expresses Rogers' attitude: for unlike the Lloyds Building, it has no hint of a conventional interior dominated by tribal rituals, but is entirely the product of an intellectual movement towards the real sources of functional truth.

Traditionally, architecture was supposed to be beautiful. It is not that the high-tech architect eschews beauty. But the beauty has to be identified with functional necessity. With Rogers, the method of construction becomes an artistic strategy, an end in itself. In the Tokyo Forum Project of 1991, for example, the spaces of use are first enclosed in a gleaming semi-transparent shell, then suspended from a metal armature, then approached by a complex of escalators. By creating this series of obviously functional elements, the building is made up of an assemblage of structural tours de force. It becomes a symbol of its own system, a chapel to progress.

However, in the design for the European Court of Human Rights (1989–94) at Strasbourg, the elements into which the complex is broken down are not the service elements as such, but spaces of use; they stand on the ground, becoming more expressive of human habitation, while the building takes its shape from the curve of a river. This increased sensitivity towards the city is also evident in the very elegant project for the Alcazar, in Marseilles (1988). Within a 7-storey height limit he inserts a wedge-shaped volume closely into the texture of the adjoining blocks, showing sensitivity both to an analytical idea of urban form and to the sense of civic propriety.

Richard Rogers, then, is a master of modern design. He will go down in posterity as the principal author of

Centre Pompidou, Paris (Piano and Rogers, 1977)

the Millennium Dome at Greenwich, a tour de force where a tent suspended from steel gantries is given the spread and authority of an immense domed space. His designs continue to exploit the cutting edge of architectural technology, as with the Headquarters for the Lloyd's Register of Shipping and the new Terminal 5 at Heathrow Airport. His Channel 4 building is not so different from any other office building, but it does articulate its parts clearly, and its skyline is dominated by TV aerials which are working parts of the programme. He now has an immense list of projects around the world.   RMa

Rogers, R(ichard), *Architecture—a Modern View* (1990)
Powell, K(enneth) (ed.), *Richard Rogers* (1994)

Roman Doric order A slender, more ornate version of Greek *Doric. What they have in common are *triglyphs in the *frieze, *mutules in the *soffit of the *corona and *guttae below the taenia, and *capitals comprising an *abacus supported by *mouldings, though rather more pronounced and ornate. Unlike the Greek, Roman Doric may sometimes but not always include a base to the column, which may or may not be fluted. It differs from the Tuscan, which, as described by *Vitruvius, is more primitive, the columns being set further apart as though carrying a timber lintel or architrave, and this is plain, lacking a frieze of triglyphs.   APQ

Romanesque A style of medieval architecture, founded on debased classical Roman forms, which developed in the Frankish kingdoms of western Europe in the 10th century and remained standard within the Latin church until slowly superseded by Gothic after the mid 12th century. Like all the Christian styles that grew out of Roman architecture in the 4th and later centuries, Romanesque employed round arches, circular or rectangular piers, tunnel-vaults and groin-vaults, but lacked the classical sense of order, proportion, and symmetry that governed its

Maria Laach Abbey Church,
near Andernach, Rhineland-
Palatinate, Germany
(1093–1156)

predecessor. It grew out of the intervening Carolingian architecture, which had consciously revived Roman forms both through an awareness that *Romanitas* and *Christianitas* were indivisible, and as a symbol of imperial intent.

Just as Byzantine architecture employed a debased form of Corinthian capital, so too did Romanesque in its scalloped capitals with primitive volutes that appear widely in the 11th century, and would develop into the crocket and waterleaf capitals of the 12th. Where Roman material could be robbed, it was reused, and if this were carved or formed architectural parts, such as arches, it served the double purpose of physical provision and of legitimizing this with its reference to Rome. Where Roman ruins were in abundance, they could provide an immediate model. This is nowhere better exemplified than in the Burgundian town of Autun (*c*.1120–32), where the fluted pilasters that decorate the two surviving Roman gates are the model for detailing the gallery in the cathedral. This reference to the fount of Christianity is particularly suited to churches, although it appears again in the clerestory windows of Burgundy's more prosperous houses as the style descended to affluent citizens through emulation.

Romanesque rapidly became ubiquitous in western Christendom, appearing in an immediately recognizable form, despite local variations, as far apart as Sicily, Spain, and Scotland (and later known in Britain as *Norman owing to its introduction as a result of the Norman Conquest). This form applied both to its debased classical detailing and imperfect construction. The widespread basilican form of churches, particularly those that contained stone vaults, produced problems in design that the Romans had been able to solve through the use of cement and their superior constructional skills, neither of which were available to Romanesque masons.

As Romanesque churches became larger, so their construction became heavier, particularly in those parts of Europe north of the Alps where good building stone was hard to obtain. Having lost the ability to manufacture cement, masons made do with mortar instead, which was both less strong and less durable. As their walls and piers became thicker so as to bear heavier weights, they were increasingly constructed from mortared rubble faced in stone, a more dense material overall than the concrete mixture of tufa, brick, and cement used by the Romans. This compromised the structure, causing many Romanesque buildings to fail as the mortar turned to dust. Only lighter construction would solve the problem, since cement was not to be rediscovered until the Industrial Revolution, but that needed either the fine, hard stone that was available in Italy, or the introduction of the superseding Gothic style.

The construction of roofs caused particular problems. These were often roofed with timber trusses, just as Roman basilicas had been, but, as in Rome, stone tunnel vaults were introduced, to provide an element of fireproofing as well as magnificence. The vaults would usually run longitudinally down nave and choir, a practice well established in Christian northern Spain by the mid 9th century. Sometimes these were articulated by projecting transverse arches, bay by bay, as exemplified in some of the 11th-century Burgundian *pilgrimage churches.

Very rarely the tunnel vaults might run across each bay between clerestory windows as they do in part of St Philibert, Tournus (c.950–1120), but it was much commoner to combine such transverse vaults with a longitudinal vault to form a groin-vault. By the 11th century these were commonly used so as to embrace clerestory windows at the level of the vault, or in crypts to incorporate the arcades running down their length, which would otherwise interfere with the progress of a tunnel-vault. The longitudinal tunnel and each transverse tunnel intersected to form an edge or groin. The Romans had introduced vaults like this for several large buildings, such as the 2nd-century baths at Leptis Magna in modern Libya.

So the groin-vault was revived, for example already c.1000 in the narthex at Tournus, and the crypt of the nearby Auxerre Cathedral (c.1030). When the bays were accurately laid out and square in plan, as they were at Leptis Magna, the groin itself would be a straight diagonal curve, but this was often not so in Romanesque buildings as a result of inaccuracy in setting-out. One way out of this problem, found in France, particularly the south-west, was to fill the bay with a shallow dome, thus avoiding the groins altogether. This was taken to extreme lengths in the domed cathedrals at Angloulême (begun c.1105) and Périgueux (after 1120). Another, more commonly adopted way was to hide the irregularities, and perhaps also to extend the articulation introduced by the projecting transverse arches by adding projecting ribs to the groins, as was undertaken on occasion in the 1070s and wholesale in the rib-vaulting of Durham Cathedral from 1095. The notion that these ribs are structural and support the remainder of the vault is mistaken, as was demonstrated by accidental bombing in World War II, when ribs fell out but webs remained. Indeed the individual stones of the ribs are not always cut so as to join each other perpendicularly to the line of the rib, but may sometimes by cut diagonally, as occurs at Durham, and hence would be unsound were they serving as structural arches. APQ

Armi, C. Edson, *Design and Construction in Romanesque Architecture* (2004)

Bodington, Oliver E., *The Romance* [i.e. Romanesque] *Churches of France* (1925)

Romanesque Revival A style of architecture found mainly in France, Germany, and the United States from about 1825 to 1900, at first based on two superficial characteristics of the *Romanesque, the semicircular arch and the barrel vault. The earliest example is von Klenze's Allerheiligen-Hofkirche, Munich (1826–37), followed by churches of *Vaudoyer and *Vaudremer. To this point they would have been hardly worth a footnote in the confusing history of 19th-century revivals, but in the work of H. H. *Richardson, the primeval and gargantuan aspects of the original Romanesque were a powerful stimulus to a highly inventive architecture. PG

Curran, K., *The Romanesque Revival* (2003)

Romania Roman domination of Romania ('Dacia Felix') from AD 106 to 271 left little architectural imprint. Subsequently, brick architecture was practically abandoned during 900 years of migration and invasion, but flourished from the 12th century onwards. The Tatar-Mongol invasion of 1242 caused considerable destruction, but Christian architecture revived rapidly, with the restoration (1247–90) of the old Cathedral at Alba Iulia, *Romanesque in its main elements, but with Gothic vaults.

Architecture developed in Wallachia from the middle of the 14th century, in a great variety of forms, some rarely found elsewhere, such as the alternating courses of stone and brick seen at St Nicholas, Curtea de Arge (1364–77). During the same period, Gothic architecture in Transylvanian architecture, such as Oradea Cathedral (1343–72), may show the influence of the *Parler family. But in the following century far more churches were built in Moldavia, most of which employed an unusual vaulting system of superimposed pendentives. The most well-known buildings in Bukovina (northern Moldavia) are the handful of monastery churches, dating from c.1487 to c.1530. However, they are notable for their external wall paintings, not their architecture, which is extremely plain.

In Translyvania during the 17th and 18th centuries, because of the Hungarian prohibition of stone churches, churches for both the Orthodox and Uniate faiths were built entirely in wood. Narrow and tall (the spire of Surdesti reaches 72 m, or 236 ft), they are among the finest all-wood constructions built anywhere (cf. STAVE CHURCHES).

By contrast the 18th and 19th centuries in Romania as a whole saw little of note, apart from some routine exercises in *Eclecticism (e.g. the Town Hall, Oradea, 1899–1904). Neoclassicism found a rather late, gargantuan expression in the House of Parliament and the People's Palace, Bucharest (completed 1989). PG

Romano, Giulio *See* GIULIO ROMANO.

Romberg, Frederick *See* GROUNDS, ROMBERG, AND BOYD.

Rome and the Roman Empire Together with that of ancient Greece, the art and architecture of ancient Rome forms the basis of the classical style. The distinctive feature of Roman architecture is that it strove to achieve a practical advancement of civilization that, by comparison, puts Greek architecture into the realm of dreams.

Stemming from similar beginnings, Roman architecture developed a wider vocabulary of forms, could command greater resources of materials, and developed its buildings in a notably comprehensive way. A comparison of two civic centres makes this clear at once. The Acropolis of Athens, originally the citadel of a thriving community and ultimately a shrine to its gods expressing civic pride, is nevertheless a loose aggregation of individual buildings, each one orientated, as is necessary with temples, in a determined way, but with no specific relationship to any other one, save for suitably filling an available space. The Trajan Forum in Rome is a large rectangular site with a symmetrically arranged pair of semicircles opening off each long side into which were set, axially, the vast Basilica of Ulpia with, before it, a public open space entered through a formal gateway, and, secluded behind it, a symmetrical arrangement of temples, shrines, and a library, while, beyond one of the semicircles, lies the famous Trajan's Markets.

The Roman state emerged in central Italy much as Greek culture had emerged some five centuries earlier in a society whose first notable architectural achievements lay in its foundation of towns and devotion to deities. Primitive *Etruscan temples, the forerunners of Roman ones, were comparable to early Greek megaron temples in comprising a cell or *naos and a porch or portico. Significant differences emerged. The roofs of Etruscan temples projected far beyond the walls without support, whereas the Greeks employed a peristyle of columns to support the overhanging eaves of their temples. Etruscan temples were single-ended, whereas Greek temples became symmetrically double-ended with an entrance for the naos at the front and another for a treasury at the rear. These two factors combined led Greek temples to be set upon a stepped base or crepidoma, which, like the peristyle, extended together with its steps on all four sides. The Etruscan temple, meanwhile, only had steps at the front, thus accentuating the entrance in a clearly axial way.

While both prototypes originated in timber buildings, when the Greeks substituted stone, they reduced the span of the lintels, column by column, to make up for stone's lack of tensile strength, whereas the Etruscan temple made its substitution stage by stage in such a way that stone columns, in still bearing timber lintels, were set further apart—in fact, in Vitruvius' description of an Etruscan temple, about twice as far apart as in a Greek temple. These features, amounting to an axial stepped front entrance, widely spaced columns supporting the portico, and overhanging eaves, characterize the resulting Tuscan order, all nicely reproduced in the Etruscan temple set in the grounds of the Villa Giulia, Rome, and suggested by the archaeology of temples excavated nearby at Cosa and Norba.

How Roman architecture would have developed if left to itself is an open question, but the conquest of Greek colonies in the 3rd century BC and the consequent discovery of the full panoply of the *Doric, *Ionic, and *Corinthian orders profoundly influenced its course. An admixture of Tuscan and Greek Doric led to the Roman Doric order, and the Ionic and Corinthian orders Rome simply annexed to itself. So much for detail and proportion, but the axial approach to a temple, with steps at the front leading up to its entrance, remained unaffected by Greek temple plans, as the 2nd-century temple of Fortuna Virilis in Rome clearly shows, despite its Corinthian order.

This temple exhibits another Roman tendency. The cell and portico of Etruscan temples are clearly defined separate parts of the whole, while in Greek temples the sense of totality is obscured by the continuation of the portico's order as a peristyle down the sides of the cell to the portico at the further end. At Fortuna Virilis, the Corinthian order continues down the side of the cell as attached half columns to produce a pseudo-peristyle. The order has ceased to be structural, thus abandoning its origins in favour of a decorative purpose as a means of articulating the sides and rear of the cell.

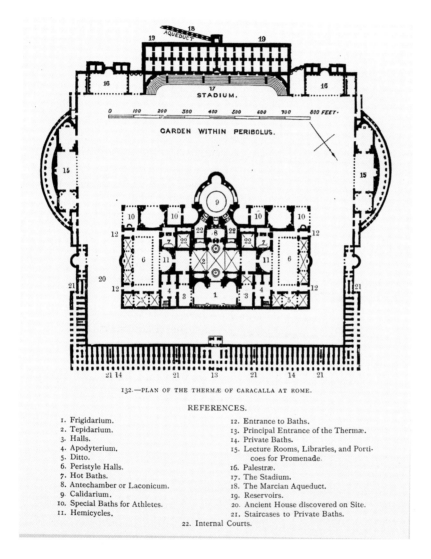

GARDEN WITHIN PERIBOLUS.

132.—PLAN OF THE THERMÆ OF CARACALLA AT ROME.

REFERENCES.

1. Frigidarium.
2. Tepidarium.
3. Halls.
4. Apodyterium.
5. Ditto.
6. Peristyle Halls.
7. Hot Baths.
8. Antechamber or Laconicum.
9. Calidarium.
10. Special Baths for Athletes.
11. Hemicycles.

12. Entrance to Baths.
13. Principal Entrance of the Thermæ.
14. Private Baths.
15. Lecture Rooms, Libraries, and Porticoes for Promenade.
16. Palestræ.
17. The Stadium.
18. The Marcian Aqueduct.
19. Reservoirs.
20. Ancient House discovered on Site.
21. Staircases to Private Baths.
22. Internal Courts.

Baths of Caracalla, Rome
(AD 206–17)

The axial approach to Fortuna Virilis became established practice, at the similar Maison Carrée (*c*.19 BC) at Nîmes in the south of France, and again in the temple of Antoninus and Faustina, Rome (begun AD 141). More significantly, the axial approach was elaborated at Tivoli, where the temple of Hercules Victor (*c*.50 BC) was emphasized by raising it on a high podium and setting it in an architectural framework of arcaded wings and imposing flights of stairs. The Sanctuary of Fortune (*c*.80 BC) at Palestrina went one step further in this respect, being all but lost backstage in a set of epic Hollywood proportions. The orders were liberally scattered around, and there was clearly no overall attempt to control them with overriding proportions, but symmetrical axiality did control the overall planning, as it would do for Trajan's Forum, and that required a fine sense of urban design.

The ruins of the Sanctuary of Fortune reveal the way its scenic constructions were mounted on a hillside using round arches to support its various parts. There was nothing new in arches—the Egyptians had used them thousands of years previously, and the Greeks used them too, even if they did not care for the arched form. The Romans made them their own. This brought utilitarian benefits to the construction in the 2nd century BC of the Porticus Æmilia, an immense range of warehouses based on the repetition of similar units with canted arches, and, more spectacularly in the late 1st century, of the Pont du Gard, the most famous of large numbers of aqueducts that brought the water of life to numerous Roman towns and cities, including Rome itself. Spanning a deep defile, the Pont du Gard comprises three superimposed bridges, each one an arcade of round arches constructed from huge blocks of finely cut, unmortared masonry. Its engineering was hardly equalled until the railway age two millennia later, its utilitarian architectural form, in modern eyes, entirely appropriate to its wild setting. The aqueduct at Segovia was similarly engineered, perhaps because Rome considered its Spanish cities equally wild. But when Rome was supplied by the Claudian waterworks (AD 53), whose aqueducts threaded through the city, some obstacles warranted full architectural treatment, notably where the Porta Maggiore, which has the form of a triumphal arch, carried the water channel across a major road.

How far the Romans could take the use of arches is well exemplified by the Theatre of Marcellus, Rome (*c*.13 or 11 BC). Unlike the Greeks, who turned the public performance of stories into acted drama, and consequently exploited hillside bowls for their theatres by setting them out with regularly spaced segmental tiers of seats, as at Epidaurus (*c*.350 BC), and adding before them a built-up scene behind the stage, the Romans integrated all the various elements of stage and auditorium into a single architectural composition. Hence the Theatre of Marcellus has rising semicircular tiers of seats raised upon radiating arched wedges which embrace entrances, staircases, and public access. The semicircular exterior rises through 2 storeys, which reflect the arched interior in a series of arched openings, and these are articulated by an attached order, Roman Doric for the ground storey, Ionic for the upper. The Greeks had already mounted one tier of columns on another, but these were usually of the same order, the upper ones only being somewhat smaller, a surprisingly casual solution compared with the sophisticated solution used here, which exploits the more slender form of the Ionic as a suitable mount above the sturdy Doric below. So, not only was the potential of an attached order for articulation exploited upwards as well as lengthwise, it was also married to the arch as a means of forming a suitable architectural frame. The aim was integration, integration of the individual arches and of the 2 storeys, just as the auditorium, stage, and scene were integrated as a single building rather than being separate parts of an additive whole.

This potential was carried further in the triumphal arch. The practice of returning armies, flushed with victory, to march into town through the gates in the walls was formalized by setting up arches through which the army might march, together with its captive booty. The arch itself would comprise a tall, wide opening, suitable for cavalry and chariots, flanked by

Colosseum, Rome
(AD c. 70–80)

lower, narrower openings for foot soldiers. The solid piers carrying the arches and the superstructure would be carved with symbolic representations of the campaign, replete with trophies of arms and inscriptions recording the triumphant events. Such is the arch at Orange erected shortly after AD 21 in southern France to commemorate Julius Caesar's conquest of Gaul, its projecting centre and corners being articulated by attached columns, an entablature and central pediment. The Arch of Septimius Severus, Rome (AD 203), is more complex: the three parts are framed by a single order of columns set on pedestals, which support an entablature over the entire arch; meanwhile the imposts that carry the springing of the central arch continue outwards across the side arches as the base of a lesser entablature above them, nicely integrating the three parts together. This definitive form became highly influential, determining the design of the Arch of Constantine (AD 315), and being adapted in the Renaissance as a means of expressing a building's tripartite section in a particularly monumental way. However far the *triumphal arch may generally symbolize a distasteful element of Roman imperialism, the Arch of Constantine, for all its reused pagan decoration, celebrates a victory won under the sign of the cross and, with the Edict of Milan (313), the triumph of Christianity over paganism as the Empire's recognized religion.

Triumphal arches were made of stone, as befitted the needs of their civic role. This was not a constructional necessity, however. The earliest surviving Egyptian arches are made of so unlikely a material as unbaked earthen brick. The Romans did rather better through their invention of cement, a mixture of lime and clay, which, when treated with water, undergoes a chemical reaction causing it to set into a hard rock-like substance with powerful binding qualities. Mixed with sand and an aggregate such as lightweight volcanic tufa it forms concrete, in which

strength and lightness combine. Used as a jointing material with fired clay bricks, strength and lightness again combine.

An arch of concrete clearly had many advantages, and just such arches gave the Theatre of Marcellus its structural base. More famous by far was the greatest of all theatres, the double theatre in Rome known as the Flavian amphitheatre, and popularly as the Colosseum (AD c.70–80). Built of tufa and brick, set in concrete and faced with stone, its rising oval tiers of seats are supported by piers carrying radial and circumferential arches and are served by staircases leading to eighty exits or *vomitoria*, which, altogether, allowed an audience of 50,000 to leave in just a few minutes. Its central stage or arena, which accommodated spectacles such as the gladiatorial contests favoured by the ancient Romans, was built over the contestants' quarters and could be flooded for mock sea battles. The exterior, like the Theatre of Marcellus, comprised storeys of arches right around the oval perimeter, though with a third storey, this being articulated with a Corinthian order on account of its being progressively more slender than the Ionic and Doric. Once again, this use of the orders entered the canon of classical architecture and passed down to the Renaissance and the modern world.

Long before Rome adopted Christianity, it had developed the classical temple in two notable ways to glorify its pagan deities. The less characteristic of these has nevertheless achieved the greater renown thanks to its better preservation and subsequent influence on the Renaissance. This is the marriage of a pedimented portico to a tholos of unprecedented size. If the circular form of the tholos as it descended from the early example at Delphi be taken to represent perfection, it found ready use in Rome dedicated to Vesta and her attendant virgins. The temples dedicated to her by the Tiber and in the Forum at Rome (1st century BC), and again at Tivoli, like that at Delphi, incorporated peristyles, but the Pantheon is far too large for that.

Maison Carrée, Nîmes, France
(269–16 BC)

Built AD *c*.120–25 to glorify all the gods of Rome,
possibly to the Emperor Hadrian's design, its circular
form was a symbolic representation of their universal
power and perfection of human character (as indeed it
was also suitably symbolic of the perfection of the
Virgin Mary, to whom the Pantheon was later
rededicated). The huge portico and the start of what
might be an orthodox rectangular temple, but is no
more than a pronaos, once projected into the square
from surrounding arcades rather than standing alone as
they do today. Despite their magnificence, they are but
the introduction to what was until the 20th century the
greatest of domed structures, thanks to the benefits of
concrete laced with brick relieving arches. With a
diameter of 43.3 m (144 ft), only modern reinforced
concrete could at last topple it from its supreme
position, and then in terms of size, but not majesty.
Comprising a drum carrying a dome, notionally an arch
rotated about its crown to form a circle, it was finished
outside with pilasters and gilded bronze, long since
looted, and inside with a facing of various coloured
marbles. The lower storey of the drum is penetrated
internally by deep recesses with pairs of columns *in
antis*, and smaller niches, framed by projecting
tabernacles, which together contained statues of the
major and minor gods. The upper storey has a
continuous blind arcade of Corinthian pilasters with
further niches, or blind windows, set over the
tabernacles below. The interior of the coffered dome
was plastered and decorated with stucco ornaments,
reaching up to an oculus, open to the sky as now, that
provided the main source of light.

This unusual temple in all its magnificence has
survived in better condition than any other monument
of the Roman period, and so attracted Palladio that he
devoted nine plates to it in his *I Quattro Libri*, and built
his own modest version at Maser, thus opening the way
to countless further versions. In its own day, its plastic
modelling was a portent of things to come, the marble
facing of the concrete core a means of adding a *gravitas*

appropriate to its enshrined deities. It would have been unthinkable for the Romans to leave the constructional brick and concrete bare. This and countless other surviving monuments imply that the concept of 'truth to materials' had no meaning to them and that, to their eyes, beauty did not reside in the speechless sublimity of a rough material that weathers poorly, stains readily, and is generally a monotonous grey.

Complex planning, whether of palaces, villas, or civic buildings, was already established by the 1st century AD. As the empire expanded into territories far from Rome, it developed multiracial qualities in which the ancient official gods shared house with those revered locally. This was part of a policy of assimilation and adaptation designed to ensure that peoples from any part of the empire could enjoy the benefits of Roman culture, including the *lex Romana*, yet at the same time not lose their own identity. Hence, the Temple of Jupiter Heliopolitanus at Baalbek in modern Lebanon combines the two deities in one building, which is thus adorned with both bulls and lions whose manes are carved like the rays of the sun.

The complex of temples begun at Baalbek in the 1st century AD continued into the second with the vast Temple of Bacchus—the Romans, like most powerful nations, were easily tempted by the grandiose, and had the constructional techniques thanks to concrete to achieve it—and terminated in the 3rd century with the forecourt buildings. These provided the complex of framing ranges of the kind already achieved *c*.80 BC in the Sanctuary of Fortune at Palestrina, but now with the plastic modelling that was a feature of later Roman architecture. Rather like the interior of the Pantheon, but on the grandest scale, this is characterized by its curved recesses, all obscured by columns *in antis* that continue the order of pilasters that articulates the whole. This trend towards increasing complexity is already evident in the mid 2nd century, notably in the two extraordinary rock-cut quasi-façades at Petra in

modern Jordan. Both are of 2 storeys, that of the Treasury being in the form of a hexastyle portico with the four central columns placed forward of the outer two and carrying a pediment. The upper storey is similarly hexastyle, but set back to the line of the outer columns below and starting off as though this time to carry a full-width pediment. However, the central two columns are missing and the pediment is correspondingly cut short to be replaced by a tholos which, like a circular three-dimensional tabernacle, frames a niche and statue; its columns exactly replace the missing two, and its conical roof similarly replaces the missing centre of the pediment.

The second quasi-façade, that of the Mausoleum of ed-Deir, elaborates the Treasury's design: the lower storey is an essay in projection and recession, the entablature having a complex rhythm in the spacing of its attached columns, which frame a central entrance and niches left and right; the upper storey again has a tholos replacing the centre of a pedimented entablature, which here frames niches complementing those below. A final example of this desire for contrast that can be achieved from classical elements by stretching the rules, if not actually breaking them, is the 3rd-century Temple of Venus at Baalbek. It is a small-scale variation on the theme of the Pantheon, namely a tholos with an entrance portico, but significantly incorporating a circular peristyle, as do the original at Delphi and its later Roman descendants dedicated to Vesta. Instead of eighteen columns, as has the Temple of Vesta on the Tiber, the temple of Venus sets off as though with eight, placed rather far apart, but the four columns of one half are nicely married to the columns of the tetrastyle portico instead. A more significant difference lies in the treatment of the crowning entablature, which, instead of being circular, curves inwards between the supporting columns, making a contrasting play between convex and concave of a teasing delicacy that a modern mind might find entirely appropriate to the female charms of the goddess to whom the temple is dedicated.

Late Roman architecture spread the classical ideal right across western and southern Europe, north Africa and the Levant, certainly as far as Mesopotamia, where the palace at Hatra in modern Iraq is far from the easternmost sign of Rome's influence. That ideal, like all ideals, lost the spring-like qualities of ancient Greece through a process of adaptation and elaboration to attain a high summer in its 3rd-century quasi-Baroque form. Continuity was nevertheless a guiding light. For example Diocletian's Palace at Split (*c*.300), on the Dalmatian coast of modern Bosnia, was based on an ancient plan with the comparatively new feature of round arches carried directly over a capital by curving the entablature upward. No doubt that arch-conservative *Vitruvius would have disapproved, but this feature was no more than an obvious development of a style that gladly embraced arches and brought them into the classical fold. The 4th century, with its adoption of Christianity and the removal of the capital from Rome to *Byzantium, could well have brought far more radical change, but classical ways were too strong to be simply overturned. The Arch of Constantine is as fine a symbol of continuity in a changing world as architecture can show, as well as being dedicated to what became a profound change in people's religious beliefs.

Even the barbarian invasions of the 5th century did no more than bring further modifications, despite the chronic poverty that came in their wake. Byzantine and Early Christian architecture, and, for that matter, the Romanesque of the west, were indeed just that, modifications to suit new needs and beliefs. It is a very modern belief that every period needs an architecture of its own that expresses the spirit of the age. So far as Rome was concerned, roots mattered for all its innovations and achievements, and the idea that the architect should be trained in these, as so fully

(and at times obscurely) expressed in Vitruvius' *De Architectura*, has a permanence that is the whole basis of civilization.   APQ

Wilson Jones, M., *Principles of Roman Architecture* (2000)

roofs The weatherproof coverings of buildings. Early roofs were thatched, a word now associated with straw or reed, materials once so common that they took the word 'thatch' for themselves, although it originates from the Old German *Dach*, a roof. Roofs come in all sorts of shapes and sizes, executed in all kinds of materials, depending on local taste and resources, and to some extent climate. They must be a shield equally against sun and rain, and exert a moderating influence on extremes of temperature. Thatch does all that admirably. Primitive buildings are often round, have conical roofs clad in thatch, and so are efficient and sound. Modern buildings are often rectangular, have flat roofs of reinforced concrete, and are often inefficient and unsound—an interesting paradox. These would be better pitched, and could thus take many forms and any sort of cladding.

A single-pitched or monopitch roof is simply a single slope. A lean-to roof has a single pitch, with the apex of the roof leaning against a wall which rises above it. The common double-pitched roof has two opposed pitched sections meeting at a ridge. If this is gabled, it terminates in an upward extension of an end wall to form a gable. A saddleback roof is a common gabled roof set over a tower. A gambrel roof is one where the lower part has a steeper pitch than the upper part. A hipped roof is usually of four slopes, which meet at an angle, rising from the corners to a ridge, thus forming hips. A half-hip starts like a gable, but the upper part is hipped, and, conversely, a gablet starts with hips, but these terminate shortly below the ridge to support a small gable. A mansard roof, like a gambrel, is usually hipped with a double pitch to its opposing slopes, or each of its four slopes, the lower ones being steeper than the upper ones. (*Mansart, incidentally, was not responsible for this form, though he did combine steeply pitched roofs and a flat roof above). A helm, or Rhenish helm (it is common in the Rhineland) is a roof set diagonally on a gabled tower with four similar inclined diamond-shaped faces, each rising from a corner between two adjacent gables to form a pointed top. Complex plans are roofed using combinations of these forms, as are large buildings, but there may be problems. A deep plan may be roofed by two adjacent double-pitched roofs, but that produces a gully between them. A frequent source of woe, it may be alleviated by making the gully higher than the outer eaves, forming an M, and sloping it gently to improve drainage. A different way, employing four hipped slopes with an inner well, again produces problems that may be solved by spanning the ridges with a flat.

These roofs may be covered in any kind of material, though individual materials have their strengths and weaknesses. Straw thatch has the advantage of being fairly light and readily worked to cover any shape as though poured on, so the roof structure may be flimsy and irregular, and the thatch may curve over dormer windows like an eyebrow. Its insulating qualities are superb, but it is flammable and a dreadful hazard. Once so cheap as to be associated with poverty, it is now prized for traditional, picturesque qualities, even though its durability is seldom more than forty or fifty years, and it is expensive. Stone or slate may last three times as long, but angles are harder to form, and the roof structure must be strong and regular. It is poor for insulation, but there is an improvement when it is laid on a base of straw. Sometimes stone is graded from large to small as it rises, but angles require another material, such as lead or tile. Lead can be beaten to any shape—it is good for domes—and is long-lasting, but expensive. Tile, which is fairly cheap and light, is now probably the most popular roof covering of all: it can be specially shaped for ridges and hips, and also gullies, and with care laid on any roof. But its insulation is poor.

Choice of material may determine pitch. Generally, the denser the roofing material, the lower the pitch of its roof should be, and the heavier its supporting trusses. The steepest pitches of around 50–60 degrees, common in the Middle Ages, suit thatch, tile, and slate, but these are all satisfactory on the lower pitches of 35–45 degrees, which better suit heavy stone and lead. Lead tends to creep if the pitch is too great and is well suited to low pitches or indeed no pitch at all. Tile comes in various shapes: flat peg-tiles need a decent pitch to ensure that the roof drains, but curved Roman tiles, which act like a gutter, tend to slip if the pitch is steep.

As well as tarred paper, the Industrial Revolution brought iron and glass to roofs, these finding a growing niche together to satisfy the need for glasshouses to protect tender plants. Such was the roof and indeed the whole of Burton's Palm House at Kew (1845–8), and this was soon taken up for *Paxton's Crystal Palace (1850–51). Closer to the practical benefits of the revolution was William Barlow's St Pancras railway station train-shed roof (1868), a slightly pointed glazed curve executed in cast iron, which could rise and fall as the metal expanded and contracted with changes in temperature, and for twenty years held the record for the world's greatest clear span at 74 m (243 ft). At much the same time, another miracle of industrial technology was Charles *Barry's Houses of Parliament (designed 1836) being roofed with iron slab-tiles as a means of fireproofing. Finally cloth, the material of tents and the roof of wandering herdsmen from Arabian deserts to American prairies, when plastic-coated and tightly hung from wires became the fashionable roof of modern pavilions, culminating in the biggest tent of them all, Richard Rogers' Millennium Dome at Greenwich.   APQ

Rose, Willem Nicolaas (1801–77) Dutch architect and engineer. In 1839 he became Rotterdam's city architect, where from 1843 he started on important large projects to modernize the city (traffic infrastructure, waterworks, parks, city extension), and thus become the pioneer of Dutch modern urbanism. He was an innovative architect, the first in the Netherlands to experiment with new building materials, techniques, and types (Coolsingel hospital, 1838–40). He published numerous articles about architectural theory and technical subjects.   AVdW (trans. CVE)

rose window A circular window with radiating tracery set in a regular repeating pattern, usually cusped or otherwise flowing. Round windows were elaborated early in the 12th century by the addition of foils around their circumference, and spokes, in the form of columns and capitals, radiating from a central hub like a wheel, thus forming a roundel of tapering lancets. In about 1196 the design of the west window of Chartres Cathedral (executed *c.*1216) comprised an inner foiled circle, an outer ring with twelve spokes, and twelve further rings outside, like elaborate plate tracery. The short step from wheel to rose started in the west front of Notre Dame, Paris (*c.*1220), which has an inner ring of twelve spokes, and an outer ring of twenty-four, and was completed some twenty years later in the west front of Reims, where the spokes are slimmer and lack capitals, and each segment has a traceried head.   APQ

Rossellino, Bernardo (1407/10?–64) Italian sculptor and architect, born Bernardo Gambarelli. Early sculptural works like the tomb of Leonardo Bruni (S. Croce, Florence, 1446–8) demonstrate his attention to architectural forms and classical details. His most important commission was the reconstruction (1459–64) of the birthplace of Pope Pius II, renamed Pienza. Rossellino redesigned the central piazza and the buildings that frame it, creating a harmonious ensemble that includes the Palazzo Piccolomini and the Cathedral, modelled on German hall churches but with a classicizing façade. The Palazzo Piccolomini design relates directly to that of the Palazzo Rucellai, Florence, generally attributed to Leon Battista Alberti but on which Rossellino may have participated. The façade articulation of the Pienza palace consists of superimposed pilasters on three of its sides, with a distinctive 3-storey loggia incorporated on the garden elevation.   ACH

Rossetti, Biagio (1447?–1516) Italian architect and military engineer. He is best known for his design of the Addizione (1492), a sizable expansion of Ferrara, and for the palaces and churches he designed within it. The Palazzo dei Diamanti (begun 1493), named after its façade of projecting faceted blocks, stands at the intersection of the two major streets of the new urban quarter. The distinctive Istrian stone façade incorporates ornamented pilasters and a projecting balcony to emphasize its corner. For the palaces on the remaining three corners of the intersection, Rossetti combined stone accents with the brick that is traditional for the city's architecture. In church designs Rossetti incorporated Tuscan and local forms. The modular bays and overall plan of San Francesco (1494) recall Brunelleschi's church of San Lorenzo, Florence, but Rossetti incorporated domes on pendentives and high windows to create a luminous interior.   ACH

Rossi, Aldo (1931–97) Italian architect, theorist, and writer. His first book, *The Architecture of the City* (1966), which placed a strong emphasis on the historic specificity of city architecture, aimed to be a 'preliminary evaluation' of the legacy of Modernism, which placed a strong emphasis on the historic specificity of city architecture. His practice bears a puzzling relationship to his theory, as the rather elementary drawings of the first decade of his work are transformed into repetitive blank façades, punched through by windows, regardless of the building type or historic context: social housing (Gallaratese Milan, 1969–74); a cemetery building (San Cataldo Cemetery, Modena, 1980–85); a theatre (Carlo Felice New Theatre, Genoa 1983–93, with Gardella); and a hotel (Il Palazzo Hotel, Fukuoka, Japan). It is equally difficult to understand the acclaim Rossi received from the architectural press for his Teatro del Mondo (Venice Biennale, 1980), a rather toy-like building bringing together dissociated elements (e.g. gables) from Venetian buildings. PG

Rossi, Carlo (Karl Ivanovich) (1775–1849) Russian architect. The culminating genius of neoclassicism in St Petersburg, Rossi excelled both as an architect and as a city planner who succeeded in creating a sense of *ensemble* among the city's disparate styles. Imbued with Roman monumentalism, his work is as much a part of the fabric of St Petersburg as the palaces of *Rastrelli.

After studying in Italy (1802–3), his major work began with a rebuilding of *Quarenghi's imperial palace on Elagin Island (1818–22), followed by the opulent Mikhailovsky Palace (1819–25; now the Russian Museum). Rossi's largest project was the General Staff Building (1819–29), with a monumental arch linking Palace Square to Nevsky Prospekt. His Mikhailovsky Palace, Alexandrine Theatre (1828–32), and Senate and Holy Synod (1829–34) played a dominant role in creating major urban squares. WCB

Rossi, Giovanni Antonio de' (1616–95) Italian architect. He was unable to transcend the financial and stylistic limitations of his period, so that his work is usually refined in its details and pedestrian in its larger-scale organization. The main exception is the Palazzo d'Aste (1658–65), Rome, with its unusually tall proportions responding to the cramped site. The plan was also adapted ingeniously to the site, as it consisted of a long, narrow vestibule forming the spine of the building, and connecting a side entrance with the staircase. The Palazzo Altieri (1650, extended 1670), with its monotonous series of pediments, is more typical of his palace designs. His ecclesiastical work was mainly limited to restorations, apart from S. Maria in Campo Marzio, Rome (1682–5), skilfully adapted to the narrow streets and small piazza in which it is set. PG

Roth, Alfred (1903–98) Swiss architect. After working on the Weissenhof housing exhibition (1927) in Stuttgart with *Le Corbusier and on the Neubühl housing estate (1930), Roth opened his practice in Zurich in 1932. The two International Style Doldertal apartment buildings (1935/36) in Zurich, built together with Emil Roth and Marcel Breuer for Sigfried Giedion, are his best known work. Roth's book *The New Architecture* (1940) championed Functionalism. As editor of the periodical *Das Werk* and Professor at the Eidgenössische Technische Hochschule, Roth's main achievement was in promoting modern school buildings and architecture abroad. CB

rotunda A building circular in plan, and a cylinder in elevation, usually surmounted by a dome, as in the Pantheon at *Rome, or Paris (*see* SOUFFLOT). PG

Roux-Dutut, Pierre (1919–) French architect. *See* AFRICA (WEST AFRICA).

Rudolph, Paul Marvin (1918–97) US architect. His first works adapted the Functionalism he had learned (and later repudiated) under *Gropius at Harvard to the warm climate of Florida (the Healy Guest House, 1948; the Wheelan House, 1951, both near Sarasota). On a larger scale, the Sarasota High School (1958–9) shows a continuing attachment to the conventions

of Modernism in his use of the *brise-soleil* (*see* LE
CORBUSIER).

Searching for the expressive possibilities denied by a
narrowly *functionalist approach, Rudolph designed a
highly complicated building, the School of Art and
Architecture, Yale University (1958–65), perhaps as a
kind of test piece. Within its 6 storeys are 36 different
levels, though the complexity of their interlocking
volumes (which house a studio, exhibition space,
and library set around the glass-roofed centre) is not
apparent on the exterior. What is apparent is the
texture of the *in situ* concrete. Unlike the simple
expression of board formwork used by the *Brutalists,
a ribbed and hammered surface creates a complex
texture. In the Temple Street garage, New Haven
(1959–62), the long horizontal lines create an effect
of monumentality, unusual for this building type.

From the early 1960s, his practice designed at a
much larger scale (e.g. the Government Centre
complex, Boston, 1962–71), but many of his projects
were not realized.   PG

Rundbogenstil an architectural style based on the
structural form of the round arch that found widespread
popularity from the early 1830s in Germany and, later,
in Scandinavian countries and the United States. The
principles of the Rundbogenstil were developed first
and most rigorously by the architect Heinrich Hübsch
(1795–1863) in his influential book *In What Style Should
We Build?* (1828; English translation 1992). Although
Hübsch found inspiration in structures like the
Rhineland Abbey Church of Maria Laach (begun 1093),
he conceived of the Rundbogenstil in opposition to the
notion of stylistic repetition, and therefore as a response
to the contemporary demands of climate, building
materials, and construction. Hübsch's Technische
Hochschule in Karlsruhe (1833–6), Trinkhalle in
Baden-Baden (1837–40), and theatre in Karlsruhe
(1851–3) provided built confirmation of the principles

developed in his writing. The projects of Alexis de
Chateauneuf in Hamburg, August Andreae in
Hanover, Johann Claudius von Lassaulx near Koblenz,
and Friedrich von *Gärtner in Munich attest to the
spread of the Rundbogenstil across Germany.   AN

Ruskin, John (1817–1900) architectural and social
critic. Drawing was Ruskin's way in to architecture,
and the artist Samuel Prout helped him to see texture
and weathering. These influences turned him against
the classical and Renaissance traditions towards an
organic vision of building. *The Poetry of Architecture*,
published serially in 1838–9, reflected the ideal of
harmonizing buildings and landscape from the
Picturesque Movement.

After 1845, North Italian Romanesque and Gothic
captured his attention. *The Seven Lamps of Architecture*
(1849) valued moral qualities and the independent spirit
of the workman. Contemporaries justifiably assumed
that Ruskin was influenced by Pugin, which he denied.
Both were appalled by the materialistic signs of
Victorian progress, such as the railways, and Ruskin
condemned the Crystal Palace as a 'cucumber frame'.

The Stones of Venice (3 vols., 1851–3) is a rather
diverse text, combining evocation, analysis and
moralizing. The section 'The Nature of Gothic' from
Book II has often been taken separately as an expression
of Ruskin's central beliefs, and was praised by William
*Morris. Here he developed his theory of structural
polychromy, that colour should be inherent in the
material used, rather than a superficial decoration: in
his own words, '. . . the school of incrusted architecture
is *the only one in which perfect and chromatic decoration is
possible . . .*' (*Stones of Venice*, Book II, p.98.)

While Ruskin came to deplore the influence of
The Stones of Venice on contemporary architecture, he
participated with Henry Acland in shaping the details of
*Deane and Woodward's Oxford University Museum
(1855–9), especially the carving of capitals and window

surrounds. He was initially tolerant of the iron and glass structure in the courtyard, but the whole experience turned him against future active engagement in building projects.

Ruskin's later political and economic writings, such as *Unto this Last* (1862) and *Fors Clavigera* (1871–84), influenced the radical aestheticism of the *Arts and Crafts movement.   AP

Brooks, M. W., *John Ruskin and Victorian Architecture* (1989)

Russia (pre-Soviet) Almost nothing is known of pre-Christian architecture among the eastern Slavs, but with the acceptance of Orthodox Christianity (988), the construction of *Byzantine-inspired masonry churches spread rapidly to cities such as Kiev and Novgorod. The largest was Kiev's Cathedral of Divine Wisdom (1037–50s); other major churches of this period include the Sophia Cathedral in Novgorod (1045–52), the Cathedral of the Transfiguration of the Saviour in Chernigov (1031–50s), and the Cathedral of the Dormition at the Kiev Cave Monastery (1073–8, destroyed 1941).

Regardless of size, the churches adhered to a plan known as the 'inscribed cross', a central dome raised above a square plan. The interior bays were delineated on the exterior by pilasters culminating in curved gables whose shape reflected the barrel vaulting of the interior. The application of stucco to church walls, typically built of thin brick, rough stone, and heavy mortar, began toward the end of the 12th century.

The other centre of architecture in pre-Mongol Rus was the Vladimir-Suzdal principality, whose limestone churches were distinguished by carved decoration and precision of design. The first of these churches was the Transfiguration in Pereslavl-Zalessky (1152–7); the most important, the Cathedral of the Dormition, Vladimir (1158–60; enlarged 1185–9).

After the Mongol invasion (1237–41), church construction sharply declined. By the middle of

the 14th century, masonry construction revived, particularly in Novgorod, exemplified in a distinct local style with steeply pitched trefoil roofs. Moscow also enjoyed an architectural revival in the construction of limestone churches, but not until the last quarter of the 15th century did the major monuments of the Kremlin take shape under the direction of Italian masters imported by Ivan III.

In the 16th century, Moscow's brick votive churches displayed boldly inventive designs, also with Italian influence. The Church of the Ascension at Kolomenskoe (1530–32) defined the 'tent' (*shatior*) tower form, while the Decapitation of John the Baptist at Diakovo (*c.*1550) exemplified another form of the tower church. These prototypes were combined in the most spectacular and famous of Russian churches, popularly known as Vasily (Basil) the Blessed (1550–61), Red Square. The structure consists of a central tent tower, surrounded by eight tower churches. Polychrome onion domes were added at the turn of the 17th century, while attached structures and much of the painted decoration appeared throughout the 17th century. The latter part of the 16th century also saw the building of major brick fortresses, most notably the citadel at Smolensk (1595–1602), by Fedor Kon.

After the depredations of the Time of Troubles (1605–13), the building of masonry churches occurred on an unprecedented scale during the reign of Tsar Aleksei (1645–76). The proliferation of lavishly ornamented churches occurred throughout Muscovy, especially in Yaroslavl. In a related development, many of Moscow's monasteries were rebuilt in the late 17th century, as was the great monastery at Sergiev Posad, 71 km (44 miles) to the north-east.

As Russia experienced increased contact with the West through Ukraine and northern Europe, elements of the Baroque appeared in numerous churches commissioned primarily by the Naryshkin

Church of the Transfiguration,
Kizhi, Russia (18th century)

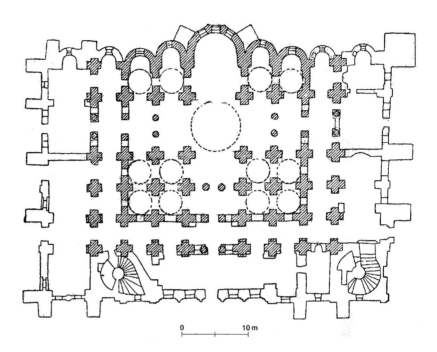

Cathedral of St Sophia,
known as 'Divine Wisdom',
Kiev, Ukraine (1037–50s)

0   10 m

and Sheremetev families on estates surrounding
Moscow. Examples of the 'Naryshkin Baroque' show
a revival of the tower church form. During the
17th century, the use of brick in secular construction
increased, mainly in Moscow, with its brick residences
(*palaty*) and the tiered Sukharev Tower (1692–1701).

The assimilation of Western architectural forms
increased radically during the reign of Peter I (1694–
1725). At this stage, St Petersburg's architecture owed
much to the northern European Baroque, particularly
in Sweden and Holland. The stuccoed brick walls of the
city's Baroque buildings were painted, with white trim
for window surrounds and other details.

*Rastrelli defined the high Baroque style during
the reigns of Anne (1730–40) and Elizabeth (1741–61).
Among his major projects were Elizabeth's Summer
Palace (1741–3, destroyed), the Stroganov Palace

(1752–4), the final version of the Winter Palace
(1754–64), and the Smolny Convent with its
Resurrection Cathedral (1748–64). He also enlarged
the existing Imperial palaces at Peterhof (1746–52)
and Tsarskoe Selo (1748–56). During this period
Russian architects such as Zemtzov (1688–1743) and
*Chevakinsky (1713–80), contributed significantly to
the city's development, the latter's masterpiece, the
Cathedral of St Nicholas (1753–62), rivalling the best
work of Rastrelli.

With the support of Catherine, a constellation of
architects endowed St Petersburg during the second
half of the 18th century with a grandeur inspired by
classical Rome and Palladianism. The two most
important architects were the Italians: *Rinaldi
(*c*.1710–94), a pioneer in the transition from the
Baroque to neoclassicism, and *Quarenghi (1744–1817),

who developed neoclassical architecture in both imperial estates and in numerous state commissions. Palladianism was represented by Charles *Cameron (*c.*1740–1812), in his work at Pavlovsk and Tsarskoe Selo.

Other major architects of late-18th-century St Petersburg include *Starov (1745–1808), whose understated Classicism in the design of the Tauride Palace (1738–9) was widely adopted as a model for estate houses. Voronikhin (1759–1814) created a still more obvious example of the Roman influence in his Cathedral of the Kazan Mother of God (1801–11), with its sweeping colonnade attached to the north (Nevsky Prospekt) façade. Similarly, Thomas de Thomon (1760–1813) used the temples at Paestum as a model for the Bourse (1805–10), on the tip of Vasilevsky Island. The Bourse was used by Tsar Alexander (r.1801–25) as a focus for an interconnecting system of architectural *ensembles* and public space throughout the centre of St Petersburg. The rebuilding of the Admiralty (1806–23) by Zakharov (1761–1811) reaffirmed that structure and its spire as dominant elements in the city plan. The culmination of the imperial design fell to Carlo Rossi (1776–1849) who created four major *ensembles* around a palace, a theatre, and government buildings. St Petersburg's other master of late neoclassicism, Stasov (1769–1848), built a number of churches, including the Icon of the Saviour (1817–23), with the attached building of the Court Stables extending on either side along the Moika Canal.

Neoclassicism in Moscow appeared primarily in houses and other institutions built by the nobility and wealthy merchants. Talented serf architects built many of the grand estate houses, but the most prominent designers of mansions and churches were Matvey Fedorovich Kazakov (1738–1812), Rodion Rodionovich Kazakov (1755–1803), and *Bazhenov (1737?–99). It is assumed that Bazhenov designed the Pashkov House, and also, at the request of Catherine II,

a grandiose plan for rebuilding the Kremlin in the neoclassical style.

During the reign of Nicholas I, classical unity in St Petersburg yielded to Eclecticism and innovations in construction engineering, both of which are evident in the final version of St Isaac's Cathedral (1818–58) by *Montferrand (1786–1858), and in mid-19th-century palaces by Shtakenshneider (1802–65). More significant was the Russo-Byzantine style, supported by Nicholas I and implemented by Ton (1794–1881), builder of the Great Kremlin Palace (1838–49). The major work in this style, which prevailed in church architecture throughout the century, was his Church of Christ the Redeemer (1837–83, destroyed).

Secular architecture in St Petersburg and Moscow during the mid 19th century was largely an eclectic combination of various periods in the history of Western architecture, but by the 1870s there arose a new national style based on decorative elements from 16th- and 17th-century Muscovy and on motifs from folk art and traditional wooden architecture. Major examples of the Russian style in Moscow include the Historical Museum (1874–83) by Shervud (1833–97); the Moscow City Duma (1890–92) by Chichagov (1835–94); and the Upper Trading Rows (1889–93) by Pomerantsev (1848–1918). In St Petersburg, the Russian style was used by Parland (1845–92) for the Church of the Resurrection of the Saviour (1883–1907).

The 'new style' or *style moderne* which arose in Russian architecture at the turn of the 20th century included a number of stylistic tendencies. Its main emphasis was on the innovative use of materials such as glass, iron, and glazed brick in functional yet highly aesthetic designs. The style flourished above all in Moscow, where its leading practitioner was *Shekhtel' (1859–1926). Other leading modernist architects of the period included Kekushev (1863–1919), Erikhson, and Walcot, all involved in one of the largest and most significant *moderne* buildings in Russia, the Hotel

Metropole (1899–1905). In St Petersburg, the *style moderne* appeared primarily in the design of apartment complexes, but also in commercial buildings, such as the Eliseev emporium and theatre (1902–4).

By about 1910, the *style moderne* had yielded to, or merged with, a more severe form of stripped Classicism, known in Russia as *neoklassitsizm*. Architects in St Petersburg were especially receptive to this revival, which they applied to almost every major structural type, including banks, hotels (notably the Hotel Astoria, 1911–12), department stores, and private houses. In Moscow the revival followed a similar pattern, even including one of the first 'skyscrapers' (the Northern Insurance Company Building, 1909–11).

In contrast to their US contemporaries, Russian architects made little use of the skeletal frame in the design of large buildings, but applied the techniques of reinforced concrete construction, with considerable proficiency. The economic chaos engendered in Russia by World War I proved catastrophic for building activity, and the ensuing revolution and civil war brought construction to a halt.   WCB

Brumfield, W., *A History of Russian Architecture* (2nd edn, 2004)

Brumfield, W., *The Origins of Modernism in Russian Architecture* (1995)
Rappoport, A., *Building the Churches of Kievan Russia* (1995)

Russia, Soviet period (1917–91) *See* SOVIET UNION, RUSSIA.

rustication The exaggerated treatment of masonry to give a rustic, primitive or unusually strong appearance as a result of its jointing or surface texture, usually by deeply inset jointing.

Forms include: banded rustication, in which the horizontal joints are emphasized by cut channels of square or V-section; Cyclopean or rock-faced rustication, in which large blocks of rubble-faced stone are laid in regular courses with regular intervals between the individual equal-sized stones; diamond-pointed rustication, in which the individual stones are dressed with a shallow pyramidal face; glacial rustication, in which the face of each stone is carved to represent icicles or stalactites; smooth rustication, in which the stones are finely dressed flat and the joints are emphasized by narrow grooves between each stone; and vermiculated rustication, in which the face of each stone has a texture like worm-casts.   APQ

Saarinen, Eero (1910–61) Finnish architect, son of Eliel. Following his father's success in the *Chicago Tribune* competition, he moved to the United States, where he was to spend the rest of his life.

Eero worked with Norman Bel Geddes in New York and then with his father, before establishing his own practice after World War II.

With the completion of the vast new Technical Centre for General Motors in 1956 his practice flourished and Saarinen received numerous commissions to design large buildings for industry and education as well as embassies and airports. In this work he actively sought out the particularities of his client and their project as inspiration to develop an approach that, when combined with rational research and explorations of the potential of materials, generated 'a style for the job'. It was an approach in sharp contrast to the ideas of universal space and the liberating frame advocated by *Mies van der Rohe which were pervasive at the time.

Saarinen's design for the TWA Terminal in New York, constructed of reinforced concrete, explored the sculptural potential of architecture in an attempt to create a building which simulated flight and suggested lightness. Constructed of reinforced concrete it was followed in quick succession by numerous other buildings, each seemingly radically different from the next—the Ingalls Hockey Rink at Yale, an auditorium and chapel at MIT, corporate headquarters buildings for CBS and John Deere, the Gateway Arch in St Louis, Dulles Airport in Washington DC, and new American embassies in Oslo and London.

Eero Saarinen died at the age of 51, and, although he oversaw the design and construction of an extraordinary range of buildings, his suddenly shortened career robbed modern architecture of a powerful and unpredictable source of inspiration. BC

Saarinen, Eliel (1873–1950) Finnish architect. His career can be divided into two parts: his activity in Finland, and then in the US from 1923. From 1896 to 1907 he was in practice with *Gesellius and Lindgren. Their fusion of elements from Finnish medieval monuments with those of Art Nouveau and Jugendstil served the needs of both private and public clients well, ensuring a prolific and high quality output during the activity of the office. The projects were always signed by all three members. Among their projects are the Pohjola Insurance Company Building (Helsinki, 1901), Olofsborg apartment block (Helsinki, 1902), their own studio and home complex Hvitträsk (Kirkkonummi, 1904), and the Finnish National Museum (Helsinki, 1902–14). During this period Saarinen had emerged as a member of the cultural and artistic elite striving for a modern, independent Finnish culture (*see* NATIONAL ROMANTICISM).

Modernity and urbanism dictated the design of the Helsinki Railway Station (1904–16), a project carried out by Saarinen alone, and which he continued to work on until 1911. His understanding of large-scale urban planning is evident in his forward-looking scheme for the Munkkiniemi-Haaga township from 1916 (vicinity of Helsinki, not realized).

In 1922 Saarinen won second prize in the international competition for the *Chicago Tribune* building with a proposal which stressed the verticality of the tall edifice. Encouraged, the Saarinen family moved to the US in 1923. Soon the Detroit newspaper magnate Henry Booth contracted him as the architect of the Cranbrook community of education in Bloomfield Hills. After Saarinen built Cranbrook

School for Boys (1925), he was the head and architect of the community, now expanded into Cranbrook Academy of Art, until his death. From the late 1930s he worked together with his son Eero *Saarinen (1910–61). PKO

Hausen, Marika *et al.*, *Eliel Saarinen. Projects 1896–1923* (1990)

Sacchetti, Giovanni Battista (1700–64) Italian architect. Initially Sacchetti assisted *Juvarra with the preparation of models and drawings, moving to Spain after the latter's death (1736). He brought to completion the latter's design for the centre of the garden front of the La Granja palace, San Ildefonso, near Segovia (1736–42). In 1738 he revised Juvarra's design for the Royal Palace, Madrid, to meet the new requirements of a changed site and a reduction in size to one quarter of the original plan. He raised the whole building (completed in 1757) on a massive rusticated basement, and successfully integrated the main building not only with a rather awkward site, but also with the levels of existing buildings, streets, and courtyards. PG

Safdie, Moshe (1938–) Israeli-born Canadian architect, urbanist, author, and educator, who moved to Canada at the age of 15. His principal office (since 1978) is in Boston with branches in Jerusalem, Montreal, and Toronto. At the age of 24, his graduation thesis—a prefabricated housing complex—was selected for construction at Expo 67 in Montreal; 'Habitat 67' became a 20th-century icon, but his other innovative designs for prefabricated housing projects were not realized.

His important works include the National Gallery, Ottawa (1988), and Vancouver Library Square (1995) in Canada; the master plan for the new town of Modi'in, Yad Vashem Holocaust Museum (2005) in Jerusalem, and Terminal 3, Ben-Gurion International Airport

(2004), in Israel; and Skirball Cultural Centre, LA, and the Peace Headquarters, Washington DC (completion due 2009), in the United States.

In 1990 Safdie donated his archive as an ongoing bequest to the Canadian Architecture Collection at McGill. Safdie has published influential books and articles, among them: *Beyond Habitat* (1970), *The City after the Automobile* (1987), and *Jerusalem: The Future of the Past* (1989).   ML

Sakakura, Junzô (1901–69) Japanese architect. After working for Le Corbusier from 1931 to 1936, Sakakura gained world prominence at the 1937 International Exposition in Paris through his design of the Japanese Pavilion, integrating his master's formal ideas with Japanese *sukiya* aesthetics as found in the Katsura Imperial Villa. He subsequently designed the Kamakura Museum of Modern Art (1951), celebrated for its integration of a 2-storey modern form into the historical context of the adjacent Hachimangu shrine. His later work was marked by large-scale public commissions, such as the Brutalist concrete town hall in Hashima (1959) and railway terminal transportation/ retail complexes in the Tokyo districts of Shibuya (1951–60) and Shinjuku (1966–7).   KTO

Saljuqs The Saljuqs of central Asia converted to Islam in c.1037. One branch of the tribe ruled over Iran, Iraq, and Syria, from 1038 to 1194; the other, known as the Saljuqs of Rum, dominated Anatolia from 1077 to 1307. As part of a great artistic efflorescence, the Iranian branch (*see* *Iran, Saljuqs) created one of the world's greatest architectures; that of the Saljuqs of Rum, if not reaching the same heights, is of considerable interest.

In Anatolia, the Saljuqs built in Erzurum, and Sivas, but it was Konya which became the capital of political and cultural strength. This was due in part to the mystic philosopher Jalal al-Din Rumi (d.1273) who founded the Mevlevi order of dervishes.

Saljuq architecture was durable and aesthetically stimulating. Both qualities were due to local craftsmen trained to build in stone and carve eloquent symbolic decoration. Doorways were framed by elaborate carving, so as to give monumental portals a more graceful aspect, but only rarely was such carving found on the side walls and around the windows (one exception is the Gök (Blue) Madrasa, Sivas, 1271–2).

Saljuq culture created functional but finely proportioned madrasas or colleges of higher learning, vital to cultural life, and mosques. The Karatay madrasa at Konya (1251–2) is one example. Richly endowed with glazed tiles, it also has a dramatic façade in black and white marble. Above the city are the palace and the Ala'ettin Mosque (begun 1252), which includes a later columned hall and outstanding minbar. Ala'ettin was a great advance on the initial example at Sivas, and had fifty piers to support a mud and rafter roof. But later madrasas at Sivas were built by teams of master craftsmen who carved the monumental gateways with symbols as well as floral designs, while pairs of glazed minarets in brick flanked the gateways. The student cells, courtyard, and lecture hall were handsomely proportioned, if austere. An unusual form found in madrasas is the 'two minarets' (*çifte minareli*) type, in which two towers rise from either side of a sculpted portal. Examples are the Çifte Minareli madrasas at Erzurum (*c*.1250) and Sivas (1271–2), and the Gök (Blue) Madrasa, Sivas (1271–2).

The rather plain but beautifully cut masonry of the Saljuqs was very suited to two particular types of utilitarian structures: caravanserais and bridges. Caravanserais were fortresses with courtyards and cattle stalls, royal apartments and dormitories, which were akin to cathedrals. They were vital for trade along the great caravan routes into Asia. The Sultan Han at Aksaray (1229) is but one example of their monumentality. The same discipline built many bridges that still survive, leaping from rock to rock;

small arches reduced the main, often elegant span to proportions in some cases still able to support the weight of international traffic.

Saljuq tomb towers (*türbe* or *kümbet*) are of 2 storeys: the lower floor housed the coffin, the upper a mosque, surmounted by a low flat dome or a conical roof. There are several examples in Kayseri, notably the Döner Kumbet (*c*.1275), Kayseri, with its carved magic birds and spirits. The conical roof tends to be the usual type further east, as in the several examples in Erzurum.

One unique monument is the mosque and hospital of the vassal Müngücüks of Divrik, *c*.1228. The mosque ceiling is a galaxy of carved panels. The austere hospital creates awe out of shadow, while the stone woodland of the portal, crowned with stars, depicts men hiding in the foliage.   GG/PG

Salmona, Rogelio (1924–) French-born

Colombian architect, who studied in Bogotá and then worked for ten years with Le Corbusier. Returning to Colombia in 1958, he tackled the housing shortage by designing various residential complexes, the most important being El Polo (1959–62), with Guillermo Bermúdez, Las Torres del Parque (1895–7), and, with different collaborators, the Nueva Santa Fe community centre (1994–6). He revived the use of exposed brick and the courtyard, developing a meticulous and original architectural style. His major works include the Modern Art Museum (1974), the Fontana Gymnasium (1992), the National Archive building (1992), the Vice-Presidency building (1994), the National University Postgraduate School in Bogotá (1996–8), the Quimbaya Museum (1985) in Armenia, and many houses. Of particular interest is the Casa de Huespedes Ilustres in Cartagena (1981), in which local stone is used to excellent effect to create a welcoming yet impressive context, achieving exceptional integration into the environment.   LNM (trans. KL)

Salvin, Anthony (1799–1881) English architect.

Prolific and long-lived, Salvin was a pupil of Nash, and is known for his country houses, Tudor and Jacobean in style, and his castles. The early Mamhead, Devon (1823–38), and Moreby Hall, Yorkshire (1828–32), both Tudor, led to his tour de force, Harlaxton Manor, Lincolnshire (1831–8), as prodigious as its Elizabethan models. Later works are dull, and even the romantic drama of his Peckforton Castle, Cheshire (1844–52), a credibly medieval stronghold, does not quite match it. His churches, which attracted favourable attention in the 1840s, detract from his status as the builder of over seventy houses and the restorer of many castles.   APQ

sandstone is geologically defined as a type of rock

usually formed of sand and quartz particles, though it may include other minerals, such as feldspar and mica. However, it is not always easy to distinguish from *limestone, as some sandstones have a high calcite content, and some limestones (e.g. Ketton) are coloured pink. As a further indication of the complexity of the subject, some of the Old Red and New Red sandstones are not in fact red.

Sandstone was used for the cores of the temples of ancient Egypt from the New Kingdom period, but otherwise not much favoured in antiquity. The widest variety of sandstones used for building is to be found in England, which, fortunately, is very well documented, more so than for any other country (see Alec Clifton-Taylor, *The Pattern of English Building*, 1962, chapter 5). Their pre-eminent quality is the variety and beauty of their colours. At Great Malvern Priory (*c*.1420ff.) can be seen almost the entire range: brown, pink, grey, and pale green.

New Red sandstone is very vulnerable to the English weather. The principal cathedrals built of this sandstone type—Hereford, Lichfield, Worcester, and Carlisle—do not wear well. In his *Recollections*, Sir George Gilbert *Scott reported (1868) that at Chester '…the external stonework was...horribly and lamentably decayed... like a mouldering sandstone cliff.' In this case, his much criticized *conservation and restoration work was undeniably necessary if the building was to survive. But, however careful the conservation work, this type of sandstone decays within a century. The Carboniferous sandstones, which are much more durable, are used mainly in the north of England, notably for Hardwick Hall.

For the more refined architecture of English *country houses (see also PALLADIANISM), though stone was the most prestigious material, sandstone was used far less frequently than limestone, possibly because its vibrant colours distracted from the contemplation of form. If sandstone was used, the preference may have been for the more discreet grey-pink varieties, as at Houghton Hall, Norfolk (1721), or Berrington Hall, Herefordshire (1778–c.1781).

In England sandstone is rarely found in combination, and is too close in colour to brick to achieve the satisfactory contrast of Portland stone (see LIMESTONE) and brick. But in India, orange-red sandstone, which has the additional advantage of being a fairly homogenous colour, was used most effectively with marble, or slate, or other stones such as corandel; so that was its most appropriate context. Most of India's sandstone is found in Rajasthan, so the cities of Jaipur have many ornate buildings of sandstone (such as the Palace of the Wind); it was used in the fort of Jaiselmer, and the material is very appropriate in this desert setting.

However, the most distinguished sandstone architecture is found outside this area, in Delhi and the abandoned city of Fatehpur Sikri. In Delhi, Humayun's tomb (completed 1571) is constructed of red sandstone, with white marble edges. At Fatehpur Sikri, the Buland Darvaza gateway (c.1585?) uses fawn-coloured sandstone to outline the frame. Favoured by the aridity of the area, the red sandstone of the Diwan-I Am has a beautifully carved façade, incorporating sandscreens. The colour may have been chosen to emphasize the majesty of the enthroned emperor, as he sat facing east, the rising sun suggesting that he was an emanation of divine light.   PG

Sanfelice, Ferdinando (1675–1748) Italian architect. Although Sanfelice built numerous churches in and around Naples, his most original designs were for *palazzi, in particular their staircases. Previous Neapolitan architects had made a feature of open staircases, but they were usually placed in a subordinate position such as the corner of the courtyard. Sanfelice made the staircases the most important feature, immediately attracting the attention of the visitor entering through the porte cochère.

In his own Palazzo Sanfelice (1723–8), the staircase occupies the whole of the side of the courtyard opposite the porte cochère and rises the full height of the building. He was able to make the staircase seem almost transparent, because it began with two flights running parallel with the façade, to left and right, leaving the central space open, with a view through to the garden. This arrangement was both spectacular and practical, as the staircases not only provided direct access to the living apartments, but eventually led to a stately approach to the main salone.

Even more spectacular examples are found at the Palazzo Serra di Cassano (1719–c.1730), where he rounded off the corners of the rectangular courtyard, so as to give even further emphasis to the entrance to the staircases; and at the Palazzo Capuano, in which, responding to a long narrow site, Sanfelice made the staircase octagonal in plan.   PG

Sangallo family Italian architects. Seven members of the da Sangallo family were architects, the most eminent being the following three (in chronological order).

Sangallo, Giuliano da (1445–1516) designed one
of the earliest *Renaissance villas, Villa Medici,
Poggio a Caiano (c.1480–97). The H-shaped plan was
symmetrically inscribed inside a square; and for the
first time, the entrance was marked by a classical
temple front. However, the design is not entirely
successful, as the rather squat temple front displaces the
side windows too much to the edges of the building.
His plan for Santa Maria delle Carceri, Prato (1484–91),
is also innovative, as it is the first Renaissance building
planned as a Greek cross with a domed drum. Giuliano
designed an interesting façade for the Palazzo Gondi
(1489–1504), which has the most subtly graduated
rustication of any Florentine *palazzo.

**Sangallo, Antonio di Francesco di Bartolo
Giamberti da, the Elder** (c.1460–1534) carried out
many works of *military architecture, but only one
major ecclesiastical building, the church of Madonna di
S. Biagio, Montepulciano (begun 1518). The barrel-
vaulted Greek cross carries a dome on a high drum,
but of the four towers planned, only one was built.
The architect aimed at an effect of solidity by means of
massive Doric pilasters, but compared to the work of
his contemporary, *Bramante, the church lacks
grandeur.

Sangallo, Antonio da, the Younger (1484–1546)
was one of the foremost military architects of the
period, but by comparison his civil architecture is no
more than competent.

After the death of *Raphael in 1520, he became joint
architect for St Peter's, with *Peruzzi. Sole architect
from 1536, his ideas were embodied in a wooden model
(1538–43), which fortunately remained unbuilt. A
rather fussy central façade of several heights, flanked by
towers rising in several storeys, and a relatively
insignificant dome, the design completely lacked the
sense of grandeur required for the greatest church in
Christendom and evident in the work of *Bramante
and *Michelangelo.

His best-known secular work was the Palazzo
Farnese (1534–46). This was a difficult commission:
a flat-fronted façade over 70 m (230 ft) long, set in an
open piazza, with a central portal of no great size.
Sangallo tried to avoid monotony by varying the
pediments over the *piano nobile* windows, but
without success. In his defence, it has to be said that
Michaelangelo's brief intervention after 1546 probably
made the *palazzo* look even more ponderous.   PG

Sanmicheli, Michele (c.1487–1559) Italian
architect and engineer. A prolific and wide-ranging
architect, Sanmicheli's work is characterized by a
powerful Roman Renaissance style. Together with
Falconetto and *Giulio Romano, he brought the
vocabulary of the High Roman Renaissance to
northern Italy, and particularly to the Venetian
Republic.

He was trained as a mason in his native Verona, and
was further educated in Rome. In 1509 he was master
at Orvieto cathedral, where he completed the façade.
A brief appointment as inspector of fortifications for
the Papal States was followed by his return to Verona
(1526), where he was patronized by several leading
families, for whom he designed palaces. Palazzo
Pompei (c.1530) is disciplined and restrained, but with
Palazzo Canossa (begun c.1530) his style began to
develop a characteristic richness, with rustication and
Mannerist detailing in the manner of Romano. Palazzo
Bevilacqua (c.1530–35) has the first Renaissance façade
in Verona all of stone, with complex rhythms and rich
detailing. It also has the prominent rustication to the
ground storey which was to become a prominent
feature of his military architecture.

In the middle of his career, Sanmicheli designed two
prominent palaces for Venice. Palazzo Corner at San
Polo (c.1550) has a difficult site, with one corner facing
the spacious Campo San Polo, but the extremely tall
water façade dominates the nearby canal, with

Palazzo Grimani, Grand Canal, Venice (Michele Sanmicheli, 1559–70s)

superimposed Serlian windows to the *piani nobili*. The majestic Palazzo Grimani (1559–early 1570s) on the Grand Canal at San Luca has an ingenious plan, its basic symmetry adapted skilfully to the asymmetrical site. Its grandiose façade has three tall *Corinthian orders, with both single and paired columns.

Sanmicheli's eclectic creativity is seen most clearly in his churches. The Pellegrini Chapel at San Bernardino, Verona (*c.*1527) is a remarkable work, circular on plan, and with an interior modelled on the Pantheon. The austere exterior gives little idea of the richness within, even the coffered cupola being screened by a simple pitched roof. His interest in centralized church forms was continued with the cupola for San Giorgio in Braida, Verona (1535), another coffered dome raised on

a tall drum, and with the tempietto for the Verona Lazzaretto (begun 1549), where a tall drum and cupola are surrounded by a low classical colonnade. This was the forerunner of Sanmicheli's greatest ecclesiastical work, the pilgrimage church of the Madonna di Campagna, outside Verona (1559). Here, the same basic architectonic elements as those at the Lazzaretto are disposed on a truly monumental scale; the simple massing of the exterior is relieved solely by the spacious colonnade and the tall windows lighting the drum. The interior is equally spare and imposing.

Sanmicheli is best known today for his many works of military architecture, where his powerful style was perfectly appropriate. The early Porta Nuova (city gate) at Verona (*c.*1530) was followed by the even more impressive Porta Palio (1547); both are indebted to the Mannerism of Romano, but have a noble presence that is purely Sanmicheli's own. In 1535 he was appointed military architect to the Venetian Republic, and for many years designed fortifications for Venice's possessions, both on the Terraferma and overseas. Among the latter were fortifications at Corfu, Crete, and Cyprus, and the imposing city gate at Zara. In Venice he designed the sea-fort at Sant'Andrea, guarding the entry into the lagoon. All of these works evince his mature Renaissance style, with refined, powerfully modelled forms, reflecting the naval power of the Serenissima. Sanmicheli's work influenced considerably the young Andrea Palladio, who trained in nearby Vicenza; it was also highly influential in the neoclassical era.   RJG

Puppi, L., *Michele Sanmicheli, architetto* (1986)

Sansovino, Jacopo d'Antonio Tatti (1486–
1570) Italian architect and sculptor, and one of the central figures of the High Renaissance in Venice. He was recognized almost solely as a sculptor until he fled Rome in 1527 and settled in Venice for the rest of his life. There his architectural skills developed rapidly,

and in 1529 he was appointed chief surveyor to the Procurators of San Marco, responsible for the church and the buildings around the piazza; he retained the post until his death.

His reputation as an architect rests on three buildings in the centre of Venice, the new Zecca (mint), the Library of San Marco and the *loggetta* at the base of the campanile. The Zecca (begun 1535) is a powerfully modelled work, all of Istrian stone, with strong rustication to its 2 storeys (the third was added later). The *loggetta* and the Library were conceived together, both for the Procurators. Sansovino persuaded them to agree to widening the piazza, thereby rendering the campanile free-standing, and permitting the Library also to be constructed as a free-standing structure. It is generally considered his masterpiece, a richly detailed essay in the High Renaissance style, with a Doric ground storey and an Ionic *piano nobile*. *Palladio considered it the finest building since ancient times. The superb first-floor reading room was decorated partly by Titian, a close friend and associate. The *loggetta*, a meeting-place for the nobility, was completed in 1542 and gains in richness of materials what it lacks in dimensions. Its decoration included four bronze statues by Sansovino himself.

Sansovino designed two major palaces in Venice, the Dolfin (later Manin) at Rialto (begun 1538) and the Corner at San Maurizio (begun 1545). The former has a regular, disciplined façade with (unusually) a public quay covered by a colonnade along the front. The Palazzo Corner has one of the most monumental and imposing façades in the city. The tripartite plan is highly traditional in Venice, but Sansovino treats the façade as a virtually free-standing screen, with two superimposed *piani nobili*, and detailing that already anticipates the Baroque of *Longhena.

He also designed several churches in Venice, including the monastic house of San Francesco della Vigna (begun 1534, with a later façade by Palladio), and

three parish churches, San Martino (*c.*1540), San Zulian (1553), and San Gimignano (1557, destroyed). The churches are less impressive than his public works, although each responded to its unique site, and demonstrated his range and versatility. He also designed one outstanding villa, the Villa Garzoni, near Padua (1537–40) at Pontecasale, an imposing fusion of the palazzo and the rural villa.

Sansovino had a profound influence on the architects and sculptors of the Baroque, above all on *Longhena.   RJG

Howard, D(eborah), *Jacopo Sansovino: architecture and patronage in Renaissance Venice* (1975)

Sant'Elia, Antonio (1888–1916) Italian architect, whose drawings of power plants, railway stations, and high-rise apartment buildings defined *Futurism in architecture. Sant'Elia's few realized works, such as the Villa Elisi in San Maurizio (1912), combined the Stile Liberty of Giuseppe *Sommaruga with the architecture of the Wagnerschule. The same year he founded the Nuove Tendenze group, with whom his drawings of the utopian Città Nuova were exhibited in 1914. His published statement for the exhibition later became the 'Manifesto dell'architettura futurista', the avant-garde artistic movement that he joined and with whom he tragically chose to fight in World War I.   BLM

Santini-Aichel, Jan Blažej (1677–1723) Czech architect. His brief career, and under a dozen major buildings, nevertheless evince the most original ideas among central European architects of his generation.

Santini was born into a Prague family of masons. After apprenticeship to J. B. Mathey, an apostle of Roman ideas, and a three-year journey to Italy, he was taken up as a designer by the Bohemian upper class and the abbots of mainly Cistercian monasteries.

His work in Prague, such as the Thun and Morzin palaces and his own house, although forceful, does not stand out. In 1700 he began the abbey at nearby Zbraslav, and his personal manner began to show in sharp spare detail; the tripartite plan of his chapel at Panenské Břežany (1705–7) testifies to his enthusiasm for *Borromini; similarities suggest that he worked from 1710 to 1714 on the pretty pilgrimage church at Bílá Hora. His ultimate direction was apparent in the remodelling of the abbey church at Sedlec (1703–8) with functionless free Gothic forms in vaulting and façade. In about 1706 he began the rebuilding of the abbey church at Žd'aìr, again with Gothic detail.

The grandiose plans which he drew up in about 1710 for the abbey at Plasy were only slowly and partially realized. But the same patron commissioned the pilgrimage church of Mariaìnskaì Tynice (1710/20–64) on a Greek cross plan with five shallow domes on very tall piers. His grandest work followed, the rebuilding of the abbey church at Kladruby (1711–26) with more free Gothic inside and out, and on top a spectacularly spiky dome like some great artichoke. His last Gothic renovation, freer still in detail, was that of the church at Želiv (1714–20).

The last five years of his career were dominated by three great 'Baroque' commissions, the pilgrimage church at Křtiny (1718–50), the hilltop house of Chlumec nad Cidlinou (1721–3), and the priory church at Rajhrad (1722–30). Křtiny is a compacted Greek cross with arms whose sub-domes merge into a great central dome. Rajhrad has three tall shallow-domed spaces made into a grand procession by elaborate piers. The cylindrical core of Chlumec is flanked by three equal four-sided wings and a double staircase, a Fischerian 'Lustschloss' raised to an extraordinary power.

Santini's most extraordinary works are back at Žd'aìr: the cemetery with its undulating wall and chapels of about 1715, and the pilgrimage church on the Green Hill (1719–22). Its forms are pointed, but no Gothic was ever like this, with its central vaulted decagon flanked by five oval major chapels alternating with five triangular minor ones. From a Borrominiesque plan he set off in the direction of Gehry.

Santini's genius showed, too, in a host of lesser buildings for his major patrons. His continued attachment to the wall contrasts with the Dientzenhofer's use of the 'wall-pillar' system. But for his early death he might have created yet more audacious spaces; as it stands, his work shows how original the best architects of his time could be.　DBK

Horyna, M., *Jan Blažej Santini-Aichel* (in Czech with German summary, 1998)

Sardinia Architecture in Sardinia achieved distinction in two widely separated periods: the Nuragic (*c*.1400–500 BC, *nuraghe); and the period of domination by Pisa (*c*.1050–1200).

Under Pisan control, a number of interesting *Romanesque churches were built, mainly in the west of the island. In some of their details they follow Pisan models, but otherwise they are quite distinctive. In the earlier period (roughly till 1150), churches always follow a simple basilican plan, but the façades are quite outstanding—well cut stones of various hues, delicate arcading, and in some cases an attached *campanile. Good examples are Santa Maria del Regno, Ardara (before 1065–1107); and San Nicola di Othana, Ottana (before 1160). Subsequently, the churches approach mainland prototypes more closely, with bands of black and white stone, and more elaborately carved stone patterns in the façades (San Pietro di Sorres, Borutta, second half of the 12th century). The most elaborate church of this type, with its colonettes, pediment, and three-arched portico at the western end, is Santissima Trinità di Saccarga, Codrongianos (second half of the 12th century), which gains in dramatic effect from the isolated rural setting.　PG

Saudi Arabia has transformed itself architecturally in less than four decades from one of the most underdeveloped countries in the world to one in which leading international architects compete with each other in large-scale and high-technological solutions. Its enormous oil revenues have enabled the government to engage in large-scale developments in terms of administrative, educational, religious, and cultural activities as well as in numerous palaces for the ruling families. Buildings for sport are rare, and often remain as unbuilt projects, or if built are not particularly distinguished.

Outstanding among the buildings for the government are the Palaces for the King and the Crown Prince in Jeddah (Kenzô *Tange, 1977–82) and the project for the King's Offices in Riyadh by Frei Otto and Rolf Gutbrod (1974–8). Convincing structures for the Ministry of Foreign Affairs were the designs in Jeddah by Arthur Erickson (1980) and in Riyadh by the Danish architect Henning Larsen (1982–4).

Great emphasis was given to educational buildings and new universities, beginning with the University of Petroleum and Minerals in Dammam by the American firm Caudill, Rowlett, and Scott (1964–71). The largest new campus was the King Saud University in Riyadh by Hellmuth, Obata, and Kassabaum in collaboration with several other firms (1964–82).

Among the new buildings for religious purposes are: the Mosque and Conference Centre in Mecca (Frei Otto and Rolf Gutbrod, 1969–74); the mosque of the King Khalid International Airport (Hellmuth Obata and Kassabaum, 1983); the Island Mosque in Jeddah (Abdel Wahed El-Wakil, 1986); and the mosque in Dharan (Zuhair Fayez, 1997). Outstanding among the new hospitals is the King Khalid Eye Specialist Hospital in Riyadh by the American firm of Caudill, Rowlett, and Scott (1983).

The design for the Towaiq Palace in Riyadh (Frei Otto, with Omrania, 1981–3) employed programmatically historic and environmental features. By contrast, residential architecture at a smaller scale is the least solved building typology, with only a few experimental buildings, by Stephen Yakeley (near Riyadh, 1990), Pier Luigi Nervi (Dammam, 1977), and Speerplan (Riyadh, 1987).

Office buildings and hotels in Saudi Arabia have been mostly shaped by foreign architects, many of them introducing the characteristics of the country of their origin. Skidmore, Owings, and Merrill's National Commercial Bank in Jeddah (1981–4) is one of the most spectacular examples. Combinations of hotels and conference centres which adapt various elements of the local tradition are found in Riyadh (Trevor Dannatt, 1973) and in Mecca (Frei Otto and Rolf Gutbrod, 1969–74).

Exceptional solutions have been found for markets, water towers, and airports, such as the numerous water towers in Riyadh (Sune Lindstroem in collaboration with Dyckerhoff and Widman), the airports in Dharan (Minoru Yamasaki, 1963), Jeddah (Skidmore, Owings, and Merrill, 1978–1984), and Riyadh (Hellmuth, Obata, and Kassabaum, 1985). UK

Kultermann, U., 'Contemporary Arab Architecture: The Architects in Saudi Arabia', *Mimar* 16, 1985

Sauvage, Frédéric-Henri (1873–1932) French architect. His early work, such as the Villa Majorelle, Nancy (1898–1901), was a luxurious bourgeois house in a version of the Art Nouveau style, but from 1903 he turned his attention to the provision of cheap housing for the working classes. His first venture, in rue Trétaigne, Paris, included extensive communal facilities. Sauvage then began an interesting series of experiments with set-back terraced houses, culminating in the rue Vavin, Paris (1912). After 1918, he seemed to become more interested in the technological than the social aspect of building, his final design being the prefabricated metal and glass department store, the Magasins Decré, Nantes (1931, destroyed). PG

scale In other contexts, 'scale' and 'size' are synonymous, but in relation to architecture it is important to preserve the distinction that 'size' refers to how large a building *is* in reality, 'scale' to how large it *appears* to the onlooker. 'Scale' is also sometimes confused with '*proportion', which concerns the relation *between* the dimensions of a form, rather than how large a form (which may mean a part of a building or the whole) appears to be, judged by a visible or assumed standard of comparison. The distinction between 'size' and 'scale' is one of the most important differences between architecture and engineering: the engineer is concerned to calculate how large a structure must be to fulfil its function, the architect how large a structure must appear to be to meet both functional and visual requirements.

To gauge the scale of a building or an element, the onlooker has to be able to refer to other elements of a known, standard size as measuring devices: either the human figure or conventionally accepted building elements. In classical architecture, the latter role is filled by the *orders.

In some very simple types of architecture, most notably the pyramids of ancient Egypt, at a medium distance it is difficult to grasp the size of the structure, because there is no element of scale. The pyramids only display such an element when the individual stones are seen close to.

Many buildings are seen or intended to be seen from a relatively close distance. In this case, setting the scale is relatively straightforward, particularly when the building consists of a central, dominant block flanked by wings. A classic example is *Vanbrugh's Blenheim Palace. The central block is made to appear much larger than it is by the disposition of the columns in the portico, and the high attic storey rising immediately behind it; and this appearance is further enhanced by the flanking small-scale colonnades, which lead to larger-scale pavilions on a scale corresponding to that of the central block. The differentiation of scales serves the purpose of endowing the Palace with grandeur, a quality noticeably absent in Versailles, where repeated additions of similar scaled blocks serve only dullness.

A more difficult problem, in fact one which is strictly speaking insoluble, is posed by a building which is approached from a considerable distance. A good example of a compromise solution is Garnier's Paris Opéra. From a distance, the dominant scale is set by a large unbroken mass (the stage loft), which is continued throughout the building, so that it does not look too diminutive; in close-up, the lower storeys have a scheme of subdivision which impresses on the passer-by a more human scale. In the approach sequence to the Taj Mahal, a different stratagem is adopted. From a distance, it is clear that it is a large building, as measured by the two small domes and the double curve of the central dome. But when viewers are so close that they cannot see the whole of the flat face, the fine scale of the wall detailing means that the arches are perceived as being very large indeed.

Within a building, height is more important than either width or length. Raising the height has a much more perceptible effect on scale than increasing either the length or the width of a room. *Palladio's villas are outstanding examples of designs in which the rooms are not only finely proportioned but, mainly because of a careful attention to room heights, are also completely adapted to a human scale.

Architects can also manipulate scale in order to create *illusions of greater or lesser height. But they can also make mistakes about scale, as Maderno did at St Peter's, Rome: 'Its great nave is divided into only four bays, and the proportions and ornaments of these, borrowed generally from external architecture, are so gigantic that no one can realize the true dimensions of the church but by the study of the plan.' (Fergusson, J., *The Illustrated Handbook of Architecture*, 1855, p.xliii.)

Modern technology has created great problems of scale, particularly with very tall buildings such as *skyscrapers. But even for much smaller buildings, the majority of modernist architects were so preoccupied with other problems that they did not pay any attention to architectural composition, of which scale is a key component. The only significant exception is Le Corbusier, who not only explored the problems of scale and proportion in theory (Le Modulor, 1948), but in one case, the Marseille Unité d'Habitation, put his theory into practice. Using a small modular unit, Le Corbusier gave scale to the 17-storey slab, by alternating large and small divisions, and by marking off a mid-height division of three floors.   PG

Licklider, H., Architectural Scale (1965)

Scamozzi, Vincenzo (1552–1616) Italian architect and theorist. Author of the last of the Renaissance treatises, the rather pedantic L'Idea dell Architettura Universale (published 1615), his architecture was rather derivative of the work of *Palladio. His villas Vettor Pisani, near Vicenza (1575–8), and Molin, near Padua (1597), were not very good copies of Palladio's Villa Rotonda, in that the temple front/flight of steps did not appear on all four sides of the building, and the dome was much more awkward, being either hexagonal or punctuated by windows. His proposal to add a third storey to *Sansovino's Procuratie Nuove was only partially implemented.   PG

Scarpa, Carlo (1906–78) Italian architect and designer, whose diverse production is grounded in a careful attention to detail and to the experience of each individual architectural moment. Scarpa's drawings are a compelling testimony to these interests, and to the highly eccentric design process in which his decisions were constantly re-evaluated during the course of construction. His work is also marked by a divergent set of references, from Japanese architecture and

culture to the artistic movements of De *Stijl and the Vienna *Secession, and the organic architecture of Frank Lloyd *Wright.

Scarpa's sporadic early career was marked by the establishment of several important collaborations, including his work with the Murano Capellini (1927–30) and Venini glassworks (1933–47), for whom he became an artistic consultant. He also began his teaching career during these years at the Istituto Universitario di Architettura in Venice (1926–76), where he eventually became director (1972–4). Following World War II, his work openly explored the tension between expressing the poetics of the architectural object and responding to the 'reality' of the historical past. This tension is particularly evident in a series of exhibition designs that included displays in the Uffizi Gallery in Florence (1954–6, with Ignazio Gardella and Giovanni *Michelucci) and the painting galleries of the Museo Correr in Venice (1957–60). His interest in the display of objects combined with an acute sense of detail in projects like the extension to the Canova plaster gallery in Possagno (1955–7) and the Fondazione Querini Stampalia in Venice (1961–3). Scarpa's masterwork from this period is unquestionably his long collaboration with the Castelvecchio Museum in Verona (1956–64, 1969–75), where a series of individual interventions within a medieval castle provide a narrative thread that draws the museum visitor through the gallery spaces.

Scarpa's interest in establishing a dialectical tension between a contemporary architectural intervention and a historical context extends to non-museum projects like his Olivetti Showroom in Venice (1957–8). This quality is further explored in one of his larger urban projects, the Banca Popolare di Verona, Verona (1973–8, project completed by Arrigo Rudi), where the subtle misalignment of the interior of the building with the exterior façade creates a powerful dialogue between inside and outside. A final masterwork of

Scarpa, the Brion Cemetery at Asolo (1969–78), extends his interests to encompass architecture and landscape.   BLM

Dal Co, F., and Mazzariol, G., *Carlo Scarpa: The Complete Works* (1984)

Scharoun, Hans (1893–1972) German architect. Scharoun was the most significant German modernist to establish himself before the Nazi takeover, to remain in Germany, then re-emerge to a major career in the 1950s and 1960s. He was also the foremost German exponent of Organic Architecture.

He spent his childhood in Bremerhaven and studied architecture in Berlin from 1912, then spent the war years on reconstruction work in East Prussia. He stayed at Insterburg until 1925, but after the October Revolution of 1918 he joined Bruno *Taut's Expressionist circle. Through the 'Glass Chain' correspondence, he contributed some of the best-known watercolours to the movement.

The early 1920s saw publication of inventive competition designs, and in 1925 he was appointed to a chair at the progressive Breslau Arts Academy. In 1926 he was elected to Der Ring, and he sought increasing contacts with Berlin, where he lived permanently from 1930. Though he had built traditional housing in East Prussia, his modernist work remained on paper until the Stuttgart Weissenhofsiedlung of 1927. Scharoun's unusual corner house was not universally appreciated, but it was followed up with an ingenious block of flats at the Breslau Werkbund Exhibition in 1929, including the daring departures from the right-angle in plan which were to become his trademark. This confirmed his reputation as a bold new talent, and he completed several housing projects in Berlin, including a substantial part of Siemensstadt, for which he also drew the master plan. In 1932 he built the Schminke House at Löbau in Saxony, experimenting with an oblique stair and discovering a new kind of dynamic interior space that was developed in his later work.

This was his last essay in the early modernist idiom, for as it was completed the Nazis came to power. Scharoun remained in Berlin, earning a living by working for others but putting his creative energy into a remarkable series of private houses. They were traditional on the outside to conform with Nazi planning controls, yet they had daring plans, and the spaces within were of unprecedented fluidity. During this difficult period he consolidated his friendship with the architect and theorist Hugo *Häring, an important influence on his later work, and he helped with Häring's art school, Kunst und Werk.

After the war Scharoun was able to re-emerge with a consolidated architectural philosophy and renewed energy, but had to wait to see his ideas realized. In 1946 he was made City Architect of Berlin, but lost the post for political reasons before any of his plans were fulfilled. From the late 1940s he won major competitions, but again his designs remained unbuilt, the most tragic case being the theatre for Kassel of 1952–3, abandoned after site work had started. Scharoun had to wait until 1963 to see a major public building completed: the Philharmonie in Berlin, a competition winner of 1956. This revolutionary concert hall, with terraces of seats surrounding the orchestra on all sides and a contrasting labyrinthine foyer, has become world famous and proved to be the most successful new model for this building type in the 20th century. It was a turning point in Scharoun's career, confirming his credibility, helping assure that subsequent competition designs such as the Berlin State Library (1964–79) and the Wolfsburg Theatre (1965–73) were completed, and bringing him commissions such as the German Maritime Museum in Bremerhaven and the German Embassy in Brasilia. Until his death in 1972, he had as much work as he could handle, and

Philharmonic, Berlin, Germany (Hans Scharoun, 1963)

several projects were completed posthumously, including additions to the Philharmonie such as the Chamber Music Hall and Museum of Musical Instruments finished by his partner Edgar Wisniewski. While the Philharmonie was under construction two other projects were realized, each of which became a crucial prototype for a series of later works: the Geschwister Scholl school at Lünen (1958–62) and the housing blocks Romeo and Juliet at Stuttgart (1956–9). Both demonstrated Scharoun's concern with an almost aggressive articulation of parts, allowing each classroom or dwelling a strong individual identity which the user could comprehend. The parts of a building had to be like individuals in a democracy: contributing to the whole yet retaining strong identities of their own.

In a period when most architects allowed space to be dictated by the construction grid, Scharoun's work stood out in its specificity and individuality. He was a well-known figure in Germany of the 1950s and 1960s, attracting many pupils and followers, but his work exerted further influence on younger architects of the 1980s and 1990s once the tyranny of technical discipline had been broken, allowing a new interest in responsive irregularity and free planning.   PBJ

Blundell Jones, P., *Hans Scharoun* (1995)

Scheerbart, Paul (1863–1915) A German Expressionist writer whose many novels and short stories dealt with a visionary glass architecture. His *Glass Architecture* (1914) is best known, but others, such as *Grey Cloth and Ten Percent White* (1914), are more typical of his quirky mix of Symbolist subversiveness and synaesthetic effects, together with a dry sense of irony. His protagonist, the architect of the future, changes the old world of brick and dark interiors into a sparkling, polychromatic, mobile glass fantasy in which these effects assume a transformative power.

808

Scheerbart's closeness to Berlin anarchists is reflected in his political novellas, which promote pacifism and criticize the war machine of the state. Through his contact with Herwarth Walden's *Der Sturm* periodical and gallery he met the architect Bruno *Taut. Through Taut's leadership of several post-war Expressionist groups, such as the Work Council on the Arts and the Glass Chain, many of his writings were circulated among Expressionist architects.   RHB

Schickhardt, Heinrich (1558–1635) German
architect, who was an important pioneer in bringing Renaissance architecture to Germany. His earliest works were alterations to existing buildings. At Esslingen he added an ashlar façade (1586–9) to the half-timbered town hall. The Neuer Bau (1611), an extension to the Altes Schloss, Stuttgart, solved the problem of applying Renaissance details, such as cornices and string courses, and classicizing proportions, to the kind of building for which there were few Italian precedents, i.e. one which housed three functions—the stables, a banqueting hall, and an armoury.

Schickhardt laid out the new town of Freudenstadt (from 1599), which is more impressive for its monumental spaces, such as the town square (219 × 216 m or 718 × 709 ft), than for its architecture. The buildings—the market hall, the town hall, the hospital, and the church, all set at the corners of the square—are of a fairly traditional kind, with steeply pitched roofs and plain facades.   PG

Schindler, Rudolph Michael (1887–1953)
Austrian-born US architect. He invented his own form of modern architecture, 'Space Architecture', focused on the articulation of complex interior spaces, modulated by natural light and integrated with the landscape. His work consisted largely of small residential projects in southern California,

Lovell beach house, Newport Beach, California (Rudolph Schindler, 1923–6)

characterized by their individual responses to site and client, their experimental use of materials and forms, and their widely varying vocabularies.

Educated in Vienna, Schindler studied with Otto *Wagner and Adolf *Loos, and was much impressed by Loos's rejection of applied ornament and his idea of the primacy of three-dimensional interior space. However, Schindler was drawn to the United States by Frank Lloyd *Wright's ideas about a horizontal architecture reaching out to the landscape, so from 1918 Schindler worked for Wright, who sent him to Los Angeles in 1920 where he settled, building his own house and studio on King's Road (1921–2).

In 1912 Schindler wrote 'Modern Architecture: a Program', a manifesto in which he declared that new developments in materials and construction methods had freed architecture from design based on structural forms; now architects could design with 'space, climate, light, mood'. Schindler's work demonstrated consistent spatial qualities and characteristics over the course of his career: articulated sections with a unifying door-height datum and extensive use of clerestory glazing; a figure / ground balance between building and landscape, frequently employing L-shaped plans;

diagonal organizations and corner windows. Schindler wrote extensively about design, construction, and practice; in 'Space Architecture' (*Dune Forum*, February 1934, pp.44–6), he distinguished himself from the more dogmatic functionalists of the *International Style, and in later articles described his proportional system, his modification of standard construction techniques, and his ideas about character, colour, light, and texture.

In the 1920s Schindler experimented with concrete construction, first in his own house of concrete slabs and redwood framing. The house was radical in every way, from its integration of indoor and outdoor spaces to its exposed construction materials and its lack of conventional rooms for adults. Other concrete experiments included the Howe house, Los Angeles (1925), with double-cantilevered redwood roof framing, and the Lovell beach house, Newport (1923–6), Schindler's best-known project, in which five articulated concrete frames hold up a 2-storey living space.

Concrete proved too expensive for Schindler's clients in the 1930s Depression, mostly middle-class intellectuals and artists with more taste than money. In response, as Schindler worked as his own contractor, he developed an inexpensive form of modern architecture made of wood frame and stucco, developing a vocabulary that he called 'plaster-skin design', which featured abstract interlocking volumes with complex built-in furniture, largely of stained plywood, contrasting with the plaster. Notable examples include the Oliver house (1933–4) with a low-pitched gable roof, the Walker house (1935–6) with a series of sloping roofs, and the Wilson house (1935–9) with an inverted gable, all in Los Angeles. Schindler continued to experiment with roof forms and materials after World War II. The green sloping textured wood roof and walls of the Kallis house (1946), the blue translucent fiberglass gable roof of the Tischler house (1949–50), and the shifting geometries and translucent roof panels of the Skolnik house (1950–52), all in Los Angeles, were dynamic, yet very livable in, works with subtly varying light conditions and a unique relationship to their settings.

Small budgets, Schindler's willingness to experiment, and his desire continually to reinvent his architecture led to an uneven output, but the best demonstrated Schindler's fertile imagination and originality. His work influenced several generations of southern California architects, including Frank *Gehry, Franklin Israel, and Michael Rotondi.   JES

Sarnitz, A., *R. M. Schindler, Architect 1887–1953* (1988)
Sheine, J., *R. M. Schindler* (2001)

Schinkel, Karl Friedrich (1781–1841) The pre-eminent German architect of the 19th century.

The beginning of Schinkel's career was interrupted by the Napoleonic wars and their immediate aftermath, forcing him to concentrate his efforts on paintings, stage set designs, dioramas, and panoramas. These projects prefigured the scenographic principles central to his architecture. During this period, Schinkel participated in the resurgence in Prussia of a patriotic and romantic interest in medieval architecture, culminating in his iron war monument in the form of a Gothic pinnacle on the Kreuzberg overlooking Berlin (1818–21).

Starting with his 1817 plan for the comprehensive reorganization of Berlin's central spaces, Schinkel devoted his most active years to transforming the Prussian capital into a renewed cultural centre on a monumental scale. His first important building in Berlin was the Neue Wache (1817–18). With its portico and robust Doric columns, it is an early example of Schinkel's use of classical forms. The building is set back from the Unter den Linden boulevard, creating a stage-like plaza for the Prussian guards.

Schinkel's Schauspielhaus (1818–21), located nearby on the Gendarmenmarkt, sits on a rusticated podium

Altes Museum, Berlin (Karl Schinkel, 1822–30)

that, also like a stage, raises it above the surrounding urban landscape. Inspired by experiments in theatre reform by architects like Friedrich *Gilly, the building's auditorium recalls a semicircular Greek amphitheatre. A structural grid articulated by a system of pilaster supports and horizontal entablatures gives unity to the building's fire-proof stone-clad masses, and, by representing the structural purity of classical Greek trabeation, enforces the theatre's cultural importance through its very composition.

His nearby Altes Museum (1822–30) is organized around two interior courtyards and a great central Pantheon-like rotunda. A monumental Greek stoa with double-height Ionic columns stretches across the building's entire front elevation. In addition to a rich programme of frescoes, the stoa screens a striking public staircase from which Prussian citizens could gain a dramatic view onto the public Lustgarten. Seen from his earlier Schlossbrücke (1819–24), the outline of the museum provided a visual anchor for the scenographic succession of overlapping volumes created by Schinkel's more sober customs administration buildings (1829–32).

The simple and largely undecorated brick elevations of Schinkel's Friedrich-Werderische Church in Berlin

(1824–30) establish a synthesis of Gothic construction and classical repose, and allow the interior logic of the building to show through to its bold exterior massing.

In satisfying both banal requirements and poetic aims, Schinkel's Berlin projects developed out of his interest in architecture as the continuation by human activity of the constructive activity of nature. At the same time, he continued this theme in the intimate relationship between architecture and landscape characteristic of countryside projects like Schloss Tegel (1820–24), a villa and museum for Wilhelm von Humboldt and his collection of antiquities. The villa is bisected by a classical vestibule, and combines the oriels, tower, and sloped roof of an existing 16th-century entrance front with new elevations organized according to a pilaster system inspired by the Schauspielhaus.

Schinkel also designed a group of country retreats with the landscape designer Peter Joseph Lenné for King Friedrich Wilhelm III and his sons. At Schloss Glienicke (1824–32), Schloss Charlottenhof (1826–33), and the Court Gardener's House in the Charlottenhof Park (1829–33), Schinkel orchestrated a picturesque architectural landscape along the Havel river near Potsdam and Sanssouci.

In addition to his responsibilities as Oberbaudirektor, Schinkel was also devoted during the 1830s to an investigation of the historical evolution of fundamental structural forms. Intended for his never-completed *Architectural Textbook*, this research assumed a progressive view of architectural history that rejected stylistic revivalism in favour of generating a new architecture capable of synthesizing the disparate traditions of the past in light of new industrial materials and the expanding demands of the Prussian public.

Along with his proposals for a bazaar on Unter den Linden (1827) and a new royal library (1835), Schinkel's Bauakademie building in Berlin (1831–6) marked most clearly this search for architectural synthesis. Housing administrative offices, an architectural school, and a private dwelling for Schinkel himself, the Bauakademie was the first masonry-framed building in Prussia. The building incorporated many features of the textile mills that Schinkel visited during his trip to the British Isles in 1826 (see his *The English Journey: Journal of a Visit to France and Britain in 1826*, published in 1993). Massive vertical pillars and brick courses between the Bauakademie's floors established an exterior grid that gave expression to the building's interior vaulted constructional system. The building's four façades were covered entirely in naked brick with a rich terracotta decorative programme. With ground-floor shops on three sides, the Bauakademie assumed a prominent position in the evolving public landscape of central Berlin.

Although he continued to design a variety of buildings in the farthest reaches of the Prussian provinces, Schinkel's unbuilt projects for a palace for King Otto on the Acropolis in Athens (1834) and for Schloss Orianda on the Crimean Sea (1838) remain the most influential and visionary designs of his late career.   AN

Bergdoll, B., *Karl Friedrich Schinkel: An Architect for Prussia* (1994)

Schlaich, Jorg (1934–) German engineer, a significant figure in the endless quest for lightness and increased efficiency. Schlaich designed a series of structures which explore the potential of wide-spanning tensile structures and steel cable nets. Developed in 1974 for a 181 m (594 ft) high cable net cooling tower at Schmehausen nuclear power station, Schlaich went on to use similar techniques in his designs for solar power stations. A research prototype, constructed at Manzanares in Spain, combined a lightweight, cable supported, transparent, 250 m (820 ft) diameter canopy beneath which air was warmed by the sun and, rising by convection through a 200 m (656 ft) high metal chimney, was subsequently transformed into electricity by air-powered turbines. More recently a more advanced version has been planned for construction in Australia.

With the engineering firm of Schlaich, Bergermann, and Partner, he has also been responsible for the design of new infrastructure—bridges, railway stations, towers, and covered public spaces—in Europe and the Middle East. Most notably these have included the glazed roofs over courtyards at the DZ Bank in Berlin and the Hotel Kempinski at Munich Airport, completed in 1999 and 1994 respectively.   BC

Schlaun, Johann Conrad (Konrad) (1695–1773) German architect and engineer. Although mainly working in the provincial obscurity of Münster, Schlaun designed a series of original buildings. He was particularly adept at integrating abstract geometrical forms with their surroundings. The hunting-lodge at Clemenswerth, near Sögel (c.1736–50) is a small 2-storey building, set in the middle of a ring of 8 pavilions, each of which forms the terminus of an avenue. In his other designs, he was able, with great ingenuity, to insert his designs into rather awkwardly shaped sites. For instance, the six-pointed star shape of the Clemenskirche, Münster (1745–53), is wedged into a triangular space. The Erbdrostenhof, Münster (1745–7), is also fitted into a triangle, but by means of concave shapes, and similarly creates some rather awkwardly shaped internal spaces. For his own houses in or near Münster, the Rüschhaus (1745–8) and the Schlaunhaus (1753–5), he abandoned the Baroque conceits, perhaps devised only to satisfy his patrons, in favour of a version of local traditions, rural and urban.   PG

Schlüter, Andreas (c.1659–1714) German architect and sculptor. Schlüter succeeded *Nering as the leading architect in Berlin, but was nowhere near as prolific. His one major design was the Royal Palace (begun 1698). At the centre of a long, flat façade, Schlüter placed a massive triumphal arch carrying a hemispherical dome—a powerful conceit to express Frederick's aspiration to become the king of a state. Each side of the inner courtyard had a projecting centre, expressing a staircase. The main staircase, on the eastern side, was celebrated by a screen of free-standing columns carrying sculpture.

Little is known about his other significant Berlin commissions, the foundry (1698) behind the Zeughaus and the Wartenberg Palace (1702–4), but it is known that his architectural career in Berlin ended abruptly and in misfortune. The tower called the Munzturm, which he had planned as a landmark, had to be demolished in 1706, as it was on the point of collapsing; and in 1707 the king's *maison de plaisance* at Freienwalde did not weather a heavy storm. Regrettably Schlüter's structural expertise did not match his powers of sculptural invention.   PG

schools, to 1870 A type of school different from the colleges of Winchester (1382) and Eton (1440) and the military or naval academies for the wealthy elite emerged during the Industrial Revolution: the endowed schools for the poor. This new type had intellectual and political roots in French Encyclopaedism, Enlightenment philosophy (especially that of Rousseau), the reforming spirit of European Absolutist regimes, and the republican ideology of the French and American Revolutions. Once the ideology of machine production was added, a new model of education emerged aptly described by Coleridge's metaphor: 'An incomparable machine—a vast moral steam engine' (1817). At its core were order, harmony, virtue, and production.

Education and work Of course production and education had long been linked. In 1677 Yarranton described and drew plans for a settlement for the rural poor, with spinning schools conducted in a large work-room with a central 'little Box like a Pulpit'. Around the edges were benches '... as they are in our Playhouses'—that is, tiered—on which about 200 children were seated, spinning. On the Box in the centre '... sits the Grand Mistress with a long white wand in her hand.' In silence, she tapped any idle child and, if this was not enough, she rang a little bell fixed to the Box out of which came a woman who took the child away to be chastised in 'another room'.

Yarranton's scheme uncannily foreshadowed key features of the 'vast moral steam engine':

1 the inverted theatre—perfect visibility for surveillance and control, the stage now being the domain of the observer, the auditorium that of the observed
2 discipline—its source and its place of execution being hidden
3 silence
4 productive work
5 hierarchy—mistress, punitive woman, child
6 religious symbolism—the pulpit.

Ordered work was also present in poor houses and *workhouses. A 1786 review defines workhouses as

'Nurseries of Religion, Virtue and Industry'; and all those listed had schoolrooms and workshops. The 1774 enabling Act for the new St Marylebone workhouse specified that, besides the usual inmates, it had to admit the infant poor to be educated 'in habits of industry, religion and honesty'.

After the Reformation some parish and endowed grammar schools disappeared, while others became independent. The landed gentry were eager to endow new grammar schools and petty schools for the poor. However Charity schools, with a prototype in Westminster (1688), were absorbing the greatest proportion of the benefactions. Here, apart from religion, reading, writing, and arithmetic, there was training in manual work. The Society for the Propagation of Christian Knowledge (SPCK, founded in 1699) claimed, falsely, that it had created these schools; nevertheless it did promote them and shifted the balance between education and work in favour of the latter. By the 1720s it was effectively sponsoring workhouses and industrial schools marked by coercion and harsh discipline. The Scottish SPCK (founded 1709) operated on similar lines, and by 1758 had set up 167 industrial schools, where boys were taught blacksmithing, shoemaking, and agriculture, and girls spinning, knitting, and sewing.

At this time various rural agricultural schools were also being promoted, to which poor, and often 'disorderly', children were to be exiled, in order for pastoral innocence to overcome urban depravity.

Paradoxically, with increasing industrialization, industrial schools almost disappeared (by 1865 only 30 were left in England and 19 in Scotland), to be replaced by huge *workhouse schools, built under the 1834 New Poor Law, and after further legislation in 1857 and 1866, by reformatory (penal) schools.

The Sunday school Another institution was growing simultaneously—the Sunday school. Starting in Gloucester in 1781, these developed rapidly, sponsored by the churches. Mostly the schools were held in churches, church halls, chapels, or houses. But some were purpose built, the earliest in School Street in Dublin (1798), where a 3-storey building had 2 large school rooms, one each for boys and girls, with separate entrance stairs from the street, and small classrooms. This strict segregation between the sexes became a hallmark of these schools' spatial strategy.

The first English school was at Friars Mount (1802), Bethnal Green, for 1,000 children. But it was in the north of England that, over a period of a mere thirteen years, the largest and most splendid Sunday schools appeared. The first in Stockport (1805) for 3,000 children, with later extensions for 5,000, was a 4-storey mill-like structure, with a ground and first floor of classrooms, one each for boys and girls. The second and third floors, which read as 2 storeys on the exterior, in fact contained a double-height galleried 'large room', with rows of raked seats, used for the entire school's interdenominational services of hymn singing and Bible readings. The linguistic camouflage which avoided 'church', 'chapel', or 'meeting room' was intended to calm the fears of the churches that their own worship would be supplanted. This stratagem matched the architectural camouflage which hid the presence of a 2-storey hall by expressing it externally as two single floors. Macclesfield's still extant Sunday school (1813), and Manchester's in Bennett Street (1818), followed the Stockport model.

The monitorial school The scene was set for the 19th century's greatest educational experiment: the monitorial school. Two people independently conceived it. One, Andrew Bell, in 1797 set up a school in Fort St George in Madras, where he used boys of 11 to 14 as 'teachers', and others of 7 to 11 as 'assistant teachers' to teach classes of 9–34 boys in a school of

200. Pairs of boys, one in the role of teacher and one in that of scholar, taught each other, under the eye of an 'assistant teacher'; these were supervised by 'teachers'; the 'teachers' were under the surveillance of three schoolmasters, who were controlled by the superintendent. 'After this manner the school teaches itself' (Bell). This is the prototypical text of the 'monitorial' system: mechanical efficiency, economy, military-style order and hierarchy, and the all-seeing, all-knowing controller.

Bell tried to persuade David Dale to adopt the system at New Lanark, and then set up his first English school in Aldgate. By 1811 the National Society for Promoting the Education of the Poor in the Principles of the Established Church was formed, under Church of England sponsorship, and the model school in Baldwin's Gardens, Holborn (1811–13), was built. The boys' schoolroom measured 18 by 18 m (59 × 59 ft), whilst the girls' was 18 × 12 m (59 × 39 ft). The former had fixed benches facing the outer walls for writing, and loose benches in the centre, which could be formed into large 'U' shapes for reading and arithmetic, with the monitors standing in the fourth, open side. The girls' room had large sewing tables in addition. Bell ranked the children by performance: the genius and the dunderhead paired in equivalent and opposite locations at the ends of the U, with intermediate ability pairs along the sides. These pairs were pitted against each other—for 'emulation'; as performance changed, children were moved up or down, thus moving space in the competition—'place-capturing'. Bell held that one master could conduct ten schools of 1,000 scholars each in this '. . . intellectual and moral engine'. An admiring commentator in 1809 compared Bell to Adam Smith: 'It is the division of labour in his schools, that leaves the master the easy task of directing the movements of the whole machine instead of toiling ineffectually at a single part. The principle in manufactories and in schools is the same.'

After 1804 National Schools were built all over Britain, some for as many as 1,000 children, and abroad in Nova Scotia, Cape Town, Barbados, and also in British and Russian army barracks.

The second innovator, Joseph Lancaster, experimented in a Southwark Sunday school in 1798, and then moved to Borough Road where by 1799 he taught 130 boys and girls using monitors. He built his first school at Borough Road in 1801, for 700 children, soon enlarged to 1,000 and then 1,200 capacity. Here there were long parallel fixed desks, with a monitor at the head of each, looking after 'drafts' of 12–20 boys. Periodically the monitor took his 'draft' to the sides of the room, to stand in semicircles around posts on which were hung spelling cards or numbers.

The Lancasterian system was favoured by Quakers, Dissenters, and Utilitarians. In 1810 a body which eventually became the British and Foreign School Society was formed, to build 'British' schools all over Britain. In France, Russia, and America this system flourished till the 1840s.

Bell and Lancaster, and both Societies, published numerous manuals, plans, curricular guides, and designs for equipment. These deeply influenced pedagogic practice and school design for the rest of the century. In Scotland, when David Stow started his programme of infant and primary education in Glasgow in 1816, many of the monitorial features were used. Equally, Stow used the teaching 'gallery', developed by Samuel Wilderspin for 'simultaneous' infant teaching (i.e. teaching the whole school), in Spitalfields in 1820. When the government first allocated public money for school building in 1833, it did so through the two Societies. By 1839 it started publishing its own model plans, each also capable of being adapted for use by the two systems.

There was considerable cross-fertilization between the monitorial schools and industrial and workhouse schools which were being built within the massive *workhouse building programme after the 1834 New Poor Law.

In fact there was no fundamental change in legislation, pedagogy, or design till the radical 1870 Education Act was passed.   TM

Markus, Thomas A., *Buildings and Power* (1993)

schools, from 1870 The 1870 Act established School Boards responsible for providing schools for all children between the ages of 5 and 13. Within a decade thousands of new schools had been built all over the country, the demand being most urgent in London, where places for 112,000 children had to be provided. Fortunately, architects rose to the occasion, not only in terms of quantity, but of quality.

The first of the new schools was at Eel Brook Common, Fulham, London (Basil *Champneys, 1872), establishing the familiar building type noticed a generation later by Sir Arthur Conan Doyle. Even the unobservant Watson did not need Sherlock Holmes's admonition:

'Look at those big isolated clumps of buildings
    rising up about the slates, like brick islands in
    a lead coloured sea.'
'The Board Schools.'
'Lighthouses, m boy!'
('The Naval Treaty')

Most of the Board Schools in London (over 250 between 1872 and 1884) were designed by E. R. Robson, who set out the ideas he had derived from his study of schools in Germany and the United States in *School Architecture* (1874). He advocated, and practised, a combination of simple planning, innovations in service technology (ducted ventilation, and in the larger schools a form of central heating), and a distinctive façade.

On each floor there was a hall, classrooms, lavatories, cloakrooms, and teachers' rooms. Each classroom was well lit, from the child's left-hand side,

at a standard ratio (5:1, floor area:glass), with quite tall ceilings (4.27 m or 14 ft high). This plan was repeated on as many as four floors, since some schools accommodated up to 1,500 children. Because of the planning requirements, and (usually) constricted sites, the Board Schools acquired their familiar silhouette—obvious even to Dr Watson: tall buildings with (for the period) large areas of windows, and prominently ribbed chimneys. Robson made the best of the cheap materials he was obliged to use: over a basic frame of stock bricks, he laid panels of differently coloured brickwork, or the occasional cartouche of moulded brick always recording the date of the school and sometimes decorated with a sunflower or other Arts and Crafts motifs. The *Queen Anne revival touches—gables for the dormer ends—are quite incidental to the basic design.

During the next period, 1900–40, innovative school design was dominated by the needs of hygiene—in particular of providing cross-ventilation, and flooding the classrooms with as much sunlight as possible, as a prophylactic against the widespread incidence of tuberculosis. The first open-air school was at Charlottenburg, Berlin (1904), which consisted of a single-storey pavilion, in which the side wall of the classrooms was completely open. Consequently, the plan consisted of parallel rows of south-facing classrooms in a finger plan.

In the 1930s, the modernist version of this type (*see* DUDOK) introduced flat roofs, and such a large area lit by metal windows and glazed corner staircases that there was even a danger of over-glazing (for example, Kemnal Manor Upper School, Bexley, 1934–8). A modern 'image', but the layout of identical classrooms off a corridor followed the Board School plan, expressing the conservatism of the educational thought of the period.

In one case only, at Impington Village College, Cambridgeshire (Maxwell *Fry and Walter *Gropius, 1938–40), did pioneering educationalism find architectural expression. The village colleges were

Green Lanes Junior School, Croxley Green, Hertfordshire (C. H. Aslin, 1952)

a combination of community centre and schools for both children and adults.

In the post-war period, an unusual combination of circumstances, which only occurred in Britain, led to a unique experiment in school design—one which attracted worldwide admiration and was repeated in hardly any other building type. From 1944, the Ministry of Education foresaw the need for a rapid expansion in school building, and called for 'standardized construction' to meet the need; in response, an idealistic group of architects, led by Stirrat Johnson-Marshall (1912–81), was prepared to carry out extensive research, not only into the technology of construction, but to designing spaces and equipment (even the washbasins) in consultation with education officers and teachers, to meet the needs of the users. The result was the Hertfordshire schools, beginning with Burleigh Infants School, Cheshunt (1947). By 1952 the system had produced 100 schools, using a standard grid system, which allowed a measure of flexibility. Similar principles

were subsequently applied by CLASP (Consortium of Local Authorities' Special Programme, from 1957), to the larger scale required by secondary schools.

The strong sense of social responsibility of all concerned is greatly to be prized, but were the schools perhaps too architecturally self-effacing? Only in the use of colour in the interiors did the architects seem to be much concerned with visual effect, but mainly for the benefit of the children. Fortunately, it was possible to have socially responsible and visually attractive buildings, such as the Danegrove Infants School (ACP, 1950–51), Brandlehow School, Putney, London (*Goldfinger, 1950–51), Hallfield School, Paddington, London (*Lasdun, 1953–5), Mayfield School, Wandsworth, London (*Powell and Moya, 1955), and Bousfield School, South Kensington, London (Chamberlin, Powell, and Bon, 1954–6).

At the other extreme, the *Smithsons' Hunstanton Secondary Modern School (1951–4), with its evident inspiration from Mies, and starkly exposed steel, concrete, and service systems, was with much justification stigmatized by a contemporary critic (Colin Boyne) as '...a formalist structure which will please only the architects...concerned more with satisfying their personal design sense than with achieving a humanist, functional architecture.' Forty years later, in a completely changed political climate, it is the Smithsons' approach which has prevailed (the Heinz-Galiski School, Berlin, by Zvi Hecker, 1990–95; Morella Boarding School, Morella, Spain, by Enric Miralles, 1986–93).   PG

> See also JACOBSEN, ARNE.
>
> Saint, A., *Towards a Social Architecture: the role of school-building in post-war England* (1987)

Schultz, R. Weir (1860–1951) Scottish architect. *See* ARTS AND CRAFTS.

Schütte-Lihotzky, Grete (1897–2000) Austrian architect. *See* AUSTRIA, 1900–2000.

Schwanzer, Karl (1918–75) Austrian architect. *See* AUSTRIA, 1900–2000.

Schwarz, Rudolf (1897–1961) German architect, one of the few German modernists involved in church architecture, whose work is often rather unfairly overlooked. He first worked with Dominikus *Böhm, who greatly influenced his first building, St Fronlichnam, Aachen (1928–30). With its white walls, it could be regarded from some angles as a typically modernist scheme; but in his post-war designs, Schwarz far surpassed his mentor. A prominent Roman Catholic involved in the liturgical reform movement (see *Vom Bau der Kirche*, English translation 1958), most of his churches aim to gather the congregation around all sides of the altar (the ring), or on three sides, leaving a fourth open (the open ring). He used reinforced concrete, brick, and glass walls with great ingenuity

to express the plan (see St Anna, Düren, 1951–6; the Holy Family, Oberhausen, 1956–8; St Anthony, Essen, 1956–9; Maria Königin, Rotenbühl, 1959).   PG

Scotland A common thread throughout the history of Scottish architecture since the Neolithic era has been provided by the geology and the equable, wet climate, and thus also by some fundamental approaches to construction, especially the use of stone construction in various forms. The first significant need and capacity to begin shaping a 'built environment' on the present-day territory of Scotland came with the appearance of farming from around 4000 BC. Initially, the principal built structures were religious ones: collective tombs, or elaborate circular ritual sites. In the Iron Age, from around 700 BC, there was seemingly a new awareness of locality, territory and the 'home', reflected in a proliferation of high-status structures for everyday life. These were dominated by circular plan-forms, and this roundhouse formula diversified and reached monumental proportions in the form of tall stone 'brochs'—circular buildings profiled like a modern cooling tower.

Early Christian religious architecture was mostly modest in scale, but in the newly unified Scottish nation of the 11th century onwards, the vast wealth of the international Roman church allowed the building of massive monastic or cathedral complexes. From the 14th century, there was an explosion in the secular building of 'show-castles' and 'palaces', intended not for military defence but as symbols of landed or royal authority.

After the Reformation and the 1603 union of the crowns, the most important patrons were the landed classes, with their country houses and castles—although there was also the beginning of a more dignified, monumental stone architecture in towns, beginning with early-17th-century Edinburgh, in projects such as the new Parliament House (1632–8) and the palace-like George Heriot's Hospital (1628–93).

The two dominant Scottish designers of the late 17th century were Sir William *Bruce and James Smith (c.1645–1731). Architecturally, just as in wider cultural terms, Renaissance ideals of order and humanist learning became gradually more pervasive. The entrenched image of the Scottish castle reigned supreme until the 1660s, as seen in towers such as Craigievar; but from the 1670s onwards, buildings and landscaping became integrated within a single ethos of classical order, as exemplified in Bruce's own palazzo-like mansion at Kinross (1679–93).

The transformation of the rural and urban environment rose to a frenzy during the 18th century in the so-called 'Improvement' movement, which strove to establish spatial order, through the reshaping of the old farming landscape and the building of hundreds of planned new settlements. Later in the century, this utilitarian rationalism provoked a creative counter-reaction in the form of the Romantic movement, emphasizing the irrational qualities of nature. The most important Scottish urban Improvement project was Edinburgh New Town—a new, high-class residential suburb to the north of the old town, planned in 1766–7 on axial lines by the young James Craig (1744–95). Early architects were prominent in this drive for Improvement, as exemplified by the indefatigable entrepreneurial enterprises of William *Adam. One of his sons, Robert *Adam, went much further, developing the first international, modern 'architectural personality', by using direct archaeological research into Roman antiquity to work out his own personal eclectic styles—classical and romantic-castellated.

As the pace of modernization quickened and its scope broadened further, the Improvement ethos of restless innovation and creativity became all-pervasive. The meanings of buildings, including the elevated, almost sacred status of the new, grand secular institutions, were expressed through the connotations of different styles. Of all these meanings, the most direct and elevated was that of national identity. Scotland's aspiration to a special status within Britain and the empire was expressed at first through the dignity of neo-Greek Classicism. Then, stimulated by the romantic writings of Walter Scott, emphasis shifted to the castellated Scottish Baronial, pioneered by Scott in his Borders retreat at Abbotsford (1817–23) and exploited in numerous massive country houses by William *Burn and his younger partner, David *Bryce.

But it was the explosive growth of the cities that dominated 19th-century Scottish architecture. Glasgow was the undisputed powerhouse of Victorian Scotland, and its energy was mirrored in its ferociously diverse classical architecture. The most original and impassioned path, developing the Adam formula of individual architectural 'personality', was ploughed by Alexander *Thomson, who peopled the Glasgow townscape with an exotic mixture of churches, commercial buildings, and housing in an idiosyncratic Greek style. In more conservative Edinburgh, the years after 1810 saw the 'Grecianizing' of the New Town. The most prestigious projects of the period were designed by the three leaders of Edinburgh neoclassicism: William Henry *Playfair, William *Burn and Thomas *Hamilton.

In the last two decades of the 19th century, Glasgow architects such as J. J. *Burnet looked to the French Beaux Arts system as a way of giving monumental buildings a more rational and consistent character; whereas in Edinburgh, the emphasis was on the moral wholeness of the 'artistic home', in the movement of 'Traditionalism', led by R. Rowand *Anderson and Robert *Lorimer.

For most of the 20th century, Scottish architecture was dominated by a violent reaction against the Victorian era, and by a drastic shift towards a collective modern world of disciplined mass movements. At first, the turn-of-century diversity continued, and was even heightened in the individualism of Charles Rennie *Mackintosh, whose work continued the Aesthetic Movement revolt from public monumentality towards the subjective refuge of the home, now through a highly charged, all-embracing artistic vision. But the chief trend was a disciplined, classical 'return to order', led by J. J. *Burnet and his main partner, Thomas Tait (1882–1954), as exemplified in their monumental St Andrew's House government headquarters in Edinburgh (1937–9).

After World War II, the triumph of the Modern Movement in the 'crusade' for social reconstruction spawned several offshoots. The most ambitious came from the modern regional planners of the new town of Cumbernauld, with its avant-garde and internationally renowned dense 'cluster' plan, and its multi-level ('megastructural') town centre of 1963–7. The most influential individual Scottish modernist architects were Robert *Matthew (chief designer of the London Royal Festival Hall and New Zealand House) and the more romantic Basil *Spence (architect of Coventry Cathedral, 1951–62).

By the 1970s, the scale and pace of reconstruction had fuelled a growing conservationist revulsion against modernist architecture. Eventually, a new architectural movement of postmodernism arose, overtly stressing façades, styles, and the inspiration of the past. In contrast to the vast horizons of Modernism, it concentrated on bringing a mixed-use vitality to the inner city, as in projects by Elder and Cannon and Page and Park for Glasgow's neglected 'Merchant City'.

When, eventually, the demands for a Home Rule parliament were met in May 1999, the inevitable architectural consequence was an upsurge in the rhetoric of Scottish identity. But all such cultural efforts now had to be played out against the unpromising backdrop of rampant global capitalism. The disorienting results of this were clear in the executed Holyrood parliament design by Catalan architect Enric Miralles (1955–2000), with its 'iconic modernist' foregrounding of metaphors of branded identity stemming from the individual architect-personality.　　　MGl

Glendinning, M., and MacKechnie, A., *Scottish Architecture* (2004)

Howard, D(eborah), *Scottish Architecture: Reformation to Restoration* (1995)

Scott, Sir George Gilbert (1811–78) The dominant architect in Britain in the third quarter of the 19th century. He was responsible for over 900 works, of which 400 were restorations, including most of the English cathedrals. He maintained the largest architects' office at the time, with about 36 staff. His designs were often in a recognizable High Victorian Gothic style, such as the Midland Grand Hotel at St Pancras (1865), but the extent of his practice meant that its quality varied. His *Personal and Professional Recollections* (published 1879, reissued 1995), after his death, reveal his approach to work and his intense Christianity.

He was articled to James Edmeston (1791–1867) of Bishopsgate in 1827, when his father dismissed a suggestion that he could rise to the top of his profession. But that was Scott's ambition and he pursued it with a lifetime of relentless energy.

Edmeston gave Scott a solid grounding in technology. In 1833 he designed his first houses and in 1835 started designing *workhouses; in 1838 he took on William Bonython Moffatt (1812–82) as a partner, and they produced 40 or so workhouses across England.

He became involved in church building and restoration, fell under *Pugin's influence, and three years after its formation joined the Cambridge Camden Society (later the Ecclesiological Society). He established his Gothic credentials with the Society in 1841 by winning a competition to rebuild St Giles'

Church, Camberwell, and in 1844 he won another competition to rebuild St Nicholas' Church in Hamburg. This success had nothing to do with Moffatt, but owed much to G. E. *Street, who entered the office to work on the church. The partnership with Moffatt ended in 1845.

In 1857 he published *Remarks on Secular and Domestic Architecture*, showing how Gothic could be used for secular buildings. This led to Kelham Hall, Nottinghamshire (1858), but his determination to produce a Gothic scheme for the Foreign Office (1860) resulted in confrontation with the Prime Minister, Lord Palmerston. Scott reluctantly produced today's fine classical-style building. In 1862 he won the Albert Memorial competition with a design that delighted Queen Victoria, and in 1872 he was one of the few architects of his generation to be knighted.

To his friends he was modest and affable, to his clients efficient and businesslike, but in his closing years he was attacked for failing to carry out the principles advocated in his *A Plea for the Faithful Restoration of our Ancient Churches* (1850). The numerous architects who passed through his office included *Bodley, *Jackson, and his sons George Gilbert junior and John Oldrid *Scott.   ILT

Scott, Sir Giles Gilbert (1880–1960) English

architect. The second son of George Gilbert Scott junior and grandson of Sir George Gilbert Scott, Giles Gilbert Scott was articled to Temple Moore and set up practice in 1903. He immediately won the competition to design the new Church of England cathedral in Liverpool, but since Scott was still in his early twenties, G. F. *Bodley, one of the assessors, was associated with the design during the first four years of its execution from 1904. His nobly massed Gothic conception, which he developed and modified over the years, was finally completed in 1980. A similar monumentality, though treated more classically, imbues his Cambridge

University Library (1931–2) and William Booth Memorial Training College, Southwark (1932), both of which, like the cathedral, are dominated by central towers. A similar feature, though in fact a chimney-stack, dominates his Bankside Power Station (1957–60, now Tate Modern), which otherwise follows the pattern Scott initiated as consultant for Battersea Power Station (1929–35, 1944–55). Though lacking the boldness of these designs, his Memorial Court, Clare College, Cambridge (1923–34), new Bodleian Library, Oxford (1936–46), and Guildhall Building, London (1954–8), demonstrate a plain but sensitive Classicism, though this appears at its endearing best in his designs for the cast-iron GPO telephone kiosks (K2, 1924; K6, 1935).   APQ

Scott, John Oldrid (1841–1913) English

architect, Sir George Gilbert Scott's second son, who is remembered as the perpetuator of his father's architecture into the 20th century.

In 1860 he entered his father's office as a pupil and assisted him on many projects. They collaborated on the Berlin Reichstag competition of 1872, but he also worked independently. His most notable work was the Greek Orthodox cathedral of St Sophia in London, which he designed in the Byzantine style in 1877.

After his father's death he continued the practice, largely working in his father's increasingly outmoded style, such as an unsuccessful entry for the Liverpool Cathedral competition of 1901.   ILT

Scott, Michael (1905–89) One of Ireland's leading

20th-century architects. To the forefront of the Modern Movement in Ireland, his early works include county hospitals at Portlaoise (1933–40) and Tullamore (1934–42) (with then partner, Norman Good), his own house, 'Geragh' (1937–8) in Sandycove, Co. Dublin, and the much-lauded 'Shamrock' Pavilion at the New York World's Fair (1939).

Following the war, Scott's practice came to dominate the Irish architectural scene for over three decades. Significant works of the period include the iconic Busáras (1944–53) (Dublin Bus Station), and Donnybrook Bus Garage (1946–51), designed in conjunction with the engineer Ove Arup. From the late 1950s, collaboration with architects Robin Walker and Ronnie Tallon saw the practice shift towards Miesian principles demonstrated at the Radio Telifis Éireann complex (1959–62, 1967) and Carroll's Factory, Dundalk (1967–9). RM

scuola A building type uniquely associated with Venice. Scuole were lay religious confraternities, which flourished in the Venetian Republic from the 15th century. Membership was voluntary, and was open to all classes of society.

They fell into two principal groups, the Scuole Grandi and the Scuole Piccole. The Scuole Grandi originally numbered only three (San Marco, Santa Maria della Carità, San Giovanni Evangelista), but by the fall of the Republic (1797) there were seven. During the 15th and 16th centuries, each Scuola Grande built imposing new buildings for its membership, in which masses were held and general assemblies of the 600 members took place; they also undertook charitable works and dispensed alms. The Scuole Grandi employed outstanding architects to design their new buildings: that of San Marco was designed by Pietro Solari Lombardo and Mauro Coducci; that of the Misericordia was by Sansovino; and that of San Rocco by Scarpagnino and others. The Scuola always contained a great hall on the first floor, the *sala capitolare*, for general assemblies, together with a much smaller hall, the *albergo*, where the governing board met, and where relics and valuables were kept.

They commissioned important cycles of paintings to decorate the two halls, all from the leading artists of the time, many of whom, such as Giovanni Bellini, were also members of the Scuole. The Scuola Grande di San Rocco, for example, is decorated almost entirely by Tintoretto. The much more numerous Scuole Piccole ('minor scuole') numbered several dozen, and often simply assembled at a chapel within a parish church; others built modest assembly halls for their members. Two of the wealthiest Scuole Piccole, that of San Todaro and the Carmini, built themselves impressive accommodation (the latter was designed by Baldassare Longhena and decorated by Giambattista Tiepolo), and were 'promoted' to the status of Scuole Grandi in the 18th century. RJG

Secessionism A term used by contemporary critics and later by historians to refer to a tendency in the architecture of Vienna and the Habsburg Empire, characterized by ahistoricism and decorative vegetal motifs. The name derives from the Vienna Secession, an artists' association founded in 1897 under the leadership of Gustav Klimt. Several progressive architects were members of the Secession, including Joseph Maria *Olbrich, Josef *Hoffmann and Otto *Wagner. The Secession members themselves were adamant that there was in fact no such thing as Secessionism, that is, no one style that the entire group embraced, in architecture or the other arts. Instead, the group saw itself as being united only by the ideals of artistic freedom, originality, and sincerity.

The building most closely associated with the Vienna Secession was its exhibition hall, designed by Olbrich and completed in 1898. The Secession building is interesting for its flexible exhibition space and its experimental combination of realism, symbolism, and Eastern and vernacular influences. But the aspect of the building that was most immediately influential was the treatment of the exterior surfaces: white-washed plaster inscribed with organic motifs, including abstract whiplash lines and stylized laurel trees and wreaths, all emphatically flat. Over the next five years, such surface treatment was very fashionable across the Habsburg Empire, especially for residential and commercial buildings, usually by little-known architects. It is this derivative use of surface treatments that was referred to at the time as 'Secessionistic'. The term used by those close to the Secession was 'false Secession'.

Historians of the period have tended to use the term Secessionism more widely to refer to the Austrian version of Jugendstil. This encompasses all the work of Olbrich, the early 'organic' work of Josef *Hoffmann, and aspects of the architecture of the students of Otto *Wagner.   LET

section The internal vertical arrangement of a building, or a drawing of the same made as if an imaginary perpendicular cut were taken through a building to reveal its interior and profile. A longitudinal section is a vertical cut through the length of a building, a transverse or cross section is a vertical cut through the width or breadth of a building.

The section of the choir of Reims cathedral showing the flying buttress system in *Villard de Honnecourt's book of drawings (c.1225–35) (f.32r, Bibliothèque Nationale, Paris) is the earliest extant example of a section. The section was perfected by later mason-architects and by the artist-architects of the Italian Renaissance, in particular Bramante in his project for the cupola of St Peter's, Rome (c.1505). Domes, cupolas, variable room heights, and schemes of interior decoration all made sections more necessary.

A section is also the profile of a moulding or other building part as it would appear if cut through vertically, or a drawing of the same.   JL

Sedding, John Dando (1838–91) English architect. One of *Street's many successful pupils, (1858–65), Sedding worked with his brother in Penzance before removing in 1875 to London, where he became closely associated with the *Arts and Crafts movement, designing furniture, ornaments, and embroidery, as well as buildings. His churches, often in a free *Perpendicular and finely fitted-out by his colleagues, include: St Martin, Low Marple, Cheshire (1870); St Clement, Boscombe, Hampshire (1873–93); All Saints, Falmouth, Cornwall (1887–90); and in London: Holy Redeemer, Clerkenwell (1887–8); Holy Trinity, Sloane Square (1888–90); and St Peter, Ealing (1892). Sedding also wrote *Garden Craft, Old and New* (1891), and *Art and Handicraft* (1893).   APQ

Seddon, John Pollard (1827–1906) English architect, who began practice in 1852 in partnership with John Prichard at Llandaff, working on houses and churches in a vigorous Puginian Gothic. As well as several church restorations, his original designs include Southerndown Hotel (subsequently a Sunshine Home), Glamorgan (1852–3), and Ettington Park, the most important Victorian country house in Warwickshire (1858–62, with Prichard). In 1862 he left Prichard and removed to London, where he built Powell Almshouses, Fulham (1869), and St Paul, Hammersmith (1882), as well as St James, Great Yarmouth, Norfolk (1870–78), St Mary, Ullenhall, Warwickshire (1875), St Andrew, Adforton, Herefordshire (1875), and the grandiose neo-Romanesque St Catherine, Hoarwithy, Herefordshire (c.1885). He wrote several books, most notably *Progress in Art and Architecture* (1852).   APQ

Seidler, Harry (1923–) Australian architect. Born in Vienna, after escaping Hitler's annexation of Austria, he studied at the University of Manitoba and Harvard University, and worked for Oscar *Niemeyer in Rio de Janeiro. His parents in 1948 asked him to join them in Australia where in 1949 he designed their house now known as the Rose Seidler House. This building initiated four decades of works of international quality.

Riverside Centre, Brisbane, Australia (Harry Seidler, 1988)

His work has changed the Sydney skyline, more particularly with Australia Square (1967) and the MLC Centre (1978), a 65-storey office tower. His proposals for Blues Point in North Sydney in 1962 were controversial, with a major redevelopment using point and slab box in the Roehampton tradition. Only one tower was built of this huge scheme. He completed a distinguished tower on the Brisbane River, the Riverside Centre (1988), which has engagement to both the street and the river. The polished façades of the tower have freely ordered 2-storey cut-out balconies. Seidler's house (1967), in a bushland setting in Sydney, has four suspended concrete bridges zoning

active and passive ocupations. Seidler has completed distinguished buildings in Mexico, Hong Kong, and most recently in Vienna, Wohnpark Neue Donau (1998) and Hochhaus Neue Donau (2001).   LN

Seifert, Richard (1910–2001) English architect. From the early 1960s, his knowledge of planning law, and his reputation for speedy construction based on a sound grasp of modern technology, made him the ideal architect for speculators wishing to build tall office blocks. The very names of his 1960s schemes express the contemporary optimism about technology and tall buildings—Orbit House, Southwark; Space House, Kingsway; Telstar House, Southwark; and Planet House, Baker Street (all in London). The best of his buildings, such as Tolworth Tower (Kingston, 1962–4), and the highly prominent Centre Point, right in the centre of London (1961–6), used pre-cast concrete in angular, rather sculptural forms.   PG

Selva, Giannantonio (1751–1819) Italian architect. In the 1780s and 1790s, Selva designed Palladian villas in Venice and the Veneto, and in the 1800s several neoclassical churches in the same region. But his best-known work is the *opera house of Teatro La Fenice, Venice (1790–92). Unusually for an opera house of that period, the building has two significant façades, one towards the canal, consisting of a portico with five round-headed arches, the other, the main entrance, consisting of a tetrastyle portico.   PG

Semper, Gottfried (1803–79) German architect, art critic, and professor of architecture. Semper's career neatly falls into three stages of practice, theory, and a return to design.

His architectural training consisted of two stays in Paris in the late 1820s, where he attended a private school run by Franz Christian Gau (1790–1854). In 1830 Semper embarked on a tour of the south, highlighted by his visit to Greece. His findings of Greek polychromy prompted his first publication, *Preliminary Remarks on Polychrome Architecture and Sculpture in Antiquity* (1834). In the same year he received a chair at the Dresden Academy of Fine Arts.

The Dresden years were happy ones. Artistically, the city was one of the most vibrant in Europe, and Semper's innovative design for the Dresden Royal Theatre (1838–41) catapulted him into prominence. He followed with the Villa Rosa (1839), Dresden Art Gallery (1839–55), and Oppenheim Palace (1845–8)—all in a refined Renaissance vocabulary. Political unrest meanwhile intervened, and in 1849 Semper and his friend Richard Wagner, both of whom supported national unification, were forced to flee Germany.

Next came Semper's years as a political refugee. His dire circumstances improved only in the summer of 1852 when Henry Cole hired him to teach metal arts at the reformed Department of Practical Art—the forerunner to the Victoria and Albert Museum in London. In 1855 Semper became the first professor of architecture at the new Polytechnikum (now the Eidgenössische Technische Hochschule) in Zurich.

During these difficult years Semper compiled most of his writings on architecture. In *The Four Elements of Architecture* (1851; English translation 1989), he suggested that architecture's formal motives—the hearth, mounding, roofing, and walling—could be found in the technical arts of ceramics, masonry, carpentry, and textiles. Crucial to his deliberations was the notion of 'dressing' (*Bekleidung*), which was the textile or spatial motive for the wall. In *Science, Industry, and Art* (1852), Semper carried out a critique of the Great Exhibition of 1851 and concluded that the current crisis in the arts was at heart a stylistic one, induced by the superabundance of means and speculative forces: the progenitors of fashion in the new industrial society.

Semper's most compelling book, *Style in the Technical or Tectonic Arts, or Practical Aesthetics* (1860–63; English translation 2004), both summarized his ideas of the previous decade and carried forward his research into architecture's symbolic underpinnings. Semper's deliberations on the psychological meaning of form, the 'masking for reality in the arts', and architectural 'space' set the course of Germanic discussions for the next forty years. In this regard the links between Semper and German modernists of the early 20th century cannot be overstated.

Semper returned to practice with his designs for the Zurich Polytechnikum (1858–63) and Munich Festspielhaus (1864–7), the latter spectacularly planned (but never built) to house Wagner's Ring Cycle. In 1869 he designed (with Karl von Hasenauer) a vast cultural complex in Vienna. He also built his second Dresden theatre (1870–78) after the first had been destroyed by fire. Semper was now celebrated throughout a recently unified Germany as the country's greatest architect and as someone who had paid dearly for his politics. A young Friedrich Nietzsche was strongly attracted to his ideas, as was the succeeding generation of German architects. The gulf between his approach to practice and his theory, however, was never successfully bridged. HFM

Herrmann, Wolfgang, *Gottfried Semper* (1984)
Mallgrave, H. F., *Gottfried Semper* (1996)

Sens, William of (d.1180) French mason. 'A most cunning craftsman in wood and stone', William of Sens was called to England to initiate the reconstruction of Canterbury Cathedral following the destructive fire of 1174. Within three years he had remodelled the choir, making it the most important work in England in the new Gothic style, but in 1177 he was crippled in a fall from scaffolding, and returned to France, paving the way for his successor William Englishman to complete the stylistic innovations. APQ

Serbia Byzantine, Romanesque, and Gothic churches of the pre-Ottoman period, some with proto-Renaissance frescoes, have survived to the present day. Under Ottoman domination (1389–1805) no work of great significance was produced. The neo-Byzantine style, in tandem with European Eclecticism after 1805, was followed by Imperialist Classicism in the works of Russian emigrant architects and their Serbian imitators (e.g. National Bank, Belgrade, K. Jovanovic, 1889).

The Modern Movement confronted local conservatism, but even so there were some outstanding buildings in that spirit: a private house (1929) by B. Kojic, his own house (1930) by M. Zlokovic, both in Belgrade, and Government Offices in Novi Sad (1937–40) by D. Brašovan. The Communists (1945–90) imposed their own priorities, inspired initially by 'Socialist Realism'. The 1960s were characterized by more freedom; good examples are the Ministry of Defence, by N. Dobrovic (1954/63); the Museum of Modern Art, by I. Raspopovic (1965); and the National Library, by I. Kurtovic (1973), all in Belgrade.

With the dissolution of Yugoslavia, Serbia remained isolated, and succumbed to architectural kitsch. A few creative projects, however, have cropped up in Belgrade: the office block 'Zepter' (B. Mitrovic and V. Milunovic, 1996), and an apartment block (B. Mitrovic, 2000). VT

Serlio, Sebastiano (1475–1555) Italian architect and theorist, who wrote a series of highly influential treatises, aiming to demonstrate to architects how *Vitruvius' rules could be applied to current problems (*see* THEORIES OF ARCHITECTURE (RENAISSANCE)). The treatises dealt with the following subjects.

Book IV (published in 1537) was probably the most important, as it was the first codification of the *orders and a good example of the applicability of Serlio's ideas

to practice. In the context of illustrating ideas for the façades of Venetian palaces, he devised the Serlian or *Venetian window, which allowed sufficient light to penetrate into deep interiors. Book III (1540) illustrated the buildings of antiquity, mainly of Rome. Book 1 (1545) was concerned with geometry; Book II (1545) dealt with perspective, including several illustrations for stage designs; Book V (1547) illustrated a selection of temples, to provide ideas for contemporary church architecture; Book VI (written perhaps in 1541, but not published until 1966) and Book VII (1575) gave examples of a wide range of domestic architecture.

His only surviving major work was the chateau of Ancy-le-Franc (1541–50), a rather bleak building which, because of the client's requirements, seems to incorporate few of his theoretical recommendations.

PG

Sert, Josep Lluís (1902–83) Catalan architect. In 1927 he was asked to work with Le Corbusier in his Paris studio, the beginning of a long association. When the Republic was elected in 1931, a massive social building programme began under the direction of a Modern Movement group called GATCPAC, led by Sert and his colleague Josep Torres Clavé.

They built schools, hospitals, worker housing, and TB clinics (Central Dispensary, 1935). Sert designed long-lasting buildings with great sensitivity, and many are still in use (Casa Bloc, 1936). Building continued well into the Civil War, which began in 1936 (Spanish Pavilion, Paris Expo, 1937), during which Torres Clavé was captured and executed.

Towards the end of the war Sert fled to New York. He practised throughout the Americas, and is particularly known for his private houses and work on university buildings at MIT, Boston, where he joined a group of European émigrés and became an international figure, even designing the US Embassy building in Baghdad (1960). Among his finest and most complex works for the arts are the Maeght Foundation in France (1964) and Mir Foundation in Barcelona (1975).   EDC

Freixa, J., *Josep Ll. Sert* (1980)

Servandoni, Giovanni Niccolò Geronimo

(1695–1766) Franco-Italian architect, designer of theatre and festival decorations. In 1732 he won the competition to design the west façade of St Sulpice, Paris (the nave and aisles had already been completed), with a scheme he revised twice, in *c.*1736 and 1750, subsequently much altered. The screen of two superimposed orders is definitely his design, but their awkward relation to the two rather stumpy towers was certainly not intended. His vision of a large square entered by a triumphal arch, the kind of magnificent spectacle he was so skilled at creating, was begun (1754) but rapidly set aside for financial reasons.   PG

services *See* ELECTRICS AND ELECTRONIC SERVICING; ENGINEERING SERVICES.

Severus (*fl.*AD 64) Roman architect, known from Tacitus and Suetonius as the architect employed by Nero to rebuild his Domus Aurea on the Esquiline Hill after the disastrous fire in Rome of AD 64. Incorporating extensive suites of lavishly finished rooms, ingeniously lit from indirect sources, and integrated into spacious gardens, it gave Nero the satisfaction of 'beginning to be housed like a human being'. Severus and his engineer assistant Celer also worked on a project for a canal linking Lake Avernus with the Tiber, and he may have also been more generally involved in the rebuilding of Rome after the fire, and have written the city's new building code.   APQ

severy synonymous with *web, the panels between the *ribs in a *vault.   PG

Sharon, Arieh (1900–84) born in Poland, and emigrated to Palestine in 1920. Arieh Sharon was among the founders of Kibbutz Gan Shmuel. In 1926–9 he studied at the Bauhaus, and from 1929 to 1931 he worked in Hannes Meyer's office. In 1932 he returned to Palestine and became a pioneer of the International Style. He won planning competitions for eight complexes of cooperative workers' residences in Tel Aviv in the 1930s. Sharon convinced the residents not to follow the conventional trend of living in small houses, and instead created large, elongated apartment buildings, making it possible to build internal gardens and give residents greater privacy. In the 1940s he built extensively in kibbutzim (collective agricultural settlements). When the state of Israel was established, he was appointed Chief Architect and head of the Planning Division in the Prime Minister's Office, where the National Plan, regional plans, and master plans for twenty new towns were drafted. In 1954 he returned to architectural work in his office, in partnership with Benjamin Idelson and later with his son Eldar. His office specialized in building hospitals, residential projects, and public buildings.   ML

Sharon, Arieh, *Kibbutz and Bauhaus, An Architect's Way in a New Land* (1976)

Shaw, Richard Norman (1831–1912) English architect, among the most influential of the final quarter of the 19th century. Shaw trained at the Royal Academy schools under C. R. *Cockerell, and worked under William *Burn for seven years. He and his friend William Eden *Nesfield worked briefly for Anthony *Salvin, after which Shaw left in 1859 to become *Street's chief assistant. By 1863 Shaw and Nesfield shared an office in London. They had travelled extensively in the Weald of Sussex and Kent, observing especially the traditional architecture of the region's farmhouses, and now put this to good use for Shaw's first commissions for substantial country houses for

827

wealthy clients. He was not the first to be influenced from this direction: the mild medievalizing of his colleague Philip *Webb, notably in William *Morris's Red House at Bexleyheath, and the small houses of many of the earlier generation had already turned to traditional forms. But Shaw's resulting Old English style, with its half-timbering, tile-hanging, gables, hips, and tall chimney-stacks, as exemplified by Glen Andred (1866–8) and Leyswood (1866–73), Sussex, and Grim's Dyke, Harrow Weald, London (1870–72), now overtook their early, more modest ventures in this style to venture into the realm of romantic magnificence, culminating at Cragside, Northumberland (1870–72).

Very soon Shaw took up a less hectic traditional style. Realizing that his previous creations were not suitable for the more formal buildings of the city, he began to adopt the easy-going forms characteristic of the late 17th and early 18th centuries, sometimes with a stripy mixture of brick and Portland stone, and even Scottish Baronial features, and others such as shaped gables from Holland and the Low Countries. This became known as 'Queen Anne' and was an immediate success in burgeoning self-conscious suburbs, as at 6 Ellerdale Road, Hampstead, London (1874–6), and widely at Bedford Park (1877–80) in west London. It was well suited to commercial and official buildings, such as New Zealand Chambers, City of London (1871–3, demolished), Alliance Assurance Offices, London (1881–3), New Scotland Yard, London (1886–90), and, in Liverpool, White Star Offices (1895–8) and Royal Insurance Offices (1896–1902). Similarly he applied it to his innovative blocks of flats for professional people that began with Albert Hall Mansions, London (1876–81). Needless to say, Queen Anne soon superseded Old English in Shaw's country houses, such as Bryanston, Dorset (1889–94), and Lowther Lodge, Kensington (1872–5), a country house despite its London address.

Old English and Queen Anne between them were the architectural foundation of the *Arts and Crafts movement, many of whose members were Shaw's assistants at one time. They were seen from within the senior ranks of the profession, which was still devoted to formal Gothic and classical, as a ginger group working outside, bent on promoting the 'smirks and leers and romps of naughty Queen Anne'. But Gothic had nearly had its day domestically, and, though still the style in the 1880s for churches, Shaw modified his Gothic accordingly at Bedford Park, where his church of St Michael is a far cry from his early Holy Trinity, Bingley, Yorkshire (1864–8, demolished), which still showed the influence of Street.

As the 20th century dawned, Shaw's Queen Anne style gradually developed into a free neo-Georgian, archly known as 'Wrenaissance', in which classical forms added a solid measure of gravity. This is already apparent at Chesters (1890–94), a severe but wonderfully massed country house in Northumberland and a precursor of some of Lutyens' most successful houses. It came into full bloom in Portland House, London (1907–8), where he pioneered the use of reinforced concrete, and above all his Piccadilly Hotel, London (1905–8), which has more than a dash of imperialism in its spirit.   APQ

Saint, A., *Richard Norman Shaw* (1976)

Shekhtel', Fedor Osipovich (1859–1926) Russian architect and designer. Among Russian architects at the turn of the 20th century, he was unique in adopting a modernist aesthetic.

His first work in this idiom, with extensive use of the decorative arts, was his house for Stepan Rabushinsky (1900–02). But the other major residence he designed in this period, for Alexandra Derozhinskaia (1901), rejects elaborate decoration in favour of a monumental definition of mass and space.

In public architecture, Shekhtel' designed some of Moscow's most important buildings, such as the Moscow Art Theatre (1902) and the Yaroslavl Railway Station (1902), with a modernized interpretation of traditional decorative elements known as the 'neo-Russian' style. For commercial architecture, Shekhtel' pioneered the use of glazed brick, plate glass, and reinforced concrete, in structures that included the Moscow Insurance Society on Old Square (1901), the Riabushinsky Brothers Bank (1903), the building of the Riabushinsky newspaper, *Utro Rossii* (1907), and the Moscow Merchants' Society.

In the final phase of his career, Shekhtel' devised new interpretations of retrospective styles, such as the neoclassical revival for his own house in Moscow (1909), and the museum in Taganrog dedicated to his friend Chekhov (1910).   WCB

shell structures are *vaults which follow the same structural principle as an eggshell, i.e. the material is extremely thin in relation to the surface area, giving an extremely high strength–weight ratio. In traditional masonry a *fan vault follows this principle, but very thin light-weight shells which curve in more than one direction (like a saddle) were made possible by the development of reinforced *concrete and an understanding of the geometry involved.

Unlike other modern developments in structures, such as *trusses or *space frames, shell structures have great expressive possibilities. These possibilities were not exploited by the first shell structure, the market hall at Frankfurt am Main (Martin Elsasser, 1927), but *Torroja y Miret's designs for the Market Hall, Algeciras (1933), and the roof at La Zarzuela racecourse, Milan (1935), as well as *Maillart's hall at Zurich (1938–9), show an increasing refinement towards elegant and slender forms.

In the 1950s more extravagant forms were used. *Candela Outeriño was perhaps most interested in

technical virtuosity, so he devised the thinnest concrete shell (only 15 mm or just over half an inch at the apex) for the Cosmic Ray pavilion, Mexico (1951), and twisted 'columns' for the Church of the Miraculous Virgin, Mexico City (1955). However, in the latter case, and in the wave-like restaurant of Los Manantiales, Xochimilo, Mexico (1958), he used the simplest form for modelling and constructing, the hyperbolic parabola.

Shell structures permit the purely sculptural approach to form typical of some modernists, an approach exemplified in two buildings by Eero *Saarinen. The Kresge Auditorium, MIT (1952–6), in which the roof is one-eighth of a full sphere, is structurally dysfunctional, in that it requires large subterranean concrete buttresses. The soaring roofs of the TWA Terminal at Kennedy International Airport, New York (1956–62), use a purely sculptural form to symbolize the idea of wings and flight.

More functionally satisfactory applications are to be found in *bus garages (e.g. Michael *Scott's Donnybrook Bus Garage, completed 1952) and factories (the Brynmawr Rubber Factory, *Architects Co-Partnership, with *Arup as engineer, 1947–52; the Canteen, Rhône-Poulenc-Rorer, Dagenham, by Edward Mills, 1943–53), in which a concrete shell roof allows a large space to be lit from one end to the other by natural light, while adopting a variety of forms (segmental arches, domes, and waves, respectively). Perhaps the most satisfactory combination of the functional and the expressive is to be found in *Nervi's Palazzetto dello Sport (1956–7).   PG

Sheppard, Sir Richard Herbert (1910–82) and **Robson Geoffrey** (1918–91) English architects, their partnership formed in 1947. In the 1950s and 1960s, Sheppard and Robson effectively applied the vocabulary of mainstream Modernism, inspired by Le Corbusier's Maisons Jaoul, to a series of schools, technical colleges, and universities. Their outstanding works are the Halls of Residence, Imperial College, London (1957–65), adopting the staircase model of Oxford and Cambridge *colleges, and Churchill College, Cambridge (1960–68), borrowing the traditional quadrangle from the same source.

Other notable schemes are the West Midlands College of Education, Walsall, Staffordshire (1964–72), and City University, St John Street, Clerkenwell, London (1969–76).   PG

shikhara The tower of a North Indian temple. *See* INDIAN SUB-CONTINENT (NORTHERN TEMPLES).

Shinohara, Kazuo (1925–2006) Japanese architect, educator, and theorist. Trained initially in mathematics, Shinohara established himself at the Tokyo Institute of Technology (TIT) designing some 30 houses between 1958 and 1978. His early house designs such as the Umbrella house (1961) focused on symbolic space abstracted from conceptual methods of 17th-century precedents. His subsequent designs shifted to geometrical strategies of inorganic forms through 'cubes' and 'fissures' and then to a pursuit of 'savagery' seen in his space-machine-like Centennial Anniversary Hall at TIT (1987).   KTO

Shinto shrines *See* JAPAN, TO 1912 (SHINTO SHRINES).

shops and stores (UK) Shops of the Roman period have been excavated in English towns, but the oldest surviving examples are medieval. Most medieval shops occupied ground-floor rooms in the street ranges of timber-framed houses, and although examples can be found throughout England, they are concentrated in East Anglia, where wealth declined after the 16th century and shops were preserved by being absorbed into dwellings. Medieval shops are characterized by unglazed, arched openings, which were closed by

wooden shutters out of business hours. Since many shops also functioned as workshops, these openings would have admitted light for craftsmen, as well as providing a stall-board for tradesmen.

The form and style of shops changed little between the 13th and the 17th centuries, and their size remained extremely small by modern standards. It was the introduction of the wooden-framed glazed shopfront from the Netherlands, in the middle of the 17th century, that transformed shop design throughout much of western Europe. By the mid 18th century bow-fronted shopfronts with classical details and small-paned glazing were the height of fashion, and some good examples can still be seen on the streets of Bath and London. Interiors of high-class shops, equipped with mirrors, screens, and chandeliers, became increasingly ornate. At the same time, shops grew in size, extending backwards through the ground floors of buildings, where they were lit by skylights and lanterns. By the end of the century some had even extended vertically, on to upper floors, and were distinguished from smaller shops by the imposing labels 'warehouse' and 'emporium'. One celebrated example of a 2-storey shop was Schomberg House on Pall Mall, which has been described as the first department store because it stocked an unusually wide range of goods. Another remarkable late-18th-century shop was James Lackington's bookshop (1789–91) on Finsbury Square, London, which had a rotunda ringed by cast-iron galleries. Aside from their shopfronts, however, there was little to distinguish the frontages of 18th- and early-19th-century retail establishments from domestic façades.

The streetscapes of medieval and early modern towns had included purpose-built rows of shops. These were greatly surpassed in scale and grandeur by John *Nash's Regent Street (1819–23), driven through central London in the years following the Napoleonic wars. Its wide pavements and Quadrant colonnade

Peter Jones department store, Sloane Square, Chelsea, London (Slater and Moberly, 1939)

were designed to accommodate shopping as part of a leisurely promenade, while the upper floors of the stuccoed buildings provided lodgings. Contemporary with Regent Street, and inspired by Paris's famous Palais Royal, were several new arcades and bazaars which gathered traders under one roof and sought to attract a fashionable clientele. In London's Burlington Arcade (1818), small but exquisite shops lined a long corridor lit by skylights. Bazaars provided a very different shopping environment, with counters arranged in large rooms or saloons, some with galleries and vaults, not unlike modern department stores.

Technological advances, especially in the manufacture of glass and cast iron, had a tremendous impact on the appearance of shops and stores in the 19th century, encouraging the emergence of a distinctly commercial style of street architecture. As plate glass became more affordable, shop windows grew larger, and glazing bars became increasingly slender. Despite

the predominance of Classicism, some shopfronts were executed in novel Egyptian, Gothic or 'Elizabethan' styles. By the 1840s shopfronts, and even complete façades, could be manufactured in iron. The cast-iron façades of Manhattan stores were emulated in provincial towns and cities throughout Great Britain, and arcaded examples can still be seen in Glasgow, Norwich, and elsewhere. This type of façade was particularly favoured by ironmongers and furniture dealers.

While effective lifts (elevators) made upper-floor shopping a more viable proposition from the 1870s, structural ironwork enabled interiors to become more spacious. Iron was also used for galleries and roofs. The best examples of this can be seen in Victorian arcades and market halls rather than in drapery and department stores which, architecturally, remained very conservative. The French style of *grand magasin*— with vast spaces surrounded by galleries and crowned by glazed vaults, typified by the Bon Marché and Galeries Lafayette in Paris—was adopted for some prominent Scottish stores, such as Wylie and Lochhead's and Jenner's, in Glasgow and Edinburgh respectively. But English storekeepers remained rooted in the tradition of the draper's shop, continuing to accommodate staff on upper floors, and it was only in the 1890s that modestly sized galleries were incorporated into new London department stores, such as Harrods. The magnificent scale of the French *grand magasin* was experienced in London for the first time in 1912, when Whiteley's unveiled its new store in Bayswater.

Shopping at the lower end of the social spectrum changed greatly in the course of the 19th century. Many market places were superseded by enclosed halls, and from the 1860s and 1870s there was a huge increase in the numbers of shops which catered for working-class customers. Co-operative shops and stores proliferated, as did commercial multiple or branch shops. While co-operatives were divided into departments selling different categories of goods, touching on all aspects of life, multiples tended to specialize, often very narrowly.

By this time, shops belonging to different types of tradesmen had adopted distinctive designs, suiting their retail methods and showing off their goods to best advantage. The shops of butchers and fishmongers, for example, had wide sash windows which could be thrown up to reveal a display of meat or fish on a cool marble slab, while interiors were lined with decorative glazed tiles. Jewellers favoured fixed plate-glass windows which could be secured by strong shutters, and glittering interiors with glass-fronted cases and shining mahogany cabinets. Chemists' windows incorporated shelves for carboys, and their interiors were lined by rows of glass bottles and small wooden drawers. In the 1890s, Boots the chemist became one of the first multiple retailers to produce a house style, conceived by the architect A. N. Bromley, which

embraced the design of the entire building, and not just the shopfront.

By the start of the 20th century the appreciation of Georgian shopfronts was influencing new designs, such as Hatchard's bow-fronted Piccadilly shopfront. Historicism affected the design of stores, as well as shopfronts. Boots and WH Smith erected a number of mock timber-framed stores in the early 20th century, and both firms undertook the restoration of genuinely medieval timber-framed buildings. However, following the opening of Selfridges and the arrival of Woolworths, just before World War I, most new stores turned their backs on English and Continental models, instead taking their inspiration from America. It was the USA which had developed stores with expansive open-plan floors that dispensed with light-wells and relied on electric lighting, the first important example being Carson, Pirie, Scott in Chicago, designed by Louis *Sullivan. In general, luxurious London stores such as Liberty's (1922–4) continued to build galleries, while more economically minded middle-market stores, desiring to devote as much floor space as possible to display, preferred the open-plan system. Stores of all types, however, were now built in steel, and many emulated Selfridges' façade, with its vertical accent and metal panelling. Examples include Clery's in Dublin (1922) and hundreds of branches of Marks and Spencer's and Burton's, which were erected on high streets throughout Great Britain and Ireland in the 1920s and 1930s.

A rather austere neoclassicism prevailed in shop design until 1925, when the Paris Exposition Internationale des Arts Décoratifs et Industriels Modernes introduced retail architects to what we now call *Art Deco. In Great Britain, its chief exponent was Joseph *Emberton, whose extravagant designs for Austin Reed and Lotus and Delta unfortunately do not survive. The more restrained language of International Modernism, including the 'streamline moderne' style (often, confusingly, described as Art Deco), was introduced to England by émigré architects such as Ernö Goldfinger and Walter Gropius. As they became unfashionable after World War II, very few Art Deco or moderne shopfronts have survived in anything but a fragmentary state. Intact examples such as Fox's umbrella shop in London, with its Vitrolite fascia, chrome trim, neon signage, and curved reflective glass windows, are rarities.

By the 1930s Joseph Emberton was designing buildings in an International Modern style, undoubtedly inspired by Erich *Mendelsohn's German stores. One of Emberton's most successful buildings, Simpson's of Piccadilly (opened 1936), had a strong horizontality and sophisticated lighting that was clearly indebted to Mendelsohn, in particular to the Herpich store in Berlin and the Schocken department stores. Although Simpson's relied on lifts and an elegant staircase, escalators were becoming increasingly popular. The first escalator in England had been installed in Harrods in 1898, but the first full installation, serving all floors, was erected in the new D. H. Evans store on Oxford Street, London (Louis Blanc, 1934–7). Escalators proved much more successful than stairs or lifts in developing the potential of upper floors, and manipulating customer flow through a building, although lifts more usefully served top-floor restaurants.

In the late 1940s and early 1950s, efforts were concentrated on rebuilding the hundreds of stores that had been destroyed by enemy action. The design of these buildings was prefigured by a handful of avant-garde stores of the late 1930s, such as Peter Jones in London (William Crabtree with Slater and Moberley and C. H. Reilly, opened 1939), which was one of the first to have a curtain wall. Many post-war stores, however, dispensed almost entirely with glazing, presenting blind walls—clad in unprepossessing modern materials, such as moulded concrete block—to

the shopping street. This was the retailers' preference, as windows interfered with perimeter displays and, moreover, were made redundant by reliable artificial lighting and air conditioning. Interiors were bland and classless, and the prevailing distaste for ornamentation led many older businesses to strip out their staircases and galleries, and to conceal plasterwork and rooflights behind suspended ceilings. Like the US-style precincts and malls which were soon springing up all over the country, new stores sometimes included car parks for customers.

A number of attractive shopfronts were erected in the contemporary style of the late 1950s and early 1960s, and many old shopfronts were transformed by psychedelic paint during the 'Swinging Sixties'. However, throughout much of the 1960s and 1970s, plain, aluminium-framed shopfronts, with illuminated plastic fascias, were ubiquitous. The perception that high streets had been ruined by bad, cheap architecture triggered nostalgia for the pre-war period, encouraging notions of a golden age of shopping, and strengthening the budding conservation movement. At first, arcading and brickwork were applied, somewhat incongruously, to severely modern designs. Then, by 1980, traditional shop designs—in particular designs of Georgian and Victorian inspiration, complete with glazing bars and classicizing detail—began to appear on high streets up and down the country. This 'heritage revival' affected not just shops, but also the furnishings of shopping streets, from benches and bus stops to hanging basket brackets.

'Heritage' shop design was quickly denounced by modernist architects, and even by the conservation lobby itself, which criticized incorrect glazing bars, appliqué mouldings, and inappropriate wood stain. Since the late 1980s, a minimalist (or quasi-industrial) modern style has dominated, both for high-fashion metropolitan boutiques and high street chain stores. In such designs, unbroken sheets of glass often provide a direct view into neutral interiors, without the barrier fabricated by traditional window displays. If there is a display, it generally conveys an image, rather than presenting an array of merchandise; if there is signage, it is discreet. The minimalist glass frontage can be applied to shops and stores of any size, one of the first department stores to adopt this style being the Harvey Nichols branch in Leeds (Brooker Flynn Architects, 1995); a more recent example is Marks and Spencer's Manchester store (BDP, 2000).

In the 1980s, the first indication that department stores were seeking to recapture some of their lost glamour was the return of the galleried light-well, an architectural device which continued to be closely associated with this building type despite the impact of post-war functionalism. When Whiteley's suffered the fate of many old department stores by being converted into a mall (1989), its well and galleries were restored to their Edwardian glory, minus their original colour. Similar structures, usually doubling as escalator halls, were built in other stores, such as Dickens and Jones on Regent Street. Meanwhile, Mohamed Al Fayed bucked the trend towards cool, light interiors by initiating the extravagant refurbishment of Harrods (begun 1987), in a sumptuous Egyptian style.

More recently, Selfridges has attempted to rejuvenate the department store. As well as refurbishing the Edwardian Oxford Street store, the firm has developed a chain of provincial stores. The most dynamic of these is a landmark building in the Birmingham Bull Ring (Future Systems, 2003). Its bulbous exterior is coated in shining aluminium discs. The curvaceous shape is echoed inside the building, in the noisy atrium and galleries which reinterpret the conventional department store interior. 'Brand cathedrals' such as NikeTown at Oxford Circus (BDP, 1999) are in a similar vein.

Shops and stores are the most ephemeral of all building types. The ultimate architectural fashion victims, their need to remain up-to-date ensures that even the most expensive schemes, by the most renowned architects, have fleeting lifespans.　KAM

Morrison, Kathryn A., *English Shops and Shopping: An Architectural History* (2003)

Shreve, Raymond (1877–1946) Canadian architect, **Harmon, Arthur Loomis** (1878–1958) and **Lamb, William Frederick** (1883–1952) US architects. *See* SKYSCRAPERS.

Sicily Apart from the rock tombs set in the cliffs at Pantàlica, there are few remaining buildings of the original inhabitants, the Sicels, and the architectural history of Sicily begins with the arrival of the Greeks in the 6th century BC.

Sicily was the most prosperous of the Greek colonies. There are substantial remains of temples from the cities of Agrigento and Selinunte (destroyed in 406 and 409 BC respectively). All the temples are of the *Doric order, but compared to the ultimate in Doric refinement, the Parthenon, Athens (447–438 BC), they are very unwieldy. For example the Temple of Olympian Zeus (?480–450 BC), Agrigento, the largest temple ever built in the Doric style, covers an area almost three times that of the Parthenon, and the columns are almost twice as tall (17 m or 56 ft). The impression of gigantic size is reinforced by the 38 atlantides each 7.6 m (25 ft) high, which carried the heavy entablature. Selinunte has five large temples, now mostly in ruins. The only temple surviving from the city of Segesta (c.424–416 BC) is misleadingly primitivist in its rather isolated hilly site, as it was never finished.

Under Roman rule (c.212 BC–AD 476) public architecture was of low priority, with the exception of the amphitheatre (1st century AD) and the theatre (now in ruins) at Tindari. But the splendid mosaics at Piazza Armerina (AD c.320) imply that at the end of this period villa architecture was flourishing.

S. Giorgio, Ragusa Ibla, Sicily
(Rosario Gagliardi, 1744)

The rule of Byzantium (535–827) and Islam (827–1061) brought prosperity, especially to Palermo, but seem to have created no significant buildings, or at least none which have survived. But the Norman rulers (1061–1194) achieved a remarkable synthesis of Christian and Muslim forms in architecture as well as the other arts, in both sacred buildings, e.g. the Cappella Palatina (1131–40) and San Giovanni degli Eremiti with its fine domes, and secular, e.g. the palace of La Zisa (1165–80), all in Palermo. But the only element of the cathedral of Monreale (Palermo, c.1175–89) to survive in its original form, apart from a vast area of mosaics, is the apsidal east end with blind arcading, a distinctly oriental feature. From this period, the only significant building outside Palermo is the cathedral at Cefalù (1131–c.1240), which is entirely Romanesque.

Neither the rule of the Spanish viceroys (from 1415) nor the Renaissance had much impact upon Sicilian architecture. Palermo was relatively untouched by the Baroque, but in the south-east of the island it is a different matter. Much rebuilding followed the earthquake of 1693, resulting in some of the greatest masterpieces of the late Baroque to be found anywhere in Europe. The pre-existing local tradition of the three-arched belfry, rather than the *campanile or the

835

Roman Baroque use of the pediment to crown a façade, gave architects the possibility of dramatically emphasizing the central element in their church designs. Noto was completely rebuilt as a planned town, with the design of churches carefully considered for scenic effect, a tendency carried even further with the work of *Gagliardi at Módica and Ragusa. The topography of central Catania did not offer so many possibilities, yet *Vaccarini succeeded in integrating into curved façades another pre-existing design requirement, the west end nuns' choir or belevedere. On the flat site of Syracuse, such dramatic effects cannot be expected. Even so, the façade of the Cathedral (Andrea Palma, 1728–54) is competently detailed (cf. *Rainaldi's S. Maria in Campitelli). As late as the 1760s, *Ittar designed two Baroque churches in Catania, the last works of more than local significance.   PG

Blunt, A., *Sicilian Baroque* (1968)

signal boxes   British railway signal boxes from the pre-1919 era show distinct regional variations on the basic type of brick base supporting a wooden box, decorated with barge boards and finials. The gradual electrification of Southern Railways (from 1925) and the introduction of colour signalling required a new type of box, a requirement sometimes met by a vaguely modern concrete structure, with an overhanging oval roof. In a later programme of electrification, on the Euston to Birmingham line, the Birmingham New Street signal box (Hamilton and Bicknell, 1964–6) is a *Brutalist masterpiece: banded pre-cast concrete panels are surmounted by a massive slab roof.

Herzog and de Meuron designed two signal boxes at Basel (1994, 1998–9) in which a concrete core is wrapped in copper strips, to protect the electronic equipment inside the box. The latter is a strikingly twisted shape, as it makes the transition from a trapezoidal ground plan, dictated by the site, into a rectangular working area.   PG

Siloé, Diego de   (*c.*1495–1563) Spanish architect and sculptor. His first architectural work was the Escalera Dora, Burgos Cathedral (1519–23), an internal staircase which is the first in Spain to follow a classically monumental form, although it is overloaded with lavish, *Plateresque ornament.

Granada Cathedral (begun 1529) follows a traditional hall-church plan of double aisles, but the Gothic piers are replaced by rich Corinthian columns, clustered to form a compound pier, and raised on high pedestals. The resulting impression is one of great stability, and clearly delineated spaces, de Siloé having considerably minimized the merely decorative emphasis of his earlier works.

The courtyard arcades of the Colegio Fonseca, Salamanca (1529–34), reduce ornament even further. The ground level consists of fluted pilasters articulating slim piers; the flat upper arches are carried by a more robust-looking structure.

His other works include a number of churches, of which the most outstanding is El Salvador, Ubeda (1536–56).   PG

Silsbee, Joseph Lyman   (1848–1913) US architect. *See* WRIGHT, FRANK LLOYD.

Simpson, Archibald   (1790–1847) Scottish architect. Aberdeen's foremost architect of the early 19th century, Simpson, along with John Smith (1781–1852), helped shape the burgeoning 'Granite City', through such Grecian *ensembles* as King Street (1816–30). By 1840 Simpson, like David *Hamilton, had adopted a more florid Classicism, exemplified in his North of Scotland Bank office of 1839–42, with its sumptuous quadrant portico. His country houses included the classical Crimonmogate (1825) and Stracathro (1827), and the Italian villa-style Thainstone (1840).   MGl

Aberdeen Civic Society, *Archibald Simpson* (1978)

Sinan (*c*.1494–1588) Turkish architect. Recruited into the *Ottoman Empire's elite janissary corps, he soon joined the army where he achieved a rapid success. There are few accounts of his life, but clearly he was seen to be a talented engineer. At one point he was chief catapult commander, but he was to build roads, causeways, bridges, and even barges to transport armaments and stores the length of Lake Van in north-eastern Turkey.

Eventually, he was posted to the royal guard with a senior rank and so became known to the Sultan, Süleyman I (r.1520–66) and his viziers. His military career took him all over the empire. He clearly took note of the many monuments. Retiring at age 47 found him working on small mosques, but very soon the Imperial Architect died, leaving no major work behind him, and Sinan was immediately appointed in his place.

Although trained as an engineer, it was Sinan's great achievement to raise Ottoman architecture to a level beyond the expressive but limited structures of civil and military engineering. Yet even long after he was appointed as Architect, his interest in engineering remained undiminished. His epitaph gave pride of place to his bridge at Büyükçekmice (*c*.1566–7) where in 1563 Süleyman had been trapped by floods when hunting. The marshes simply swallowed stone or any foundation. Sinan's solution was to create three great islands across which beautiful arches rise and fall.

The post of Architect was of junior ministerial rank with responsibility for maintaining roads and pavements and all royal buildings, not least Topkapısaray. He had to be expert in ordering supplies of all the materials for new mosques, palaces, and fortifications, and make sure that they arrived on time. Clerks kept detailed accounts for marble columns, lead for roofing, and every saddlebag and nail, quite apart from wages.

He was a managerial genius and a perfectionist. One example is the catalogue compiled throughout the empire, in every byway as well as public places, of all the marble or stone columns and capitals from the past. Exact measurements, the type of marble, from porphyry to limestone, its colour and condition: thus future architects had a vital guide, while the columns themselves, buried in soft earth, awaited their new functions.

He had 70 students who, after graduation as architects, were set to work from his plans to build a mass of monuments in Anatolia and elsewhere in the empire, many of which are attributed to him although he could never have seen them. A good example is the Muradiye Mosque at Manesa (north-east of Izmir, completed *c*.1586), where problems with the steep hillside brought architects back to consult, and produced a mosque like none other.

In Constantinople itself, Sinan's first large-scale work was the Şehzade complex (1543–8), which included a mosque, courtyard, and türbe. In his own words an 'apprentice work', it almost solves the problem of creating a large (about 40 m or 131 ft square) centralized space under the mosque dome. His aim was to create a space in which as many of the worshippers as possible could see the *mihrab and follow the imam during prayer.

At the Süleymaniye complex (mosque completed 1550–57), he organized a much larger space (58.5 × 57.5 m, or 192 × 188½ ft) with great confidence, by placing the buttresses of the piers in the walls. The mosque was at the centre of many buildings (including a hospital, madrasas, and shops), which are a union of style and function, sensitively placed on the site. The four minarets are placed with classical symmetry, so that the whole complex dominates the city when seen from below.

He could also work at a smaller scale (10 m or 33 ft square) in the Sokullu Mehmet Paşa mosque (1571–2), in which the delicacy of his invention matches the finest Iznik tile wall ever created.

But Sinan's greatest mosque was that of Süleyman's son, Selim II (r.1566–74) at Edirne (1569–75). Like many cathedrals, its great dome and four minarets, over 70 m (230 ft) tall, can be seen from afar when approaching the town, more especially from Greece. The essence of its beauty lies in the logic of its structure and its play of light and shade throughout the day. The width of the space under the dome equals that of the *Byzantine Hagia Sophia, but there is more than technical achievement. The dome is supported by eight enormous piers, set into the walls, so that the space under the dome remains free. This space is ingeniously organized, so that the *mihrab is recessed in a dramatic manner, and brilliantly lit by the glowing colours of the tile panels. Ottoman architecture had reached its climax, a worthy rival to its Byzantine forerunner.   GG

Necipoglu, G., *The Age of Sinan: architectural culture of the Ottoman Empire* (2005)
Kuran, Aptullah, *Sinan* (1987)

Singapore

Singapore   From 1819 to 1867 Singapore was a trading post of the British East India Company. Many of the earliest buildings were constructed by migrants from China and India and include Fuk Tak Ch'i Temple (1835) and Sri Mariamman Temple (1843). One of the oldest surviving architect-designed buildings is the Armenian Church (1835) by G. D. Coleman.

In 1867 Singapore became a Crown Colony. The Singapore Cricket Club (1888) and Raffles Hotel (1886) were the focus of colonial life. Both had substantial additions designed by Swan and MacLaren. Buildings erected for Chinese entrepreneurs included the Tan Yeok Nee House (1885). Several dignified civic buildings were constructed including City Hall (1926–9) by A. Gordon and F. D. Meadows. Modernism arrived in the 1930s and is exemplified by Kallang Airport (1937) by the Public Works Department.

In 1959 the island achieved self-government and in 1965 became an independent sovereign state. The National Trades Union Congress Conference Hall (1961–5) designed by the Malayan Architects Co-Partnership, People's Park Complex (1970–73) by Design Partnership, and Jurong Town Hall (1970) by Architects Team 3 all expressed the spirit of the time.

I. M. *Pei's appointment as designer for the OCBC Tower (1975) marked the beginning of a trend to commission foreign architects for major projects. The Colonnade (1985) by Paul Rudolph, Singapore Indoor Stadium (1990) by Kenzô *Tange, and Temasek Polytechnic (1995) represent the architecture of this period. Resistance to the influx of foreign firms came from William Lim with Tampines North Community Centre (1989) and Tay Kheng Soon with Kandang Kerbau Hospital (1988–97).   RP

Powell, R(obert), *Singapore Architecture: A Short History* (2003)

Siren, Heikki and Kaija

Siren, Heikki (1918–) and **Kaija** (1920–) husband and wife Finnish architects, whose blend of modernist and classicist principles made a unique contribution to post-1945 Finnish Modernism.

Buildings that exemplify this remarkable approach include the Kotontie Terrace Housing, Tapiola (1954), the Concert Hall, Lahti (1954), the Conference Palace for Baghdad, Iraq (1984), and, most notably, the Chapel for the Technical University, Otaniemi (1957), where architecture, nature, and spirituality are one, an achievement on a par with *Le Corbusier's Ronchamp. The architects' own Private Retreat on the Island of Ingonso (1966) confirms the correspondence between Japanese and Finnish minimalism in the interpretation of nature.   MQ

Siren, John Sigfrid ('Jukka')

Siren, John Sigfrid ('Jukka') (1889–1961) Finnish architect, whose reputation rests on a single, monumental building: the Finnish Parliament Building,

Helsinki (1927–31), a celebration of the Nordic Classic Style. Its giant entry columns hint at impending National Socialism, clearly at odds with Finland's new freedom and independence. Every detail of architecture, furniture, and sculpture freezes Finland's first democratic assembly into a theatre of pretension. It was born out of its time and style, because his contemporary Alvar *Aalto was already turning to Modernism.   MQ

Siza, Álvaro (Álvaro Joaquim Melo Siza Viera) (1933–) Portuguese architect. His earliest work was in a traditional *Regionalist vein and includes four private houses (1954–7), a parish centre (1956), and the Carneiro de Melo House (1957–8) in Mantosinhos. His unadorned, minimalist, exposed concrete in the Boa Nova Tea House (1958–63), situated along the Atlantic Coast in Leça de Palmeira, is the first in a series of works that follow the example of Alvar Aalto's 'geological' manner, rather than vernacular-based regionalist Säynätsalo City Hall (1949–52). They break down the usual single building mass into distinct units with mono-pitched roofs linked by stepped paths and platforms and exhibiting a remarkable sculptural sensitivity to the irregular, terraced site. His Ocean Swimming Pool in Leça de Palmeira (1961–6) and his Rocha Ribeiro House in Maia (1962–9) are also designed as aggregates of exposed concrete structures, remarkably well integrated into the shifting levels of the topography. From the early 1970s on, he received a large number of housing commissions which he also carried out with vernacular references. His first projects, the Bouça housing quarter (1973–7) and the São Victor District Rehabilitation (1974–7), both in Porto for the national housing association, followed in the wake of the revolution in Portugal in 1974. They were carried out with the participation of the inner city's residents' association, and based on the *ilha*, a kind of housing typical of traditional Porto. The white

stucco and patios of his 2-storeyed houses in Quinta da Malagueira Residential District (Evora, 1977–1995), also recalling the local vernacular, form a new residential district with 30,000 inhabitants. His first major foreign housing commission was for a mixed-use commercial housing project, the Corner Building, Elders' Club, and Kindergarten (Kreuzberg, Berlin, 1980–84, 1986–8) followed by the Residential Settlement in Schilderswijk in The Hague, Netherlands (1989). In 1988 he received the first of his high profile, monumental commissions, starting with the Oporto Faculty of Architecture (1987–93), in which he once more took up the fragmented articulation of the building elements of his early works, and then the granite-clad Galician Centre of Contemporary Art in Santiago de Compostela (1988–95). These were followed by his Portuguese Pavilion in Lisbon (1996–8), with its long-span reinforced concrete canopy, and the never-completed Stedelijk Museum (1995).   AT

Frampton, K., *Álvaro Siza: Complete Works* (2000)
Testa, P., *Álvaro Siza* (1996)

Skidmore, Louis (1897–1962), Owings, Nathaniel Alexander (1903–84), and Merrill, John Ogden (1896–1975) US architects, who formed SOM in 1936, the very model of US corporate Modernism. Following the business model of large integrated teams, SOM offered a complete service, to deal with all aspects of building, from architectural design, engineering, and structures to interior design and the use of graphics, ironically enough re-assuming roles divested by architects a half-century before in their quest for professional respectability. Within about twenty years of its foundation, SOM had offices in four different cities (in turn, Chicago, New York, San Francisco, and Portland, Oregon), with over 1,000 employees, at a time when a 'large' European office numbered about 30 staff.

Faculty of Architecture,
Oporto University, Portugal
(Alvaro Siza, 1987–93)

Its architectural reputation and approach to design was established by Lever House, New York (1952), designed by Gordon Bunshaft. A glass box of the kind that *Mies van der Rohe yearned to build, it was a design of great simplicity and elegance: a lower podium, relatively in scale with the street, its pilotis opening up the space to pedestrians, lay at the base of a curtain wall of aluminium and plate glass. It was the first successful 'glass box', without setbacks, so different in profile from most previous skyscrapers. It was an easy formula to vulgarize, especially once the temptation to thrust far beyond the modest 21 storeys of the original was embraced by other architectural firms.

However, SOM itself continued to experiment with structures, using reinforced concrete (e.g. the Hartford Building, Chicago, 1971), or a method of using tubular forms which allowed the construction of very tall buildings, such as the 442 m (1,450 ft) high Sears Tower, Chicago (1974). The firm's output has continued unabated, adapting tall office buildings to hot climates (the National Commercial Bank, Jeddah, 1981–4), but as the Broadgate and Canary Wharf developments in London (1990s) show, with perhaps less sensitivity to local context.   PG

skyscrapers first appeared in New York during the mid 1870s. The development of the fireproofed metal supporting skeleton, however, took place in Chicago during the 1880s (*see* CHICAGO SCHOOL), beginning with the Home Insurance Building (1884–5). It obviated the need for load-bearing walls, and so fulfilled the new demand in the city for flexible office spaces filled with natural light. In the Tacoma Building (1885, 1887–9), *Holabird and Roche refined the skeleton with terracotta cladding as a system, allowing more light. Louis *Sullivan made the skyscraper a 'proud and soaring thing' with energetic verticals and distinctive nature-inspired ornament. He linked his Wainwright

Building (1891) in St Louis and Guaranty Building (1896) in Buffalo with American democratic ideals.

By 1896, the Chicago innovations (*see* BURNHAM AND ROOT) were fully incorporated into New York building practice with Bruce Price's 92 m (303 ft) American Surety Building (1894–6), supported throughout by a riveted and portal-braced steel skeleton. Within a decade, New York-based corporations were competing for height with conspicuous trademark towers. Cass *Gilbert's 55-storey, 241 m (792 ft) Woolworth Building (1910–13) surpassed the 186 m (612 ft) Singer Tower (Ernest *Flagg, 1906–8) as the tallest in the world and epitomized the 'skyscraper Gothic' style.

New York's Zoning Resolution of 1916 engendered setback forms that during the 1920s distinguished the city as the world's representative modern metropolis. The steel frame underwent simplification and refinement as a system of construction. The Chrysler Building (William Van Alen, 1928–9) featured gargoyles inspired by hood ornaments, friezes of hubcaps, and a chrome-nickel steel 'vertex' and stainless steel spire; it exemplified the era's delight in Art Deco urban theatrics. But the Empire State Building, at 85 storeys and 378 m (1,239 ft) (Shreve, Lamb, and Harmon and H. G. Balcom, 1929–31) surpassed the Chrysler, and with a chrome-nickel steel 'mooring mast' exploited the advertising potentials of the world's newest record for height.

The skyscrapers of the 1950s, built after the hiatus following the Depression and World War II, fulfilled the new demand for open work environments with fluorescently lit, column-free interiors. Prestige office buildings such as the Lever House (*Skidmore, Owings, and Merrill, 1951–2) were sheathed with exquisite glass curtain walls and sited in plazas as objects within the city. The Seagram Building (*Mies van der Rohe, 1954–8), a finely proportioned volume poised above a piercingly empty plaza, had elevations featuring I-beams of bronze. It projected a glamorous and timeless image of modern corporate life.

To create still larger column-free interiors in skyscrapers of great height, engineers developed the 'hollow tube' conceptual model for structural design in the early 1960s. The World Trade Centre's twin 110-storey towers in New York (Yamasaki *et al.*, 1962–76, destroyed 2001) at 415 and 417 m (1,362 and 1,368 ft) set a new record. New permutations of the hollow tube appeared in the John Hancock Centre and Sears Tower, both in Chicago (Fazlur Khan, SOM, 1965–70, 1968–74). The Sears Tower, a bundled cluster of nine tubes that successively diminish in height as they rise to 110 storeys and 443 m (1,454 ft), claimed the title of world's tallest and reinstated Chicago as a centre of innovative skyscraper design.

Outside the United States, the skyscraper serves as the most visible marker of modernity and the desire for recognition within the global marketplace. The 452 m (1,483 ft) Petronas Towers in Kuala Lumpur, Malaysia (Cesar *Pelli with Thornton-Tomasetti, 1993–7), at completion the world's tallest, create a distinctive skyline signature for the city.   GF

Goldberger, P., *The Skyscraper* (1981)

Landau, S.B., and Condit, C., *Rise of the New York Skyscraper 1865–1913* (1996)

Willis, C., *Form Follows Finance* (1995)

slate A fine-grained rock which can easily be split into thin slabs, to be used as a roof or wall covering. It was used in England for roofs from the 12th century, and perhaps a little later in France, where it was used much more adventurously for curves and sometimes at an almost vertical pitch. Welsh slate can be set on roofs at a very low pitch (22–26 degrees). Hence, from the middle of the 18th century, it held great appeal for architects, who often preferred to hide their roofs, an awkward element of a classicizing design, behind a parapet.

Slate is an unjustly neglected material in modern buildings, an honourable exception being the Maritime Museum, Falmouth (M. J. Long, 2002), where grey-green Delabole-type slates are used in the traditional manner: the courses diminish in size from the cornice to the roof line.   PG

Slovenia was dominated by Romanesque (Church in Sticna, 1156) and Gothic architecture (13th-century houses in Piran and Koper, and the Cathedral in Koper). The Renaissance flourished in the coastal region.

Franciscan and Ursulin churches, and the Cathedral in Ljubljana, with the manor in Dornava (17th century) gave Slovenia a Baroque image. Private houses in Ljubljana, Maribor, Koper, and Piran are examples of Classicism.

Historicism in the 19th century was interrupted by the arrival from Vienna to Ljubljana of Maks Fabiani, Jože *Plečnik, and Janez Jager. Fabiani's work possessed a strict architectural expression.

Jože Plečnik (1872–1957) dominated Slovene architecture for 50 years, but his influence has left his successors in an isolated position vis-à-vis the Modern Movement.

Ivan Vurnik was preoccupied with the vernacular (workers' housing, Maribor), whilst Vladimir Šubic's 'Skyscraper' (1933) and Stanko Rohrman's Hotel Slon (1937), both in Ljubljana, were characterized by commercial Modernism.

The Modernism of the National Assembly (Vinko Glanz), the Press Centre (Branko Kocmut) in Ljubljana, and Hotel Slavija (Milan Cernigoj) in Maribor have a 'revisionist' flavour.

Slovene architecture now follows general European trends.   PT

Smirke, Sir Robert (1780–1867) English architect. Training under George *Dance, junior led Smirke to the Royal Academy Schools and a Grand Tour (1801–5). He published his extensive record of the Morea as *Specimens of Continental Architecture* (1806). Well connected, he was soon designing houses for Sir Robert Peel. As an official in the Office of Works from 1813, he was commissioned to design the British Museum, London (1823–46), his best-known work. His extensive private practice included county halls for Gloucestershire (1814–16), Herefordshire (1815–17), and Perthshire (1815–19) and clubs such as the United Services Club, Westminster (1817–19, destroyed). This success owed more to his professional thoroughness and reliability than any unusual flair in design. His technical ability was manifest in his use of concrete foundations and load-bearing iron beams. As a result of this he was often commissioned to complete buildings that were beyond the competence of the architects who had designed them. In public buildings he favoured the classical Greek style, repeating ad nauseam the Ionic order of the temple on the Illisus. By contrast his country houses were less set in a classical straitjacket, some being castellated, like Eastnor Castle, Herefordshire (1812–20), others Tudor or Jacobean, like Cultoquhey House, Perthshire (*c.*1820), and Drayton Manor, Staffordshire (1831–5).   APQ

Smirke, Sydney (1798–1877) English architect. Brother of Sir Robert Smirke, 'Little Syd' was trained by him and later assisted him. His independent works, generally in a pleasing classical or Italianate style, include Shoreham Custom House (later Town Hall), Sussex (1830); portico and domes of Bethlehem Hospital (later Imperial War Museum), Lambeth, London (1838–40); The Rocks, Uckfield, Sussex (1838); the Conservative Club, Westminster (1843–5, with George Basevi); St John, Loughton, Essex (1846); Reading Room, British Museum, London (1852–7); Brookwood cemetery, Surrey (1854, with William Tite); Dr Johnson's Building, Inner Temple, London

(1857–8); and King Edward's School, Wormley, Surrey (1867).   APQ

Smith, Francis (1672–1738) and **William** (1661–1724) Brothers, English architects, and builders. Pre-eminent among architect-craftsmen, Francis Smith became named 'of Warwick' thanks to his and William's rebuilding of Warwick after the fire of 1694. As a thoroughly reliable builder, he established an immense practice working on country houses, many to his own design, such as Chicheley Hall, Buckinghamshire (1719–25), and Sutton Scarsdale, Derbyshire (1719–24).   APQ

Smithson, Alison (1928–93) and **Peter Denham** (1923–2007) Husband and wife English architects and theorists, who formed a professional partnership in 1950. The Smithsons played a leading role in the theoretical debates over Modernism in the 1950s and 1960s, with their books *Ordinariness and Light* (1970) and *Without Rhetoric* (1973).

Their completed work had a curiously staccato character, as if every design embodied quite a different approach. Each design would be widely acclaimed, but did not lead to any further commissions of the same type. The partnership won the competition for Smithdon School, Hunstanton, Norfolk (1951–4), with a design all too obviously inspired by *Mies van der Rohe: a steel frame with exposed corner detailing. A harsh and noisy environment, laid out on a purely formal plan, the scheme is an architect's self-indulgence, particularly compared to the contemporary programme of the Hertfordshire *schools.

Much of their theoretical writing was concerned with the relationship between architecture and the city. Unfortunately, the Smithsons had only one opportunity to design buildings *and* their surroundings, but the result is a masterpiece: the *Economist* buildings, St James's, London (1962–4). The three hexagonal towers

are not only interesting in themselves, because
of the texture of their Portland roach cladding and the
integration of the service cores into the main building,
but because of the interlocking external spaces they
create.

Almost twenty years after they had put forward
the idea, the Smithsons had the opportunity of creating
'streets in the sky', at the Robin Hood Gardens Estate,
London (1972). In each of the two long parallel blocks
there were 'streets' on every third floor. But because of
the rapid deterioration of the exposed concrete finishes,
the buildings' grim exteriors cannot be redeemed
by the 'street' layout.   PG

Smythson, Robert (1534/5–1614) English
architect; trained as a stonemason, but the first English
architect to be so described. Smythson first emerges by
name with four masons in 1568 at Longleat, Wiltshire,
where Sir John Thynne was building from 1547; by
1575 Smythson had recast the house as an exemplar of
exuberant symmetrical Elizabethan taste. In 1580 he
began Wollaton Hall, Nottinghamshire (completed in
1588), which combines the romantic chivalry of a castle
with vigorous massing and Mannerist detail. Stylistic
attributions include Worksop Manor (c.1575,
burnt 1761); Hardwick Hall, Derbyshire (1590–97);
Barlborough Hall, Derbyshire (1583); and Worksop
Manor Lodge, Nottinghamshire (c.1594–5).   APQ

Soane, Sir John (1753–1837) English architect. The
son of an obscure bricklayer, Soane rose to become
Surveyor (in reality, architect) to the Bank of England
by the age of 35, and by the last decade of his life was
the senior figure of the architectural profession.

In 1768 he joined the office of the architect
George *Dance, junior (1741–1825). Although his
precise role within Dance's office is unknown, Soane
worked on commissions such as Pitzhanger Manor and
Newgate Gaol.

Soane then (1772) moved to the office of Henry
Holland, and five years later was awarded the Gold
Medal of the Royal Academy and a three-year travel
scholarship. In March 1778 he set off for Italy, via Paris.
First-hand experience of the monuments of classical
antiquity, across southern France, Rome, and in the
Grecian outposts of southern Italy and Sicily, was a
revelation; he also studied the architecture and
engineering of every period as he travelled through
France, Switzerland, and Italy.

Returning home (1780) in the expectation of a
lucrative commission from the Bishop of Derry (the 4th
Earl of Bristol), Soane found himself summarily
dismissed without payment or apology by his mercurial
patron. At first he was forced to depend on small
commissions, but quickly built up an enviable country
house practice. Up to this point Soane's architecture
was confidently neoclassical, in the mainstream mould
of late Georgian country house architects from Holland
himself to James *Wyatt or James *Paine.

His career now took a dramatic turn when, owing to
his City of London connections, he was commissioned
to remodel the Bank of England. Events in France were
unfolding which placed the Bank of England at the
heart of national life, beyond palaces and parliaments.

The Bank had a complex and continually changing
set of requirements. Soane's brilliance was to embellish
the plan continually in an effective and functional way.
He designed public banking halls and private offices,
passages and vestibules, and rebuilt Robert *Taylor's
drum-shaped Rotunda (1794–5), articulating his
impressive Pantheon-like structure with lunettes,
top-lighting and niches around the walls. At the very
heart of the site was Lothbury Court, above the storage
vaults for gold bullion. Here he designed a massive
*triumphal arch (1798–9), modelled on the Arch of
Constantine in Rome. The entire site was wrapped
by screen walls, massive and unpierced. Soane's belief
in an *architecture parlante, a classical architecture

The 3% Consols Office, Bank of England, City of London (Sir John Soane, 1799)

which expressed its purpose, was epitomized at the Bank.

Solutions worked out in early phases of work at the Bank or for himself were applied to houses designed for two Prime Ministers and a roll-call of leading figures in national life, in innovative public buildings such as Dulwich Picture Gallery (1811–14), and the Infirmary and other additions to Wren's Royal Chelsea Hospital (1809 onwards), and later in various departments of state, including the Law Courts attached to Westminster Hall (1824).

The Soane family, with their two sons John and George, moved into a new house at 12 Lincoln's Inn Fields in 1792. This house, and later its neighbours at nos. 13 and 14, were together to become Soane's 'laboratory' in which he continually refined and reworked his increasingly idiosyncratic architectural vocabulary. Almost every motif in his repertoire can be found in the confined yet extraordinary spaces of a pair of London terraced houses successively transformed

over half a life-time. Classical detail in his hands was stripped down to essentials, even inverted (as in his famous grooved pilaster strips), while his desire to suffuse interiors with overhead natural light led him to attenuate structure, to the point at which it appears to be legerdemain. The vaulting which floats overhead in his exquisite mirrored breakfast room at no. 13 Lincoln's Inn Fields almost suggests weightlessness.

In 1800 he also acquired Pitzhanger Manor, where he had worked for Dance; here he transformed a modest country villa behind an elevation in the form of a triumphal arch. Soane believed passionately in the hierarchies and absolutes of the classical canon, expounding his ideas in the lectures he gave at the Royal Academy after his appointment as Professor of Architecture in 1806.

When Soane could not build he turned to print. He designed on paper a triumphal route through London, linking the monarch to parliament, and published a steady stream of volumes under his name from youth to old age, often righting the wrongs he felt he had suffered. His legacy has proved difficult to estimate, but paradoxically his work has become increasingly influential in recent years. John Soane demonstrated that an architectural language thoroughly understood can become the basis for reinterpretation, even improvisation, within the guidelines of that vocabulary. GMD

Darley, G., *John Soane; An Accidental Romantic* (1999)

soffit The underside of any architectural element, such as an arch (when it is called an intrados), architrave, or lintel. In classical architecture, the soffit of a Greek Doric cornice was usually decorated with little more than guttae, but in Roman usage this was greatly elaborated. The soffits of arches in Early Christian and Byzantine architecture were often decorated with plaster patterns or symbols or might be finished in mosaic. APQ

solar The medieval term for a domestic upper chamber or bower, intended for private use. Unlike a bower, which might be detached, it was often built adjacent to an open hall or another room, and could equally be above service rooms or ground-floor chambers, or the uppermost room in a tower. APQ

Solari, Santino (1576–1646) Italian-born architect and sculptor, active in Austria. He is known for two particular works, which are sometimes regarded as important in transplanting the early Baroque north of the Alps. Schloss Hellbrunn, near Salzburg (1613–19), is definitely post-Gothic, with its symmetrical plan, clearly marked string courses, and a horizontal orientation. The influential Salzburg Cathedral (1614–28) has a *basilica plan, one of the first successful uses of the tall drum / dome combination outside Italy, and twin towers. PG

Soleri, Paolo (1919–) A visionary and experimental Italian-born architect, artist, bell-maker, and radical urban theorist, who introduced a concept termed 'Arcology' (Architecture and Ecology). His first major building was a ceramics factory at Vietri-sul-Mare, Italy (1953). In the USA he designed an experimental Dome House (with Mark Mills), before commencing designs for earth- and silt-based structures at the Cosanti Foundation, Scottsdale, Arizona. His 'Mesa City' project and a series of experimental bridge designs led to the development of his principles of Arcology, culminating in the creation of his experimental city, Arcosanti, Cordes Junction, Arizona, and the publication of *Arcology: The City in the Image of Man* (1960). DS

Solomonic (Salomonic) **column** A spirally fluted or shaped column, commonly believed to derive from Solomon's Temple. First in use in about 1300 in Italy, for example on the façade of Orvieto Cathedral, Bernini famously supported his baldacchino (1626–33) in St Peter's, Rome, on four giant Solomonic columns, thus paving the way for their general use in Baroque churches. APQ

SOM *See* SKIDMORE, OWINGS, AND MERRILL.

Sommaruga, Giuseppe (1869–1917) Italian architect. His Palazzo Castiglioni, Milan (1901–3), is one of the leading examples of the Stile Liberty (*see also* NEO-LIBERTY), sometimes confused with Art Nouveau, with which it does not have much in common. Sommaruga loaded a rather conventional flat-fronted 7-bay façade with an abundance of coarsely sculpted contorted human figures over the entrance and above the windows of the *piano nobile*. He built a series of villas for the Milanese bourgeoisie, one of which, the Palazzino Comi (1906), showed a more promising façade design, with a considerable reduction in ornament and a massing of cubic forms.   PG

See SANT-ELIA.

Sonck, Lars (1870–1956) Finnish architect. From 1894 he created a highly personal, modern idiom in timber architecture, partly drawing on the vernacular tradition. In unison with the prevailing patriotically tuned movement in all the arts in Finland, he turned to Finnish medieval monuments as one source for his large-scale projects from 1900 onwards. His Tampere Cathedral (1900–07), with a rough-hewn granite exterior, is one of the key monuments of its era in the whole Nordic realm. Here the medieval ingredients are fused with current influence from Art Nouveau and Jugendstil. During the next five years Sonck designed a series of buildings for Helsinki which lie at the heart of the so-called Finnish *National Romantic period, including the Privatbanken premises (1904), Eira Hospital (1904), and the Telephone Exchange Company Building (1905). Like most leading Finnish architects, Sonck abandoned the medievalist overtones and the picturesque effects abruptly around 1905. His Kallio Church (1906–12) was rigidly axial and symmetrical. A similar tendency is evident in the Mortgage Society Building (1908) and the Stock Exchange Building (1911), both applying a smooth granite surface combined with classicist features.   PKO

Korvenmaa, P., *Innovation versus Tradition* (1991)

Soufflot, Jacques Germain (1713–80) French architect, pioneer of neoclassicism. Settling in Lyon in the 1740s, he developed a private practice (which produced Hôtels Denis and Parent, and Châteaux La Rivette, Bourbon, Oullins), and was commissioned to design the vast Hôtel Dieu (1741) and the Loge du Change (1747). If the latter is Palladian in precept but Mannerist in detail, the former is Baroque in scale but restrained in ornament, classical in its extended horizontals but fashionably French in its central pavilion.

In 1751 Soufflot was called on to accompany the future Marquis de Marigny, director-general of royal buildings, on his formative trip to Italy. On his return Soufflot lectured on classical theory, Gothic structure, Baroque techniques, and archaeological excavation, and applied his knowledge of the innovative royal theatre at Turin to the design of the free-standing Lyon Opéra (1754). Summoned to Paris by Marigny—for whom he had worked at Roule and Menars—he was appointed controller of the royal works (1756) and admitted to the Academy. His most important building is Sainte-Geneviève (now the Panthéon, 1757–90) where he revived Greek Doric in the crypt, developed *Perrault's experiments in basilican trabeation for the main volume—uniting Gothic lightness with the *noble simplicité* of the Greeks to the satisfaction of the *Enlightenment—and referred to Wren's St Paul's in London for the controversial dome.   CT

South Africa *See* AFRICA (SOUTH AFRICA).

Soviet Union, Russia (1917–91). The chaos of war (1914–17), revolution (1917), and Civil War (1918–20) meant that there was virtually no new building during this period, a situation which barely altered with the partial revival of the economy following the introduction of the New Economic Policy (1921). For the time being, the unprecedented opportunities for rational city planning and mass housing provided by the decree of 20 August 1918, abolishing the right to private ownership in landed property, remained unutilized.

But for the first seven years of the new regime, there was an outpouring of formal innovation in sculpture, graphic designs, and theatre sets. All these experiments focused on abstract forms, liberated from decorative or

847

historic precedents, with an emphasis on regular shapes lying in different planes, so as to give an impression of multiple perspectives. Typical of the discrepancy between utopian striving and harsh reality was Tatlin's Monument to the Third International (1919), built as a model only 2 m (6.5 ft) high, but intended to reach 400 m (1,312 ft).

Could these formal experiments be the basis for real architecture? The question was first answered by the *Vesnin brothers, then by the other supporters of *Constructivism. Their first two projects, the Moscow Palace of Labour competition (1923) and the Leningrad Pravda office (1924), were unexecuted, but highly influential. Using reinforced concrete and glass, the Vesnins created a building rather like a stage set, in which basic geometric forms are combined with symbols of new technology, such as radio masts and docking ports for airships.

The Vesnins were joined by the leading theorist of Constructivism, Moisei *Ginzburg, author of its leading text *Style and Epoch* (1924), which advocated using modern technology and mass production to create new types of space for new social tasks. The next seven years were intellectually dominated by Constructivists, although they did not have many opportunities to build, other than: the *workers' clubs; buildings by the Vesnins; the *Izvestia* building, Moscow (Barkhin, 1925–27); and the planetarium, Moscow (Barshch and Siniavskii, 1927–9). These buildings are the purest type of Constructivism, embodying basic geometric forms (the circle, the cylinder), whereas the more straightforwardly functional type is represented by Ginzburg's Narkomfin apartment house, Moscow (1928–30). Outside Moscow and Leningrad, there are significant works in Kharkov (the State Industry building, by Serafimov *et al.*, 1926–8), and Sverdlovsk city centre. Although *Melnikov was not formally associated with the Constructivists, his work showed a similar interest in abstract forms.

Constructivist architecture was widely admired by the European avant-garde. During this period there were not only frequent contacts between Soviet architects and the outside world, but at least two architects, Mendelsohn and Le Corbusier, had designs realized in the Soviet Union.

The former's Red Banner textile factory, Moscow (1925–7), is rather a conventional exercise using the rounded corners later to be familiar in his store designs, but Le Corbusier's Tsentrosoiuz, Moscow (Central Union of Consumers' Co-Operative, 1929–36) was altogether more ambitious. The planned technology of circulating heated or cooled air within the double glazing of the façade was far too advanced for European, let alone Soviet, industry at this period. The interior shows a surprising application of the *promenade architecturale*, following a series of spiral ramps.

The crucial event marking the end of the dominance of Constructivism was the Palace of Soviets competition, Moscow (announced 1931). Leading European architects were invited to enter, but in the middle of 1933 the project was awarded to a team led by Boris Iofan. A stepped-back structure rising to 315 m (1,033 ft) was to be surmounted by a 100 m (328 ft) tall statue of Lenin. By 1940, construction of the lowest stage, a steel frame, had begun, but with the onset of war the megalomaniac structure was abandoned.

The main reason for the sudden eclipse of Constructivism after about 1932 was that its forms were too abstract for a state which wished to celebrate the economic and political successes of the First Five Year Plan (completed 1932). Undoubtedly this was the key factor at the time, but it should it also be remembered that the Constructivist buildings suffered from a number of shortcomings. Most were poorly finished; those like the Narkinform flats which experimented with new communal ways of living were perhaps too much ahead of their time; and most Constructivist architecture paid little attention to site or context.

Structure of the inner crossing, the Panthéon, Paris (Jacques-Germain Soufflot, 1757–90)

However, the uninventive Classicism of the period 1932–55, even that labelled as 'proletarian *Classicism' by its proponents, such as Ivan Fomin (1872–1936), was in purely architectural terms a disappointing successor. At that time, the only society in the world which was in a position to implement the social agenda of *Modernism on a large scale actually took a great step backwards artistically by adopting pre-capitalist architectural forms.

The first sign of the new trend, Zholtovsky's apartment house on Mokhovaya Street, Moscow (1933–4), was a slightly larger, otherwise entirely literal version of Palladio's Loggia del Capitanio (1571). On a much larger scale, the main library of the Soviet Union, the Lenin Library, Moscow (Schuko and Gelfreikh, 1928–40), was not a literal copy, but a monumental exercise in stripped Classicism. But it is important not to exaggerate the importance of this trend, since relatively few buildings of this type were built by the end of the 1930s. In fact the most significant achievements of this period are the factories designed by Albert *Kahn, the epitome of functionalism, and the opulent *metro stations built in a variety of historical styles.

The architecture of the period from the end of World War II to the collapse of the Soviet Union is not well documented, and compared to the brief efflorescence of Constructivism has been almost entirely overlooked by critics and architects in the West, possibly motivated by political prejudice.

The devastation of World War II meant that mass housing was an urgent priority. For almost a decade new housing had to yield to other priorities, industrial and military. However, resources could still be found for prestige buildings, such as the seven landmark buildings located at key points in Moscow (1947ff.), including the new buildings of the Moscow State University on the Lenin Hills (Rudnev et al., 1949–53). Technically they were more advanced, but visually were crass, rather similar to the Woolworth Building, New York (see GILBERT, CASS).

From 1948 the Industrial Construction Bureau, directed by the engineer Vitaly Lagutenko with the involvement of the architect Mikhaily Posokhin, began to research methods of *prefabrication, using standardized components. At first, this approach was adopted on a mass scale for factories, but not for housing. The application of these methods to housing began at the end of the 1950s and continued until the collapse of the Soviet Union. The first schemes (from 1961) were 5 storeys high, built with a very small range of identical rectangular standard units. By the mid 1970s, as in the Yasenevo estate, Moscow for 220,000 residents (Belopolsky et al., 1975), many blocks reached 22–25 storeys, and used a much wider range of units.

The Soviet housing experiment was a success unmatched anywhere else in the world, in terms of efficiency, because of the scale of production, and social justice, in providing very cheap basic accommodation for the working class. However, the difficult, purely architectural problems of avoiding drabness and monotony when operating under these design constraints, and of providing internal spaces which were imaginatively designed as well as functional, were usually not confronted. It was only possible to overcome the monotony of such huge complexes of standard designs when the terrain itself was distinctive enough to offer the opportunity of *picturesque siting, such as by an artificial lake or on a slope or knoll.

In the purely architectural sphere of public buildings (clubs, congress buildings, theatres, sports buildings), monumentalism was abandoned in favour of a rather low-key Modernism. The leading architect of Soviet Modernism, Mikhail Posokhin, established his position with the Moscow Palace of Congresses (1961; now the State Kremlin Palace), an innocuous glass and concrete box, inserted not too insensitively into its historical context.

Hotels and sports complexes showed the most distinctive approach to architecture. The first of the new type of *hotels was the Rossiya Hotel, Moscow (Chechulin, 1962–9), like others of its type, difficult to distinguish from contemporary hotels elsewhere. By 1980 the Izmailovo, five 30-storey buildings, was then the largest hotel in Europe. The state's commitment to sports buildings meant that there were fewer restrictions on costs, and some of the most interesting modernist designs are for sports stadia, such as the Central Lenin stadium, Moscow (Vlasov *et al.*, 1955–6). The soaring lines of the Velotrek bicycle-racing stadium, Krylatskoe, Moscow (Voronina *et al.*, 1978–9), are made possible by a complex steel frame roof structure. But, perhaps as a sign of the regime's weakening self-confidence, from the end of the 1970s many prestige schemes were carried out by foreign firms and their architects.

During this period, the social achievements of mass housing and certain types of civic building were not matched by high architectural quality. Even the best Soviet buildings gained little recognition abroad, unlike their Constructivist predecessors. Ironically, it is many of the latter which have been destroyed or dismantled in the newly capitalist Russia. PG

Ikonnikov, A., *Russian Architecture of the Soviet Period* (1988)

space Pre-modernist architects and theorists used the term quite prosaically as a synonym for 'volume' or 'void'. However, 'space' became a defining concept of most versions of Modernism by appropriating a philosophical category, the Kantian notion that space is a transcendent aesthetic category. It was in this sense that 'space' became one of the central concepts of the orthodox version of Modernism, beginning with *Loos ('The Principle of Cladding', 1898) and formalized by Sigfried Giedion, the spokesman of the abstract, formalizing tendency within Modernism (*see* CIAM; MODERNISM), in his book *Space, Time and Architecture* (1941).

The pioneer of the modernist concept of space was Gottfried *Semper in his book *Der Stil* (1860–63; translated as *Style in the Technical or Tectonic Arts, or Practical Aesthetics*, 2004). He argued that the purpose of structures, such as walls, was formally to represent and make visible the enclosed space, as space 'in itself', a mental construct. The versatility of the concept derives from its twofold meaning in German, the language of most of the early theorists of Modernism. 'Raum' can signify both a material enclosure ('a room') or a philosophical idea ('a small section of infinite space').

In practice, the attempt to create abstract 'space' in this sense, independently of the purposes of the space, so that the same space could be used for apartment blocks, offices, or exhibition buildings, is typical of certain strands of Modernism (*see* MIES VAN DER ROHE; MODERNISM, TO 1975 (A NEW MANDATE)). A more positive use is to exploit the structural possibilities of modern materials to create spaces which can easily be reconfigured (*see* RIETVELD).

Yet for the user, and indeed for the onlooker, what is more important is not that architecture embodies an abstract concept of space, but that it creates a perceptible sense of space, or spaciousness. To create this sense of space requires a command of *scale, i.e. it is possible to give a sense of spaciousness or a feeling of space while using quite small volumes. Unfortunately, this is one of the traditional skills of architects which few, if any, modernist architects have been interested in acquiring. PG

Forty, A., *Words and Buildings* (2000)

space frames In essence, *trusses in more than one plane. Space frames were first developed for aeroplanes in the early 1900s, but their first application to architecture was conceived by Buckminster *Fuller in the 1950s. Advances in the computer analysis of their structural behaviour made their widespread use feasible, as in *Foster's design for Stansted Airport. PG

Spain, medieval Unlike the rest of western
Europe, medieval Spain developed a split personality
as a result of the Muslim conquest of 711–18, leaving
only the north-west in Christian hands. The next seven
centuries slowly reversed this, so that by the end of
the Middle Ages Spain had been entirely recaptured.
Consequently it not only has imported Christian and
Muslim architecture but also both *Mozarabic, a
mixture of the two, and Mudéjar, Christian architecture
in an entirely Muslim style. All took on a Spanish
flavour.

Fragments of pre-Muslim Spain at S. Juan Bautista at
Baños de Cerrato (661) and S. Pedro de Nave have an
agglomerative pattern that continued in northern
churches such as the cruciform S. Julián de los Prados
at Oviedo (c.830). The former royal hall that became
S. María de Naranco (843–50) has strong affinities with
the Carolingian palace at Goslar, its main hall and
adjacent rooms being set over tunnel-vaulted
undercrofts, and tunnel-vaults appear again at the
basilican S. Miguel de Linio (founded 848) and Sta
Cristina de Lena (probably after 905).

In 786 Muslim architecture got into its stride with
the Mosque of Cordoba, whose grid of arcaded bays
grew until they comprised nineteen naves separated by
striped horseshoe arches. Refugee monks copied these
arches in their Mozarabic basilican church of S. Miguel
de Escalada (912–13). They appear again in the more
recognizably Romanesque S. Michel de Cuxa (955–74)
in Catalonia, with its apsidal transept chapels, and in
S. Pere de Roda (consecrated 1022), which also has
an apse and ambulatory. The pilgrimage church of
Santiago de Compostela (begun c.1075) is firmly in the
French tradition right through to the inspired carving
of the Pórtico de la Gloria (1188). Zamora Cathedral
and the Old Cathedral at Salamanca have domes
(c.1174–1200) a little like those of south-west France,
but distinctly naturalized. Muslim influence was not yet
done: Moorish masons worked successfully in brick,

Burgos Cathedral, Spain (1221ff.)

and this continued as Christians pressed forward, for
instance in the 12th-century Mudéjar style of S. Tirso at
Sahagún, which has horseshoe arches set in rectangular
panels around its three eastern apses and a tall, broad
crossing tower with four stages of pointed arches.

Gothic arrived in French form at Burgos
Cathedral (1221 onwards), which was completed with
open western spires (begun 1442) of German design,
and an open traceried star in the vault of its Capilla del
Condestable (1482–94). Léon Cathedral (c.1255) is
again French in spirit, but Barcelona Cathedral (1298
onwards) modified this by adapting the Germanic form

of a hall-church, employing a very wide nave, and raising the windows high in the aisles to reduce the glare of Mediterranean sun. Palma Cathedral (begun 1306) took this one stage further, progressively reducing the width between nave and choir, and between choir and Lady chapel. Girona Cathedral again was started in French fashion with an apsidal choir with radiating chapels, but completed (1407) uniquely with a nave whose unprecedented width of 23 m (74 ft) embraced both choir and its aisles.   APQ

Bevan, B., *History of Spanish Architecture* (1938)

Dodds, J., *Architecture and Ideology in Early Medieval Spain* (1990)

Harvey, J.H., *The Cathedrals of Spain* (1957)

Whitehill, W. M., *Spanish Romanesque of the 11th century* (1941)

Spain, post-medieval The history of Spanish architecture from the reconquest of the Muslim territories (1492) until the end of the 19th century is rather unrewarding. Few if any buildings are of European let alone international distinction; there are no Spanish treatises on architecture of more than local significance; and, as if to parallel this lack of creativity, architectural history itself is poorly documented, with hardly any general accounts or monographs, leaving the attribution and visual analysis of many works undecided.

Certain general features can be identified. Architecture was almost entirely restricted to two building types, churches and royal palaces. Each province retained certain distinctive characteristics, and there was hardly any national diffusion of architectural ideas. The capital city itself has a very small proportion of the nation's significant architecture, and the difference from, say, Paris or Rome, is very marked. Compared to other countries, Spain always seemed to be something of a backwater: Gothic lasted much longer, well into the 16th century; the Baroque had a

minimal impact in the 17th century; neoclassicism appeared only in its more arid forms; and in the 19th century, there was hardly any equivalent of the historicist styles so prevalent elsewhere.

1490–1600 Work continued almost throughout this period on additions to earlier cathedrals, such as Toledo (*see* EGAS, ENRIQUE DE), and Burgos (*see* SILOE, DIEGO DE), and new cathedrals were begun at Segovia, Salamanca, and Granada. In general, the designs were structurally conservative, but included two features which were to be of continuing significance in the development of Spanish religious architecture.

Great attention was paid to the lavish use of ornament, both internally (on altarpieces) and externally (on portals and window frames), a type of decoration known as the *Plateresque. In terms of plan, the cathedral at Granada (begun 1529) used the *chevet for a new purpose: the ostentatious display of the sacred Host, a gesture of defiance against the church's Protestant and Muslim opponents.

During this period, the Italian Renaissance made only a limited impact upon Spain, confined to two Royal palaces, where its influence was restricted to the minimizing of ornament, rather than an interest in proportions or in using the orders to organize a well-articulated façade. Charles V's palace at the Alhambra, Granada (1527–68), with its large circular courtyard of two superimposed classical orders and a classical façade, was a deliberate intrusion into the already existing Muslim palace.

For the palace and monastery of the Escorial (1563–84), King Philip II's instructions to his architect, *Herrera, 'Above all, do not forget what I have told you—simplicity of form, severity in the whole nobility without arrogance, majesty without ostentation,' temporarily checked the tendency to decorative excess, a tendency which the king may have considered too closely associated with his rebellious Muslim subjects.

The Escorial had few imitators, perhaps fortunately, because it is one of the most monotonous palaces in the whole of Europe.

1600–1880 From about 1600, Spain entered a long period of economic and political decline. Culturally, it was a golden age for theatre (Lope de Vega and Calderón) and painting (Zurbarán and Velàzquez), but not for architecture, as building virtually ceased for the first quarter of this period.

When building revived, from about 1675, architects' creativity focused not so much on the façade or the plan as on altarpieces and their settings in elements of buildings peculiar to Spain: the *camarín* (a chamber for the display of relics) and the *sagrario* (a separate chapel for the exposure of the Host; *see* HURTADO, FRANCISCO). Forms rarely used elsewhere (e.g. the *estípite) or combinations of forms (the estípite, the *Solomonic column and fragmentary architectural details) are combined in a fantastic manner. Indeed, in some cases, particularly in eastern Spain, the façades of buildings, particularly the doorways, can be considered as a kind of extruded altarpiece (*see* FIGUEROA, LEONARDO DE; RIBERA, PEDRO DE). A local variation is the *Churrigueresque, a cruder repetition of the Plateresque of almost two centuries earlier. During the whole period, the *Baroque, strictly interpreted as the use of movement in façades to make a scenographic effect, was not employed, with the exceptions of the cathedral of Murcia (Jaime Bort, 1736–49) and one entrance to the cathedral of Valencia.

The accession of the Bourbon dynasty in 1700 did not have an immediate architectural result, for it was not until 1735 that plans for a new royal palace in Madrid were drawn up, by Juvarra. After his death, the size of the planned building (completed 1757) was reduced by three-quarters, and the site was changed. The design by his successor, *Sacchetti, was only in part successful, being of rather awkward proportions,

though responding well to its site. Royal influence upon architecture was more by decree than by example, with the stipulation (from 1755) that the designs for public buildings must meet the approval of the Royal Academy of Fine Arts (established in 1752). The approved style of the Academy was neoclassicism, not an unusual choice at the period, but perhaps also supported because of its superficial similarity to the severe style adopted at the Escorial, almost two centuries earlier.

The first exponents of the Spanish version of neoclassicism were undoubtedly the most capable. Ventura Rodríguez Tizón (1717–85), a convert to the style, used his position as Director of the Royal Academy, and other official positions, to assign architectural commissions, as well as contributing numerous designs of his own. The Prado Museum (1787–9) by Juan de Villanueva (1739–1811) represents a more sophisticated approach.

Neoclassicism continued to be the dominant style until the middle of the 19th century, but Spain's continuing economic enfeeblement offered little opportunity for building for the rest of the century: only a handful of works, all rather undistinguished revival or *national romanticist architecture. The great exception is Barcelona, from the 1880s.   PG

Kubler, G., and Soria, M., *Art and Architecture in Spain and Portugal and their American dominions, 1500 to 1800* (1959)

Spain, modern (1875–present)

MODERNISME
NOUCENTISME TO RATIONALISM
FRANCO'S NEOCLASSICISM TO MODERNISM
MODERN RATIONALISM

Throughout the modern period in Spain, architectural styles and movements have often expressed regional identity and political change. The late 19th century went from monarchy to republic and back to monarchy, and there was widespread political unrest and regional dissent, particularly while the Basque country and Catalonia were undergoing massive industrial progress. The industrial bourgeoisie displayed their wealth through commissioning architecture and design, encouraging new expressions of regional values.

Modernisme So, unlike other European countries at the time, the trend was away from cohesive expressions of national pride. A revival of Catalan culture in the late 19th century was the first step in the expression of regional identity. This movement, called *Modernisme* (in Spain, what we call Modernism is called *Rationalism*), lasted 50 years and encompassed architecture, beginning with explorations in medieval Gothic—influenced by the writings of Viollet-le-Duc—and Islamic traditions, which permeate most corners of Spain. Lluís Domenech í Montaner, who worked closely with Gaudí, investigated Gothic construction and Arab and Mudéjar forms in his Hospital de la Santa Cruz, la Ciudadela Restaurant (1888), and the stunning Palau de la Música Catalana (1907). These architects were influenced by the concurrent Art Nouveau, Jugendstil, and Arts and Crafts movements around Europe, in a reaction against the banality of mass production and for 'art into industry'. Most were also propelled by more or less socialist beliefs along the lines of William Morris, who was widely read.

In Valencia, *Modernisme* was expressed ebulliently in buildings, but due to economic restraints often of poor quality brick or rubble and adobe construction. These use the scale and appearance of contemporaneous Catalan town houses and apartments, but are profligate with brightly painted stucco relief work in organic forms. Sadly, many of these crumbled away and have not survived.

Noucentisme to rationalism Eventually the enlightened factory owners who had patronized Gaudí and his

peers left their political ambitions and sense of social responsibility behind as the country became engulfed in yet another dark political period, with strikes, riots, and finally a military coup. Expressions of regional pride were stamped on, and in 1923 Primo de Rivera became dictator. His government was based in Barcelona, and his choice of national expression was *Noucentisme*, a simplified and effete version of neoclassical architecture decorated with classical motifs to denote eternal values. He built Madrid University City, and his plan for the 1929 World Expo—which attracted the controversial Mies German Pavilion—included Pueblo Español, still existing today, a mini-village of regional styles which reduced traditions to kitsch.

After his removal by General Election in 1929, the elected Second Republican government quickly allied itself with the Modern Movement. The group of architects was focused around *Sert and Torres Clavé, and in a short space of five years succeeded in planning and building social housing, clinics, hospitals, TB clinics, replanning Barcelona (Diagonal, with Le Corbusier), and addressing the grinding poverty and ill-health of the working class, most of whom were illiterate. This programme continued into the Civil War (1936–9).

Franco's neoclassicism to Modernism The first ten years of the Franco regime (1939–49) saw yet another search for identity through architecture (see Emma Dent Coad, *Constructing a Nation*, forthcoming). Franco wished to authenticate his position, having elaborate family trees drawn up to show dubious royal links, and similarly wished to express his authority and aspirations with appropriate architecture in imperial style (Airforce Ministry, 1947), triumphal arches, and monuments. The ensuing debate, all published and some written by Franco himself, with support from the Royal Academy, focused on Roman Classicism—Greek being associated with pagan worship. Rationalism was associated with leftist politics and generally reviled,

855

with some buildings actually being boarded up. A whole generation of Modern Movement architects, up to 200, had fled the country, many to the US or South America, a few to the Soviet Union. Despite Franco's best efforts and the intriguing rhetoric, no buildings of architectural merit emerged.

The transition from this period to an acceptance of Rationalism removed from its original political context came with the selection of Francisco Cabrero's design for the Sindicatos (trades union building, 1949) headquarters in Madrid, its austere and imposing presence facing that of the Prado Museum. That same year a design for a villa by *Coderch (Casa Garriga-Nogués, Sitges, 1947) was spotted by Gio Ponti in an exhibition in Barcelona, and hailed as the new direction for Spain. Thence for the next 30 years the Modern Movement was tolerated or embraced, much as in the UK, as a symbol of 'being modern', and used for public housing (often designed by Falangist architects), in commercial buildings (Banco de Bilbao, by Saenz de Oiza, 1971), and sophisticated private houses (Casa Valdecasas, by Javier Carvajal, 1966). Some of the most interesting work was for holiday apartments during the tourist boom of the 1960s (La Manzanera, Calpe, by Bofill, 1964). That tasteless monument to Franco's megalomania, the Valley of the Fallen (Muguruza, 1949), built by slave labour, was most appropriately Franco's final destination when he died in 1975.

Modern rationalism After the 'transition' from dictatorship to democracy, Spain embraced the Modern Movement and transformed the country, architecturally as well as politically, through a programme of social reform, infrastructural projects and public buildings that have catapulted Spanish architects into the international forefront.

The Ministry of Culture re-established state support for the arts and private sponsorship, fostering a new generation of cultural buildings that began with Rafael Moneo's Museum of Mérida (1984), the huge Reina Sofia Centre in Madrid (1986 and 1992), and the Instituto Valenciano de Arte Moderno (Salvadores, 1986). Train stations and bus terminals were also modernized, with Santa Justa Station in Seville (Cruz and Ortiz, 1987) one of the first award-winning designs.

Many of the major infrastructural transformations were focused on 1992, when Barcelona hosted the Olympics, Seville the World Expo, and Madrid was Cultural Capital of Europe. In Barcelona architecture was popularized, with every new bar performing architectural feats (Miralles, Arribas). The city, its parks, and its relationship with the sea were transformed (masterplanning by MBM Arquitectes). Similarly in Seville the city was transformed, and the Expo site saw an amazing six-month exhibition of the best of regional, national, and international architecture. Madrid celebrated the arrival of the Thyssen-Bornemisza art collection with the discreet and dignified Moneo building.

Elsewhere schools (Concepción School, Barcelona, Zazurca, 1991), religious organizations, and private clients (Casa Gaspar, Campo Baeza, 1991) were commissioning the best possible Modern architects in an enviable competition between cities, regions, and organizations to be chosen for the cover of international architectural publications. Many of these are the natural successors of the earlier generation, and readily acknowledge the influence of the likes of Coderch í Sentmenat and of Sert. After a short economic downturn, Spain continues to amaze the international community with its daring and innovative architectural commissions, such as the extensive (and expensive) City of Science in Valencia (Calatrava), or the redevelopment of Bilbao.   EDC

spandrel The roughly triangular space between arches or the ribs of a vault, or, by extension, a similar space formed by other structural members.   PG

Speer, Albert (1905–81) Hitler's principal architect from 1934. Speer designed and built only a few major buildings: a remodelled Chancellery for Hitler (1937–8), an exhibition building in Paris (1937), and the Zeppelinfeld Stadium (1934–7), part of the Party Congress Grounds in Nuremberg. In close collaboration with Hitler, he also projected a group of grandiose buildings and boulevards for central Berlin.

Speer's executed buildings were relatively modest in scale. They were neoclassical in their detailing, extremely axial and symmetrical, with exaggeratedly thick walls, vertical proportions, and an appearance of accessibility. Their detailing may have owed something to the work of Peter Behrens, of Speer's mentor Heinrich *Tessenow, and of *Troost, whom Speer called 'my second teacher'. Despite Hitler's strictures against modern construction methods, Speer usually employed a steel and concrete framework faced in limestone. His buildings belonged to the general type of 'stripped Classicism' that appeared everywhere in Europe and the United States in the 1930s (see FASCISM), though they were colder and bleaker looking than most similar buildings elsewhere.

But Speer's buildings differed from similar buildings in other countries in their uses and in their theatrical impact. In his memoirs, Speer wrote that he was most proud of his designs and choreography for the Party Congress Grounds. Here bright flags by day and searchlights by night (Speer called these his 'cathedral of light') echoed and dramatized the vertical piers of the grandstand, and framed the complex marching patterns of thousands of Nazi delegates inside, chanting their affirmation of the new German racial community on its way to war.

As Minister of Armaments and War Production (1942–5), Speer became one of the most powerful men in the Nazi government, planning transport networks, monitoring the industrial effort, allocating forced labour and building materials, resettling Jewish populations, and overseeing some aspects of the design of concentration camps. Speer's architecture and his politics continued to serve the same ends.   BML

Lane, Barbara Miller, *Architecture and Politics in Germany 1918–1945* (1985)

Spence, Sir Basil Urwin (1907–76) English architect. Spence's tentative and perhaps reluctant acceptance of Modernism was probably the reason why his designs were the acceptable face of contemporary architecture. In his first major work, the rebuilding of the Cathedral Church of St Michael, Coventry (1950–51), Spence showed his sensitivity to context, and his interest in modern art. He kept intact the ruins of the old cathedral, linked to the new work by a high porch, and by the use of a similar material, rose-red sandstone. The building was a showcase for the artists Piper, Reyntiens, Epstein, and Sutherland.

The cathedral immediately enjoyed a worldwide reputation, and by the 1960s Spence soon had a very extensive practice, usually involving large-scale works in the public sector. For his most successful work, a series of low-rise buildings at the University of Sussex (from 1960), Spence used a combination of pink brick walls and segmental arches of pre-cast concrete which harmonized well with the downland site. Much of the success of the scheme is due to his cooperation with the landscape architect Sylvia Crowe.

Among Spence's other works deserving of mention are: three small churches in Coventry, St Chad's, St John the Divine, St Oswald's (1955–7); two churches in Sheffield, St Paul (1958–9) and St Catherine of Siena (1958–60), for their experiments with space and light, particularly at the east end; Swiss Cottage Library, London (1963–4), for its open planning; and Brooke House, Basildon (1960–62), which uses very tall pilotis to give the building a commanding appearance.

His final works are rather a shock, since they lack any of the qualities of sensitivity found in his earlier

857

work. The British Embassy, Rome (1971), seems (next to Michelangelo's Porta Pia) quite indifferent to its context; and the Home Office Building (1971–6) is a heavy-topped *Brutalist building, rather crudely detailed.

PG

spire A tall pyramidal or conical feature rising from a tower or turret, particularly of a church, and analogous with the steep conical roof of a mosque's minaret. Spires are usually made of either stone, or timber clad in lead, copper, tile, or shingle. There are many forms: a broach spire has a square base converted into an octagonal section by means of triangular faces set point downward on each corner; a *flèche*, or spirelet, is very slender and comparatively light, usually rising from a roof; a needle spire is thin and rises from the centre of a tower well within the parapet; a splayed-foot spire is broached, the lower part of whose cardinal faces are splayed out so as to rise from the parapet or to overhang the tower thus forming eaves.

While the early stair and bell towers of Romanesque churches might have tall pyramidal or conical roofs, these only attain the verticality of a spire after 1100, for example at St Philibert, Tournus (after 1120). The advent of Gothic with its emphasis on verticality sent the spire heavenward, often being taller than the tower on which it is mounted, and sometimes so integrated that the junction of the two parts is obscured. The classic example is the south-west tower and spire of Chartres Cathedral (begun 1142), where the tower rises through three square stages to a fourth octagonal stage with steeply roofed projecting tabernacles on each face that partly obscure the base of the octagonal spire mounted above. Later spires, particularly in Germany, elaborated this theme, notably at Freiburg im Breisgau (1275–c.1340), where the faces of the spire are formed from open, traceried panels. Spires came back into their own in Baroque architecture, whose characteristic sense of drama and contrast favoured such inventions

as Wren's towers and spires for his City churches and St Paul's. Spires are an outstanding feature of English *parish churches, the most outstanding being found in Lincolnshire.

APQ

sports buildings

HISTORY
SWIMMING POOLS
STADIA AND SPORTS GROUNDS
INDOOR ARENAS
ICE RINKS
SPORTS HALLS
EDUCATIONAL FACILITIES
SPORTS PAVILIONS
SPECIALIST INDOOR SPORTS BUILDINGS

History The earliest sports buildings were the facilities at Olympia in ancient Greece, which was the forerunner of today's Olympic Games. Roman arenas such as the Colosseum were used for contests, and the Hippodrome in Rome was used for horse and chariot racing. Later came the bullrings, largely in Spanish-speaking countries (the earliest 'modern' bullring was in 1789, in the Granada area).

In the Middle Ages, jousting and military sports such as archery were prevalent. Real tennis emerged in France and the UK. Some of the old courts are still in existence (e.g. Hampton Court). Forms of cricket and football were played, but with local rules, and often the organization was unstructured.

However, the mid 19th century saw conditions arise to set the scene for the development of sport as we largely understand it today. These conditions were: mass transport by rail and sea, created by the Industrial Revolution, which enabled people to travel; the establishment of the rules of modern sport, mostly by universities and by the colonial forces; and the need for exercise and leisure which has grown with prosperity and the pressures of industrial life.

In 1896 Baron de Coubertin revived the ancient Olympic Games. The 20th century saw steady growth into the kind of facilities we know today. The main changes have taken place since World War II.

The main types of sports buildings to be dealt with in this entry are: swimming pools; stadia and sports grounds; indoor arenas; ice rinks; sports halls; educational facilities; sports pavilions; multi-purpose facilities; and specialist indoor sports buildings.

All these types can be divided into two or three categories, which may overlap: facilities for active participation, for spectating, or for leisure.

Integrated with these facilities are the needs of people with disabilities, the recognition of which has largely taken place since World War II. In 1948, at Stoke Mandeville Hospital in the UK, Sir Ludwig Guttman, a surgeon dealing with spinal injuries incurred during World War II, organized the first Games for wheelchair-bound people.

Sir Ludwig had realized that people in wheelchairs benefited from the exercise that sport brought, and also that morale and spirits were raised by the adrenalin. Previously they had been considered incapable of using sports equipment or entering into open competition. In 1960 the 'Disabled Games' were held in Rome, in the same stadium as the main Olympics, and in the same year. Now the Paralympics is an established, large-scale event. These changes have focused not only on the top athletes: local, regional, and national facilities all have to cater for both participants and spectators with disabilities.

Swimming pools   The pool as a constructed facility arrived in the 19th century with the coming of the Industrial Revolution.

The first pools were built not for competitive sport but out of a desire for cleanliness; they were associated with baths and washhouses, which is why they were called swimming baths. At first, the water was only changed when it became unhygienic, but from about 1909 onwards, it was filtered and purified.

The demand for swimming has changed, and can probably be categorized under three headings: competition and training; health and fitness; and leisure. Consequently, there are several often overlapping types of swimming pools: Olympic standard 50 m (164 ft) pools with provision for diving and spectator facilities; large-scale regional pools, some of which have diving and spectator facilities; local community pools (probably 25 m or 20 m (82 or 65½ ft) in length); school and college pools; 'leisure' pools, including both public sector and hotel pools, but the largest type being water parks in tourist areas; and finally private pools.

The 'leisure' pool, first built in the 1960s, was based on the recognition that many users came not to swim, but to splash around and enjoy themselves informally. Learner (or teaching) pools arrived at this time, again to reflect the need for shallow water to allow young children to play and learn to swim. Leisure pools also changed the architectural character of all pools, from white tiled rectangular halls with a hygienic atmosphere into more imaginative interiors which are attractive to the wider public. They experimented with free shapes for the pool, but the main changes have been towards more colour, more texture, better acoustics, and more exciting structures.

Indoor swimming pools are one of the most demanding and difficult of building types: high humidity, high temperatures, and the use of chemicals in water purification all mean a challenge for the design team of architect, services engineer, and structural engineer. There have been many disasters, including the collapse of entire buildings. In the UK, firms such as Faulkner Browns have combined a deep knowledge of the building type with research and development.

Stadia and sports grounds   The stadium of today is a facility where spectators surround a central outdoor

859

activity area (usually for field sports or athletics). It can vary greatly in size, the very largest holding 80,000 spectators or more. The word 'ground' is also used to denote a stadium, but can also refer to outdoor playing facilities without spectators.

The first purpose-built Olympic stadium was built in London for the 1908 Games, and could hold 100,000 spectators. The growth of stadia in the UK focused around football, and to a lesser extent rugby and cricket. They were largely designed by engineers, the most famous being Archibald Leitch. However, the stadiums of today were influenced by the crowd problems of the last part of the 20th century. A series of disasters, at the Heysel Stadium in Belgium (1985), a fatal fire at Bradford (1985), and Hillsborough, Sheffield (1989), accompanied by a climate of crowd violence, caused the authorities to look at the design criteria for safety. All major stadia became all seated. At the same time, spectators were looking for rising standards of comfort and amenity in comparison with their predecessors.

Not only does the modern stadium have to provide a much higher standard of comfort, but it also has to be designed for a much wider range of uses. Developments in grass pitch technology mean that more intensive use is possible, and also combinations of rugby and soccer, previously thought impossible, are taking place. Concerts and other entertainments are being held in the stadia: at the Toronto Skydome, the Millennium Stadium in Cardiff, and the Ajax Stadium in Amsterdam, the roofs can be closed to create an interior space capable of greater multi-purpose use.

There is certainly potential for exciting structures. The magnificent roofs built for the Munich Olympics in 1972 by Frei Otto set the scene for structures of great beauty. The Wembley Arch and the Cardiff Millennium Stadium are examples of what are perhaps the new icons of our cities. The Mound Stand at Lord's Cricket Ground, London (1987), by Michael Hopkins is

an elegant structure with a lightweight membrane roof. The Sydney Olympic stadium (Bligh Voller Nield, 2000; now the Telstra Stadium) is a highpoint in stadium design. These examples reinforce the trend to build stadia in central locations, served by public transport. Designers like HOK Sport Architecture have tended to specialize in these complex buildings.

Indoor arenas Though 'arena' derives from the Latin for 'sand' (used in Roman arenas to absorb blood), the term is now used to denote an indoor spectator facility.

Historic examples of the modern arena include the Albert Hall in London, not designed for sports use but frequently used for tennis and movement and dance. Its oval shape mirrors the Roman Colosseum. Perhaps the most famous arena is Madison Square Gardens, in New York, well known for boxing. Wembley Arena, built in 1926, was a structure in reinforced concrete designed by Sir Owen Williams.

Arenas meet similar criteria to stadia, i.e. a central activity space surrounded by spectator seating. The central space will vary in size depending on the activities to be included. The most common sports requirements will be for basketball, ice-skating, indoor athletics, five-a-side football, tennis, soccer 6 from the USA, and others. Larger facilities might be used for show jumping and some motor-based sports.

A structure published in 1989 by the GB Sports Council suggested the following sizes: scales 1 and 2 with a central space of 100 × 50 m (328 × 164 ft), large enough for indoor athletics, with scale 1 having seating for a minimum of 8,000 spectators; scale 3 with a central space of 64 × 34 m (210 × 111½ ft), large enough for ice hockey, tennis, basketball, and many other sports, with a minimum of 5,000 seats. However, the commercial demands of multi-purpose use would suggest 15,000–20,000 spectators for arts and entertainment uses. The London Millennium Dome is being provided with such an arena space.

Ice rinks Artificial ice-skating facilities can be provided both indoor and outdoor (the latter are only practical in winter climates). They can be permanent in indoor buildings, or temporary in both indoor and outdoor situations. Skating for pleasure and for competition can be provided in the same building, or can be created separately. Competitive skating evolved in three major forms: ice hockey; speed skating; and figure skating.

For ice hockey, the usual ice pad size is 60 m × 30 m (197 × 98 ft) with rounded corners (or 56 m × 26 m (184 × 85 ft) for regional smaller-scale facilities). The pad is surrounded by spectator seats on all four sides.

The number of seats will vary greatly. In Canada, where ice hockey is the national sport, numbers of 20–30,000 are common for the big teams. In the UK spectator capacities will be in the order of 10–12,000.

Ice rinks can be provided as permanent features in purpose-built form, or provided temporarily in multi-purpose arenas. Some indoor ice rinks are closed in summer and can be used for other purposes, e.g. exhibitions, shows. The ice pad can be temporarily created in other indoor spectator buildings. The challenge for the designer is, wherever possible, to create a facility that can change and adapt to need. The Haakonshall Arena in Lillehammer, Norway, is a good example.

Speed skating arenas are generally built only for Olympic-scale events, though training and practice facilities may be required. The large scale of the building, housing a 200 m track, usually demands consideration of alternative uses. Elegant examples are the Palasport speed skating oval, Turin, and the 'Viking Ship' Arena in Hamar, Norway. Both have planned for multi-purpose uses.

The late 1980s saw developments in skating facilities that are free-shaped for leisure use, incorporating features such as islands, slopes, and even artificial snowstorms.

Sports halls These are indoor spaces capable of housing a number of sports. They are sometimes confused with gymnasiums. Although they have overlapping functions, a gymnasium is usually a space fitted out with specialist equipment, whereas a sports hall is an open multi-purpose sports space with larger dimensions.

The growth of indoor sport after World War II led to the introduction of the sports hall. The most famous example of an elegant structure is the Palazzetto dello Sport, by *Nervi (1960). Because of the variety of sports, and in the levels of standard in these sports (e.g. national/international through county/club to casual/recreational), the sizes will vary depending on need. The Sports Council in the UK has used scales such as large, medium, small, and community. It is vital, however, that a large sports storage area is provided with direct access to the hall, to permit a range of equipment to be accommodated. This initially should be as large as 20% of the playing area. Most sports halls will cater for participation needs, but some seating may be provided. This will always be in a movable, retractable form that can be opened out when needed.

Multi-purpose use has to be mentioned, particularly where the hall is the largest and best space in a small community. Use has included dog shows, election meetings, local concerts, and a variety of other needs. Obviously this creates difficulties in a building primarily designed for sports use (protection of the floor will be an obvious factor), but it is a reality of life that these demands will occur, sometimes to earn extra income. The challenge for the designer is to create a building that can respond to change over its life.

Educational facilities In the 19th century, sport in schools began in various ways. At Rugby School, William Webb Ellis famously picked up the ball and ran, beginning the game of rugby. *Mens sana in corpore sano* was the inspiration for education. Much thinking was developed from military sources. Germany led the way in the teaching and development of gymnastics. By the early 20th century every secondary school in Britain had a gymnasium, and playing fields. The universities were the founding ground for many sports during the late 19th century.

Sports buildings for educational use can be examined under four headings: primary schools; secondary schools; universities and further education; and joint provision between education and the adult community.

In primary schools, exercise and sport are usually provided for in a multi-use hall and in outside fields and hard surface areas. In secondary schools also, Physical Education is a compulsory part of the curriculum; normal provision will be a gymnasium equipped with wall bars and gymnastic equipment, and outdoor pitches, plus artificial surfaces for games such as netball and tennis.

For universities, there is a great variety of provision. Loughborough University, for example, has a School of Sport and Exercise Sciences, so has superb facilities. All universities will have some kind of playing fields. In the USA sport has a high place on the university campus. Many of the large stadia for American football will be found at universities. The level of indoor facilities for fitness and recreation is also very high.

Sports facilities jointly provided for education and the adult community have seen a major advance since World War II. The concept arose from new thinking: how can the community use the school facilities when they are empty in the evenings, weekends, and school holidays? Why not enhance these school facilities to provide a dual function, raising the size and quality for adult use, that in turn raises the quality for schools? The same thinking has been applied in certain university and further education campuses.

Sports pavilions Although there were no doubt examples in history that might loosely fall into this category, it is the 19th century when the familiar pavilion format begins. It coincides with the growth of organized sport.

The following sports require pavilions: golf, cricket, football (soccer), rugby, tennis, and athletics; there may be other smaller sports to be catered for, often grouped with other sports. Combinations of summer and winter sports within the same building are common, e.g. football and rugby with cricket.

In all cases, multi-purpose use needs to be considered, so that full use can be made of the building where appropriate, e.g. because of their high quality, golf club buildings can be hired out for social occasions.

The golf pavilion is probably the most luxurious type. Typically it includes the following accommodation: entrance, reception, offices, shop, professionals' office, changing rooms, lavatories, showers (male and female), committee room, bar, restaurant, and groundsman's rooms (which may be separate).

Although the oldest type of facility, cricket has simple needs: merely rooms for changing, a social room, with a kitchen, and preferably a balcony or covered area overlooking the pitch. Tennis pavilions tend to be similar, except that both male and female changing rooms will be needed. Larger tennis centres will have more elaborate facilities, e.g. restaurant and bar, tennis professionals' room, and shop. Athletics pavilions also show the same characteristics, except that the number of changing places needs to be calculated from the usage of the facility.

Football (soccer) and rugby may require the most elementary facilities. A public authority building might contain just changing, showering and lavatories (one unit per team), with perhaps a minimal social area. A larger club pavilion might in addition have a bar, social room, kitchen (large enough to prepare meals), a physiotherapy room, and a viewing terrace. In all cases, the finishes need to be tough and floor surfaces able to be hosed down.

A modern sports pavilion should have in mind flexibility of use, to enable the building to cope with new trends and new challenges in sport, but also to allow the management to programme uses when the building is idle. These will include social events, meals, and even weddings. This, together with the higher aspirations of society generally, means a higher quality of design, materials and accommodation.

Many indoor sports buildings are sport-specific, i.e. they are built to the requirements of the sport or activity for which it will be used. Examples would be a badminton centre, a gymnastics centre, or a tennis centre. However, multi-purpose buildings have economic advantages, and are more readily adaptable as uses of buildings change: sports change in popularity and new activities emerge. Therefore the building that is easy to adapt for different purposes becomes desirable to users and operators.

Specialist indoor sports buildings Velodromes are cycling tracks with banked profiles. They have been outdoor (e.g. Herne Hill, London) but are now generally to be found indoor, because of the requirements for a wooden track and the difficulties of protecting this from weather. The most common track length is 250 m. The banked profile, particularly the ends of the track, make this a largely specialist facility, and it is also difficult to provide good sight lines for spectators.

More and more indoor tennis is being played in specialist centres. Because of the intensity of use there is no usual provision for any other purpose, but other racquet sports are often linked, e.g. squash courts and badminton courts.

There has been a growth in indoor bowls, in specialist centres. Because the bowls green is such a specialist artificial surface, it cannot be used for other purposes.

The rapid rise of the public's search for exercise and a healthier lifestyle has led to a huge surge in the creation of fitness centres. These are often private sector initiatives, linked to a high standard of provision. They are fitted with a sophisticated range of fitness equipment, together with facilities such as sauna baths, pools and Jacuzzis in the larger centres. 		GJ

John, G., and Sheard, R., *Stadia* (2000)

squinch A series of gradually projecting superimposed arches, rising from the corners of a square, by means of which a dome can be placed over a square base. The squinch is structurally adequate, but visually awkward, and the perfected solution to the problem is provided by the *pendentive. 		PG

Sri Lanka The close proximity of Sri Lanka to India has resulted in continuing influence from its larger neighbour, with most of its population coming from southern India (the best known being the Tamils), a historical source of conflict that remains to this day. Sri Lankan Buddhism was primarily Theravada (the 'path of the elders'), the more conservative or traditional form also widely followed across most of South East Asia. The geography and proximity to Indian trade routes meant Buddhism often arrived in South East Asia via Sri Lanka. The best preserved Buddhist monuments are located around medieval capitals, such as Anuradhapura and Polonnaruva, in the central part of the island. As in India, the earliest architecture would have been in wood, but the reconstructed Sri Lankan monuments that remain today reveal an evolution and a sophistication that diverged from Indian sources, in both style and choice of building materials. Through the use of vaulted brick construction (generally with corbelled vaulting), circular shrines, the limited use of decorative elements, including fewer stone sculptures, and local details such as the semicircular 'moonstone', the Sri Lankan Buddhist architecture style evolved distinct from the early Indian sources. It has been noted that Sri Lankan

863

sculpture is subordinated to architectural forms, the opposite of the Indian tradition.

Although most extant remains date from the 2nd millennium, some of the earliest references in Buddhist history are associated with Sri Lanka, including ancient Pali literary sources and links with India's first Buddhist ruler, Ashoka. The sacred bodhi tree in Anuradhapura is believed to be the descendant of the original planted over 2,300 years ago by Ashoka's son. In fact, a type of construction was designed that housed that tree, the pillared bodhi-ghara, open to the sky and flanked by four images of the meditating Buddha. This same *hypostyle form of construction is also found as part of *stupa complexes, repeating the pillared halls (that once supported a roof) that flank the main stupa.

The most distinctive feature of Sri Lankan architecture is the stupa (dagaba or cetiya), and the most dramatic example the reconstructed monument at Anuradhapura, whose origin likely dates to the 3rd century BC. Its antecedents derive from early Indian versions, as found at Sanchi and Amaravati, but the developed Sri Lankan stupa is notable for its larger main hemispherical body (anda), surmounted by a prominent square structure, and finally the tapering series of umbrellas (harmika). Instead of elaborate gateways (toranas) and carved railings, small shrines or relic halls were directly attached to the stupa, with additional examples sited nearby, including the open pillared hall, repeating the construction that encloses the sacred bodhi tree. The limited evidence of wall painting suggests liturgical purposes rather than surface embellishment. The immense Sri Lankan version of the stupa succeeds in communicating a sense of calm, through its largely undecorated mass, befitting the Theravada form of Buddhism, with the emphasis upon simplicity, meditation, and serenity. This variation upon the early Indian stupa was influential across South East Asia, with related examples found in Burma, Cambodia, and Thailand.

The relatively few images and visual simplicity of Theravada Buddhism did not totally prohibit architectural decoration, rather it seemed to cause it to be concentrated into a few limited areas. An interesting and early feature of Sri Lankan architecture is the decorated stone threshold, a half circle placed at the base of the stairs leading to various buildings. Known as 'moonstones', these are elaborately carved surfaces, consisting of concentric rows of images of animals (lions, horses, bulls, and elephants), separate rows of geese, and in between elaborate floral patterns, including lotus leaves. All these images are well documented in Buddhist cultures, but only in Sri Lanka are they compressed into such a humble location, although carved with exquisite skill and detail.   RF

Staal, Jan Frederik (1879–1940) Dutch architect, a gifted and independent architect of the *Amsterdam School who deserves fuller recognition. While working for his building contractor father, Staal met A. J. Kropholler, with whom he set up a practice in 1902. Their work was strongly influence by *Berlage, with much expressed brickwork. After the partnership broke up in 1910, Staal found his own more romantic voice, epitomized by houses at Park Meerwijk in Bergen of 1916–18. In their functional articulation and overt symbolism—two deliberately boat-like—they mark the high-point of Dutch Expressionism. Urban housing schemes of the 1920s followed, with folding planes of brickwork and projecting bays or turrets extending the vocabulary of Michael de Klerk. This expressive period culminated in Staal's Dutch Pavilion at the Paris Exhibition of Decorated Arts (1925), an eclectic marriage of modernist space with a hand-wrought brick gable. The more restrained Amsterdam Telegraph building (1927–30) and Aalsmeer Auction House (1927–30) show Staal at his peak: exploiting irregular sites with ingenious massing, articulating planes, and surfaces, yet maintaining builderly control.

His magnum opus, the Rotterdam Exchange of 1928–40, which suffered endless delays and changes of programme, witnesses a late swing towards 'objectivity' that did not make his last work more lovable. PBJ

stables Until the invention of the steam engine, and then the internal combustion engine, the horse was people's primary motive power on land. Horses were fundamental to farming, transport, warfare, and hunting. Though horses do not need shelter in the wild, people found it convenient for reasons of practicality, security, and display to keep the horse in purpose-built accommodation. Consequently, stables were an important building type, often housing scores, sometimes thousands, of horses.

Stables allowed horses to be put easily and efficiently to work. Stables meant that the horses were to hand when needed and conveniently fed, watered, and groomed. They also kept the horses secure, as the best creatures have always been expensive and highly prized. Though the best medieval stables were large and sophisticated, significant advances in stable design can be identified in the late 16th and late 18th centuries. These coincided with major developments in horsebreeding, first the introduction of the coach horse and then the thoroughbred. New, expensive types of horse needed careful husbandry, and marked improvements can be traced both through the contemporary literature and through the physical and documentary evidence of the stables.

Much of the history of the stable can thus be written in terms of practicality. How can stables be kept well ventilated without encouraging draughts? What form of flooring and drainage should they have? Should they have partitions, and if so of what sort, and fixed partitions, or hanging bales? What is the best design and material for the rack and manger? How many horses should be kept together? What other ancillary elements should be included, e.g. harness

room, feed store, groom's rooms, coach houses, hayloft?

But stables have always been about more than simple utility. Horses were symbols of status and connoisseurship. The better class of stable, and that might include the stables of the great London brewery companies as well as those of monarchs or landowners, were also designed as places of display, to show horses off to their best advantage. For this reason stables have been treated with an architectural dignity found only very rarely in buildings designed for other animals. This can be seen both in the external quality of the stable building and in the dignity of the interiors, particularly the fittings. The best country-house stables are of a quality that can rival the house itself and need to be understood as an extension of the rooms of parade, not as utilitarian, essentially agricultural buildings. GW

See also RIDING HOUSES.

Worsley, G., *The British Stable* (2004)

stadia *See* SPORTS BUILDINGS (STADIA).

stained glass Glass that has been coloured, either during the process of firing or by adding translucent pigment such as paint to form patterns or pictures, characteristically used in the churches north of the Alps to depict biblical and other figures and scenes. Glass was first used for windows in Roman times, and, although the preserve of the rich, was also used in the first Christian churches and often coloured. The process of fitting together pieces of differently coloured glass within a lead frame to form patterns slowly developed, and only in the 11th century were figurative pictures built up by painting the glass, thus putting the art on a par with mural painting. The heyday of stained glass coincided with the first phase of Gothic, when the still surviving large windows at St Denis and Ste Chapelle, Paris, and of cathedrals at Chartres, Bourges, and Le Mans in France, and Canterbury and York in England were filled with deeply coloured scenes of the highest artistry. Florence and Siena followed, but later glass north of the Alps became lighter and more realistic and detailed in what it depicted, so that by the 16th century, notably at King's College Chapel, Cambridge, these qualities subdued the earlier glowing effect of its colours. APQ

stairs, staircases, and ramps Stairs have been found in some of the oldest known buildings. Besides providing access, stairs have been used for defence, for status, for ritual, for prayers, for ceremony, and for many other purposes. For example, monumental stairs, such as the immense double staircase leading to the great Hall of Xerxes, Persepolis, emphasized the power of the state and the ruler. Vast compositions of stairs, such as the *ziggurats of Mesopotamia and pre-Columbian pyramids, were often built for communal, religious, and ritual purposes. Elevating temples and important buildings onto platforms at the top of steps made them appear more imposing.

The spiral, or helical, stair, where steps ascend around a central newel or well, was an innovative invention. It was useful not only for access, but for defence, since the stairs could be blocked easily. They were often built within the massive walls of the fortress, occupying comparatively little space and weakening the carcass under attack less than orthogonal layouts. However, most of these ancient stairs were precipitous, dark, and uninviting.

As military architecture changed, the staircase became more an instrument of communication than defence. In the castles of the powerful, the stairs were freed from the walls and enclosed in towers or turrets constructed solely for the purpose. Stairs were also used to satisfy the growing desire for privacy, to avoid crossing one room to gain access to another, to provide separate communication between apartments or suites

on different floors, or for secrecy. So the number of staircases grew in proportion to the number of apartments. The palace at Chambord contains about 25 spirals.

Spiral stairs are difficult to build and awkward and restricting to use. This made them less desirable where defence was no longer one of the main functions. Dogleg stairs, which are almost as compact, soon began to replace them. The dogleg was interesting also because it enables the exit and entry points to be located almost directly above each other, permitting floor plans to be regularized with rooms over rooms and the whole plan to be repeated if necessary.

Later, stairs were freed from their enclosing walls and set into their own stair halls. Opening the stairwell ensured that the whole stair can be seen, giving it greater emphasis in the building. The diagonal line of the exposed stair, the only major sloping plane in the composition of horizontal and vertical planes, forms a strong visual connection between the two floors. The stair connects the two levels, visually and functionally, with a spatial generosity that accentuates its significance within the building composition. For example, Bartolomeo Bianco in Genoa allowed the stair in the Palazzo dell'Università (1630–36) to be seen from a distance and enjoyed as both a decorative object in space and the means for visually connecting spaces.

When formal access to the *piano nobile* became customary, the status of the building was expressed as much by a monumental stair in its hall as by the façade and the reception rooms. The stair hall (*Treppenhaus*) became a scenographic presence with spatial exuberance as demonstrated in the palaces of Wurzburg (*see* NEUMANN, JOHANN BALTHASAR), Pommersfelden, Bruhl, and Bruchsal (where the stair hall is the largest room in the palace). Visiting dignitaries were often received on the stair, and this was an indication of their rank and social position.

Calvaries The steps leading to the choir in some churches were symbolically significant, reminding worshippers of Christ's ascent to Calvary; the frequent use of fifteen steps to the choir represented the fifteen virtues. Some famous stairs encourage ascending pilgrims to strive towards a worthy goal: the best known of these is the Scala Sancti in the Palatine Chapel of the Popes, in Rome. External flights of steps have also been built for Calvaries, such as the granite staircase leading to the Bom Jesus do Monte, Braga, Portugal (begun 1722), where thousands of pilgrims ascend the monumental stair at Whitsun following a Way of the Cross. At Lamego, Portugal, there are *azulejo* representations of the Stations of the Cross on each landing.

Ramps There are numerous impressive uses of ramps. Antonio da *Sangallo's extraordinary double spiral ramp at Orvieto was built so that animals carrying water up from a deep well and animals descending to the well will not meet and will not have to turn around at the top or bottom. The internal ramps at the Palazzo Ducale, Urbino (*c*.1470), and at the Villa Caprarola (*Vignola, 1559ff.) allowed the passage of horses as well as people. *Michelangelo's stepped ramp (*cordonata*) for the newly designed Campidoglio, in Rome, invites the visitor both physically and visually to ascend to the courtyard.

In many ways, ramps are like stairs, but they do not constitute such a visual or physical barrier between adjoining levels. However, because their slope is gradual, they occupy more space. The ramp was an important element in the *promenade architecturale*. At the Villa Savoie, Poissy, and at Chandigarh, Le Corbusier showed that dogleg ramps could be used to liberate the vertical visual flow of space. In the Guggenheim Museum in New York City, Frank Lloyd *Wright used a vast well surrounded by an access ramp to lead people through the exhibits.

Because of the physical effort required for stair climbing, until the end of the 19th century (*see* CHICAGO SCHOOL) the height of most practical buildings was limited to about six floors. The development of lifts fundamentally changed this, so the urban form of cities freed from this constraint was transformed and grew into the familiar tower blocks of the contemporary urban landscape.

Finally, stairs have a history of being the locus of many serious falls. From the records of injuries in many countries, it is clear that steps and stairs are the most hazardous component of the built environment, causing many deaths and injuries. The reasons for this dismal statistic are manifold, and often the causes are avoidable. JAT

> Templer, J. A., *The Staircase: Studies of Hazards, Falls, and Safer Design* (1992)

Stam, Mart (Martinus Adrianus) (1899–1986) Dutch architect and urban designer. A modernist with radical social ideas, Stam produced projects and a few built works during the 1920s, among them the van Nelle factory, Rotterdam (together with van der Vlugt and Brinkmann), terraced housing at the Weissenhof exhibition, Stuttgart, and the Hellerhof housing estate, Frankfurt. In his spare, lean architecture, he exposed steel or reinforced concrete frames to demonstrate their structural truth and accommodate change. He was a founder and active member of *CIAM, headed the left-wing architectural organization *de 8 en Opbouw*, and edited the radical publication *ABC, Beiträge zum Bauen*, which advocated a hardline Functionalism. During the early 1930s he worked with Ernst *May in the Soviet Union, planning new cities. He eventually returned to Amsterdam, where he ran a private practice until retiring in 1966. CO

Stark, William (1770–1813) Scottish architect. *See* HOSPITALS, TO 1850 (RADIAL AND CRUCIFORM PLANS).

Starov, Ivan Yegorovich (1745–1808) Russian architect, influential in St Petersburg's transition from the Baroque to the neoclassical.

After four years in the Paris studio of de *Wailly, and travel in Italy (1766–8), Starov returned to St Petersburg. During the 1770s, he designed country mansions in the environs of St Petersburg, Moscow, and Tula.

His first major project in St Petersburg was the Cathedral of the Trinity at the Alexander Nevsky Monastery (1776–80s). Catherine personally approved the Roman basilical design, with a great ribbed dome that suggests the work of *Soufflot, particularly Ste Geneviève (the Panthéon). His most influential project was the Tauride Palace (1783–9), a model of elegant simplicity, which was widely imitated in the design of Russian estate houses. WCB

Stasov, Vasily Petrovich (1769–1848) The most productive Russian architect in the concluding phase of neoclassicism. Following his appointment in 1817 as supervisor of palace construction in St Petersburg, Stasov designed state buildings such as the Pavlovskii Regiment Barracks (1817–21), the Coachman's Market (1817–19), the Imperial Stables (1817–23), and the Military Provision Warehouse (1829–31) in Moscow. He endowed each of these prosaic structures with monumental form through bold use of the Doric order. Among his churches, the Cathedral of the Transfiguration (1828–9) and the Trinity-Izmailovsky Cathedral (1828–35), with five massive domes, are landmarks in late neoclassical St Petersburg. Other exercises in imperial grandeur include the Narva Triumphal Gates (1827–34) and the Moscow Triumphal Gates (1834–8), built at St Petersburg's southern entrances to commemorate Russian victories over France and Turkey respectively. WCB

stave churches These are a type of wooden church constructed with vertical timbers rather than horizontal logs, found mainly in Norway. The Norwegian word *stav* (a pole or pillar) is used to mean either the corner posts of a building or free-standing masts supporting a roof. Timber churches in medieval Norway were overwhelmingly of the stave type, of which there were about 700. Today only 27 (mostly incorporating later changes) survive. One stave church (Hedared) survives in Sweden.

Stave churches fall into two main groups. Smaller, single-nave churches (Hedared; Holtålen, in Trondheim Folk Museum) have no aisles and no separating masts. The larger, aisled churches (Borgund; Gol, in the Norwegian Folk Museum, Oslo) have tall masts which divided the narrow perimeter aisles from the nave and support the elevated upper part of the nave. Surrounding ambulatories were added later to many churches in both groups.

Glue and metal nails were avoided in construction and foundations were minimal. In aisleless churches the foundation beams, laid on edge to support vertical plank walling, were joined at the corners and clamped together by corner posts slotted over them. In aisled churches foundation beams were arranged as a rectangular, chassis-like base frame of flat sleepers in parallel pairs, notched over each other at intersections, and extended at the corners to support ground sills for the aisle walls. The superstructure, braced by diagonal crosses, was raised on tall masts up to 11 m (36 ft) high and covered by a series of steeply pitched roofs. Each piece of timber was precisely cut to ensure a perfect fit whilst allowing the building to move and so take up the climatic and structural stresses.

Decoration was important. Apart from the profuse and intricate carving often found on entrance portals (Urnes; Hedal), delicate carving was also incorporated on structural components such as mast tops, cross bracing, and quadrant bracketing. Borgund has elaborate dragon carvings and six tiers of roofs, and, as the only stave church to have survived

Stave church, Borgund, Norway (12th century)

unchanged, was a model for the restoration of other stave churches.

Stave churches were conceived as structures able to 'float' on the surface and 'give' with the wind: in this and in their use of intricate interlaced decoration, dragon heads, and their method of erecting masts, they continued the earlier tradition of fine craftsmanship found in Viking ships.   JBH

Bugge, G., and Norberg-Schulz, C., *Stave and Loft in Norway* (1990)

steel Technically, steel is an alloy of iron and carbon (between 0.02% and 2.04% by weight). It has been manufactured in small quantities since antiquity, but it was only with the invention of the Bessemer process (patented 1855) that steel could be manufactured cheaply in large quantities. Not only is the tensile strength of steel about five times that of wrought *iron, it is the first material in human history which has sufficient tensile strength to permit the construction of very wide spans, without intermediate supports. On the other hand, steel has two important drawbacks: it requires fire-proofing and protection against corrosion (cf. reinforced CONCRETE).

The first and indeed in some ways the defining experiments in the engineering of steel frame construction and the architectural expression of the new material took place in Chicago (*see* CHICAGO SCHOOL), from about 1880. The structural principles of the steel frame were worked out by William Le Baron *Jenney, who may also have designed the first structural framed *skyscraper, the Home Insurance Building (1884), which used steel in the upper 6 of the 10 storeys. Thereafter the technological problem of developing the use of steel was quite straightforward, but the issue of how to give architectural expression to a steel frame was more difficult.

At first sight, a steel frame looks like a simple case of trabeation (post-and-beam), but on a much larger scale.

In fact, it is not, since it is a cage formed of cubes, with the beam of equal visual weight to the post; and it has a marked horizontal emphasis, since the beam is much longer than the post. In theory, Root (*see* BURNHAM AND ROOT) argued that to load the frame with lavish ornament was useless, as the most important factors were a sense of mass and proportion; and Louis *Sullivan famously (and misleadingly) argued that 'form follows function', and that tall buildings should be insistently vertical.

For the most part, their practice was quite different. Their façades (e.g. Sullivan's Wainwright Building, St Louis, 1890–91 and Guaranty Building, Buffalo, 1894–5; Burnham and Root's Rookery Building, Chicago, 1885–8), which followed the classical formula of base/capital/column, masked the structural characteristics of the underlying frame. Furthermore, Sullivan's buildings in particular were overloaded with ornament.

But their ideas did subsequently find expression, in two very elegant Chicago constructions, the Gage Building (*Holabird and Roche, 1898–9), and the Reliance Building (Burnham and Root, 1890–95). In fact, these buildings represented a high point, since for almost fifty years great technological progress was matched by visual regression, as the frames became cluttered with historicist or Art Deco details (representative examples being the Woolworth Building, by Cass *Gilbert, 1910–23, and the Chrysler Building, William van Alen, 1929, both in New York).

Europe lagged about twenty years behind the United States, but eventually steel frames were used not only for offices and for shops and stores, the main building types in Chicago, but for factories (*Behrens AEG Turbine Factory, 1909;) and hotels (*Mewès and Davis, Ritz Hotel, 1903–6). However, beginning in 1906 with the Pierce factory, Buffalo, it was a US architect, Albert *Kahn, who developed the use of very wide spans in 1-storey, roof-lit factories, which made assembly-line production possible. Within a generation, one of his factories, the Glenn Martin Aircraft Plant, Maryland (1937), was covered by a flat roof of an immense span, 91 m (300 feet).

During the 1920s there occurred the next major technical development in the use of steel that had significant consequences for design: the invention of welding. Rivets, gusset plates, and bolts were no longer necessary, so it became possible to produce angled forms, or straight sections in smooth, clean lines. Kahn was again the pioneer in designing varied roof profiles, for different functional purposes.

But modernist architects were much more attracted by the other possibility, the pure, abstract lines and surfaces made possible by the use of welding. The pure line as a framework for other materials, such as glass, or glass/cement, can be seen in the work of Pierre *Chareau (the Maison de Verre, Paris, 1932) and Richard Neutra (the Lovell House, Los Angeles, 1929); the foremost advocate of unclad steel was *Mies van der Rohe.

His first large-scale building (its precursor was the Illinois Institute of Technology campus, Chicago, 1945) to display the abstract virtues of black-painted steel was the Lake Shore Drive apartments, Chicago (1948–51). The building seems to exemplify his famous aphorisms, 'Less is more', 'Almost nothing', but in reality, in order to fireproof the structure, I-beams of the columns and mullions were added on to the already existing façade, as appliqué. However, Mies had established the dominant pattern for the steel frame, quickly copied elsewhere, even in steel-rationed England (Hunstanton School, Norfolk, *Smithsons).

The 1950s was also a decade of experimentation for the use of steel in small houses. In 1945, the Californian magazine Arts and Architecture announced the 'Case Study' programme, to illustrate cases (and not just ideas) of houses built in steel, with particular emphasis on *prefabrication and duplication, to which the material seemed ideally suited. One of the earliest and perhaps the most successful was the *Eames House. In all, about 25 were built, mainly in California. Their reputation may be undeservedly high, because of the brilliant photographs of Julius Shulman (e.g. the Stahl House, Los Angeles, Pierre Koenig, 1960; see PHOTOGRAPHY, ARCHITECTURAL). Quite different from the rather stick-like Californian houses, rather reminiscent of timber construction, were the Farnsworth House (Mies van der Rohe, 1946–51) and the Glass House (*Johnson, 1949).

Alternatives to the conventional model tended to be employed in only a handful of buildings. The problem of fireproofing can be solved by constructing the frame of tubular members as an exoskeleton, i.e. external to the main building. This method was apparently first used in the 64-storey United States Steel Corporation Building, in Pittsburgh, where the frame is a grid, or, in the more futurist-looking frames of the Centre Pompidou, Paris (*Rogers, 1977), or Bush Lane House, Cannon Street, London (*Arup, 1976).

Another solution is to suspend the building from a steel mast, either on the model of a suspension bridge, as in *Nervi's uncharacteristically inelegant Burgo Paper Mill, Mantua, Italy (1961–3), or on the model of the cable-stayed bridge. The forms of masted structures subsequently became less dependent upon bridge design, and articulated the exposed steel structure of tension rod, vertical mast, and horizontal beam much more clearly (the Renault Distribution Centre, Swindon, *Foster, 1980; the Fleetguard Manufacturing and Distribution Centre, Quimper, Rogers, 1979–81).

Attempts have been made to enliven the rather starkly diagrammatic form of the Miesian steel frame by the use of CorTen steel which 'weathers' to a rust colour: the Cummins Engine Factory, Darlington (Roche and Dinkeloo, 1964–6); John Winter's own house, in London (1969) used Cor-Ten on a very simple grid. Cor-Ten steel oxidizes to a purplish-brown colour within about five years.　PG

　　See also FULLER, BUCKMINSTER; EAMES, CHARLES; JOHNSON, PHILIP.

　　Jackson, N(eil), *The Modern Steel House* (1996)

Steindl, Imre　(1839–1902) Hungarian architect. *See* HOUSES OF PARLIAMENT.

stele　An upright, free-standing slab or block of stone. Carved or inscribed, it may serve as a gravestone, or the decorative stone mounted on the ridge of a pediment, answering to the terminal *antefixum*. The term more loosely applies to any slab of stone bearing an inscription, such as a plaque.　APQ

Stevenson, John James　(1831–1908) Scottish architect. *See* QUEEN ANNE REVIVAL.

Stijl, De　A group of mainly Dutch painters and architects who for some time cherished the same more or less related ideals about art and society, and published them in the journal *De Stijl* (1917–31). Its founder, Theo van *Doesburg, was the central figure; with his death, *De Stijl* and the coherence between its collaborators came to an end. In the early stage (1917–22), apart from van Doesburg, there were the painters Piet Mondrian, Bart van der Leck, and Vilmos Huszár; the sculptor Georges Vantongerloo; and the architects Jacobus J. P. *Oud, Robert van't *Hoff, Gerrit Th. *Rietveld, and Jan Wils. The second phase began at the end of 1922, without Oud, Van't Hoff, and Wils, because their contacts with van Doesburg had, for various reasons, become rather problematic. Rietveld stayed. Together with young Cor van *Eesteren, van Doesburg began a search for the ideal synthesis of painting and architecture.

　　De Stijl went public when the *Amsterdam School had become too showy. In the first issue of *De Stijl* Oud presented the Amsterdam School as 'decadent in principle' (because based on an individualistic aesthetic), whereas the creation of a modern style should be based on 'the universal'. In this style a street and a city would no longer be a random collection of individual houses, but a 'monumental' modern order of housing blocks with a strong rhythm of form and space, devoid of 'impure' particular elements. Therefore the sloping roof (or 'fake' roof) would have given way to concrete constructions with flat roofs: a demand that was crucial for budding international Modernism.

　　It is ironic that despite its 'universal' and collectivist programme, the architecture of De Stijl looks much more divergent than that of the Amsterdam School. The architects were too diverse to realize a collective ideal. To determine the idea of 'the' *stijl*, Wils was too much an average architect, Van't Hoff too much a dreamer, Rietveld too much a quiet genius of furniture-making, van Eesteren the architect too much an average designer, and Oud despite his self-assurance too much a doubter. The consistency and impact of De Stijl were the achievement of two painters apart from van Doesburg, in particular Mondrian, who formulated and visualized 'new imaging' (*nieuwe beelding*), a concept he himself, using a French translation, called *néo-plasticisme*, but which in fact meant 'a new way of creating an image', an expression of a new, all-embracing culture for a new, enlightened society.　AVDW (trans. CVE)

　　Blotkamp, C. (ed.), *De beginjaren van De Stijl 1917–1922* (1982)
　　Blotkamp, C. (ed.), *De vervolgjaren van De Stijl 1922–1932* (1996)

Stile Littorio　A term used by architects and critics to refer to the official architecture of the Fascist regime in Italy (1922–43)—the word 'Littorio' referring to one of the emblems of the Fascist Party. In particular it has been associated with the stripped down monumental

Classicism of major public commissions proposed for and built in Rome. The idea of a Stile Littorio was a counterpoint to the efforts of young architects in the early 1930s to have Rationalist architecture installed as the official Fascist style. Although the first use of the term came with the publication of the results of the first competition for the Palazzo del Littorio of 1934, it was with the design and construction of the Città Universitaria in Rome (1932–5) that a relatively unitary neoclassical style was first implemented on a large scale. The Palazzo del Littorio, originally to be located along the Via dell'Impero, was, however, the first national competition where Italian architects were asked to design a monumentally scaled image for the Fascist state. While the architects of this competition did not provide a unitary response, this project and the later series of competitions related to the Esposizione Universale di Roma (1937–42) did move Italian architects towards a more overtly monumental and symbolic style.   BLM

Stirling, Sir James (1924–92) British architect. During the 1950s and 1960s, his designs typified a move away from a rigid application of *Modernism. In the next two decades, unlike contemporaries such as *Foster and *Rogers, who focused on the development of the technological basis of Modernism (*see* HIGH TECH), he was the only major English architect of his generation to move decisively towards *postmodernism.

His first significant work, in partnership with James *Gowan (1923–   ), was a small block of flats at Ham Common, west London (1957–8). Inspired by *Le Corbusier's Maisons Jaoul, its directly expressive use of common materials, stock brick and concrete, was regarded (though not by its designers) as one of the first instances of *Brutalism.

The partnership's next design, the Leicester University Engineering Building (1960–63), attracted

Engineering Building, Leicester University, England (Stirling & Gowan, 1960–63)

worldwide attention. The brief was to provide workshops for heavy machinery, laboratories, and lecture theatres, all placed on an awkward site on the edge of a public park. Their ingenious solution was a glass and red brick building in the heroic manner of *Constructivist architects such as *Melnikov. Nonetheless, the design still operated within the limits of *Functionalism: a clear correspondence between façade and plan, and the use of industrial materials (red bricks and patent glazing). However, unlike Stirling's

873

later buildings, it was technologically unadventurous. It used well-tested materials, and, apart from the glazing systems, it was made on site and not prefabricated.

The partnership dissolved in 1963. While Gowan continued to work with brick and glass, but at a smaller scale, only Stirling's next two commissions (with Michael Wilford, his partner from 1964 till his death) were in this idiom, and also at a larger scale: the History Faculty Building, Cambridge (1964–7), and the Florey Building, Queen's College, Oxford (1966–71). The distinctive character of Stirling's Modernism can best be seen at Cambridge, where in some ways it is a deliberate *riposte* to the gentle *picturesque of the nearby Raised Faculty Buildings by Casson, or the sensitive orthodox-modernist approach of *Powell and Moya's Cripps Building, St John's College.

Many architects would have made a successful career out of developing minor variations along the same theme, but Stirling moved restlessly on, using prefabricated concrete units for the first time (student accommodation at St Andrews University, 1968ff.) and prefabricated glass reinforced polyester (the Olivetti Training School, Haslemere, Surrey, 1970–72; the Southgate housing estate, Runcorn, Lancashire, 1969ff., his only design for social housing). In the latter two cases, he began his first experiments with bright colours, such as lime green, mauve, and red.

Although highly rated by other modernists, his buildings were a technical disaster. They all suffered variously from leaks, poor insulation, and defective acoustics, to the extent that the Southgate estate was demolished in the 1990s, and the others required considerable repair work. The major causes were undoubtedly cuts in already inadequate budgets, hasty construction, and the inexperience of the contractors, but Stirling's egotistical concern with technological experimentation was partly to blame. Stirling's reputation suffered, so that he built only two more major buildings in England, and his next commission anywhere did not arrive until 1977.

When it did, it was a major surprise: the Neue Staatsgalerie, Stuttgart (1977–84). The Staatsgalerie was the first in a new wave of *museums and art galleries, 'signature' buildings which did not so much provide a setting for the gallery's collection, as draw attention to the building as a way of giving a city a new 'image'. The design was cleverly fitted into the existing urban fabric, rather than set as an isolated monument in the conventional modernist manner. It consists of a round sculpture court, an entrance hall lit by an undulating glass wall with bright green glazing bars, and ramps which lead up to the galleries. The banded stone used throughout the scheme, the numerous references to the work of German neoclassical architects such as *Schinkel, and the glass wall were instantly recognizable images.

For the rest of his career, Stirling had numerous commissions, two of which may be singled out as typical.

The Clore Building, Tate Britain, London (1980–86), attracted much controversy for its use of solid over void and other devices, suggesting an interest in Mannerism. More evident to the general public was its use of bright colours, particularly green. It is hard to judge Stirling's intentions in using colour, since at this period he wrote so little about his ideas (see *Writings on Architecture*, 1998, ed. R. Maxwell).

His final design was for a 5-storey office building, No. 1 Poultry, City of London (1986–98). In a prominent site, its banded stone in buff and pink is visually quite unrelated to the neighbouring buildings, as are its variety of historical references. Nor is there any clear relationship between the plan, the façades, or the function. Perhaps it has a metaphorical connection to the Midland Bank opposite by *Lutyens, who was also interested in what he called the 'High Game' of architecture. Stirling's untimely death cut short a career which was still developing in new directions.   PG

stoa In ancient Greek architecture a portico or roofed colonnade, which might be of far greater length than width and incorporate 2 storeys. The restoration of just such a stoa in the Athenian Forum is used to house an archaeological museum. Although suited to many uses, such as a market place, the great Stoa Poikile (or Painted Portico) in Athens achieved immortality as the place where Zeno of Citium founded his school of philosophy (*c*.310 BC), his students consequently being known as Stoics. The type appears in Roman and Byzantine architecture, and is similar to a medieval cloister range or Renaissance loggia.   APQ

Stone, Edward Durrell (1902–78) US architect. For the first twenty years of his career, Stone's designs made quite a significant contribution to the development of US Modernism. The Mandel house, Bedford Falls, NY (1933), was one of the first modernist houses on the east coast; he designed sections of the Radio City Music Hall, and with Philip Goodwin (1885–1958) was responsible for the Museum of Modern Art, or MoMA (1938–9).

Thereafter his work assumed an increasingly formal, almost classicizing, tendency. The US Embassy, Delhi (1954) established the pattern, followed by the Kennedy Center for the Performing Arts, Washington DC (1961–71). The Embassy retained a modernist concern for simple box-like structures, but organized on an axial plan and surrounded by thin, unornamented columns. On a much larger scale, the General Motors Building, NYC (1968), favours marble cladding and bay windows rather than the steel and glass streamlined façades of his first period. Neither making overt historic references, nor expressing a rationalist approach to structure or plan, his work is an enigma to modernists and postmodernists alike.   PG

strainer arch An arch set within an opening so as to resist inward pressure from the side members. Such

arches are famously employed across all four transept openings at Wells Cathedral (*c*.1338–40), where they are in the form of a symmetrical scissor, or one arch standing upside down on an identical arch.   APQ

strapwork Decoration comprising interlaced bands, sometimes edged and studded as though representing leather straps, common in the late 16th and early 17th centuries on furniture and panelling as well as in stone architecturally. Commonly used to surround a chimney-piece or achievement of arms, strapwork sometimes forms an open parapet.   APQ

Strauven, Gustave (1878–1919) Belgian architect. *See* ART NOUVEAU; BELGIUM, MODERN.

Street, George Edmund (1824–81) English architect. A leading High Victorian Gothic Revivalist, Street assisted George *Gilbert Scott (1844–9) before becoming Diocesan Architect of Oxford in 1850. That year, he toured France and Italy, and thereafter regularly visited the Continent, finding sublimity and solace, like *Ruskin, in the Alps. He published his account of northern Italy in *Brick and Marble Architecture in the Middle Ages* (1855), and his *Some Account of Gothic Architecture in Spain* (1865) became a standard work. He saw Gothic evolving for the needs of modern buildings. His own style matured with the vigorous, Italianate St James the Less, Westminster (1859–61), the simpler sharp angles and rugged verticality of St Philip and St James, Oxford (1858–65), and St Mary Magdalene, Paddington (1865–78), churches which reflected the current ethos of 'muscular Christianity'. In addition to numerous restorations, he built vicarages and estate cottages, as well as St Peter, Bournemouth, Hampshire (1858–65), St John, Torquay, Devon (1862–85), the Crimean Memorial Church, Istanbul (1863–8), St Saviour, Eastbourne, Sussex (1867–8), St John the Divine, Kennington, London (1870–74), and also

St Margaret's Convent, East Grinstead, Sussex (1865–74). These are in many ways eclectic: his early steeples could be Italian campaniles, whereas later ones are far closer to Normandy. His pleasure in colour settled into the 'streaky bacon' effect of red brick and Bath stone. He favoured apsidal chancels with a clutch of buttresses more for vigorous effect than structural necessity, sometimes haphazardly tacked on to the canted ends of naves akin to *Butterfield's.

Street employed several assistants, but, believing that 'three-fourths of the poetry of building lies in its minor details', worked on these himself. William *Morris and John Dando *Sedding worked briefly in his office,; Philip *Webb and Norman *Shaw were successive Chief Assistants. It was in his office that the late Victorian style was born, though he did not take part in it himself. He was too busy, having entered the badly managed competition for new Royal Courts of Justice in London in 1866. The site was changed, and, after coming second, he was declared winner and asked to adapt his reduced Gothic design to incorporate some of *Waterhouse's plan. Begun 1874, it was completed in 1882 shortly after he had died from nervous exhaustion hastened by overwork and his excessive conscientiousness and inability to delegate.   APQ

Street, A. E., *Memoir of George Edmund Street* (1888)

Strickland, William (1788–1854) US architect.

The artistically gifted youth was apprenticed briefly to Benjamin Henry *Latrobe (1764–1820) in Delaware before returning to Philadelphia where, at 19, he designed a Gothic-style Masonic Hall (1808–11, demolished). He subsequently won the competition for the Second Bank of the United States, in Doric with two temple fronts imitating the Parthenon. Latrobe accused Strickland of stealing the design from him. Prominently sited on fashionable Chestnut Street, Philadelphia, the *bank (1818–24) became one of the most famous buildings in the country and

played a key role in launching the *Greek Revival nationwide.

In 1825 the Franklin Institute sent Strickland to England to study canals and railways, and on his return he engaged in several engineering projects, including the Delaware Breakwater (begun 1829). His innovative United States Naval Asylum, Philadelphia (1826–9), used iron for its long piazzas. In a flurry of commissions, Strickland gave Philadelphia a series of landmarks, including places of worship, theatres, the replacement steeple for Independence Hall (1828; an early example of historic preservation), and the elegant Merchants' Exchange (1832–4), with a curving portico reminiscent of the work of John *Nash in London. After another trip to England and the Continent (1838) and a fallow period, he concluded his career with the Tennessee State Capitol on a hilltop in Nashville (1845–59), which repeats the Greek Revival theme of a Choragic Monument of Lysicrates tower, already used on the Merchants' Exchange. Strickland is buried in the capitol, his masterpiece. Like his mentor, Latrobe, Strickland exemplified the architect–engineer fighting hard for professional stature in the young republic, and he was president of the short-lived but promising American Institution of Architects (1836–7).   WBM

Gilchrist, A. A., *William Strickland* (1950)

structural forms Forms in which the strengths and stiffnesses of construction materials are exploited to meet needs for spanning, enclosure, and support.

Architecture is primarily an art of spatial enclosure. This has always called for structural forms capable of spanning over a void and, unless these have sat directly on the ground, for other forms to provide them with support. There have also been needs for bridging over gaps in the support and for further forms to complete the vertical enclosure if this was not already adequately provided by the support. Moreover the support has had not only to bear the weights of the spanning and bridging forms; it has also had to resist any horizontal thrusts exerted by these forms and any other horizontal loads or disturbances such as wind or earthquake. Spanning and bridging forms are considered first in what follows, and then their supports. (*See* BRIDGES; CONSTRUCTION MATERIALS; CONSTRUCTION PROCESS.) Foundations, having only an indirect influence on architectural choice, are not considered.

1) Possible spanning forms up to about 1800 With the materials available before the 19th century, the choice of spanning and bridging forms that did not exert horizontal thrusts was limited to simple beams of timber or stone and simple *trusses. These could be supported by timber posts, stone columns, or piers or walls of brickwork, stone, or Roman concrete. Provided that these had a firm base and that the beams or trusses were well seated on them, the only other requirement was some provision to avoid lateral movement due to disturbances such as wind or earthquake.

Arches, vaults, and domes of brick, stone, Roman concrete, or framed in timber were alternative forms that all did exert horizontal thrusts. To contain them as well as resisting the other possible disturbances it was necessary to provide further resistance, either by more substantial supports or by the use of ties. The structural behaviour of these thrusting forms is nevertheless simpler. They will therefore be considered first with only a brief look at earlier approximations to them before turning to the non-thrusting ones.

i) true arches In a true masonry arch, at least above the haunches, the individual wedge-shaped blocks or voussoirs are set radially in relation to the centre or centres of curvature of the under surface to give one another mutual support, and they usually require temporary support there during construction. On completion the arch supports itself, and the loads imposed on it, by a compressive thrust that follows

a curve within its depth. At its supports this acts horizontally as well as vertically. The magnitude of the horizontal component in relation to the total vertical load depends on the flatness of this curve, and hence on both the flatness of the *soffit and the depth of the arch. The flatter the curve, the greater is this component for a given loading. Any giving way to it by the supports may also change it because it will be accommodated by several splayed openings or effective hinges through which the curve will then have to pass. Since the whole compression will be concentrated at these hinges on the narrow lines of contact, the average stress has to remain far below the full strength of the material if this is not to split and perhaps precipitate slips at the joints. Arch rings were usually deep enough, however, to avoid a resulting collapse. Indeed experience of this forgiving character allowed a fairly free choice of soffit profiles.

ii) Barrel, groined, and ribbed vaults Much the same behaviour is characteristic of space-enclosing forms like barrel, groined, and ribbed *vaults. When uniformly supported throughout its length, the barrel vault is merely an arch extended laterally and behaves in almost the same way. In a groined vault, two barrel vaults cross, meeting at their crowns but with those parts inside the groins or lines of intersection missing. The internal thrusts are then channelled to the feet of the groins, which are the stiffest parts of the vault. In a masonry or brick ribbed vault, ribs projecting below the vault carry some of the thrusts. The actual proportion depends on the precise way in which the intervening vault severies join the ribs, on relative stiffnesses, and on the sequence of construction. But it is not usually of much importance. This characteristic was exploited in two further developments. In one, notably by *Guarini (1624–83), some of the severies were omitted leaving only the rib cage. In the other, notably in some central European late Gothic vaults, advantage was taken of the continuity of the vault surface by interrupting the ribs in seemingly impossible ways.

iii) Domes In true *domes, with the masonry bed joints more or less at right angles to the soffit, the behaviour of any radial vertical section is like that of an arch, and would always exert an outward thrust at the base but for the simultaneous presence of ring-like horizontal courses. Those towards the top will be in compression throughout construction. Both then, and later if there is an open eye, they can thus act as supports for the incomplete radial arches. Lower down, this compression changes progressively to tension as construction proceeds, and this tension can contain the thrusts if the material can resist them. However, it is unlikely that sufficient tension was ever mobilized in any but the smallest masonry dome, on account of both the limited tensile strength of the stone and the fact that, unless the blocks are cramped together, it can be transmitted from block to block only by blocks above and below through friction or shear in the bed joints. Although there was more likelihood initially of sufficient tensile resistance in smallish domes of brickwork or Roman concrete, they also now usually exhibit substantial radial cracking. Outward thrusts would have developed as soon as this occurred.

iv) False arches and domes Even in earlier approximations to true arches, horizontal thrusts usually arose. They certainly did so when there were only two blocks of stone leaning on one another as an inverted V. When successive courses of horizontally bedded stone projected towards one another on each side of a gap until it was reduced sufficiently to be bridged by a single further block, such a thrust could be avoided only if the gap was a small one and the over-sailing courses were so constructed that on each side they would independently be amply stable in spite

of the overhangs. Otherwise they would lean towards one another until stabilized by the thrust.

Irrespective of span, false domes of any span could be constructed with successive over-sailing courses in much the same way, and even more easily, because each complete course was a continuous ring, and hence not liable to collapse inwards. On the other hand, if the profile was like that of a true dome and not more conical or spire-like, there would be a tendency for the lower courses to burst outwards as construction advanced. To curb this tendency it was necessary to add weight on the exterior, as was typically done by piling earth around it, as at Mycenae.

v) Beams The beam is a non-thrusting form because, in spite of its simple rectilinear geometry, it acts internally as a shallow arch whose thrust is neutralized by mirror-image tensions, also within its depth. It usually spanned simply between end supports, but the mirror-image tensions when bending in the opposite sense allowed it also to project freely beyond a support, either as an independent cantilever if restrained from rotating there or if similarly restrained as a continuation of the main span. When it is cantilevered beyond a support or continuously over one, and bends there in the opposite sense, compression becomes tension, and tension becomes compression. Most beams were either straight lengths of timber or monoliths of a good stone such as marble or granite. When not used as found, timber was usually dressed to a rectangular cross section and stone lintels were almost always similarly dressed. This was structurally very wasteful because it meant that the full strength of the material was brought into play only near midspan and, even there, only near the face subject to tension. This severely limited feasible spans when stone was used. With timber, the much lower stiffness of the material meant that the limit was more likely to be reached when there was too much deflection.

vi) Roof trusses and timber counterparts of the arched masonry forms Where a timber beam was too short or not strong enough for the loading, a simple truss was a possible alternative. In this, two inclined rafter-like lengths of timber spanned the gap as an inverted V and their feet were connected by a third length which served as a tie to absorb the horizontal thrust that they exerted and prevent them from spreading. The chief limitations then arose from the difficulty of effectively transferring the tension in the tie to the inclined members and transferring it from one length of timber to another if a single length was not long enough. As in all traditional timber joints, cutting into the cross section reduced the effective strength, and there was a further limitation because load was transferred in the joint by shear along the grain, which timber is ill fitted to resist.

Efficient timber roof trusses were nevertheless built from at least Roman times and continued to be built in Italy and later in France, although they did not appear in England until even later. There, whether through cautious indecision or more deliberately, what should have been the tie was long used partly as a beam to carry an upright member supporting the heads of the rafters—a practice that is reflected in the still current terms 'tie *beam*' for the former and 'crown *post*' for the latter—when this member also should have been a tie to reduce sag of the main tie. Over the unusually wide span of Westminster Hall (1394–1402) a thrusting arch was actually the principal support, relegating the associated *hammerbeam 'truss' to a secondary role.

Since timber rarely grew in a fully arched form, the timber arch usually had to be constructed of numerous lengths assembled into an arch. Simply butting individual lengths against one another could have led to collapse. To prevent it, several arch-like sets of timbers had to be connected to one another with their joints staggered, as they were at Westminster, so that rotation was always prevented by the bending strength and stiffness of adjacent members. Thanks to this bending stiffness, there was more freedom in choosing the profile than there was for a masonry arch, and shallower profiles were usual. When, in 16th-century France, suitable long lengths of timber were becoming scarce, a form closer to that of the masonry arch was adopted, using shorter but deeper and fairly thin pieces of timber side by side. This would have allowed more rotation at the joints than in the masonry counterpart, resulting in a correspondingly restricted choice of profile.

2) Provisions for support up to about 1800
Structures with only non-thrusting spanning elements required only vertical support if this support had a firm base and there were no disturbances such as wind or earthquake. It could be provided by timber posts or stone columns of roughly circular or rectangular cross section, or by piers or walls of brick or stone and of almost any desired cross section.

In practice, some resistance to possible lateral displacements was always called for. In stone column-and-beam structures it was provided most readily by adopting sufficiently sturdy proportions for the columns and ensuring well-dressed bearing surfaces at their feet and heads, as in some early Egyptian temples (26th century BC and later) and even in the much later 5-storey Panch Mahal at Fatehpur Sikri (AD 1575). Standing on firm bases, they were stabilized by a slight lifting of their centres of gravity in any rocking movement. With more widely spaced slender columns, as in the great audience halls at Persepolis (between 521 and 465 BC), there was more need for the bracing provided there by enclosing walls.

In all but the smallest timber post-and-beam structures, the necessary resistance could be assured by enclosing walls, infills of masonry, or equivalent diagonal bracing. Knee braces of the joints between posts and beams were possibly the commonest way of preventing stability-threatening relative rotations. If they were present on both windward and leeward sides of the posts, those in compression could be relied upon even if, as was likely, the others went slack. A notable alternative was adopted first in China and then in Japan. Here, these joints were given a measure of rigidity by elaborating them into multi-level sets of brackets. These projected increasing distances from the heads of the posts and were alternately in line with one set of beams and another set at right angles to it.

Since early arches over openings in a continuous wall were of short span, the wall itself provided ample resistance to their thrusts, even when they were given a flat soffit. Early barrel vaults, whether truly arched or corbelled, had their thrusts similarly resisted by the thick low walls between which they spanned or the massive masonry of the pyramid, ziggurat, or Eastern temple in which they were embedded.

When wider spanning arches or barrel, groined, or ribbed vaults were supported only on isolated piers, resistance was less readily assured. The piers would be subjected to oblique loads and their response to them would have depended a good deal on the character of the masonry, brickwork, or concrete. The best resistance was to be expected from the solid, excellent cut masonry of Roman and early Byzantine times. Much less was to be expected when large quantities of mortar were used, or when good masonry was only a facing to a weak rubble fill. Collapse could then be forestalled only by adding buttresses or iron ties. For this reason external *flying buttresses became characteristic of tall Gothic churches and cathedrals whose main piers were usually bowed outwards very visibly by the oblique and eccentric loads they bore. Even earlier, extra buttressing had been required during construction of the large church of Hagia Sophia (532–7) in spite of the excellent construction and seemingly ample cross sections of the lower parts of the main piers supporting its dome and the cramping

together of the blocks of the cornices. Contributory factors here were the use of brickwork with thick mortar joints for the original interconnections of the piers and for their upward continuations, and the too speedy construction of this brickwork.

The alternative to buttressing the piers was to use iron ties near the springing levels. This was done most frequently in Italy, perhaps partly because wind loads—which could be resisted only by buttresses on the lee side—were lower there than they were further west. The timber 'ties' commonly found in small later Byzantine churches could have restrained possible inward movements of the piers in the later stages of an earthquake as well as perhaps helping to resist the moderate thrusts of their vaulting systems.

For the earliest, mostly false, domes the necessary resistance was provided directly by the ground on which they were built. For later domes, constructed well above ground level, the alternatives were broadly similar to those for other arched forms except that the thrusts to be resisted were not only those of the dome itself. They included also the usually larger thrusts exerted by the arches and squinches or pendentives of the supporting structure if this was not simply a solid ground-based drum. Tying of the dome itself had to be circumferential. Cramping together the blocks of the cornice in which it stood was an early form of such tying, but was usually unlikely to have been really adequate. Circumferential timber ties, also of doubtfully adequate strength, were built into at least some early brick domes in Iran. Stronger and more durable iron ties were usually required, and it became normal practice from the early 17th century to install them around larger domes during their construction.

3) Possible spanning forms after about
1800 Choice became wider after the late 18th century with the development of new materials as strong in tension as in compression, a more reliable and stronger

*concrete, the use of *steel reinforcement to overcome the tensile weakness of this concrete, new construction techniques, and new jointing possibilities including the use of new glues for jointing timber.

Cross sections and self weight could be greatly reduced, thereby allowing greater spans with reduced horizontal thrusts. Buildings could also rise to greater heights thanks to new ways of resisting tendencies to lateral movement or elastic buckling. These new possibilities led however to some blurring of the earlier distinctions between clearly defined elements as they were subsumed into more complex total forms. Much must therefore be omitted from the following outline.

i) Arches, vaults, and shells When cast iron replaced masonry or timber in arches, chiefly in bridge arches, it had little influence on the forms adopted. These mostly replicated timber prototypes, initially even with similar joints. But when wrought *iron and then steel became available, their much higher tensile strengths allowed changes. Different and more efficient cross sections were adopted and their bending strengths and stiffnesses could be fully exploited thanks to new jointing techniques. Greater spans became possible with less need for a profile that conformed fairly closely to a compressive thrust line determined by the expected loading. Much the same happened when reinforced concrete was used, except that solid cross sections with reinforcement appropriately distributed through them usually remained preferable. Laminated timber continued to be used throughout the 19th century in the same ways as before and continued to suffer from poor durability in the open even when protected, as in the covered bridges of central Europe and North America. The later 20th-century form, with thinner laminations bonded by more durable glues, could however be used in much the same way as steel except that it usually called for constant solid cross sections.

The chief new possibilities were the thin reinforced concrete *shell and corresponding grids of relatively thin timber laths. Both were more versatile counterparts of the heavier masonry or concrete dome or vault.

Even when the masonry dome was tied circumferentially to contain its thrust, it invariably cracked as a result of a spreading of its supports. It therefore required a thickness appropriate to an arch of similar span. A suitably reinforced domical concrete shell can be much thinner if there are no large concentrated loads, because the reinforcement can both resist all tension and coerce the radial compressions to follow the curvature of the surface irrespective of the profile. The only limit is set by a need to avoid local buckling.

Appropriately distributed reinforcement can also allow not only forms like barrels, but also others that were previously possible only on a very small scale, to do more than span in simple arching compression. A barrel form, or even a folded plate, can be made to span as a beam or cantilever if it is suitably supported at isolated positions along its length, and saddle-like forms such as the hyperbolic paraboloid (with convex curvature in one direction and concave in the other) can span between their low points by arching compression in the first direction and tension in the other.

However, choice is not unrestricted. Curvature must be continuous, and appropriate edge support is always required at the shell boundaries. Geometry also has to be matched to the requirements of the anticipated range of loading if a uniform thickness, much less than masonry would require, is to be adequate. If it is not, local thickening is necessary, and local ribbed support is needed if the curvature is discontinuous, as it was in the shells that *Utzon initially proposed for Sydney Opera House (1960).

ii) Beams, slabs, and shear walls The casting process did away with the need for an inefficient solid rectangular cross section for beams. An I-shaped cross section with a bottom flange much wider than the top one was much better matched to the internal bending stresses and the comparatively low tensile strength of 19th-century cast iron. Cast-iron beams could also be easily made deeper towards the centre to match the greater bending moment there when the beam was simply supported at both ends. To make an incombustible floor, adjacent beams could be spanned by brick jack-arches (flattish barrel vaults) with their thrusts absorbed by iron tie rods.

Wrought iron, and then various qualities of steel, allowed the rolling of new and even more efficient cross sections without the restriction on length imposed by casting. Top and bottom flanges were now made of equal width to take advantage of the now equal tensile and compressive strengths. As well as cantilevering beyond their supports when desired, longer beams could also be made to span continuously over supports, thereby considerably reducing the bending moments at midspan. Where standard rolled sections were not adequate, larger sections, including tubular ones, could be built up using the newly developed techniques of riveting and later of welding. As these built-up forms became larger, chiefly in bridges, narrow stiffeners were added to prevent buckling of thin webs and thin plates in compression flanges.

Reinforced concrete could serve in much the same roles without the restriction to a few standard cross sections of constant depth that arose with rolled steel. It also allowed a greater choice of cross section and profile to match strength and stiffness to need, and made possible for the first time the casting of relatively thin slabs of any desired width. Suitably reinforced, these could span simultaneously in more than one direction, either between beams or directly between isolated supporting columns. They could also resist horizontal loads tending to distort them in their own plane. When serving as a continuous floor, this latter characteristic allowed them to distribute wind loads between all the columns carrying the floor. Up-ended as walls and suitably reinforced, they could alternatively resist horizontal loads acting in their own planes as mentioned in the final section below.

iii) Trusses, space frames, and framed counterparts of other spanning forms The design of wide spanning trusses benefited chiefly from the availability of steel with a tensile strength to match its compressive strength, and from joints better able to transmit the tensions, though a clearer understanding of the way in which loads were distributed through the members of the truss was called for to take full advantage of it.

Before this understanding was acquired, many new designs for both timber and iron or both together were proposed, especially in North America in response to early-19th-century bridging needs. They all had far more members than were really necessary. As analytical ability grew and there were requirements also for wider spanning roof trusses, these designs were followed first by simpler, easily analysed ones with pinned joints, just the right number of members, and a clear differentiation between ties and struts, and then by more economical ones sometimes calling for rigid joints. For a considerable time they nevertheless still envisaged the behaviour as being essentially planar, even when parallel triangulated bridge trusses spanning in vertical planes to resist vertical loads were connected to one another by horizontal diagonal bracing to resist horizontal loads.

The final development in this respect, more relevant to buildings and calling for more complex analysis of the forces in the members, has been what is known as the space frame. Its members are deliberately arranged and connected in such a way that all share in resisting any force acting on the frame. Several meet at each joint, often at varying angles to one another, and their connection is facilitated by new types of joint often made of cast steel. It usually serves as a counterpart to a beam or reinforced concrete slab, but can also serve as a counterpart to a space-enclosing form like a reinforced concrete shell. In the domical form, the pattern of framing previously adopted—in which radiating sets of arched ribs were linked by horizontal hoops—is typically replaced by an overall triangulated mesh such as that seen in Buckminster *Fuller's geodesic domes.

iv) Cable nets and tensile membranes A new departure has been the use of networks of cables, made from cold-drawn high-tensile steel wire, to support the first of two far larger counterparts of traditional tents. Initially networks of cables carrying a weathering surface spanned between suitably curved edge beams. More recently it has been usual for similar networks to span between heavier cables which are themselves slung between a number of isolated pylons and ground anchorages. All the cables must be in sufficient tension to maintain the geometry of the whole network without excessive billowing in the wind. This calls for them to have opposite curvatures in different directions as in the saddle-shaped shell. The difference from the shell is that, to obtain the necessary tension throughout, even those with arch-like curvature must be placed initially in tension. This is done by applying additional tension to the set with the opposite curvature.

In one sense there is again a much greater freedom than with masonry in choosing the geometry. But it is still not an unlimited freedom. It is more limited than with the reinforced concrete shell because it is not possible to vary the thickness to match the expected loading. It must be exercised largely in choosing the principal points of support and the boundaries of the networks. To allow the use of cables of constant cross section, a strict discipline must then be observed in the choice of network geometry and intersection points. Already, for the pioneering roofs for the Munich Olympic stadia (1972), the precision required could be achieved only with the aid of a powerful computer.

In the closer counterpart of the traditional tent, durable high-tensile fabrics span in much the same ways as suspended cable networks. They must be similarly pre-stressed through boundary cables, with tension in the direction of arching curvature acting against an enhanced natural tension in the other direction, and the choice of geometry is similarly circumscribed. Indeed it is even more circumscribed on account of the different ways in which the fabric responds to loading in the directions of warp and weft. A precisely determined geometry is again essential if the stresses are to be kept as uniform as possible. This calls for precise cutting of the fabric, with the additional difficulty that narrow strips of a surface continuously curved in all directions cannot be unrolled completely flat.

As an alternative to being hung from pylons, such fabrics can be given a form which, except in any waisted regions, curves in the same way in all directions. Unless it is double-skinned and inflated in contiguous arch-like sections, this form must have its shape maintained, like that of a hot-air balloon, by an internal air pressure sufficiently in excess of external pressures at all times to produce tension throughout. Since the required tension increases rapidly as the curvature is reduced, it is usually increased locally throughout by adding a cable network above the fabric.

4) Provisions for support after about 1800 With this last form, the whole nature of the structure has changed. It is almost a purely tensile one—the antithesis of most early structures which act largely in compression. It must be tied down against the internal pressure. But a counterpart to the normal support acting in compression is also required. This is an air pump. Hitherto this air-supported form has been an economical way of meeting some fairly straightforward requirements for temporary shelter. But will it ever be recognized as architecture?

Other new means of support for wide-span structures do not depart as radically from earlier ones. They still differ according to whether the spanning forms do or do not exert horizontal loads, but not to the same extent as previously because the thrusts exerted by arching forms are more readily contained by reinforcement, especially if this is pre-stressed. If they are not so contained, suitably inclined supports of either tubular steel or reinforced concrete usually serve the purpose. With non-thrusting space frames or beam grids a full assurance of stability is best provided by limiting rotations at the head of the supports. This is done by means of rigid, usually welded, joints at the column heads, or by adopting a different type of support. A V-shaped design, or a three-dimensionally forked one, as at Naples Central Railway Station (c.1958) and the Stuttgart Airport terminal building (1992), best serve this purpose.

The chief developments calling for further consideration are those that arise in multi-storey buildings from needs to resist wind- and earthquake-induced loads, rather than from thrusts generated within the building. One limit to doing so by relying on the in-plane stiffness of masonry walls was reached in the Monadnock Building in Chicago (1889) when the wall thickness then deemed necessary to support the weight of the structure above led to far too much of the total floor area being filled at the foot with masonry. With modern brickwork, and more so with reinforced concrete, this limit has been much increased, but not sufficiently, even with the latter, to justify much reliance on it as more than a supplementary source of resistance.

In early iron-framed structures with cast-iron beams and columns, the columns were cross-shaped or hollow circular in cross section to make better use of the material than a solid rectangular section would have done. But the joints at the column heads were no stiffer than those in earlier timber framing. Wrought-iron columns usually had I-shaped cross sections which differed from those adopted for beams only in having sturdier flanges. Riveting made more rigid joints possible, although the necessary cleats between column and beam did still allow some play. After steel-supplanted wrought iron, the subsequent introduction of welding finally made completely rigid joints feasible and the portal frame—a beam supported by two columns—became a basic component of both wide-span and multi-storey structures.

In single-storey frames of this type, such as those in the Crown Hall of the Illinois Institute of Technology in Chicago (*Mies van der Rohe, 1956), horizontal thrusts do arise because the frame is effectively an arch whose profile is able to depart so far from that of the usual arch by virtue of the bending stiffnesses of both beam and columns. But in multi-storey frames the thrusts are absorbed by the beams below, acting as ties. The columns and beams together then resist any horizontal loads imposed from outside by all bending in S-shaped curves, with a consequent small horizontal movement at each storey. If they provide the only resistance, a height is eventually reached at which the movements become excessive. The number of columns in each storey has little effect on this height because each frame responds in the same way, the total side load being simply distributed between the frames by the floors in the way mentioned earlier.

Three ways have been devised to raise the limit without simply beefing up the frame members as the walls were beefed up in the Monadnock Building. One is to arrange for part of the load to be resisted by the inherently stiffer reinforced concrete walls of lift shafts and stair wells, as became common in the 1950s. A second is to reduce the bending of the beams by making them proportionately deeper and stiffer, ideally to the extent that the columns effectively bend only as one much stiffer tubular column, as was first done in the New York World Trade Centre (1967–72). The third is to abandon the portal-frame unit in each storey and use instead much stiffer triangulated external trusses as the principal supports, as was done in the Chicago Hancock Building (1969). Numerous variations have since been played on these three possibilities.   RJM

Mainstone, R. J., *Developments in Structural Form* (2nd edn, 1998)

structural principles   These are the ways in which an understanding of structural needs and behaviour has been brought to bear on the structural aspects of design.

1) Structural needs   The principles to be considered here are those directed towards achieving *firmitas*, the first requisite of good building in the Vitruvian triad of '*firmitas, utilitas et venustas*' (*De Architectura*, Bk1, ch.3) or 'commodity, firmness, and delight' as rendered by Sir Henry Wotton (*The Elements of Architecture*, 1624).

What Vitruvius referred to as *firmitas* would then have been chiefly the ability of the structure to support its own weight and any loads imposed on it by users and the environment. Today, user-imposed loads and even environmental ones tend to be proportionately larger as structures become lighter. Deformations under these loads also call for more attention. If, for instance, the whole structure sways in the wind, this must not jeopardize stability, disrupt services, cause excessive damage to finishes, or alarm the occupants. During construction, loads on the incomplete structure will mostly be smaller. But, with parts missing, they must still be safely supported.

These requirements are met chiefly by ensuring throughout that all loads are balanced right down to the foundations by the resistances opposed to them,

and that there is adequate stiffness throughout. It may be necessary also to ensure that the energy imparted by repetitively varying loads like those due to wind, continuous traffic, or a major earthquake are safely dissipated.

Ensuring this balance has always been partly a matter of the choice of overall structural geometry—of the way in which the elements of the structure are disposed in space and connected to one another—and partly a matter of choices of the geometry, the materials used for them, and any other characteristics of the elements and their interconnections that confer strength and stiffness. The possible range of the latter choices has greatly increased in recent times, and so has their importance.

2) Early principles   Millennia ago, repeated trial and error would have shown that some ways of assembling rocks or logs found lying on the ground would be stable while others would not, and again that some rocks or logs would bear the loads upon them while others might split or buckle. A rock jammed between two others would stand as a rudimentary arch. Two logs propped against one another as an inverted V might likewise remain standing—but only if they did not together collapse sideways. A third leaning against them at the peak could prevent this collapse.

Further experience with other and more complex forms, including the experience gained as construction proceeded, would have given a broad intuitive understanding of the structural responses brought into play—mostly at that time direct compression, perhaps some bending, and sometimes a limited amount of direct tension in cramps and ties—and of the situations in which they arose and the ability of different materials and forms to withstand them. This would have provided some basis for rational choice in place of blind trial and error, but not yet a sufficiently precise basis to yield more explicit principles of design.

The principles that then emerged as guides to future design were of two kinds. One set were derived directly from past experiences of success and failure. They were either simple numerical rules or simple geometric constructions for determining such things as the desirable width of a foundation, the width of wall required to buttress the thrust of an arch of given profile, or the width of a rib. The others were various geometric disciplines based on simple regular figures like the square and equilateral triangle. These probably began as no more than convenient techniques for setting out a ground plan or marking out a block of stone for cutting. But when they came to be used in design they seem, at least sometimes, to have been given greater authority by Platonic ideas of cosmic order based on the five regular solids. However, since they would have retained their value in setting out, and would have been relevant also to *venustas*, it is difficult now to say quite how widely they were regarded as structural guides. They also had a serious shortcoming in that, in themselves, they gave no clear indication as to how they should be applied.

3) First changes More widely valid guides to design had to break free from a direct dependence on prior experience of success and failure. This called for both precise concepts of the forces involved and a fuller understanding of the conditions of balance between forces. These were arrived at only gradually over a long period. They applied initially only to self-weight loading, and to responses that could be considered entirely in terms of direct compressions and direct tensions in any tie members—limitations which were not then unduly restrictive.

Archimedes (287–212 BC) had codified the laws of the balance for vertically acting weights in his *On the equilibrium of planes*. Leonardo (1452–1519) much later visualized non-vertical forces as acting through inclined cords attached to the balance arm. The cords passed over pulleys and carried weights at their free ends both to apply and, at the same time, measure the forces. A precise fully generalized concept of a force acting in any direction was arrived at only when Newton (1642–1727) defined it in terms of the acceleration that it would produce. Varignon and Bernouilli then laid the foundations for modern static analysis by formulating in 1717 and 1725 the related principles of virtual work and the triangle of forces.

Application of these principles to actual built structures still called for much simplified, idealized models. After a false start in 1712 by La Hire, Couplet in 1730 successfully modelled the hinging deformation of a masonry arch about to collapse and its thrust on its supporting piers, and thereby arrived at a better estimate of the width required to maintain stability than had been given by the earlier empirical purely geometric rules. Application to pin-jointed roof and bridge trusses followed.

However, the insights thus gained were not in themselves unequivocal guides to design. Judgements had to be made about such matters as the likelihood of future yielding of the supports and how closely, in the arch or indeed any vaulted structure, the thrust line could safely approach the surface of the masonry. The latter would depend on local stresses where the hinging could occur. But gravity loading due to the self weight of such structures (and for that reason determined chiefly by the structure's geometry) still greatly exceeded other loads, and the stresses in the masonry to which it gave rise were usually low enough not to call for a further criterion setting a safe limit.

4) Subsequent changes A different situation arose when loads other than self weight became more important and new materials stronger in tension and bending were introduced and widely employed. Precise estimates of the likely additional loads were then called for, plus both a fuller understanding of the structural responses to them and separate criteria for acceptable responses. In what follows we shall look first at the growths in understanding of responses and ability to predict them, and only then at the further needs.

Early attempts by Galileo (1564–1642) and others to predict bending strengths by considering the internal stresses were not wholly successful. Thus when iron beams were introduced in place of timber in the late 18th century to reduce fire risks in mill buildings and then to carry heavier loads, their bending strengths could for some time be determined only by proof testing. But from the early 19th century it became possible to predict both strengths and stiffnesses in terms of the stresses developed. Later it became possible also to predict safe loads on columns and struts, taking into account also the risk of buckling.

The next major advance was the development of predictive techniques that recognized the part played by relative stiffnesses and consequent relative lengthening, shortening, or bending of the members in determining how loads would be resisted, both in complete structures, and in composite structural elements, when geometry alone allowed more than one possibility. All reinforced and pre-stressed concrete elements are examples of the former, and the latter include all pin-jointed trusses with more than the minimum number of members for full triangulation and all but the simplest rigid-jointed frames.

By the early 20th century a start had been made on analysing the behaviour of reinforced and pre-stressed concrete elements. It had also become possible to arrive, by successive approximations, at sufficiently accurate estimates of the distribution of bending under static or quasi-static loading in the columns and beams of rigid-jointed structures like tall building frames.

The analytical techniques used then have now been superseded by more versatile ones that exploit the ability of numerical computers to solve rapidly large numbers of simultaneous algebraic equations, the most powerful and versatile being that known as the finite element method. This notionally breaks down any structure into linked small finite elements, each with characteristics representative of those of the real structure in the corresponding location. Displacements are calculated for the loading that is of interest. Other measures of response such as stress distributions are then derived from them. Structural forms such as fabric and cable-net tension roofs, whose behaviour could earlier be checked only approximately by building prototypes or suitable reduced-scale models, have thereby been brought within the scope of much more precise, purely numerical, analysis.

The chief further recent advance here has been in relation to dynamic situations in which there are rapid repetitive variations in loading. These include the moving loads of heavy traffic on a bridge, wind loads, and loads due to earthquake. Even in themselves some of these loads can be influenced by characteristics of the structure on which they act that have no effect on static loading. Their influence on traffic loading is usually small. But wind loading is much influenced by the shape of the obstacle that is presented to the wind's free flow, and earthquake loading is greatly influenced by the structure's inertia or reluctance to follow the ground movements as its foundations are pushed rapidly to and fro and (usually to a lesser extent) up and down. They must therefore be specified initially not as loads but as wind speeds or ground accelerations, leaving the loads to be derived from them. In addition, the response to all three depends not only on the stiffnesses of the structure but also on its natural frequencies of vibration in relation to the frequencies with which the load varies. When it varies roughly in tune with a predominant natural frequency, the response can be much magnified. Great strides have now been made in predicting these loads and analysing the responses of at least the types of structure most frequently built today, much assisted again by the new finite-element computational tool.

Suitable measures of likely loads, or the disturbances producing them, have called for separate studies. They began some two centuries ago with measurements of wind speeds and wind pressures. These early studies have been followed by numerous others of the loads imposed by traffic and other users, of ground accelerations due to earthquakes, of temperature variations, etc., all of them linked, as appropriate, to the types of use and/or the locations at which they are to be expected.

The first criteria of acceptable response were essentially stress criteria. Maximum design stresses were specified that typically incorporated large factors of safety on the stresses measured on test specimens of the materials to be used. These stress criteria have since been largely supplanted by criteria specifying required strengths, maximum deflections, and permissible dynamic responses, and the ways in which these should be estimated.

Typically, design loadings and criteria of acceptable response are now laid down in codes of either recommended or mandatory practice. These still do not make the design of a new building or bridge a purely routine exercise, and they can even be ignored if there are good reasons for adopting different criteria. Either way, judgements are still required, though these tend to be of different kinds from those called for earlier. Moreover the new underlying principles are neutral in respect of both *utilitas* and *venustas*, as also are codes based on them except perhaps in respect of some aspects of *utilitas*. Just how they act nevertheless still depends a good deal not only on the designer's imagination but also on his personal and essentially intuitive understanding of the loads, the conditions of balance, and the development of the necessary resistances. No rules can do away with a need for these.   RJM

Benvenuto, E., *An Introduction to the History of Structural Mechanics* (1991)

Mainstone, R. J., 'Structural theory and design before 1742' in *Structure in Architecture: History, Design, and Innovation* (1999; previously published in *Architectural Review* 1968, pp. 303–10)

Mainstone, R. J., *Developments in Structural Form* (2nd edn, 1998)

Timoshenko, S. P., *History of Strength of Materials* (1953)

Stuart, James (1713–88) English architect. Dubbed 'Athenian' on account of his ground-breaking visit to Athens with Nicholas *Revett in 1751 and eventual publication of *The Antiquities of Athens* (1762), Stuart significantly widened the current perception of Classicism which hitherto had been almost entirely focused on Rome. His innovatory Greek Doric temple of 1759 at Hagley Park, Worcestershire, was the first fruit of the visit, and his rebuilding of the chapel at Greenwich Hospital (1780–88) a fine exemplar of Grecian detail.   APQ

stucco In Italy, stucco is synonymous with a rendering, specifically of fine lime-plaster, which can be shaped and moulded into the most ornate interior decoration of walls and ceilings. In Britain, that is known simply as plaster; stucco, by distinction, is generally understood to mean any weather-proof plaster used externally. Its origins lie in an attempt to rediscover Roman cement in the 18th century, with the aim of replacing common plaster with a composition that would be more durable and resemble stone. The market was soon flooded with many patented stuccos which claimed these qualities as a result of employing a specific recipe including clay and cement as well as lime and other ingredients in various proportions: Parker's Roman cement, Liardet's patent cement, Wark's patent composition are just a few.

Stucco came into its own after the 1774 London Building Act reduced the amount of woodwork on the outside of houses as a measure to counter the risk of fire. So, with decorative wooden porches and cornices forbidden by law, other forms of decoration became desirable. Cast iron and stucco were at hand, stucco stepping in as a finishing material for applied pilasters, entablatures, and other decoration, and indeed as a finish for entire façades, its showy characteristics probably best exploited by John *Nash. Not only could it provide architectural decoration far more cheaply than carved stone, it could also cover over poor brickwork—in fact little better than brick rubble and mortar—and successfully hide a multitude of sins with a veneer far more hard-wearing than ordinary plaster. Stucco did indeed have a greyish brown colour that could be mistaken for stone, and at first it was therefore left unpainted. But since its rough surface readily stained and collected soot, not long passed before it was coated with smooth-surfaced oil-based paint. Thus it attained a desirability that, despite some lows, is as high as ever today. APQ

stupa Known across Asia by various names, it is one of the three main types of Buddhist buildings (along with the residence hall or *vihara*, and the hall of worship or *chaitya-griha*), but the stupa remains Buddhism's most distinctive and recognizable architectural monument. The original Indian stupa, also known as the pagoda, began as a humble Brahmanical burial mound, initially shaped by hand, and it retained both this basic shape as well as its sacred purpose (*see* INDIAN SUBCONTINENT (BUDDHISM)). On one level the stupa typically functions as a repository for a sacred object, be it an image, a humble begging bowl once used by a venerable priest, the ashes of an auspicious Buddhist, or the most holy of objects—the actual physical remains of the historical Buddha, such as his ashes or a tooth. Thus, a stupa or pagoda can

function similarly to a reliquary in Christian history, albeit as a work of architecture rather than a mobile receptacle for auspicious objects. The traditional stupa remained a solid construction throughout most of its history, to be circumambulated and worshipped from outside. It was not only a unique architectural shape, but functioned on several religious levels, as a repository of sacred objects, a didactic vehicle for education as well as a sacred entity unto itself. In the history of religious architecture, it remains remarkable, if not unique, for its longevity, over 2,000 years, embodying many of the core values of an entire religious system.

The stupa also is a symbol of the sacred Mt Meru, the Brahmanic abode of the gods. To Buddhists a stupa is Mt Meru and the visual embodiment of an entire cosmology, including an axial orientation, with steps, platforms, niches with images of deities, and a measured progression from the profane world on into the sacred realms of the highest deities. Stupas can range in size from miniature replicas only 30 cm (12 inches) tall, to exhaustively detailed, enormous architectural achievements such as the Bayon in Cambodia and the colossal Borobadur in Indonesia.

As Buddhism expanded across Asia, variations did occur, notably the use of different building materials, best known being the use of wood in Japan, with some reserving interior areas for images. The choice of building material naturally influences aspects of style. The wide eaves so familiar among Japanese wooden pagodas cannot be duplicated with the stone preferred in Korea, or the bricks widely popular in China. Likewise, stupas built with stone and brick, well known in South East Asia, feature surface decoration, including stone reliefs, fired and polychromed tiles and wall paintings. While in some east Asian temple construction the pagoda no longer dominated the compound, it nevertheless retained its familiar shape and sanctity.

Stupa, Borobadur, Java (AD ?800)

Given its longevity and range of building materials across all the cultures of Asia (Buddhism is the only religion to enjoy pan-Asian success), the Buddhist stupa has followed a fairly consistent design. Most of the major elements can be seen among the oldest examples, such as the reconstructed stupas at Sanchi, the thousands of Burmese cetiyas, the white-plastered clay chortens of Tibet, or the simple and direct stone pagodas of Korea. Typically, the stupa consists of several distinct parts. The largest, a hemispherical shaped body (the *anda*), is raised upon a low platform, usually of stone, with a single pillar emerging from the top. This pillar is surmounted by circular discs (umbrellas) and enclosed by a square set of railings. The pillar refers to the axis of the universe, and the umbrellas can be likened to the traditional Indian custom of honour for auspicious individuals, a practice still seen in modern times. This construction is often surrounded by various fences and gateways that accentuate the axial, symmetrical orientation as well as providing areas for didactic messages. Various symbolic meanings are associated with the many parts, such as the levels of the heavens, as well as numerous cosmological associations, especially multiples of the number three, such as the three umbrellas atop the pillar representing the Three Jewels of Buddhism: the Buddha, the Law, and the monastic gatherings of the monks.   RF

stylobate A continuous solid base or platform on which a colonnade stands. It may have the form of a dwarf wall and serve as a notional partition, dividing, for example, the two parts of a megaron. More usually it serves to block entry into an otherwise open arcade, or confine it to one specific interval between its columns.   APQ

Suger (1081–1151) Abbot of St Denis. Abbot Suger was not an architect or a mason, but certainly an initiator of the rebuilding of the royal abbey church of St Denis, Paris (*c*.1135–44), in which the west end and, more significantly, the apse and ambulatory incorporated a new lightness of construction made possible by the use of pointed arches, rib-vaults and flying buttresses, thus inaugurating if not inventing

*Gothic architecture. Suger wrote a commentary on these works, but mentioned neither these innovations nor their designer. APQ

Sullivan, Louis Henry (1856–1924) US architect. Sullivan looms without peer as an architectural draftsman, ornamental designer, and inspirational author and leader in Chicago in the late 19th and early 20th centuries, but his reputation as an architect—as a maker of spaces—has been greatly inflated. His patchy education included a brief stay at the Massachusetts Institute of Technology, briefer periods in the office of Frank *Furness (1839–1912) in Philadelphia and William Le Baron *Jenney (1832–1907) in Chicago, and a year more or less in attendance at the Ecole des *Beaux-Arts in Paris. By 1875 he was back in Chicago and by 1883 had become a partner in the firm of Dankmar Adler (1844–1900) and Sullivan, one of the leading offices of what came to be called the *Chicago School of architecture.

Adler was 12 years Sullivan's senior and head of an established architectural practice, a gifted planner as well as an innovative structural and acoustical engineer, and it was he who attracted the clients. As a rule Sullivan ran the artistic side of the enterprise. Adler and Sullivan flourished until the older man left in 1895, and without him Sullivan's career declined from designing ornamental façades for major urban skyscrapers to sketching small commissions for banks and houses in out of the way places. His role as the inspiration for a group of younger architects led by Frank Lloyd *Wright, who had worked in the Adler and Sullivan office, and his publications, including 'The Tall Office Building Artistically Considered' (1901), *The Autobiography of an Idea* (1924), and *A System of Architectural Ornament* (1924), underpin his continuing reputation.

On several commercial façades of the 1880s in Chicago, Sullivan leaned on the conventionalized ornamental style he had learned in Furness's office. For the details and *parti* of the exterior of the firm's first major commission, the massive Auditorium Building (1887–90), whose complex plan (including auditorium, hotel, and office building), cutting edge structural technology, and acoustical excellence Adler engineered, Sullivan turned to powerful round-arched load-bearing masonry forms inspired by H. H. *Richardson's recently finished and neighbouring Marshall Field Wholesale Store. The Wainwright Building in St Louis (1890–91), the Stock Exchange in Chicago (1893–4, demolished), the Guaranty Building in Buffalo (1894–6), and, after Adler left the firm, the first sections of the Schlesinger and Mayer Department Store (later Carson, Pirie, Scott) in Chicago (1898–1903), and the Bayard Building in New York (1898), all helped shape the image of the Chicago School as commercial, urban, and modern. Sullivan's later small-town banks, especially the National Farmers' Bank (1906–8) in Owatonna, Minnesota, are exquisite architectural bijoux, but compared to his earlier work in major cities they exemplify the unravelling of his life and the rustication of his career.

Sullivan's inflated reputation rests in part on his statement in 'The Tall Office Building' that 'form ever follows function, and that is the law'. This is the source for the oft repeated, mindlessly alliterative, and reductive 'form follows function' of 20th-century modernists who failed to notice that he was speaking metaphorically about the relationship between architecture and nature, not about a mechanical equation. It rests in part also on his presumed 'solution' to the problem of tall building design for which he claims in his *Autobiography* to have found the perfect formula, 'one that admits of no exception'. This was the use of continuous vertical piers rising up the façade of a skyscraper to proclaim that it is 'a proud and soaring thing'. But an analysis of the tall buildings Sullivan designed shows no standard solution, while the designs fail to reflect function other than in the metaphorical way in which Sullivan meant it. In the 'Tall Office Building' he ignores the structural frame and mechanical systems such as elevators to concentrate on a classical external *parti* of base, shaft, and capital and ornament that poetically expresses growth in nature. So his façades rarely follow the continuous rectangular armature of piers and spandrels that is the essential expression of the early skyscraper.

Sullivan's true genius is on display in the original drawings for his *System of Architectural Ornament*. Here are some of the most brilliant free-hand sketches ever executed by an architect. He looked to nearly a century of theory of decorative design based on a Platonic view of nature that characterizes the works of Owen *Jones, Frank Furness, and many others, but infused these patterns of conventionalization with a forceful vitality, a spirit of organic growth, that electrified the page. This energy carried over into terracotta and cast-iron ornament on buildings such as the Guaranty Building in Buffalo or the entrance to the Schlesinger and Mayer store in Chicago. JFO'G

Andrew, D(avid) S., *Louis Sullivan and the Polemics of Modern Architecture* (1985)

O'Gorman, J(ames) F., *Three American Architects: Richardson, Sullivan, and Wright, 1865–1915* (1991)

Twombly, R(obert), *Louis Sullivan: The Life and Work* (1986)

Sumerians *See* MESOPOTAMIA.

supermarkets (UK) The architecture of present-day supermarkets in the UK has developed from the long tradition of rows of *shops located in the high street to large stand-alone structures that occupy their own sites and, in some cases, are now designed to support the development of housing and new communities. Initially British companies emulated American supermarket systems like Clarence Saunders' Piggly Wiggly Stores (1916).

In the UK, increasingly popular supermarket retailing resulted in the need for larger premises. Disused cinema sites were a temporary solution to the problem (Morrisons, 1960), but by the 1970s increased demand necessitated even larger stores and forced companies to develop supermarkets on out of town and brown field sites. Sainsbury's first out of town store was opened near Cambridge in 1974. As suitable sites became difficult to acquire, companies undertook to restore listed or significant buildings for store development, probably the best known being Tesco's restoration of the Hoover Building in 1995.

From the 1970s, as supermarket trading continued to expand rapidly, the design of stores can be roughly divided into two categories. The first, ubiquitous during the 1980s and early 1990s, was apparently inspired by red brick English farm buildings and is often referred to as the 'Essex Barn'. The original store was designed for Asda in South Woodham Ferrers, Essex, in 1977. This design was popular as it fulfilled many criteria necessary for successful development. It was an ideal shape, long and low, to house a standard supermarket layout. Its pitched roof could be used to house machinery necessary for services. It was easy to accommodate the need to include mandatory vernacular features or materials in the design and construction. The design was also popular with customers (and town planners) who liked the metaphor of a building stocked with food suggesting a rural idyll from the past.

During the 1980s and 1990s, in addition to their standard stores, Sainsbury's commissioned a group of high-profile architects to design flagship buildings: their high-tech Camden Town store (1988) designed by Nicholas *Grimshaw and the 'green' Millennium store in Greenwich (1999) being the most extreme examples. Although innovative in the context of supermarket design, none was as extreme as Best Supermarkets *trompe l'œil* designs in the USA.

The second, more recent style, which began to emerge in the 1990s, could be described as a modernist or neo-modernist design, and included the use of large areas of glass supported by a steel framework, often leaving structural elements and service ducts exposed. These designs were not as popular as the 'Essex Barn' which, by the end of the century, was being referred to as 'traditional' supermarket design.

Tesco began to pioneer modernist designs in the late 1990s and also produced flagship stores, including Sir Richard MacCormac's design for Ludlow in Shropshire (1999). These designs reinforced the company's progressive approach to retailing and their position as the leading UK supermarket company. Their buildings were perceived not merely as shops but as 'machines for shopping in'.   AK

sustainable architecture

ENVIRONMENTAL DESIGN
ARCHITECTURE AND NATURE
ARCHITECTURE AND ENVIRONMENTALISM
THE PLURALITY OF SUSTAINABLE ARCHITECTURE
THE AESTHETICS OF SUSTAINABLE ARCHITECTURE

The term 'sustainable architecture' has come to be used as a shorthand version of 'environmentally sustainable architecture', more or less synonymous with 'green architecture', 'bioclimatic architecture', and 'ecological architecture'. These alternatives have the advantage of immediately indicating their focus of interest in a way that the phrase 'sustainable architecture' does not. Sustainability has a much broader remit, and refers to a 'triple bottom line' of economic, social, and now environmental sustainability. As architecture has been concerned with economic and social sustainability at least since the Modern Movement of the early 20th century, it is the environmental third of the triple bottom line that is perceived as new within architecture, and which is

generally understood to be implicit in the phrase 'sustainable architecture'.

Environmental design Whatever the name, the intention is the same: to establish a more cooperative, less environmentally damaging relationship between buildings and biosphere, primarily through the reduction or abolition of fossil fuels in the construction and operation of buildings. This requires adopting a 'whole life' strategy for the building, taking into consideration its conception, running, and eventual demolition. In the construction of a building, the law of the 'Three Rs' is paramount: reduce, reuse, recycle. The first ensures that the waste of building materials is kept to a minimum (reduce); the second that the building envelope, and the invested energy it represents, functions for as long as possible (reuse); and the third that at the end of its natural life, a building has been constructed in such a way that its components or materials can be easily disassembled and used elsewhere (recycle). In the operation of a building, a two-pronged strategy applies: first, minimizing energy demand through the design of the building envelope (e.g. increased insulation, orientation, i.e. protection from wind, exposure to sun etc.); and second, supplying the remaining demand, as far as possible, with renewable energies (sun, wind, water, biomass, geothermal).

Architecture and nature Architecture's relation to nature is as old as architecture, from the imitation of organic forms (*see* ORGANIC ARCHITECTURE) to rules for the healthy siting of a dwelling or settlement in the landscape (as set out in the 1st century BC by *Vitruvius), to the extrapolation of proportional systems from natural objects (by *Alberti (1404–72) in the *Renaissance). It was not until the exponential growth of the European Industrial Revolution during the 19th century that this generally respectful

BedZED (Beddington Zero Energy Development) Housing, Sutton, Surrey (Bill Dunster, 2002)

relationship between the built environment and nature was threatened. By the late 19th century, industrialization and its new materials had come to dominate building construction, and architects all over Europe and America began addressing the technical and formal implications of its arrival (for example, *Ruskin, *Semper, and *Viollet-le-Duc in France). By the early 20th century, there were architects who embraced the change, for example Le Corbusier in *Vers une architecture* (1923) and Walter Gropius in *The New Architecture and the Bauhaus* (1935), and architects who were more ambivalent, for example Frank Lloyd Wright in *The Natural House* (1954) and Richard Neutra in *Mystery and Realities of the Site* (1951).

Architecture and environmentalism The distance between built culture and the natural environment continued to increase during the second half of the 20th century, as building technology made claims on a fully controllable, mechanically maintained internal environment (see Reyner Banham, *The Architecture of the Well-tempered Environment*, 1969; ENVIRONMENTAL CONTROL). This involved a shift away from the traditional *vernacular strategy of making the building envelope do most of the mediating between inside and outside— for example, heavy walls and small openings in hot dry climates—and towards making mechanical systems do the work. The result was *air conditioning, central *heating and artificial *lighting systems burning excessive amounts of fossil fuels in an attempt to make climatically unsuitable buildings tolerable to be in. This 'active' approach to environmental control dominated, but did not entirely typify architectural Modernism. From Alvar *Aalto in Finland to Luis *Barragán in Mexico, there were architects acutely sensitive to the need for climate-responsive design (see *The Other Tradition of Modern Architecture*, 1995, by C. St John Wilson, and *The New Eco-architecture*, 2002, by C. Porteous).

Nevertheless, mainstream architectural production went unchallenged until the oil crisis of 1973 coincided with a burgeoning environmental movement to

894

produce what was called 'green architecture'. The emphasis then was on autonomy, like the pioneering 'Autarkic House' designed by a team led by Alex Pike at Cambridge University in the early 1970s. This processed its own waste, and supplied its own power needs with a wind turbine and photovoltaic panels (that convert solar radiation to electricity). Other early examples of green architecture made no use of high technology, seeing it as the cause of all environmental problems and not their solution. It is this 'low tech' approach, and its accompanying rejection of modernity which still typifies 'green architecture' (see D. Pearson, *The Natural House Book*, 1991).

The plurality of sustainable architecture

What is remarkable about sustainable architecture over a generation later is the variety of means pursued to achieve the same end: a more symbiotic relationship between built and natural environments. These means can be divided into three categories: passive, active, and hybrid.

Passive sustainable architecture uses no mechanical or high-tech means to maintain a certain level of interior comfort. The building envelope is manipulated in ways that draw on the environmental techniques of climatically appropriate traditional vernacular architecture, for example, the work of Hassan *Fathy in Egypt, Brenda and Robert Vale in England, and early Ken *Yeang in Malaysia.

Active sustainable architecture, as its name suggests, is the opposite, using mechanical and high-tech systems to achieve a much greater—and faster—response to environmental stress. Such an approach can be found in the earlier environmentally inflected work of those architects who used to be dubbed *high tech—such as *Rogers, *Foster, or *Grimshaw—and are now dubbed 'eco-tech' (see C. Slessor, *Eco-tech*, 1997). Though energy was generated from renewable sources in these buildings, mechanical and digital systems

controlled its use throughout what was often still a sealed building.

This active approach is almost non-existent now, even among 'eco-tech' architects, the dominant strategy being a hybrid one of passive techniques and active systems. In Europe, mainstream sustainable architecture presents a wealth of architectural solutions that combine, for example, passive solar heating (sun through glazing) with active PVs, and passive natural ventilation with active flywheels and heat recovery systems. The European Union, because of its environmental legislation, is particularly rich in architecture experimenting with hybrid environmental strategies, for example, the work of Mecanoo Architects (Holland), *Hopkins (England), Jourda and Perraudin (France), Renzo *Piano (Italy), and Thomas Herzog (Germany).

The aesthetics of sustainable architecture

Representationally, rather than operationally, sustainable architecture is highly contested between those who believe that a new practice should be as revolutionary aesthetically as it is functionally (e.g. MVRVD Architects), and those who think environmental design is one concern among many for the architect and should not be allowed to dictate form-making (e.g. Mario Cucinella Architects). Whatever the view, there is a concern that 'greenwash' does not come to typify sustainable architecture. This is the adding of certain environmental devices to a building to signify an environmental sustainability that is not in fact there. In such cases, the highly visible grass roof or photovoltaic panels or wind cowels are not part of an integrated environmental strategy, but cosmetic. Where these are the result of a rigorous environmental analysis, however, the result is a kind of environmental *Functionalism. Bill Dunster's BedZED (Beddington Zero Energy Development), Sutton, Surrey, in which rows of glazed south-facing houses are ordered by the desire for solar gain, is an example of the aesthetic effect of an uncompromising aesthetic agenda.

Sustainable architecture will continue to develop in a plurality of ways, from the most rigorous environmentally to the most arresting aesthetically. Energy efficiency requirements will also continue to vary worldwide, from countries where there are none, to the European Union where there are increasingly demanding environmental directives that translate into increasingly demanding Building Regulations in member states. Quantified targets, like the number of kilowatt hours of electricity burned per square metre of building, are, and will remain, the best way to assess the energy efficiency of a building, but this is no guarantee of architectural quality, which requires that at least as much attention be given to social and aesthetic criteria.   SKH

Edwards, B.W., *Green Architecture—An International Comparison* (2001)

Hagan, S., *Taking Shape* (2001)

Hawkes, D., Macdonald, J., Steemers, K., *The Selective Environment* (2001)

Phillips, C., *Sustainable Place* (2003)

Swart, Pieter de   (1709–72) Dutch architect. He began his career as a master carpenter in Breda in 1737, with ephemeral installations for the entry of Prince William IV of Orange. After attending Jacques-François Blondel's Ecole des Arts in Paris he became architect to the Stadholder, but their joint attempts to recreate a court architecture never left the drawing board. De Swart then became a successful designer for the circle of the nobility and Catholic institutions, combining classicist exteriors with Rococo interior decorations, notably in The Hague with Lange Vijverberg 14–16 (1755), Lange Voorhout 74 (1760), Korte Voorhout 3 (1766, now the Royal Theatre).   FS

Sweden, medieval   After Sweden's conversion to Christianity (9th–10th century), Sweden's earliest

churches are *stave churches of splined vertical logs. One such church is at Hedared, Västergötland (originally *c.*1020, though the present building dates from *c.*1500). Less usual are the detached timber bell towers of the period, impressive for their lack of cladding.

The earliest stone churches are simple and austere, even with the aisled, cruciform plans of St Olaf, Sigtuna (*c.*1100–35), and the former cathedral of Gamla Uppsala (probably after 1258). The greater Lund Cathedral (consecrated 1146) is derived from the German Romanesque of Speier, and Husaby, Skaraborg (*c.*1150), has a form of westwork. Gothic arrived with a French designer and the apse, ambulatory, and radiating chapels of Uppsala Cathedral (begun 1287). While this influence remained, German hall-churches determined the form of the nave of Linköping Cathedral (*c.*1300), although St Peter's, Malmö, is basilican in form. With the growing influence of the Baltic in the late Middle Ages, north Germany increasingly affected Swedish practice, especially in the net-vaulting of Strängnäs and Västerås Cathedrals. Other buildings which should be mentioned are the Cistercian monasteries of Alvastra (Östergötland, 1143–85) and Varnhem (Västergötland, 1150s–13th century).

Domestic architecture evolved from the frequent use of a single-room house of horizontal timbers, reminiscent of the ancient megaron, to more complicated 1- or 2-storey houses of timber-jointing or half-timber constructions.   APQ/TF

Sweden, 1500–2000

16th century   After Sweden turned Lutheran (1527–), the Church lost its position as a patron of art and architecture. Its role was taken over by Gustav Vasa (r.1523–60) and his sons, who concentrated on rebuilding medieval royal castles as Stockholm and

City Library, Stockholm, Sweden (Erik Gunnar Asplund, 1927)

Kalmar or erecting new ones as Gripsholm (1537–), Vadstena (c.1550), and Uppsala (1549–). While King Gustav stressed the military aspects, ramparts with cannon-towers or angular bastions, his sons Erik XIV (r.1560–68) and Johan III (r.1568–92) developed these enterprises into monumental residences with traits both of Italian and north European Renaissance: elaborate tower helms, classical portals, and stuccoed interiors.

Johan III was particularly interested in vast building projects. Compared with medieval-looking Gripsholm with its tall, circular towers, Johan's enlargement of Uppsala and Svartsjö (demolished) near Stockholm became highly original creations: Uppsala with its remarkable stuccowork inside and out; and Svartsjö, a rectangular house, to which was added a circular, arcaded courtyard in front, and a large dome-covered rotunda, probably Pantheon-inspired, on the rear side, and seven towers with lanterns and spires. Johan also

took up church building in Stockholm and created chapels in the royal castles. They showed a curious mixture of Gothic and Renaissance elements.

17th–19th centuries When Sweden emerged as a great power during the first half of the 17th century, the high nobility became the dominant builders. The Swedish government had been concerned about receiving foreign diplomats for the funeral of Gustav II Adolf in 1634 because of the lack of modern, representative accommodation. During the lengthy minorities of Kristina (1632–4) and Karl XI (1660–72), the nobility ruled the country and were inclined to conspicuous display, both to emphasize their leading position and to give Sweden a dignified architectural, modern appearance, consistent with its military and political status.

Thus they erected stately private palaces in rapidly growing Stockholm and mansions on their country

897

estates. This building boom also coincided with the government's zest for creating new towns and remodelling old ones. All these activities were documented in the topographic work *Svecia Antiqua et Hodierna* (1667–1715), which aimed to show that Sweden was as important in culture as it was in politics. Beside the nobility, the new dynasty of Karl X Gustav (1654–60) planned vast projects, his dowager queen Hedvig Eleonora becoming the most important patron of art and architecture in Sweden, evidently to enhance the importance of the royal family. The Drottningholm and Strömsholm palaces (*see* TESSIN, NICODEMUS, THE ELDER) are the outstanding legacy of this period.

The nobility were equally active. Chancellor Axel Oxenstierna built a country house, Tidö (1625–45), based on a French chateau plan: a rectangular house with a courtyard closed by lower wings and with elaborate sculpted portals and gable fronts. Oxenstierna also initiated the construction of the Stockholm Riddarhuset or Palace of Nobles (1641–74; *see* JEAN DE LA VALLÉE), with Dutch Palladian giant pilasters on a monumental scale. The biggest noble complex of the century was General Wrangel's Skokloster Castle, Uppland (1654–71), of a royal grandeur with its four tall wings around an arcaded courtyard and four octagonal corner towers. For churches, architects turned away from the previous combination of traditional Gothic and Renaissance elements to Italian-inspired solutions such as Kalmar Cathedral (by Tessin the Elder) and the centrally planned Stockholm churches by de la Vallée.

The Russian victory at Poltava (1709) marked the end of Sweden's half-century as a great power, but building activity continued, if at rather a reduced pace. The main enterprise up to the 1750s was the completion of the Stockholm Royal Palace, first by Tessin the Younger, then by *Hårleman. He initiated the new Office of the Surveyor-General, regulating official and, later on, church building projects. A typical representative of the Age of Enlightenment, Hårleman wanted to rationalize, economize, and enforce a French-inspired 'good taste' in Swedish architecture.

Together with Carl Fredrik Adelcrantz (1717–96), Hårleman dealt with projects ranging from royal palaces to simple, practical tasks such as model designs for unpretentious countryside parish churches, bridges or lighthouses. But Adelcrantz's best known works are the Chinese *maison de plaisance* and the theatre at Drottningholm (1760s). His Stockholm Opera House for Gustav III (1777–82, demolished) was French-inspired, but also continued the Swedish Palladian trend of the 17th century.

The final quarter of the 18th century saw a marked change in architectural taste. The Stockholm Merchants' Exchange (1773–8) by Erik Palmstedt has rounded corners and a balustraded roof surmounted by a lantern. He also designed King Gustav's court theatre at Gripsholm (1780s) as a domed, semicircular Ionic temple, cleverly placed inside one of Gustav Vasa's massive, circular towers. After Gustav III's travels in Italy and France (1783–4), a stern, neoclassical architecture was introduced at the Botanical Institute in Uppsala (Olof Tempelman and Louis Jean Desprez, 1787–1807), with plain walls and a heavy Greek Doric temple front as its only dominant ornament. King Gustav became quite obsessed with such weighty, Doric creations, as did the theorist Ehrensvärd.

For the first half of the 19th century, Sweden remained mainly rural with a slow urban development. Traditional commissions such as churches, private mansions, and state buildings continued as before.

Fredrik Blom designed the Barracks of the Royal Equestrian Guards (1805–17) and the Karl Johan Church on Skeppsholmen (1824–42), both of them in Stockholm. The former is plain and sternly monumental with its centre topped by a closed attic storey. The octagonal church with short cross-arms, dome, and slender lantern is one of many contemporary variations on the Roman Pantheon.

Blom also received international renown for his movable houses, constructed of prefabricated wooden elements and iron bolts. Carl Fredrik Sundvall started a new library—Carolina Rediviva—for Uppsala University (1819–41). It had a monumental position on the upper end of one of the main streets, overlooking the town. The façade is essentially modelled on the north front of the Stockholm Royal Palace, perhaps to emphasize a connection with the new Bernadotte dynasty.

With the introduction of railways in the 1850s and the rise of industry, the population began to move into the larger cities. A new series of building types—railway stations, hospitals, prisons, schools, museums, and apartment blocks—were now required.

Thus Adolf Wilhelm Edelsvärd, architect of the state railways 1855–95, designed stations of various sizes, for example, in Stockholm, Gothenburg, Uppsala. Fredrik Wilhelm Scholander built the lyceum for boys in Uppsala (1864–9), which exercised a marked influence on later Swedish school buildings because of its overall planning—wide classroom windows and modern heating system. Helgo *Zettervall was active both as a church restorer and as architect of many public and private commissions.

The University Building in Uppsala (1878–87) by Herman Teodor Holmgren contains a great central hall with double flights of stairs, surrounding galleries, and coffered cupolas supported on pendentives. It is one of the very finest creations in 19th-century Sweden. Thanks to railway transport, brick or stone could now be used more frequently, as can be seen in the university exterior and in works by Isak Gustaf Clason, e.g. in his Nordic Museum, Stockholm (1889–1907), an early example of *National Romanticism.

20th century In the first two decades, it was the public buildings of Stockholm, by Ferdinand *Boberg, Carl Westman, and Ragnar *Östberg, which dominated the architectural scene. Westman's Courthouse (1909–15) is an outstanding example of National Romanticism, its heavy silhouette harking back to the 16th-century Vadstena Castle. But because of its dramatic position by the harbourside, and its architectural quality, it is Östberg's Town Hall (1911–23) which is the outstanding achievement, so rapidly gained an international reputation and influence.

But the movement of National Romanticism had run its course, and the younger generation of architects were more interested in technological and social developments. The technological influence of US architecture is seen in the steel and concrete Myrstedt and Stern Store in Stockholm (Ernst Stenhammar, 1908–10), and the Chicago-inspired King's Towers (Sven Wallander and Ivar Callmander, 1919–25), sometimes claimed to be Europe's first skyscrapers.

The leadership of the Modern Movement, with its commitment to social as well as technological progress, was assumed by *Asplund through one short-lived work: the Stockholm Exhibition of 1930. He was also creator, with Sigurd *Lewerentz, of the Woodland Cemetery at Enskede in the south of the city. Social housing now came to the fore in the work of Uno Åhrén and Sven *Markelius. The more advanced settlements were concentrated in Stockholm and its surroundings. Modernism also extended to other building types, such as L. M. Ericsson's industrial plant in Midsommarkransen, which combined factory, offices, and amenities for the personnel with rows of apartment houses. The architect, Ture Wennerholm, gave the plant its characteristic touch by means of two cylindrical, glazed staircases interrupting the horizontal bands of windows (1930s–40s).

In the 1950s the community of Vällingby near Stockholm was planned and built by a group of architects as a self-sustained project with its own working-places, dwellings, and urban centre.

Beside the housing projects, culminating in the 'million programme' of the 1960s and 1970s, smaller-scale church building has been a characteristic since the 1950s, such as Lewerentz's S. Petri Church in Klippan, Skane (1964–6), and Carl Nyren's parish church in Gottsunda near Uppsala (1976–9). The former is an abstract brick block with refined detailing and an undulating skyline, the latter a postmodern wooden, free and witty variation on a vernacular tradition.

Official or public buildings of the same periods are Artur von Schmalensee's Town Hall in the mining centre of Kiruna, Norrbotten (1959), Peter Celsing's State Bank building as part of a comprehensive Stockholm project (1968–76), and Ralph *Erskine's Stockholm University Library (1981–3). The Kiruna Town Hall combines a brick-faced block with a transparent steel-cage tower. Celsing's bank building is a tall slab, clad with rough-hewn black rustication as a modernist version of the neo-Renaissance of earlier bank palaces. Erskine's library is a fanciful mixture of *Constructivist and *Brutalist elements. Major enterprises of the 1980s and 1990s are the Globen arena in Johanneshov and the Modern Museum on Skeppsholmen, Stockholm, the latter by the Spanish architect Rafael *Moneo Vallés. The sports and concert arena, shaped as an enormous sphere, is surrounded by office buildings. As a contrast, the museum is a low-keyed complex, designed to accommodate discreetly the given topography with its older buildings.   TF

Andersson, H. O., and Bedoire, F., *Swedish Architecture. Drawings 1640–1970* (1986)

Kidder Smith, G. E., *Sweden Builds* (1957)

Paulsson, T., *Scandinavian Architecture* (1957)

swimming baths *See* SPORTS BUILDINGS (SWIMMING POOLS).

Switzerland There are four designated UNESCO World Heritage Sites in Switzerland representing the country's historic tradition and varying cultural influences. The 9th-century convent of St Johann in Mustair, founded by Charlemagne; the 15th-century fortifications of Bellinzona, built by the Dukes of Milan to keep out Swiss confederates descending from the north; the exuberant Baroque convent and library of St Gall demonstrating an unbroken line of Christian influence from the arrival of Irish missionaries in the 5th century; and the old town of Berne, an exceptionally well preserved medieval city with uniform rows of patrician houses whose Rococo sandstone facades date from the 18th century. Other historic highlights include the Gothic cathedral of Lausanne, relating to similar structures in Burgundy, and the Baroque abbey of Einsiedeln, influenced by neighbouring Vorarlberg.

The Baroque is also represented in the profane architecture of the 17th and 18th centuries when waves of religious refugees from France fled to the towns of western Switzerland, bringing with them their knowledge of watch-making techniques, and to Basle and Zurich with the secrets of the silk industry. A well-off aristocracy without a court built town *palais* such as the urbane solution of row houses at the rue des Granges 2,4,6,8 (begun 1760) in Geneva or the elegant Rococo Hôtel de Peyron (1765–8) in Neuchâtel, as well as country houses of the French chateau type such as the hipped-roof Schloss Thunstetten (1711) near Berne.

The popular image of Switzerland as a country of wooden chalets, although none too differentiated, is not completely wrong. Until the creation of modern Switzerland in the mid 19th century, most of the population lived in the country. The dearth of good pastureland in this mountainous terrain led to families moving up and down the slopes up to seven times a year finding fodder for their animals. Buildings for these annual peregrinations included numerous temporary storage units and shelters. Emphasis was placed on practical solutions that withstood the tests of weather and time and on teamwork that discouraged individuality. In the Swiss midlands, these vernacular buildings have traditionally been made of wood and provide the basis for what, in the 19th century, became internationally known as the 'Chalet Style'. In Italian and French-speaking Switzerland, buildings are nearly uniformly made of stone. These agricultural buildings still dot the landscape of mountain Switzerland and, when not abandoned, are often renovated into holiday homes.

The harnessing of the country's plentiful Alpine water gave Switzerland the power to run the many textile industries that employed 50% of the country's 19th-century population and resulted in new factories and workers' housing, the remnants of which are currently being built over into fashionable lofts or cultural centres. Newly accrued wealth, however, did not result in bombastic architectural outpourings. Rather, the Swiss remained true to their reticent tradition, building small neoclassical homes and humanistic institutions such as Karl Moser's Kunsthaus (1910) and Gottfried *Semper's neo-Renaissance Technische Hochschule (1859–64) in Zurich. The one exception to this rule is hotel architecture, such as the turreted Grandhotel Giessbach, Brienz (Horace Davinet, 1875 and 1883), built expressly to bring luxury and comfort to tourists beginning to explore the hoary Alpine world.

The general modesty and understatement of this society continues to characterize Swiss architecture today, often resulting in works of great quality that have found no acclaim outside architectural circles. Neither the perfect cinema Le Paris in Geneva by Marc Saugey (1957–9), nor the elegant Bleicherweg office building in Zurich by O. R. Salvisberg (1939–40), both still in use, brought its architect international acclaim. In fact, Switzerland has rather discouraged stardom, a trait that led *Le Corbusier from La Chaux-de-Fonds to exchange his citizenship and nearly be eliminated from this entry, except for his 1928 founding of the seminal *CIAM at La Sarraz.

Swiss architecture is most adventurous when it overcomes the country's near-impossible topography. Robert *Maillart's breath-taking concrete Salginatobel Bridge (1929–30) is echoed and even trumped by Rino Tami's stretch of Ticino *autostrada* (1963–83), arguably the most beautiful expressway in Europe. Tami's design work has been continued by Flora Ruchat, who, together with Aurelio Galfetti and Ivo Trümpy, created one of Switzerland's best public swimming areas (1967–70) in Bellinzona. In one continuous ramp, the *bagno* Bellinzona simultaneously unites the city with the Maggia River, organizes swimmers, and offers shelter for changing rooms and a cafe. In another aquatic context, Hans Hofmann's locks at Birsfelden (1951), a felicitous combination of public park and Rhine shipping system, allows walkers, skaters, and cyclists to cross over the river while small freighters, using the locks, pass underneath. This sophisticated combined use of levels is also exhibited in Pierre Bonnet's Couverture des Voies (1999), where a community centre, studio and office buildings, parks and a bike path, are all built on the thin concrete roof of a high-speed train tunnel in Geneva.

In a country where land costs are high and 70% of the population have long been renters rather than homeowners, housing developments and co-operatives, some of them quite radical in their aims, have been an architectural issue since the onset of industrialization transferred the population from the country to the city. Hannes *Meyer's Freidorf near Basle (1921), its module based on the standard bed length, launched his pre-Bauhaus career. Hans Bernoulli, architect of hundreds of simple four-room row houses with eat-in kitchens in Basle, was stripped of his ETH professorship in 1938 for proposing state ownership of land as a means of reducing rents. Maurice Braillard's Maison Ronde (1928–30) in Geneva offered an alternative to pure functionalism while providing livable, low-cost spaces. Kitchens, for example, were positioned so that mothers could see their children playing in the crescent-shaped courtyard below them. Newer examples of this concern with affordable living space are offered by Michael Alder's Luzernerring apartments (1991–3) and Diener + Diener's Hammer Siedlung (1978–81), both in Basle. But collective housing has also effectively been put to middle-class use, as evidenced in the Neubühl colony (1930–32) outside Zurich by the young team of Haefeli, Moser, Steiger, together with Artaria and Schmidt, and Atelier 5's stepped concrete Halen (1957–61) development near Berne.

Beginning with the Tendenza Ticinese in the 1970s, a movement bringing Italian-speaking Switzerland's architecture to the fore, issues other than that of architectural form have begun to take precedence. To keep the village centre alive, Luigi Snozzi's heroic twenty-year work in Monte Carasso regrouped public architecture in and around a rebuilt medieval cloister now housing the primary school, community rooms, and a cafe. By choosing the labour-intensive materials of stone and wood at hand rather than importing new building technology, Gion Caminada has, in the face of depressing rural depopulation, injected civic pride and workplaces into his home town of Vrin in the Grisons. His small wake building (2002) is a finely crafted update on traditional mourning architecture. Ecological concerns are perhaps best exemplified in the work of the Metron office, Brugg, founded 1965. Eschewing high-tech solutions and avoiding building products that pollute the environment, Metron has made an *oeuvre* out of row housing such as the wood-clad Siedlung Oepfelbau in Stetten, Canton Aargau (1986), and the re-use for housing of redundant buildings such as a former chocolate factory in Aarau (1987/1988).

Local and national Swiss governments contribute greatly to architecture by sponsoring competitions such as that for schoolhouse programmes in the Ticino beginning in the 1960s. A 1990s Basle schoolhouse programme was specially planned to give young architects the chance of gaining a toehold in the face of intense architectural competition in that city: Miller + Maranta's Volta Schulhaus, a pristine white structure set on the foundations of disused oil tanks, was one result. The national Holz 2000 programme aimed to encourage building in wood, so stimulating industry in heavily forested rural areas where jobs are scarce. Bauart's 'smallhouse', a prefabricated wooden modular construction, emerged under its aegis.

Although most Swiss still cling to their rural image, Switzerland today is being built up rapidly. About 1 sq m (1.12 sq yard) of land is currently being built over per second. Urban environments are becoming more densely populated, and urban conglomerations that reach across national borders—around the cities of Basle, Geneva, and Lugano—are already a reality. In the meantime, Alpine settlements, those upon which the traditional image of Switzerland is based, are being abandoned and forest is beginning to reclaim the Alps. Switzerland's democratic tradition, whereby each commune can make its own separate decisions, seems to hamper any modern large-scale decision-making. Perhaps the new ETH teaching studio in Basle founded in 2002 by *Herzog and de Meuron, Roger Diener, and Marcel Meili will be able to find a way out of this conundrum.   CB

Allenspach, C., *Architecture in Switzerland: Building in the 19th and 20th Centuries* (1999)

Gubler, J., *Nationalisme et internationalisme dans l'architecture moderne de la Suisse* (2nd edn, 1988)

Reinle, A., and Gantner, J., *Kunstgeschichte der Schweiz* (3 vols., 1958–65)

Ruegg, A. (ed.), *Swiss Furniture and Interiors in the 20th Century* (2002)

symmetry When referring to architecture, this term is used in two distinct senses. As first used, by *Vitruvius, it is a direct translation from the Greek, meaning '…a proper agreement between the members of the work itself, and relation between the different parts and the whole general scheme, in accordance with a certain part selected as a standard' (*De Architectura*, Book I, chapter 2, section 4). The term seems to have been first used in the modern sense, i.e. identical to its use in mathematics, by *Alberti: '…the Members on the right side shall exactly answer on the left'—such an exact correspondence of elements became almost a defining feature of *neoclassicism and *Beaux Arts design.   PG

synagogue The prototype of the synagogue in the Greco–Roman world was the *bouleuterion*, or in Roman times the basilica. The plan was a long hall, divided by two rows of columns into a central nave and two aisles. The columns supported a gallery, but there is no evidence of the use of separate sections for women. The orientation of the building was towards Jerusalem, and the location was on the town's highest point. The exteriors were in a dumpy Roman colonial style, with a central entrance and two side doors on the front elevation. Over a hundred sites (3rd–8th centuries AD) have been identified in Israel, with the earliest concentrations in the north, but with notable examples at Baram and Capernaum. Major diaspora structures were erected at Alexandria (destroyed AD *c*.115), Sardis in Asia Minor, with a basilica 122 m (400 ft) long, holding a thousand congregants, and Dura Europos in Syria, which had four walls frescoed with biblical scenes.

In the medieval period, the architecture reflects that in general use at the time. For example, the synagogue at Worms (1175, destroyed), in the Upper Rhein district of Germany, was a Romanesque structure with a men's prayer hall that was a roughly rectangular room, with its roof based on a system of groined vaults springing from two columns on the long axis of the plan. Women were housed in a separate room abutted against the north wall.

The real jewel of medieval synagogue architecture is the Altneu building in Prague, completely Gothic in detailing. Women were accommodated in neighbouring annexes, with slits in the stone walls to permit a restricted view through, though the diminished congregation nowadays allows them in at the back of the rectangular prayer hall. The vaulted ceiling displays five ribs in each section, to avoid showing the form of a cross. The vaults rise from two octagonal piers which articulate the chamber.

Moorish Spain was a land where the Jews prospered. There must have been many synagogues in Islamic times, but the only surviving ones date from the *Reconquista*, and are in *Mudéjar style. The most notable examples are in Toledo and Cordoba. The Transito synagogue of Cordoba sports a stucco frieze into which is set a line of verses from the Psalms, in square-letter Hebrew. A strapwork frieze bears the Arabic words for 'happiness and prosperity', while badges feature a castle and three towers, perhaps the arms of the founder. This feudal blazonry, the Arabic mottoes, and the Hebrew Bible quotations represent three cultural traditions, co-existing in harmony.

Renaissance learning and the architecture it evoked had a profound effect on the Jews of Italy. The synagogues of Padua, Venice, and Rome, though extremely discreet on the exterior, exhibited within the full gamut of Renaissance and, later, Baroque display. In Venice and Rome, the Jews were confined to a single building. Marvels of architectural convergence, however, succeeded in compressing five synagogues into a single structure.

The classical style spread from Italy to northern Europe, and in Amsterdam reached its paragon in the mighty Great Portuguese Synagogue, designed by Elias Bouman (1675). The splendid interior, 38 by 26 m

(125 by 85 ft) has a barrel-vaulted nave roof supported by four colossal unfluted Ionic columns of Bremen stone. It can accommodate 1,227 men and 440 women.

A modest offspring of the Amsterdam synagogue was built by Joseph Avis for the Sefardi community at Bevis Marks in the city of London, opening in 1701, less than fifty years after Cromwell had readmitted Jews to England. The restrained classical style is comparable to that of Wren's city churches, as is that of the Touro synagogue in Newport, Rhode Island (1759–63), the oldest surviving synagogue in North America.

A strange rustic transfiguration of Baroque architecture was achieved in the wooden synagogues of the forested lands of eastern Europe. Most of these were burned by the Germans in World War II, but old photographs and architectural drawings recapture the effects. The most accomplished example was found at Wolno, near Grodno in Belarus (early 18th century), where the ark is flanked by the two halves of a double-headed eagle, and the interior features a succession of curvilinear spandrels tumbling down like a wooden cascade.

The later 19th century, from 1860 onwards, was the golden age of synagogue building. Even the most reactionary regimes were granting Jews civil rights, and their rising prosperity found expression in the construction of imposing synagogues. Three of the greatest 19th-century schemes were erected in Paris, Budapest, and Berlin. In Paris, Alfred Aldophe designed an amazing Romanesque cathedral (1861–74), completed with barrel-vaulted bays, soaring piers, a domed apse, and an enormous triforium storey, to provide a huge ladies' gallery, where the *mondaines* of Parisian Jewish society would sit, arrayed in the latest fashions. In Budapest, the ladies' gallery was likewise enormous, extending into 2 storeys in Ludwig von Förster's great synagogue (1854–9), the largest synagogue in Europe, accommodating 3,000 worshippers. Edward Knoblauch's Moorish-style

building in Berlin (1859–66) had gaslights installed in the spaces between the double glazing panes, clear outside and coloured within.

The 19th century brought a new movement in the Jewish religion: Reformism, which had a direct effect on the architecture of synagogues. In Reform synagogues men and women could sit together, which obviated the need for gallery accommodation. The Reform movement originated in Germany, but its greatest spread was achieved in the United States, which gradually superseded Russia as the country of the greatest Jewish settlement.

The style of the 19th century was historicist, frequently with an oriental trend, sometimes Moorish, which had a bizarre effect, for example, in the immense Islamic concoction in Florence, the birthplace of Renaissance architecture. The 20th century produced some notable ventures in the Modern style. An early example is Sir Owen Williams' synagogue at Dollis Hill, London (1937), where the walls are folded in accordion pleats, permitting the ladies' galleries to run through without supporting columns obstructing the space below.

In the United States, Erich *Mendelsohn built a series of synagogues with movable walls that could expand the prayer space threefold for the occasions of the High Holy Days. In Israel, Heinz Rua's synagogue at the Givat Ram campus of the Hebrew University suggests the cerebral activity of prayer by roofing the concrete structure in the shape of a brain pan. Finally, the postmodern style of Norman Jaffé's Gates of the Grove synagogue at Easthampton, New York (1987), recalls the wooden synagogues of Poland in a series of cascading skylit gables.   HM

Meek, H. A., *The Synagogue* (1995)

Syria, historic Because of its particular location, sharply bounded by mountains (the Taurus range, to the north), the sea (the Mediterranean, to the west), rivers (the Tigris and Euphrates, to the east), and desert (the Great Arabian Desert, to the south), Syria was occupied by the most important civilizations of the ancient world: Mesopotamian, Roman, Byzantine, Islamic, and Christian.

In every case, Syrian architecture tended to assume quite a different, often a superior, form to that of the 'home' civilization. However, this generalization does not apply to the two particular cases of indigenous architecture. The conical-shaped huts made of mud-brick in some of the villages east of Aleppo may have been built since *c*.3750 BC. Nothing quite like this 'beehive' shape is found in any other *vernacular architecture. The excavations at Tell Ras Shamra, north of Latakia, revealed the city of Ugarit, within which the vast Royal Palace, built in several stages between the 15th and 13th centuries BC, covered nearly 7,000 sq m (8,372 sq yards).

Roman Palmyra flourished for over two centuries until it was abandoned in AD 273. The profits levied on the caravan trade funded an impressive series of palaces and temples. The local limestone was easily carved into more exuberant forms of the *Corinthian order than those found in Rome, but the really distinctive feature of Palmyra was the extensive colonnaded streets, perhaps following the model of Antioch (AD 14–37, subsequently destroyed by earthquake). The colonnades, almost 1.6 km (1 mile) long, are made up of four or five rows of gigantic columns, over 15 m (50 ft) high. The streets are not as long as those of Apameia, in northern Syria (destroyed by earthquake, AD 116) nor is the plan as regular as Leptis Magna (*see* LIBYA, HISTORIC), which in other respects Palmyra resembles. The irregularity was dictated by the location of the water sources within the oasis.

Numerous village churches survive from the *Byzantine period (AD *c*.313–634). In Syria, architecture was more of a mason's art—the carving of wide scrolls at the base of the window frames, the stylized capitals—than perhaps anywhere else in Byzantium. The buildings are modelled on small rural houses, with two doors in the south (or main) façade, usually the most decorated, one reserved for men, the other for women. Larger churches may have had more complex plans. The basilica of St Symeon (Qal'at Sim'an, AD 476–80) combined a 28 m (92 ft) diameter octagon and a Greek cross, though this may be a particular case, as the layout was determined by the requirement to incorporate the saint's pillar as the focal point.

For the only time in its history, under the Umayyads (AD 661–750; *see also* PALESTINE, HISTORIC) Syria was not a province or a satellite. Their rule was celebrated in the Great Mosque, Damascus (706–15). For the first time, a *mosque was an instrument of political and religious propaganda, being built over the site of Syrian, Roman, and Byzantine religious buildings. The walls of the great courtyard (about 100 × 57 m or 328 × 187 ft) are decorated by an extensive programme of mosaics, which may represent an idealized view of Damascus; the gable end of the transept on the south side gives an impression of regal power (*see* IRAQ, HISTORIC).

The finest examples of Saracenic and of French *military architecture are to be found in Syria. The Saracenic fortress of Aleppo (*c*.1146ff.) has a forbidding glacis of finely cut stone and a monumental entrance block, with three gateways. Their opponents, the *Crusaders, faced such a shortage of manpower that their castles had to be as massively impregnable as possible. The evidence that they succeeded can be seen in perhaps the finest castle in the world, the Krak des Chevaliers (1142ff.). By comparison, the Crusaders' religious buildings, such as the cathedral of the Templars' headquarters at Tortosa, were unremarkable.   PG

Fedden, R., *Syria and Lebanon* (1965)

Syria, modern Contemporary architecture seeks to revive the great tradition which goes back five millennia to the Phoenicians. But it is also dominated

by foreign, mostly French influences, manifested—
for example—in the French Cultural Centre by Jose
Oubrerie (1981–6) and his project for the Palace of
Congress in Damascus of 1983. The Italian architect
Luigi Barbara built the Sheraton Hotel in Damascus in
1978, with the aim of reviving old Syrian traditions.
Realistic and innovative contributions came from the
Polish architect Wojciech Zablocki, who designed the
Sport City in Latakia in 1982–7, containing sports halls,
a training stadium, a swimming pool, tennis facilities, a
medical centre, children's parks, and a yacht club. The
central stadium in particular, with its dynamic tent
roof, is an outstanding achievement for establishing a
harmony between past and present. Zablocki also built
a number of residences near Damascus, in which in a
different way elements of the past are revitalized.

Among the rare attempts by Syrian architects to
continue the local vernacular tradition are the works
by Bourhan Tayara, Aladine Lolah, and the Muhanna
Brothers. Tayara built the School of Architecture in
Damascus, apartment blocks in Damascus, and the
Marine Research Centre in Latakia. Aladine Lolah
worked out projects for the Presidential Palace in
Damascus in 1970, still unbuilt, and for a mosque
in the civic centre in Aleppo in 1979–83. Closest to the
vernacular Syrian tradition are the houses by Raif and
Rafi Muhanna in the Der'a Province built between 1978
and 1980. The material of these buildings is natural
stone in a cost-saving manner as well as part of a
continued tradition.   UK

system building *See* PREFABRICATION.

Tait, Thomas Smith *See* BURNET AND TAIT.

Talman, William (1650–1719) English architect. Emerging from obscure origins as a rival of *Wren's, Talman had a successful career building country houses, despite self-inflicted damage resulting from his querulous nature. He made enemies at the Office of Works from Wren downwards, and, according to *Vanbrugh, his relations with private clients ended in 'vexation and disappointment'. Yet he was pre-eminent in gaining Whig patronage in the 1680s and 1690s until Vanbrugh entered the fray. He had the ability to apply Wren's palace style, as exemplified by Hampton Court, to such noble houses as Chatsworth, Derbyshire, where he rebuilt the south and east fronts (1687–96) with undeniable majesty, and fitted it out with similar quality. The south front has 2 equal storeys over a rusticated basement, its three terminal bays embraced by giant Doric pilasters, and an entablature and balustrade parapet concealing the roof. Similar qualities appear at the earlier Thoresby House, Nottinghamshire, (1685–7, burnt 1745), though his authorship is unclear. APQ

Tange, Kenzô (1913–2005) Japanese architect. Tange's development to become one of the most important architects of post-war Japan reflected the nation's reconstruction and rise to become an industrial leader. Having graduated from Tokyo University in 1938 and worked briefly for Kunio *Maekawa, Tange began his career by seeking to combine Modernism with forms of traditional Japanese architecture in projects such as the winning competition entry for a memorial to the creation of the Great East Asia Co-prosperity Sphere at Mount Fuji (1942, unbuilt). Following World War II, Tange produced a master plan for Hiroshima (1946–7) and won first prize in the Hiroshima Peace Centre design competition (1949–55). As a leading participant in the 'tradition debate', Tange combined details from traditional Japanese design with elements from Le Corbusier, such as pilotis, in his design of the central Peace Memorial Museum. He further expressed traditional wooden post-and-beam construction as minimal modern design in his own residence (1953) and also in reinforced concrete in the 8-storey Kagawa Prefectural Government office building (1955–8). The end of the period of post-war reconstruction in Japan came to be symbolized by the 1964 Tokyo Olympics and Tange's designs for the sweeping, asymmetrically composed tensile roofed National Gymnasia (1961–4).

Following soaring growth in Tokyo, Tange's interest increasingly focused on urban planning, proposing his 1960 plan for extending the Japanese capital out into Tokyo Bay as a linear, megastructural system of transportation, offices, and residential clusters. Focusing on the change and growth of the city, Tange's scheme inspired and was further developed by younger *Metabolist architects, many of whom had worked with Tange. While the utopian urban plans of Tange and the Metabolists were unbuilt, Tange realized urban-scale schemes such as the Communications Centre in Kofu (1967) and the Expo '70 master plan and space-frame roofed Festival Plaza.

Despite the quantity and international scope of Tange's subsequent projects, his late projects did not surpass the creative intensity of his early ones. Tange's urban design schemes included a reconstruction project for Skopje City Centre (1965–6), Fiera District Centre, Bologna (1971–4), and the Yerba Buena Centre plan for San Francisco (1967–8). His extensive projects in the Middle East include work in Iran, Saudi Arabia, and Qatar. Returning to Tokyo, Tange's late career is highlighted by a dramatic shift to embrace postmodernism in his competition-winning design for a 243 m (797 ft) twin tower Tokyo City Hall (1986–92) reminiscent of a Gothic cathedral.   KTO

Bettinotti, M., *Kenzô Tange* (in Italian, 1996)
Kultermann, U., *Kenzô Tange* (1970)

Taniguchi, Yoshirô (1904–79) Japanese architect and educator. Taniguchi established his reputation with the design of his functionalist Hydraulics Laboratory (1932) at the Tokyo Institute of Technology after having criticized *Bunriha* architects for their privileging aesthetic pursuits over practical concerns. His post-war work reflects traditional Japanese precedents in the Tôson Memorial Hall (1947), and the neoclassical sensitivity of Karl Freidrich Schinkel and Heinrich Tessenow in works such as the Department of Medicine at Keio University (1951).   KTO

tas-de-charge This is the lowest course of a vault or arch laid horizontally and bonded into the wall, rather like a corbel, as a means of increasing the stability of the courses above and reducing their outward thrust. Characteristic of *Gothic vaults, it normally consists of a single stone, lying directly on the impost or capital and founded deep within the wall, which is carved on its outer face with whatever mouldings are applied to the ribs. On it are mounted the ribs themselves, the lowest lying flat above it, but wedge-shaped above so as to follow the radius of curvature of the arch. The weight of the wall over its inner half counteracts the weight of the arch stones on its outer half, as though it is a cantilever.   APQ

Taut, Bruno (1880–1938) German architect. He was a leading figure in the *Expressionist Movement in Germany 1918–20, and later chief architect to the

GEHAG building society, Berlin. During exile in the 1930s, Taut was a key European interpreter of the architecture of *Japan.

Born in remote East Prussia, Taut studied architecture in Munich under the great contemporary architect and teacher Theodor *Fischer, who taught that buildings should respond to site and show regional character. On completing his studies, he worked for Fischer for four years, then in 1908 moved to Berlin where he designed housing. He made his name with two exhibition buildings: the Steel Pavilion at Leipzig of 1913 and Glass Pavilion at the Werkbund Exhibition in Cologne of 1914. The latter was highly original in its imaginative use of glass, its effect far exceeding its small size. It included inscriptions by Paul *Scheerbart, the poet of glass, and paved the way for the crystalline obsessions of the Expressionists, where again Taut was in the forefront.

Following the November Revolution of 1918, Taut was a founder member of the Arbeitsrat für Kunst (Art Soviet), a society of architects and artists who sought new forms for the coming new society. His work at this stage centred on drawn images published in his own magazine *Frühlicht*, and his books *Die Stadtkrone* and *Alpine Architektur*. He also managed the 'Glass Chain' correspondence to which younger architects like Hans *Scharoun and Hermann Finsterlin contributed now famous drawings. Although in the end almost nothing was realized, this was a crucial period of inspiration.

In 1921 Taut was appointed City Architect of Magdeburg, a potentially important position, but the economic crisis left little to be done. Undaunted, he cheered up the city with a radical repainting programme, of which little record remains, though eventually his design for a cattle-auction hall was built. He had not ceased to write, and books like *Die neue Wohnung* (1924) and *Der neue Wohnbau* (1927) argued for a revolution in housing. In 1924 he was appointed to the leadership of the design office for GEHAG, the

leading Berlin building society, were he remained until 1932, supervising altogether the construction of around 12,000 dwellings. These included Onkel Toms Hütte in Zehlendorf and the Hufeisensiedlung in Britz, which remain among the most famous *Siedlungen* of the period. Again Taut showed his strong interest in colour with daring painting schemes only recently rediscovered through restoration. The year 1929 saw the publication of *Die neue Baukunst*, a perceptive history of the Modern Movement, and in 1931 Taut became Professor at Berlin's Technische Hochschule.

His long association with the political left and an extended visit to the Soviet Union in 1932 made him an enemy of the Nazis, and he was warned on his return to Berlin immediately to flee the country. He took up an invitation to visit Japan where he remained until 1936, studying and writing about Japanese culture and design, and winning international recognition for the 17th-century Katsura Palace. Though revered and successful, he failed to win significant design commissions, so in 1936 took up an offer of a post in Turkey. He became chief architect to the Ministry of Education, building several schools and an interesting house for himself, concerned to adapt his designs to the place and climate. He also produced projects for a theatre, a parliament, and various other public buildings, but this promising third career was cut short by his early death at the age of 58.   PBJ

Boyd Whyte, I., *Bruno Taut and the Architecture of Activism* (1982)

Speidel, M., *Bruno Taut, Natur und Fantasie* (in German, 1994)

Taut, Max (1884–1967) German architect. During the Weimar period he was far more productive than contemporaries such as *Gropius and *Mies who later became far better known; but his commitment to a socially progressive Modernism was far more definite. He believed in the straightforward expression of structure (usually formed of reinforced concrete, with large areas of glass infill), as evident in a series of buildings for the German Printers Union, Berlin (1922–5, with Mart *Stam), the Federation of German Trades Unions (Frankfurt-am-Main, 1931), and the Co-Operative Department Store (Berlin, 1932). He also designed two schools, which showed capable planning skills: the Dorotheen Lyceum (Berlin, 1927); and a group of schools linked together around a courtyard. In the post-war period he concentrated on large-scale housing (e.g. the Reuter-Siedlung, Bonn, 1948–52).   PG

Taylor, Sir Robert (1714–88) English monumental mason and architect. Following study in Rome, Taylor carved a number of monuments and the pediment of the City Mansion House, London. Lacking talent, he turned to architecture and success, the first of his country houses being Harleyford Manor, Buckinghamshire (c.1755). As surveyor to the Bank of England he provided new buildings both for the bank (1766–88, mostly demolished), and for City merchants, such as Grafton House, Piccadilly (1760, demolished) and Danson Park, Bexleyheath, London (1760–65). A Palladian by inclination, Taylor could plan ingeniously and design compact but convenient houses such as 37 Dover Street, London, Asgill House, Richmond, London (1760–65). His Purbrook House, Hampshire (1770, demolished), apparently included the first atrium of the classical revival.   APQ

Tecton See LUBETKIN, BERTHOLD.

Telford, Thomas (1757–1834) Scottish engineer. Inspired by rapid industrial progress at the end of the 18th century, and with the increasing availability of cast iron, Telford developed designs for radically different structures. He came to attention with a proposal for a bridge across the Thames in London which used cast iron to create a single span of 183 m (600 ft). Telford

was the builder of more than 1,287 km (800 miles) of road, three bridges over the Severn, warehouses at St Katherine's Docks in London (1825–8), canals, and two impressive aqueducts, at Longdon-upon-Tern, Shropshire (1794, in cast iron), and Pont-y-Cysyllte, near Llangollen, Wales (1795–1805). Telford also explored other systems of construction, and between 1819 and 1826 built two chain suspension bridges, over the Menai Straits and River Conway. Of his many other buildings, St Mary's church, Bridgnorth, Shropshire (1792), is perhaps the best, as a competent exercise in *neoclassicism.   BC

temenos A piece of ground surrounding or adjacent to a Greek or other temple, and hence a sacred enclosure.   APQ

tempietto Literally 'a small temple', usually circular in form, as in *Bramante's tempietto next to San Pietro in Montorio, Rome.   PG

temples, fire See ZOROASTRIAN ARCHITECTURE.

temples, Hindu Hinduism emerged in the first half of the 1st millennium CE from a Brahmanical reform process prompted by the success of Mahayana Buddhism. The faith centres on a Trinity embracing the powers of Creation, Preservation, and Destruction personified as Brahma, Vishnu, and Shiva; but sectarian devotion focuses predominantly on Vishnu or Shiva—who descend from pre-Brahmanical native deities associated respectively with the sun and death. The efficacy of worship depends on the intercession of the *shakti* (the consort and activator of the deity) who derives from the age-old cult of the Mother Goddess as the feminine power of fertility and abundance (see INDIAN SUBCONTINENT (RELIGIOUS AND SPIRITUAL INFLUENCES)).

The deity whose grace is invoked for salvation is worshipped in the form of an image or symbol sanctified to be fitting for the god's residence. The product of a syncretic process and embracing a wide range of roles and powers, the multiple identities of the Hindu deity in a multiplicity of forms distance the icon—never a mere image but a potential seat of grace—from the realities of this inadequate world of appearances. Beyond super-human power, represented by a multiplicity of organs, identity is primarily established in the attributes of a particular manifestation of the deity, from his/her vehicle or weapons, to the whole corpus of fertility symbolism deriving from the pre-Vedic 'water cosmology'.

As in the earliest native cults, worship is primarily the sacrifice of service and sustenance, by the individual worshipper as he wills, or, more regularly at the four principal states of the sun, by the priest whose caste and consecration fit him to represent the community as a whole. The Hindus evolved the most elaborate ritual: like a supreme personage, the deity incumbent in its image is awakened from the sleep of non-manifestation, greeted with flowers, accommodated, bathed, anointed, dressed, adorned, fed, honoured in accordance with the ritual of circumambulation, entertained with dancing, confined with his wife and paraded through the town in a car (*ratha*) on festival holidays.

As worship (*puja*) is not congregational, in practice it requires the provision of little more than a cella (*mulaprasada*) and a porch (*praggriva*) to house the image and shelter the individual worshipper or priest—as in Temple 17 at Sanchi (*c*.450). However, in addition to a cella, a porch, and a pavilion (*mandapa*) large enough for ritual dancing or banqueting, there are many other buildings—especially in the great temple cities of the south, such as Srirangam and Madurai. The temple is the centre of intellectual and artistic endeavours, promoting the development of painting, sculpture, architecture, and the performing arts, as well as philosophy and theology. As the nucleus of the community, as school, hostel, hospice, and hospital, its

expansion over the centuries catered for priests, the poor, and pupils, as well as the bureaucracy sustaining its endowments, managing its estates, administering its charities, and employing its servants. However, the conception of the Hindu temple goes far beyond mere practicalities.

Though a princely patron might be as interested in fame as in the spiritual welfare of his subjects, the building of a temple was a sacrificial act earning the builder merit in accordance with the permanence of the work. The Vedic ideal of the constitution of the Progenitor—the Purusha—still governed the exercise, though the theatre of worship (*puja*) rather than the flame of the sacrifice (*yajna*) was to rise from its base. Thus the formula for sacred building (*vastupurushamandala*) remained the first concern of the Hindu science of architecture (*vastushastra*).

The place of contact between man and God is identified with the form of the universe; the moment of imprinting the ground with the diagram (*mandala*) to be followed is the subject of astrological calculation; and at all phases of construction the sanctity implicit in the forms is secured by strictly defined ritual. Indeed, the persistence of the Vedic ideal ensured a strong measure of consistency in the conception of the temple throughout the subcontinent, despite regional differences—of which the broadest is not uncontroversially distinguished between the 'Nagara' of the north and the 'Dravidian' of the south.

The temple is a place of pilgrimage. Ideally, pilgrimage is to the Holy Waters at a spiritual 'fording place' (*tirtha*) providing purifying and regenerative passage through those waters as initiation to salvation: the temple is a *tirtha* and its natural site is by the sacred waters of a river—often, in practice, in the vicinity of the grove or pool of some time-honoured *yaksha*. Whether or not water is present on a site whose auspiciousness is indicated by some sign of divine favour, it is ritually introduced to the sanctum in a pot or pitcher (*kumbha* or *kalasha*) during the consecration rites. In any event, a tank is constructed to collect water for the obligatory ritual ablution.

As the house of the god, and the theatre of the sacrifice of service and sustenance, the temple is a place of epiphany where the operation of the god's grace, his descent from transcendence, is effected through the *shakti*. Thus its sanctum, penetrable only by the priest competent to invoke divine conjunction, is called 'womb chamber' (*garbha-griha*) because the interaction of *shakti* and deity, the gestation of grace, takes place there: nothing asserts this more potently than the 'amorous couples' (*mithunas*) of the portal and the phallus (*lingam*) which provide the prime focus for devotion to Shiva within.

The culmination of the momentum developed along the ground plane, in the *garbha-griha* for the priest, around it in circumambulation for the lay devotee, represents one great strand in the Indian tradition, following the precedent set by the Buddhists in particular in creating or adapting caves as wombs of grace. This is reflected also in the hewing of the complex exterior ordonnance and iconographical programme from assembled block-work or even from the living rock itself. Though the mastery of masonry and the ability to handle widely differing hard and soft stone is a key to the development of the major schools of Hindu temple architecture, representation rather than structural innovation was always the main concern of Hindu builders.

In the conception of what was to be represented in the mass itself, the other great strand of the Hindu tradition concerns itself with a vertical momentum. If the geometrical formula of the *mandala* provides the key to its planning, the temple is constructed as the manifestation of the Purusha's towering residence invested by the hierarchy of the gods in accordance with the *mandala* to which the sculpture provides the

key: as far as the accidents of survival testify, the process began at Deogarh, if not Aihole.

Brahma is usually personified as Shiva or Vishnu, sustainers of Brahma, the living presence (*jiva*) in the symbol or image of the Brahmasthana—the *garbha-griha*. *Shakti* permeates the temple from the water pot (*kumbha*) at its base to the pitcher/vase (*kalasha*) which forms its finial. Personified as the consort of the dedicatee, the *shakti* motivates the *jiva* to emanation as Divine Grace to endow the devotee at the portal and to manifestation in blind doors (*ghanadvaras*) at the cardinal projections to its mass as the principal accessory aspects of deity (*parshva devatas*). Maturity was to accommodate many images in multiple recessions and projections, but the essentials were the three persons of the trinity, *avatars* of Vishnu, faculties of Shiva, the *shakti* herself—or their symbols.

Hand in hand with the consequent development of the iconographic programme, which itself went hand in hand with the development of devotional Hinduism as it had for Mahayana Buddhism, went the endowment of structural form with symbolic value. For Buddhists and Hindus alike—as, indeed, for the Jains too—the elements of the traditional timber structural system provide the basic armature not only of aesthetic unity but of *shakti* symbolism. Lotus and pot (*padma* and *kumbha*) informed the evolution of the socle from a simple stepped stylobate; and the same motifs enriched the petrified trabeation: the tasselled binding which once protected timber posts from splitting was first translated into the *kumbha* and then into the *kalasha* with trailing foliage, the Bowl of Plenty (*purnakalasha*).

The *purnakalasha* naturally takes its place, too, in the portals whose succession symbolizes passage through the 'Fording Place' to the new life generated in the *garbha-griha*. Each portal has several frames, originating in branches (*shakha*) tied together for strength: the inclusion of an architectonic frame is not invariable but the others, rising from the River Goddesses Ganga and Yamuna, are always incised with images of fecundity—notably lush creepers (*patra-lata*) of *padma* origin and *mithunas*. Thus the *thirta*, the Theatre of Grace, the reconstituted Purusha, pulsating with the power of *shakti* is infused with the regenerative essence of the waters throughout.

The process of symbolic transformation is most dramatically illustrated in the evolution of the superstructure. Initially of superimposed slabs, this was first modelled (at Deogarh *c*.500) on the multi-storeyed *prasada*, the residential palace pavilion or its monastic derivative (*vimana*). This approach survived in the 'Dravidian' south where the storeys were marked by open terraces bordered with cell-like pavilions (and called *vimana*): the process may be traced from its inception at Mahaballipuram to its apogee at Tanjore via Pattadakal and the astonishing rock-cut Kailasa temple at Ellora. 'Nagara' maturity achieved a series of progressively abstract permutations which reflect the imagery of the mountain—specifically Kailasa of Shiva or Vishnu's Vaikuntha—encountered in the *shastras* from the very earliest reference to the superstructure of temples: the masterpieces of Bhubaneshwar, Udayapur, Khajuraho, and Ranakpur are the supreme surviving examples. A synthesis of the southern and the northern was ingeniously effected in the central Indian Deccan at several sites, of which Lakkundi and Somanathpur are outstanding.

The Hindu temple abroad Ubiquitous in native and imported guises in Nepal, the Hindu temple is relatively rare elsewhere in the Himalayas, Burma, Thailand, and Sri Lanka, where Buddhism has long sustained pre-eminence. However, Hindus made an important contribution to the development of architecture in Java and Bali, and an unparalleled one in Khmer domains. In these rich lands the natives worshipped the spirits of the waters and the mountain,

and ambitious rulers of foreign origin—like the Indian emigrées who first established kingdoms there—would naturally seek to identify themselves with such spirits, asserting their own divinity. To a Hindu pretender the waters would be identified with the primordial ocean from which the tree of life sprang forth through Varunya's navel and to the floor of which Indra pegged his *stambha* to prop the sky from the earth. And the mountain would be identified with cosmic Meru, itself identified with that *axis mundi*. It is this imagery that provides the key to understanding the imperial buildings of the Khmers. They went further than the Indians who inspired them: they needed to construct models of the cosmos centred on Meru in distant Jambudvipa; the Indians built on Jambudvipa itself.   CT

Hindu temples in Bengal Following the Mughal conquest of Bengal in 1575, there occurred a general cultural revival and, paradoxically enough, a Hindu religious revival. In architecture, a regional style emerges in Bengal for the first time, combining some traditional Islamic techniques (arches, vaults, and domes) with local materials, especially brick and terracotta, and an element of the vernacular hut form, the curved cornice, bamboo forming elastically under tension.

Temples were built until the beginning of the 19th century, though the highpoint in terms of architectural achievement was about 1700–50. Almost all the significant examples are to be found in the alluvial delta of the Ganges. The various temple types were classified in great detail by David McCutchion, in research published after his death (*Brick Temples of Bengal*, 1983; see also Dani, A. H., *Muslim Architecture in Bengal*, 1961). Most of these types showed Bengali architects' continuing attachment to the towered forms of Orissa, in particular the pinnacled or *ratna* (jewel) type, which has a more or less flat roof surmounted by one or more towers. The outstanding example is the Kantaji

913

Temple, Kantanagar (1704–22), which had six pinnacles before their destruction by an earthquake in 1897.   PG

temples, Jain The revelation of the 'Way of the Conquerors' (*jinas*), followed by the Jainas since the 6th century BC, is credited to Vardhamana, son of Siddhartha, a chief of the Jnatrika clan. In about 510 BC, towards the age of 30, he renounced his family and became a sannyasin associating with the Nirgrantha sect of ascetics, whose name his own followers later took. After thirteen years of wandering and privation, completely destitute even of clothing, he achieved Enlightenment and became a *jina*. The Mahavira ('Great Hero') to his converts, he spent the rest of his life in the Ganges valley proclaiming his ascetic doctrine concerned with the preservation of the intrinsically blissful soul through the renunciation of violent action. Motivated by the interaction of souls, the universe passes through an infinite series of cycles in which progress and decline are marked by the appearance at regular intervals of twelve 'Righteous conquerors of the Four Corners' (*Chakravatins*) and twenty-four guides to their way. These are the 'fordmakers' (*Tirthankaras*), creating a ford across the river of human suffering, of which Mahavira was the twenty-fourth of our aeon.

The Mahavira left no scripture, and attempts at formulating a canon of doctrine some two hundred years after his death led to schism between those who insisted on nudity (Digambaras) and those who permitted minimal clothing (Shvetambaras). Though Jains are to be found all over India, they were never numerous and ultimately tended to congregate in the south and north-west: the Digambaras around Mysore, the Shvetambaras in Rajastan, Gujarat, and Kathiawar, where they benefited from official patronage under the Solanki dynasty from the 11th to the 13th centuries.

Ministers of the Solanki rulers themselves were responsible for the great Dilwara series of Jain shrines at Mt Abu inaugurated by the Vimala-Vasahi early in the 11th century and completed by the Lunar-Vashahi 200 years later. This extraordinary achievement echoed through other mountain fastnesses in Kathiawar and Gujarat—notably Kumbheria, Satrunjaya, and Mt Girnar—and is reflected in such exquisite Rajasthani fort-temples as the Salindheshvara at Chitor. Here, as elsewhere in India, the Jains drew directly on the Hindu repertory of forms, reorganizing them to cater for their devotion to multiple *Tirthankaras*.

As in the typical orthodox Hindu shrine of the region, the main elements are a cella with ambulatory preceded by closed and open halls aligned east–west on a platform. But the Jaina works are distinguished from their Brahmanical counterparts by the extremely rich Jaina iconography, and the row of miniature cellas housing repeated images of all the *Tirthankaras* on the edge of the platform. A sumptuous open hall of nine squares was usually inserted into the court. The culmination was the four-faced (*chaturmukha*) temple with multi-storey halls succeeding one another before all four sides of a cella enshrining a four-faced image of the *Jina*. The earliest surviving example is the Dharana-Vihara at Ranakpur. Indirectly lit, infused by the opalescent sheen of the local Arasa marble, the open hall beyond the western entrance is the chief glory of Jaina architecture.   CT

Tengbom, Ivar Justus (1878–1968) Swedish architect. His work follows the main trends of Swedish architecture in the generation following *c*.1910—*National Romanticism, modern *Classicism, and *Modernism.

The brick-faced Högalid Church, Stockholm (1917–23), with its twin eastern towers, is reminiscent of Visby cathedral on Gotland (mainly 13th century). By contrast, the Stockholm Concert Hall (1923–6) is a closed cubic volume with a recessed attic storey and a giant, extended colonnade in front. Perhaps following the lead of *Asplund, Tengbom then turned to a radical Modernism, with the Esselte Printing House, Stockholm (with N. Ahrbom, 1928–34), a concrete and glass building, 10 storeys tall, with the final 3 storeys recessed step-wise. The wall surfaces between rows of steel-framed windows were designed to be covered with illuminated advertisement signs.   TF

tenia (taenia) A narrow projecting fillet between a Doric architrave and frieze on which the *triglyphs are mounted and from which the *guttae hang.   APQ

terraced houses 'A terrace of houses' is a peculiarly British expression which does not make much sense (even its precise definition is somewhat unclear) unless one knows about its origins. It was in the 18th century when London builders and architects provided an overall classical dress for a group of houses, so that their *ensemble* looked somewhat like a French Baroque palace (e.g. part of Robert *Adam's Adelphi development, the 'Royal Terras' of 1768, situated on a podium above the Thames). The smartest 'terraces' sported a central accent as well as projections for the houses at either end; lesser terraces simply impressed through the overall repetition and regularity in all their details. During the early 19th century the grand terrace peaked in the developments around Regent's Park, London (architect John *Nash), and the fashion lasted somewhat longer in Glasgow and Edinburgh. Thereafter the type ceased to be fashionable and was replaced by the more suburban-looking semi-detached or detached house.

During the 18th and especially the 19th centuries most large urban centres in Europe adopted the many-storeyed block of flats as the common form of dwelling. But a few areas held out and continued with the traditional urban row house, especially the Low Countries, stretching from north-west Germany to northern France. Above all England (but not Scotland)

eschewed large blocks of flats for a long time and varied the row house tradition, down to the smallest possible units, such as the 'back-to-backs'. From England row houses were transplanted to the East Coast of the USA from Boston to Baltimore, and further to Australia. However, an erosion of the type took place, in that in the largest town centres, such as Amsterdam and New York, a row house merely pretended to be one house, but was in fact subdivided horizontally into apartments. In inner London this happened, too, but on the whole the English resorted to their spread-out suburbs where it was still economic to house one family each in endless strings of houses. In strong contrast to the Low Countries, where the façade of each house in the row was designed to look slightly different, the English row houses conformed with the principle of order and unity, i.e. each house looks exactly like the next. By the later 19th century economic factors like the mass manufacture of identical elements also played a role. All this finally sealed the fate of the terrace, by about 1900; for an Arts and Crafts mode of thinking the look of endless rows of terraced houses was nothing but a tasteless bore. For many decades Britain shunned them, but, like much of Europe, later revived the type.   SM

Muthesius, S., *The English Terraced House* (1984)

terracotta means 'baked earth', and is a clay product closely allied to brick, used in the construction of walls and decorative features, and as a fireproofing material. In its production, clay is mixed with pulverized ceramic and water, after which the mixture is left to rest before being pressed into moulds. The moulded blocks are fired at temperatures of 800–1200 °C, resulting in a high degree of vitrification and hence of durability.

Apart from its resilience and strength, the main virtue of terracotta is that it can be mass produced, yet also be decoratively carved and moulded. It therefore particularly appealed to 19th-century designers who hoped to establish a distinctive and colourful urban architecture. Its drawback is that every feature has to be designed in detail in advance to allow for the moulds to be made and production completed: the finished blocks cannot be cut or altered.

Terracotta was used by the ancient Greeks and Romans and was revived in 15th-century Italy. That revival spread to other European countries, but it was not until the 18th century that its full potential began to be appreciated. In England, Eleanor Coade started producing a version of terracotta in 1769, which was marketed as a substitute for carved stonework (*see* COADE STONE). Its production ceased in the 1830s, but was gradually superseded by the widespread manufacture of terracotta by other firms.

In the 19th century many architects who made the pilgrimage to Italy returned as devotees of terracotta, most of all in Germany in the 1830s. Buildings such as K. F. *Schinkel's Bauakademie Berlin (1831–6) maximized its virtues as a decorative material. As part of the German influence in England in the mid 19th century, or directly from Italian sources, English architects took up the cause, most of all in the design of the institutions and museums of South Kensington. At the Victoria and Albert Museum (1861–9) and the Royal Albert Hall (1867–71), façades were composed of terracotta and brick, then at the Natural History Museum (1873–81) Alfred *Waterhouse went one step further by constructing the entire exterior and interior elevations in terracotta.

In the late 19th century, terracotta reached its height of popularity in England, especially for commercial buildings, theatres, and pubs. Its popularity also spread to North America, where it was first used extensively at the Museum of Fine Arts, Boston (1870–76). Many of the most famous early skyscrapers were extensively clad in terracotta, for instance the Wainwright Building, St Louis (1890–91), and the Woolworth Building, New York (1910–13). But equally significant

was the use of terracotta tiles and hollow blocks to fireproof their steelwork structures.

In recent years, terracotta has mainly been used in restoration projects where the original material has failed, or been damaged, or as tiles in cladding panels. The potential risks in its production process detract from its more widespread adoption in building projects.   RT

Stratton, M., *The Terracotta Revival* (1993)

Terragni, Giuseppe (1904–43) Italian architect who has been most closely associated with the movement of Italian Rationalism. In fact, other than Antonio *Sant'Elia, he is the most celebrated Italian architect to appear in most general histories of modern architecture.

Terragni signed the first of four manifestos of the Gruppo 7 along with Ubaldo Castagnoli, *Figini and Pollini, Guido Frette, Sebastiano Larco, and Carlo Enrico Rava. His involvement in the polemical activities of the Gruppo 7 was quickly followed by his participation in the Werkbundausstellung in Stuttgart in 1927 and the first and second Rationalist exhibitions in Rome (1928 and 1931).

At the same time Terragni opened a practice in Como with his brother Attilio, one of their first commissions being the Novocomum apartment building in Como (1927–8)—a project whose cubic massing is reminiscent of early Constructivist works. His development of a rationalist language for architecture continued through a series of residential projects in Milan, such as the Casa Rustici (1933–5, with Pietro Lingeri), his participation in building exhibitions like the Casa sul lago per l'artista for the fifth Triennale in Milan (1933), and his continuing work in Como, like his poetically inclined Asilio infantile Sant'Elia (1936–7).

In the early 1930s, Terragni embarked on a series of projects that directly served the political exigencies of the Fascist state. The first of these was a series of

Casa del Fascio, Piazza del Popolo, Como, Italy (Giuseppe Terragni, 1936)

interior display spaces in the Mostra della Rivoluzione Fascista, held in Rome in 1932, such as his Futurist-inspired 'Sala del '22'. The most significant built work, however, was his Casa del Fascio in Como (1932–6), a brilliant essay on the application of a rigorous system of geometric proportioning to the design of an abstract cubic composition. Inspired by Mussolini's statement that Fascism was 'a glass house', Terragni developed a series of meeting rooms and office spaces whose transparent relationship to an enclosed indoor courtyard was in turn linked to an outdoor assembly space in front of the main façade. Though never executed, the façade was to contain a photomontage of Fascist imagery, including a portrait of Mussolini. Two later projects by Terragni, his Scheme A for the Palazzo del Littorio competition (1934, with Lingeri *et al.*) and his Danteum Project (1938, with Lingeri), brought his concern for representing the Fascist state to new poetic heights. Despite his death during World War II, the interest in his work continued after the war and he was

the first Italian architect whose work from the 1930s was given substantial critical attention.   BLM

Ciucci, G. (ed.), *Giuseppe Terragni: Opera Completa* (1996)

terre pisé   Earth is one of the most ancient of building materials, and in ancient times its use was developed in many ways. It could be puddled and piled up, or pre-formed into bricks and laid, but the most sophisticated method was to use shuttering in a way similar to that used for concrete today. Extensively practised in France, hence its name, this method is known as *terre pisé* or simply *pisé*, meaning beaten or kneaded earth. Earth or clay, mixed with gravel and sometimes a binding material such as straw, bramble or animal hair, is beaten down between shutter boards, 1 m (3 ft) at a time, into a dense, compact, self-supporting mass. As it hardens, the boards are removed to a higher level as the wall is built up. It consequently differs from the commoner way of using earth in Britain, known as cob or wychert, and adobe in the Americas, which is normally wetted and piled up, then when dry scraped to produce a flat surface. As is general with earth, *pisé* was used for cottages, barns and other poor rustic buildings, but in the Levant and North Africa its use from ancient times was for better multi-storeyed buildings. Lutyens' Marsh Court (1901–4) uses a variant of rammed earth in which chalk is added to the mixture.   APQ

Tessenow, Heinrich (1876–1950) German architect, influential especially through his writings and through his teaching at the Technische Hochschule in Berlin-Charlottenburg (1926–41). Tessenow's writings on the design of small, single-family houses emphasized the importance of craftsmanship (*Housebuilding*, 1916, in German; trans. 1989), a modest scale, and a pre-industrial village ideal. Here and in his teaching he stressed simplification above every other design goal. His best-known buildings were his classicizing Dalcroze

Institute, a school of dance at Dresden-Hellerau (1912, a design that produced great conflict with Richard Riemerschmid, Hermann Muthesius, and Theodor Fischer, because its severe neoclassicism was out of keeping with the other Hellerau buildings), his Heinrich Schütz School in Kassel (1927–30), his Stadtbad Mitte in Berlin (1927), and his remodelling of Schinkel's Neue Wache in Berlin (1931). At the Berlin Technische Hochschule, Tessenow was the mentor of Albert Speer, who always professed great admiration for him. Tessenow, however, disapproved of Speer's buildings, and he received scarcely any commissions during the Nazi period. Postmodernist architects have been enthusiastic about Tessenow's work; his writings and buildings have been extensively published since the 1970s. BML

De Michelis, M., *Heinrich Tessenow* (1991)

Tessin, Nicodemus, the Elder (1615–81) Swedish architect. His main works were: the royal palaces of Drottningholm (1662ff.) and Strömsholm; Kalmar Cathedral (1660–c.1702); the State Bank Building, Stockholm (1675–82); and palaces and mansions for the nobility. Tessin's buildings show a dignified restraint with complex and heavy roofs and walls framed by colossal pilasters or lesenes, inspired by French and Roman models. In the State Bank he mirrors the stern Roman fronts of Palazzo Farnese or Borghese. Similarly, Kalmar Cathedral with four corner towers and four scrolled gable fronts is dependent on Roman late-16th- and early-17th-century models. Drottningholm Palace has a main block flanked by two square courtyards surrounded by lower wings, corner pavilions and a domed octagon at each end of the complex. Originally, the main block carried a big lantern with a royal crown to emphasize the centre of the vast *ensemble*. The monumental and richly decorated central stairway runs through the height of the building. TF

Tessin, Nicodemus, the Younger (1654–1728) Swedish architect, much influenced by Italian 16th- and 17th-century and contemporary French models, the last-mentioned especially for room planning. His main contribution is the Stockholm Royal Palace (1690–1754). Other more important works include his own Stockholm residence (1696–1700) and the country mansion of Steninge (1694–8).

The Royal Palace was based partly on *Bernini's Louvre project, partly on the Farnese and Borghese palaces, Rome. Characteristic of this four-winged complex is the varying treatment of its façades, each clearly relating to and dominating the surrounding cityscape, for which Tessin made extensive but unexecuted plans, including a domed church, and a large arsenal building. The architect's work matches the nearby Palace on a small scale, cleverly adapted to its narrow, irregular site. The centrepiece of the mansion of Seninge was varied in his grandly scaled country palace, Roissy, near Paris (demolished), whereas his ambitious projects for the Paris Louvre and Versailles remained unrealized.

Nicodemus Tessin the Younger is probably the internationally best known Swedish architect before the 20th century, and was most important for Sweden's Italian and French contacts with art and architecture.

TF

Testa, Clorindo (1923–) Italian-born Argentine architect and painter. He gained international recognition for the construction of the Bank of London and South America, Buenos Aires (1959–66), using an exposed concrete structure. Other works of significance in Buenos Aires include the boldly original National Library (1962), the Central Naval Hospital (1970), the Recoleta Cultural Centre (1970), and the Paz Sigiar Auditorium (1993–6), as well as some attractive residential buildings.

LNM (trans. KL)

Teulon, Samuel Sanders (1812–73) English architect. Starting practice in 1838, Teulon helped George Porter design the Watermen's Almshouses, Penge, London (1840–41), in an already hectic Tudor Gothic style that reappeared more strongly in his own Drapers' Almshouses, Islington (1842–3, demolished). His model village of estate cottages at Thorney, Cambridgeshire (1843–63), and cottages for Crown labourers, Windsor (1854), are less marked in style. At the same time he designed Tortworth Court, Gloucestershire (1849–52), in an emphatic Gothic that he carried into his churches. The most characteristic of these are marked by multicoloured brickwork and masonry, the jagged edges of cogging courses and florid carving, heavy plate tracery and bold massing. At his peak, as exemplified in London by St Mark, Silvertown (1860–62), St Mary, Ealing (remodelled 1866–74), and St Stephen's, Hampstead (1868–71), his churches rank amongst the most colourful and wilfully imaginative of the Victorian period, but many others are so dull as to seem from another hand.   APQ

Thailand As a distinct style, Thai Buddhist architecture developed rather late. The religion was established in the region well before AD 1000, but it was not until the 13th century, with the emergence of the Sukhothai Kingdom (formed following the migrations of Tai peoples from China), that a characteristic Thai artistic mode emerged. Thai style appeared similar to the Indian and Sri Lankan styles—the latter admired throughout most of South East Asia as a purer form of Buddhism, and reflecting Khmer architecture, a direct result of Cambodian hegemony in the region (some of the finest Khmer remains are at Pimai, in Thailand proper). Early inscriptions at Sukhothai indicate that Singhalese craftsmen carried out some of the actual construction.

Wood was thought to have originally been the favoured material, as it was among the earliest Buddhist monuments elsewhere, but the passage of time saw buildings of such a fugitive material replaced by more permanent methods. What often does remain are the brick podiums which once supported those wooden buildings. In more recent times, wood has returned as a popular element, and continues as a significant aspect of contemporary Thai design. Ruins of Buddhist structures and restored stupas are found across Thailand, constructed in styles reflecting those varied sources. Most are composed of mortared brick (a favourite Singhalese method), also laterite (widely used in Cambodia), and trimmed with stucco with remnants of the original polychrome. The Sri Lankan sources are especially evident in the tall, bell-shaped stupas (Thai: chedi) that came to be the dominant element by the 15th century, though remains at Lopburi indicate the form had a long history in the region. As the capital moved from Sukhothai and on to Ayudhya and finally to Bangkok, the buildings increased in richness and decorative elements, due in part to increasing Chinese influence. As with much of the architecture of South East Asia, the Indian belief in the cosmological role of Meru, the sacred mountain, was a central theme. Thus the temple is the centre of the universe, the elements of the complex are oriented to the cardinal directions, and the central stupa dominates the compound, the latter the most notable and expressive aspect of Thai architecture.

The Sukhothai builders, though influenced by Khmer techniques and decorative choices, also retained elements of the earlier Dvaravati period (from the middle of the 1st millennium AD) especially in the use of brick construction, and the numerous stucco niches with their terracotta figures. Although the widespread damage from the wars with Burma decimated Sukhothai monuments, reconstructions that continue many of the earlier modes of construction can be found, notably among the later monuments at Ayudhya.

Si Satchanalai stupa, central Thailand (?15th century)

Best known, and continuing into modern times, is the tall *stupa, with its lotus bud spire, a particular contribution of Sukhothai builders. These soaring stupas dominate a temple complex, and the form is repeated on corners of the square base that supports the main spire. The overall shape derives from forms originating in India, but especially from the bell-shaped style favoured in Sri Lanka. In Thai hands, these towering monuments, typically constructed of brick and stucco, many with laterite cores, were at times embellished with fired tiles, some encircled by elephant protomes, with the entire assemblage erected upon a multi-tiered base. It was common to build new construction over the ruins of older stupas, and portions of several can sometimes be seen, though the sanctity of many prevents excavation down to earlier structures. In Bangkok the great Nakhon Pathom stupa, 114 m (375 ft) tall and dating from the early 20th century, is thought to have been constructed over much earlier, possibly Dvaravati remains. These

towering stupas—likened to a minaret by some scholars—commanded a rectangular precinct, with the main entrance to the east, although some Thai temples instead feature a set of three towers as the dominant architectural motif, an arrangement favoured among Khmer designs. A chaitya hall often dominated the east–west axis, with subsidiary buildings (the mandapas, housing relics or major images, and viharas, the assembly halls, as found elsewhere in Buddhist temples) just off the longitudinal plan, and ever less rigid in their placement as the complex grew.

Many of these large buildings were made of wood or masonry, with nave-shaped interiors and roofs supported by pillars, again made of wood or masonry. The rectangular white buildings, wrapped with a row of tall pillars, under large wooden roofs covered with multi-hued tiles (that appear to be sliding one beyond the other), and finished with projecting serpent-like stylized creatures at the corners, are a hallmark of the religious complex. It is not unusual for excavators to discover hundreds of smaller ruins, monuments erected by the wealthy in proximity to the major buildings, a pattern well established in Indian Buddhist temples and proof again of the importance of imperial support to the success of the faith. Following the Burmese sack of Ayudhya in 1767, Thai architecture came to emphasize decorative elements, especially refined surface patterns. During the subsequent two centuries, and due in part to increasing Chinese influence, greater use of wood and surface decoration resulted in ever more graceful reflections of traditional styles.

A fundamental aspect of Buddhism is its didactic function. Across Asia, Buddhist architecture has provided an opportunity, literally a place to communicate the tenets of the faith. Buildings are designed with niches to display deities (often of enormous size), and areas are set aside for primary images, all typically enhanced by architectural devices that control the light. Due especially to the Theravadin form of Buddhism of Thailand, the display of narrative painting is critical, although the practice is widely known notably from the 1st century at Ajanta in India (and slightly later in Sri Lanka) and nearly as old from outlying regions of central Asia into western China. Due to the losses over time, relatively little architectural decoration remains, and modern-day visitors typically view ancient Buddhist monuments with little or no evidence of what was originally a fundamental element of its design.

Extant wall painting in Thailand (most not older than the 18th century) indicates the widespread use of murals, typically devoted to popular Theravadin didactic themes. The styles of these murals reflect the native fascination with colourful, elaborate and richly patterned designs, but stylized to a greater extent than their Indian counterparts. This quality gives Thai wall painting—as is also true of Sukhothai sculpture—an affinity with modern art, and these graceful, linear and strongly abstract styles that serve to set Thai art further apart from the Buddhist art of the region. What Westerners might consider 'stylized' or as an esthetic departure from the visual norm, a Buddhist would feel was the capturing of the essence of the sacred, thus worthy of devotion, avoiding having simply to repeat the mere appearance of the physical world. When Thai Buddhist architecture displays its narrative wall paintings, the impact is closer to what the architects, working under the direction of the monks, have created for centuries. Because so much of this blend of structure and harmonious decoration can still be seen today in Thailand, one is given a glimpse into the Buddhist past, where the function of architecture is first to facilitate the communication of the tenets of the faith, providing a setting for worship and education and a setting for sculpture and painting, all in the service of the faith.　　　　RF

thatch So ubiquitously were roofs covered in vegetable materials in the earlier Middle Ages, that roofing, regardless of the material used, and the old word for roof, taken from the German *Dach*, became synonymous. In medieval Britain a roof could be thatched in slate or tile, but today thatch is confined to vegetable materials, and only wheat straw and water reed are in regular use. The straw or reed is prepared on the ground by wetting it to make it pliable, then formed into tight bunches. These are laid on the roof, either in horizontal courses, higher ones overlapping the one below, or in vertical courses, each tightly butting against its neighbour. Gables, hips, and ridges need extra bunches to build them up, and gutters, dormer windows, and chimney-stacks are similarly treated to ensure waterproofing. In Britain methods of thatching vary, so that thatch may have a brief or extended life depending on how it is laid. The highest quality of workmanship in England is probably in eastern counties, where, combined with a favourably dry climate and relatively high-pitched roofs, wheat straw thatch may commonly last for 35 years, and water reed even longer, though it is more expensive.

APQ

theatres, worldwide

The archaeological record There are two distinctly different and parallel, but equally important, traditions concerning the theatre buildings of classical antiquity: the outdoor theatre and the roofed theatre (*theatrum tectum*). Historically our knowledge of the architectural mutations of the classical Roman outdoor theatre was limited to *Vitruvius and archaeology.

But this turns out to be only half the story. The only serious mention of the roofed theatre in the readily available literature was in Margarete Bieber's *The History of the Greek and Roman Theater* (2nd edn, 1961). It was not until Professor Izenour's research, based on a wide range of sources (published in *The Roofed Theatres of Classical Antiquity*, 1992), that a serious effort was made to establish the tradition of the roofed theatres as being of equal value and as important as the outdoor theatres.

The outdoor theatre Referred to as *ikria* this was in all probability a three-sided temporary wooden risked-seating structure, surrounding a trapezoid-shaped orchestra, erected on the occasion of the Pan Athenai and Linean drama festivals in the Athenean Agora. On this occasion that structure collapsed, the probable reason for the theatre being moved to a permanent hillside site on the south slope of the Acropolis. It can also be noted that the flowering of the Greek tragic trilogy and the Attic comedy was over before the Lycurgan theatre of Dionysus was moved to its permanent site on the south slope.

However, in the beginning there was little effort at creating the classical, symmetrically hollowed-out,

bermed hillside auditorium, the remains of which we see today. The archaeological evidence for the 'archaic' hillside-supported auditoria was found at sites outside Athens, for example, the early-5th-century BC archaic hillside theatre at Thorikos, some 40 km (25 miles) south of Athens.

During the late decades of the 5th century BC, the outdoor theatre very quickly mutated into the architect-designed, classic, stone masonry constructed, outdoor Graeco-Hellenistic theatre which completed with a *skene*, flanked by a right and a left *parodos*, a circular orchestra fronting a symmetrical three-quarter-round-enveloping auditorium. Located in the Peloponnese, the Graeco-Hellenistic theatre at Epidaurus (340 BC) is the most perfectly preserved and unmodified example of the genre to survive.

However, the Lycurgan theatre was extensively remodelled by the Romans. Exhaustive study of this and other similar sites clearly indicates that the design of the classical Graeco-Hellenistic theatre went through a continuing, dual-faceted purposeful afterlife that by way of Roman remodellings finally mutated into the Roman theatre.

The Romans who succeeded the Greeks designed a type of theatre professedly derived from the Greek model which is described in detail by Vitruvius. In the meantime, playwriting had also changed. Greek drama was three-dimensional and was played in the round (the orchestra). Roman drama, two-dimensional and linear, was played confrontationally on a shallow, raised stage in which the popular comedies of Plautus and Terence were produced to the delight of an empire-wide paying audience.

Design of the Roman theatre followed suit. The auditorium was now smaller, more intimate and closer to the raised stage, steeper and half-round with a randomly seated orchestra which was terminated in a wood-framed-roofed, shallow raised stage backed by an enormous permanent stage set in masonry (the *skene*

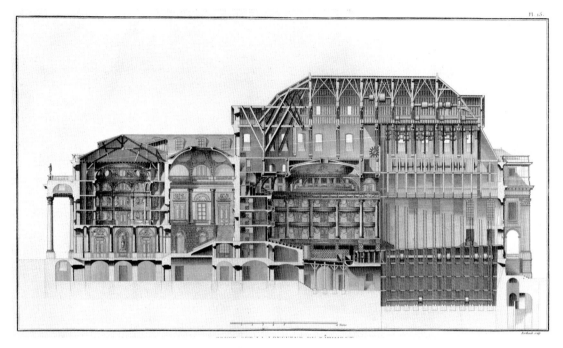

Longitudinal section: Grand Théâtre, Bordeaux, France (Victor Louis, 1780)

frons). On many occasions the auditorium was also roofed by a tension structured rope-rigged *velarium* (canvas awning), as at Aspendos (Turkey).

In parallel with the development of the large Roman outdoor public theatre, the Romans also built a smaller-scaled (outdoor-indoor) theatre. This size and type of theatre was designated in the literature of the time as an *odeum*. In light of the evolving archaeological evidence, particularly that on the Herodes Atticus site in Athens (AD 162), this style of theatre is best described as a hybrid. Proportionally the design is identical to the conventional Roman public outdoor theatre. The auditorium is reduced in size but it is considerably larger than the fully roofed outdoor theatre (*theatrum tectum*), also identified as an *odeum*.

With but few exceptions (notably Epidaurus), the older Graeco-Hellenistic theatres were remodelled by the Romans in two distinct stages.

The first remodelling straightened out the sides of the orchestra, which was then cut approximately in half. The movement forward of the shallow raised stage placed the audience in the confrontational relationship of the Roman public theatre.

In the second remodelling of the Hellenistic theatres, as well as many of the large Roman theatres located in those provincial cities of the Empire not equipped with a permanent oval-shaped arena, these initial remodellings were further transformed into half-round arenas. In its present state, the Lycurgan theatre yields clear evidence of the second Roman remodelling, which show that in the second remodelling the orchestra was surrounded by a barbed metallic fence rising out of a low stone masonry wall. This barrier, for the protection of the audience, converted the theatre into an arena for staging the more popular entertainments featuring 'man to wild animal' and 'man to man' gladiatorial combat. These final remodellings converted ('dead ended' is the better term) most of the Graeco-Hellenistic as well as many of the Roman outdoor theatres from buildings previously devoted to dramatic performances to buildings for the popular frivolous entertainments for Populus Romanus; this transition could well have prompted the acid comment *cum* sociological lament about 'bread and circuses', from the Latin poet Juvenal.

The roofed theatre Not mentioned by *Vitruvius, but a parallel development of the outdoor theatre and also dating from the 5th century BC, are the remains of the walls and the column bases of a roofed theatre, the Odeum of Pericles (435 BC). Because the mainland Greeks were structurally limited to knowledge of post-and-beam construction for spanning space, this mode of construction placed severe seating, seeing, and hearing limitations on the interior of a public auditorium. This limitation is quite evident in the Odeum of Pericles.

Development of the clear-spanned auditorium free of columns did not occur until the discovery of structural triangulation and the consequent invention of the timber truss, a discovery placed somewhere in the Middle East in the 4th and 5th centuries BC. Use of the timber truss in the design of clear-spanned auditoria for public assembly occurred in the Greek colonies of Ionia, in what is now Anatolia. The type of building in which the truss was first used was either a *bouleuterion* or an *ecclesiasterion*, meeting houses (auditoria) for either a magisterial or an elected governing body (an ecclesia or a boule respectively) of a city state. An example with rectilinear seating on three sides is to be found at Priene, *c*.200 BC.

The ultimate development and proliferation of the clear-spanned roofed theatre (*theatrum tectum*) throughout the Mediterranean basin was carried out by the Romans. An elegant example of Roman building in the early imperial style is the theatre sited in the Athenian Agora, in which the 'common-sense' lengthening of the seating radius and 'lateral truncation' of the seat bank provide comfortable (30 degree) sight lines to and direct hearing lines from the stage for all seats in a rectangular auditorium.

The post-classical theatre Returning to the odeum of Herodes Atticus: the continuing mutation of classical theatre design did not occur until after a hiatus of 1,100 years. From the fall of Rome, no theatres were built until the revival of classical theatre design in the waning decades of the High Renaissance. When the building of theatres was resumed, the architects copied the Roman confrontational style of theatre design embodying a smaller-scaled but still exteriorized version of the Roman (outdoor) theatre as a lightweight wooden secondary structure under a fake-painted sky within a masonry-walled heavy timber truss-roofed primary structure.

They were also misguided in matters of acoustics by their literal acceptance of Vitruvian dicta. The performing arts of drama, opera, dance, concert, and recital were variously accommodated by means of continuing modified U-shaped seat-banked auditoria that eventually fronted on a mechanically equipped proscenium stage. However, thirty years elapsed between *Scamozzi's shallow three-dimensional, forced-perspective, multi-vista stage which he added to *Palladio's Teatro Olimpico, Vicenza (1585), and the initial deep mechanized proscenium stage for handling movable scenery at the Teatro Farnese by Aleotti (1618).

Over approximately the next century, the half-round socially contiguous seat bank of the Roman outdoor theatre auditorium, now facing an ever more elaborately mechanized proscenium stage, was initially transformed into an elongated U, then into a series of ovoids, circles, contorted bell-shapes and horseshoe-shapes in plan. In order to retain the seating capacity at maximum, the section was divided into segments, rising higher and higher, in the balconied, socially stratified, royal box-centred auditorium of the Baroque and Rococo court theatre, of which an outstanding example is the Opéra de Versailles, by A.-J. *Gabriel.

During the 18th and 19th centuries, horseshoe-shaped, stacked-balconied public theatre auditoria in this mode with an ever-increasing number of seats with no view at all onto the stage was the dominant design type—little short of an outright fraud, but architecturally *de rigueur*. Continuing public theatre design in this mode became simply a matter of frivolous architectural extrapolation in size and in a variety of styles to accommodate an enlarged, now paying public audience. In particular, auditorium *acoustics were a hit or miss proposition.

For the next two hundred years, hardly without exception, Western theatre design in a variety of architectural styles was held captive to this Italianate model. Except for the engineering application of scientific *acoustics, electric lighting, and self-contained mechanical *heating and *air conditioning systems, the 20th-century practice of architecture in this mode is simply more of the same. It fronts an enlarged theatre-engineered stage, which is effectively an increasingly more complex electro mechanical-hydraulic driven and electrically powered incandescent-lighted production machine.

During the 18th century, apart from two isolated examples—the small provincial Drottningholm Court Theatre, Stockholm, and the equally small theatre at Lauchstadt, for the Duke of Weimar—further development and exploitation of long radii, truncated-seating geometry in the design of the seated auditorium facing a proscenium stage, did not occur until the creation of the Bayreuth Festspielhaus (1876).

This theatre, designed by the architect Otto Bruckwald (1841–1904), with the guidance of and under the supervision of Wagner's theatre design and engineering consultant Carl Brandt, was intended by Wagner to be the festival theatre for definitive productions of his music dramas. It was his often-stated intention to design a festival theatre that signalled a return to the classical festival theatre of ancient Greece.

However, because of Wagner's insistence that every member of the audience should be able to have a clear sight of the stage, and the symphony orchestra's being relocated into a deep covered-over pit where it could be heard but not seen, the final result missed Wagner's intention by a wide margin. Instead of the outdoor festival theatre of Greece, the design of the Festspielhaus, unknown to Wagner and his collaborators, virtually copied the long-lost Roman odeum (*teatrum tectum*) of Agrippa in the Athenian Agora.

The closed loop Italian and the open truncated Bayreuth styles of Western theatre design became worldwide in the 20th century. Due principally to the emergence of the theatre-design-engineering and the acoustics consultant, design of auditoria also became more technologically oriented. Inclusion of these disciplines in the graduate curricula of the universities and technical schools has also given rise to a proliferation of the multiple-use theatre, theatre-in-the-round, and the black-box theatre, as well as re-emergence of the three-quarter surround or thrust stage theatre and the adaptation of found spaces to theatrical purposes. Overall these disciplines have exerted a profound influence on theatre design. GI

Izenour, George C., *Theatre Design* (1996)

theatres in Britain The open-air playhouses that appeared in Shoreditch and on Bankside from 1576 onwards constituted the first complete generation of substantial, purpose-built public theatres in Europe since antiquity. They were a logical development from the tradition of inn-yard and baiting arena performances, but represented a major advance into specialized theatre form: timber-framed, mostly polygonal on plan, with seated galleries around an open yard for standing 'groundlings'. The stage, thrusting to the centre of the yard, was not designed for visual illusion. The attention of the audience was focused on action and words.

Indoor 'private' theatres of the same period had their physical forms dictated by the shape of pre-existing rooms. The indoor environment called for a different style of performance and allowed more sophisticated effects, but the stages themselves remained open, a continuation of the space occupied by the audience. Painted frontispieces framing changeable perspective scenery, and elaborate mechanical effects, were introduced by Inigo Jones in spectacular court masques (for which his Whitehall Banqueting House, 1619–22, was specifically designed), but these innovations did not, for the time being, transform general theatrical practice.

The cessation of overt theatrical performance during the Commonwealth effectively killed off the roofless 'wooden O' (Shakespeare's apt metonymy) as a building type. The Restoration was followed by the granting of Royal patents to two theatre companies, creating a duopoly that was to hamper competition and restrict theatre building (but to dwindling effect) until 1843. The first Restoration theatres looked to the Continent, adopting the scenic stage developed in Italy, but without wholeheartedly following Continental models. In at least one respect, they clung to earlier tradition. *Wren's design for a playhouse, believed to be the Drury Lane theatre of 1674, shows a fan-shaped auditorium with a benched seating area (the pit) with a raked floor, two galleries at the rear, and converging side walls with boxes divided by pilasters. There is a deep perspective stage, but the action takes place on a forestage (proscenium) extending halfway toward the gallery fronts and having doors of entry on each side. There is no structural proscenium wall.

The intimate contact with the audience made possible by such an arrangement was exploited by British actors for more than 150 years. Over the whole period, the forestage steadily retreated, but the hundreds of rectangular barn-like circuit theatres built in country towns in the late 18th and early 19th centuries represented a distillation of the native theatre form. Their deceptively simple 'pit, boxes, and gallery' geometry, with conventional 'stock' scenery set behind

an acting area, furnished with proscenium doors and extending into the auditorium, was as perfectly adapted to the acting style of the Georgian era as the Bankside theatres had been to their own time.

Until the second half of the 20th century, British theatres were wholly commercial, having to survive without the patronage enjoyed by most of their European counterparts. They tended, consequently, to experiment cautiously with varieties of U-shaped or horseshoe auditorium form, rarely aiming for or achieving monumentality either in design or siting. The processes of rebuilding the two metropolitan patent theatres (Covent Garden and Drury Lane) by Henry *Holland in the 1790s were, nevertheless, major architectural events, and were followed in those houses and elsewhere by further attempts (with widely varying success in theatrical terms) by a roll call of architects distinguished in other fields.

Britain's first specialist theatre architect was Samuel Beazley (1786–1851), who was also a playwright. He designed theatres 'to serve the purpose of the drama' rather than to follow the latest architectural fashion. His neoclassical designs were, nevertheless, architecturally distinguished as well as being highly effective in theatrical terms.

Throughout the first half of the 19th century a growing taste for spectacle led to the continuing decline of the intimate playhouse, the elimination of the forestage, and a retreat of the action into the scene, until the two worlds of audience and actor were completely separated by the proscenium frame. In the popular theatre the melodrama, pantomime, burlesque, and extravaganza took visual spectacle to new heights, the stage machinist and scenic artist becoming as important to success as the writers and performers. The picture stage concept was, however, given its most complete expression in C. J. Phipps's remodelling of Nash's Haymarket in 1880, where a gold four-sided frame was created for Squire

Bancroft's intimate drawing-room plays and their realistic scenery.

That century also saw the rise of a new form of entertainment house, the music hall. A well-established tradition of tavern concerts had entered a new phase by the 1840s and 1850s, in which modest singing rooms were overtaken by ambitious halls, bigger than their parent pubs. They presented chairman-led, professional entertainments in the form of individual turns, mainly vocal, with comic singers 'in character' increasingly featured. The earliest music halls were rectangular, usually with a single, straight-sided balcony and an open concert stage. Supper tables and benched areas were encircled by promenades in which patrons came and went as in a bar room, rather than a theatre. Bars and serveries opened into the auditorium. For the performance, audibility rather than perfect visibility was the overriding requirement.

A number of influences converged to reshape the music halls into theatrical form, including the desire to present popular ballets, which demanded improved sightlines. By the 1890s the two building types were indistinguishable, the metamorphosis from platform stage music hall to proscenium stage variety theatre being further accelerated by regulatory pressures.

Theatres had long been recognized as inherently unsafe places in which lives were regularly lost as a result of fire or disorderly flight. The revolutionary expansion of construction and safety controls, which took place between 1880 and 1900, coincided with an unprecedented surge in theatre building in which many old theatres were replaced and hundreds of new ones appeared throughout the country, calling into existence a new generation of specialist theatre architects, amongst whom Frank *Matcham was the unchallenged leader.

All the 'boom' theatres of the late Victorian and Edwardian years were of the solidly established proscenium form, with elaborate box compositions linked on either side to undivided balcony tiers. They were decorated in a highly eclectic manner, achieving an unprecedented degree of opulence and warmth of embrace. The audience remained socially divided, as it always had been, but nearly all parts of the house enjoyed good sightlines and improved standards of comfort as well as exemplary means of escape. Pressure for increased capacities sometimes led to deep balcony overhangs, resulting in imperfect views from the rear of the pit (today's rear stalls), but the theatres of this generation that have survived remain popular with modern performers and audiences.

Until the 1890s all theatres, however varied their plan forms and decorative treatments, were of short-span timber and cast-iron construction. Rings of columns supporting the tiers could, to an extent, be disguised, but their unavoidable presence imposed a powerful discipline on design. Only when columns were finally eliminated by steel beams spanning the auditorium from side to side were architects of the later Matcham era released to indulge even greater flights of fancy.

Theatre building between the two world wars, a period dominated by the development of the cinema, was at a low ebb. Those few dedicated theatres that were built adopted a variety of fashionable decoration schemes, but hardly moved from multi-tier proscenium form. The influence of *cinema design was evident in their 'all-face-forward' seating, which made for nearly perfect sighting, but left naked sidewalls. The best inventions of this period had their own delights, but few of them matched the intense theatrical atmosphere generated by their (at the time no longer admired) predecessors. When the attempt was made at Stratford-on-Avon (the Shakespeare Memorial Theatre, 1932) to design an adaptable modern theatre, taking the advice of an array of experts, the result was a chilly hybrid.

The years from 1950 to 1970 saw a massive destruction of old theatres and the appearance of a generation of supposedly multiple-use but depressingly untheatrical civic halls, relieved by a few innovative designs like Moro's Nottingham Playhouse (1963) and Ham's Leatherhead Thorndike (1969). From the late1970s there was much activity in reviving neglected and disused old theatres, the success of which, despite a prevailing urge to 'escape' from the proscenium frame, led to a re-examination of the virtues of theatre designs of the past. Historicism is not a feature of modern theatre architecture (it is certainly not evident in the unaffected clarity of *Lasdun's Royal National, 1976) but neither is the past completely rejected. The thrust stage has been reinvented, the horseshoe has been reinterpreted, and the courtyard theatre has proved to be a highly effective model for intimate modern playhouses, while theatre-in-the-round represents simultaneously the most revolutionary and the most basic of all forms.   JE

Earl, J., *The Theatres Trust Guide to British Theatres* (2000)
Glasstone, V., *Victorian and Edwardian Theatres* (1975)

theories of architecture

ANTIQUITY
MIDDLE AGES
RENAISSANCE
1600–1750
1750–1880
1880–2000

Architectural theory is the interface between the architect, the client, the builder, and the public. Whereas painting or sculpture is often a solitary process, in architecture the design has to be approved by the client, executed by the builder, and appreciated by the public. Architectural theory therefore does not only consist of design principles, but also offers a critical vocabulary and strategies of interpretation.

Antiquity In the Western world until the 1880s architectural theory consisted, with a few notable

exceptions, of a series of commentaries, revisions, translations, and illustrations of *De Architectura* by *Vitruvius, the only surviving architectural treatise from classical antiquity, written *c*.30–20 BC. The topics he addressed provided the agenda for practically all subsequent treatises: architecture defined as a *scientia*, that is a rational activity guided by rules and knowledge both specific to architecture and derived from other disciplines such as mathematics or rhetoric; the education of the architect; the principles of architectural beauty; the *orders, their meanings, and the rules of decorum guiding their use, advising for instance the use of the sturdy *Doric for temples devoted to warlike gods; building types, and some civil engineering. His stress on decorum, of what is fitting for a particular function, public, or occasion, implies a consideration of buildings in their social and religious context.

Western architectural theory until the 1880s is also inextricably linked with *Classicism. Classicism, in the sense that artworks or a style from the past are held up as the model for the present, was first formulated by the Roman teacher of rhetoric Quintilian in his *Institutio oratoria* (AD *c*.80), when he proposed the development of Greek sculpture towards ever greater lifelikeness as a model for rhetorical style. Vitruvius' treatment of temple design and aesthetics is based on a similar conviction of the superiority of Greek art of the 5th and 4th centuries BC. The very fact that Vitruvius, like Aristotle on dramatic poetry and rhetoric before him, had succeeded in writing a text formulating the general rules and principles of building proved that architecture was not a craft, but a *scientia*, that is an activity based on general principles. This reliance on theory to claim that a practice is an art is a defining characteristic of Classicism from antiquity to the 20th century. The existence of Vitruvius' treatise demonstrated that architecture was a teachable activity. During the Renaissance this would encourage Renaissance humanists such as Leon Battista *Alberti to write treatises on architecture *all'antica*.

Vitruvius, and all architectural treatises of the classical tradition after him, singled out the importance of the architect as the intellectual author of the design, supervising the entire process from first sketches to finished building, and the architectural object with its technical, aesthetic, and stylistic properties. The reactions of the public or the meanings of a building are rarely discussed in the classical tradition, but received much more attention in other traditions of architectural thought, such as that developed in England before the introduction of neo-Palladianism *c*.1715.

In the great emphasis it places upon temple design and the orders, Vitruvius' book reflects Greek and Roman building practice until the 2nd century BC. Innovation, such as the use of concrete and vaulting, took place in domestic or non-traditional building types: amphitheatres, baths, and theatres. These are not included in Vitruvius, who drew largely on his own experience as a military engineer and the books, now lost, of the Greek architects Hermogenes and Ictinus about their temples' proportion systems. Vitruvius therefore presented an essentially Hellenistic outlook, not a representative reflection of contemporary building practices. His main concern was not with the practical tasks of the architect (surveying, design, calculations of materials and costs, and supervising the building site), but with architecture considered in its most general form, including everything touching human physical, social, and intellectual life. Ultimately he considered all architecture to be created by nature. He therefore devoted much time to the abstract scientific principles underlying design. As a result his book is important as a record of ancient scientific knowledge, but made it also more suitable for people who wanted to understand architecture, than as a handbook for architects. This may explain why little reference was made to him during the Roman Empire, although he was the main source for the handbook by Marcus Cetius Faventinus written AD *c*.300.

Middle Ages During the Middle Ages Vitruvius was copied across Europe, as the large numbers of surviving manuscripts testify. The text became damaged and the illustrations, if they actually existed, were lost. But architecture was a frequent topic in medieval theology and philosophy. The Byzantine theologian Maximus the Confessor (580–661) declared that church building was an image of heaven, in which God becomes manifest as light, thereby uniting neo-Platonic visions of God as light with an aesthetic experience. His *Mystagogia* was read in Saint Denis, and in the 12th century by Suger, the builder of Cluny III. It illustrates an important aspect of Western thought about architecture: that its medium was not always the treatise, but could be part of philosophical, theological, or political discourse, for instance in descriptions of buildings such as the Byzantine Procopius' *On Justinian's Buildings* (*c*.553–5). Generally the focus is here on architecture's metaphorical meanings.

Other important sources of architectural thought were the lexica by Isidore of Seville (d. 636) and Hrabanus Maurus (780–856). Isidore's *Encyclopaedia* analysed architecture, following Vitruvius, in terms of planning, building, and beauty based on ornament and decorum, distinguishing between the practical and functional aspects of architecture and its more formal aspects. In his *Etymologiae* he preserved the Latin artistic and architectural vocabulary, thereby offering Renaissance humanists the rudiments of their artistic theories. He also argued that the world's beauty and order of the cosmos testify to the divine order of the world. Hrabanus Maurus' *De universo* also united etymology with theological speculation, calling the universe a book written by the finger of God.

These ways of thinking were much elaborated in the 12th and 13th centuries, which saw the flowering of scholastic system building and Gothic architecture. The Benedictine Suger (1081–1151) left a record of his involvement in the Gothic choir of Saint Denis

(1140–43), the *Libellus de consecratione ecclesiae Sancti Dionysii*. This is a gradual revelation of Suger's vision of the church as an image of divine harmony, built to edify the spectators. At the same time Hugo of St Victor (1096–1141) wrote the first medieval treatise on beauty, in which the neo-Platonic view of the aesthetic experience as an intuitive experience of God is continued. Robert Grosseteste (1168–1253) compared God to an architect, echoing a comparison already made by the Greek church father Basilios the Great (329–79) in his *Homilies*: life is a visit to the workshop of a divine artist, where he has exhibited his works for us to admire. This view of architecture as a reflection of the divinely ordered universe would be repeated and elaborated in scholastic circles throughout the high Middle Ages on the basis of Plato's *Timaeus* and neo-Platonic light metaphysics. Building on Vitruvius' metrological discussion of the *homo quadratus*, the divine mathematical proportions of the universe were attributed to the human body. In Thomas Aquinas' *Summa*, architecture is used to illustrate divine creation: just as the design of a house exists in the mind of the architect, which he then uses to give form to the actual house, the idea of the entire world pre-existed in God's mind before it was created, because the universe was not created without plan. This is a very influential comparison, recurring for instance in Federico Zuccaro's *Idea de' pittori, scultori et architetti* (1607).

Although it is difficult to establish direct causal connections between this way of thinking and the design of the great cathedrals of this period, their design does reflect the interest in geometry and light. Geometric design was actually based on the procedures of *ad quadratum* and *ad triangulum* as described in *Villard de Honnecourt's manuscript (c.1235) and Matthaeus Roriczer's *Büchlein von der Finalen Gerechtigkeit*, printed in Regensburg in 1486, which offers instruction in the geometrical design of finials. St Stephen's Cathedral in Vienna (c.1450–1500) is based

on the procedure *ad quadratum*; the choir of Cologne cathedral on that of *ad triangulum*; their basis may be found in a passage in Vitruvius' Book 9, where he describes the geometrical construction of ground plans.

Renaissance The discovery of a superior copy of Vitruvius by the humanist Poggio Bracciolini in 1416 was not an isolated phenomenon; complete manuscripts of Cicero's *De oratore* and *De officiis*, Quintilian's *Institutio oratoria*, and the major ancient historians were rediscovered at the same time. The renewed interest in ancient texts was part of what Petrarca and Vasari called the 'Rinascità', a movement rooted in the growing independence of Italian city states which increased the demand for the skills and knowledge needed in self-governance: rhetoric for public speaking, political thought for statesmen and their educators. Cicero's Latin became the model for cultured language, and humanists endeavoured to revive not only the literature, but also the architecture of ancient Greece and Rome. To understand Vitruvius and connect him to the evidence of Roman ruins proved to be an arduous task, which would take almost 150 years. The first Renaissance treatise was *De re aedificatoria* by Leon Battista *Alberti (1404–72), substantially completed c.1452, and published in 1486. It started as a translation with commentary of Vitruvius, but halfway through Alberti had to give this up because of Vitruvius' idiosyncratic and badly preserved text, and lack of coherent structure. Instead it evolved into a systematic treatment of the principles, both practical and aesthetic, of architecture considered as an art essential to civilized society.

The next phase in the development of Renaissance architectural theory consisted of a series of attempts to produce reliable and usable Italian Vitruvius editions: in 1486 the first Latin edition was published, followed by the illustrated versions of Fra Giocondo (1511) and Cesare Cesariano (1521). The most ambitious project, instigated by Pope Julius II, was to combine a translation of Vitruvius with measured drawings of all ancient monuments in Rome, to be produced by a team led by Raphael. The only results, however, were Raphael's Letter to Leo X, the first attempt to give an historical overview of Western architecture, and fragments of the translation by Fabio Calvo. The most complete Renaissance Vitruvius edition was produced by the Venetian humanist Daniel Barbaro, who collaborated with *Palladio in producing a Latin edition with very extensive Italian commentary in 1567.

Meanwhile the Bolognese architect Sebastiano *Serlio had produced a treatise in several instalments from 1537 to 1575, whose format and content was to be very influential, as is testified by the great number of translations and pirate editions that started to appear shortly after its publication. This was intended for the practising architect and painter, and therefore focused on design and its presentation. Book IV (1537) offered the first synthesis of all available knowledge of the classical orders in the form of a single plate presenting them together in a proportionate series. Serlio's treatise and its immense success across Europe are inextricably linked with the medium he used. Instead of Alberti's unillustrated manuscript or the lavish, hand-made illustrations in Francesco di Giorgio's versions of Vitruvius, Serlio chose the relatively cheap and simple medium of the woodcut, in which he integrated image and text on the page. This enabled him to compress large amounts of complex information in one image combining sections, enlargements of details, and general views. It also allowed for cheap and quick dissemination across Europe. Palladio's *I Quattro Libri di Architettura* (1570) used the same highly perspicuous presentation for Roman monuments and his own designs. It became the standard for classical design across Europe and the colonies. In *Vignola's *La Regola delle cinque ordini* (1562) the image became the chief medium of architectural theory, reduced here to the

correct use of the five orders. With this short book the codification of the orders reached its completion, and the calculation of proportions was much simplified. Whereas Alberti and Barbaro offered a theory of architecture that included its aesthetic and philosophical aspects, Vignola narrowed down his subject matter to the practicalities of architectural design.

1600–1750 *Scamozzi's *Idea dell'Architettura Universale* (Venice, 1615) was the last major Renaissance architectural treatise. Until the 1750s no radically new treatises were published in Italy. Instead the centre of theoretical debate moved to France. Starting with Alberti, Renaissance architectural theory had been based on a combination of archaeological investigation and the study of ancient literature, history, and science to understand the visible remains of classical culture. In the 17th century it became increasingly clear that the major Renaissance theorists not only contradicted themselves about the proportions of the orders and their use, but also did not conform with ancient ruins. In 1671 the Académie Royale d'Architecture was founded in Paris to establish the rules of classical design: to determine the correct proportions of the orders and define good taste. These rules should be derived from a study of Roman buildings and the treatises. This double approach immediately led to problems, because the measurements of Roman buildings conflicted with the measures given in the treatises. Requests sent by the Académie to Rome for new measurements of key monuments (resulting for instance in Antoine Desgodetz' *Edifices Antiques de Rome, dessinés et mesurés très exactement*, 1682) did not help, because they conflicted both with each other and the treatises. The unsatisfactory solution adopted by the Académie, and recorded in the *Cours d'Architecture* by Nicolas-François Blondel (1675–83), was to give precedence to the general principles of theory over the

931

inconsistencies of practice. Another approach to the problem of proportion was developed by the physician and architect Claude *Perrault (1613–88), most conspicuously in the *Ordonnance des cinq Espèces de Colonnes selon la Méthode des Anciens* (1683). His suggestion to distinguish between positive and arbitrary beauty was so thorough that it contributed in the end to the downfall of Vitruvianism because it questioned the assumption underlying the entire debate, namely that correct proportions actually exist, and that these lead inevitably to beauty in architecture. He also undermined its authority by arguing that its rules are accepted not because of their consistency or evident truth, but because of the religious veneration inspired by antique architecture.

Perrault was not alone in his rationalist attitude towards the authority of the Vitruvian tradition or the architecture of the past in general. From the 16th century, French architects had praised the ingenuity and daring of Gothic construction. Philibert *De l'Orme (1505?–70), who had introduced the theory of classical architecture in France, devoted several chapters to Gothic vaulting technique in *Le premier tome de l'architecture* of 1567. Even Nicolas-François Blondel appreciated the constructional aspect of Gothic architecture, and in 1678 the members of the Académie made several excursions to Notre-Dame in Paris, Saint-Denis, Rouen, and Chartres. In 1687 Jean-François Félibien located the origins of the Gothic in 5th-century France, and distinguished between *gothique ancien* (what we would now call Romanesque architecture) and *gothique moderne*, which began at Saint-Denis; Chartres Cathedral he declared 'among the most sumptuous [buildings] that can be seen today'. This tradition of appreciating Gothic construction was continued in the 18th century by Michel de Frémin's *Mémoires critiques d'architecture* (1702) and Jacques-Germain *Soufflot's 'Mémoire sur l'architecture gothique' (1741). Frémin favourably

compared Notre-Dame and the Sainte-Chapelle with the classical churches of St Eustache (begun 1532) and St Sulpice (begun 1645). The crudeness of the mass of pillars in St Eustache, and the squared 'monstrous' pillars of St Sulpice are criticized; but the Gothic churches are praised for their spaciousness, ample daylight, and ingenious vaulting system. Soufflot advocated serious study of Gothic structural innovation, because the large windows, open plans, lightness, and delicacy of its construction are valid models for modern church design. In both cases the structural aspect of Gothic architecture, not its ornament, was praised on rationalist and functionalist grounds.

1750–1880 Many of the arguments introduced by Perrault were to be rehearsed in the gradual dissolution of Vitruvianism's authority. Archaeological investigations of Greek architecture in Greece, Asia Minor, and Paestum questioned Renaissance versions of classical architecture. Marc-Antoine Laugier's *Essai sur l'architecture* (1753) was a powerful plea to return to a use of the orders based on architecture's origins in the primitive hut. At the same time the *picturesque movement made the use of a wide range of styles from all ages and countries acceptable, first in garden and landscape design, but subsequently in public architecture as well. The *Gothic Revival also contributed to the erosion of the Vitruvian stylistic monopoly, because it challenged its fundamental assumption that the only architecture worth its name was classical architecture.

The increase of archaeological knowledge and range of acceptable styles, together with the new building types, materials, and techniques that were developed in the context of the Industrial Revolution, and the social changes that followed the French Revolution and the Napoleonic Wars, led to a crisis in architectural theory around 1800 that would last until the 1880s. Vitruvianism lost its paradigmatical status, both as a building style and a format for theorizing. Style became the main issue for 19th-century architects. Historical and scientific enquiry replaced Vitruvianism. In 1828 the German architect Heinrich Hübsch published a pamphlet called *In welchem Style sollen wir bauen?* ('In which style should we build?'). An historical investigation of the development of the main Western building styles of the past was the foundation for his proposal to adapt Romanesque architecture to contemporary needs. He would be followed by many other attempts. *Pugin's and *Ruskin's pleas for the Gothic Revival, the *neoclassicism of *Schinkel, *Klenze, and *Cockerell, or the Eclecticism favoured by *Vaudoyer, all belong to the same cast of thought. Ruskin, following Pugin, added a moral dimension to architectural discourse. In *Contrasts* (1836) Pugin had connected what he considered the decay in taste of his own age with the moral decadence brought on by the Reformation and the Industrial Revolution. Ruskin went even further, presenting Gothic ornament in *The Seven Lamps of Architecture* (1849) as a means to salvation for both the architect and society, and holding up Venice's medieval piety and Renaissance decadence as a mirror to the British Empire in *Stones of Venice* (1851–3).

Next to the past, nature was another important authority and inspiration in architectural debate. That architecture should imitate nature had been a recurrent theme in Vitruvian theory, where both decorum and a building's fitness and beauty are ultimately based on nature. In the 19th century, nature was used as an inspiration in religiously inspired pleas for the Gothic. In the chapter on 'The Nature of the Gothic' in *Stones of Venice*, Ruskin analysed Gothic architecture in the way a physicist analyses the elements, as a natural phenomenon, laying out its components, and connecting these to the love of nature, capacity for transformation, and piety of the medieval mind. Nature was also used as a model by K. F. *Schinkel in

the unfinished fragments of his *Architektonisches Lehrbuch*, his Berlin successor Bötticher in *Die Tektonik der Hellenen* (1844–52 / 1874), and *Viollet-le-Duc, who continued the French tradition of appreciating the Gothic on rationalist grounds in his *Entretiens* (1863–72). They all appealed to the ever-developing character of natural forms to justify a further development of classical or Gothic forms using technical and scientific innovation.

In Gottfried *Semper's *Der Stil* (1860), historical and scientific investigation are combined. Inspired by the worldwide exhibition of arts and crafts at the Great Exhibition 1851, he drew on the latest research in historical and comparative linguistics, ethnography, and cultural anthropology to formulate a theory of style centred on the architectural representation of the four basic human crafts—weaving, ceramics, masonry, and carpentry—that provided the basis for human society. Semper never finished the final part of *Der Stil* specifically devoted to architecture. The book therefore stands as the unfinished culmination of 19th-century architectural theory, but as it was written it became isolated from architectural practice, which was increasingly determined by technical and professional developments such as the rise of civil engineering, or the strong competition offered by building speculators to traditionally trained architects. After the 1860s the debate about style died down. *Eclecticism became a strong contender for the claim to be the style of the 19th century, but in line with its character it did not produce a systematic theory. Instead the widely read *Revue de l'Architecture et des Travaux Publics*, founded in 1840 and edited by César Daly, became its forum.

The 1870s and 1880s saw the first beginnings of a significant new departure in Western architectural theory that would eventually provide the conceptual foundation for *Modernism. For the first time architecture was defined as the art that creates and shapes space, and its study was no longer conceived historically in terms of styles succeeding each other or being revived. In 1834 the German art historian Karl Schnaase had for the first time discussed the interior of Antwerp Cathedral in terms of handling space. Thus he broke with the Vitruvian tradition of considering architectural design almost exclusively in terms of groundplans, sections, and façades, of proportion and the correct handling of the orders, that is in terms of smaller parts that together make up a larger whole. Schnaase's introduction of interior space as a main focus for analysis was taken up by Burckhardt, who defined Renaissance architecture as the spatial style or *Raumstil*, and by Semper, who in *Der Stil* stressed the spatial motive of wall dressing. In 1893 the art historian August Schmarsow drew on experimental research into human perception by Wundt and Łotz to argue that we experience architecture primarily in terms of enclosure and movement through space, and that this experience is modelled on the experience of one's own body. The history of architecture should therefore be not a history of styles, but of the development of spatial feeling or *Raumgefühl*. As Schopenhauer and Bötticher had argued before him, architecture should be the dynamic, spatial representation of the conflict between support and load. Therein resides its meaning, not in the representation of function, as Schelling and Hegel and in their wake many 19th-century theorists had argued.

This psychological approach was further developed by Heinrich Wölfflin in his *Prolegomena to a Psychology of Architecture* of 1886. Drawing on the theory of empathy or *Einfühlung* he argued that the formal qualities attributed to architecture are nothing but the experience of our own bodies: will, balance, regularity, symmetry etc., projected onto buildings. Adolf Göller added an historical dimension to this approach by applying it to the history of styles. To explain stylistic change he used the concept of the memory image or *Gedächtnisbild*. We perceive architecture not primarily as composed of elements taken from historical styles,

but as an art of pure geometrical forms and the play of light and darkness. Its appreciation depends on the formation of memory images, or psychological residues of forms viewed previously. Once a style has been entirely assimilated, artists begin to look for new forms, and this process explains why all styles go through a 'Baroque' phase before they are replaced by a new, 'simple' style. Some twenty years before the advent of abstraction in the visual arts, architecture is here presented as an art dealing with pure geometrical forms, but Göller was too much preoccupied with analysing existing styles to see the importance of his theory for the development of contemporary architecture. Adolf Gurlitt did draw the implications for contemporary architecture, advocating a new abstract art that possessed a pure geometrical beauty based on geometrical forms, space handling, and the play of light and darkness. CVE

1880–2000 A new strand in theory appeared in the 1880s with the rise of the *Arts and Crafts movement. Drawing on *Ruskin's radical critique of Victorian industrial society, William *Morris argued for a socialist vision of 'Art for Everyman', i.e. that architecture should not be a privilege for the 'swinish rich', but that every worker had a right not only to a decent but also to a beautiful home (*see* MODERNISM, TO 1975 (RELATIONSHIP TO POWER)). But this idea was to lie dormant until it became a practical possibility with the victory of the Russian Revolution in 1917, the rise of a strong Communist movement in Germany of the 1920s, and the state socialist regimes of the 1940s.

The first opportunities for using modern materials occurred with the *Chicago School, but only *Sullivan wrote significantly about theory. He was not interested in space or plans, had contradictory views on ornament, was pantheistic rather than scientific, and his most famous phrase, 'form *ever* follows function', was set in the context of a hymn to nature, not to the machine or modern science ('The Tall Office Building Artistically Considered', 1896). At least Sullivan had had practical experience of the new conditions, and was reaching for an answer which could not be provided by traditional theory. The sterility of the Beaux Arts tradition is shown by Guadet's *Eléments et théorie de l'architecture* (1902–4), which has scattered insights about building types, proportion, and details, but could easily have been written at any time in the previous two centuries, since it has nothing to say about modern life.

What are the elements of a theory of modern architecture? In the pre-1920 period, the answers are partial, internally contradictory, and, because of the backwardness of European building technology, noticeably distant from the latest developments in materials and structures. The first attempt to formulate a theory of Modernism, Otto *Wagner's *Moderne Architektur* (1896), begins promisingly, by stating that the starting point for 'artistic work' can only be 'modern life' (*Preface*). His main emphasis lies on the use of materials, where, rather oddly, he argues that the modern method of construction is the replacement of blocks of stone (the 'Renaissance way of building') by thin stone panels (e.g. of granite) bolted onto a masonry wall.

Wagner's work was a dead end; not so that of *Loos. For a decade, culminating in his essay 'Ornament and Crime' (1908), he polemicized against the false starts of *Art Nouveau and *Secessionism. The evolution of culture 'means the elimination of ornament from useful objects' (1908), but in architecture he proposed, and used in his practice, not the smooth unornamented surfaces of modern materials, but traditionally luxurious marble, onyx, and fine woods. However, his advocacy of the unornamented façade was of great significance for the future.

Loos' contribution was, if anything, rather negative; a more positive, indeed messianic, view of the future

was championed by *Scheerbart's paean in praise of *glass (1914). In the same year, a momentous meeting of the *Werkbund discussed the concept of *Typisierung*, loosely translated as 'standardization'. More remote from modern technology, in one of the most backward industrial countries in Europe, Italy, the *Futurists championed an apocalyptic view of technology as the guiding inspiration of architecture (*see* SANT'ELIA).

Regrettably, the only Europeans working consistently in a modern material (reinforced *concrete), *Garnier and *Perret, wrote hardly anything in this period. Gropius' first-hand experience of the United States did not yet lead to detailed theoretical reflection. The surprising resurgence of *Beaux Arts design in the United States (*see* MCKIM, MEAD, AND WHITE) meant that drawing theoretical conclusions from the practice of the 1880s and 1890s was deferred, with one exception. Throughout his life, Frank Lloyd *Wright's theory of architecture was idiosyncratic and difficult to characterize: in this period, while vigorously rejecting the styles of *historicism, his views on *organic architecture tend to be ill-defined.

The turmoil of the 1920s saw a great outpouring of modernist theory. In *Russia: Architecture for a World Revolution* (1930), El Lissitzky argued that the basic elements of Russian architecture are tied to the social revolution following October 1917, rather than to the technological revolution, and, rather optimistically as events have turned out: 'Because of bare economic necessity the millions of workers have no love for the ornamental junk, the holy pictures, and all the thousands of useless articles that usually clutter up middle-class homes. These millions of workers must unquestionably be considered supporters of modern architecture' (1970 edition, p.157). The social aims of Modernism were also stressed in France and Germany (*see* LURÇAT; MEYER; TAUT), the countries where the communist movement was relatively strong.

Perhaps the only work of architectural theory widely known to the general public dates from this period: *Le Corbusier's *Towards a New Architecture* (1923). It is a strange miscellany, consisting of a questionable statement of the 'Engineer's Aesthetic and Architecture' (*see* ENGINEERING AND ARCHITECTURE), a naïve admiration of modern machinery, a spirited attack on the 'styles', all underpinned by a traditional view of architecture as '...the masterly, correct and magnificent play of masses brought together in light' (1987 edition p.29), with 'Three Reminders' to architects about mass, surface, and plan. Thanks to the work of his disciple Sigfried Giedion, his dominating position in *CIAM, and the support of other architects such as *Gropius, Le Corbusier's theory became the orthodoxy of *International Modern, eclipsing any alternatives (which were resuscitated by Colin St J. Wilson in *The other tradition of modern architecture*, 1995). By about 1930, modernist theory of this type had also adopted a distinctive language, relying heavily on concepts such as form, *functionalism, and *space, and dispensing with older concepts of composition and character.

In the post-war period, the modernist consensus began to fragment. At first, the discussions of theory took place within the framework of Modernism. The liveliest debates of the 1950s and 1960s took place in Britain (*see* BRUTALISM), which had made little previous contribution to contemporary theory. The debates included contributions from eminent historians such as Pevsner and Summerson, but the most original contribution was made by Rayner Banham's *Theory and Design in the First Machine Age* (1960), and *The Architecture of the Well-tempered Environment* (1969; *see* ENGINEERING SERVICES).

However, from the end of the 1960s the theoretical foundations of Modernism itself were called into question. Modernism was not attacked at its weakest point, that it neglected to work out a theory of composition, i.e. what a modernist architecture should

look like, but at its two strong points: its commitment to modern science and technology; and (in some varieties of Modernism, at least), a commitment to a socially responsible architecture. Under the guise of a supposedly 'radical' critique of Modernism, *postmodernism explicitly championed the anti-rational charms of symbolism and tacitly abandoned Modernism's social goals entirely. As such, it was perfectly adapted to the Thatcher–Reagan project of restoring the *status quo ante*. In the first decade of the new century, it is perhaps too early to decide whether a series of increasingly complex and obscurantist theories, such as Deconstructivism, have anything to offer architectural practice.   PG

Kruft, H.-W., *A History of Western Architectural Theory* (1992)

Mallgrave, H. F., *Modern Architectural Theory: a Historical Survey, 1673–1968* (2005)

Mallgrave, H. F. (ed.), *Architectural Theory* (2005)

van Eck, C. A. (ed.), *British Architectural Theory 1540–1750: An Anthology of Texts* (2003)

tholos A circular domed building or structure, usually associated with *Mycenaean architecture.   PG

Thomas de Thomon, Jean François (1760–1813) French émigré, proponent of neoclassicism in Russia. He arrived in St Petersburg in 1799, and in 1805 began work on one of the most important architectural monuments in the city, the Bourse (Stock Exchange), located at the point of Vasilevsky Island. Completed in 1810, with its peristyle of 44 Doric columns, the Bourse is based on the temples at Paestum. To emphasize its dominant role in the expanse of the Neva River between the fortress and the Winter Palace, Thomas de Thomon placed two rostral columns in front of the Bourse, with allegorical figures personifying Russia's major rivers. His other extant structure in St Petersburg is the Laval mansion (1806–10), with one of the city's most imposing neoclassical interiors. At the imperial estate of Pavlovsk he designed the mausoleum of Emperor Paul (1805–10). WCB

Thomson, Alexander (1817–75) Scottish architect. The brightest of Scotland's Victorian constellation of classical designers, Thomson was Scotland's equivalent to the impassioned and individualistic English *Gothic Revivalists—albeit working within a diametrically opposed religious denomination and architectural style: indeed, he violently attacked in 1866 the choice of an English Goth, Sir George Gilbert *Scott, to design Glasgow University. Thomson's work infused mid-Victorian entrepreneurial capitalism with an idealistic Presbyterian quest to celebrate 'eternity', combining the two in a monumental urban architecture of the Sublime.

Thomson designed a mixture of churches, commercial buildings, and housing, in a violently eclectic Greek style with numerous idiosyncratic elements. In his churches and villas, he combined massive vertical punctuations with an overall aesthetic of horizontal repetition, articulated by lines of inset piers in the *Schinkel manner, and by repetitive bands of incised ornament. His three most important churches, all for the United Presbyterians, encased conventional auditorium plans within piled-up podiums intended to evoke the 'Temple of Solomon'. At Caledonia Road (1856–7), the podium was juxtaposed with a portico and tall, austere steeple of Early Christian character. At St Vincent Street (1857–9), the steeply sloping site allowed the church to be sunk into a massive base, with temple superstructure and exotically decorated campanile alongside. The Middle Eastern theme was elaborated at Queen's Park (1867–9), whose portico was crowned by a pylon and squat dome, and which was decorated inside in a polychromatic scheme by artist Daniel Cottier (1838–91). A similar asymmetrical, towered

United Presbyterian Church, Caledonia Road, Hutchesontown, Glasgow (Alexander Thomson, 1856–7)

massiveness, and 'architectonic' polychromatic interior schemes, characterized Thomson's villas, such as Holmwood, 1857–8, whose heroic classical interior included a drawing-room frieze reproducing Flaxman's illustrations of the *Iliad*.

Thomson's urban commercial and terraced-housing architecture was different in character, as it had to fit into confined street façades and plots. Here, he downplayed any dynamic asymmetry, and instead stressed the unifying, mystical effect of repetitive horizontality. He used concealed iron reinforcements to allow long bands of window piers to be set into

937

the wall plane. His more conservative Edinburgh counterparts, such as *Bryce, still relied on the academic orders as a way of differentiating the storeys, but Thomson instead used a variety of sometimes fearsome eclectic detailing. For example, at Egyptian Halls (1871–3), a 4-storey Glasgow city-centre commercial block, he subverted the traditional palazzo into a vertical stack of glazed shopfronts and exotically columned upper storeys. In his many blocks of tenements, such as Queen's Park Terrace of 1857–60, Thomson also abandoned the orders for a freer interweaving of repetitive linear patterns, while in 1–10 Moray Place (1859), a middle-class terrace including his own home, outer pavilions were linked by a ruthlessly homogeneous row of pilastered bays. However, in the exceptionally stately composition of Great Western Terrace (from 1869), Thomson evoked the more austere neoclassicism of the earlier 19th century.

Thomson's architecture and writings, as a whole, formed part of the mid-Victorian 'neo-Sublime', with its addiction to massiveness and its incessant search for emotionalistic 'free styles' which could leave behind the everyday world of conventional historical ornament—something which anticipated the later work of *Mackintosh. But his love of horizontality and incised patterning gave his work a unity no English High Victorian Goths ever achieved, and seemed instead to presage the later work of H. H. *Richardson in America. In Glasgow, Thomson's main legacy was to legitimize Greek Classicism as the continuing mainstream of the city's architecture—as represented by the work of James Sellars (1843–88) and Hugh Barclay (1828–92) and his brother David (1846–1917). MGl

McFadzean, R., *The Life and Work of Alexander Thomson* (1979)

Stamp, G., *The Light of Truth and Beauty* (1999)

Thorpe, John (*c*.1565–1655?) English land surveyor and architect. Famously laying the first stone of Kirby Hall as a child, where his father presumably was the master mason, Thorpe served in the Office of Works as a clerk at the royal palaces (1583–1601). Thereafter he surveyed many royal estates, but expressed an interest in architecture through compiling a book of house plans. Some are surveys of existing buildings, but a few are Thorpe's own designs, including Thornton College, Lincolnshire (*c*.1607–10), Somerhill, Kent (*c*.1610–13), Audley End, Essex, where he probably designed the outer court (*c*.1615), and Aston Hall, Birmingham (1618–35). These are typical of Jacobean architecture, with a variety of classical influences at work—a Palladian plan at Somerhill, detailing at Audley End from Du Cerceau's *Livre d'architecture* and *Les plus excellents bastiments de France*—allied to a native ability to squeeze traditional arrangements into symmetrical outlines, and set up ingenious wit. APQ

Thumb family A dynasty of German architects, of whom the most important were **Michael** (*c*.1640–90) and Peter, known as **Peter II** (1681–1766). Michael's first church, Wettenhausen (1670–87), is an unremarkable transformation of an earlier building, but then he designed the first *wall-pillar churches: the pilgrimage church of Schönenberg, at Ellwangen (1682–92); and the monastery church, Obermarchtal (1686–92; *see* BEER FAMILY). He also instituted the *Vorarlberg School's typical layout of galleries connecting wall piers and forming the ceilings of side chapels, and the use of 'false' transepts, in which chapels are housed in the slight projections.

Peter II's involvement with a number of churches is not clear, but Birnau, Germany (1746–50), his masterpiece, is undoubtedly by his hand. It breaks definitively with the Vorarlberg scheme, in that, instead of the wall-pillar arrangement, the galleries, which undulate around the entire church right up to the altar, are set back against the outside wall. The overall effect, of architecture being subordinate to light and decoration, is much more like one of *Zimmermann's churches. But the exterior, in which the church, the tower, and the clergy house are integrated into one block, is much more satisfactory than Zimmermann's *Die Wies*. His design for the Library of the Benedictine Abbey of St Peter in the Black Forest (1739–53) also shows his ability to modulate simple spaces.   PG

Tibaldi, Pellegrino (1527–96) Italian painter and architect. Tibaldi's architectural career began when he moved to Milan under the protection of Archbishop Carlo Borromeo (later canonized), whose *Instructiones Fabricae et Supellectilis Ecclesiasticae* (1577) is the only significant work to show in detail how the decrees of the Council of Trent should be applied to architecture (*see* COUNTER-REFORMATION). After designing the Collegio Borromeo, Pavia (completed 1592), in which the courtyard, with its coupled Doric columns, is more successful than the colossal external façades, Tibaldi designed a number of ecclesiastical buildings in Milan: the courtyard of the Canonica, in the cathedral precinct (1565–72); S. Fedele (1572), with its typically northern plan of three separate vaulted units; S. Sebastiano (1577, completed 1617); and S. Gaudenzio, Novara (1579). Borromeo's precepts are followed in the west façade of S. Fedele, with its several niches for statues of saints, but otherwise they are not particularly evident. Indeed, the circular form of S. Sebastiano is in direct contradiction to Borromeo's ideas. After the death of Borromeo in 1584 Tibaldi lost his place, and designed no more buildings.   PG

Tibet Despite arriving relatively late, Buddhist architecture is closely related to Tibet's indigenous roots. The foundation for most Tibetan 'structures' is the nomad's tent: traditionally decorated with vivid rugs on walls and floors. Such colourful decoration is found in the interior of a Tibetan temple, with its elaborate hangings (tankas) and painted wooden pillars.

Likewise, Tibetan temple architecture follows that of the traditional farmhouse: multi-storeyed, with balconies and courtyards, and massive load-bearing walls of stone, mud-brick or rammed earth, and flat roofs. The heavy roofs of temples necessitate extra supports, and the interiors feature the requisite added columns needed for the greater weight. Instead of the cut stone architecture favoured in India, or the elaborate wooden structures of China (although early styles of Chinese bracketing were followed), Tibetan architecture presented a cubic façade, with few windows, and inward-sloping, whitewashed walls of sun-baked brick or stone, for wood was a building material in scant supply.

In the typical Buddhist custom, the Tibetan version of the stupa or pagoda (known as the chorten) also functioned as a receptacle for an auspicious object. However, as with many other Buddhist objects in this land of rich, esoteric Buddhism, it was created in more forms, sizes, and complexity. Some were of massive dimensions, such as the multi-storeyed chorten at Gyantse, with numerous statues and elaborate painted interiors, while others were created in a variety of sizes and media, including metal, wood, even butter. In Tibetan culture, the commissioning of votive chortens was especially auspicious, believed to accrue great merit to the donor. Within a Tibetan temple complex, great numbers of dome-shaped chortens would be commissioned, each atop a square, multi-level platform, their elegant shapes accentuated by a bell-shaped body that flows outward as it rises above the base, finally topped by a tower of concentric rings. This distinctive chorten, though deriving from Indian and especially neighbouring Kashmiri Buddhism, came to be associated more with Tibetan culture, and is one of the most elegant and memorable forms the Buddhist stupa assumed across Asia. Its fluid, balanced design stands with the better known wooden pagodas of Japan or the massive square Chinese examples or those gold-covered

Burmese stupas, regional examples of the single most distinctive element of Buddhist architecture.

Since the Buddhist monastery assumed the central role in Tibetan society, the focus of life and belief, the elaborate arrangement of these buildings exceeded all others, ultimately with palace and monastic architecture merging, best seen today in the fortress-like Potala in Lhasa, one of the world's best known religious structures. The orderliness of the Tibetan monastery is clear in its layout: a mandala plan, reflecting a belief in the harmony of the universe. This includes a surrounding wall, smaller structures arrayed about the main building, then the mandalic format continues upward with each floor dedicated to different religious deities and concepts. Within individual halls of worship, in response to the need to accommodate greater numbers of worshippers, the mandala-like plan can be altered by placing the altar and main images at the rear.   RF

tierceron A subsidiary vaulting *rib which rises from the springing of a *vault to the ridge without crossing it. First introduced asymmetrically in St Hugh's choir of Lincoln Cathedral (c.1200), the nave was completed (1230s) with symmetrical tiercerons. The sixteen tiercerons of each bay of Exeter's nave (c.1310–14) obscure the bay-by-bay division even further.   APQ

Tolsá, Manuel (1755–1818) Spanish sculptor and architect who, from 1771, worked in Mexico. He studied sculpture at San Carlos de Valencia, one of his important works being a statue of Carlos IV on horseback (1803). In the architectural sphere he is best known for his work on completing Mexico Cathedral and constructing the Royal Mining School (1797–1813), which consolidated the neoclassical style. He also designed the palaces of Apartado and Buenavista, the latter with original oval-shaped courtyards, and the Cabañas Hospice in Guadalajara.   LNM (trans. KL)

tools Today the architect's principal tool is the computer. A century ago it was the pen or pencil, aided by a parallel motion, ruler, and other drawing equipment. Five centuries ago, the art of architecture was not divorced from building, and the architect's tools were those of the craftsmen from whom his art had sprung. Two crafts were pre-eminent, the mason's and the carpenter's. Their tools were, respectively, the axe, chisel, and hammer, and the axe, adze, augur, chisel, drill, plane, and saw, all powered by muscle alone. To these must be added the set-square, compass, and scribe for the purposes of design alone. Drawing still played a part. The French mason *Villard de Honnecourt's sketchbook (1225–35) shows plans and elevations together with details of carving and tracery at Laon, Reims, and Chartres cathedrals, and also timber trusses, mouldings, and building machines. In 1436 a house was built in Winchester, England, according 'as the trasying schewith y drawe in a parchment skyn', and a single such drawing survives from the early 16th century, after which drawings became common. More usually contracts referred to standard bays or details, or to other buildings that provided models. How the most complicated detail was designed from overall concept to individual piece of cut timber or stone is a miracle. Details were drawn out, or scribed, on the plaster of a tracery floor, full scale, hence the square, compass, and scribe, but a master mason such as Erwin von Steinbach needed a drawing for something as complicated as his west façade of Strasbourg Cathedral. Similarly a master carpenter such as Hugh Herland had to be aware of each piece of interlocking timber for the arched *hammerbeam of his Westminster Hall roof. The ultimate tool was a lifelong understanding of a single material and the long tradition of using it.   APQ

Torroja y Miret, Eduardo (1899–1961) Spanish architect and engineer. Improved techniques for the mixing of concrete and refinements in the manufacture of steel reinforcement in the first half of the 20th century made it possible to build thinner reinforced concrete shells. By using layers of small diameter reinforcement and better quality cement, these shells, which were structurally sound and only a few centimetres thick, offered long spans without intermediate structural columns. Inspired by the work of Perret and Freyssinet, the engineer Eduardo Torroja explored the use of shells for a series of elegant industrial buildings that were built in Europe in the 1930s. The flat, barrel-vaulted shell structures that he designed for a series of waterfront sheds in Hamburg in 1931 were minimal and elegant, and these ideas were developed further in proposals for industrial and commercial buildings. His most refined schemes included a new Market Hall at Algeciras in Spain, completed in 1934, and the grandstand at Zarzuela racecourse near Madrid that was built a year later. BC

torus A large moulding with a semicircular convex profile, particularly forming part of the base of a classical column, and the reverse of a scotia, which has a semicircular concave profile, and often lies between two projecting toruses. APQ

tower A tall building, or part of a building, evidently taller than its adjacent parts, sometimes specifically a donjon or keep of a castle, from which derives the tower house. There has always been something importunate in the building of a tower, as Almighty God's petulant reaction to the earliest of towers, the Tower of Babel, suggests. No wonder—they stood for power! Roman city walls were punctuated by towers, as those of Autun in France and York in England show, but none is so redolent of power as the striped polygonal towers of the Theodosian walls of Constantinople (AD 412).

Long before towers were fully exploited in western Europe for defence, they were taken over by the church. San Lorenzo, Milan (begun c.370), has four symmetrically arranged towers, whose practical purpose is unclear. Bell towers probably originate in one supposedly added to St Peter's, Rome (754), and the earliest survivor is the Benedictine San Giovanni, Ravenna (893). The Benedictines took bell towers to Lombardy and thence to Burgundy in the 10th century, from where they spread to Western churches everywhere. Detached campaniles, an Italian speciality, include the Leaning Tower of Pisa (begun 1174), which is unusual for being circular and not particularly high, whereas most are rectangular, slender and tall. The wealth of the later Middle Ages was expressed in elaborating church towers into fantastic compositions such as the west tower of Strasbourg Cathedral, which is nearly doubled in height by its surmounting spire. Even modest towns converted their profits from wool into the masonry of a vertiginous tower.

The tower as a residence has a different origin, belonging to the years of strife following the collapse of Carolingian Europe and the appearance of mounted knights on the battlefield. The first stage was accomplished in the second quarter of the 10th century with the rebuilding of a stone hall at Doué-la-Fontaine in France, as a high basement to carry an upper chamber and thus form a strong defensible building with domestic accommodation. From this developed the donjon, keep, or tower, which embraced two or three floors of heated rooms, over a basement. It came to England at the Norman Conquest, notably with the White Tower of the Tower of London and Colchester Castle (both begun shortly after 1077). As combined strongholds and palaces, these were intended to symbolize power as well as being a means of formally wielding it. Keeps of a more or less standard pattern were raised in great numbers during the next hundred years, as Norman lords and their successors secured their grip on

England. Among these is the keep at Rochester, the tallest of all at 34.5 m (113 ft) to the top of its parapet, once with finely appointed accommodation on three floors above the basement, leaving the parapet as a fighting platform. Scotland's first keep was built at this time too, and their vertical form remained popular on both sides of the Border, for the tower-houses that responded to the hostility between the English and Scots in later centuries. Tower-houses were often entered by a stair or ladder directly into an upper storey, and set on a basement sometimes only reached from within, this giving them their defensive capability. The main and perhaps only room on the floor above served as a hall, and would have a fireplace set into a wall; there was usually a chamber in a floor above with access to a parapet which served as a lookout and, if necessary, for fighting.

Despite their evident military qualities, many keeps, notably Castle Hedingham, Essex (c.1140), lacked impregnability, and consequently seem to have been built to be used formally as expressions of chivalry. The Hôtel de la Buffette at Provins in northern France was built in the 12th century as a 3-storeyed tower, with its undercroft and lower storey vaulted, and a high degree of comfort that included large fireplaces, basins for washing, and subsidiary rooms and latrines in the thickness of the walls. The rapid transformation from serious military purpose to atavistic symbol as the badge of a noble residence came about through the understanding that a tower symbolized magnificence, even though its progenitors were the defensive towers of the internecine nobility that blooded the streets of Italian city states. So, from the time of its completion in 1435, the 4-storeyed Lollards' Tower at Lambeth Palace allowed the archbishops of Canterbury unparalleled views of Westminster. Men of lesser rank, like Sir John de Pulteney who in the 1340s graced his City inn with an embattled tower, followed what was already a century-old fashion. The only mercantile tower to

survive in England is at Clifton House, King's Lynn, where its late-16th-century 5-storeyed tower has a sweeping view of the river Ouse.

The inherent seriousness of these symbolic towers was turned to folly in the 18th century when every estate was adorned with its tower, usually one of many different kinds of eye-catchers. Lacking a medieval ruined castle, then one could be built, like Blaise Castle (1766) near Bristol. The most imposing of these follies is Peterson's Tower (1879) at Sway in the New Forest, which is 66.4 m (218 ft) high and, remarkably, built of shuttered concrete.

At precisely this time a new form of tower was coming into existence thanks to the great fire of Chicago of 1874. With the advent of iron for framing, expensive land values, and a booming economy, a solution to rebuilding the city lay in building upwards. The result was the *skyscraper, which also needed electric elevators if it were to exceed 7 storeys or the maximum height reachable by domesticated humanity. The protagonist here was William le Baron Jenney whose framed 7-storeyed First Leiter Building of 1879 was rapidly overtaken by the 16 storeys of Burham and Root's Monadnock Building (1889–91), and eventually by Bruce Graham's Sears Tower, which reached 443 m (1,454 ft) in 1974, just a century after the fire. The tower now symbolized neither military power, nor chivalry, but commerce.   APQ

tower blocks   The term 'tower block' to denote a high block of flats is mainly used in Great Britain, where high blocks appear especially prominent given the predominance of low-rise dwellings in most parts of the country. These towers also count among the most striking examples of modernist architecture. As such, they are closely related to the North American skyscraper—indeed, the first multi-storey steel-framed blocks of dwellings of the interwar period must be those lining the west side of Central Park, New York.

But it was the use of the 'tower block' not for elite private apartments but for low-rent social housing that became most common in Britain. For this, a number of very diverse socio-political and architectural factors had to come together, quite apart from the new constructional possibilities of high-rise steel and concrete. First, there was the demand for 'housing reform', which led to a massive state investment in house-building for the lower classes. Then, there was a largely Le Corbusier-inspired dislike of low-rise, low-density suburban housing, coupled with a demand to redevelop inner urban 'slum' areas—and here, a crucial impetus came with the destruction from World War II.

In the initial post-war climate of the 1940s and early 1950s, the chief pressure for the building of tower blocks in Britain came from advanced architects and social reformists: the first tower blocks rose as the proud beacons of Welfare State Britain, pioneered above all by the London County Council (LCC) and metropolitan boroughs, who employed many of the most eminent young architects of the day, such as *Powell and Moya (designers of Westminster's path-breaking Pimlico redevelopment of 1946–54); the internationally most renowned 'tower blocks' were those of the LCC architects' lavishly landscaped Roehampton project (from 1950).

The strong political and social pressures invested in multi-storey housing meant that it could not long remain the preserve of elite designers. By the late 1950s and 1960s, it was increasingly appropriated by a different welfare-state faction: the municipal politicians and engineers who advocated maximum 'output' and 'production' of new dwellings, to satisfy populist local political demands in cities such as Glasgow, Liverpool, and Dundee. In other cities, such as Birmingham or Sheffield, there was more of a balance, with both powerful city architects and strong housing politicians.

Eventually, virtually all countries in the world adopted, and many continue to build, multi-storey blocks of dwellings, for 'social housing' as well as for smart apartments. In Britain, with its violent fluctuations of housing preference, the type became suddenly and severely eclipsed in popularity. As early as the late 1950s, avant-garde housing architects had turned away from tower blocks towards dense, low-rise patterns, and from the late 1960s in England and Wales, especially following the Ronan Point collapse of 1968, public and professional opinion turned radically against them, and many blocks have since come down. More recently, however, as part of the 'iconic' or 'revived' Modernism from the late 1990s, many new tower blocks have begun to be built for fashionable private occupiers.   MGl/SM

Glendinning, M., and Muthesius, S., *Tower Block* (1994)
Ravetz, A., *Council Housing and Culture: the History of a Social Experiment* (2001)

town halls The prototype of the town hall was the Roman *basilica. This was adopted by the independent Italian cities of the Middle Ages, though with one important difference: it was mounted on an undercroft. The reason for this is likely to be a need for security, just as this need raised Ottonian imperial halls on to an upper storey. Such town halls are legion: the Palazzo Communale (begun 1280) at Piacenza may stand for them all, and the grand hall, with its immense boat-shaped timber roof, of the Palazzo della Ragione, Padua (completed *c*.1306), shows what magnificence dignified the proceedings of Italian city fathers. The arcaded ground storey of these halls was suited to the accommodation of the ancillary functions that civic authorities took to themselves, and also to the commercial activities from which their wealth sprang. These confused the arrangements, creating labyrinths within the Palazzo Pubblico at Siena and the Palazzo Vecchio at Florence as they grew after their foundation in the 1290s. Apart from an increasing number of ancillary rooms, these halls were graced by towers. An essential feature when the internecine feuds of powerful families bloodied the streets of their cities, towers stood for power, a tempting symbol that neither Siena nor Florence resisted. Just these qualities remain today, and for precisely the same reasons. Add some style to a public hall at the centre of an administrative labyrinth with a tower bearing a clock and little more need be said, the image is so potent.

As civic authority grew in the later Middle Ages, particularly through wealth derived from cloth, guilds and fraternities built themselves halls, which, as their influence gained them civic charters, became town halls in all but name. The reliance on Italian models of the Cloth Hall at Ypres, Belgium (begun 1304), is plain enough, despite rebuilding after World War I. Its arcaded ground storey, upper-level hall, and oversailing tower were repeated later in the 14th century in several Flemish town halls, despite the decline in industry, notably at Bruges, Leuven, Brussels, and Oudenarde. Their flamboyant Gothic was repeated further east in Germany, for instance at Braunschweig, Marienburg, and Breslau (now Wrocław), demonstrating that burghers could now compete with the church in matters of style.

In England civic power emerged more slowly: guilds built halls of some magnificence, usually on an upper floor, but these were small fry by comparison and few had a tower. London had its City Guildhall, with its hall set over two undercrofts (1411–25, partly rebuilt); and Norwich, which was granted full civic powers only in 1404, rebuilt its old Tollhouse as its Guildhall (1407–12). When extended, Norwich Guildhall accommodated an unchained prison for those awaiting trial at the next sessions, separate male and female debtors' prisons, a chapel, a great hall for full meetings of the town council, and also the sheriff's court, a guest hall, and a smaller hall for the use of the

Mayor's Court and the Inner Court of Aldermen. For all its modesty when set beside its Continental contemporaries, or for that matter the opulent wool churches of East Anglia, here, in effect, was one of the new breed of town hall, its Perpendicular Gothic architecture appropriately symbolizing dignified civic authority.

What the Middle Ages bequeathed to the next four centuries differed as much in style as in substance. As civic authorities took on greater responsibilities, they added fresh accommodation, sometimes piecemeal. The Town Hall at King's Lynn, Norfolk, began as the Guildhall of Holy Trinity, rebuilt in 1422–8 after a fire, typically over an undercroft, with a huge Perpendicular window to advertise its presence. This served until 1624 when a second range was built alongside, again using chequered stone and flint, but now with a Doric porch, an achievement of arms above, and a small shaped gable, behind which lies a second upper hall. In the 18th century a courthouse and assembly rooms were added at the rear, and prominently in another range on the further side of the Guildhall a gaol with cells set around the back yard. Finally, with the increase in local government's responsibilities, a whole new town hall, mainly comprising offices, was added in 1895 in Arts and Crafts Gothic. Today, the courts and gaol are housed elsewhere, the old ranges are either museums or confined to a ceremonial role, and the town hall is augmented by other premises to accommodate all its departments.

Towns and cities that flourished later, especially when this involved their first charter, made architectural statements which validated their new-found status within an ancient context. When the enlightened corporation of the old clothing town of Leeds, Yorkshire's largest by the middle of the 19th century, determined to build a new town hall to incorporate a courthouse, council chamber, public hall, ceremonial entertaining rooms, and municipal offices, it had its eye on the fresh achievements of its neighbours, particularly Bradford; so, to ensure its proper civic dignity, it employed the local man Cuthbert *Brodrick to design a magnificent giant decastyle Corinthian portico *in antis* between projecting wings, with the same order gracing an immense central clock tower based on the Mausoleum at Halicarnassus, re-interpreted in the grandest Baroque manner. Erected in 1853–8, it was the wonder of the world.

Stockholm Town Hall (1911–23, by Ragnar *Östberg) seems further from the Baroque of Leeds than the Gothic of Italy, being a 'modern traditionalist' application of 20th-century simplicity to a romantic vision of Romanesque Sweden. The century really found itself with the geometrical massing, inspired by Dutch avant-garde De *Stijl, of *Dudok's Hilversum Town Hall (1924–31), and yet, behind the brave new shapes of this impressive brick pile lurks the skeleton of an Italian public palace, tower and all. The cataclysm of World War II and the concomitant political determination that the old order should be replaced by greater social responsibility had architectural consequences of the first magnitude, finally allowing Modernism in through the front door. For all Modernism's claimed rationalism, it is interesting that the foremost town hall of post-war years, Kallmann, McKinnell, and Knowles's Boston City Hall (1962–9) in the USA, should take the then popular form of an inverted *ziggurat, expressed in the raw concrete of its *Brutalist years. By way of inexplicable contrast, Robert *Matthew, Johnson-Marshall and Partners designed Hillingdon Civic Centre, Uxbridge (1973–8), again as a ziggurat, no longer inverted, and dressed it in brick with tumbledown hipped tile roofs of neo-vernacular form. Both have an atrium—to return to Rome.   APQ

Cunningham, C(olin), *Victorian and Edwardian Town Halls* (1991)

townscape The word 'townscape' is first recorded in 1880, but its meaning is most closely associated with *Townscape* (1961), by the architectural artist and planner Gordon Cullen. With a combination of drawings and photographs, Cullen catalogued the largely accidental visual pleasures of the built environment, involving surprise, contrast, and irregularity. As he explained, '... one building is architecture but two buildings are townscape ... as soon as two buildings are juxtaposed the art of townscape is released ... [but] We are still in the elementary stage where the individual building is the be-all and end-all of planning' (*Townscape*, 1961, p.133). The 1961 book included material from a feature in the *Architectural Review*, December 1949, including an important introductory text by H. de Cronin Hastings, proprietor of the *Review*, who gave 'townscape' an anarchist political slant missing from Cullen's version, as well as a more explicit grounding in the theory of the *picturesque, 'a revolt against that old bore, Plato'. Under his pseudonym, Ivor de Wolfe, Hastings responded with his own book, *The Italian Townscape*, in 1963.

Townscape caught on, and by 1964 there was a Townscape Department of the Ministry of Housing and Local Government. The idea of a continuous historic environment was behind the innovation of 'group listing' and 'conservation areas' in the 1967 Civic Amenities Act in Britain, and the moves to preserve historic city cores such as York. Townscape and the revived picturesque were attacked by new Brutalists. Colin Rowe and Fred Koetter described townscape as 'a cult of English villages, Italian hill towns and North African casbahs, ... above all else, a matter of felicitous happenings and anonymous architecture ...' Even so, a prime *Brutalist project, the *Economist* plaza by Alison and Peter Smithson, is a perfect exemplar of townscape in its marriage of new and old, and its basis in human movement through space. As Hastings wrote in 1964, 'Townscape is something far bigger than individual buildings, modern architecture or indeed the whole professional idea of architecture and planning. It is simply the visible expression of collective life.'

The Concise Townscape, a shorter version of Cullen's book, has remained in print since 1971 and is reckoned to be a classic of planning literature. In his introduction, Cullen distanced his theory from its trivialization in widespread applications, including 'a superficial civic style of decoration using bollards and cobbles, ... traffic-free pedestrian precincts and ... the rise of conservation' (*The Concise Townscape*, 1971, p.13). AP

Townsend, Charles Harrison (1851–1928) English architect. Townsend's reputation rests on three London buildings: the Bishopsgate Institute, City of London (1894); the Whitechapel Art Gallery, 1895; and the Horniman Museum, Forest Hill (1896–1901). The plans ingeniously solve the difficulties of their narrow sites; their elevations, with turrets, broad decorative friezes, and massive arched doorways, appear to have been influenced by H. H. Richardson, in their massive simplification of form. Walter Crane and Robert Anning Bell contributed mosaic designs for his buildings (only Bell's frieze at the Horniman was executed). The interiors of these buildings, all of them altruistic institutions of popular education, were plain and rational. The church of St Mary the Virgin, Great Warley, Essex (1902–4), was his last significant work, full of craft and symbolism. AP

tracery The intersecting rib-work in the upper part of a Gothic window, or blind panel, formed by the elaboration of the mullions, and similarly the projecting interlaced work in a vault. The term was possibly first used by *Wren, who also used it for the tracing-house where it was set out.

There are many forms of tracery. The simplest, hardly tracery at all, is plate tracery, current in France, England, and elsewhere in the early Gothic of the 13th

century, which comprises a collection of geometrical shapes such as the circles and polyhedrons that make up early circular windows, or a circle set centrally over a pair of lancets with the stonework of the spandrels unpierced by further openings. Geometrical tracery, typical of England in the 13th century, is formed by a range of lancets, usually with cusped heads, similarly supporting circles, again usually cusped, but with the intervening spandrels also open and perhaps cusped. An analogous form in France is known as *Rayonnant. Intersecting tracery, again typically English, and of the 13th and 14th centuries, is formed by a range of lancets whose arches continue upwards to intersect those rising in the opposite direction. When these arches have an ogee outline, the double ogees of the intersections become of equal shape and size, thus forming reticulated tracery. A combination of the multiplicity of circles found in geometrical tracery with the ogees and generally flowing lines of reticulated tracery produces the curvilinear or flowing tracery of the 14th century. When characterized by acute points symmetrically radiating from a central shape, it is known as Kentish tracery, though found in other counties. The French equivalent is known as Flamboyant. Perpendicular tracery, used in the late 15th century and thereafter, comprises a series of repeated shapes characterized by tall, cusped panels set within a framework with a few secondary arches as a support. APQ

transept The transverse arm, usually of a church, and found in pairs between the nave and chancel, often opening off each side of a crossing, occasionally at the western end of the nave, and, in cathedrals, sometimes doubled with smaller transepts opening off the sides of the choir. Possibly originating in subsidiary spaces in early Christian basilicas to accommodate choirs, transepts offered a route to subsidiary chapels opening off their eastern side. In Jesuit churches the transepts formed chapels in their own right, one being dedicated to St Francis Loyola, the other to St Francis Xavier, the two guardian patrons of the order.   APQ

travertine A sedimentary rock formed from the precipitated deposits of hot springs of calcareous water (cf. TUFA).

In the Roman Republic travertine replaced tufa from the 1st century BC, because of its greater compressive strength, and its suitability for ornamental carving. Extensive quarries at Tivoli, near Rome, meant that travertine was much more readily available than *granite or *porphyry. The stone was used in the forum of Augustus and the temple of Fortuna Virilis, at critical load-bearing points, such as piers and arches; and from the middle of the 1st century AD formed the solid mass of walls in the Temple of Vespasian and the Colosseum.

But the really outstanding visual qualities of travertine, that it is much more easily carved than granite, and that, because the surface is pitted by small cavities and voids, it has a more varied texture than limestone, were not fully exploited until the *Baroque era. Furthermore, a variety of textures, rough or smooth, and colours, from creamy grey to gold, are readily available.

The first significant use of travertine in this period, by Carlo Maderno, for the façade of S. Susanna (1597–1603), reveals another interesting property of the material. Unlike, say, limestone or many sandstones, the strata are quite visible. Thus the clear horizontal lines of the material form an interesting counterpoint to the marked verticality of the design. Maderno's choice of a delicate golden travertine for St Peter's (1607–25) must have given the stone great prestige, apart from its evident visual advantages, and his example was followed by all the leading Roman architects for over a century. A particularly notable use of different textures of travertine occurs at S. Maria della Pace. The upper storey is considerably set back from the lower, so that it requires some kind of emphasis if it is to register with the viewer from the piazza. *Cortona achieved this effect by choosing a rough travertine with symmetrically patterned graining, which gives a very rich overall texture to the surface.

During this period, travertine was evidently considered to be rather a superior material. For his design of the façade of the Oratory of S. Filippo Neri, Borromini was instructed to use brick rather than travertine, so that the façade would not compete with that of the neighbouring church.

The use of travertine was revived in the 1930s in Italy, proving to be equally adaptable to the Modernism of *Terragni's Casa del Fascio (1936) or the modern Classicism of several buildings at the EUR, Rome. Subsequently it has continued to be an attractive and much used form of cladding. A particularly fine interior use is Louis *Kahn's Kimbell Museum in Fort Worth (1966–72).   PG

Tressini (**Trezzini**), **Domenico** (*c*.1670–1734) Swiss architect and engineer active in Russia from 1703. Hired by Peter the Great, he defined the early northern European Baroque in St Petersburg with buildings such as the Cathedral of Saints Peter and Paul (1712–33) and the Petrovsky Gate (1717–8) in the Peter-Paul Fortress (which he also planned), the Building of the Twelve Colleges (1722–42), and the Summer Palace of Peter I (1710–14). The façades of his buildings established the Petersburg practice of painted stucco over brick, with white trim for ornamental flourishes.   WCB

tribune An *apse of a *basilica where officials or priests sit; a raised platform or rostrum as may be found within an apse, or a gallery in a church, usually placed over an aisle and opening on to the upper part of the nave, choir, or chancel, and beneath the clerestory. APQ

947

Arch of Constantine, the Forum, Rome (AD 315)

triforium An arcaded wall-passage in a church, placed over an arcade and opening on to the upper part of the nave, choir, or chancel, and beneath the *clerestory where present, and not to be confused with a gallery or tribune when set over an aisle.   APQ

triglyph A stylized plate, a paraphrase in stone of a feature deriving from timber construction, notionally attached to a beam-end, in the form of three chamfered vertical bars with a V-shaped channel between them, decorating a frieze of the *Doric order and set between its *metopes and immediately over or halfway between the supporting columns.   APQ

triumphal arch An arch set up to celebrate a military triumph. The practice of victorious armies to march into town through the gates in the walls was formalized by setting up arches specifically for parades and as symbols of victory. The arch itself would comprise a tall, wide opening, suitable for cavalry and chariots, flanked by lower, narrower openings for foot soldiers. The solid piers carrying the arches and the superstructure would be carved with symbolic representations of the campaign, replete with trophies of arms and inscriptions recording the triumphant events. Such is the arch at Orange (after AD 21) in southern France commemorating Julius Caesar's conquest of Gaul. The Arch of Septimus Severus, Rome (AD 203), has three parts framed by a single order of columns set on pedestals which support an entablature, while the imposts that carry the springing of the central arch continue outwards across the side arches as the base of a lesser entablature above them, integrating the three parts together. Much

948

copied from the Renaissance onwards, triumphal arches were adapted for a multiplicity of uses, such as formal entrances to grand buildings of many kinds, as well as being used as war memorials and to commemorate victories. APQ

triumphal column like the triumphal arch, a Roman innovation. Small at first, triumphal columns could be carved with scenes of victorious struggle. Trajan's huge column (completed AD 113) is 38 m (125 ft) high, and carved with a low-relief spiral depicting his two victories over the Dacians. This and the Antonine column, erected some eighty years later, set a pattern that outlived Rome. Wren built a column in London (1671–6) to commemorate the Great Fire; Napoleon set one up in the Place Vendôme, Paris (1806–10) and another outside Boulogne (begun 1804) in honour of his achievements, and they were also used decoratively. APQ

Troost, Paul Ludwig (1879–1934) German architect and interior designer, from 1931 to 1934 Hitler's most favoured architect. His classicizing buildings in Munich, bleak, modern-looking in their lack of traditional detailing, but clumsily proportioned, began the transformation of Munich's Königsplatz, the site of fine 19th-century neoclassical buildings by Klenze and others, into a Nazi cult centre. The Königsplatz buildings included the renovation of the party headquarters, two *Führerbauten*, two 'honour temples' to Nazi dead (destroyed), and the repaving and relandscaping of the square (since largely restored). His Haus der Kunst (1933–7), to the north of the Königsplatz, initiated the process by which Hitler and the Party used official buildings for propaganda purposes. By ceremonies at the Haus der Kunst and frequent publications about the building, the Party asserted its claim to be creating a new culture and a new 'German art'. The museum was the site of the

infamous exhibition of 'Degenerate Art' in 1937, which displayed the work of all the modern artists that the Nazis promised to supplant (and whom indeed they persecuted). In propaganda, Troost's buildings, completed by his wife Gerdy, were often attributed to Hitler himself. BML

tropical architecture The term refers, in a literal sense, to all architecture located in a broad belt that encircles the globe between the Tropics of Cancer and Capricorn. However, the expression is more specifically applied to architecture in the hot/wet/humid tropics and to an architecture fashioned in response to climate and culture.

Many countries in the tropics share a common history of colonial rule, and most publications on tropical architecture have issued from academic institutions in the former colonizing countries. The notion of tropical architecture as a separate and distinct architecture can arguably be traced to the setting up of the Department of Tropical Architecture at the Architectural Association, London, as a result of an International Conference on Tropical Architecture (1953). Dr Otto Koenigsberger (1908–99) saw the perils of transferring Western building and planning methods to countries in the tropics, and the need to establish a body of knowledge for the professionals of these countries. The basic concept of the school was that 'tropical architecture cannot be a mere adaptation of temperate architecture but must evolve fresh principles derived from an understanding of tropical conditions, social and economic as well as physical'.

There is a considerable body of literature on architecture in the tropics, much of it dating from the 1950s and 1960s. Prominent among the writers were Maxwell Fry and Jane Drew who published *Tropical Architecture in the Humid Zone* (1956) and Victor Olgyay and Aladar Olgyay, authors of *Design and Climate: Bioclimatic Approach to Architectural Regionalism* (1963).

Miles Danby drew on his experience of working in Africa to publish *Grammar of Architectural Design: With Special Reference to the Tropics* (1963). More recent publications include *Tropical Urban Regionalism* (1987) by Ken *Yeang, and *Tropical Architecture: Critical Regionalism in the Age of Globalisation* (2001), edited by Alexander Tzonis, Liane Lefaivre, and Bruno Stagno.

In the 1980s, architectural discourse in the former colonial territories revolved around the notions of identity and Critical Regionalism. By the early 1990s, publications emerged such as *The Architectural Aesthetics of Tropicality* (1990) by Tay Kheng Soon, *Modern Tropical Architecture* (1997) and *The Tropical Asian House* (1996) by Robert Powell, *Contemporary Vernacular* (1998) by William Siew Wai Lim and Tan Hock Beng, and *An Architect in the Tropics* (1999) by Bruno Stagno. Tay Kheng Soon argues that, because of the equable climate in the tropics, the building enclosure can be permeable and the wall is thus not the most important element. The roof is the main feature, and the development of a tropical aesthetic is predicated on an understanding of the resultant shade and shadow. Bruno Stagno forcefully makes the point that the shadows cast by eaves, pergolas, and other elements produce a transition between the intense light of the exterior and the deep shade of the interior. Resolving this 'in-between' space becomes an important theme in tropical design.

An incalculable number of local architects in the tropics have produced solutions which respond to the imperatives of climate and culture. Western dominance of the media has meant that few have been recognized outside their own region. Exceptions include Tay Khen Soon of Singapore, whose *oeuvre* includes the Institute of Technical Education at Bishan (1994); and the Asia-based Australian architect Kerry Hill whose work is well illustrated by the Datai Hotel at Pulau Lankawi, Malaysia (1993). The Argentine-born Ernesto Bedmar, a resident of Singapore since 1984, has built a remarkable series of climatically appropriate houses, none more beautiful than the Eu House (1993).

The Malaysian architect Ken Yeang has achieved international recognition for his seminal office tower, Menara Mesiniaga in Kula Lumpur (1992), and his compatriot Jimmy C. S. Lim won accolades for the Salinger House in Selangor (1993). The work of Francesco 'Bobby' Mañosa from the Philippines has also achieved recognition, initially through publication in the now defunct architectural magazine MIMAR. His best-known work is the Mary Immaculate Parish Church in Las Piñas City, Manila (1988). Another Filipino, Rosario Encarnacion Tan, has promoted the use of renewable resources, as demonstrated in an airy bamboo house built for her own use in 1997. Mathar Bunnag from Thailand has produced several exotic tropical resorts, best illustrated by the Pankor Laut Resort (1993), while Kanika Ratanapridakul has built a tropical house in Bangkok, referred to as House U3 (1997).

In Indonesia, the Ibrahim House at Bogor (1994) by Jaya Ibrahim and the Tan House at Bandung (1993) by Tan Tjiang Ay are both superb examples of working with climate, while Takan Bebek at Sayan in Bali (1994) by the expatriate Australian Madé Wijaya is a romantic exposition in the art of design in the tropics.

On the Indian subcontinent, Charles *Correa is a revered figure whose great 'open to the sky' architecture includes the Vidhan Bhavan at Bhopal (1980–96). Rahul Mehrotra has completed a number of projects including the exemplary Shanti House at Alibag (1997), while Anupama Kundoo has designed several dwellings, including her own house at Auroville (2000). In Sri Lanka, Geoffrey *Bawa has left a substantial body of tropical architecture, including the Triton Hotel (1982) at Ahungalla. C. Anjalendran has designed a number of homes for orphans which are beautifully attuned to the tropical climate, including the SOS Children's Village, at Anaradapura (1996).

Tropical architecture is promoted in Central and South America by the Institute for Tropical Architecture based in San José, Costa Rica. The Director, Bruno Stagno, is a practising architect whose work is epitomized by the Balbina Environment Protection Centre in Minais Gerais State. In Southern Africa, the work of Michael Pearce of Zimbabwe has been widely acclaimed, particularly the Eastgate Development in Harare (1995).

The Northern Territories and Queensland in Australia host numerous excellent examples of tropical domestic architecture, including the Addisson House at Taringa (1999) by Red Addisson, the Mapleton House (1991) by Richard Leplastrier, the Rozak House at Lake Bennett (2001) by TROPPO, the T House on the Sunshine Coast (1994) by Donovan and Hill, the Poole House at Doonan (1997) by Gabriel Poole, and the Moolooba House on North Stradbrooke Island (1998) by Andresen O'Gorman.   RP

truss A triangular framework, used for spans or bracing members. Although timber trusses were used in earlier periods (e.g. Palladio's design for bridges, in *I Quattro Libri*, 1570), the widespread use of the truss developed with modern materials (iron and steel) from the middle of the 19th century (*see* STRUCTURAL FORMS (I,VI, ROOF TRUSSES; 3,III, TRUSSES)), particularly in relation to *bridge design. The triangular form of a truss is easily identifiable; but its repetitive pattern, dictated by structural necessity, has proved hard to express in an architecturally interesting manner.

Trusses formed in more than one plane are known as *space frames. (*Foster's Stansted Airport is a very clearly displayed example.)   PG

Tudor architecture The Tudor monarchy (1485–1603) is not associated with architecture in the same way as *Georgian or *Queen Anne, though there

is notable work at the beginning (*see* PERPENDICULAR) and the end (*see* COUNTRY HOUSES, ENGLAND).   PG

tufa A sedimentary rock formed from the deposits of calcareous spring water. If formed near hot springs, it is known as *travertine. It should not be confused with 'tuff' or 'tufo', also known as *peperino*, which is consolidated volcanic ash. In antiquity, because tufa is so easy to cut, it may have been one of the first materials used by the Romans for the earliest forms of ashlar walls (*see* OPUS QUADRATUM) and by the Etruscans (*c.*700 BC) for funerary chambers.

Tufa is one of the lightest stones, consequently it was used for the *webs of ribbed vaults, for instance at Canterbury Cathedral (after 1174). Because of its porosity, tufa is often used for garden buildings such as grottoes, but rarely as a building stone. Two interesting examples in England are St Andrew, Shelsley Walsh, Worcestershire (13th century), whose spongy appearance shows its weakness as an external material; and the largest English building to be constructed mainly of tufa, Berkeley Castle (mainly 14th century), where an iron admixture gives the tufa a rather unmilitary pink, red, and brown tinge. A grey variety (it also occurs in brown) is used to beautiful effect in the courtyard of *Vignola's Palazzo Farnese.   PG

Tunisia *See* AFRICA (NORTH AFRICA).

Turkey, since 1918 Modern Turkish architecture has evolved over three periods. The first (1918–1950) is one of nation-building during which the *Ottoman revivalist 'national style' of the late Empire (an eclectic combination of French academic design principles, modern building programmes, materials, and construction techniques with Ottoman/Islamic stylistic motifs like domes, arches, and tile decoration) was replaced by an austere Modernism introduced by German and central European architects invited by the new, secular republican regime after 1923. The government complex of Clemens *Holzmeister, the buildings of higher education by Ernst Egli and Bruno *Taut, and the work of Turkish modernists like Seyfi Arkan transformed Ankara into a modern national capital in the 1930s. After 1938, the desire to express state power and nationalist politics informed an increasingly heavy, monumental, and classicized Modernism (for public buildings) and a vernacular-inspired 'Turkish house' style (for private houses), with Sedad Hakkı *Eldem and Paul *Bonatz as leading architects.

The second period (1950–80), symbolically marked by the construction of *SOM's Istanbul Hilton Hotel (1952–5), corresponds to multi-party democracy, accelerated modernization, and massive urbanization, as well as a conspicuous internationalization/Americanization of Turkish architectural culture. In this period, two lasting architectural/urban phenomena came to define Turkish modernity: namely, the proliferation of reinforced concrete, slab-block, medium-rise apartments as the dominant residential typology; and the growth of poorer squatter belts around major cities as a result of mass migration from the countryside. A new generation of Turkish architects, including Abdurrahman Hancı, Turgut Cansever, Enver Tokay, Doğan Tekeli, Haluk Baysal, and Melih Bilsel, produced some of the most notable works of Turkish high Modernism, assimilating influences from both the later Le Corbusier and the corporate International Style of the US during the Cold War. In the 1970s, echoing critical and revisionist trends abroad, prolific designers like Behruz Çinici, Cengiz Bektaş, and Şevki Vanlı experimented with regionalism, new Brutalism (exposed reinforced concrete in particular), and organic architecture.

In the third period (1980 to the present), the twin forces of globalization and political Islam continue to transform the urban landscape in Turkey. The proliferation of shopping malls, international hotel chains, high-tech office towers, and gated communities are indicative of global trends and transnational consumption patterns. Expensive new residential developments involving US architectural firms (such as SOM in Etiler Maya Residences or Duany and Plater-Zyberk in Kemer Country villas in Istanbul) testify to the unprecedented internationalization of architectural practice. The lucrative market for 'Turkish house' style luxury villas (with their tile roofs and projecting window bays) is one manifestation of the pervasive postmodern penchant for discourses of identity. On the other end of the social spectrum, the boom in new mosque construction (mostly cheap derivatives of classical Ottoman precedents, especially in poorer urban fringes), is another highly visible testimony, this time to the increasing presence of Islam in a hitherto radically secular country. As the architectural scene is increasingly fragmented to respond to very different constituencies, tastes, and ideologies, a number of talented young architects like Nevzat Sayın, Han Tümertekin, and Emre Arolat stand out with the conceptual sophistication and tectonic qualities of their designs. SB

Bozdoğan, S., *Modernism and Nation Building* (2001)

Tuscan order A Roman version of the Greek *Doric but in general more primitive, and, as Vitruvius describes it, derived from an ancient type of Etruscan temple, so the gap between columns is about twice as great as in the Doric or the other orders, a residual feature of the original construction in wood of the entablature or lintel. Tuscan columns lack fluting, and sometimes but not always have a base, unlike Greek Doric, and a slightly more pronounced capital, comprising plain mouldings, like a Roman Doric capital, but its plain frieze lacks both *triglyphs and *metopes.   APQ

Tylman van Gameren *See* GAMEREN, TYLMAN VAN.

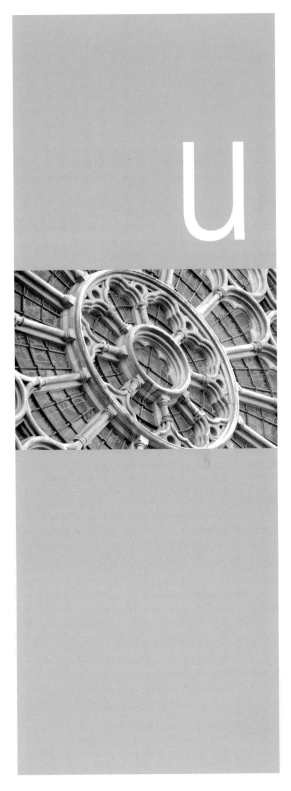

Ukraine Little is known of pre-Christian architecture among the eastern Slavs, but with the acceptance of Orthodox Christianity by Prince Vladimir of Kiev (Kyiv) in 988, the construction of *Byzantine-designed masonry churches spread rapidly. The largest of these was Kiev's thirteen-domed Cathedral of Divine Wisdom (1037?–50s), commissioned by Yaroslav the Wise. Other major churches of this period include the Cathedral of the Transfiguration of the Saviour in Chernigov (1031–50s), the Cathedral of the Dormition at the Kiev Cave Monastery (1073–8, destroyed 1941), and the Cathedral of Archangel Michael 'Golden Domes' (1108–13, destroyed 1934–6). These churches adhere to a plan known as the 'inscribed cross', consisting of a cuboid core structure with crossing main aisles whose intersection is marked by the central dome, elevated on a cylinder supported by four piers. The interior bays were delineated on the exterior by pilasters culminating in curved gables known as *zakomary*, whose shape reflected the barrel vaulting of the interior. The application of stucco to church walls, typically built of *plinthos* (thin brick), rough stone, and heavy mortar, began toward the end of the 12th century.

Smaller Kievan churches followed the inscribed-cross plan. In Chernigov similar patterns appeared in the Cathedral of Saints Boris and Gleb (1120–23) and Church of Saint Paraskeva (c.1200), although the latter is unusual for its vertical compression of structure. Most of these churches were severely damaged during the Mongol invasion of 1240, and all of them were substantially modified during the 17th and 18th centuries.

Following the Mongol invasion, the fragments of the Kievan state were divided among Poland, Lithuania, and Hungary. The expansion of Catholic influence is notable in church architecture of the 15th and 16th centuries, although the Trinity Cathedral within the massive fortress of the Trinity Monastery at Mezhirichi (15th century) displays the Byzantine style in its previous majesty.

With the reunification of the Kievan lands in the middle of the 17th century into the territory of Ukraine, Orthodox church architecture again flourished, although with strong influences from the West (Poland in particular). The so-called 'Ukrainian Baroque' is characterized by florid decorative displays and the development of cruciform church plans with a pronounced vertical character, such as the Church of Saint Nicholas in Nezhin (1668), the Cathedral of the Intercession in Kharkov (1689), and the Cathedral of the Elevation of the Cross in Poltava (1689–1709). The architecture of the major Kievan monasteries is particularly rich during this period, which extended into the 18th century.

The incorporation of Ukraine into Muscovy during the latter half of the 17th century, and subsequently into the Russian Empire, led to similarities between the architecture of Kiev, Moscow, and St Petersburg. A notable example is Kiev's Church of Saint Andrew (1747–53), designed by Bartolomeo *Rastrelli. In the late 18th and early 19th centuries, neoclassicism spread throughout Ukraine, with notable achievements in Odessa. Eclecticism characterized the latter 19th century, particularly in the design of commercial and administrative buildings in Kiev and Odessa. National revival styles appear in both secular and church architecture at the beginning of the 20th century.

The Soviet period witnessed the widespread destruction of religious monuments and the creation of massive administrative complexes in Kiev. Of greater architectural interest is Kharkov's massive State Industry Building (1925–9), one of the major products of Constructivism. In the eclectic post-Soviet era, the most striking development is the rebuilding of demolished Orthodox churches and cathedrals, especially in Kiev.   WCB

Brumfield, W., *A History of Russian Architecture* (2nd edn, 2004)

Ukraine, L'viv (Lwów, Lemberg) L'viv is the chief

city of western Ukraine; for five centuries it was the metropolis of south-eastern Poland. Little remains of its late medieval foundations. But by 1600 it had grown rich on grain exports, and began to build in a Netherlandish style of Mannerism—the Bernardine church (1600–17), the profusely decorated Kampian (1585) and Boim (1609–15) funeral chapels, and showy house fronts on the main square. Counter-Reformation style and Roman builders arrived around 1610 with the Jesuits, resulting in the collegiate church at nearby Zhovkva (1606–18) which set the fashion for 25 m (82 ft) high naves. Magnates' seats in the surrounding country culminate in the great *palazzo in fortezza* of Pidhirtsi (1635–40).

The best churches are in a forceful late Baroque: de Witte's Fischeresque façade and elongated oval dome for the Dominicans (1749–64), and Merderer/ Meretyn's Uniate Cathedral of St George (1744–63), which is exaggeratedly tall with idiosyncratic Rococo detail. The final flowering came as the capital of Austrian Galicia, with an elaborate Opera House (1897), the church of St Elizabeth (1903), Poland's biggest railway station (1904), and streets of eclectic offices and tenements well seasoned with the 'Sezession'. They still give the city's ample centre its peculiar Austro-Polish charm.   DBK

underground railway stations *See* METRO STATIONS.

United Arab Emirates *See* GULF STATES.

United States of America

Native American architecture Villages and cities emerged in the Americas from around 2000 BC onwards. These Native American civilizations marked their ceremonial centres with large earthworks or pyramids, often arranged orthogonally and symmetrically to reflect the divine perfection of the gods and the earthly control of the chiefs. In Mesoamerica, these ideas flourished in the Mayan and Teotihuacán civilizations, and culminated in the Aztec capital of Tenochtitlán (now Mexico City), which housed over 400,000 people when the Spanish invaded in 1519.

Although the area of the present day United States lay on the fringes of this major civilization, it also developed villages and towns. At its height in the 11th and 12th centuries, the Anasazi civilization had created an extensive network of villages in the semi-desert 'four corners' region of present-day Colorado, New Mexico, Arizona, and Utah. Skilfully crafted masonry structures several storeys high and containing hundreds of rooms were built in the canyons and under the cliffs. These forms later evolved into adobe pueblos that are still used in the south-west. Other North American civilizations emerged along the inland waterways of the Mississippi, Missouri, and Ohio river valleys. Most complex and extensive was the Mississippian culture, whose capital city at Cahokia (near St Louis, Illinois) at

its height in AD 1100 controlled a region from the east coast to the Great Plains, and from the Gulf of Mexico to Wisconsin. Cahokia boasted a terraced pyramid 30 m (100 ft) tall and 305 m (1,000 ft) long. These civilizations took advantage of the ancient forest covering eastern North America, and built a variety of house forms with wood sapling frames covered in thatch, birch bark, or wattle-and-daub. The cultures living in the rain forest of the north-west coast included the Haida, who constructed with heavy timber frames and massive wooden planks.

European colonies, 1500–1776 The colonists who first settled in America left Europe during a time of momentous cultural and architectural change. They reproduced all the familiar styles of the *Renaissance and the *Baroque, often more simply, and often after a considerable delay from when the style first attained prominence in the home countries.

In Mesoamerica the Spanish colonists encountered a well-established urban society with strong architectural traditions. After obliterating the symbols of the old religions, they fused their own transplanted European architectural ideas with some of the native traditions and construction techniques. In New Mexico, this fusion led to what is now known as a south-western style with pueblo-like adobe construction and colonnaded porches. In the early 18th century, a Spanish version of the Baroque appeared as rich decoration to the exteriors of mission churches in Texas. Outside the major settlements in New Orleans and Quebec, the French mostly built forts and trading posts along the inland waterways. Their lasting contribution to American design was the plantation house, well designed for the hot and humid south, with a large hipped roof sheltering a colonnaded gallery around all four sides of the house.

The British settled along the eastern seaboard, and initially constructed traditional half-timbered medieval houses with steep roofs and prominent chimneys. Later they often constructed more substantially in stone or brick, and in the prevailing British architectural styles. Masonry construction was less popular in New England, although many wooden houses were detailed to look like stone. Particularly popular in the 18th century was the Baroque style used by small English manor houses. Houses in this style typically had steep hipped roofs over a rectangular plan, with a large staircase hall in the centre, prominent chimneys, and sash windows symmetrically arranged around a classically detailed front door at the centre. Churches followed a Baroque style developed by Sir Christopher Wren for London churches, with prominent steeples decorated in successive sections of Baroque classical details.

While these Baroque styles were flourishing in America, the taste-makers in Britain in the 1720s and 1730s were already leading a revolt against the Baroque in favour of a more austere and correct Classicism inspired by the 16th-century Italian architect *Palladio. This style was termed Anglo-Palladianism, and was characterized by the use of simpler massing and detailing, and archaeologically correct Roman classical temple fronts on building façades. Pattern books helped disseminate the new style in the British colonies. The Scottish architect James *Gibbs influenced through his books many American designs with his distinctive fusion of *Palladio's rational correctness and Wren's creative interpretations.

From the American Revolution to the Civil War, 1776–1865 The American Revolution was part of a broader revolution in European culture in the latter half of the 18th century, known as the Enlightenment. Common assumptions were fundamentally reconsidered, including the justification for political power, the nature of historical development and human behaviour, and the value of reason itself.

This gave rise to a Romantic Rebellion in the arts, which celebrated emotional aesthetic qualities as opposed to the intellectual rationalism of Roman Classicism, and which favoured personal expression over correctness. The Enlightenment thinkers also created the important concept of *style*. Where the *Renaissance had conceived of history as one great ancient civilization temporarily interrupted by the Dark Ages and possessing the one correct architectural language of *Classicism, the *Enlightenment began to see history as a series of ages or phases, each with its own equally valid artistic expression or style. From the early 19th century onwards, architects in Europe and the United States felt free to draw from a richer palette of architectural traditions, including Egyptian, Greek Classicism, *Byzantine, *Romanesque, and *Gothic. Each was provided with a rationale for why it made sense for the era or the individual project. This explosion of styles in the 19th and early 20th centuries gave the entire period a distinctively eclectic character.

The Federalist style was the most popular following the American Revolution. It was based on the ideas of the fashionable rival English architects Robert *Adam and Sir William *Chambers, who had refined their understanding of Classicism through more careful studies of ancient and Palladian buildings. Distinctive characteristics of the Federalist style include oval-shaped rooms, sweeping helix staircases, and Palladian windows (a rectangular window flanked on either side with narrow windows, and topped with a semicircular or elliptical window). The American architect Charles *Bulfinch adapted from Chambers, and more indirectly from Palladio, the idea of a dome and temple front for the Massachusetts State House. This idea was also used by William Thornton for the nation's Capitol building in Washington DC, and later became a common theme for government buildings throughout the country.

Monticello, Charlottesville, Virginia (Thomas Jefferson, 1768–1809)

Thomas *Jefferson objected to the British and Baroque sources of these ideas, turning instead to the French neoclassical movement, which stressed the purity of classical forms based on the original Roman temple with a simple rectangular gable roof over a colonnade. He designed the new Virginia State Capitol as a pure classical temple. The British architect Sir John Soane sought a more radically innovative style in keeping with the revolutionary period, synthesizing and transforming elements from a variety of historical sources. The first professional American architect, Benjamin Henry *Latrobe, adopted Soane's approach for a number of projects including the Baltimore Cathedral, as did Thomas Jefferson for a substantial remodel of his own home, Monticello.

The Greek War of Independence in the 1820s inspired in Europe and America an enthusiasm for all things Greek, including an architectural *Greek Revival. The original Greek version of Classicism predated the ancient Roman adaptation, and is based purely on the temple form without Roman arches or domes. Although Greek temples, particularly the early Doric version, are less refined in proportion or detail, they expressed raw energy and an affiliation with the

origins of democracy that resonated throughout the new American republic. Robert *Mills and William *Strickland popularized the style, which eventually was used for everything from major government buildings to decoration on modest houses at the frontier.

The Industrial Revolution rapidly accelerated in the first half of the 19th century, bringing dramatic improvements in construction technology. The new technologies fundamentally changed the traditional limitations on the sizes and shapes of buildings. With the invention of gas and later electric lighting, buildings were no longer limited in width by the need for natural daylight. Iron and later steel allowed designers to abandon the ancient system of load-bearing walls in favour of lightweight frames that could be built much higher. James *Bogardus helped develop this idea, while Elisha Otis perfected the first steam elevator that would make access to tall buildings possible. In the 1830s, Chicago builders invented balloon framing for wooden structures, a lightweight and more easily constructed alternative to the ancient wood post-and-beam system.

The Industrial Revolution also brought overcrowded and dirty cities, and appalling living conditions for the factory workers. In reaction, many early-19th-century philosophers, writers, and poets advanced Romantic ideals of regaining harmony between people and with nature. Following the lead of the British architect A. W. N. *Pugin and critic John *Ruskin, they looked back to the Middle Ages as a time when these harmonies were still alive, and promoted the medieval Gothic style as the best expression of these ideals. Gothic had the further advantage for the Romantics of creating powerful emotional responses through its soaring, visually complex forms. Richard *Upjohn, James *Renwick, John Haviland, and Alexander Jackson *Davis popularized the style in America. Davis and his friend the landscape architect Andrew Jackson Downing also explored how the more picturesque Gothic concept could be applied to the design of modest houses, leading to a picturesque tradition in American house design that weaves its way to the present. Other prominent revivals before the Civil War included an Italian Classical Revival, a Baroque Revival, and a Romanesque Revival. A short-lived Egyptian Revival culminated in the Egyptian obelisk Washington Monument in Washington DC.

From the Civil War to the First World War, 1865–1918 Americans after the Civil War energetically set out to rebuild their lives, creating a brash, materialistic and individualistic mood variously called the Gilded Age or the Age of Enterprise. A Second Empire style imported from France perfectly captured the new spirit, with exuberant layers of Baroque details, aggressively projecting pavilions, and mansard roofs. Gothic Revival architects after the war chose from a more eclectic range of precedents than Pugin would have allowed, seeking more aggressive and polychromatic forms. Frank *Furness explored a highly personal style by selecting vaguely familiar forms from diverse sources, and then squashing, stretching, and combining these into unprecedented

compositions. His emphasis on free expression over tradition later inspired many modernist architects.

The extravagances of the post-war period moderated in the 1870s, due in part to economic and political changes in Europe and the United States. The British architect Richard Norman *Shaw developed an appropriate architectural expression that was not too brash but still picturesque by reviving and refining British rural vernacular medieval and urban Elizabethan and Jacobean traditions. His rural Old English style and urban Queen Anne Style merged together in the hands of the American architects, leading to the first recognizably distinct American style, the Queen Anne. Houses in this style are typically characterized by picturesque massing, broad porches across the entire front, turrets, wooden siding, and elaborate details like sunburst bargeboards, brackets, and latticework. The Centennial celebrations of 1876 led to a nostalgic Colonial Revival that has survived to the present. Another uniquely American style, the Shingle Style, emerged in this period, typified by a smooth skin of shingles wrapped over Queen Anne or Colonial forms.

Henry Hobson *Richardson helped develop both the Queen Anne and Shingle Styles, and then offered a third distinctive American architecture style so striking and influential that it has been named Richardsonian Romanesque in his honour. His version of this style is characterized by bolder, more coherent massing than his predecessors, and the dramatic use of powerful, primitive forms including giant arches for entries. Inspiring both American and British architects, the style rapidly spread throughout the country, including in the recently established towns in the mid-western prairie and inter-mountain west.

In the 1880s, in part because of the increasing influence of the *Beaux Arts school of architecture in Paris, architects became more sophisticated in their use of historical precedents. Rather than pick up pieces of traditions and assemble them, architects were

Lovell Health House, Los Angeles (Richard Neutra, 1927–9)

encouraged to seek the underlying design principles behind the traditions, and then use those principles to develop fresh and fully integrated interpretations of the traditions. They turned to more styles than ever before, including a Spanish Colonial style in California and the south-west. Most pervasive of all was a grandiose neoclassical style taught at the Ecole des Beaux-Arts and employed by the American architecture firm *McKim, Mead, and White for many major public buildings. The style spread throughout the United States, thanks in part to its use at the Columbian Exposition in Chicago in 1893. The dazzling image of large, white, formally composed public buildings grouped around a lake inspired many visitors to construct similar urban centres back home, leading to a national 'City Beautiful' movement. These powerful, imposing structures also resonated well with an America beginning to flex its muscles as a colonial and international power at the end of the century.

The Gothic Revival ideals of Pugin and Ruskin earlier in the century blossomed into an *Arts and Crafts movement in the 1880s and 1890s in Britain and the United States. In support of their favoured medieval style, the two thinkers had called for buildings derived

from their functions, honest in their structure and construction, and handcrafted rather than machine-made. The British designers *Voysey, Edwin *Lutyens, and Charles Rennie *Mackintosh, among others, moved beyond simply a revival of medieval styles, and began to strip down the traditional forms to their underlying, simple essences. The forms became so abstracted and clarified that their underlying historical precedents were no longer always obvious.

Arts and Crafts ideals in America first found full expression in Chicago, helped along in part by a building boom in the 1880s that demanded maximum financial return on investment as quickly as possible. Owners were willing to forego the niceties of traditional architectural detailing, and the architects of the later named *Chicago School, including Daniel Burnham, John Wellborn Root (*see* BURNHAM, DANIEL HUDSON, AND ROOT, JOHN WELLBORN), and Louis *Sullivan happily obliged with buildings stripped to their essence, and dramatically emphasizing the vertical direction of the increasingly taller *skyscrapers. The development of the steel frame was both inspired by—and contributed to—building taller structures more cost-effectively. Sullivan found additional inspiration in the Gothic Revival ideal of harmony with nature, and expressed this by applying richly patterned organic forms on selected surfaces of his buildings. Prominent Arts and Crafts architects for buildings other than skyscrapers around the turn of the century included Bernard *Maybeck, Julia *Morgan, the *Greene brothers Henry and Charles, and Gustav Stickley, the last-mentioned popularizing a craftsman style for houses of modest means throughout the country.

Sullivan's apprentice, Frank Lloyd *Wright, initially applied the Arts and Crafts ideals to Shingle Style and Colonial Revival forms. But after seeing the Beaux Arts Classicism and a reproduction of a Japanese temple at the Columbian Exposition in Chicago in 1893, he synthesized these diverse sources into his own distinctive invention, the Prairie Style. His historically unprecedented houses are characterized by simple abstracted forms, long low horizontal lines, shallow hip roofs with broad overhangs, and classical principles of axial and symmetrical design fused with picturesque asymmetries. Wright gained fame in Europe before America with a publication of his portfolio in Germany in 1910, inspiring a number of young European architects like Walter *Gropius and *Mies van der Rohe, who later developed the style of International Modernism. Through a career spanning almost three-quarters of a century, Wright continued to find fresh expressions in a variety of sources, always synthesizing these into buildings of unusual power and unity. He is considered by many to be the greatest American architect ever.

Between the wars, 1918–1945 World War I devastated Europe and overturned the old world order. In everything from politics to social mores and the arts, Western culture moved in two opposed directions: those who sought as rapid a return as possible to the old order, and those who saw in the chaos an opportunity to impose a new order more favourable to their own interests. The communists and the fascists, the Roaring Twenties flappers, and the prohibitions against liquor and the teaching of modern science, are all familiar examples of the extreme opposites in this period. In architecture, the differing views were played out between the traditionalists and the emerging modernists.

Most post-war American architects promoted the pre-war ideals of historical revivals, reminding people of their connections with centuries worth of civilized values before the slaughter of the war. The firm of Mellor, Meigs, and Howe interpreted vernacular domestic European styles for suburban and country house estates, and helped popularize a Tudor style for American houses that remains popular today. Styles were often chosen for their regional appropriateness, so pueblo styles were used in the south-west, Spanish Colonial and Mediterranean in California, northern Italian for mountainous Colorado.

A number of European architects after the war explicitly rejected the historical revivals, embracing instead some pre-war experiments with a modernist approach to design. The pre-war experiments had originally sought a Free Style less obviously dependent upon the traditional historical styles, and by the eve of the war this search had broadly led in two directions. One direction, championed by designers like Hermann Muthesius and Walter *Gropius, stressed the simple, rational forms abstracted from traditional architecture and expressive of the industrial products of the new machine age. The other direction, known as Expressionism and championed by designers like Bruno *Taut and Rudolf Steiner, attempted to elicit powerful emotional responses to designs typically reminiscent of dark caves or crystalline forms. Like the classical and the Gothic before them, the one stressed the rational and intellectual while the other stressed the expressive and emotional aspects of human nature.

Both views revived after the war, and in the collapsed economic conditions and social unrest of post-war Germany, both views rejected bourgeois culture and embraced socialist politics as the way to create a more just world in the wake of the war's destruction. The German Expressionists called for avant-garde artists and architects to lead a spiritual and cultural uprising, while the Swiss architect *Le Corbusier championed the rationalist cause and proposed bulldozing central Paris to make room for regular rows of austerely Modern housing blocks for the working class. Walter Gropius founded the influential *Bauhaus school of design in Germany in this period, which rejected the Ecole des Beaux-Arts reliance on historical architectural styles and substituted instead the teaching of an abstract language of vision.

These modernist views did not resonate well in the United States, which had suffered none of the destruction of the war, and whose response to the Russian Bolshevik Revolution was a Red Scare leading to communist witch-hunts. Two Viennese immigrants, Richard *Neutra and Rudolph *Schindler, designed the earliest European modernist buildings in the United States. Both trained with early modernists in Europe and then worked for Frank Lloyd Wright. They each developed designs combining Le Corbusier's simple, white planar forms and Wright's predominantly horizontal lines.

A number of post-war architects, both in Europe and the United States, sought a middle ground between the resolutely traditional forms of the revivalists and the stridently unprecedented forms of the modernists. They attempted to update traditional forms with the spirit of the modern age. One popular approach in Britain and the United States started with the venerable language of Classicism, but then stripped off the ornament to reveal its basic underlying rational forms. Proponents of stripped Classicism in the United States

included Bertram Grosvenor *Goodhue, John Russell Pope, Henry Bacon, and Paul *Cret.

Another approach turned the energy of the Jazz Age into the *Art Deco style. Starting with stripped classical forms as the basic armature, this style layered on images from German *Expressionism and Italian *Futurism including zigzags and sunbursts, capturing the frivolous and exuberant mood of the 1920s with opulent and glittery materials. The style also acquired images from Egyptian, Chinese, and Mayan sources, particularly for the new movie theatres springing up around the country. Frank Lloyd Wright explored a fusion of Maya and European modernist forms in the 1920s, although he publicly denounced the philosophies of the modernists and continued to seek distinctively American architectural expressions.

Following the stock market crash of 1929 and the ensuing worldwide Great Depression, extremes became more pronounced. A no-nonsense pragmatism replaced the frivolity of the 1920s, while the longstanding American belief in self-sufficiency was challenged by the stark reality of millions out of work through no fault of their own. Roosevelt dramatically expanded the federal government to tackle social challenges collectively, just as Fascism and Communism rose as powerful movements and bitter enemies. All turned to even more grandiose stripped Classicism as the best expression of their respective collective social and political aims, despite their fundamentally different values.

Art Deco in the Depression evolved into Art Moderne or Streamline Moderne, following the scientific efforts in the 1920s onwards to streamline the design of aeroplanes, steamships, and trains for greater efficiency. This captured the imagination of product designers and architects, who streamlined stationary objects with rounded corners, long horizontal lines, and no fussy ornament. This modern, functional look helped ease the entry of International Modernism into America. More architects began to build in this style, including the designers of a number of Roosevelt's Public Works Administration housing projects. In this period, Frank Lloyd Wright designed his most famous building—Fallingwater in Pennsylvania—by cantilevering modernist white horizontal terraces over a rocky outcropping and waterfall. European refugees in this period, including Walter Gropius, brought the modernist Bauhaus method of teaching to American schools of architecture. All ensuing generations of American architecture students would learn Modernism, not the traditional styles.

Modern and postmodern America, 1945 to the present The United States emerged from the war as the economic and political leader of the Western world. Where America had long followed European tastes and styles, in the post-war era much of the world emulated American culture, including its architecture. And now its favoured architectural style was Modern. Modernism reflected a clean break with a tumultuous recent past, while embracing a post-war enthusiasm for science, technology, and efficiency. The new modernist styles employed in the United States were still largely inspired by Europeans or European immigrants, however. Le Corbusier experimented with large, raw concrete structures after the war, leading to what was later termed a Brutalist style for similar projects throughout Europe and the United States. Le Corbusier's image of rationally ordered modernist housing blocks lined up in grassy parks inspired urban renewal projects, both in Europe to replace its bombed-out housing, as well as in the United States to rebuild its decaying inner cities. The immigrant *Mies van der Rohe fashioned another highly influential modernist style with his austere steel-framed, glass-façaded, box-like buildings. The American corporations quickly embraced his style, because it suited their

self-image as rational, efficient, powerful and not desirous of individual self-expression. Philip *Johnson and *Skidmore, Owings, and Merrill helped promulgate the style. These steel and glass skyscrapers reshaped the central core of cities, first in the United States and then throughout the world.

The expressionist strand of Modernism also revived after the war. Le Corbusier led the way with his free-form design for the Ronchamp chapel in France. Wright followed suit with his spiral Guggenheim Museum in New York, while Eero *Saarinen designed the TWA terminal like a bird in flight. Paul *Rudolph experimented with inter-penetrating rectilinear forms playfully stacked up, rejecting any functional justification for his forms other than their aesthetic qualities. Louis *Kahn also developed a language of rectilinear forms picturesquely composed, although he justified his forms with deeply introspective reflections on the nature of materials and the functional needs of the building.

Helped by inexpensive mortgages and more efficient mass housing production, and aspiring to the American dream of owning a house on its own land, middle-class Americans moved to the suburbs in vast numbers after the war. The favoured house styles were traditional, along with a new ranch style that was derived from Spanish Colonial, Craftsman, and Frank Lloyd Wright ideas. In the 1930s, Wright had developed an affordable house design he called Usonian, which merged the kitchen, dining and living rooms into one space, and which turned its back on the street in favour of a backyard patio. The post-war ranch houses embraced these ideas, spread out in low, single-storey wings, and set back from the street with a sweeping lawn reminiscent of the old manor houses. Regional shopping malls and strip malls surrounded by parking lots substituted for traditional town centres in the suburbs, now that the car almost universally replaced public transport.

Lever House, Park Avenue, New York (Gordon Bunshaft, SOM, 1952)

Post-war Modernism came under increasing attack in the cultural revolution of the 1960s, on a number of fronts. Purist modernists like the New York Five decried the expressionist tendencies, and returned to the more rationalist ideas in Le Corbusier's 1920s white houses. Buckminster *Fuller promoted more aggressively technological solutions to building problems, including his proposal to cover entire cities with geodesic domes to control their climates. Robert *Venturi objected more fundamentally to Modernism's treatment of architecture as simple form making, without reference to traditional meanings or visual complexities, and drew attention to rich meanings in the contemporary vernacular environment. Moore, Lyndon, Turnbull, and Whitaker also promoted a revival of vernacular forms updated with modern sensibilities like Pop Art. And as urban renewal bulldozed the historic centres of American cities, preservation movement arose to protect the legacy.

After the loss of the Vietnam War and the rapid decline of the manufacturing sector, America's optimism soured in the 1970s, along with its faith in technology, rational progress, and big government. Individuals began to identify less with an abstract idea like an American melting-pot, and more with local or regional cultural, economic, or ethnic groups. Many competing and often acrimonious viewpoints emerged, including in the world of architecture.

One strand of architectural thinking since the 1970s continued the revival of traditional forms started by Venturi and still predominant in the American popular culture. At first the postmodern architects, including Venturi, Charles *Moore, and Michael *Graves, explicitly revived the classical language, although they employed it jokingly and ironically with over-scaled or grossly disproportionate elements superimposed on modernist massing. This soon led to a more serious revival of traditional styles by architects like Robert Stern and the firm Duany and Plater-Zyberk. The latter, along with Peter Calthorpe, led a New Urbanist movement inspired by the European urbanist Leon Krier. The New Urbanists wish to replace the post-war car-based suburbs with traditional walking neighbourhoods complete with front porches, local shops, and more traditional house styles. The concept of regionally appropriate design was also revived, as designers like Lake/Flato Architects or Antoine Predock became more attuned to the special character and traditions of their local cultures and environments.

The other strand of architectural thinking continued with the modernist belief in forms without reference to historic styles. Some like Helmut Jahn celebrated highly expressive technological forms, while others like Cesar *Pelli wrapped their forms in mirror-like surfaces that deflected attention to the surrounding environment. Richard *Meier, one of the original New York Five, continued his explorations of the 1920s Corbusian ideal, although now much more complexly expressed. From the 1980s another group of modernists explored more deeply the sense of angst and dislocation in contemporary society. Known as the Deconstructivists in architecture, and drawing from the Deconstructionists in literary criticism, these architects, including Peter Eisenman, Morphosis, Frank *Gehry, and Daniel Libeskind, abandoned rational orthogonal geometry in favour of more complex, ambiguous, and aggressively crashing forms that created a sense of disorder and even anger. Gehry more recently evolved his forms into softer, more sensual curves, at the same time pioneering new design and construction methods using the digital technology of the aerospace industry.

MGe

Gelernter, M., *A History of American Architecture* (1999)

Jordy, William H., *Progressive and Academic Ideals at the Turn of the Twentieth Century*, vol. 4 of *American Buildings and their Architects* (1972)

Jordy, William H., *The Impact of European Modernism in the Mid-Twentieth Century*, vol. 5 of *American Buildings and their Architects* (1972)

Maynard, W. Barksdale, *Architecture in the United States, 1800–1850* (2002)

Roth, L. M., *A Concise History of American Architecture* (1979)

Scully, V., *American Architecture and Urbanism* (1969)

Upton, D., *Architecture in the United States* (1998)

Whiffen, M., and Koeper, F., *American Architecture 1607–1976* (1981)

universities The Greco–Roman 'universities' and the earliest medieval institutions, Bologna, Rome, and Paris, were so tied in with the urban fabric that practically no buildings survive from their early years. Oxford and Cambridge *colleges, the great exception

with their pseudo monastic buildings, are discussed separately. The closest parallel preserved on the Continent is the Collegium Maius of the Jagiellonian University in Cracow (15th–16th century). During the 16th to 18th centuries, universities in Spain, Portugal, and Italy (e.g. Salamanca, Coimbra, Pavia) built a mixture of monasteries and palaces. In the 19th century new universities took the form of the new type of large public building: the University of Vienna (1877–84) occupies one of the prominent positions on the Ringstrasse, alongside half a dozen other major public institutions, like the City Hall, the Austrian Parliament, the Burgtheater and the Palace of Justice. Inside the rationally planned complex there are a large number of offices, lecture halls, and the Aula, the main space for assemblies, replacing the chapel of the older universities. But even Vienna's grand university building might be mistaken for an over-large school. The same can be said of the plethora of important institutions in Continental cities of the 19th and early 20th centuries.

The modern university, at least as it has been known until the later 20th century, was well under way from the early 19th century onwards. Its research ethos was due chiefly to German efforts, the education policies to England, but its new architectural character was formulated predominantly in the USA. It was a period which saw the creation of the distinct plan types of many other modern institutions, such as hospitals and prisons. The new key term for the university in the USA was 'campus'. First used for Princeton University in the later 18th century, it signifies the spread of the varied buildings of the institution over a green site outside the town; not uniting all the functions in one impressive building, as in Continental Europe, but separating the various parts containing administration, lecture halls, the chapel, and finally student residences—a custom the Americans took from England and not from Continental Europe—all laid out in a loose but orderly manner. It had one great advantage, in that the 'campus' could easily be expanded. The first complete formulation of such a campus complex was the University of Virginia, designed by Thomas *Jefferson in 1817. The dignity of its Roman-style buildings enclosing a long lawn has rarely been surpassed.

During the 19th and early 20th centuries the Americans built a far larger number of universities and colleges, large and small, than any European country. Vast campuses varied the grandiose layouts with classical French *Beaux Arts style (University of Minnesota, Minneapolis, 1910), or a more English Gothic style (University of Chicago, 1893), or as at Stanford (1888) in a Mediterranean monastic manner. By 1900 some New England 'colleges', such as Yale and Princeton, tried to revert back to medieval England by incorporating Oxbridge college-like subsections. Even on a much tighter urban site, as in uptown Manhattan, its Columbia University (1894, by *McKim, Mead, and White) adopted the campus layout, creating a small oasis within the diverse urban fabric.

The vast expansion of the university sector after World War II brought the problem of outgrowing even the most flexible possibilities of the classical campuses, leading to the sprawl of the 'multiversity'. This was countered by more intense planning in the International Modern 'functionalist' manner, i.e. carefully allocating separate zones for each function and connecting them with a sophisticated vehicular and pedestrian communication network, as well as using much more careful forethought for the expansions.

During the 1960s finally, Europe retook some of the initiatives in university planning. It was now the period of entirely new foundations which were started up in a great many countries. In several ways England now took the lead, founding seven major new universities during the early 1960s. They took on the basic American campus model and situated it just outside their provincial urban locations. But the aim of

these proud institutions was not just, as with classical Modernism, to accommodate and move around a certain number of people efficiently in pleasant green surroundings, but also to influence their social psyche. An old debate was revived, whether students should be seen as adults or as adolescents. The old English college model tended to opt for the latter, and thus the English new universities tried to fuse the college type with the campus plan. The Universities of Kent, York, and Lancaster actually constituted themselves as a series of colleges, while Sussex, Essex, and East Anglia tried to integrate college and Oxbridge elements such as the 'quad' or the 'Oxbridge staircase' into their central complexes. Above all the architecture was meant to encourage a spirit of 'community'. The architects, working closely with the founding vice-chancellors, were certainly convinced that they had created a kind of building that was recognizable as a 'university'. Soon other countries joined this movement: Germany's Konstanz, Bochum, and Bielefeld, and Paris-Jussieu, built strong central foci within their massive campuses. The planning ideals of campus and college were supplemented with those of the small town.

Rather unexpectedly these sincere and ingenious efforts were confounded by the student revolt of the late 1960s. In a bitter campaign, the 'paternalistic' and 'brutal' architecture of the University of Essex was held to be at least partly responsible for the troubles. When expansion resumed in the 1990s (in Britain) architectural tastes had changed: no grandiose plans but, where money and outstanding designers were to hand, distinguished buildings arose, strikingly beautiful as well as user-friendly in their details. However, the question of what is specific to university architecture is hardly asked any more.   SM

Muthesius, S., *The Post War University. Utopianist Campus and College* (2000)

Turner, P. V., *Campus. An American Planning Tradition* (1984)

Upjohn, Richard (1802–1878) US architect. His masterpiece is Trinity Church, New York (1839–46), which brought *Pugin's Gothic to the American stage, though with plaster vaulting. Countless ecclesiastical commissions followed, including St Mary's Church, Burlington, New Jersey (1846–54); most were Gothic, but Upjohn was an early promoter of *Romanesque, too. Kingscote, Newport, Rhode Island (1839–41), helped popularize the Italianate villa. His book *Rural Architecture* (1852) illustrated board-and-batten chapels for small-town America. Upjohn founded the American Institute of Architects in 1857. WBM

Urartu The kingdom of Urartu was centred round Lake Van (eastern Anatolia), flourishing *c*.850–600 BC. Its principal monuments are fortresses with masonry courses averaging 1 m (39 inches) high, stepped in slightly, giving a batter. One fortress near Van has exceptionally fine limestone ashlar with dummy andesite windows, found fallen from the walls but identifiable from representations on Urartian bronzes and reliefs. These make it possible to reconstruct the mud-brick superstructure of the major fortresses, with their ornate parapets. The columned halls of various Urartian palaces may betray contacts with north-western Iran, especially Hasanlu, perhaps immediately after its sack by a Urartian army (*c*.800 BC).

The Urartian square temples of tower-like proportions are distinctive. The best preserved is the temple at the splendid late Urartian citadel of Ayanis, north of Van and overlooking the lake. This was the work of the great builder Rusa II (*c*.685–645 BC). This temple stood at one side of a large court with massive square piers having small buttresses at each corner. The interior of the sanctuary is highly ornate, with intaglio figures on wall faces and a podium of alabaster incised with elaborate designs. The whole decor is in the characteristic Urartian style, with its Assyrian overtones. CAB

Forbes, Thomas B., *Urartian Architecture* (1983)

Uruguay Separated from Argentina at the time of the independence struggles, Uruguay's capital was established in Montevideo, which developed along distinctly European lines. Noteworthy buildings include the Cathedral (1790) by Custodio Saá y Fariá, the Cabildo (*c*.1810) by Tomás Toribio, and the Solís Theatre (1841–56) by Carlos Zucchi. In the early 20th century the city spread and achieved a certain splendour with numerous commercial and administrative buildings, including the Palacio Municipal by Mauricio Cravotto. A distinguished contributor to modern developments was Eladio Dieste, the originality and audacity of whose brick structures are evident in the Atlantida Church (1959). LNM (trans. KL)

Utzon, Jørn (1918–2008) Danish architect. He drew on a variety of influences: architects such as *Aalto, *Asplund, *Mies, and Frank Lloyd *Wright, but also oriental architecture, and forms in nature such as crystalline sequences. The connecting thread was his interest in a repetitive system of standardized elements.

His first opportunity to put his ideas into practice was his own house, Hellebæk, near Elsinore, Denmark (1951–2). Its ground plan echoes Mies's Barcelona Pavilion, with its flat roof, over partly opened up or protruding brick walls.

But he achieved international recognition by winning the competition for the Sydney Opera House (1957–66). It has a solid podium for service functions carrying public auditoria and stages, covered by a cluster of curved, concrete shells, creating a multi-membered, dynamic silhouette, somewhat steeper than originally planned. This building has—naturally enough—been compared with bird's wings or, perhaps more appropriately given its harbourside setting, with the hull and sails of a ship. But given its purpose as a place for music and drama, it could perhaps also be functionally associated with the idea of sound rising and falling beneath swelling canopies. As a result of technical difficulties and political pressure, Utzon left Sydney in 1966 and the opera house was completed by other architects. Therefore he regarded the exterior only as his own work—a remarkable synthesis of poetic vision and technical difficulties.

He continued to design in Denmark. The Kingo Houses, Helsingør (1958–60), are L-shaped dwellings with a patio, linked in patterns adapted to the given topography. Traditional Danish yellow bricks and red roof tiles, topped by a forest of broad chimney-stacks, give this development the air of a friendly village. This type of overall layout became influential, and was varied by Utzon himself in the Fredensborg Terraces at Sjaelland (1962–3).

His Danish work extended beyond housing. His Bagsvaerd Church, Sjaelland (1974–6), is a most original creation, both technically and formally. The entrance front looks like a very free variation on the long side of a basilica, but the interior is oriented at right angles to it, the high clerestory of windows illuminating the main room from behind. Using prefabricated elements, the roof consists of a system of curvilinear, undulating concrete vaults, bulging into or receding from the interior as if moving freely, independent of the supporting walls.

The Bagsvaerd vaults have been interpreted as moving clouds, letting through the light of the sky. If so, they are another example of Utzon's inspiration from nature, here also with celestial overtones. Another example of this inspiration is Paustian's Furniture Store, Nordhavn, Copenhagen (Utzon Associates, 1986–7). Its front is oriented towards a harbour basin and consists of eleven columns shaped as stylized trees. Similar columns continue inside and grow taller in the middle, supporting a skylight, and then spread more sparsely towards the edges. The roof is raised upwards on the front columns, then sinks into an elongated slope down to the rear side. Thus the

exhibition area reminds one of a forest with a central glade, illuminated from above. In his sketches, Utzon started drawing beeches with their branches, then abstracted them into his Paustian columns.

He also designed the Parliament Building, Kuwait (1973–85), and his own house at Porto Petro, Mallorca (1971–3).   TF

Weston, R., *Jørn Utzon* (2002)

Uzbekistan The territory occupied by contemporary Uzbekistan contains remnants of pre-Islamic Buddhist architecture, such as the ruins of the brick Zurmala stupa (2nd century AD) near Termez. The area is best known, however, for its concentration of Islamic architectural monuments. Islamic culture was firmly implanted after the capture of Samarkand in 712.

Funerary structures play a large role in central Asian architecture, and one of the earliest extant monuments is the mausoleum of Ismali Samani (*c*.900) in Bukhara. A small cuboid structure with a hemispherical dome, the Samanid mausoleum is the first known central Asian structure to be built with fired (rather than dried) brick. Both exterior and interior display intricate brick patterns, a feature that characterizes subsequent architecture in the region on a far larger scale.

The earliest extant religious *ensemble* in Bukhara is the Poi-Kalian, consisting of the great Kalian minaret (1127) and the Masjid-i Kalian mosque (early 14th century, with additions in the 15th and 16th centuries). The Kalian mosque displays a form followed in large mosques throughout the region, with a large rectangular courtyard enclosed by a gallery arcade. The *qibla iwan*, an arched vault indicating the direction toward Mecca and containing the *mihrab* (prayer niche), is framed by a façade of ceramic tile with geometric ornamentation. The opposite end of the courtyard is marked by the entrance portal, or *peshtak*, also decorated with ceramic tile. Facing the mosque's entrance is the Miri-Arab madrasa (1535–6), a 2-storey gallery structure covered in ceramic tile and enclosing a central courtyard. Such *kosh* combinations—mosque, minaret, madrasa—continued to appear until the 18th century (several in Bukhara alone) and are among the architectural glories of Uzbekistan. The most elaborate *ensemble* is Samarkand's Registan complex, consisting of the Ulug-Bek madrasa (1417–20) and the Shir-Dor madrasa (1619–31, with remarkable ceramic ornamentation), facing each other across a cobbled square with a small minaret. A third madrasa, Tilla Kari (1641–60), is situated at right angles to the earlier structures.

The greatest concentration of funerary architecture in Uzbekistan is Samarkand's Shah-i Zinda, a necropolis whose mausoleums and shrines, situated along an ascending passage, date primarily from the late 14th and 15th centuries. Samarkand also contains two great mausoleums from the Timurid era: the Bibi-Khanym

mosque and mausoleum (1399–1404) and the Gur-Emir (1404–5, with subsequent additions) situated in the 15th-century Muhammed-Sultan complex and containing the tomb of Tamerlane.

In addition to religious architecture, cities such as Bukhara (part of the Silk Road) built elaborate commercial structures in the 15th and 16th centuries. Of particular note are trading domes devoted to specific merchandise (*taki*) and domed bazaars (*tim*).

Other major centres of architectural monuments in Uzbekistan include Tashkent, Shakhrisabz, and Babkent (with a tall minaret from the 1190s), as well as Khiva, and Kokand, which are particularly rich in 18th- and 19th-century monuments. Monumental Soviet architecture is concentrated in the capital, Tashkent, and displays a pastiche of 'national' motifs applied to largely standardized structures.   WCB

Knobloch, E., *Monuments of Central Asia* (2001)

Vaccarini, Giovanni Battista (1702–69) Italian
architect. Appointed architect to the city of Catania,
Sicily, in about 1730, Vaccarini immediately transformed
the central area around the cathedral. He improved the
Municipio (1732–58) on the north side of the cathedral
square, by introducing elements of movement on the
upper floor—canting out the window frames and the
central doorcase. In completing the façade of the
cathedral (1730–68), Vaccarini used the same devices,
but failed to create a coherent composition. However,
in his design for Palazzo Valle (*c*.1740–50), the façade is
unified by means of the central bay, in which a
ground-floor doorway is canted out and the *piano
nobile* balcony pushes forward in a convex curve.

His two other main works were a successful
response to the needs of convent churches. The
convex façade of S. Giuliano (1739–57) emphasizes
the belvedere, from which nuns watched processions
in the street. At S. Agata (1735–67) the nuns' choir is
emphasized internally, by being much higher than the
side chapels, and by becoming a feature of the façade.

PG

Vaccaro, Domenico Antonio (1681–1750) Italian
architect, who designed several churches in Naples
and its surrounding area.

Vaccaro devised some inventive solutions to the
perennial *baroque problem of reconciling the
longitudinal and central plan, in particular the use of
the octagon. In his church of the Concezione a
Montecalvario, Naples (1718–24), the central octagon is
elongated along the axis leading to the High Altar. A

continuous ambulatory surrounds the central space connecting the chapels, a very unusual plan (cf. *Longhena's Santa Maria della Salute, Venice; also instructive to compare with the work of J. M. *Fischer, though the latter does not include an ambulatory). Breaking with the Neapolitan tradition of highly coloured marble inlay, brought to perfection by *Fanzago, Vaccaro eliminated all colour, apart from the inlaid marble of the High Altar. The dome is white, and the windows in the lower part are large, so that the overall effect is one of dazzling whiteness. The façade, set on a tall plinth, with pairs of pilasters framing the single doorway, is perfectly adapted to the sightline along the narrow, sloping street on the main axis.

The culmination of Vaccaro's designing with light is S. Maria delle Grazie, Calvizzano (c.1743). All the structural lines of the dome are eliminated Here he created a spacious and luminous structure, evenly and strongly lit and painted white.   PG

Valadier, Giuseppe (1762–1839) Italian architect and urban designer. His architecture is characterized by a tentative acceptance of *neoclassicism. The façade for San Pantaleo, Rome (1806), is, for Italy, rather novel: a *Diocletian window over a pedimented doorway, the whole set in smoothly banded rustication. In a late work, the façade of San Rocco, Rome (1833–4), a temple front of paired Corinthian columns projects from a wall modelled by flat pilasters. But for the most part, Valadier's opportunities in architecture were confined to restoration, for example of the Arch of Titus (1819–21) and the Temple of Fortuna Virilis (1829–35).

In an extremely unpropitious period for Italian architecture, Valadier's most significant work was re-modelling the Piazza del Popolo, Rome (1816–20). He re-shaped the piazza as an oval, adding a series of ramps leading up the Pincian Hill to a formal garden.

See also RAINALDI.   PG

Vallée, Jean de la (1620–96) French-born architect, working in Sweden. Original and inventive, he was decisive in introducing the lessons of Roman antiquity and the Renaissance to Sweden, for example in his designs for Oxenstierna Palace, Stockholm (probably 1652–8). For the Riddarhuset or Palace of Nobles (Stockholm), he created a copper roof of an original type (1656–9). His early use of centralized plans in his Stockholm churches—Katarina (1656–95) and Hedvig Eleonora (1666–75)—also inspired later works. With its fanciful, multi-element exterior, the former became influential even outside Sweden.   TF

Vallin de la Mothe, Jean-Baptiste-Michel (1729–1800) French architect active in Russia, 1759–95. He was the first prominent architect in St Petersburg to effect the transition from the late Baroque to the neoclassical style favoured by Catherine the Great. His early projects, such as the Catholic Church of Saint Catherine (1762–83), the Merchants' Court trading centre on Nevsky Prospekt (1761–85), and the Small Hermitage (1764–75), include elements of both styles. Classical principles were applied with greater rigour in his building for the Academy of Arts (1764–88), which he designed with Alexander Kokorinov. The building's Doric porticoes above a rusticated ground floor illustrate the principle of progressive refinement in the arts. His most unusual design was the naval warehouse at New Holland (1765–80s, assisted by Savva *Chevakinsky), with its superb arch for the canal passage.   WCB

Vanbrugh, John (1664–1726) English playwright and architect. After a varied career, eventually as a renowned playwright (*The Relapse* 1696; *The Provok'd Wife* 1697), Vanbrugh's ambitions took a sudden and unexplained shift to architecture. Lacking training and an ability to draw (though he could express his ideas well enough by sketches), he made designs in 1699 for

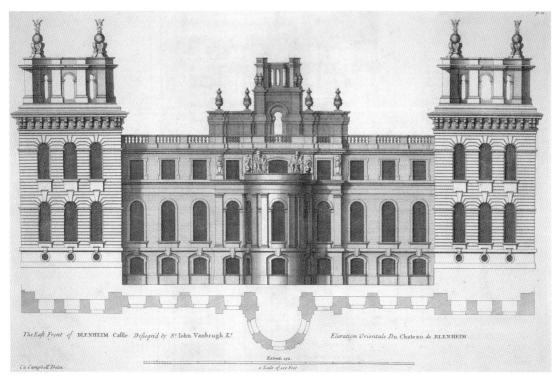

The east front, Blenheim Palace, Woodstock, Oxfordshire (John Vanbrugh, 1724)

Castle Howard, Yorkshire, which were realized with Hawksmoor's assistance as an exemplary designer and draughtsman in 1700–26. The plan, loosely following Palladio's larger villas, comprises a main block linked to service wings at the front and to a long enfilade of rooms on the garden side. Its glory is the full-height, domed entrance hall, with flanking chimney-pieces, overlooked by twin staircases and a landing gallery.

In 1704/5 he was commissioned to design an even more vast country house, Blenheim Palace, the nation's gift to the newly ennobled Duke of Marlborough for his victories over Louis XIV. Similarly planned to Castle Howard with a central *corps de logis* linked to kitchen and stable wings, it is in an even grander and more monumental Baroque style, with a giant portico for the entrance, behind which rises a vast pedimented lantern over the entrance hall. Despite this gravity, it was nevertheless lightened by numerous witty details. The grenades that serve as finials are wonderfully symbolic, just as the gilded flames that crown *Wren's Monument to the Great Fire. The clock tower over the

entrance to the kitchen court is replete with details that, taken alone, would seem wild and incongruous, perhaps reflecting Vanbrugh's own character, but together, once again conceived and executed (1705–16) with *Hawksmoor's assistance, are thoroughly at home in this extraordinary architectural *tour de force*.

Castle Howard led to Vanbrugh's appointment in 1702 to the Board of Works as Comptroller, a post he retained until his death. He subsequently worked as Wren's assistant at Greenwich, taking over from him at his retirement in 1716. Together with Hawksmoor he must have contributed extensively to Wren's masterpiece, though it is hard to unravel their individual contributions. He also became a commissioner for the building of Fifty New Churches, influencing policy but, unlike his colleague Hawksmoor, not having any of his own designs in fact accepted. His first house for himself, Goosepie House, Whitehall, has gone, but Vanbrugh Castle (1718) at Blackheath survives, though not the nearby houses he built for his brothers and sisters, as a very early revival of the castellar style, and a domestic parallel of Hawksmoor's collegiate Gothic at All Souls', Oxford.

Vanbrugh remodelled Kimbolton Castle, Huntingdonshire (1707–10), with a giant Roman Doric portico and niches between *antae*. His Kings Weston, Bristol (*c*.1710–19), though much altered, retains its crowning assemblage of chimney-stacks, linked together with miniature arches to resemble a tiny aqueduct. He rebuilt Grimsthorpe Castle, Lincolnshire (1722–6), with closely paired giant terminal columns and an entrance hall overlooked by galleries behind heavy arcades. He reinterpreted Palladio's Rotunda for his Temple of the Four Winds (1724–6) at Castle Howard, which takes the form of a cube with projecting pediments on each face and an inset dome over it. If it was his response to Campbell's outcry against the 'affected and licentious' quality of his Baroque style, it would have been out of character. His late masterpiece at Seaton Delaval, Northumberland (1720–28), enshrines all the best qualities of English Baroque. It is like a small version of Blenheim Palace, without the wings and lacking some of the more far-fetched ornament. Yet it is hardly tame, combining a sturdy and muscular attitude to Classicism, a sense of the fantastic (now heightened since the house has become a burnt-out shell), and a remarkable evocation of the Elizabethan prodigy house in its overall planning and turreted outline.

He brought the country house to an imaginative peak while not forsaking sensible planning, both of which attributes, remarkably, were recognized in France. His poignant appeal to an Elizabethan and earlier past, re-interpreted in a boldly inventive Baroque, show him as the equal of his Continental contemporaries and the heroic vanguard of the Romantic movement, yet to come.   APQ

Downes, K., *Vanbrugh* (1977)

van Campen, Jacob *See* CAMPEN, JACOB VAN.

van der Hart, Abraham *See* HART, ABRAHAM VAN DER.

van der Rohe, Mies *See* MIES VAN DER ROHE.

van de Velde, Henry *See* VELDE, HENRY VAN DE.

van Doesburg, Theo *See* DOESBURG, THEO VAN.

van Eesteren, Cor *See* EESTEREN, COR VAN.

van Eyck, Aldo *See* EYCK, ALDO VAN.

van Gendt, Adolf L. *See* GENDT, ADOLF L. VAN.

Vanvitelli, Luigi (1700–73) Italian architect. Vanvitelli's work in Rome was a failure. He destroyed the admirable proportions of Bernini's original scheme when he enlarged the Palazzo Chigi-Odescalchi (*c*.1745, with Nicola Salvi), and played a controversial part in the restoration of the dome of St Peter's (1742–8).

In 1751, he was invited by King Charles III to design the new royal palace of Caserta, 24 km (15 miles) to the north of Naples. The problem was rather daunting, as the court required 1,200 rooms. Vanvitelli designed an immense rectangular block about 253 m long by 190 m deep (830 × 623 ft), punctuated by four internal courtyards. His tame neoclassicism, with its endlessly repetitive window frames and its timid central pediment, is one of the weakest possible solutions to an extremely difficult problem.

The plan and the interior were quite a different matter. Just inside the monumental vestibule, the visitor has impressive views into the four courtyards, an imposing staircase, and a long vista into the garden with its enormous cascade.   PG

Vasconcelos, Constantino de (active 1629–68) Portuguese-born architect. *See* PERU.

Vauban, Sébastien le Prestre de (1633–1707)
French military engineer. *See* ENGINEERING AND
ARCHITECTURE.

Vaudoyer, Léon (1803–72) French architect. His
early studies in Italy and Sicily (1826–32) analysed
architecture not only in visual terms, but also as a
record of social and political evolution.

His major work, the cathedral of Ste.
Marie-Majeure at Marseilles (1855–72), offered an
opportunity to show that his theories could be embodied
in a new kind of architecture. In plan, structure, and
façade, he combined elements from both the local
styles which had succeeded each other in Marseilles
(including also Byzantine, for which there was no local
precedent) and the French *Gothic cathedral. The
façade, of banded green and white marble, is an early
demonstration of structural polychromy, especially
effective in its waterfront site.   PG

Vaudremer, Joseph-Auguste-Emile (1829–
1914) French neo-Romanesque architect. He studied
the *Early Christian and *Romanesque architecture of
Italy and followed his older contemporaries, especially
Léon *Vaudoyer (Marseilles Cathedral, 1852) and C.
Naissant (Notre Dame de la Gare, Paris, 1855) in
reviving the latter style for his Parisian churches of
Saint-Pierre de Montrouge (1862) and the somewhat
less austere Notre Dame d'Auteuil (1883).   CT

vaults A vault is a roof or ceiling, usually in brick,
concrete, or stone, built according to the principle of
the arch (*see* STRUCTURAL FORMS (1 ii) BARREL, GROINED
AND RIBBED VAULTS)).

Roman experiments in vaulting form the basis of
nearly all forms of vaulting until the invention of
reinforced concrete. The simplest type is the barrel or
tunnel vault, essentially a series of round-headed or
segmental arches set along an axis. It is structurally
sound, since the thrust is uniform along the
length of the vault, and easy to construct, since once
the first section has been built, the centring can be
moved and re-used for the next section. The earliest
buildings using this type, such as the market hall,
Ferentino (1st century BC), were rather utilitarian.
Segmental barrel vaults are found in more
distinguished buildings, such as Nero's
Golden House (AD 64–8).

The inherent limitations of the barrel vault were that
only narrow spans were possible, so that the vault was
only suitable for square bays and the resultant spaces
were rather dark. The adoption of the *dome solved
the first problem, but to open windows in the sides of
the dome was too risky, and lighting could only be
provided by the oculus at the top. To overcome these
limitations, the Romans developed the groined vault,
in which two barrel vaults intersect at right angles.
The groins, i.e. the lines of intersection, carry much of
the vault's thrust and weight, allowing the wall to be
pierced for lighting, and for the sides of the bay to be
open. The construction was made possible by their
mastery of concrete, in which brick was embedded
along the lines of the groins.

Together with the dome, the range of vaults at
their disposal allowed the Romans to plan sequences
of spaces, particularly in their designs for *baths. In the
Baths of Caracalla (AD 212–16), a groined vault was
used for the *frigidarium*, which stood on the cross-axes,
and was open on four sides. The barrel vaults at the
sides, with coffered ceilings pierced by large windows
in the walls, provided the lighting. The apogee of
Roman vault construction was reached at the Basilica
of Constantine, also known as the Basilica of Maxentius
(begun AD 307). Three groined vaults cover a central
space, 80 m long and 25 m wide (262 × 82 ft), rising to
an extraordinary 35 m (115 ft) high, heights never
reached by vaults until almost 1,000 years later in the
*Gothic period.

The secret of concrete construction vanished with the collapse of the Roman Empire. While the West languished in technological backwardness, ribbed brick vaults were invented in Iran (*see also* IRAQ, HISTORIC). The 200 vaults built by the *Saljuqs in the Jami Masjid, Isfahan (11th century), are a veritable grammar of vault forms.

In western Europe, almost another two centuries passed until the revival of the barrel vault in *France during the *Romanesque period. The earliest examples, such as the Abbey of Saint-Martin-du-Canigou (AD 1001–26) demonstrate the massiveness which was to be an enduring feature of Romanesque architecture. The banded barrel vault, in which an additional arch was introduced at intervals, had several advantages: it was easier to erect, as it could be constructed in stages, using the same centring; it provided additional stiffening to the vault; and the band relieved the unarticulated monotony of the tunnel-like ceiling. This type of vault was perhaps first introduced at Sainte-Foy, Conques (c.1050–c.1120); and is most visually effective at Ste Madeleine, Vézelay (1120–36), where, used in conjunction with a groined vault, the band was picked out in dark and light stone. But none of the varieties of barrel vault allowed for the creation of well-lit spaces.

The solution to the problem lay with the *rib vault, probably first used at Durham Cathedral at the beginning of the 12th century. It is easy to construct since the diagonal arches (the ribs) need little centring; and the supporting walls can safely be pierced by windows. The first type constructed in this manner was the sexpartite vault, in which the ribs divided the area between the transverse arches into six parts. Sexpartite vaulting was well adapted to Norman thick wall structure, as at St Etienne (c.1120) and La Trinité, Caen (c.1130), or to external wall buttressing as at Laon Cathedral (c.1157ff.), but was made redundant by the invention of the *flying buttress in c.1175 and replaced by the quadripartite vault. The new system of construction was first used at Chartres (c.1194) and was followed for about a century.

For reasons which are unclear, from about 1290 there emerged a tendency to use vaults in a purely decorative, even anti-structural manner. In lierne vaults (from the French *lier*, to link), secondary ribs connect the main ribs. The earliest examples are English—Pershore Abbey (c.1290), the cathedrals of Bristol, Ely, and Wells (1300–c.1330)—but, after an interval of over fifty years, they became a standard element in European late Gothic. *Fan vaults exhibit a pattern of delicate tracery, a tribute to the virtuoso skills of the mason, but are of little architectural consequence, unlike *diamond vaults, one of the most striking achievements of Gothic architecture.

Until the era of modern materials, there are no further structural innovations in the use of vaults. The barrel vault on a Roman scale and with coffering on the surface was re-introduced by Alberti at S. Andrea, Mantua (begun 1470). In the baroque period, vaults are often made of lath-and-plaster, serving merely as canvases for frescoes, particularly in south Germany (though, by way of exception, J. M. *Fischer did experiment with masonry vaults). Or, as in the work of *Guarini and *Vittone, vaults were used primarily to create lighting effects. A supposedly new type, Guastavino or timbrel vaulting, introduced into the US by Rafael Guastavino (1842–1908), which uses interlocking terracotta tiles, in fact follows a traditional Catalan method. However, even in the 20th century, traditional masonry vaulting was still capable of great expressive power, as can be seen in the coffered barrel vault at Pennsylvania Station, New York (*McKim, Mead, and White, 1902–10).

The invention of reinforced concrete and a more scientific understanding of how structures work enabled the development of vaults designed as *shell structures.   PG

Velde, Henry van de (1863–1957) Belgian architect. Before 1914, he was one of the most significant figures in the development of 20th-century architecture, enjoying international renown as a theoretician and designer. In his first design, his own house, Bloemenwerf (Uccle, Brussels, 1895), the plastic qualities of his later work are not yet evident. His work differs from that of his contemporary, *Horta, in that it does not show a sophisticated control of space, being rather two-dimensional, in line with his graphic design. Nor is he attracted by the restlessness of the modern city, preferring instead the purity and simplicity of rural life.

A central element in his Art Nouveau approach is the principle of the expressive line which not only expresses the dynamic and vital earthly force of creation but at the same time guarantees the unity of the designs as a *Gesamtkunstwerk*. During his stay in Weimar, Germany (1900–17), van de Velde designed several buildings (the Nietzsche-Archiv, the Kunstbewerbeschule) and decorative interiors in the Art Nouveau manner. He also joined the *Deutscher Werkbund, for which he designed the Theatre for the Werkbund exhibition (1914, demolished). His predilection for curvilinear forms and for individual artistic creativity led to a controversy with Muthesius, who considered rectilinear uniformity to be more appropriate for industrial design. After moving to Switzerland (1917–20) and to the Netherlands (Kröller-Müller museum, 1920–26) he returned to Belgium. Although van de Velde abandoned the principle of the *Gesamtkunstwerk* in favour of Modernism, he did not follow a hard line. Projects like La Nouvelle Maison (Tervuren, 1927), House Wolfers (Elsene, Brussels, 1930), and even the more urban project, the University Library in Ghent (1933–6), do not aim to create a dematerialized or abstract architecture.   YS

Venetian or Palladian window A symmetrical tripartite window, the central light arched and wider than the outer lights, often employing classical features such as columns acting as mullions with a cornice above. Not in fact Venetian, but used most emphatically by Palladio for the arcades of his Basilica at Vicenza (1549), the Venetian window found greater favour in the work of *Bramante, *Raphael, and *Scamozzi. Inigo Jones brought it to England, using it for the Queen's Chapel, Westminster (1623–7). *Hawksmoor took it up quirkily at All Souls' Library, Oxford (begun 1716), where he gave it Gothic dress outside, but its commonest usage was among the 18th-century Palladians.   APQ

Venice Venice's architectural history has been profoundly affected by its location and topography. Its site is an archipelago of around 100 islands in the centre of a shallow tidal lagoon. During the 5th–7th centuries it became a place of refuge from the 'barbarian' invasions of Italy. In AD 810 Venice became capital of the confederation of settlements that evolved into the Venetian Republic. The lagoon offered security, but presented many difficulties, including sourcing building materials and constructing foundations. The earliest buildings were of timber; later, bricks were made on the adjacent mainland, and stone came from Istria, a Venetian possession.

After the acquisition of the body of St Mark in AD 829, the city developed rapidly. Culturally, Venice retained close ties with Byzantium; the architecture of San Marco reflects this, although the Romanesque style was also influential. The city became a dense matrix of island-parishes, each with its church and square. By the 12th century the dominant typology was the 'palazzo-fontego', combining the residence of a noble family with the functions of warehouse and business offices. Since defence was not a consideration, these structures were characteristically open, with spacious arcades; several have survived, although heavily restored: Ca' Loredan, the Fondaco dei Turchi. Most early churches

San Marco and the Doge's
Palace, Venice (1094/1450)

were brick basilicas, with a freestanding bell-tower: Torcello cathedral, in the lagoon (mostly 11th century), is an early survivor.

Venice's wealth and power grew in the 13th and 14th centuries, primarily based on Mediterranean trade, with colonies in Cyprus, Crete, and the Aegean. Many monastic orders were established; the Dominicans and Franciscans built large new churches in a characteristic late Gothic style, all in brick, with stone detailing and open timber-trussed roofs. In the early quattrocento Venice established an empire on the Italian mainland, extending as far west as Bergamo. The resulting wealth was reflected in many fine palaces, with elegant stone tracery, symmetrical façades, and internal courtyards with open staircases; most have a tripartite plan, with a long central hall. Dozens have survived, including Ca' Foscari and the Ca' d'Oro. The reconstruction of the Palazzo Ducale (begun 1340, second phase begun 1422)

marks the apogee of the Venetian Gothic style, a unique response to the requirements of the Republic's form of government, and to its context on the edge of the lagoon.

The early Renaissance is marked by several influences: the works of *Alberti and *Brunelleschi; the continuing influence of the East; and the classical Roman legacy. The principal exponents were Pietro Solari Lombardo and Mauro *Coducci. Lombardo was initially a sculptor, but his S. Maria dei Miracoli is a brilliant solution on an extremely restricted site, with architecture and sculpture perfectly integrated. Coducci represents a more 'Brunelleschian' approach, and is noted for two contributions: the development of the palace façade; and the design of refined, centrally planned churches. The former culminates at the monumental Palazzo Vendramin Calergi, the latter at Santa Maria Formosa, a masterful series of hierarchical internal spaces. Several Scuole Grandi were rebuilt on a lavish scale, using the finest architects and artists of the era, including Coducci and the Bellinis.

The High Renaissance is represented by *Sansovino, *Sanmicheli, and *Palladio. Each made a distinctive contribution; Sanmicheli's powerfully modelled style (Palazzo Grimani) reflects his background as a military engineer. Sansovino arrived from Rome in 1527, and disseminated Roman principles of design, based on studying the classical legacy. His principal contributions were at San Marco, where he designed the new Mint (Zecca) and the Biblioteca Marciana, incorporating the widening of the Piazza San Marco. Palladio's works include three churches: San Francesco della Vigna, San Giorgio, and Il Redentore. Each became a new monumental element in the fabric of the city. The 16th century also saw extensive reclamation around the city's perimeter, notably at the Zattere and the Fondamente Nuove, increasing space, and reflecting the spirit of the age of urban improvements.

Baldassare *Longhena was the outstanding Venetian Baroque architect. He designed many palaces, of which two are outstanding: Ca' Rezzonico and Palazzo Pesaro, grandiose, self-confident, and extremely expensive. Santa Maria della Salute is his ecclesiastical equivalent: a monumental masterpiece of theatricality, dominating the entrance to the Grand Canal. Longhena's followers built several other notable Baroque churches: Sardi's Santa Maria del Giglio and his façade for Longhena's Scalzi; and Tremignon's San Moisè. All respond to the lagoon's light in their rich modelling, while representing the wealth of their noble benefactors. After the Baroque, the age of Enlightenment is represented in the work of Massari (the cool monumentality of Palazzo Grassi), Tommaso Temanza (La Maddalena), and Andrea Tirali (San Nicolo da Tolentino).

The Republic capitulated to Napoleon in 1797; for 50 years Venice was passed between France and Austria, finally joining unified Italy in 1866. The early 19th century was an era of eclecticism, with Gothic and Byzantine revivals as well as industrial architecture at Murano and the Giudecca. The arrival of the railway in 1846 ended Venice's isolation from the mainland. Considerable damage was inflicted in the 19th century by works of 'improvement', involving reclaiming canals and the cutting of new streets (the Strada Nuova).

The development of the Lido in the early 20th century led to a new typology, the grand hotel, represented by the Excelsior, in an eclectic Moorish style. The road bridge joined the rail causeway in 1930–33, terminating with a new 'white modern' multi-storey car park. The development of the industrial zone at Porto Marghera resulted in serious problems of environmental degradation. The 20th century is represented by the pavilions in the Biennale gardens, with works by Stirling, Josef Hoffmann, and Alvar Aalto. Inappropriate modern buildings have been balanced by the sensitive interventions of Carlo Scarpa, notably at Palazzo Querini Stampalia. Recent housing by Giancarlo de Carlo at Mazzorbo reinterprets the traditional vernacular of the lagoon villages. The city remains beset by flooding and the damaging effects of mass tourism, although there have been prodigious efforts of restoration since the disastrous floods in 1966. RJG

Goy, R. J., *Venice: the City and its Architecture* (1997)

Howard, D(eborah), *The Architectural History of Venice* (2002)

Lorenzetti, G., *Venice and its Lagoon* (1975)

Venturi, Robert Charles (1925–) US architect.

He came to fame with a contextual theory of architecture first demonstrated in the Vanna Venturi House (1959–64) and the Guild House (1961–6) in Philadelphia, and then articulated in *Complexity and Contradiction in Architecture* (1966).

Rethinking the lessons of his mentor, the architect Louis *Kahn (1901–74), Venturi rejected modernist claims to originality and autonomy of design in favour of ordinary and conventional forms which could mediate between a building's internal constraints of programme and its external constraints of physical, social, and historical context. This produced a rhetorically complex architecture of the 'building-board', in which a building's façade results from the 'contrast between the inside and the outside'.

Working with Denise Scott Brown, Venturi next analysed the urbanism of the American strip and its architecture of the 'decorated shed' in *Learning from Las Vegas* (1972, with Steven Izenour). The Sainsbury Wing, National Gallery, London (1991), is the best example outside the United States of Venturi and Scott-Brown's contextual approach to design.   CCM

Brownlee, D., DeLong, D., Hiesinger, K., *Out of the Ordinary* (2001)

vernacular architecture

Introduction: defining the vernacular The buildings that we customarily term 'architecture' represent only a minute fraction of the buildings of the world. No one knows exactly what that fraction might be, nor do we even know how many buildings there are as a whole. But it is likely that less than 5% of the world's buildings were and are architect-designed, and even if we include those created by the true 'architects'

or 'master-builders', the combined total is probably little more than 10% in total. *So what are the remainder, the majority of the world's buildings?* To which in broad terms we may reply that they are 'vernacular architecture'. That isn't likely to satisfy the educationalists and the architects, much less the politicians, in whose training there was little or no mention of the term. Inevitably, the questions arise:

What is vernacular architecture? What does the term mean? Why don't we call it what it is: primitive or folk building? Such adjectives as 'primitive', 'naïve', 'folk', 'intuitive' or 'native', and other attempts at identifying the buildings of people in different cultures, represent a superior, and largely Western, view. They are patronizing and simplistic, making little or no attempt at understanding the nature of the buildings or why whey are constructed in ways that are far removed from those of Western traditional or modern design. *So, what does it mean?*

The term 'vernacular' is applied to the language of the people of a culture, as distinct from the formal and specialized language of the educated elite. 'Vernacular architecture' may therefore be seen as 'the architectural language of the people' designed and built by the people of a culture for themselves and for their own use. *How about suburban and speculative building—is that vernacular when it is designed for the people?* This, it may be explained, is 'popular architecture', built *for* the people, but not *by* the people; it is not determined by their values nor to accommodate the spatial needs of the cultures for whom they have been erected, but by generalized ideas about their functional requirements.

If 'architecture' is designed by architects, and vernacular architecture is the buildings of the people—where do functional buildings like factories or warehouses fit in? Granted, they are often designed by architects, or by engineers and 'master builders'. Generally, we would identify them as 'functional architecture' (*see* FUNCTIONAL TRADITION, THE) although some examples built by

Masai structure, Kenya

communities for their own use can be considered as 'vernacular'. Vernacular architecture is rarely influenced by 'polite' or 'elite' architecture. Yet there are exceptions, such as the influence of Georgian symmetry on some buildings, and its use of classical proportions for windows and doors. Such questions are raised in the following discussion.

Economy and society *Under what circumstances are vernacular buildings constructed?* Making built structures implies sedentarism and settlement, which depends upon access to water, and suitable land for building and production. Therefore, vernacular buildings are usually constructed where there are resources for subsistence economies, such as small-scale fishing, the raising and pasturing of sheep, goats, cattle or other animals, or for working on the land as farmers in agriculture, raising edible plants and producing crops. So at one level they will build largely

to meet the nature of their 'economy', and at another level to meet the social needs of their families and communities.

If they are working together, presumably their houses are near each other. So how are vernacular buildings arranged? There are different kinds of arrangement, or settlement. Farmers may live in separate farmhouses on the farmers' respective lands. In these cases the settlements are 'dispersed', but it is more customary for houses to be grouped together, in small hamlets, villages, townships and eventually even in urban communities.

Have any attempts at classifying them been made? Some may be arranged in a 'linear' row, especially where they may follow a river or a road, as is often the case in central China, or they may be 'clustered' together, as is common in most parts of the world, for reasons of family relationships or for security, for instance. Often, as in England, these clustered

979

settlements may be 'nuclear', gathered around a church or manor house. Others have roads radiating from them, or converging on them: these are 'nodal' settlements.

Do these types occur in all parts of the world? They are very widespread, but linear settlements are usually to be found on communication routes of one kind or another, while nodal settlements are frequently market centres. But their form and size depend on many other factors, such as the size of the population, their relationships with neighbouring communities, their age, and the capacity of the land to support a population of particular size. *And what influences that?* Many factors help determine the size and form of a settlement, such as the nature of the natural environment. As we have noted, access to fresh water is essential, and this may be possible beside rivers, or only if wells are sunk. Settlements tend to be small in mountainous regions, though larger in the valleys, as in Nepal; they may be dispersed in the plains and steppe as in Russia and movable in the deserts, as is the case with the nomadic peoples of the Arabian peninsula. Prevailing climates are also important, influencing the kind of economy that is possible, which is often also affected or limited by the seasons—the monsoon period in India, for instance.

This helps explain the significance of economy, landscape and climate on settlements, but how do the 'social needs of families and communities' affect their nature? Apart from the pragmatic and functional aspects of the form of the settlement in relation to its economy and these environmental considerations, there are many factors that are important to every cultural group, that help to definite its character. These may include their religious beliefs and customs, and their related value systems. Some parts of the settlement may be sacred and others, such as cemeteries, may also be sanctified. Social structures are especially significant, with the buildings of the people of higher status often having required positions. So class and caste, gender and ancestry, may all be reflected in the settlement pattern and the forms of the buildings. Their size may be affected by marriage customs, such as exogamous marriage, when sons or daughters move to the dwellings of the in-laws.

If it is possible to identify these kinds of influence on vernacular settlement and architecture, why are they so varied, and not broadly similar within the classifications? Over a period of time, usually of at least three generations, traditions evolve which reinforce the characteristics noted above. For instance, mosques and communities in Islamic cultures of the Middle East are very different from the mosques and settlements of Muslim South East Asia. We may sometimes identify them by their political definitions, but cultures in countries such as India, the Philippines, or Indonesia can be numbered in their hundreds, and each one has a different tradition of building: its own vernacular architecture.

Building types and functions *Given that they are culturally different, aren't certain buildings common in type all over the world? Aren't housing needs fundamentally the same?* Although all cultures need dwellings, they take different forms dependent on the nature of the cultures that build them. One kind may be for a single nuclear family unit, as is common in western Europe and North America and the former 'colonies'. Another may be the 'compound', as can be found in northern India and sub-Saharan Africa, with individual dwelling units and stores constructed by each family within an encompassing wall. Some so-called 'house societies' build very large structures which house several families, as is found among the jungle peoples of the western Amazon. Others, such as the Iban of the great island of Borneo, build 'long-houses' which accommodate many families, each living in their own house unit but sharing communal spaces for work and leisure along their entire length.

These long-houses may be exceptional, but aren't most vernacular dwellings built as single-cell, 1-storey structures? It is true that single-storey buildings are to be found in most regions of the world, if there is sufficient land available. They are common among many agricultural societies, but some, as in Lower Saxony, build structures which have 2- or 3-storey dwellings at one end and with immense, single-volume spaces for the incorporation of animal stalls, stables, and stands for farm equipment at the other. Farms with long-standing territorial claims on the land may have been single-storeyed at first, with a second storey and loft above built at a later date. A farmhouse with a living-space developed from a large hall, bedrooms, kitchen, and scullery could be found in most parts of Europe. They may be differently serviced, with large cooking and heating stoves being widely used in eastern Europe and Scandinavia, where 'box beds' with cupboard-like doors were also customary. In compact villages and townships, houses are generally on two or three floors, served by stair-flights or winding stairs, the roofs sometimes being used for bedrooms illuminated by 'dormer' windows, and the ground floors may have shops.

Shops? That raises the question 'What other types of vernacular buildings are there?' There aren't any vernacular fire stations or airports, so what else do they build? The first buildings constructed after the dwellings are those that relate to the economy. For pastoral or herding economies these may consist of simple walled but roofless 'folds' or 'pounds' for protecting sheep or goats. Larger and stronger structures may be constructed for heavier animals: stables for horses with individual stalls and eating troughs or 'mangers' for each one, or accommodation for cows (in Scotland, 'byres'). Draught animals like shire horses, oxen, or yaks may be sheltered in separate structures, as are bulls, the walls and pillars curved to prevent the animals damaging themselves. Two-wheeled carts,

four-wheeled wagons and tractors may be garaged in open-fronted sheds, while ploughs, harrows and other farming equipment and tools will be stored in secure outbuildings.

Agricultural economies usually require barns or large stores for the crops. Some may have a 'threshing floor' where the corn may be 'threshed' with flails to separate the 'wheat from the chaff'. A 'threshold' may be inserted in the main doorway to prevent the loss of the threshed grain—the origin of the symbolic 'threshold' in many societies. Stores for particular field crops such as barley, rye, maize corn, and cellars for root crops such as yams, potatoes, swedes, turnips and many others, may be constructed according to the nature of the economy. Some stores are raised on mushroom-shaped 'staddle stones' or other frames to prevent rodents from getting at the crop, while others are raised to avoid the deleterious effects of damp. Loading openings may be differently placed from those used for obtaining the grain or other crop. Hay ricks and straw ricks, singular and often cylindrical granaries, are among the many kinds of farming structures that are to be found in every continent. The types of barns vary greatly, from the round barns of Illinois to the 'bank barns' of Austria and many other countries where hillsides provide access to the upper floors of barns built into the slopes.

So what about other supporting structures, as well as those of other economies? Do they have special buildings? They are too numerous to list. But some examples might include beehives and bee-skips, pigsties, pigeon lofts and dovecotes. Specialized buildings for certain crafts and building processes were also extensively constructed, including sawpits or sawing trestles for converting logs into planks, which are still used, for example, in Java. Lime kilns and lime pits were widespread, while stone-dressing sheds, blacksmithies, carpenters' shops and many other building-craft units are common. Different occupations require different buildings, such as the boat sheds, net and tackle stores of fishermen, as well as their open-sided fish gutting sheds. As for ancillary but necessary sanitary and cleansing structures, outdoor privies, wall-hung *garderobes*, bathing cells and communal washing places are widespread but little documented.

And the shops? These may be open and dismountable stalls in the markets of countless communities, open only on certain days. In their permanent forms shops are characteristic of nodal villages and townships. The 'shophouses' of Chinese migrants and settlers throughout South East Asia are among the most noted types. With relatively narrow frontages they are many rooms deep, with spaces allocated to living and to the receiving and storing as well as the selling of merchandise. In more urban settings land is less freely available and costlier at the centre of a nuclear settlement. Narrow frontages may reduce the rental, so shop-houses of a depth which includes both corridor and courtyard are customary.

That implies particular plans for their function, and raises the question 'Do vernacular builders work from plans?' If not, how do they know what arrangement to use? In the case of the shops these are often largely determined by the available space; from medieval times 'burgage plots', or pieces of land of similar or identical width and length, were of limited availability in the towns. To a considerable extent these exercised a control on the plans, especially where stores had to be accessible. Opportunities for more variety were apparently greater in the open country, but in every region particular types and arrangements can be detected, a testament to the working efficiency of traditional building types, adapted to the specific requirements of a site. Variants may be subtle, but significant for a householder and family, while being in accord with the norms of the local tradition.

How do they arrive at the house plans? Why are some dwellings circular in plan? Aren't they unsuitable for the furniture, such as beds and tables? The plans of individual structures are determined partly by the use to which the buildings are to be put, and partly by the nature of the materials used. Square and rectangular plans can be achieved with lengths of timber, but circular plans are difficult with wood, without skilled craftsmanship and the expenditure of a considerable amount of time. One-to-one plans are often drawn upon the ground with the material to be used, or a manageable equivalent, such as poles. In square-planned buildings the furniture is usually made of wood and it fits relatively easily if the spaces are large enough. Sometimes, as in Ireland and parts of France, some of the furniture, such as tables, is made to fold down against a wall, to be opened when needed for use. Built-in furniture is not uncommon in some traditions, such as the box-beds of Scandinavia and central/eastern Europe, sometimes built over broad drawers, or the roof of a cellar stairway.

Circular plans are often drawn out by the simple use of a peg and length of rope. In the case of circular plan dwelling units, they are usually constructed of moulded clay, which makes them as strong as the pottery that they resemble. Couch beds, steps, platforms for utensils and for serving food are also frequently moulded in the clay, often as extensions from the wall.

Talking of extensions, is there any principle governing them? The plans and forms of many building traditions have changed and continue do so over time. Additional spaces may be required as families increase, and occupations may make greater demands in terms of storage. An entrance porch is quite commonly added in some traditions, with access to a storage area over the porch being possible without entering the domestic area. In many regions, such as Valencia province in Spain, and in numerous maritime areas, a room over the entrance hall and porch may have a full-size door opening which enables the loading of produce onto a waiting vehicle. Other extensions may be constructed at the side or rear of a dwelling, often under a pentice, or 'lean-to' monopitch roof. The roof structure is usually of wood but the walls may be of timber, brick, or stone, retaining the overall rectangular plan with add-ons.

Presumably they aren't possible with circular-plan buildings? It is true that such extensions are not easily achieved on circular-plan buildings, although twin-cylinder dwellings were developed by the rural Hausa of Nigeria and certain Indian societies. However, cultures using circular-planned cylindrical units generally place them in an enclosed space, or 'compound', which may take several other structures of a similar kind but of different sizes, for the accommodation of other members of the household, or for storing grain, stabling animals and other uses.

So why did circular plan buildings evolve? They are among the oldest of plan types; Paleolithic and Bronze Age buildings frequently had circular plans, judging from the archaeological evidence, such as the two thousand or so Bronze Age sites on Dartmoor alone, apart from those in Brittany and elsewhere in Europe. There appear to be several reasons for this persistent circular plan. One is that drawing the plan with rope and stick can be achieved very quickly. Many nomadic peoples still use circular-plan structures, with straight or curved poles converging at the apex, like the *tipi* of the Native American peoples of the Great Plains, or the temporary shelters of several peoples of the 'Horn of Africa'. Such structures require the minimum of joints. Many permanent buildings also have circular plans. Often they will have a conical roof, with radiating poles resting on the circular walls. Such *rondavels*, as they are termed in South Africa, are 'cone-and-cylinder' constructions which are to be found among many South African peoples, like the Sotho. The cylindrical walls are often constructed of packed clay, and have the character of pottery.

Living in caves and tents *What about cave dwellings? Perhaps they are not vernacular architecture because they are not constructed?* In the strictest sense that is probably true, but 'found architecture' may be regarded as a separate category. *But what can be called 'found' architecture?* To consider this we have to go back to the beginnings of mankind. Where did early human beings live? Where were they living when their cultural differentiations evolved? *Are you thinking of 'cave men'—and cave paintings, for instance?* Indeed, and cave dwellings are not to be ignored, or considered only as part of our primeval past. On the contrary, they are fascinating because they represent the oldest traditions in human accommodation which still survive and are still in use.

But they aren't used nowadays, are they? The estimates of over 60 million cave dwellers today are probably too low, as some 40 million people live in caves in China alone. There are a great many different kinds of cave dwelling in China, some being in natural caves, others excavated from the loess soil. They are very common in Shanxi and Hunan provinces, but many are to be found in other regions, too. A particular type is the 'shaft' cave dwelling: a deep pit is excavated to a depth equivalent to a 3-storey house; then caves are excavated into the walls of the pit, and deep under the surrounding land. After excavation, they are often closed in with a frontal wall, which will have both a door and a high-level light and air ventilation grid. Scores of such shafts may be excavated, but the land above can still be used for cultivation, or for pasturing animals. The method is so practical and economical with natural resources that in China 'constructed caves' are built almost in imitation of rows of cave dwellings in a rock wall. They are built with barrel-vault roofs, and then covered with large quantities of mud and rock, which provide the roof pasture. Caves of the shaft type are also to be found in Matmata in southern Tunisia and in western Libya. They too have dwellings carved out of the rock walls, sometimes with carved stairs within, leading to an upper floor.

Do you find both the natural and the excavated caves together? This is quite common, but probably the most spectacular examples are in Cappadocia, in central Anatolia, Turkey. In this region the landscape is weird, with tall pinnacles of soft rock which in some instances are as high as a skyscraper. Some have natural caves, but the majority of caves have been enlarged, excavated, hollowed out, and sculptured in many different ways. Centuries ago the cave complexes were dug by Christians fleeing from persecution. They carved them in the internal form of great churches, painted with devotional murals. Today many farmers carve out their own dwellings, granaries, bird houses, and stables. Their houses are usually on at least two levels, pecked out with an adze by the farmers themselves. In this area there are two 'underground cities', large complexes of dwellings on many levels below ground. But these are no longer used.

What about Europe: are there any cave dwellings there? There certainly are. Many are to be seen in the Canary Islands, generally well made and tidily kept by their occupiers. There are also large complexes of cave dwellings in mainland Spain, those of Guadix, for example. This is a hilly region north of Seville, and the houses are of great variety and originality, carved out of the rock face, with the debris from the carving used to build auxiliary walls or stores, etc. A lot of chimneys are to be seen rising from them. They were occupied largely by Gypsies, as were those of Granada which were made just beyond the limits of the city wall. Others are to be found at Cuevas de Almanzora in Andalusia, and at Paterna near Valencia, where a forest of chimneys and ventilators dot the town square like a chessboard. They mark the dwellings dug out underneath the plaza.

Anywhere else in Europe? Of course. Many are still occupied in places such as Brantôme (the Dordogne,

France), near Saumur (France), or Matera in southern Italy. Often they do not appear like caves, for the carved façades have been made up and painted to look like conventional houses in front of a rock face. But behind the façades they are cave dwellings. Others are to be found in different countries—those in Kinver, Staffordshire, England, were still occupied in the 1970s.

Are there any other examples of found architecture? A related type is the 'rock shelter', more of an opening in the rock, like a large mouth, than a cave. Some rock shelters are of immense size, and centuries ago a whole village might be protected in one rock shelter, as was the case with Native Americans in Colorado and Arizona in the United States, as in Mesa Verde and Canyon de Chelly. But they are not used for living in now.

And any others? How about trees? There is not a lot of evidence of trees being used for housing, though there are some examples in New Guinea, and a few in southern central Africa. Perhaps the greatest use of trees for dwelling has been in the Philippines, especially on Mindanao island. But these rare examples have seldom been documented.

People had to travel a lot in those early times before agriculture. But they spread all over the world, so how did they make their shelters? Often they made them once, and then travelled with them, as nomadic peoples still do. Some nomad groups were hunters and gatherers, tracking down animals where they could, and collecting those nuts, roots, and leaves which they found edible. The Bushmen people, also called the San or the Basarwa, of Namibia and Botswana, were such nomads until very recently. They would build their shelters out of brushwood, covered with grass. Often they would dismantle the simple hut after use and leave it, rather than be encumbered by carrying its parts. But many others had domesticated animals like camels, and used them to carry the framework. Often the women assemble the frame and then cover it with skins, or mats made of grass, as do the Gabra of Kenya, and many other similar peoples.

When I think of nomads I think of tents. How are tents used? We have already mentioned the *tipi* of the Native Americans of the plains, with their cone of crossed poles providing the frame. This would be covered with a big tent cloth. They were originally made of bison (buffalo) skins, but for a long time they have been made of canvas strips, sewn together in a great arc, with extensions to make the flaps into which long poles are inserted to regulate the opening at the peak, for ventilation or smoke emission. *But no longer used?* They were still used by the Blackfeet in the 1930s, and recently there has been a return to tradition by some 'nations'. The *tipi* is still an important symbolic building and frequently seen at 'Pow-Wows', or inter-tribal gatherings. This form of tent structure is also used by the Sami (Lapp) of northern Scandinavia.

What about those that are called 'black tents'? This is the type which is to be found with many variations in the Middle East and North Africa. It consists of a 'velum', or large tent cover, which is made of strips of cloth from wool or goat hair. The strips are woven on ground looms by the women, and they are then sewn together along their edges. The cloth is the main protection against the desert sun when the nomads stop travelling. It is held up, in some instances, by poles which support a ridge-piece, or two or three ridge-pieces in line. Among peoples like the Lurs or Quashgai of Iran, the tents are box-like in form, but some Bedouin tents are broader and lower in contour, with poles of different length to provide the form of the tent-cloth. The cloth is held in tension across the ridge by ropes attached to the edges, which are held in position by pegs driven into the ground. Some tribes have bands of coarse webbing stretched across the ridge and pegged in position, over which the tent-cloth is laid. *How are they carried?* In most instances, the tent-using tribes are camel nomads, and the camels

carry the burden. The women assemble and dismantle the tents, which they own, and which they renew by weaving freestrips to replace old ones in sequence.

Why do they use a black tent when it is so hot in the desert? If the strips are washed, they lose the natural oils which are important for flexibility, and necessary in sudden rains as they contract and close up the weave, making it water-resistant. But the Touareg, who use a similar tent, do not sew woven cloths but use the skins of dead camels for their covers. *What about the yurt?* Among the most widely distributed building types, the *yurt* is employed by nomads from the Caspian Sea to Outer Mongolia, where it is called a *ger*; the type has several different names, but most are similarly built on a circular plan. Lattices of sticks held with leather thongs are opened out and about six are used to define the circle, the ends being attached to a door-frame. From this lattice ring poles are inclined to support a hoop at the crest of a domed or conical roof. It makes a most effective shelter and may be used for two or three months on one site in the steppe or hills, before the nomads move on with their herds.

Are there many nomads today? Probably a few million, but they form a very small proportion of the world's population, the majority of whom live in settlements with permanent buildings, which we should consider now.

Buildings of earth and stone *Soil, rock, and timber—they've all been mentioned in connection with dwellings. So what about the importance of materials?* There is little, if anything, that is more fundamental to the form, strength, and durability of a vernacular building, or of its parts and the spaces they define, than the materials from which it is constructed. We have seen that the environment is important to the process of settling, but the environment is also a major determinant of materials. The landforms may be shaped by rocks and stone, the humidity, rainfall or soils. Soils in turn may vary greatly, whether they are desertic and sandy, clay and muddy, friable or compactible, fertile or not. Most indigenous cultures employ the materials that are available to their settlements, developing methods of using them to achieve the accommodations they need. As the capacity of some materials is limited, this may require both ingenuity and compromise, the builders responding creatively to the qualities of the materials they obtain.

Which materials are most commonly used? Earth is the most readily available and the most widely used material. At least a third of all the world's buildings are constructed substantially of earth, and if one bears in mind that brick is basically earth, some would argue that more than half the buildings in the world are of earth in one form or another.

But if it differs so much, what methods are most appropriate? Over the centuries, even over millennia, cultures have learned how best to make the earth type prevailing in their area suitable for construction. If the earth is laterite it has a high proportion of iron in it, and it hardens like concrete when exposed to the air. Laterites are common in west Africa, and methods have been developed for compacting or moulding it. Desert soils can be compacted by the technique of 'rammed earth' (*see* TERRE PISÉ), where earth within a wooden frame is tamped until it is hard. Then the frame can be removed and used for the tamping of the next section of earth wall.

What about earth bricks? One method widely used in the Middle East is that of adobe, or earth compressed in wooden moulds to make adobes, or bricks, which are dried in the sun. Sometimes a natural fibre or aggregate is mixed with it, as in the old adage 'You can't make bricks without straw.' Clay is also used for a method common in northern Europe, called 'wattle and daub'—a lattice of wattles, or thin sticks, into which mud is forced and the whole is plastered over with mud plaster. The frame is of timber, usually oak.

That means that wood is important even when building with earth? Often it is, and especially for spanning the walls to make a roof and, often, a ceiling. Houses which are built mainly of earth have good thermal properties.

You mean that they are 'warm in winter and cool in summer'? Exactly. The reason is not the temperature of the earth itself, which can vary, but rather the transmission time of the external temperature through thick walls of earth to the interior. A wall may be heated by the sun during the day, but by the time the heat has passed through the wall to the interior, the exterior is cool and the interior warmed by the transmitted heat. In the winter, internal heat from a domestic fire is retained and only very slowly transmitted to the exterior. Thermally it is very good. But it is a compression material, which means it can take a great deal of weight, and is also heavy in itself, so upper layers compress the clay layers below.

Isn't that good? Yes it is, but it has very little tensile strength, so earth is not easily used to span a space, as it will collapse easily. Certain methods can be used, including one of making dried blocks of earth for walls, which are then shaped with a vaulted, slightly narrower base than top dimensions, so that they can be stacked in the form of an arch. This means that a space can be spanned and the weight is transmitted to the feet of the arch which rest on the outside walls. A succession of these arches, with blocks of slightly different dimensions so that they interlock, together create a vault.

Earth can be found almost anywhere, so it must be a useful material. True, but the various earths have properties of their own, and some are suitable for making very high buildings, up to 10 storeys or so, as in the Yemen or parts of Morocco. But others have different particle sizes, or binding materials like slate fragments in them, which mean that they perform in diverse ways which the vernacular builders have discovered over generations, each developing the methods most suitable for building with the material they find. *Are there any other problems with earth buildings?* Yes, the principal one being the porosity of earth which allows water to penetrate it, and its tendency to collapse if over-saturated. For this reason, earth buildings may be 'rendered' with a thin layer of plaster, which helps keep the rain out and sheds it from the surface. Lime plaster is often used and gypsum plaster, where it can be found, being used on walls and vaults in northern Tunisia, for instance. Gypsum sometimes has deposits of other minerals in it, which makes it very strong when used in construction, clay walls being supported between columns of gypsum in the Ademuz region of Valencia, Spain.

How about rocks? Isn't stone even more useful for building? Where it is readily available, stone may often be used in vernacular buildings. But even in a big city like London, which has thousands of old stone buildings, the stone had to be brought there from the Cotswolds, or from Portland in Dorset, transported over considerable distances. So it is often available only for prestigious architecture of the wealthy and the powerful. Yet, as in the Cotswolds, and many parts of England on the limestone belt which spreads from Devon to Yorkshire, lumps of stone of convenient size for vernacular building may be found. It may have to be worked with tools, which demands time and the appropriate skills. 'Ashlar' is stone building constructed of 'dressed', or squared and trimmed stone blocks. Rubble stone of irregular shapes is cheaper, sometimes being supported by ashlar construction at the corners where walls meet or end.

What is 'dry stone walling' then? The term refers to the process, there being no mixing of mortar with water. This type of building is believed to be very ancient, dating from the Bronze Age in much of Europe. It is admired for its simplicity, economy and for being built by skilled workers. Domes are often constructed in dry stone over circular- or square-plan single cells. Some

are parabolic rather than semicircular in section, giving greater head-room and transferring the weight even more effectively to the walls. Parabolic constructions can also be found made of earth blocks, as in Harran in eastern Turkey and parts of Syria. They are similar in structure but are made with a mud mortar, as are virtually all mud block buildings.

How about bricks? Aren't they the same? Bricks are often of very similar size, and are generally horizontal blocks of earth which have been shaped by hand, or pressed into moulds. They are usually of the same dimensions in any one situation, even though brick sizes differ in various countries. They are 'fired' or 'burnt' in a special oven, known as a brick kiln, which makes them hard and suitable for making regular constructions of all shapes and sizes. The kiln might be of the 'clamp' type, being made of the bricks that are going to be fired, and is dismantled after the firing has taken place. This type is found in places like Sudan, or north India, where brick building may have been developed by colonists. A large and efficient type is the 'Bull's trench' kiln, which is constructed on a circular or oval plan, and is continually in use.

So how old is 'fired' brick construction? Fired bricks were certainly used by the Romans, who may have been responsible for their widespread distribution in Europe and the Middle East. They were little known in Britain until the 14th century, when the Dutch techniques of brick building were introduced. Like blocks of stone, bricks are usually laid in 'bonds' or particular patterns that ensure greater stability to the walls. Usually they may alternate 'stretchers', or bricks laid lengthwise, with 'headers', or bricks that are laid to the depth of the wall thickness. Many patterns using these methods are employed, often used decoratively and always in a manner that ensures that there are no continuous cracks between layers of bricks which might make the wall vulnerable to collapse. Usually the bricks are adhered to each other by the use of mortar, often a lime-based material, applied with a trowel to the contacting surfaces.

Timber, grasses and palms *Earth may be one of the world's most available materials, but it's lifeless. What about the living resources, like trees and grasses?* They are fundamental, and they come in literally tens of thousands of varieties. Conifers are softwood species which often grow in mountainous regions, and are to be found extensively in the Nordic countries and in central and eastern Europe. In those areas there is a strong timber building system—horizontal log construction, known also as *Blockbau*, and more commonly, as 'log cabin'. It is a compression system, with the combined weight of the logs laid on top of each other to make a wall. Where one wall meets another the logs are 'notched', so that each log sits in the notch of another. These have to be cut, which may be done simply with axes.

Over time skills are developed in the making of the notching, like the 'dovetail', which ensure that there are few gaps between logs, and the joints are secure at the corners.

Do they take the bark off first? Sometimes, but many buildings are made of round logs with the bark still on. This helps to close gaps between logs, which are also packed with moss, earth, or small stones. If the builders have the tools and the time, they may strip off the bark and 'square' the timbers, making flat walls, though they are still notched at the corners. Often the log building will be lifted on piers of stone or other material to prevent the interiors from rising damp. *Who first thought of the log cabin?* We don't know, but it is likely that it originated in Russia and spread from there. Perhaps the most remarkable log buildings are to be found in northern Russia, including the great log churches of Kizhi island.

When Europeans colonized North America they brought their building techniques with them, but for pioneers the quickest building method for a permanent structure was log construction, probably introduced by Scandinavians but also by Germans and central Europeans. The British never used the system at home, but they rapidly adopted it in the new American territories. Regional techniques developed, such as the 'Red River' method used in Canada, where trimmed logs are dropped between slotted vertical corner posts, so that notching is not necessary and the building has no projecting ends of logs.

Did any people use logs vertically for their building, or were they always horizontal? Almost all log construction is horizontal, but in Australia where the eucalyptus 'gum tree' is common, 'slabbys' or slab huts of vertical split logs were constructed (*see also* STAVE CHURCHES). This method was also employed in the building of many of the great woolsheds used for housing and shearing sheep. *Wood is used all over the world, but in a great many parts it isn't in the log cabin form. So what about the other systems?* First, we should note that log construction is found in Turkey, and places as far removed from Europe as Kashmir. There is evidence that in the past it was employed in Japan. But Japanese vernacular architecture is usually constructed using timber framing, and this is evident even in very prestigious buildings like the Katsura Palace.

Generally we find framing systems use hardwoods, which have both compressive and tensile strength, so that they can be used in many ways. Oak is particularly appreciated in Britain where it was cut and carved while still 'green' and then allowed to twist or take any natural form as it dried out. When used in the structure it became increasingly hard, 'like iron' as owners often say.

Ash is another hardwood much used in Europe, but also in north Africa and western Asia. After removing the bark, the hardwoods can be sawn lengthwise to produce a variety of building elements of different lengths and thicknesses. These can be assembled by cutting 'joints' which may be of the 'mortise-and-tenon', 'scarf', 'lap', or other types, depending on the framework to be used and the loads or stresses it may take. Hardwoods have both compressive and tensile strength, so that they can be used in many ways. Most systems employ posts at corners and intervals along the walls, which are linked by horizontal beams at both the sill and eaves levels. To ensure stability, corner bracing and diagonal braces that make use of the principle of the rigidity of triangulation are employed. In the English timber-frame tradition this was often used decoratively.

Was decoration usual? Grid-like framing is used in some central European traditions, most dramatically in Lower Saxony, Germany. The spaces between the grid components are filled with wattle-and-daub or brick 'nogging', and in Germany with decorative brick patterns of various kinds, often with many on the same building. But the wooden framing was often decorated as well, with carved ornamentation especially on specific details. Since this was more expensive, it is usually to be found on the houses of the wealthier merchants. In many cases, in Britain, across Europe, and even in Venice, we may see houses with their upper levels 'jettied' or projecting, their walls being supported by cross beams, the ends of which are often carved.

What about the roofs? Did they use logs? Occasionally on smaller buildings we may find log roofs, but generally the roof is framed in timber. The roof frame customarily makes use of triangulation, the inclination of the side roof planes being at 30 to 45 degrees, and meeting at a ridge. But in some traditions a succession of roof 'trusses' is used, with rafters meeting but not necessarily supporting a ridge. Depending on factors such as weight, spans, wind, and snow-loads, among others, central 'king-posts', wind-braces, and other elements maybe employed; purlins, or horizontal beams used lengthwise at intervals along the roof

planes, strengthen the structure and give support for the roof cladding.

Well-clad buildings *What is used for cladding?* As in all aspects of the vernacular, the cladding system employed depends on the materials that are available. Thatching, or the use of grasses, straw, and leaves for roof covering is widely applied. In Europe this was frequently of wheat straw, gathered after harvest. It was still widely used until mechanization on the farms destroyed the wheat straw. Other grasses are used, and rushes or reeds are effectively employed. In other parts of the world, as in much of South East Asia, palm thatch is used, the palm fronds being re-sewn so that they all face in one direction to produce a 'tile'. The tiles are then laid horizontally, partly overlapping the layer below—similar to the layering of straw thatch. Other kinds of thatching exist, such as the use of leaves. In central Africa the *mongongo* leaves are frequently used, as they are large and flat, and they shed water readily. In some parts of the world, including Indonesia, lengths of thin bamboo may be used like thatch for roof cladding.

Is bamboo used for anything else? Definitely; it is one of the world's most widely used materials, although it often grows in areas where it is used very little, as in much of the Amazon basin. Technically bamboo is a grass, and is a major building material throughout South East Asia, the Pacific islands, and many other regions: Ecuador and Colombia in South America for instance. Bamboo is a tensile material, which makes it ideal for bending, or for use in spanning roofs. Some varieties are thin and cane-like; others are thicker with some even having stems as thick as tree trunks. They are unique in being light, but naturally formed in chambers, which gives them their strength and flexibility. On some Pacific islands buildings are almost exclusively of bamboo, which provides the supporting frame, the roof spans, and interwoven covers for roofs and walls. It is also used for wall cladding, or as shutters which can be rolled as the weather or the temperature changes. Unlike hardwoods, bamboos grow quickly, so they make an excellent renewable resource.

Is wood used for cladding, and any other materials? In regions where there are great forests, as in much of central Europe and the United States, especially in the Appalachianss, flat boards of wood are used, known as 'shingles' and in the United States as 'shakes'. Basically, they are boards as little as 5 cm or up to 20 cm (2–8 inches) wide, which are affixed to battens attached to the roof rafters with wooden pegs; nails may be sharper and stronger, but they rust over time and cease to hold the shingles in position. Like thatch, they are placed in layers, and overlap up to two-thirds of the layer below. This ensures protection from water seepage after rain or snow, and also adds weight to resist the effect of wind. *How are the shingles made?* The shake-maker uses an axe to split the shakes off a log, held on end. They can be made by sawing, but it takes more time.

Shingles sound as if they are like wooden tiles. Exactly, they are the equivalent of flat clay tiles. They are not as vulnerable to fire as thatch, but fired clay tiles are fire resistant. The Romans were probably responsible for their spread; Roman, Spanish, and Chinese tiles are usually semicircular in section, and are laid with the curved vault-form uppermost, and with a linking inverted tile laid between. This ensures that there is no gap to let rainwater on to the roof: it drains into the inverted tiles and flows into a 'gutter' or into a barrel to be saved. So that they can be laid in layers, tiles are often slightly tapered, enabling the next layer to fit over them. A simpler form of tile became common, which was flat but which often had a lip at one end so that it could be hung over the roof battens. These produce a flatter surface, and we can see them extensively used on suburban housing, as well as in the vernacular.

Are there any other types of cladding? Several, though most use similar principles. Slates, for instance, are tiles

of natural slate which can be split in thin sheets—we see these in the vernacular traditions of Wales, Cornwall, Quercy in southern France, and wherever slate occurs. Limestone is also sometimes used, depending on the type of stone. In the Cotswolds of England, blocks of stone would be stood in the open air during winter, and water poured over them frequently. This caused them to freeze in icy conditions, and to split into sections which made useful roof tiles ('Stonesfield slate'). But there are many other types of cladding—made from interwoven broad strips of flattened bamboo for instance, as found in the Pacific islands. Again, it's the availability of the resource that is significant.

Why is cladding so important? All buildings are constructed to provide shelter, no matter what other functions they serve, so cladding is important. Ideally, it should be a good insulation against extreme heat or cold, it should take and discharge the loads of snow or heavy rain and hail, but it also should offer protection against high winds. It may have to cover a simple conical or pitched roof, but often it has to accommodate differing roof profiles or extensions to a building, without being vulnerable at the meeting of building forms.

For example? Where thatch and stone meet has to be very skilfully crafted. A thatched roof might meet a gable wall, or a chimney might project through the thatch, each causing a problem of water penetration. Stone chimneys on old thatched buildings often have projecting ledges of stone or slate. These are to throw the rainwater away from the most vulnerable point. The same technique is used, for example, in the Asir region of south-western Arabia, where layers of projecting stone slabs or tiles cast shade on the walls and help to keep them cool, and also repel water from the mud walls in seasonal rains.

So climate is significant in its effect on the design of vernacular buildings. As climates differ, so do the building methods that come to terms with climate in specific cases. It may be a matter of the overall design of the building. For example, in many parts of the Middle East, including the traditional housing of Iraq, the house may be constructed around a central courtyard. This provides a shaded area at all times of the day, and a form of loggia may be constructed in the parts that receive the most sun. Often the building form plays a considerable part in climate modification. Cubic houses with square plan and flat roofs are found in hot, dry regions, where the form offers the least exposure to the sun, and simple gargoyles release the water from the roof in the rare rains. Painting the walls white, as in southern Spain or the Greek islands, helps to reflect the sunlight and keep the interiors cool. A structure called a *badgir* or 'wind-scoop' can be found on the roofs of buildings from Egypt to Pakistan. It gathers cool air from above the roof and transmits it to lower levels of the interior, and then exhausts it.

So what about people who live in hot and humid regions? Air circulation is very important, and the buildings are often raised on poles or 'stilts' to get the benefit of air movement. Open roof gables ensure the movement of air, but the roof slopes help shed storm-water. In climates such as you may find in South East Asia and the Philippines, such methods are common. The stilt houses are also effective in protecting people in seasonal floods, and you may find these too in tropical South America. Some cultures build houses on piles over lake or sea water, especially if they have a fishing economy.

But floods can be disastrous. What can be done about disasters? Very little can be done about disasters, except to defend the buildings against them. This may mean careful siting of houses so that they are not vulnerable to landslips or volcanic eruptions, as is the case in Central America. Certain regions are known to be seismic and prone to earthquakes, but their occurrence is still unpredictable. People in some vulnerable areas

have developed techniques to meet the impact of earthquakes: in Kashmir, for instance, a form of log construction is used which permits a 'loose fit', allowing a building to receive a seismic shock without collapsing.

What about earth construction and the terrible loss of life and buildings in earthquakes in Tangshan in China and Bam in Iran? Could nothing be done?

As we have noted, earth is among the most widely used of materials, but it can be vulnerable to heavy flooding, as in Bangladesh, or to earthquakes. Much research was done on this in the 1980s, and various methods were recommended of economically making earth buildings safer, such as using wire mesh in the mud construction, which greatly reduces the risk of collapse. But little notice was taken of these suggestions, and of course they have to be communicated to the vulnerable cultures, who must be assisted in introducing them to their traditional techniques. *So how are these traditions passed on?*

Passing on traditions This is a fundamental issue, and it relates to the persistence of traditions and the means by which they are passed on to successive generations. We cannot be sure how long the Inuit have been building iglus, because they are ephemeral by nature, melting with the snows. But we do have archaeological evidence of the use of cave dwellings in the Ice Age, and much on the building of structures in stone and earth in different parts of the world. There is biblical evidence of the antiquity of tents, and much to reveal that some traditions go back hundreds, even thousands, of years. This is because the functions, the forms, the preparation of the materials, the skills and techniques in using them, and the underlying significance and meaning of the buildings to those who use them, have been 'handed down'. The phrase covers many means of transmission.

What kinds of means would they use? Depending in part on what is being transmitted, an elder may instruct a member of a younger generation verbally. But he or she is more likely to demonstrate, or to instruct by doing, encouraging the novice to imitate but also to learn why such a method or function is employed. Often devices are used to aid the memory; songs or catches may be sung, maxims and axioms recited and repeated, 'tricks of the trade' shown and explained.

Isn't all that rather boring? No, because it assists the younger members of a culture, a tribe, or a sub-cultural group to respect those with knowledge and ability, and it makes them proud when they achieve the effects for themselves. Admittedly some things may be drudgery, such as preparing the floor in a rondavel, but other techniques induce delight in craftsmanship, and on a larger plane they gain a sense of identity with the group.

Surely the sense of identity is reinforced by other means: decoration, for example. True, but it is, by definition, different for every culture. Many of the world cultures use decoration, not merely to make their houses more attractive, but because the decorations have meaning for the group. In some instances the decoration may be very bold and large. Among the best known are the paintings of the façades and the courtyard walls of the Ndebele of southern Africa. These are painted by the women, who may re-paint them every year, using cheap house paints, or sometimes mixing their own. The motifs they use vary greatly, depending on the family and what it values. For instance, some have images based on the buildings of the cities—but they prefer to live where they are.

It seems that there are more decorated buildings in Africa than elsewhere. There are certainly many peoples that do use decoration, like the Sotho, who probably influence other peoples like the Tswana and the Pedi. Often they use zoomorphic, or animal, shapes and motifs, but abstract and geometric patterns are also popular. To do this the walls need to be smoothly rendered with clay to take the paint, although some

peoples who build with blocks of stone or adobe use them in a patterned way, for example with chevrons. *So what do the patterns mean?* That depends on the society concerned. Chevrons or zigzag rows often signify water among some groups, especially if it is scarce. Others use the chevron to symbolize fire, while for another South African tribe, the Shona, they symbolize women and their domain. *Are some motifs or designs used throughout the world?* Certain shapes can be traced in most continents, like the star, the wheel, the spiral for example. All these have a centre and a periphery, and in most instances a radial character too, which is sometimes a clue to their meaning. But we attach our own meanings to shapes, which can be very different from those of other cultures. Consider the swastika: because of its use by the Nazis it is still associated with evil in many Western countries. Yet it has been employed for at least four millennia, in every part of Asia as a symbol of good fortune, and among the Hindus as symbolic of Vishnu. Like virtually all other motifs, whether they are derived from the heavens, animals, flowers, or human attributes, they may be painted, moulded, carved or a combination of these.

But why don't some cultures use decoration or ornament? Certain materials and structures do not encourage decoration. Bamboo, for example, cannot be carved, but flattened strips can be woven and may have a meaning that we don't recognize. Many cultures make buildings entirely of adobe blocks or rammed earth, while others employ interwoven canes or reeds. These do not always inhibit decoration: we can even see grass or reed thatch used decoratively on the ridges of houses in Britain. Mural painting, or painting on walls apart from colour-wash, is traditionally quite rare in western Europe, although in parts of eastern Europe, such as Romania, such decoration was widespread.

But if they don't use decoration does it mean that the buildings don't have any symbolic meaning? Not at all. For most cultures their buildings have meaning and often this is profound, as is obviously the case with the places of worship of many religions. Though our attention is frequently drawn to the major cathedrals and mosques, we should be aware that country churches and chapels, village mosques and Hindu temples, and many forms of shrines throughout the world are as significant in their symbolism and sacred values as the large-scale buildings that are recorded in architectural histories. But even the simplest of houses may have cosmic associations: the roof or ceiling corresponding with the sky or the heavens, and the walls, particularly in a circular-plan dwelling, symbolizing the earth and the limits of the horizon. Such cosmic symbolism is characteristic of the *hogan*, or dwelling of the Navajo, a Native American people in Arizona. This may be built of logs, poles and earth, blocks of stone, or modern materials, but it carries this cosmic meaning.

A number of cultures, especially those which build large conical roofs, place particular emphasis on a central pole or column, sometimes known as the *axis mundi*, the axis of the world, which links the heavens with the earth. Some buildings are anthropomorphic, like the great meeting houses of the Maori of New Zealand, which represent the ancestor of the tribal group, with the ridge seen as the central spine, the rafters as the ribs, and the barge-boards that define the roof at the façade being viewed as the arms and hands. They are very richly carved, as well as being painted, while inside there are supporting figures that symbolize the ancestral lineage of each family, and panels in between woven by the women which have many associated meanings. *Do they depend on the past or are they still being built?* The meanings are part of the traditions, and are passed on to succeeding generations, and as the Maori are regaining their lands new meeting-houses are being built, with the carving tradition kept very much alive.

But if that is so, why have so many traditions died? They have been lost, where this is the case, because the younger generation has often been obliged to leave the home-site and live in the destitute fringes of the city. They have not been driven to do so by the members of their society, but by economic forces which serve the multi-nationals, the West, and the interests which have sought globalization at the expense of rural and indigenous peoples. In the process, local skills, techniques, and values have been threatened and frequently lost. In some of the informal settlements encircling the cities of the developing world contact has been maintained with the homelands, and in such instances skills and forms have been transmitted to the peri-urban edge, as was the case in the *gecekondus* of Turkey. But the drive towards multiple replication of mass housing, such as we are witnessing in China, with no reference to the desires or traditions of the peoples concerned is proving to be highly damaging.

Would conservation of vernacular architecture make a difference? No doubt it would, but the decision as to what is conserved is usually made on aesthetic grounds, or on the 'importance' of the building in its scale, its history of the person or people associated with it. This places the emphasis on the wealthy and the historic or the beautiful in the eyes of the conservationist, and does not help the ordinary people and their buildings; in fact it may work against them and their interests. *Do open-air museums compensate for this?* Only to a limited extent. They certainly help people to respect aspects of the vernacular, although the tendency is often to conserve the special and the finest, which tends to devalue the more common forms of building. But the main problem with such museums is that they are nostalgic, often with staff dressed in period costumes. They are always looking back at the past rather than at the present, let alone the future of the vernacular. *How about world heritage sites?* Those which conserve vernacular settlements, such as Hongcun in Anhui, China, or Visby island in Denmark, undoubtedly give a greater sense of the reality of places, because people are still living and working in them, though largely for the tourist trade. Eco-museums that are active in their use of traditional means of production might be more effective, but few of these are likely to address the needs of communities in the future.

Architects and the vernacular *Does that have a bearing on the work of architects?* Absolutely. It is extremely important that architects are properly and thoroughly informed on vernacular traditions, so that they can relate to them in their introduction of new buildings. This is especially important today as architectural practices are becoming increasingly international. It is essential that architectural education confronts these issues. *Isn't it the case that many architects are interested in vernacular architecture and have been influenced by it?* Yes, it is true that highly influential architects like Frank Lloyd Wright and Le Corbusier wrote approvingly of vernacular traditions in their experience, and encouraged students to study them. Unfortunately, they gave little indication of how this was to be done. It was not until after World War II that certain architects gave more than passing attention to vernacular traditions (for example, Bernard Rudofsky, *Architecture Without Architects*, 1964). Since then, architects such as Alvaro Siza, Geoffrey Bawa, Laurie Baker, Aldo van Eyck, Imre Makovecz, François Spoerry, and Peter Zumthor, among others, have acknowledged their indebtedness to vernacular traditions, especially those of their own countries. However, this has seldom been of benefit to those who build their own houses and struggle to keep their own traditions alive. Exceptions are the influential Egyptian architect Hasan Fathy, who wrote more about the vernacular than any other professional, and the Indian architects Charles Correa and Balkrishna Doshi, who have helped design contexts for adequately serviced sites for indigenous builders, Doshi even establishing

his Vastu-Shilpa Foundation to research the vernacular environment of Gujarat. The Aga Khan Award for Architecture has honoured a number of projects, including community participation in Jordan, Tunisia, Indonesia, and elsewhere, but though they have shown how the professional designer can help, there is much to be done in most parts of the world.

It sounds as if it is urgent, but why? Although it is ignored by most architects, by architectural education, by the media, and by politicians, the fact is that the world's population will have grown to 9 billion people or more (and not less) by 2050. That is an increase of 50% of the present population, in less than five decades. We cannot even provide clean, fresh water for half the world's population, so how are we to meet the housing needs of this massively increasing number of people— whether they are in families or single, young or old? If the world's housing is not to be reduced to millions of minimal, stereotyped, mass-produced, and culturally inappropriate repetitive units, an alternative strategy will be essential. This should be based on the positive support of indigenous, self- and community-built vernacular traditions. They have proved themselves to be sustainable, with their use of natural and renewable resources, their climatic and environmental suitability, and their capacity to adapt and change in accordance with the needs of the cultures that have produced them. With sensitive and knowledgeable concern for their traditions, a sustainable future for vernacular architecture could be assured for the benefit of all.   PO

Oliver, Paul (ed.), *The Encyclopedia of Vernacular Architecture of the World* (1997)

Oliver, Paul, *Built to Meet Needs: Cultural Issues in Vernacular Architecture* (2006)

Oliver, Paul, *Dwellings: The Vernacular House World-Wide* (2003)

Spence, R. J. S., and Cook, D. J., *Building Materials in Developing Countries* (1983)

Vesnin, Leonid (1880–1933), **Viktor** (1882–1950), and **Aleksandr** (1883–1959) Russian architects. In the early 1920s, the brothers worked on avant-garde stage designs, with a marked architectural character (e.g. for the play *The Man Who Was Thursday*). Their progression to architectural projects began with the design by all three brothers for the Moscow Palace of Labour competition (1923), which combined basic geometric forms in a complex array, together with provision for the most advanced technology—radio masts, and docking ports for airships. For the competition for the Leningrad Pravda office (1924), the Vesnins designed a tall structure of glass in a concrete frame, exposing the lift cabins and supporting information display boards. Like their theatre designs, there is a sharp contrast between the static and the mobile elements.

Given the backwardness of the building industry in the USSR, these projects were inevitably far more imaginative and influential than their built work—the Mostorg department store (Moscow 1927–9), with its awkwardly splayed corners, the club for the Society of Tsarist Political Prisoners (Moscow, 1931)—particularly in serving as examplars of *Constructivism.

After about 1932, Viktor and Aleksandr opposed the return to traditionalism to no avail. Their design for the People's Commissariat for Heavy Industry (Moscow, 1935–6) is a compromise between an undecorated frame of concrete and glass and the required superstructure of monumental colonnades and statues. PG

Vietnam Following the country's independence from China (AD 938), the already prominent role of Buddhism was enhanced. In the Ly dynasty (1010–1225) many new temples were built. Influences from China are evident in the introduction of new materials (stone), innovations in the use of trabeated structures and trusses, and the use of decorative forms, such as eaves decorated with terracotta symbols. The most outstanding building from this period is the One-Pillar or Lotus Temple (1049). The building is quite small, being only 4.2 m (14 ft) square, but, uniquely, is supported on a single column, 1.2 m (4 ft) across, the whole being intended to represent an opened lotus blossom.

During this period, the brick architecture of Champa (the central coastal district of today's Vietnam), with its distinctive use of local tree resin as a mortar, continued to flourish. Its most extensive remains are at My Son, though after extensive bombing by US forces during the Vietnam war, they are now in rather a fragmentary state.

Buddhism continued to prosper under the Tran dynasty (1225–1400) when Vietnam enjoyed a period of political stability and independence. During this period, the outstanding work is the Pho Minh or Thap Temple, Nam Dinh City (c.1262), with a 17 m (55 ft) high 14-storey brick tower, based on a stone foundation.

In the turmoil of later centuries, few significant works were created, as far as the scanty documentation allows a judgement to be made. The final achievement of the pre-colonial period was the imperial city of Hue, Emperor Gia Long's early-19th-century version of the Forbidden City of Beijing, mostly destroyed by US bombs in 1968. PG

Vignola, Giacomo Barozzi da (1507–73) Italian architect, who played a leading role in two of the most important changes of his time: the integration of architecture and landscape; and the application to architecture of the principles of the *Counter-Reformation.

For Pope Julius III he designed a retreat outside the walls of Rome, the Villa Giulia (1551–5). Along the axis of the rectangular enclosed area, about 97.5 m by 36.5 m (320 ft × 120 ft) are set a conventional 2-storey entrance building, curved round to create a semicircular courtyard; 1-storey ranges which enclose a garden; a loggia; a sunken nymphaeum (designed by *Ammannati); and the final building, merely a screen, looking out over another garden. The changes in building height, and the gradual reduction in the complexity of the structures, create a sense of balance between the architecture and its setting.

Vignola's aim to design not only buildings but also their setting was replicated on a massively greater scale at Palazzo Farnese, Caprarola, near Rome (begun 1559), but this time the relationship was one of domination. On top of an already existing fortress building, set high on a hill, a 1-storey pentagon of 51 m (167 ft) a side, together with five outworks, Vignola added 2 tall storeys, 15 m (50 ft) in height. The exterior is all power—not only the building, but the surroundings. Vignola forced a long, straight, inclined approach through the ungeometric medieval village, leading to two semicircular ramps, a trapezoidal piazza, and two rectangular ramps. The visitor to the *Gran Sala* on the *piano nobile*, formerly an open loggia but now glazed, looked out over the Farnese domains, and around at the frescoes celebrating Farnese triumphs. By contrast, the inner courtyard is very graceful. Ten pairs of columns articulate a 2-storey circular wall of round-headed arches. The wall is sharply carved in grey volcanic stone (*peperino*), and punctuated by voids, niches, balusters and urns. Vignola solves the problem of setting a circle inside a pentagon by using the awkward spaces left over for service stairs or to be filled in. The Palazzo was cleverly planned so that different rooms or suites of rooms were adapted for use at different seasons of the year.

For the somewhat megalomaniac Farnese, Vignola planned an even larger scheme in Piacenza, to include a fortress, a villa and a courtyard with a theatre (1559–68). What survives is a gaunt hulk, occupying 122 × 88 m (400 × 289 ft), only a third of its planned extent. There

were no scenic possibilities here for Vignola to exploit, as the site was flat and on the edge of a city.

Vignola designed a number of interesting churches, S. Andrea in via Flaminia, Rome (1551–3), the first church to be built with an oval dome, and S. Anna dei Palafrenieri (probably begun 1568), in which the plan of the church is an oval, culminating in his design for Il Gesù, Rome (from 1568).

The plan satisfied the demands of the *Counter-Reformation: a broad nave to hold large congregations to preach to, for which the space was also more acoustically effective; the choir was clearly separated from the nave, so as to emphasize the hieratic character of the priesthood; and the long axis was ideally suited to processions. The façade was also ideologically correct, since it had numerous statues in niches (cf. TIBALDI), but, surprisingly, a slightly different design by *della Porta was accepted. Some of the differences did not seem essential. In della Porta's design the niches were retained, but some of the statues were discarded and the façade had a slightly more vertical orientation. The crucial difference was the more acceptable covering to the space above the side chapels—della Porta's S-shaped scrolls, rather than the awkwardly attenuated virtually blank space left by Vignola.

Given the inventive character of his architectural practice, it is rather ironic that his widely influential treatise, *La Regola delli Cinque Ordini d'Architettura* (1562), focused narrowly on a stylized version of the *Orders.   PG

villa The word 'villa' was first used in ancient Rome to signify the agricultural estate and home of a wealthy man. Such houses started appearing in the Italian countryside in the second century BC, and later spread throughout the Roman Empire. They were usually one storey high, and in their simplest form consisted of a range of rooms fronted by a portico and colonnade, with wings at either end. In larger houses the rooms were arranged around one or more colonnaded courtyards, with extra courtyards for farm buildings. By the 1st century AD it had become common for wealthy townspeople to build villas as pleasure houses or second homes, often close to a city (the *villa suburbana*) or in favoured scenic locations such as the Bay of Naples. The villa at Laurentium, near Ostia, described by the younger Pliny in one of his letters (AD *c.*97–102), comes into this category, as does the villa—really a palace—built by the Emperor Hadrian near Tivoli (118–134), surrounded by magnificent gardens with spectacular waterworks. These larger villas were richly decorated internally, with mosaic floors and painted walls, and served as a setting for a life of luxurious relaxation (*otium*) interspersed with bouts of socializing and physical activity such as hunting and bathing, celebrated in the mosaic pictures at the Villa Casale near Piazza Armerina, Sicily (3rd–4th century). But even smaller villas like that at Chedworth, Gloucestershire (2nd–4th century), with their baths and mosaic floors, proclaimed an ideal of civilized rural life in which leisure played a significant part.

Villa life did not survive the collapse of the Roman Empire. The houses fell into ruin and the word itself went out of use until the Renaissance. Elements of villa life revived in the Mediterranean countries in the 13th century, in luxurious hunting lodges—of which the Emperor Frederick II's Castel de Monte in southern Italy is a good example—and in the growing practice of *villegiatura*: spending time on a rural property to avoid the stifling summer heat of a town. This practice was also popular in the Islamic world, as seen in the relatively modest, compact houses that still line the shores of the Bosphorus near Istanbul. But it was not until the 15th century in Tuscany that rural second homes began to be called villas again, or to show an architectural debt to ancient Rome. The first villas built by the Medici family near Florence, such as that at Careggi (remodelled by Michelozzo *c.*1434–50), still presented a quasi-fortified face to the outside world. But in the Villa Medici at Poggio a Caiano (Giuliano da *Sangallo, begun *c.*1480) the idea of a symmetrical, classically detailed house on a rural estate, surrounded by a formal garden, was realized for the first time.

Classically inspired villas proliferated in 16th-century Italy, and successive architects were ingenious in adapting what was known of ancient Roman villa design—chiefly through Pliny's letters and the ruins of Hadrian's Villa—to the needs of modern life. In and around Rome successive popes, cardinals, and their families constructed *villae suburbanae* with colonnaded courtyards, vaulted loggias, outdoor theatres, *nymphaea*, and grottoes (e.g. the unfinished Villa Madama, by Raphael, begun *c.*1518, and the Villa Giulia, by *Vignola and others, 1551–5). Antique relief sculptures could even be used as external decoration, as in Ammanati's remodelling of the Villa Medici (1576–86). And at the Palazzo del Tè, outside Mantua (1525–35), Raphael's pupil Giulio Romano reverted to the ancient Roman ideal of a single-storeyed villa around a courtyard, profusely decorated internally with frescoes of the gods, and surrounded by formal gardens.

Elsewhere in Italy a different ideal prevailed: that of the compact, classically proportioned house either on the edge of a city (as in Galeazzo Alessi's Villa Pallavicino at Genoa, *c.*1555), or on a rural estate. Andrea *Palladio, perhaps the most accomplished and certainly the most famous Italian Renaissance villa architect, designed both kinds of villa. His Villa Rotonda, built on a hilltop on the outskirts of Vicenza (*c.*1565–6), falls into the *villa suburbana* category, but houses like the Villa Emo at Fanzolo (*c.*1559), are surrounded by farmland and should be seen as revivals of the ancient *villa rustica* ideal. Common to both is a pervasive Classicism, proclaimed not only by porticoes reached by flights of steps, but also by their harmonic proportions, rigorous symmetry and ingenious schemes of decoration (cf. Veronese's frescoes at the

Villa Barbaro at Maser, *c.*1561). And, through his *I Quattro Libri dell' Architettura* (1570), knowledge of Palladio's villas was transmitted to later generations both within and outside Italy.

In the 17th century Italian villa design began to exert a significant influence on the domestic architecture of the rest of Europe. Compact, classically proportioned and classically detailed houses began to be built in large numbers in or near the cities of England, France, and Holland (e.g. the Mauritshuis at The Hague, by Pieter Post and Jacob van Campen, begun 1633). The Queen's House at Greenwich, begun 1616 by Inigo *Jones, who had been to Italy at least twice, was in effect an Italianate *villa suburbana*, and Jones's influence pervaded the domestic architecture of late-17th-century England. The publication of an English version of Palladio's *I Quattro Libri* in 1715, together with a revival of interest in Jones, contributed to a renewed surge of villa-building in 18th-century Britain, exemplified by Lord Burlington's villa at Chiswick, near London (1725–9), with its garden deliberately designed to evoke the memory of antique landscapes. From Britain the ideal of the neo-Palladian villa as a rural retreat for a cultivated gentleman and his family spread to Ireland, and also to America (e.g. Thomas Jefferson's Monticello, Virginia, 1770–1808). In Continental Europe too, monarchs and courtiers built relatively small classically inspired houses—not always called villas—as places of retreat in the gardens of their vast baroque palaces, such as Mme de Pompadour's Petit Trianon at Versailles, by Ange-Jacques *Gabriel (1762–8).

Towards the end of the 18th century more and more wealthy merchants throughout Europe and North America began to build suburban houses in landscaped grounds as a means of escaping the growing cities. To cater for the expanding market, architects such as John Plaw (1746–1820) published books of designs for villas, and in the early 19th century such books proliferated, influencing countless middle-class suburban villa builders on both sides of the Atlantic. The 19th-century villas were often designed with irregular plans and picturesquely composed exteriors: characteristics exploited with great panache by John Nash (e.g. Cronkhill, an Italianate *villa rustica* in Shropshire, *c.*1803), by Karl Friedrich *Schinkel (e.g. the gardener's house at Charlottenhof, Potsdam, 1829–33), and by Alexander ('Greek') Thomson (e.g. Holmwood, Glasgow, 1857–8). There were also Gothic villas: Horace Walpole's Strawberry Hill at Twickenham, begun in 1750, is an early example; the Red House at Bexleyheath, designed by Philip Webb for William Morris in 1859, a later one. But by the end of the 19th century Gothic had given way to less overtly medievalist styles: Arts and Crafts (as in the 'weekend houses' with which Edwin Lutyens and C. F. A. Voysey made their reputations), and Art Nouveau, seen in the suburban villas designed by the Vienna Sezession architects and their counterparts in every European country. Charles Rennie Mackintosh's Hill House at Helensburgh, near Glasgow (1902–3), combines elements of both styles.

By the end of the 19th century villa settlements had sprung up in the suburbs of British, American, and to a lesser extent European cities, causing the seriously rich to retreat further into the countryside and often to eschew the word villa altogether. In the first half of the 20th century the ideal of a small suburban house in its own garden became fully democratized: a process that is still continuing throughout the developed world. Meanwhile a new generation of architects succeeded in reinterpreting the classical villa ideal in uncompromisingly modernist terms, shorn of the decorative or historicist motifs found in most suburban houses. In the years between the two World Wars the pioneers of modernist architecture all designed villas as occasional residences for wealthy, progressive patrons: Le Corbusier (Villa Savoye at Poissy, 1929–31); Mies van der Rohe (Tugendhat House at Brno,

Czech Republic, 1930); Alvar Aalto (Villa Mairea, Finland, 1938); and Frank Lloyd Wright (Falling Water, Pennsylvania, 1936). These buildings have become part of the canon of modern architecture, influencing the design of detached, architect-designed houses down to the present day. But in recent times the word villa has become attached not so much to this kind of house as to a holiday home, especially in the Mediterranean. In this way it remains true to its ancient leisured, escapist and even classical connotations. GT

Ackermann, James S., *The Villa* (1990)
Coffin, D., *The Villa in the Life of Renaissance Rome* (1979)
Holberton, P., *Palladio's Villas: Life in the Renaissance Countryside* (1990)
Percival, J., *The Roman Villa* (2nd edn, 1988)

Villagrán García, José (1901–82) Regarded as the father of contemporary Mexican architecture, he built the Granja Sanitaria (Hygiene Institute) at Popotla (1925), the first Functionalist work, meanwhile gaining recognition as a pioneer thanks to his university lectures in the theory of architecture (1926–82), and his writings. His main concern was with the architecture of hospitals and schools, so he was responsible for the Tuberculosis Hospital at Huipulco (1929), the National Institute of Cardiology (1937), and the Gea Gonzáles Hospital (1942); and he organized the National Plan for Schools, including works such as the Costa Rica School (1944). He also built office blocks, cinemas, hotels, and the markets of San Cosme and San Lucas (1954).

LNM (trans. KL)

Villanueva, Carlos Raúl (1900–75) English-born Venezuelan architect who studied in Paris at the Ecole des Beaux-Arts and the Institut d'Urbanisme. Buildings constructed in the eclectic style included the Maracay Bull Ring (1931), and the Art Gallery and Natural Sciences Museum (1935–7). His first work in a modernist style was the Gran Colombia School (1939).

He built housing estates: El Silencio (1941), El Paraíso (1952), 23 de Enero (1954–7), in Caracas; and General Rafael Urdaneta (1943), in Maracaibo. His main contribution is the campus of the Central University of Venezuela (1944–75), created with a deep understanding of tropical conditions, as reflected in the selection of the most appropriate materials and finishes, as well as the most suitable technologies, including bold concrete structures and incorporating works by well-known artists. Other buildings include the La Salle Foundation (1961–4), the Venezuela Pavilion in Montreal (1967), and the Jesús Soto museum in Ciudad Bolivar (1970–73). LNM (trans. KL)

Villanueva, Juan de (1739–1811) Spanish architect. Trained at the Royal Academy, Madrid, which promoted *neoclassicism as an official style, in 1768 he was appointed director of architecture at the Escorial, giving him an intimate knowledge of the severe manner of *Herrera. His designs for a series of casinos at the Escorial and the Aranjuez Palace express the unadorned style he had derived from both sources. On a much larger scale, his design for the Prado Museum, Madrid (1787–9), represents his most significant work. Behind a six-columned Doric portico, the elements of the building are laid out as separate units, in the orthodox neoclassical manner. PG

Villard de Honnecourt (*fl.*1225–35) French mason. Villard, who probably worked at Cambrai Cathedral and possibly Reims, is celebrated for his *Carnet*. Its 33 folios of annotated drawings include Laon, Reims, and Chartres Cathedrals, and other churches, with plans and elevations together with details of carving and tracery. Further architectural drawings show timber trusses (perhaps including a *hammerbeam truss) and mouldings, together with building machines. Other drawings depict saints and other figures in a wide variety of poses, some drawn from life, others from sculpture, as well as grotesques and animals, all with a prolix freedom that helps to explain how medieval masons conceived their work. APQ

Vinci, Leonardo da *See* LEONARDO DA VINCI.

Vingboons, Philips (1607–78) Dutch architect, regarded as the most important Amsterdam architect of the 17th century, partly on the basis of his own publications. Trained as a painter like *Post and *Van Campen, he adapted Italian Renaissance treatises, fashionable with the Amsterdam elite, to furnish a model for the idiosyncratic shape of their houses. His *halsgevel* (neck gable) was constructed to facilitate the application of the classical orders to the narrow, high and heavily glazed façades of the three-bay canalside house. In the planning of the home he established a standard ground plan. FS

Viollet-le-Duc, Eugène Emmanuel (1814–79) French architect and theorist, leading promoter of the *Gothic revival. After a brief architectural apprenticeship as a youth, he travelled extensively throughout the 1830s to study and record the medieval heritage of France and Italy. On his return to his native Paris he was entrusted by the new Commission des Monuments Historiques—established in 1837 in reaction to the devastation wrought by the Revolution—to undertake restoration work at Vézelay (1840). He devoted most of the next three decades to numerous similar commissions: notably for Notre Dame and the Sainte-Chapelle in Paris and at Saint-Denis from the mid 1840s, Carcassonne and Clermont-Ferrand in the 1850s, the Château de Pierrefonds for Napoleon III from 1857, and throughout the 1860s and well into the 1870s the cathedrals of Amiens and Reims, Saint-Sernin in Toulouse, and the walls of Avignon. In addition to building and decorating his own house

(68 rue Condorcet) he worked for private clients on palaces in Paris and chateaux across France: notably Ambrières-les-Vallées, Mayenne (from 1857), and La Flachère, Rhône (from 1862). He built and furnished several churches, most notably St Gimer at Carcassonne (from 1854) and Saint Denis-de-l'Estrée at Saint Denis (from 1864).

He translated his antiquarian studies into practice not only to secure the essential and improve stability but with a passion for stylistic unity: uncharacteristic of organic development, this often transcended the findings of his initial archaeological investigation, so that in general his buildings have been less well received than his books. He also translated his theory with a somewhat messianic didacticism, aimed principally at promoting Gothic structural functionalism in opposition to eclecticism in general and the Renaissance tastes of the Ecole des Beaux-Arts establishment in particular (he had a troubled tenure of the Ecole's chair of history briefly in 1863). Critical dictionaries on both French architecture (1854–68) and furniture (1858–75) were accompanied by his major publication, *Entretiens sur l'architecture* (1863–72) and supplemented by works aimed at the layman (*Histoire d'une maison*, 1873).

In the *Entretiens* he wrote: 'In architecture, there are two necessary ways of being true … according to the *programme* and true according to the *methods of construction* … purely artistic questions of symmetry and apparent form are only secondary conditions.' He also sought to establish the organic massing of the medieval castle as a supreme exemplar of functionalism and Gothic fusion of structure and ornament as a paradigm of the scientific rationalism essential to architectural design: rationalism, certainly, was not new to the French tradition but most immediately Viollet could draw on Durand's teaching in the opening decades of the century at the Ecole Polytechnique. Further, he maintained that the High Gothic approach of the early 13th century was singularly appropriate to the promotion of skeletal iron and, ultimately, ferro-concrete structure in the industrial age. Saint-Denis-de-l'Estrée is perhaps the most significant of his rare attempts to put his theory into practice in building: its highly systematic design could well have lent itself to the pre-fabrication at least of the Gothicized structure. CT

> Bercé, F., and Foucart, B., *Viollet-le-Duc, Architect, Artist, Master of Historic Preservation* (1988)

Viscardi, Giovanni Antonio (1645–1713)

Swiss–Italian architect. He was of equal importance to *Zuccalli in introducing the Baroque into southern Germany, although his main works are churches, not secular buildings. His skill lay in creating compact yet dramatic spaces; his façade designs are less impressive. The pilgrimage church (1700–10) of Mariahilf in Freystadt, near Nuremberg, combines a circle, octagon, and cross, which, however, do not distract the viewer from seeing the altar, gripped by Solomonic columns, fill the end walls of the apse. The cliff-like west façade, with 2 storeys of tall columns, lacks subtlety or a sense of movement. The plan of the Dreifaltigkeitskirche (Holy Trinity), Munich (1711–18), shows how the longitudinal axis (for processions) can be combined with a central space for common worship. Like the earlier church, the west façade has no towers, but by making the central bay thrust forward, Viscardi reduced the effect of monumentality. PG

Visconti, Louis-Tullius-Joachim (1791–1853)

Italian-born architect, commissioned by Napoleon III in 1852 to extend the Louvre westwards in two parallel ranges, each articulated by three pavilions. Visconti's designs were somewhat ponderous, but he at least intended to respect the modest scale and restrained decoration of *Lescot's courtyard façade. His successor, *Lefuel, showed no such *finesse*, burdening the façades

with cumbersome ornament and sculpture, doubtless more to the taste of the Empress Eugénie. PG

Vitruvian scroll

A classical ornament, like a *guilloche, in the form of a running frieze of curly waves with a scrolled crest, rather like a volute, sometimes called running dog. Palladio illustrates it decorating the Temple of Mars Ultor in Rome. APQ

Vitruvius Pollio, Marcus (*fl.*46 BC–AD 25)

Roman architect and writer. Vitruvius wrote his treatise *De Architectura* early in the 1st century AD. It is the only work on architecture to survive from the ancient world, so has been copied and recopied since the Renaissance, inspiring the writing of numerous other treatises in emulation, notably by *Alberti and *Palladio.

Marcus Vitruvius Pollio was of little consequence in his own day. He served under Julius Caesar in the African War of 46 BC and later in Spain as a military engineer. According to his own account, he was the builder of a basilica at Fano, now lost, but well enough described for its plan to be readily understood. In old age he wrote the treatise that made his name, and dedicated it to Caesar Augustus.

The oldest copy, probably made at Jarrow in the 8th century, is now in the British Museum. A further sixteen copies are to be found at various other European libraries, the one at St Gallen, Switzerland, being 'discovered' in 1414 by Poggio Bracciolini, thus inspiring the architects of the Renaissance. The first printed edition appeared in Rome *c*.1486, and several more editions were published in the following century together with translations and commentaries.

Occasionally obscure and often laboured, the text is backward-looking, an attempt to re-affirm already out-of-date architectural ideals. Nevertheless Vitruvius's division of architecture into 'firmness', 'convenience', and 'delight' stands all tests. His first issue is the overwhelming importance of order, symmetry, and proportion as established by the Greeks and inherited by Rome. Secondly he stresses the human-oriented origins of these qualities. Taken together, these notions were a revelation equally to architects and humanists. They have been the foundation of classical architecture ever since. Indeed, the importance that Vitruvius invested in education, in architectural principles, and, finally, in understanding the qualities of building materials, is the very foundation of all architecture. APQ

Vittone, Bernardo Antonio (1702–70) Italian architect. The last important Baroque architect on the Italian mainland, Vittone was best suited to the design of small, centralized churches, of which over 30 were built, most of them in small towns around Turin. The ideal designs depicted in his books, *Istruzione elementari per indirizzo de'giovani allo studio dell'Architettura Civile* (2 vols., Lugano, 1760) and *Istruzione diverse concernanti l'officio dell'Architetto Civile* (Lugano, 1766), suggest that he might not have been capable of handling large masses with much assurance.

Whereas *Guarini used a series of interlacing domes in order to create perspective *illusions of greater height, Vittone's structural purpose was to control light to focus the spectator's attention on the figures in the frescoes of his vaulted domes. As the spectator looks up into the vaults, he seems to see the saints at the mystical moment of translation into the celestial realm.

In the first design of this kind, the small chapel of Santa Maria della Visitazione, Vallinotto (1738), Vittone used three vaults and a double dome, set over a hexagonal plan. In the *Istruzione diverse* he described the vaults as '...[placed] one above the other, all pierced and open such that the viewer in the church may see the spaces that exist between them and enjoy, with the aid of light that is introduced by unseen windows, the variety of the [heavenly] hierarchies represented in these vaults increasing gradually to the top of the lantern where the Holy Trinity is seen.' The frescoes themselves were intended to be seen in diminishing perspective, to reinforce the illusion of a very tall structure.

At San Bernardino in Chieri (1741), though forced to insert a more traditional domed form into an existing building, Vittone created a much lighter structure than the traditional ribbed dome, by increasing the number of supports from eight to twenty. The open structure, pierced with light flowing through the vaults and pendentives, appears to hang weightlessly above the chapels. The culmination of these experiments in this the first phase of his career is found at Santa Chiara at Brà (1742). Here Vittone uses a structure not immediately comprehensible by the spectator, two vaults one above the other, but the purpose is the same: to create an illusion of the luminous infinity which is the dwelling place of the saints and angels. Each sector of the vault has an opening through which the earth-bound spectator sees a vision of saints and angels. The fragile shell of the vault separates a comprehensibly built space from an ethereal realm which seems to defy the laws of structure. More prosaically, as in all Vittone's buildings, these complex structures are built of brick and stucco, partly for economy, and partly because Vittone did not apparently have sufficient knowledge of stereotomy to make their construction possible in masonry.

Although Vittone's structures are unusual, they are not unprecedented. Paradoxically, his only structural innovation, gouging out a space in the pendentives to insert windows, for a different kind of lighting, leads to an awkward result, as can be seen at the chapel of the Albergo di Carità at Carignano (1744) and the church of S. Maria in Piazza in Turin (1751–4).

Far more successful was his belated concern to set his buildings in their space. In most cases, exteriors, usually or brick and stucco, are the exact expression of interior forms, quite regardless of the immediate setting. The best example of the change in his later work is the church of S. Michele in Rivarolo Canavese (1759). The street itself was widened to give the building prominence; the church entrance is set back from the street and two curved lower pavilions project from the portico to act as a frame. In this case, Vittone's use of brick is especially effective.   PG

volute A spiral scroll. The defining decorative feature of an Ionic capital, volutes are also part of a Composite capital, and, smaller, a Corinthian capital, as well as being used in other contexts in classical decoration, for instance on the side faces of brackets and the inner termination of a swan-neck pediment.   APQ

von Erlach, Fischer *See* FISCHER VON ERLACH, JOHNANN BERNHARD.

Vorarlberg School A name given subsequently to the work of several inter-related families, the *Beers, *Moosbruggers, and *Thumbs, based in the Forest of Bregenz district in the Austrian region of Vorarlberg. The School was influential in southern Germany and Switzerland for about fifty years, starting from its prototype, Obermarchtal (Franz *Beer, 1686–92), which showed its main characteristics: longitudinal plans; the use of deep, solid-looking *wall-pillars, faced by pilasters and linked by galleries; naves wider than choirs; and vestigial transepts accommodating side-chapels, rather than creating a centralized space. Frescoes and statuary groups are of little importance, and unlike the slightly later churches by the *Asams, are integrated into the architectural framework.

In many cases, particularly Holzen (Franz Beer, 1696–1704), the massive wall-pillars create rather a ponderous effect, and tend to diminish the apparent width of the nave. To offset these disadvantages, two

expedients were adopted. At Rheinau (Franz Beer, 1704–11), St Urban (Franz Beer, 1711–36), the galleries were set back from the pilasters, rather than flush, as elsewhere, or were concave, as at Weingarten (*Moosbrugger and others, 1714–24); and the pilasters were given a much more decorative treatment.

The School's architects designed striking and distinctive interiors, but paid only perfunctory attention to exteriors. They usually had two rather ordinary towers (Irsee, Bavaria, 1699–1704, by Franz Beer, is an exception), but so did many non-Vorarlberg designs of this period; and were otherwise plain to the point of ugliness (St Katherinenthal, Switzerland, Johann Michael Beer, 1732–5).   PG

Voronikhin, Andrei Nikiforovich (1759–1814) Russian architect, proponent of neoclassicism. A former serf of Count Alexander Stroganov, he was not a prolific builder, but by virtue of extraordinary talent and the support of the Stroganov family, he obtained major architectural commissions in St Petersburg at the turn of the 19th century. The most imposing of these is the massive Cathedral of the Kazan Mother of God on Nevsky Prospekt (1801–11), with debts to the Basilica of St Peter in Rome (the curving double colonnade) and Soufflot's Ste Geneviève. His other major extant structure in Petersburg is the Mining Institute (1806–11), whose Greek Doric dodecastyle portico forms a dominant feature of the Neva River embankment of Vasilevsky Island. He also designed important additions to the park ensembles at the imperial estates of Peterhof and Pavlovsk.   WCB

voussoir A wedge-shaped stone or brick that, together with other similar ones, forms an arch. Its sides are normally shaped so as to follow the radius of the curve of the arch, and thus attain maximum stability without recourse to dowels or mortar.   APQ

Voysey, Charles Francis Annesley (1857–1941)
English architect and designer. Voysey was articled to
the Gothic Revivalist J. P. *Seddon in 1874 and worked
for George *Devey, a domestic architect specializing in
the picturesque, until 1881, when he set up his own
practice. He produced a number of wallpaper designs
with bold clear patterns taken from nature, and
designed furniture based on simple oak planking. He
specified his own lock plates and other architectural
ironmongery for his houses, often incorporating a heart
motif. These designs appear close in character to Art
Nouveau, but in common with other Arts and Crafts
designers, Voysey rejected the self-conscious originality
of this movement. In 1884, Voysey joined the Art
Workers Guild, becoming Master in 1924.

In the 1890s, Voysey's architectural practice began to
flourish. Two town houses in Hans Road, Kensington
(1891–2), were plain but well proportioned and planned.
Houses such as New Place, Haslemere, Hampshire,
for the publisher Arthur Methuen, and Norney,
Shackleford, Surrey (both of 1897), covered in white
render, with slate roofs, simplified windows and bays,
low ceilings and simple beams measuring the space,
show the style that seldom varied in Voysey's work.
According to Herman Muthesius, he refused to work
for clients who would not accept low ceilings, adding
that 'low rooms always look comfortable and give the
room a compact, unified appearance'. The calm
influence of horizontals was dominant. The style
was especially apt in the Lake District where at
Windermere (1898) Voysey built Broadleys and
Moor Crag, the latter one of his least self-conscious
efforts. His own house, The Orchard, Chorleywood,
Hertfordshire (1899), was a demonstration of his ideals
of living with fresh air, sunlight, bright clear colours,
white woodwork, and fruit trees around the house.
The author H. G. Wells, who described Voysey as
'that pioneer in the escape from the small snobbish
villa residence to the bright and comfortable

pseudo-cottage', was influenced by his own Voysey
house at Sandgate, Kent (1899), to become interested
in the reform of interior design. Although most
Voysey houses have a strong family likeness, each was
experimental in plan, adapted to client and site. The
designs were widely published, especially in early
numbers of *The Studio*, and a reductive and often
over-ornamented version of Voysey's style influenced
the design of suburban speculative houses from
1900 to World War II.

Voysey's non-domestic designs included the
wallpaper warehouse for Sanderson's in Chiswick.
He characterized his style as Gothic, on account of its
northern forms, despite the lack of pointed arches.
He called classicism 'a crutch for fools', but as it
began to infiltrate the Arts and Crafts movement in the
Edwardian period, his commissions began to tail off.
He was 'discovered' by the poet John Betjeman around
1930, and celebrated as a pioneer of Modernism,
something he strongly repudiated, being conservative
by instinct and opposed to communal movements.
Even so, his ideal of serenity in domestic interiors may
well have influenced the trend of English Modernism.
His writings (for example, *Individuality*, 1915) reveal a
mixture of common sense, prejudice, and spirituality.

AP

Hitchmough, W., *C. F. A. Voysey* (1995)

Vries, Hans Vredeman de (1527–1606) Dutch
architect, known for his treasuries of architectural
ornament, which include *Architectura* (1577), *Variae
Architecturae Formae* (1601), and *Perspective* (1604). They
were inspired by a fashion which spread via the court of
Charles V and his successor Philip II to the southern
Netherlands (Belgium), as part of a northern European
Renaissance. De Vries was a designer as well as a
talented compiler, drawing from the work of Antwerp
artists such as Pieter Coecke van Aelst and Cornelis
*Floris, and adding his own architectural emphasis. FS

Wagner, Otto (1841–1918) Austrian architect. Having produced historicist designs since the 1860s, he came to international prominence in the mid 1890s as one of the first to advocate a 'modern' approach to architecture.

Major projects of his career before 1890 include a Venetian Gothic synagogue for Budapest (1868) and, in a style he called 'free Renaissance', the offices of the Länderbank (1882) and his own villa (1886) in Vienna. In 1880 he produced a set of drawings for a vast imaginary cultural complex called 'Artibus', in which he experimented with *Beaux Arts planning and demonstrated his ambition to design on a quasi-urban scale.

In 1894 Wagner was appointed professor of architecture at the Vienna Academy of Fine Arts, and in his inaugural address of that year he called upon architects to reject academic historicism and take inspiration from the challenges of modern life. This was a message reiterated in his *Modern Architecture* (1896, English translation 1988), which was published in multiple editions and received international attention. Inspired by the example of Gottfried *Semper, Wagner advocated a synthesis between close attention to purpose and material considerations on the one hand and, on the other, a sense of the 'inner truth' of a commission, expressed through monumental axial planning, symbolism, and stylized references to historical precedent.

Wagner embraced the energy and speed of the metropolis, and sought to bring old-fashioned Vienna closer to the example of Paris. In his role as artistic adviser to the public authorities building a new municipal rail system (the *Stadtbahn*, 1894–1900), he and his office (which included Josef *Hoffmann and Joseph Maria *Olbrich) were responsible for station and bridge designs which used a simple and consistent vocabulary of white-washed plaster, red brick, and green-painted iron to knit together visually disparate sections of the city.

With the two adjoining blocks on the Linke Wienzeile (1898), Wagner reinvented the Viennese apartment block façade, rejecting the elaboration of the *piano nobile* as a misleading hangover from the past. Instead, he designed 'democratic' façades, of flat tiles or plaster, expressing the reality of the apartment block as a collection of equal rented units.

His two best known projects were designed almost simultaneously: St Leopold's, the chapel of the Vienna psychiatric hospital (1902–7), and the Vienna headquarters of the Austrian Postal Savings Bank (1903–7 with an addition 1909–11). The former used advanced building technology and new lightweight materials to create a light-filled, hygienic updating of the Baroque centralized domed church. It was the focal point of what counts as Wagner's only self-contained urban plan, his site plan for the hospital's complex of 60 buildings.

The Postal Savings Bank is the single architectural project in which all of Wagner's preoccupations are united. The plan demonstrates a thorough analysis of the bank's complex functions; 'modern' materials (especially aluminium) and building technologies are used demonstratively throughout; and Wagner imbues the whole with a powerful monumentality, especially in the central banking hall with its glass roof and basilical plan.   LET

Graf, O.A., *Otto Wagner* (vols. 1–2, 1985)

Wailly, Charles de (1730–98) French architect. His alterations to the garden front of the Hôtel de Voyer

showed a certain interest in placing more emphasis on the façade than on interior planning, by using the Greek *Ionic order, rare in France, and heavier rustication than usual with his contemporaries. After some small or uncompleted projects, and apparently unwilling to work for the Court, where he was nominally employed, he found his *métier* in theatre design. With his friend M. J. *Peyre, he designed the Théâtre de France (1768–82, now the Théâtre de l'Odéon). In sympathy with the naturalism of a contemporary playwright such as Beaumarchais, the clever plan, with its nearly circular auditorium, brought the audience close to the actors. The theatre also provided unprecedented comfort to both the audience and their waiting servants. The façade is rather severe, with a portico of unfluted columns, but is beautifully integrated with the equally plain façades of the semicircular Place de l'Odéon.   PG

Wales Much of the architecture of Wales has been strongly affected by activity beyond its borders. For instance, the Romans built a series of quadrangular forts (Cardiff) and towns (Caerwent), the occasional amphitheatre (Caerleon), and villas. An important unifying feature during much of the post-Roman period was the early Christian church. *Monasteries, each comprising a number of small buildings enclosed within a curvilinear *llan* (churchyard) wall, were established in mainly coastal areas. Although the buildings, mostly of wood, have disappeared, the sites of many early churches can still be identified by the circular or elliptical *llan* in which they were set. Stone structures may well have utilized corbelled vaults—as in surviving wells—similar to those found in early Irish oratories.

The Normans erected castles, mostly of the motte-and-bailey type, but also in stone (Chepstow, 1067), and built churches and monasteries of a type familiar in England. By the early 13th century the

Anglo-Norman Marcher lords dominated the southern coastal areas. To maintain their control they rebuilt many of their castles as the less vulnerable round keep type (Pembroke, c.1200)—probably inspired by the castles of northern France. The Welsh princes defended their territory with castles, often on rocky, inland locations, and copied Marcher lords' round keeps, particularly in the south (Dinefwr). In the north, designs were more varied with examples of rectangular (Dolwyddelan), D-shape (Ewloe) and round (Dolbadarn) keeps.

Following punitive campaigns in 1277 and 1282–3, the English king, Edward I, built a chain of powerful castles, in two phases, on or near the coast, from Flint to Aberystwyth, which incorporated the latest developments in *military architecture. Beaumaris (begun 1295) was a classic example of the concentric plan, while Caernarfon (begun 1283) was designed as a showy demonstration of imperial power, inspired by the Roman walls of Constantinople.

As population increased in the 13th century, the more important churches were enlarged by adding aisles, separated from the nave by arcades of slender piers, and linked by tall, pointed arches. Towards the end of the 15th century, increasing wealth allowed many existing churches to be extended and embellished with fine, timber-panelled ceilings. Intricately carved rood-screens (many of which have survived in isolated places) were important features. In the north, splendid new churches were erected with elaborately ornamented towers and large windows occupying all the space between wall buttresses.

By the 14th century the need for military fortifications had declined and the castle gradually gave way to the great house, as at Tretower where a new house, with central hall open to the roof, was erected near the earlier castle. The wealthiest landowners built extravagantly. Between 1330 and 1350 Bishop Gower erected splendid palaces (St David's; Swansea;

Lamphey), with main rooms above vaulted undercrofts and decorative, arcaded parapets. During the 15th century the most ambitious work was the rebuilding of Raglan as a military strongpoint (the hexagonal Great Tower) combined with elegant courtyard planning.

Most domestic buildings, apart from great houses, belonged to an unpretentious *vernacular tradition. The cruck-framed, single-storey hall-house, heated by an open fire, appears to have been the dominant type over most areas (except in the south-west) until the late 15th century. In upland areas the longhouse—with both family and cattle under the same roof, divided by a central service passage—was common.

During the 16th century the E-shaped plan, with projecting wings and central porch, became fashionable for larger houses, allowing symmetrical front elevations. Greater prosperity provided opportunities for extensive rebuilding. Carew Castle was extended with a magnificent new wing incorporating giant windows articulated by semicircular bays. Crow-stepped gables from the Netherlands were introduced at Plas Clough, and became a popular feature in northern Wales. Renaissance architecture was hesitantly introduced, first at Old Beaupre, with a gatehouse in debased classical form in 1586, then fourteen years later with an elaborate porch incorporating three tiers of classical columns. An underlying current of romanticism during the 18th century made its presence felt in architecture, especially through the picturesque movement, with Thomas Johnes (at Hafod) and John Nash (Rheola) among its earliest exponents.

Architecturally, the 19th century was an era of historicism. Towns developed rapidly, particularly in the iron-making districts and coalfields. Occasionally, industrial buildings were designed to impress as in the Egyptian 'temples' of the ironworks at Rhymni, but generally they were basic and functional. At Tredegar (1809–18), the first planned industrial town in Britain, the buildings remained utilitarian. The 'castles' of the newly-rich entrepreneurs and industrialists were a different matter. They were often ostentatiously 'Gothic' (Cyfarthfa Castle; Cardiff Castle; Gwyrych Castle). Larger educational buildings also tended to be either revived Gothic (University College, Aberystwyth) or Tudor (St David's College, Lampeter) in style. Ecclesiastical architecture was divided. While Romanesque was used early in the century, Gothic in all its varieties remained the most popular style for the established church, and was used by John Prichard in his imaginative rebuilding of Llandaf Cathedral. Nonconformist chapels were—apart from the early, long-wall type—predominately classical in style, reflecting, perhaps, a less ostentatious attitude by the majority of Welsh worshippers.

During the early 20th century there were forays into the Arts and Crafts movement by H. L. North in northern Wales, and Art Nouveau by J. C. Carter in southern Wales. Earlier styles continued to be revived, however, especially for public buildings: for example, Jacobean university colleges (Bangor, 1911), classical for the National Museum, Cardiff (1910–27). In the period after World War I, architecture began to evolve in a different direction, marked by a watering-down of period details, which resulted in austere buildings—such as those by Sir Percy Thomas—with a superficial feel of Modernism. Functionalism, characterized by unadorned geometrical forms, made brief appearances in the 1930s, mainly in the shape of welfare buildings. During the second half of the century the rationalist approach to design gave way to the more expressionist or allusive buildings of the 1960s and 1970s. JBH

Hilling J. B., *The Historic Architecture of Wales* (1976)
Smith P., *Houses of the Welsh Countryside* (2nd edn, 1988)

Wallis, Thomas (1873–1953), **Gilbert** (unknown) and **Partners** English architects. *See* ART DECO.

wall-pillar A buttress supporting a vault or ceiling, placed inside a church rather than against an outside wall (*see* BUTTRESS); essentially a Late Gothic structure. Most commonly found in south German churches (literally *Wandpfeilerkirchen*; *see also* VORARLBERG SCHOOL), the wall-pillar is usually pierced to allow the formation of side chapels, and, at the next level, often carries a gallery. PG

Walter, Thomas Ustick (1804–87) US architect. In a long career in his native Philadelphia, Walter made important contributions in *Greek Revival and other styles. After an apprenticeship as a mason and training with William *Strickland, he looked to John *Haviland for precedents in designing Moyamensing Prison (1831–5, demolished). The commission for the $2m Girard College (1833–48) brought early fame. Walter was sent to Europe to study innovative technologies, including iron. The lessons of Girard were applied to the extension of the United States Capitol and its magnificent cast-iron dome (1850–63). Old age found him impoverished, drafting details for John McArthur's Philadelphia City Hall. WMB

Ware, Isaac (1704–66) English architect. Reputedly educated under Lord *Burlington's guidance and trained by Thomas Ripley, Ware gained the first of several posts in 1728 in the Office of Works. He published *Designs of Inigo Jones* in 1731, his celebrated translation of Palladio's *Four Books on Architecture* in 1738, and *A Complete Body of Architecture* in 1756–7. His first independent commission was in 1733, followed by Clifton Hall House, Bristol (1746–50), and Chesterfield House, London (1748–9, demolished). APQ

Ware, William Robert (1832–1915) and **Van Brunt, Henry** (1832–1903) US architects and critics. In their practice, Van Brunt was recognized as the designer, while Ware was the authority on architectural education and theory. Their work tended to a rather dutiful application of period styles to churches (the First Church, Boston, 1856–7) or university buildings (the Episcopal Theological School, Cambridge, Mass., 1869–80; Weld Hall, Harvard, 1871–2). The Memorial Hall, Harvard (1865–78), which used an ecclesiastical plan to combine a dining-hall (the nave), theatre (the chancel), and a Civil War memorial (a rather abbreviated transept), is a fine example of *Gothic Revival. Their only functional innovation to meet the needs of the modern age was Gere Hall, Harvard University Library (1876–7), the first use in the US of the stack principle for storing books. PG

warehouses Although they have some functional and visual similarities to *factories, they are treated here as a separate building type.

In classical antiquity, the Romans built large warehouses for storing grain at Porticus Aemilia (193 BC), and at the main port for Rome, Ostia. These were usually built of concrete, with no hint of architectural distinction.

The European warehouse type, which remained unchanged for two centuries from c.1700, has the following characteristics: it may be as high as 6 storeys, to make the most economical use of water frontages; the façades are completely regular, the windows not much more than holes in the wall (a fact disapprovingly noted by *Schinkel, in his English journey of 1826); and a vertical emphasis is given by the larger openings of the doors through which goods are hoisted. However, some modernists admired this kind of building as an example of the *functional tradition in design.

In London and Liverpool, the construction of enclosed dock basins, in which the warehouse was separated from the water by a quay, seems to have inspired architects to give the ground floor of the warehouse a more dramatic form. Examples include the West India Dock, London (George Gwilt, begun 1800), St Katherine's Dock, London (Philip Hardwick, begun 1827), and the Albert Dock, Liverpool (Jesse Hartley, 1841–5), where cyclopean Doric columns both emphasize the monumental character of the structure they carry, and create a quayside loggia.

Reyner Banham's *A Concrete Atlantis* (1986) showed how the tradition of warehouse design achieved a final late flowering in Buffalo, USA, at the turn of the 19th century. The detailing of window frames, window openings, and the corners of buildings, using different types of brick, achieved a high level of competence. Brick was followed by the imaginative use of the reinforced concrete frame, as in the end elevations of the Larkin Company (1911), divided into five bays of unequal width, a break with the usual uniformity of the planning of warehouse bays.

The vertically oriented multi-storey warehouse no longer had a rationale following a cluster of innovations from the late 1950s: the container; the fork-life truck; pallet racking systems; and automation. The first example of the warehouse as a serviced shed was for the Brunswig Drug Company, Los Angeles (1960). Except in rare instances, such as *Foster's Renault distribution centre, Swindon (1980–82)—in this case because the building was intended to provide publicity for the company's products—this type of warehouse offers the architect few opportunities to display other than technical skills. PG

Wastell, John (d.1515) English mason. Working mainly in the eastern counties, Wastell was among the most significant of late medieval designers. From 1485 he was working on King's College chapel, and built the fan vault. In 1494–7 he built Bell Harry, the central tower of Canterbury Cathedral, notably with a stone-faced brick core. He worked in his home town of Bury St Edmunds, both on the abbey and from 1503

1009

completely rebuilding the church of St James (now the cathedral).   APQ

Waterhouse, Alfred (1830–1905) English architect. Following articles in Manchester, Waterhouse travelled in France, Germany, and Italy, gaining a wide experience of Gothic architecture that would stand him in good stead. He established his practice in Manchester in 1856, where he stayed until 1865, when he moved to London. His career was enormously successful thanks to his professional skills, admirable planning, and happy use of well-handled Gothic motifs. His first triumph was to win a competition for Assize Courts in Manchester, which he designed with consummate planning and elevations in a free Gothic. Built in 1859–64, this encouraged him to enter competitions for many other public buildings of a similar kind, notably for Manchester Town Hall in 1867. Again he won, and his design, built in 1868–77, unlike the Assize Courts, has survived as a prized public building. Built on a triangular site, its nearly symmetrical front is given over to a Reception Room and Banqueting Room on one side and the Mayor's Parlour and Council Chamber on the other side of a tall clock tower which rises over a ceremonial entrance. The two other sides contain offices reached by an internal corridor running from broad spiral staircases in each corner. Meanwhile a great formal staircase behind the entrance leads to a large Public Hall, which fills the centre of the triangle. His assured and efficient planning and suitably towered and gabled Gothic are complemented by a proprietary system of fireproof concrete vaults supported by wrought-iron beams. Meanwhile the services are fully integrated into the structure, with warmth provided by heating coils in the basement rising up the newel staircases to wherever it is needed.

This success led to others of an ever widening character. Other town halls include Municipal Buildings, Reading (1872–5), and Hove Town Hall, Sussex (1882). His university buildings include ranges at Balliol College, Oxford (1866–8), and Caius College, Cambridge (1870), and all of Girton College, Cambridge (1873). He built offices for the Prudential Assurance Company in most large towns, with its Head Office in Holborn, London (1879, and 1899–1906), executed in bright red terracotta which he made his own. His prominent landmarks include the Natural History Museum, South Kensington (1873–81) and St Paul's School, Hammersmith, London (1881–5, demolished). The last years of his career were occupied with the National Liberal Club, Whitehall Place, London (1885–7), Royal Infirmary, Liverpool (1887), Metropole Hotel, Brighton (1888), and University College Hospital, London (1897–1906), after which his son Paul Waterhouse continued, completing many of his father's works.   APQ

Cunningham, C., and Waterhouse P., *Alfred Waterhouse* (1992)

Wealden house A medieval timber-framed hall-house, common in Kent and Sussex, whose three-part plan of hall and 2-storeyed, jettied end blocks is set beneath an overall roof. Because the upper floors of the high-end chamber and low-end services blocks are jettied like suppressed wings forward of the hall, this appears recessed between them and beneath the continuous roof, whose eaves are usually supported at this point by prominent curved braces. This arrangement, which derives from that of a hall with projecting wings, first appears south of Maidstone, Kent, in the 1380s, and may be a consequence of local yeomen's prosperity (notwithstanding a possible Wealden in Winchester, dated to 1339/40). The majority of some thousand survivors of the type were built in the late 15th century, and are common in Wealden Kent, but less so in Sussex, and rare elsewhere. An urban variation, lacking one jettied end, is more scattered, several examples being found in the Midlands.   APQ

weathering of buildings Once completed, all buildings are subject to a gradual process of erosion by the elements—wind, sun, rain, and snow. Generally this process is regarded as harmful, because it detracts from a building's original appearance through discolouration and the break-up of materials. Weathering also has more serious consequences, because ultimately it can destroy a building's exterior protection and structural integrity.

But the effects of weathering can be beneficial. Materials mellow with age, reflecting not just their erosion but also the slow accumulation of sediments and marks of use. People enjoy old buildings because they are imbued with such signs of age: they even find pleasure in ruins, where the destructive effects of weathering predominate.

In Britain and northern Europe the main impacts of weather come from rain and snow. Water penetration is particularly destructive because, by inducing various forms of rot, it can destroy a building's structure; it can also ruin a building's contents. Many features of traditional construction can be said to originate in the need to throw water from a building—pitched roofs, projecting eaves, sills, and hoodmoulds. The cornice at the top of an external wall is designed to protect the wall below from rain, and may include a dripmould to help that function. The huge overhanging eaves of Swiss and German houses are intended to provide the same kind of protection, against snow as well as rain.

However good the roof and eaves, the external wall may need further protection, especially if it incorporates timber-framing. Hence the use of tile-cladding or weather-boarding (clapboard in the US), also stucco and various forms of render. These coverings have the advantage that they can be regularly renewed, returning the building to a semblance of its original appearance. The same is true of painted finishes on all external features.

Occasionally buildings have been designed to improve with age. It has been argued that the use of rustication and other features in Renaissance architecture took account of the long-term effects of staining and dirt on façades. And in recent years the use of Cor-Ten, a steel alloy which improves in appearance as its surface oxidizes, has found favour. Copper is another material which is used in the knowledge that its surface will change over time.

Whereas much traditional construction took account of weathering, the Modern Movement had as its ideal the design of smooth, flat elevations which were intended to keep their perfect finish throughout the life of the building. Part of the disenchantment with such designs was because they were easily defiled and eroded by the weather, and required more frequent and fundamental overhaul than expected.

The need to learn from such mistakes has been underlined in recent years by the advocates of sustainable design. They insist on the need to take account of climatic and environmental conditions, and to maximize benefits from the changing weather to create comfortable lower-energy buildings. RT

Mostafavi, M., and Leatherbarrow, D., *On Weathering* (1993)

web or severy The panel between the *ribs of a *vault. In French *Gothic, the webs normally run parallel to the line of the nave arcade, whereas in England they are set at right angles. The structural reason was that in France the web courses were laid on top of the ribs, whereas in England the webs were rebated into the ribs. Thus in the French examples the webs assume a more clearly warped shape, marking out the difference between web and rib. But given that the webs are usually at least 18 m (60 ft) distant from the spectator on the pavement, the difference is not usually significant.

In *Guarini's churches, S. Lorenzo (1668–87) and the Holy Shroud (1667–90), the webs were omitted, to achieve a particular lighting effect.   PG

Webb, Sir Aston (1849–1930) English architect. A year of Continental travel, often in association with Edward Ingress Bell, preceded the start of Webb's practice in 1873. He designed many important public buildings whose solid Baroque style well suited the times. His first major work, the Victoria and Albert Museum, Kensington (1891, built 1899–1909), lacks overall cohesion. The French Protestant Church, Westminster (1893), his favourite work, has living accommodation in a pretty Flemish Gothic street front, with narrow oriels, and a steep gable carrying a lantern. Mumford's Flour Mill, Greenwich (1897), is as majestic as his Victoria Memorial, Westminster (1900–01), the start of improvements that led to the Admiralty Arch (1911), which cleverly hides a change of axis into the Mall, and the refronting of Buckingham Palace (1913), converting Blore's façade into a Portland stone essay in French *Beaux Arts—but buttoned up, like the public face of the monarchy. Birmingham University, Edgbaston (1900–09), made red brick synonymous with higher education.   APQ

Webb, John (1611–72) English architect. His career fell awkwardly in the political and architectural interregnum between Charles I/Inigo *Jones and Charles II/Christopher *Wren. His portico in the *Corinthian order for The Vyne, Hampshire (1654–6), the first portico attached to a domestic building in England, has the air of an experiment, since its white attenuated form lies incongruously in the middle of ranges of patterned red brickwork. But the façade of Amesbury House (1661, destroyed 1830), with the rustication rising through 2 storeys, pressing a very low storey finial under the cornice, and with giant statues on the pediment, is an assured, if rather awkward composition. For the eastern section of the King Charles block, Greenwich Palace (1662–9), Webb again used overpowering rustication, in conjunction with giant pilasters—a building which is in sight of the comparatively unarticulated Queen's House by Inigo Jones, and to which it is perhaps a deliberate riposte.   PG

Webb, Philip Speakman (1831–1915) English architect and designer. Like many architects associated with the *Arts and Crafts movement, Webb worked in Street's office, meeting William Morris and other similarly minded artists. In 1856 he joined Morris and designed jewellery, embroidery, stained glass, and furniture. In 1859 he built Red House, Bexleyheath, for Morris in a free style whose extended plan embraces the traditional forms of the late Middle Ages through to the 18th century. His few architectural works remain highly influential for their well-judged stylistic simplicity, which seems to enshrine eternal domestic virtues. These apply equally to town and country, notably at Fairmile, Cobham, Surrey (1860); 1 Palace Green, Kensington (1863); 91–101 Worship Street, Shoreditch, London (1863); 19 Lincoln's Inn Fields, Holborn (1868); 55 Glebe Place, Chelsea (1869); Upwood Gorse, Caterham, Surrey (1873); Smeaton Manor, Great Smeaton, Yorkshire (1875–8); East Rounton School, Yorkshire (1876); Clouds, East Knoyle, Wiltshire (1879); offices for Dorman Long, Middlesbrough, Yorkshire (1883); Coneyhurst, Ewhurst, Surrey (1886); Standen, East Grinstead, Sussex (1891–4); and Hurlands, Puttenham, Surrey (1898). With *Morris he was a founder in 1877 of the Society for the Protection of Ancient Buildings, which advocated careful repair rather than wholesale restoration, particularly of churches. This set them and many other free-thinkers against much of the established architectural profession.   APQ

Weed, Robert Law (1897–1961) US architect. *See* CAR PARKS MULTI-STOREY, AND GARAGES.

Weinbrenner, Friedrich (1766–1826) German architect. From his earliest proposals for Karlsruhe's Marktplatz in 1791, Weinbrenner's career was intimately linked to the development of that city. He created a unified urban composition within the radiating Baroque axes of the city's original 1715 plan, through interventions like the Schloss Strasse, a triumphal route composed of a series of linked spaces punctuated by monuments. Although the bold façade of his Karlsruhe synagogue (1798–1806) employs a synthesis of Gothic, Egyptian, and ancient Greek forms, Weinbrenner's designs for the Karlsruhe Town Hall (1806–20), Palace of the Margrave (1805–13), Protestant City Church (1806–16), Residenztheater (1807–8), Catholic Church of St Stephan (1807–14), and Mint (1826–7) all assume a more strict Classicism. Weinbrenner also founded an important school of architecture in his own house, where, through lessons based on his *Architectural Textbook* (1810–19), the importance of drawing, construction methods, and an idealized view of classical architecture were emphasized.   AN

Wells Coates *See* COATES, WELLS.

westwork The developed west end of a *Romanesque church in which a large range is set before the west end of the nave. It comprises an open entrance loggia or an enclosed anteroom, and an upper room, sometimes containing an altar, which is usually open to the nave and, on each side, to a continuation of the galleries above the aisles. This may be reached by flanking newels, set in turrets, and the whole is usually crowned by a broad tower. The earliest westwork was at St Riquier, northern France (*c.*790–800), and it became common in Germany, for instance at Speyer Cathedral (complete 1062).   APQ

Wiebenga, Jan Gerko (1886–1974) Dutch engineer. *See* DUIKER, JOHANNES.

Wilkins, William (1778–1839) English architect. Quickly established as a leader of the *Greek Revival, by his design for Grange Park, Hampshire (1805–9), Wilkins won a competition for Downing College, Cambridge (1807–20). His numerous Greek designs for prominent public buildings, such as the United Services Club, Westminster (1817–19, demolished), culminated in the new National Gallery (1832–8). His country houses bowed to the current taste for Tudor Gothic at Dalmeny House, West Lothian (1814–17), a style he also applied to New Court, Trinity College, Cambridge (1821–3). Despite these successes, his fine draughtsmanship failed to conceal an essentially two-dimensional mind.   APQ

William of Sens *See* SENS, WILLIAM OF.

Williams, Sir (Evan) Owen (1890–1969) English engineer. If anyone personified *Le Corbusier's views on the 'engineer's aesthetic' (*see* ENGINEERING AND ARCHITECTURE) it was Sir Owen Williams. His first work, as consulting engineer at Wembley Stadium (1924), did no more than show his facility with reinforced concrete, but in the 1930s he designed a series of buildings which had few precedents in European *Modernism. At the former Pioneer *Health Centre, Peckham, London (1935), Williams used his engineering flair to set a swimming pool on the first floor, and glazed the main frame to make the activities of the centre visible to the public. A similar interest in transparency was evident in the office buildings for the *Daily Express* in Fleet Street, London (1931), and Manchester (1938), with its *curtain wall of translucent black glass Vitrolite panels, the joints concealed by chromium strips and rounded corners; and the Wets Factory (1930–32) and the Drys Factory (1935–8), for

Boots, Nottingham, which used a mushroom-shaped structure.

Some of his post-war work—Technical Block A, British Overseas Airways Corporation, Heathrow (1950–55), the M1 motorway bridges (1959), and 'Spaghetti Junction', Birmingham (1967–72)—showed the limitations of large-scale engineering without *finesse* at its smaller scale. But he made a welcome return to pre-war form in the *Daily Mirror* Building, Holborn, London (1958–61), a curtain wall of scarlet glass.　　PG

Williams-Ellis, Sir Clough (1883–1978) Anglo-Welsh architect.

Famous for the Italianate hotel village of Portmeirion, Gwynedd, which he began to build and operate in 1926 in the territory of his Williams forebears, Clough Williams-Ellis was one of the most prominent architects of his time, even if he would never have claimed weight as a designer. In fact, his life's philosophy was based on a kind of dedicated levity that found its proper place in the interwar years.

Williams-Ellis was strongly influenced by Swedish Classicism at the 1923 Gothenberg Exhibition, and by the decorative revival of 18th-century styles in England. He built private houses (Llangoed Castle, Powys, 1913; Cornwell Manor, Oxfordshire, 1938; Nantclwyd Hall, Clwyd, redesigned 1956–74), school buildings (at Bishop's Stortford College, 1924, Chatham House, and Stowe School, 1925), and housing in private estate villages, such as Cushenden, Co. Antrim (1926), and Cornwell. The Fishponds Restaurant, Cobham, Kent, a simple timber design, was the closest he came to the Modern Movement. The Italianate garden of his home at Plas Brondanw, Gwynedd, is especially fine.

Williams-Ellis was a great campaigner for the environment in Britain, through books, articles, lectures, and campaigns to save buildings and landscape. He was driven by left-leaning politics and a belief in 'more fun for more people'.　　AP

Haslam, R., *Clough Williams-Ellis* (1996)

Wills, Frank (1822–57) English-born architect.
See CANADA.

Wilson, Charles (1810–63) Scottish architect.

One of the chief Glasgow architects of the mid 19th century, and a follower of David *Hamilton, Wilson vigorously developed Hamilton's rich Greco–Romanesque idiom in a series of monumental urban buildings, adding a dash of the *Rundbogenstil. His key works are concentrated in Glasgow's residential west end, where the tall Lombardic towers of his Free Church College (1856–61) crown the imposing Woodlands Hill development (from 1855). Woodlands Hill's variegated classical terraces—centred on Wilson's own stately, rusticated Park Circus—look down on Wilson's sumptuous neo-Renaissance Queen's Rooms (1857–8), just to the south.　　MGl

Wilson, Sir Colin St John (1922–2007)

English architect: a fierce, scholarly opponent of the *International Style, *high tech, and *postmodernism, and proponent of architecture grounded in human values and psychological, as well as physical, needs. His life's work culminated in his design for the British Library, St Pancras (with M. J. Long, 1997), one of the UK's largest buildings and its only major architectural monument of the later 20th century. Much criticized during design and construction, it has been highly acclaimed since opening, particularly by its users.

Wilson joined Leslie *Martin in Cambridge in 1956, teaching at the university and designing together a student residence, Harvey Court, Cambridge (1962), and the Manor Road Libraries, Oxford (1964). Both buildings were based on research into the geometrical potential of built form in relation to function, as was their design for a library for the British Museum (1964). Innovatory research into user needs and function also underlay Wilson's proposals for another enormous

Interior, British Library, London (Colin St J. Wilson, 1970ff.)

building of strong regular geometrical form, the Liverpool Civic and Social Centre (1969), commissioned in 1965 but abandoned in 1972.

Unfashionably, most of his buildings are of brick, of which there were early contrasting explorations in Cambridge, in the closed cubic form of his extension to the School of Architecture (1958), proportioned according to the Golden Section, and the open, cross-wall, organically ordered William Stone Building (1963), a student residence.

Wilson devoted 37 continuous years' work to the British Library, from the original commission as the British Museum Library in Bloomsbury; it would not have been built without his tenacity. During this time there were profound changes in his architectural language, from architecture as order to an ordered architecture of place and occasion, prefigured in designs for houses in Cambridge, 2 & 2A, Grantchester Road (1964) and Spring House (1966), and explored in his teaching at Cambridge as Professor of Architecture (1975–89) and in his writing.

Particularly significant among his essays, all republished in *Architectural Reflections* (1992), were 'The Ethics of Architecture' (1992), propounding architecture as a practical art as opposed to a fine art; and 'The Natural Imagination' (1989), expounding a necessary resonance between degrees of enclosure and deeply seated psychological needs. In 'The Other Tradition' (1995), he explored the argument for an organic architecture responding to an extension of the functional requirement into the psychological realm, seen in the work of *Aalto, *Lewerentz, *Asplund, and *Häring, who influenced Wilson's development of his language, and were themselves influenced by the 19th-century English Free School, the design principles of which Wilson cites as a motivating force behind the design of the British Library.   RJS

Stonehouse, R., *The Architecture of the British Library at St Pancras* (2004)
Stonehouse, R., *Colin St J. Wilson* (2008)

windows Openings in a wall, designed to let in light to an enclosed space, to provide a view outside from the interior, or for ventilation.

Originally, large windows could usually be shuttered or, if expensive, be filled with a translucent material such as horn or mica. Roman building made full use of not only windows but also glass to fill them. Glass had been used since prehistoric times for vessels and ornaments, but Seneca said that the Romans were first using glass for filling windows by AD 65. The failure of Rome in the 5th century removed many building skills, one being window glazing. Indeed, in western Europe glazed windows became a preserve of the rich for another millennium. According to Bede, Benedict Biscop was the first to introduce into England 'builders of stone edifices and makers of glass for windows', but their purpose was to furnish churches, the craftsmen being sent in 674–5 expressly to build in the Roman manner. Church windows developed thereafter, particularly after the Conquest, with its concomitant increase in wealth and church building. This resulted in an ever increasing size of window. They could be partitioned vertically by mullions into separate lights, and, similarly, could be partitioned horizontally by transoms. The upper part could continue the mullions upwards into elaborate tracery, reaching a peak in such huge windows as that filling the east end of Gloucester Cathedral (c.1350–60), which has thirteen major and minor mullions, and seven stages of transoms. Simultaneously the glass was coloured to produce a whole new decorative art form.

Windows seem to have been universal in all but the meanest houses long before the Conquest. These openings were no more than rectangular gaps in walls, which, if more than about 600 mm (2 ft) wide, were protected by vertical bars and perhaps closed by hinged or sliding shutters. Glazed windows were unknown in Southampton's 12th-century houses, many of which had round-headed two-light windows with a central shaft and a round relieving arch above, and a deep internal splayed reveal, of a Romanesque pattern common in Europe, and these were simply shuttered. Many ordinary houses may have turned to translucent oilcloth or parchment as a poor response to the problem of keeping out harsh weather but not light, as in the brighter Levant windows, which were filled with bone, mica, or translucent stone. Reed or withy mats

could achieve the same effect, but, like cloth curtains, they were probably more likely to be hung behind glazed windows.

The widespread use of glass in domestic windows probably dates only from the 13th century, and then seems to have descended the social scale until, at the end of the Middle Ages, quite ordinary houses had a glazed window or two. Because of their framed construction, late medieval timber houses might have long bands of windows, the upper parts carved with tracery, just like the stone windows of a church. These windows might extend across much of the front of a house, and be joined by windows of less depth but reaching the same height, known as clerestories, so that the whole elevation was fenestrated. Glass was expensive, so the more one used, the more one showed one's wealth, and the more esteem reflected on the building. Akin to the vast areas of glass in late medieval churches, large domestic windows remained the fashion well into the 17th century. It was then fashion, particularly for all things classical, which reduced the size of windows, rather more, one suspects, than the realization that large windows made interiors uncomfortably bright, caused precious dyes to fade, and aggravated the fluctuations of temperature within, due to the poor insulating qualities of glass.

When the advances of the Industrial Revolution improved the transparency of window glass and allowed it to be made in ever larger sheets, size again took on an element of esteem, regardless of other utilitarian considerations. Widely used for orangeries and conservatories, glazed windows became ever larger, achieving a spectacular success in the Crystal Palace, which was all window. Forgetting its problematic insulation, architects hung a whole architectural theory on the notion that light meant life, and one could not have too much of it. Thus the Modern Movement embraced large windows, going as far as cladding whole buildings in glass, ignoring any problems of heat gain or loss.

Considering the structuring and fastening of windows: in the later Middle Ages windows were sometimes made in the form of casements, hinged vertically so that part could open, either inward or outward. The casement itself comprised a flanged iron frame with the individual panes or quarries of glass set into lead cames, which fitted into the frame and would be tied down to slim saddle-bars that spanned the frame for extra support. In the 1680s a new form of window arrangement came into use. Known as a sash, it took the form of a sliding glazed panel, like a shutter, that slid open vertically or less usually horizontally. Vertical sashes took the form of pairs, an outer upper one, and a lower inner one, eventually being counterbalanced by weights. Since they did not project when open, they were of especial advantage where space was restricted, and so were quickly adopted in towns.

Windows derive their forms from their various functions. Opening pairs of glazed windows that reach the ground are known as French windows after their introduction by Hardouin-Mansart at Versailles in the 1680s. A bay window is simply one that projects, and if it is of round plan it is known as a bow window, or as a canted bay if its sides project diagonally. A more elaborate form, known as an oriel, adds status to a particularly grand room or to a hall where it will light the high table, and balance the porch sheltering the entrance at the low end, and it may either rise from the ground, or be corbelled out, or be supported on brackets. A dormer window, so-called as it often lights a sleeping room, projects from the roof, either over the eaves or a parapet, or from the roof itself, and has a roof of its own.   APQ

Wittgenstein, Ludwig (1889–1951) Engineer, architect, and philosopher. Between 1927 and 1929, at the instigation of his sister, Margaret Stoneborough,

Ludwig Wittgenstein designed her family house in Vienna, first in collaboration with the Viennese architect and student of Adolf Loos, Paul Engelmann, then single-handedly. Having initially trained as an engineer, Wittgenstein designed for the house a number of ingenious mechanical devices, including an elevator, all the locks, a dumbwaiter, convection heating under the floor, and retractable iron curtains on the east side of the ground floor. Stylistically, the house is much more radical in its bareness and lack of symmetry and proportion than any of its contemporaries. During the war the house was abandoned by the family through the Nazi occupation, and subsequently it fell into disrepair and Wittgenstein's role in its design was forgotten. Hans Hollein first made public the authorship of the house in an article of 1969, ultimately saving it from demolition.   LL

Wijdeveld, P., *Ludwig Wittgenstein, Architect* (1994)

Wolff, Jacob, the Elder (*c*.1546–1612) German mason. An early exponent of Renaissance motifs in southern Germany, Wolff is best known for the magnificent Pellerhaus he built for Martin Peller in Nuremburg (1602–7, destroyed), which combined three heavily rusticated but otherwise restrained and well-proportioned storeys of a kind Peller had observed in Venice, with a richly decorated, steep, 3-storeyed shaped gable. Less exuberantly finished is his connecting range (1600–07) that forms a long courtyard between the wings of the Marienburg Castle above Würzburg.   APQ

women architects Architects who are female invariably reject the term 'woman architect' as an identity, and the antiquated 'lady architect' is considered unprofessional and defunct. Nevertheless, women have been, and are, positioned differently within architectural practice and the profession in terms of hierarchies of gender, power, and visibility, and therefore have a distinct and significant experience and history.

Increasingly from the 16th to the 19th century, women's participation evolved into the role of architect in the amateur tradition, which encompassed theory and design. Directed by philanthropic and social concerns throughout the 19th century, women in architectural production attained professional status by 1900. Women architects in Scandinavia were in the vanguard of education and professional practice. Today, women work at all levels of architecture from principal partners to the most junior members of design teams, in a broad range of activities, which include teaching, writing, and research, as well as designing buildings. Long hours, low pay, and a highly gendered work culture impact negatively on women's experience and contribution, but their outstanding individual achievement remains in stubborn contrast to their overall under-representation in the design process and in the profession (c.14% in Britain in 2005).

The entry of women into the profession began in the late 19th century in Europe and American, but in both developed and developing countries it is mainly a 20th-century story. Although the first woman members of the AIA (Louise Béthune, 1888) and the RIBA (Ethel Charles, 1898) trained in the traditional way in an architect's office, pupillage was highly problematic for women. Crucially, the rise of formal, systematic architectural education facilitated women's access to architecture. As early as 1890, Signe Hornborg was granted a degree in architecture in Finland, while the prestigious Ecole des Beaux-Arts, Paris, awarded a diploma in architecture to the American Julia *Morgan in 1902. By the 1920s and 1930s, substantial numbers of women trained in schools of architecture.

Countries in the British Empire (later Commonwealth) provided substantial commissions for British women, but they lacked the visibility of work at home. Jane Drew joined local conditions of practice to

the principles of Modernism across Africa, the Middle East, and most notably at Chandigarh, India (housing, school, women's college and nurses' home, 1951–6). In post-colonial countries, the education of women as architects served as markers and vehicles of modernity and new national identities. As elsewhere, architects such as Eulie Chowdhury (India) and Minnette De Silva (Sri Lanka) acted as role models for younger women. The unity of modern architecture and indigenous arts struck a cross-cultural chord among diverse architects, including De Silva, Lina Bo Bardi (Brazil), and Pravina Mehta (India). In the Middle East, architecture is often a preferred profession for women whose extended families and networks of friends and neighbours assist with childcare and domestic work. Nonetheless, in countries such as Botswana, women's traditional power as builders was reduced by modernization and the transfer of housing to professional architects.

Modernism was attractive to many women in architecture who identified its 'clean sweep of the past' and its call for a better world with improved conditions for all. Grete Schütte-Lihotzky's 'Frankfurt kitchen' (1926) and Zoja Dumengji 's Infective Disease Hospital, Zagreb (1935), embodied Modernism's social programme and scientific functionalism. In her unexecuted community buildings (1930s), Eileen *Gray investigated the social and political possibilities of modernist design, while her carefully considered houses, E-1027, Roquebrune (1926–9), and Tempe à Pailla, Castellar (1932–4), brought a profoundly humane sensibility to the new materials and modernist space. Elizabeth Scott employed a more conservative Modernism at the Shakespeare Memorial Theatre, Stratford-upon-Avon (1932), which was seen as a victory for all women and as evidence of their ability to design and win large-scale public commissions.

With the advance of the Welfare State, opportunities for women in the public sector proliferated. Government and local authority offices gave architects scope to design social architecture, most importantly mass housing and schools, informed by progressive architectural and social ideas (Rosemary Stjernstedt, LCC's Alton East, Roehampton, 1950). The ambition and scale was remarkable. At Hunstanton School (1949–54), Alison and Peter Smithson proffered an experimental 'Brutalist' rethinking of Modernism, while Mary Medd played a leading role in Hertfordshire's innovative programme of school building. Today in Britain the pendulum has swung away, but in France a vigorous public sector clientele exists to provide work which is the cornerstone of many women's practices.

Heralded by Patti Hopkins' Royal Gold Medal (joint winner, 1994), the groundswell of high profile projects and accolades in recent years culminated when Zaha Hadid became the first woman to win the Pritzker Prize, 'the Nobel Prize of Architecture' (2003). International reputations are not however unfamiliar territory for many contemporary women: Gae Aulenti transformed thinking about the reuse of historic buildings for art museums at the Musée d'Orsay, Paris (1986), while a cult following and the use of industrialized materials in a precise, highly refined manner unites the architecture of Itsuko Hasegawa, Eva Jiricna, and Odile Decq.

Although dominated by the star system, contemporary architecture is fundamentally collaborative. One characteristic form of women's collective practice, the feminist co-operative, was demonstrated most fully by Matrix at the Jagonari Asian Women's Centre, London (1984). Their collaborations emphasized the process of design over the end product (of the building) by involving the client or user group and by sharing professional power and expertise. The ubiquitous husband and wife team expresses shared interests and the urgent need to negotiate personal and professional lives through flexible working. A global phenomenon, these teams represent architects of all ages, working in a range of building types, from Denise Scott Brown/Robert Venturi in Philadelphia to Karla Kowalski/Michael Szyszkowitz in Graz. However, competing with the reputation of prominent male collaborators proved a long road for Marion Mahony (Frank Lloyd Wright), Charlotte Perriand (Le Corbusier), and Lilly Reich (Mies).   LW

Lorenz, C., *Women in Architecture: A Contemporary Perspective* (1990)

Museum of Finnish Architecture, *Profiles: Pioneering Women Architects from Finland* (1983)

Toy, M. (ed.), *The Architect: Women in Contemporary Architecture* (2001)

Walker, L. (ed.), *Women Architects: Their Work* (1984)

wood/timber   Wood is normally used for light construction, for detailing and finishing, and such fixtures and fittings as floorboards, doors, panels, and cornices, while timber is normally used for heavy structural parts, such as posts, beams, and rafters. Two different crafts of working wood and timber emerged in medieval Europe, namely that of the joiner and that of the carpenter. Add to these the woodmen responsible for the growth and upkeep of supplies, and the merchants who procured abroad what could not be found at home, and a major building industry emerges.

No building material contrasts more greatly with inert stone, brick, and earth than live timber. Most houses around the world are built in timber, and practically every building employs wood or timber in some part of its fabric. Unlike the inert materials it lacks permanence, so the archaeological record of its use is less clear. This shows that in comparatively backward places such as prehistoric Britain wood had a major role in building from the first, as it seems to have done in much of the world. It is relatively easy to make a strong wooden or timber structure if the single prerequisite of enough trees is at hand. This was usually the case to begin with, but by the 4th millennium BC agriculture in Britain was advancing so rapidly that clearances were denuding the landscape of its natural woodland. Trees were so extensively used in manufacturing and building as well as for implements and fuel that woodland was specially managed to ensure adequate supplies. Coppicing, a process whereby trunks were cut just above ground and allowed to regenerate by growing new shoots that could be harvested almost indefinitely, produced straight poles, ideal for light building work as well as for fencing and fuel. The ancient trackways of Somerset were built from cultivated and coppiced trees, a practice of woodland management that continued until the Industrial Revolution killed off traditional crafts.

Early houses were roughly built and often round in plan, wooden stakes being driven into the ground, according to their archaeological traces, by implication to support some kind of wattle and daub walling. Interspersed among them, there might be more substantial timber poles, which allowed the walls to be raised higher and could support a ring beam, and above that a conical thatched roof. In wider buildings, there was an inner ring of posts to support the roof, and these had the advantage of being set into earth that remained relatively dry, thus reducing the onset of rot. The archaeological record of prehistoric Britain suggests that the bulk of Bronze Age and Iron Age houses were built in this form. The round shape not only gave them enough strength to bear the weight of the roof, but also served well against the pressure of the wind. Such houses seem to have been almost universal. The round *usha* of Tihama farmers in Saudi Arabia is first recorded three and a half millennia ago. Similarly the *fale tele* of Samoa is the largest form of Polynesian round house that was common two thousand years ago. The Hutu of Rwanda still build round houses of an ageless traditional form. Less usual is the Zulu *indlu* of Natal, whose domical shape is based on hoops of withies

radiating from the forked top of a central pole. It is a short step to the *tipi* of the North American plains, a conical tent that was at once strong and readily movable, thanks to four tall poles that support its substructure, and animal hide cladding. The analagous Yurt of the Mongolian steppes does a similar job, but with a structure of willow lattice lashed to a wooden ring that supports a low conical roof.

Where timber was plentiful it was used to construct mass walls rather than framed walls. The trunks were butted together, either vertically or horizontally, to make a heavy strong wall that only needed an earthen filling to block the draught from penetrating small gaps. Horizontal logs are generally used for rectangular buildings, and, although vertical logs could be set in the ground to form any shape, they normally are used for rectangular buildings too. Vertical timber walling or stave-walling was common in northern Europe, but is comparatively rare because the timbers, when set in the ground, are prone to rot as indicated by the restored stave-walls of Greensted church, Essex (*c.*1060–1100). When mounted on a damp-proof sill they have a better chance. A more sophisticated form was to use planks instead of raw logs, and slot these into the sills and plates of a framed building, such as Borgund church (*c.*11150) in Norway. Vertical timber walling, though localized, is widespread. The Maoris of New Zealand traditionally build *whare*, a cluster of houses constructed from closely set vertical poles, which lean inwards slightly and are protected outside by overhanging eaves of bullrush thatch and inside by bracken. When logs are laid horizontally to form walls, the ends of the logs of adjacent walls are either lapped over each other at the angle, or butted against a corner post. The more primitive form of lapping the ends is typical of the Russian peasants' traditional *izba*, and appears widely in Scandinavia as well. It was probably Swedish settlers who took the form across the Atlantic when they settled in Delaware in the 1630s, and provided the prototype of the log cabin of the mid-west. In Switzerland the typical Alpine farmhouse is made of readily available fir logs, sometimes butted against corner posts, sometimes lapped over each other, the two methods often appearing in the same house. A plain, low-pitched roof with heavy overhanging eaves keeps off winter snow and provides plenty of space outside the walls for drying crops, sheltering animals, and storing firewood. Each valley has a characteristic variation on the basic pattern.

Timbers could be used roughly and unsquared like this, poles being simply lashed together. But squared timber, joined by lap-joints and mortises and tenons, is far more efficient, as such timbers can be quickly erected into a substantial frame. The techniques were well developed in prehistoric times, as surviving fragments of Bronze Age structures at Flag Fen, Peterborough, show. These long predate the sophisticated methods of framing known to the Romans, who were masters of all forms of building. The development of joinery meant that a few weeks could see the erection of a large hall, and this could be deconstructed as quickly, for its timbers to be reused elsewhere. This was a cheaper way of building than in stone, and in many places no more expensive than earth. Timber could be carved with mouldings or figurative sculpture, just as stone could, and its posts, studs, and braces could be disposed in pleasing patterns that implied status and conspicuous expenditure.

Timber-framed buildings are found throughout the world, some using hard wood, others soft, some with sophisticated carpentry, others with little more than lap-joints. The framed houses of western Europe depend on forms of carpentry that quickly developed in the 12th and 13th centuries to become not only efficient structurally, but also a status-symbol that is as potent today as it was during their heyday. All kinds of regional variations mark the houses of France and Germany: the framed houses of the Landes, for

instance, are clearly different from those of Normandy. In England two basic kinds of frame appear, and separate schools of carpentry in the western Midlands, the north and the south-east. Framed houses with far greater variations than these appear all round the world, adapted to many different terrains. The framed houses of Sri Lanka are comparatively light but use the abundant hard wood of tropical forests, and the frames are set directly on the ground. In Java, by distinction, the frames are typically raised on low stones, which not only keep them above the wet soil but also allow a flow of cool air beneath the house, which helps ameliorate the hot humid climate. This is taken to an extreme in various parts of the tropics where the houses are raised on piles over water. Such houses are common around the islands of Indonesia and along its river estuaries, generally around the South China Sea, and also in mainland China. They can be found, for example, in southern Yunnan, along the Mekong River and its tributaries. Here, the ground floor is for livestock with the living space above. Similarly in Africa, the Toffinou tribe of Dahomey, who inhabit the shores of tidal Lake Nokwé, build their houses on tall piles, using timber from the mangrove forests of the hinterland, as well as bamboo and palm leaves. In southern Chile the inhabitants of the Chiloé archipelago build similarly, so arranging their *palafitos* that they stand well clear of the water at low tide, but at high tide form a landing stage for their fishing boats. The Annamese of Vietnam's mountain chain go one stage further: they use fine-grained hard wood for their rectangular houses, which are built on floating rafts so that they can move around the mountain lakes like houseboats, following the fish on which their economy is based.

In Britain the paramount building timber was oak, the finest hard wood for building. When especially long and stout timber was needed, this would come from mature trees chosen from parks or forests. For more ordinary buildings, the trunks of younger, standard trees generally served. These grew naturally in woods and hedges, but so great did the demand for building timber become, that they were eventually cultivated in managed woodland, where they grew quickly and straight upwards among underwood. From the 13th century onwards, this demand set builders to look abroad for supplies, particularly of timber from wildwood, which had become scarce in England and Wales. The Baltic became a traditional source of supply, mainly of broad flat timbers used for wall planking and floor boards. While the craft of carpentry produced magnificent timber buildings right through the Middle Ages, its skills only turned in the 12th and 13th centuries to the development of frames that could have a chance of long-term survival.

Before that, timber buildings depended on posts for their support, which were possibly squared, like their predecessors in Roman Britain, and had lap-joints and perhaps mortises and tenons so as to form a sound frame. But, because the timbers were set into holes in the ground, the firmness this gained was at the cost of a short life, owing to the onset of rot. An alternative building method employed timber planks, which were set up vertically in trenches and arranged in various ways to support either horizontal planks and boards, or an infilling of wattles daubed with an earthen mixture. This method of building was widespread, appearing across the North Sea and near the Baltic coast, where it may have originated, and it seems to have lasted until at least the 13th century and probably longer.

As carpenters refined their techniques in the 13th century by carefully jointing the horizontal and vertical timbers, and triangulating their joints with braces, a rigid timber frame could be constructed on pad-stones or timber sills that formed a waterproof base. In the first instance this was achieved through a multiplicity of braces and several extremely long timbers. But, during the 13th century, carpenters progressively reduced the number and length of these separate timbers, and

employed types of joint that were more efficient. This left no room for mistake: it was no longer possible to add parts to an assembled frame if these had been forgotten during the proper stage of their assembly. But this immediately removed the old problem of decay, since rot could be avoided, as well as providing economies in timber.

The earliest buildings framed by these new methods adopted a wide centre divided by arcades of stout posts from lower and narrower aisles. One of the first great surviving aisled halls was built for the bishop's palace at Hereford with timber felled in 1179. The all-important junction of a vertical post and the wall-plate or arcade-plate that it supported in the longitudinal plane and the tie it supported in the lateral plane was crucial to stability. The means by which this was achieved seems to have been entirely of English origin. During the 13th century carpenters devised an ingenious compound joint that employed a lower mortise and tenon to hold the post and plate, and an upper mortise and tenon to hold the tie, which was then lap-dovetailed over the plate, thus clamping it in place. This practice so satisfied carpenters that it lasted some 600 years. No other method was so universally applied in Britain, despite others being common on the Continent. It indeed worked well, but shrinkage of the green timber as it dried out could strain the joints to such an extent that the head of the post might split. Yet this compound joint became an essential feature of the carpenter's grammar, seemingly understood without question equally by the woodmen who produced the timber and the carpenters who cut it.

Lateral stability in these early aisled structures was provided by bracing together the centre and aisles with very long straight timbers, and applying large numbers of subsidiary timbers to add a degree of stiffening. During the 13th century carpenters learnt how to dispense with these and frame their buildings and roofs with fewer, shorter timbers of uniform section or scantling, which greatly eased the problems of supply and their ability to mass-produce buildings. This inaugurated the so-called common-rafter roof, which comprises pairs of rafters, pegged at their apex and often braced by collars about a third of the way down, all made from timber of common scantling. Although arcades enhanced the status of the wide halls where they had first been developed, arcade-posts interfered with the internal space, and so were slowly abandoned in the later Middle Ages in nearly all buildings that did not need to have a span of more than about 6.5 m (22 ft), or the length of a readily available beam of oak. This left at its simplest a timber box, framed on a rectangle of sill-beams, with four corner posts that carried the weight of all above, namely wall-plates and tie-beams, all suitably braced together, and, mounted on them, the roof frame and rafters.

This box-frame became one of two basic forms of timber building from the late 13th century onwards. It comprised a series of bays that could extend lengthwise as far as desired, or bays that could be arranged to form angles, making winged plans shaped like an L, a T, or an H. This bay system links the structure with the plan in an immediately comprehensible way that is not found in other forms of building, whether of timber or stone.

An important development in box-framing, which had all the advantages of a highly visible status symbol, allowed a frame to accommodate an upper floor. It was achieved by tenoning the inner end of each floor-joist firmly to a bridging-piece or *bressumer and simply resting its outer end on a second bressumer at the front and projecting it forward to produce an overhang or jetty, which would advertise the existence of the upper floor, and, since these were still not universal, confer a fashionable degree of status. First used in crowded towns where upper floors became a necessity, jetties appear at the same time on the Continent, so the idea may well be an import.

An alternative method of framing bays, which again came into prominence in the 13th century, carried the weight of the roof independently of the walls on a cranked A-frame. This comprised a pair of curved or elbowed timbers, known as crucks, joined together at the apex and braced by a collar. A series of cruck-pairs, linked by lengthwise timbers carried on their backs, formed the basic frame of a cruck building. Unlike the box-frame, the cruck frame is inherently stable transversely and has little need of either extensive bracing or sophisticated joinery. Despite these advantages, crucks serve best in relatively small buildings, otherwise they must be very stout and long if they are to do their job. The availability of suitable timber therefore set limits to their use. While they can reach a little over 10 m (33 ft), as they do at Pershore Abbey's unequalled barn at Leigh Court, Worcestershire, this needs massive bowed timbers of a similar length to its great span, and with a maximum scantling of well over 0.5 m (1½ ft). Such timbers were way beyond what woodmen could quickly cultivate, and very large cruck-framed buildings are consequently rare. Even ordinary crucks of, say, 6 m (about 20 ft) in length probably came not from the young trees of managed woodland, but from the trunks and a low curving branch of more aged trees that had to be specially selected. Crucks could, nevertheless, be used and reused because they could be as easily dismounted as raised.

Although there were further developments in timber framing after the 14th century, these were few and of little importance when compared with what had been achieved since the 12th century. Only the onset of industrialization brought significant change. This mostly centred around the use of standardized trusses cut from imported Baltic soft wood, mostly fir and pine, and the use of iron nails, screws, and straps to secure their joints. One major form of timber construction did emerge, and this was the balloon frame. It was designed to use soft wood cut to a single uniform scantling, which was then assembled into structural wall and floor panels that were rigid enough when joined together to bear the weight of a similarly panelled roof, thus forming a balloon. Although English migrants took their old methods of timber framing with them to America as they colonized New England, it was the balloon frame that colonized the New World. APQ

Berg, Arne, *Architecture in Wood* (1971)

Buxton, D., *The Wooden Churches of Eastern Europe* (1981)

Wood, John senior (1704–54) and **John** junior (1728–81) British architects, of Bath. The elder Wood began the architectural transformation of Bath, developing Queen Square (completed 1734) and pressing ahead with his scheme for a Circus and Forum, and designing Prior Park (1735–48). The Circus, a miniature, inside-out version of the Roman Colosseum, was completed by the younger Wood, who extended the project to the Crescent. APQ

Woods, Shadrach (1923–73) US architect, who contributed significantly to the renewal of modern architecture after World War II. He criticized the neo-monumental tendencies of the 1950s, by introducing the concepts of 'Stem' (1960) and 'Web' (1962) which stressed the importance of change and circulation in buildings in sustaining open social interaction and maximization of choice.

After studying engineering, literature, and philosophy, he worked for Le Corbusier (1948), and then co-directed with Georges Candilis ATBAT-Afrique, Northern Africa (1951–4), developing new types of regionalist social housing. He set up an architectural practice in Paris with Candilis and Alexis Josic (1954), which produced the projects most representative of his theoretical positions. Even when built, many of his innovative buildings remained powerful diagrams, except Berlin Free University

(1963), for which Jean Prouvé and Schiedhelm were collaborators.

Woods returned to the US permanently after the Paris partnership was dissolved (1969), and practised in New York (Redevelopment Plan, SoHo District, New York, 1969; Douglas Circle, Central Park, New York, 1970). He wrote numerous articles, the most significant in *Carré Bleu*, and a book, *The Man in the Street* (1975). AT

workers' clubs, Soviet Union Workers' clubs were built in large numbers in the former Soviet Union and eastern bloc countries. In the years immediately succeeding the Russian Revolution (1917), their purpose was mainly political, to serve as 'centres for mass propaganda and the development of creativity among the working class' (CPSU 12th Party Congress), but eventually their focus turned to culture and education. One of the earliest competitions (1919), for a Workers' Palace in Petrograd, set out the requirements: a large hall for meetings of 300–400 people, and theatrical events; lecture theatres and study areas; a concert hall; a gym; and a self-service restaurant.

Architecturally, the most interesting examples were built in the Soviet Union in the 1920s, particularly the five clubs by *Melnikov, all in Moscow: the Rusakov; the Gorky; the Kauchuk; the Frunze; and the Burevestnik (all between 1926 and 1929). Melnikov took great pains to design spaces which could be used for a variety of uses, and his façade designs, although they appear somewhat arbitrary, are designed to express the interior spaces. For example at the Rusakov club (1927–9), the three massive wedges projecting above the glazed façade support the slope which carries the theatre's seating.

Whereas Melnikov tended to gather diverse spaces into one volume, Il'ya Golosov emphasized one major element, such as the glazed cylinder at the corner of the Zuev Club, Moscow (1927–8), to which all the other parts were subordinate. For the Railwaymen's Clubs, a standard design, a more strictly functional approach was adopted by *Ginsburg—an approach carried to its logical conclusion by Alexander and Leonid *Vesnin in the use of a pavilion layout to house buildings of various types, in a series of workers' clubs in the Baku area (end of the 1920s).

See also GENTLEMEN'S CLUBS.   PG

Khan-Magomedov, S. O., *Pioneers of Soviet Architecture* (1987)

workhouses Buildings for those unable or unwilling to work, but thus inevitably accommodating destitute, disabled, mentally handicapped or sick, elderly, old, and vagrant people, as well as orphans and petty criminals.

The Old Poor Law forced vagrants back to their native parishes, which became responsible for them. The distinction between destitution and crime gradually became blurred, and the institutions, modelled on Bristol's 1696 workhouse, became increasingly carceral. As this change intensified, the variations in the older type were reduced, as the formerly open courts were enclosed and multiple entries (e.g. for individual family units) were eliminated. The block plans were in the shape of a U, H or E, based on those of the classical country house.

Most of the 17th- and 18th-century designs were merely the pragmatic designs, of which some palatial schemes were conceived and built. The most spectacular unbuilt scheme was Henry Fielding's vision for 'a body of men united under one government in a large city' for the Middlesex County House (1753), designed by Thomas Gibson. In his design 6,000 people were to be housed in two blocks (one for men, the other for women) set around courtyards; on the central axis was a magnificent chapel. A built example of such a large formal project, rare in Britain, was the H-plan Smallburgh House of Industry in Norfolk (1785) with separate accommodation for six categories of individuals, and family rooms; a large school room; a

chapel on the central axis, and specialized workrooms. In Continental Europe such formal schemes were common, often on a cruciform plan with a chapel at the crossing, as in the case of Vittone's Ospizio di Carità at Casale Monferrato (begun 1739).

The 1834 New Poor Law introduced a much harsher regime. Groups of parishes could combine into Unions (some 600 for England and Wales) to build and run workhouses. Between 1835 and 1841 some 320 Union boards decided to build central workhouses.

By 1835 the Commissioners published model plans, designed by their architect, Sampson Kempthorne, who went on to design a number of Union workhouses. Initially they suggested separate buildings for the aged, children, able-bodied men, and women. But soon a shortage of capital and staff resulted in single, highly segregated, complexes. Kempthorne's various designs were radial, either three- or four-armed, with the master's accommodation at the centre. These plans were developed by others— notably the partnership of George Gilbert *Scott and William Bonython Moffatt, which was responsible for some forty workhouses. Their design aims, both stylistically and in planning, were to reduce what they regarded as the prison-like features of the Kempthorne models. In planning they opened up the three-armed and four-armed Kempthorne designs, with more open courtyards and detached blocks. Finally the main block became linear. But surveillance and control still retained as high a priority as in the Kempthorne models. In style they adopted the less severe Gothic, Tudor (Elizabethan), and Jacobean forms.

By mid century workhouses developed into enormous 'total' institutions, combining the functions of school, orphanage, bridewell, prison, hospital, almshouse, asylum, and factory on one site, sometimes under one roof, sometimes in a series of detached blocks.   TM

Markus, Thomas A., *Buildings and Power* (1993)

Wren, Sir Christopher (1632–1723) English
architect. A true Universal Man in the Renaissance
sense, and Britain's greatest architect, Wren brought
to architecture a feeling for assured monumentality
that regained for England a place in Europe which
had been lacking since the rebirth of Classicism some
two centuries before his arrival on the scene. Thereby
he laid the foundation for the ensuing British Baroque
style, and equally many of the subsequent classical
styles. His architecture is much copied, since it
symbolizes the particularly English qualities of an
Augustan age. Arguably he also set the course of
revived Gothic until the serious moralizing of the
19th century. An inspiration to future generations
of architects, Wren was an out-and-out professional
who understood the art of compromise. This is
evident in both of his masterpieces, St Paul's
Cathedral and the Royal Naval Hospital at
Greenwich, monuments that have never
been surpassed in Britain.

The son of a clergyman who later became Dean of
Windsor, Wren educated at Westminster School,
leaving in 1646 to spend three years in London before
going up to Wadham College, Oxford. Here he studied
mathematics and other scientific subjects, including
anatomy. He associated with the group of brilliant
scientists who formed the nucleus of what became the
Royal Society, of which Wren was himself president at
one time. His scientific interests extended to sundials
and the measurement of time, and hence astronomy.
This subject was rapidly transforming itself from arcane
speculation to rational enquiry, and would lead to
Newton's great works later in the century as well as
the practical developments in navigation which gave
Britain the key to the world's oceans. Appropriately, he
designed the Royal Observatory, Greenwich (1675–6).
Wren stayed at Oxford after graduation until 1657,
when he was appointed Professor of Astronomy at
Gresham College, London. This post he held until

St Stephen Walbrook, City of London (Sir Christopher Wren,
1680)

1661, when he returned to Oxford as Savilian
Professor of Astronomy.

Already in 1660 he was concerning himself
with architectural design, and in 1663 joined the
Commission for repairing St Paul's. His ability as a
scientific draughtsman and his love of model-making,
together with a deepening theoretical understanding of
architecture, led to two commissions for buildings, one
from his uncle to design a new chapel at Pembroke
College, Cambridge (1663–5), the other for a new
assembly hall, the Sheldonian Theatre, Oxford
(1664–9). Both show the benefits of studying the

antique, and the Sheldonian attracted great attention for the ease with which Wren spanned its wide space without internal columns.

In 1665 Wren made his only visit abroad, going to France, among other reasons 'to survey the most esteem'd Fabricks of Paris'. These included the Louvre and Vaux-le-Vicomte, the church of the Sorbonne, the Collège des Quatre Nations, and various chateaux. During this visit he was able to see the several proposals for the east front of the Louvre at the very moment when the aged *Bernini was in Paris presenting his design. 'I would have given my skin for it,' Wren recalled, 'but the old reserv'd Italian gave me but a few minutes view—I had only time to copy it in my fancy and memory.'

Wren returned in 1666 to England and the problems of restoring St Paul's when, in a short while, the Great Fire of London completely changed the circumstances of his life. His plan to rebuild the City on up-to-date utopian lines was no more than a pipe-dream; London had to be rebuilt immediately to ensure its commercial viability, and that meant on the lines of its former streets. But his designs for rebuilding the City churches, to be paid for out of a coal tax, were executed and show the extraordinary fecundity of his imagination. In total 52 churches were to be rebuilt, and for these Wren supplied designs that were not only original but also respected to varying degrees the surviving fabric of the pre-Fire churches. Thus their former medieval plan-form was adapted to suit the new needs of Protestant liturgy. Aisled plans, cruciform plans, domed plans, and combinations of these flowed from his hand from 1670 onwards, as did plans for two churches in Westminster, in both Baroque and Gothic, for his assistants to execute under his guidance.

Appointed Surveyor-General of the King's Works, Wren was greatly occupied with these churches, which formed the bulk of his early work, and paved the way for the design of his masterpiece, the rebuilding of St Paul's (1675–1710). Here his thoughts progressed through various models to the centrally planned Great Model, which was rejected as untraditional, and then to the conventional basilican design known as the Warrant Design, since it was approved by warrant. A clause to make minor amendments gave Wren his chance to replace its peculiar spire-like lantern for 'a little pomp' with the famous dome that has dominated the City skyline ever since, even at the cost of some tricky diagonal arches that span the internal piers. Similarly he was able to raise the main walls to give the cathedral the appearance of greater bulk.

His secular works were more modest, as was Chelsea Hospital (1682–92), or left incomplete, as was his rebuilding of Hampton Court (1689–94). Trinity College Library, Cambridge (1676–84), is the epitome of successful contrast, its river side being severe and plain, its court side graced by a Doric and Ionic order. Among much university building, Tom Tower at Christ Church, Oxford (1681–2), stands out for its Tudor Gothic design rising from the base of a 15th-century gatehouse. His greatest secular achievement, the Royal Naval Hospital at Greenwich (1696 onwards), was bound by compromise, resulting from the necessity of retaining Inigo *Jones's Queen's House as the undersized centrepiece of an extremely grand scheme. Here he was assisted by his two great protégés, Nicholas *Hawksmoor and John *Vanbrugh, who carried his flame forward into the 18th century with their extraordinarily robust versions of the Baroque style.   APQ

Downes, K., *The Architecture of Wren* (1982)
Sekler, E. F., *Wren and his Place in European Architecture* (1956)
Summerson, J., *Sir Christopher Wren* (1953)

Wright, Frank Lloyd (1867–1959) US architect. He produced a body of work over seven decades that was always stimulating, usually satisfying, and often superb, securing him a place among the most significant architects of the Western world. Following a year's work at a local engineering firm, Wright entered the University of Wisconsin in 1886, but left during his second semester to find a job in Chicago. He was hired by Joseph Lyman Silsbee, a leading Chicago practitioner of the 'Shingle Style', an undogmatic blend of picturesque forms and materials often combined with historic detail. Wright's initial response to the complex situation of American architecture in the 1880s resulted from this encounter; Silsbee also taught him about Japanese art.

In 1887 Wright joined the firm of Adler and Sullivan, where he met Louis H. *Sullivan, the most potent architectural influence on his career. In contrast to Silsbee's empirical approach to design, Sullivan was obsessed with architectural theory and its relationship to the meaning of style. Like a number of his European contemporaries, Sullivan devoted himself to creating a new architecture that he felt would express the modern age rather than recreate the past. For Sullivan this meant an architecture that was democratic and American, in addition to being modern. A new architecture must be organic, by which he meant that all the elements of a building should be as integral to the whole design as the parts of an organism are related to its successful adaptation. Wright appropriated this term from Sullivan but used it in a much less dogmatic way. During their six-year association, Wright became an ardent believer in Sullivan's teachings, to which he remained committed throughout his life.

In 1893 Sullivan fired Wright in a dispute over independent work, so Wright established his own practice. For the remainder of the decade he experimented with a wide variety of forms, styles, and decoration, some picturesque, others Sullivanian, with occasional forays into the historic styles, as he strove to find his own version of a modern American architecture. He was joined in this search by a group of colleagues, similarly inspired by Sullivan, who have come to be known as the Prairie School.

Mature architecture In 1900 Wright solved Sullivan's problem to his own satisfaction by producing the Prairie House, a middle-class dwelling type that synthesized the lessons from Silsbee and Sullivan, melded with aspects of Japanese architecture and the work of English Arts and Crafts architects such as Voysey and Baillie Scott. Wright's knowledge of Japanese and English work was acquired secondhand, as he had not yet travelled abroad. The type appeared in ideal form two years later at the Ward Willits house (1902), with its characteristic rectilinear forms, open interior, plaster wall surfaces trimmed with unmoulded wooden boards, central fireplace, banks of casement windows decorated with art glass, and overhanging hipped roofs. Despite the appearance of symmetry, circulation through the house is picturesque, not axial. Like many of his residences, the Willits house spreads horizontally across the flat mid-west landscape, giving rise to the erroneous notion that Wright intended to create a regional rather than a national style. Wright's early practice remained mostly residential, with the few exceptions including a steel-framed office block, the Larkin Building (1903–6), and a concrete church, Unity Temple (1905–7). In contrast to the irregular compositions of his houses, these public buildings are symmetrical; they are also separated from their environments, as opposed to the openness with which Wright's residences embrace their surroundings. Wright did not work alone; his office was run by a small band of highly talented individuals, including Walter Burley Griffin and Marion Lucy Mahony.

By the end of the decade, Wright's Prairie style had become a self-referential system of design of which the architect himself finally tired. Yet in 1908 he produced one of his masterpieces, the Frederick Robie house, a brick and stone house whose raised living floor is a connection with its rolling terrain reflected Wright's personal encounters with similar villas in Tuscany. He was then commissioned to create a large-scale public building in Chicago, Midway Gardens (1913–14), an outdoor concert garden, indoor restaurant, and private club, which summarized his accomplishment to that point, even as its expressive ornamentation heralded a change in direction for the architect. The spectacular complex revealed both Wright's keen understanding of American popular culture as well as his recent engagement with European art and culture. Wright's architectural career was then interrupted by a personal crisis, and when he was able to work again, he devoted his time to a single building: the Imperial Hotel in Tokyo, Japan (1913–22). Here he further developed the exaggerated decorated forms to produce what might be called an American Expressionism.

The 1920s saw a renewal of Wright's practice as he worked primarily in California, promoting a construction system of concrete blocks and iron rods. He called these 'textile blocks' because ornamental patterns could be impressed on the surface, like the woven patterns in textiles, uniting structure and ornamentation into a single grand surface. He had created what he called 'machine-age ornament'.

Falling Water, Bear Run, Pennsylvania (Frank Lloyd Wright, 1936)

single, continuous space with living and dining areas separated by a free-standing fireplace. When construction was underway in September 1909, Wright travelled to Europe to oversee production of a deluxe portfolio of his work (*Ausgeführte Bauten und Entwürfe von Frank Lloyd Wright*, Wasmuth, 1911).

Middle years   Returning to America's mid-west, Wright soon settled in south-west Wisconsin, where he built Taliesin, a country villa and studio whose intimate

Second golden age   By the end of the 1920s, Wright became aware of the emerging European Modernism soon to be dubbed the International Style. Wright's attempts to defend his expressive, decorated architecture fell on deaf ears, however, and he himself was the one who changed. Absorbing the ideas of his young rivals even as he rejected them, he produced one of the most extraordinary monuments of the 20th century, the country house Falling Water (1936). To the horizontal floating concrete volumes associated with Walter Gropius and Le Corbusier he wedded weighty, vertical masses of coursed limestone that tie the building to its dramatic site. Intimately

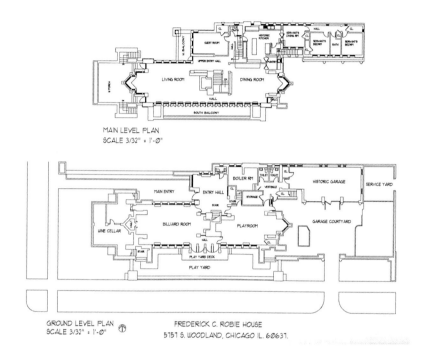

MAIN LEVEL PLAN
SCALE 3/32" = 1'-0"

GROUND LEVEL PLAN
SCALE 3/32" = 1'-0"

FREDERICK C. ROBIE HOUSE
5757 S. WOODLAND, CHICAGO IL. 60637.

Plan: Robie House, South Woodland, Chicago (Frank Lloyd Wright, 1909)

grounded to the landscape—the stream and waterfall become part of the composition—it unites nature and humanity, indoors and out, tradition and modernity into an overwhelming whole. In the same year he created an administration building for the Johnson Wax company (1936), whose superb interior space is made possible by thin 'mushroom' columns that open at their tops into horizontal 'lilypads', with the space lit by horizontal bands of translucent Pyrex tubing.

Unlike the Willits house and Unity Temple, with their similar Prairie vocabulary, Falling Water and the Johnson Wax building are wildly disparate in form and detail. Yet the basic dialectic approach remains the same: residential buildings embrace their surroundings, while public buildings are given self-reflexive interiors, detached from their contexts.

Wright's amazing confidence and energy continued unabated. In 1931, he established the Taliesin Fellowship as a school of architecture and de facto office force. He turned his attention to two of the leading issues of the European modern architects: urban planning and the low-cost house. For the one he proposed Broadacre City, an anti-urban idea for decentralizing contemporary congestion to the countryside. For the other, he devised the Usonian House, a prototype for an inexpensive if middle-class dwelling meant for the average citizen of 'Usonia' (the United States of North America).

For the next twenty years, until his death in 1959, Wright produced hundreds of designs for all building types, developing ideas he had created for Broadacre City and the Usonian House, while occasionally resurrecting unbuilt projects from his decorated period of the 1920s. The crowning achievement of his later years, the Guggenheim Museum in New York (1943–59), was completed shortly after his death. Its spiralling form makes an intentional critique of the planar wall of buildings along Fifth Avenue, while its continuous interior ramp allows visitors to descend at their leisure, concentrating on the works displayed on the outer walls, while easily absorbing the entire exhibition simply by turning around.

Wright was one of the few architects in history capable of reinventing his architecture over several generations and, in his case, through one of the greatest transformations in architectural history, the replacement of Beaux Arts methodology and historic revivalism by the educational system instituted at the Bauhaus and the rise of International Style Modernism. In the Prairie period, Wright devised an original approach to housing design that simultaneously summarized many of the leading ideas of his time. His fertile late period was a constant reminder to the architectural world that there could be an alternative Modernism to that preached by the International Style establishment. Through his personal, organic approach to design, Wright regularly produced designs that were bold and imaginative, grounded in their culture yet aesthetically superior to most of the buildings produced by his contemporaries.

PKr

Kruty, P., *Frank Lloyd Wright and Midway Gardens* (1998)
Levine, N., *The Architecture of Frank Lloyd Wright* (1995)

wrought iron *See* IRON (WROUGHT IRON).

Wu, Liangyong (1922–) Chinese architect. He studied at Cranbrook Academy of Art under Eliel *Saarinen, worked with Eero *Saarinen (G.M. Centre, Detroit, 1950), and returned to China (1951) to join the Tsinhua University, Beijing, carrying out research and teaching.

The rehabilitation of the historical Ju'er Hutong Neighbourhood of Beijing (1987–93), which gained a UN Habitat Award (1992), is his most well known project. Through it Wu developed a new prototype for urban housing, the 'basic courtyard', which preserved the original community structure in continuity with the traditional courtyard system, an 'organic replacement' rather than a conservation of the old urban tissue. To increase the density of the neighbourhood, and to provide modern standards of privacy while maintaining community, Wu used 2–3 floor walk-up apartments forming a courtyard, and recruited the fishbone circulation pattern from the southern China mansion.

Among his other projects are the National Library of Beijing (1976–87) and the restoration and redevelopment of Huitongci Temple and its environment (1985–8). Wu's approach to architecture is Critical Regionalist, committed to modernization while sustaining cultural diversity and local identity. AT

Wurster, William Wilson (1895–1973) US architect and educator. During the 1930s and early 1940s he established a successful residential practice in San Francisco, where he became the leading advocate of regional modernism in the Bay Area and northern California. His hallmark work from this period, such as the Jenson house in Berkeley (1937), the Clark house in Aptos (1937), the Grover and Stevens houses in San Francisco (1939 and 1940), and the Pope house in Orinda (1940), is distinguished by intelligent but strictly functional planning strategies, purposeful simplicity of architectural expression, and responsiveness to site and climate. In 1945 he established the San Francisco office of Wurster, Bernardi, and Emmons, which was known nationally and internationally in the 1950s and 1960s for its residential, commercial, and institutional work in the Bay Area and elsewhere. RTH

Hille, T., *Inside the Large Small House: The Residential Design Legacy of William W. Wurster* (1994)

Wyatt, James (1746–1813) English architect, the most distinguished of a family of which perhaps seventeen members became architects, and several more were associated with building in one form or another. James Wyatt went to Venice (*c*.1762) and Rome, where he made measured drawings of the dome of St Peter's. Yet his first designs show the influence of Robert and James *Adam, since he could study their influential additions to Kedleston Hall in Derbyshire. Commissions for country houses came to him, among them Gaddesden Place, Hertfordshire (1768–74), and Heaton House, Lancashire (1772), which shows the influence of Paine's work at Kedleston as well as the Adams'. But it was his design for the Pantheon in Oxford Street, London (1769–72) which made his name.

This fashionable assembly room, basilican in form with arcaded aisles and apsidal ends, opened the doors to numerous domestic commissions. It also led to public appointments, including to the Office of Works. His architectural talent, however, far outstripped his professional qualities, leading to a chaotic state of affairs in both his public and private works. Moreover, although his designs came from his drawing board with great facility and brilliance, they lacked both consistency and any sense of aesthetic conviction. With equal verve he would do both classical, like Roehampton Grove, London (1777), and Dodington Park, Gloucestershire (1798–1813), or Gothic, like the Royal Military Academy, Woolwich, London (1800–06), and Belvoir Castle, Leicestershire (1801–13). And while his designs might break new ground in their planning, as at Fonthill Abbey, Wiltshire (1796–1812, collapsed), their Gothic clothing was little more than meretricious and romantically gloomy. This brought him celebrity, but when he turned his talent toward restoration, such as the reconstruction of the east end of Durham Cathedral (after 1795), controversy was the result. APQ

Dale, A(nthony), *James Wyatt* (1956)

Wyatt, Sir Matthew Digby (1820–77) English architect, designer, and author, the cousin of James Wyatt. Digby Wyatt travelled on the Continent in 1844–6, drawing for *Specimens of Geometrical Mosaics of the Middle Ages* (1848). His interest in art led to his secretaryship of the Executive Committee for the Great Exhibition of 1851. For this he designed the Byzantine, English Gothic, Italian, Pompeiian, and Renaissance Courts at the Crystal Palace. A flow of publications including *The Industrial Arts of the Nineteenth Century* (1851–3) accompanied designs for carpets, tiles, and wallpaper, and such architectural works as Paddington Station (1854–5, with *Brunel and Owen *Jones) and the Durbar Court, India Office, Westminster (1867). APQ

Wyatt, Samuel (1737–1807) English architect, an elder brother of James Wyatt. He worked under Robert *Adam at Kedleston, becoming proficient in designing medium-sized country houses in a spare neoclassical style, notably Doddington Hall (1777–98) and Tatton Park (1785–91) in Cheshire, and others now demolished. He made alterations or decorated rooms at several others in the same style, which also admirably suited his model farm buildings at Holkham (1780–1807). In 1783–6 his celebrated Albion Mills, Blackfriars, London, was founded on a structural raft and made extensive use of cast iron, both important innovations obscured by their destruction by fire (1791). APQ

Wyatt, Thomas Henry (1807–80) a cousin of James Wyatt and the elder brother of Matthew Digby. T. H. Wyatt was for a while a partner of David Brandon. He had a large practice, as varied as the styles he employed, light-hearted youth giving way to dour old age. Wilton Church, Wiltshire (1843), is memorably Italian Romanesque; his Garrison Church, Woolwich Barracks, London (1863, partly demolished), is floridly

Venetian; St Peter, Wimblington, Cambridgeshire (1874), conventional Decorated Gothic; his early Wiltshire Assize Court, Devizes (1835), is enlightened Grecian; his late Southern Range, Brompton Hospital, London (1879–82), forbidding cliff-like Jacobean.   APQ

Wyatville, Sir Jeffry (1766–1840) English architect. Having demonstrated skill as a draughtsman, Wyatville worked for his uncle James Wyatt (1792–9), after which he built up a large country-house practice serving four dukes, a marquess, seven earls, and, from 1824, royalty. For William IV he began the transformation of Windsor Castle into a modern palace (1824–), for which he was granted the right to the name 'Wyatville', a residence in the Winchester Tower, and knighthood. Of greater professional ability than artistry, he worked in Tudor Gothic for this and Claverton House, Somerset (*c*.1820), Lilleshall Hall, Shropshire (1826–30), and also Sydney Sussex College, Cambridge (1821–2, 1831–2).   APQ

xystus Among the Ancient Greeks, a long covered portico or court used for athletic exercises, from which it passed to the Romans for whom it was an open colonnade or walk, planted with trees, and used for recreation and conversation, rather as a pergola or bower would do in later times. APQ

Yamada, Mamoru (1894–1966) Japanese architect and educator. As a co-founder of Japan's first Modern Movement in architecture, the Bunriha kenchikukai, in 1920, Yamada sought to create a distinctive public architecture, inspired by German *Expressionism. With Tetsurô *Yoshida, he became a leading architect of the Communications Ministry 1920–45, known for his landmark Tokyo Central Telegraph Building (1925), with its crowning line of parabolic arches, and the glistening white-tiled Tokyo Teishin Hospital (1937). In the post-war period, he became a lecturer and architect of Tôkai University, Tokyo. While his late designs, such as Kyoto Tower and the monumental Buddôkan (1964), designed to house judo events of the 1964 Olympics, have been criticized for their direct quotation of historic precedents, he never abandoned his individual expressive ideals.   KTO

Yamasaki, Minoru (1912–86) US-born architect. He was a mainstream Modernist, whose early reputation was established by the Lambert Air Terminal, St Louis, Missouri (1953–6), a skilled exercise in handling thin concrete shell vaults. Unfortunately for his current reputation he is also known for two buildings which are associated with disaster.

The Pruitt-Igoe estate, St Louis (1950–58), of 2,875 units was much praised at the time as a radical example of large-scale social housing. Its design faults, such as the lift system, the lack of designed outdoor space, and the 'streets in the sky' concept, contributed partly to its demise, but the main causes of its rapid disintegration lay far outside the scope of an architect's control.

Naturally, its *postmodernist critics, such as Charles Jencks, ignored such factors. The World Trade Centre (1966–74) was the apotheosis of corporate Modernism, two technologically advanced, but bland, towers isolated on a plaza.　　　　　　　　　　PG

Yeang, Ken (1948–) Malaysian architect. He set up practice in 1976 with Tengku Dato Robert Hamzah (1939–). Yeang first came to the attention of an international audience with the Roof-Roof House (1984) and IBM Plaza (1987), both in Kuala Lumpur. The latter explored the design principles for a tropical urban high-rise building. Yeang's major contribution to architecture is a formal theory and methodology for ecological design that was published as *Designing with Nature* (1995). He is the originator and inventor of the 'bioclimatic skyscraper' and he has interpreted his ecological ideas in numerous projects, the most significant being Menara Mesiniaga (1992) in Kuala Lumpur, and Menara Umno (1998) in Penang. The former received the Aga Khan Award and the RAIA International Award. Singapore National Library continues this investigation and is scheduled for completion in 2005.　　　　　　　　　　RP

　　Powell, R(obert), *Rethinking the Skyscraper: The Complete Architecture of Ken Yeang* (1999)

Yemen has better preserved vernacular architecture than that of most countries, as it was closed to outsiders until 1970. It has also a number of major Islamic monuments. A range of high mountains parallel to the Red Sea traps the monsoon rains from the Indian Ocean, inducing a mild climate in the highlands. From ancient times this region has held 80% of the population of the Arabian peninsula because, to the east and south, along the Indian Ocean, lay the groves of frankincense and myrrh which supplied Pharaonic Egypt, Greece, and Rome, taken there by caravans along the eastern edge of the mountains.

The unique midland and highland architecture of today can be traced back to pre-Islamic times. The modern, square, tower-houses seen in farms, villages, and cities today are sophisticated descendants of circular fortified farmhouses, the *nobah* or *nawbah*, which continued to be built until recently. The mild climate obviated the need to have cross-ventilation against humidity, and fertile ground was scarce, making tall, narrow houses the logical way to build. Clay was abundant and so earth construction predominated (e.g. Sada' and Shibam), but where good building stone was easily available it was preferred—in high buildings the stone being replaced by thinner, lighter walls of baked brickwork (e.g. Sana'a). The lower levels of some of these houses are extremely old.

The ground floor held animals. A mezzanine was used for the storage of grain. The first level had the family living room, in which business might be conducted and visitors initially received. On the next floor was the *diwan*, the formal room of the house, for important family occasions, childbirth, weddings, feasts, and the laying-out of the dead. The kitchen was generally up another level, with smaller rooms used mainly by the women and children. On the roof there would be at least one room used for the afternoon entertainment of close friends.

There are various building types. The earliest mosques are flat-roofed, most influenced by Persian royal halls or *apadānas*; they have elaborately moulded and decorated ceilings carried on high slender columns. The Great Mosque in Sana'a, traditionally built on the instructions of the Prophet, has arcades derived from Byzantine influence, for the largest Christian cathedral south of the Mediterranean stood nearby. The oldest public baths, pre-dating Islam, resemble provincial Roman baths. They are largely built underground to provide maximum insulation, roofed with domes and vaults, and the hot area of the bath is heated by hypocausts and flues in the walls. Caravanserais,

Houses in Sana'a, Yemen

or khans (*samsarah*), were built both with courtyards and without. Typically there were large stables for animals on the lower levels and rooms for lodgings above.

In the coastal plain along the Red Sea, besides beehive huts and tents of grass thatch with colourfully plastered interiors, there are single-storeyed, urban courtyard houses, also richly decorated internally. Finally, in the Wadi Hadramaut to the south-east are the tallest houses in all of Yemen, built of sun-dried clay brick and reaching over 30 m (98 ft) in height. RLe

> Serjeant, R. B., and Lewcock, R., *Sana'a, An Arabian Islamic City* (1983)
>
> Varanda, Fernando, *Art of Building in Yemen* (1982)

Yevele, Henry (d.1400) English mason. Of north Midland origin, Yevele was in London by 1353, working at Kennington Manor in 1357/8 and St Albans Abbey in 1359. He worked at Queenborough Castle, Kent (1361–7), possibly designing it, as later Cooling Castle (1380–81), and Nunney Castle, Somerset (*c*.1373). He designed tombs for the Black Prince, his wife, and probably for Edward III. For his successor, Richard II, he remodelled Westminster Hall (begun 1394). APQ

Yorke, Francis Reginald Stevens *See* YRM.

Yoshida, Tetsurô (1894–1956) Japanese architect, educator and author. As a leading designer with the Ministry of Communications along with Mamoru *Yamada, Yoshida designed the Tokyo Central Post Office (1931) and Osaka Central Post Office (1936), noted for their standardized, rationalist schemes suitable for Japan's climate. He became a close friend of Bruno Taut during his 1933–6 stay in Japan. In the post-war period, he was a professor at Nihon University and published books on Japanese traditional architecture and gardens. KTO

YRM founding partners Yorke, Francis Reginald Stevens (1906–62), Rosenberg, Eugene (1907–90), and Mardall, Cyril (1909–94), architects practising in England. Yorke, a prominent no-nonsense figure on the London modernist architectural scene of the 1930s, was the magnet around whom a major multi-disciplinary practice grew between the 1950s and the 1990s.

Yorke was well-known for concrete houses, and books surveying this subject. He had a softer side to his work, reflecting a background in the Arts and Crafts and a love of materials. Enthusiasm for modern art was shared by all three. Yorke was good at getting commissions, but usually steered his projects from a distance. Rosenberg, a refugee from Prague, became a hospital specialist. Mardall was half Finnish, with an interest in timber construction.

In the 1950s, the work, including many schools, was moderately picturesque, but rigour reasserted itself in Gatwick Airport (1955–8), inaugurating a Miesian stream cultivated by a young future director of the firm, Brian Henderson. His contemporary, David Allford, preferred a heavier mode, and liked to use white tile cladding, which became a trademark at Warwick University (1966). YRM collaborated on two major factory / office buildings with SOM (Boots D90, Nottingham, 1968, and Wills, Bristol, 1975). AP

> Powers, A., *In the Line of Development* (1992)

Zabłocki, Wojciech (1930–) Polish-born architect. *See* SYRIA, MODERN.

Zakharov, Andreyan Dmitriyevich (1761–1811) Russian architect. His mature work began with several pavilions (1798–1800) for the imperial estate at Gatchina. Following his appointment as Admiralty architect in 1805, he undertook projects at naval facilities in St Petersburg and at the Kronstadt naval base, where he built the neoclassical Cathedral of Saint Andrew (1806–17, not extant). His supreme legacy is the Admiralty (1806–23), originally built by Ivan Korobov (1730s) near the Winter Palace and damaged by fire in 1783. Zakharov redesigned the central spire, which rises above an Ionic peristyle with 28 allegorical statues and a heroic entrance arch flanked by statuary. Dodecastyle Doric porticoes anchor each end of the main façade (375 m or 410 yards), from which two perpendicular wings extend to the Neva River and culminate with end blocks that are rigorous statements of geometrical purity. WCB

Zehrfuss, Bernard Louis (1911–96) French architect, who rose to prominence following his association with the UNESCO headquarters building, Paris (1952–8). Unfortunately this led to his planning and design of the La Défense district, Paris—almost a caricature of modernist urbanism, a pedestrian axis lined by skyscrapers and the gigantic CNIT building (1955–8), technically superb, but a visible disfigurement of the Parisian skyline. Within Paris itself, he was responsible for further equally insensitive high-rise developments in Montparnasse (from the 1980s). PG

Zettervall, Helgo (1831–1907) Swedish architect. The influence of *Viollet-le-Duc is shown in his brilliant but controversial restorations of the cathedrals of Lund (1860–80), Uppsala (1885–93), and Skara (1886–94). His own work—for example the Oscar Fredrik's church, Gothenburg (1889–93); the University Building, Lund (1877–82); and the Bolinder House, Stockholm (luxury apartments, 1875–7)—is characterized by striking outlines, marked plasticity, and strong contrasts. The Oscar Fredrik's church is a good examplar, with its dramatically clustered group of narrow eastern towers terminated by needle-sharp spires, conical-roofed presbytery, and prominent transepts. TF

Zevaco, Jean-François (1916–2003) French architect. *See* AFRICA (WEST AFRICA).

Zholtovsky, Ivan (1876–1959) Russian architect. *See* CLASSICISM, PROLETARIAN.

ziggurat from *zigguratu*, 'height' or 'pinnacle' (Assyrian *ziqquratu*). It is a stepped tower, a feature of *Mesopotamian architecture, imitating the sacred mountains which circle the Iranian plateau. A ziggurat was not a temple, but '…a tower whose top *may reach* unto heaven…' (Genesis 11.4). There has been much speculation about the dimensions of ziggurats, but it can be stated with some confidence that the tallest early ziggurat was at Ur (*c*.2100 BC), rising to 19.6 m (64 ft). The largest remaining ziggurat is at Choga Zambil (*c*.1250 BC) in the Susa region of Iran which was originally 105 m (345 ft) square at the base, and reached an estimated 50 m (165 ft) high.

See also MESOPOTAMIA. PG

Zimbalo, Giuseppe (1620–1710) Italian architect, designer of several churches in Lecce, Apulia. The easily carved *pietra leccese*, a golden-tinted limestone, offered too great a temptation to Zimbalo, who scattered putti, fruit, garlands, and vases across his façades in disordered profusion.

However, the façades do have quite distinctive architectural elements. The central feature of the north façade of the Cathedral (1659–70) is a statue of the city's patron, S. Oronzo, framed by a round-headed arch; S. Croce (completed 1695) has a small rose window; the Celestine monastery (now the Prefettura) attached to the church has elaborate window frames set in smoothly banded rustication; and S. Maria del Rosario (1691–1728) has spirally banded columns, straight-sided, not like Solomonic columns. As far as can be ascertained, it was the only building planned by Zimbalo. Because the lateral arms of the Greek cross are much wider than the main axis leading to the altar, the central space is rather lifeless.

It is completely mistaken to regard Zimbalo as a *Baroque architect. Although the façades are richly decorated, they are all essentially flat fronts with sculpture as an *appliqué*. PG

Zimmermann, Dominikus (1685–1766) German architect. Because of his skill as a *stucchodore* and designer of altars, Zimmermann was able to create a closer harmony between architecture and decoration than any of his contemporaries—the *Asams were more interested in decoration and J. M. *Fischer in architecture. The contrast with Fischer is telling in another respect. Zimmermann's plans (1732) for the abbey church of Ottobeuren were clumsy, showing that he could not design buildings on a large scale (the nave is about 100 m or 315 ft long), whereas at this scale Fischer was in his element.

His first five churches, with his brother Johann Baptist (1680–1758) who was responsible for the frescoes, were rather hesitant. But when the brothers turned to designing pilgrimage churches—Our Lady of Sorrows, Steinhausen (1728–33), the Church of Our Lady, Günzburg, near Ulm (1736–41), and the Church of Christ Scourged, Füssen (1746–54), more popularly known as *Die Wies*, because of its meadow setting—their partnership blossomed.

In common with many other architects of pilgrimage churches of the region, Zimmermann favoured the oval plan, because it allowed pilgrims to make a procession around the walls, and to look up at the frescoes. The brilliance (literally) of his designs appeared in their planning for light and colour. Architecture, stucco, and frescoes almost dissolve into each other, to create an overall effect of glorious white light, magnified by the whiteness of the walls and the unfrescoed sections of the ceilings.

To a certain extent the first two churches are experimental, and his masterpiece, indeed one of the greatest masterpieces of the Baroque, is *Die Wies*. Colour is used both symbolically, as the red of the high altar column represents the scourged Christ, and to heighten the sense of procession through space, as the colours mount in intensity, from pale blues and yellows, towards the high altar. Every architectural form is chosen to enhance the effect of light. The lath-and-plaster vaults allow the windows to be shaped with one purpose: to cast as much light as possible at an angle throughout the whole church. Columns are used because they reflect more light than pilasters or piers. Perhaps because these were cheap buildings, financed entirely by popular subscription, the façades and the grouping of the churches with other buildings were uninspired.   PG

Bourke, P., *Baroque Churches of Central Europe* (1962)

Zoroastrian architecture
Of all religions, Zoroastrianism has made the least contribution to architecture. For the first thousand years or so after its founder Zoroaster (an Iranian, who lived at some time between 1700 and 1500 BC), the simple rituals of the seven great feasts and the corporate sacrifices were performed in the open air without any buildings, as was the funerary practice of exposing the dead to scavengers.

Zoroastrianism flourished in Iran and Azerbaijan from the 6th century BC until its suppression by Islam after about AD 651. But even as an imperial faith, under the Achaemenids (*see* IRAN), its temples for fire worship were very simple buildings. The typical form, a small square sanctuary housing the fire altar, covered by a dome carried on squinches, was probably established in the Parthian period. Many of these temples seem to have been built, particularly in south-east Iran, but now they lie in ruins or were converted into mosques. The Sasanians (AD 224–651) revitalized Zoroastrianism, building numerous fire temples, including the fabulous (perhaps in every sense) Takht-i-Taqdis (built by Khosrau II in 618, destroyed by the Byzantine emperor a decade later). The supporting structure, in which only silver and gold nails were used, was built of precious wood (cedar and teak); the dome was encrusted with rubies and lapis lazuli. Allegedly the building was able to rotate in synchrony with the sky, as a way of ensuring the timeliness of rituals.

The practice of building stone towers to carry a platform screened by a parapet upon which to expose the dead may have begun during the period of Islamic repression. One example seen by the French traveller Chardin (17th century) had no entrance, used dressed stones, and was of surprising proportions: about 10 m (35 ft) high and 29 m (95 ft) across.

In the modern era, the fire temples of the Parsees (Zoroastrians who had emigrated to Bombay) cannot be distinguished from ordinary houses. The modern fire temple Atashkadeh (*c.*1910), now the headquarters of the religion at Yazd, Iran, is likewise undistinguished.   PG

Zuccalli, Enrico (1642–1724) Italian–Swiss architect. Not a particularly talented designer, but one of the figures (*see* VISCARDI) important for introducing the Italian Baroque into Bavaria. For the Theatine church, St Kajetan, Munich (from 1674), he designed the west façade, flanked by two towers, and the dome, supported by a drum. He was much involved at the Schloss Schleissheim, outside Munich, where he designed a small pleasure palace, the Lustheim (1685), at one end of a long canal, and the east wing of the palace (1701–04) at the other. For the Ettal abbey church near Oberammergau (1709–26) he designed the west front, merely adding a Baroque form to an existing Gothic church. The awkwardness of the convex centre carrying a squat drum/dome is unfortunately emphasized by the later additions (of 1853 and 1906–7) of corner towers, which bear onion domes of different sizes. PG

Zumthor, Peter (1943–) Swiss architect who made his name with perfectly crafted wooden buildings such as the Protective Buildings for Archaeological Excavations in Chur (1985–6) and the chapel Sogn Benedetg in Sumvitg (1985–9). Sophisticated and economical, these works pointed the way for a new regional architecture in the Alps. Later larger buildings with concrete cores, e.g. the Thermal Bath in Vals (1986–96), with gneiss cladding, and the Art Museum in Bregenz, Austria (1990–97), sheathed in glass panels, are monolithic, sepulchral, grand figures celebrating their materials and the precision craftsmanship here exhibited. CB

Bibliographic Essay

No printed work can match the range and search power of the computer, which has made the traditional bibliography as a list of books and articles redundant. For this purpose, the reader is therefore referred to the following two sources:

The Royal Institute of British Architects Library online catalogue (www.architecture.com) lists works on every aspect of architecture (including particular buildings).

JSTOR (available through university libraries and some major public and private libraries) is an electronic archive of articles from a very wide range of periodicals in art and architecture.

Instead of a list, this essay recommends (or in a few cases criticizes) a much more selective list of works. The recommendations are based on the general approach to architecture explained in the *Preface*.

The reader will notice that there are some very significant gaps in the list of recommended works. These occur either because, in the Editor's opinion, he cannot recommend a work on the subject which is consistent with the approach taken by the *Companion*, or because of the tremendous imbalance in the literature. For instance, there are at least 400 books and articles on the work of Le Corbusier, but only a handful of works on some entire countries (the coverage of South America is particularly distorted in this respect). To take one year at random, in 2003 more articles were published on US architecture 1800–1950 than on the *entire* Islamic world at all periods (see the devastating critique of Eurocentrism by Robert Hillenbrand, 'Studying Islamic architecture', *Architectural History*, 2003, p.10, pp.1–18).

* Authors who have written for the *Companion* are identified by an asterisk, so that the reader can decide whether their selection is unduly partial.

Any reader who has a query about a particular subject should email the Editor, at companiontoarchitecture@hotmail.com.

Appreciating Architecture

From the many books which explain architecture for the general reader—a genre which seems to have petered out in the last 30 years—the following are the most useful:

Cullen, Gordon, *Townscape* (1961) illustrates, by text and drawings, vital lessons in how to see architecture in its context.

Gauldie, Sinclair, *Architecture* (1969) is one of an interesting series about appreciating the other arts.

Licklider, Heath, *Architectural Scale* (1965) is an exemplary analysis of one aspect of architecture, which makes one regret that there are so few books of this kind.

Rasmussen, S. E., *Experiencing Architecture* (1959) analyses every element of architecture, particularly colour and texture, with a wealth of examples.

Robertson, H., *Principles of Architectural Composition* (1924) explains how architects have traditionally regarded form and mass. It should be read in conjunction with Rasmussen, because of its lack of coverage of colour and texture.

General Works: History of Architecture

If I had to recommend only one work on this subject, it would be:

Fergusson, James, *History of Architecture in all Countries, from the Earliest Times to the Present Day* (2 vols., 1865–7) because of Fergusson's highly opinionated but well argued visual judgements, despite being quite out of date in terms of dates and attributions. Above all, Fergusson was not Eurocentric, and had catholic and generous sympathies. See below, on **India**.

The remaining works are listed alphabetically, not in order of importance.

Sir Banister Fletcher, *A History of Architecture*. There can be few books on any subject first published 1896, and reaching their 20th edition in 1996. Its great virtues are being a comprehensive reference work and having a series of useful and complete drawings (plans / elevations / sections). Perhaps for the non-architect the drawings may look a little technical and forbidding; and the format of the text as a series of descriptions of individual buildings makes it difficult for the authors to set out a line of argument.

Benton, T. *et al.*, *History of Architecture and Design 1890–1939* (1975). This series of textbooks (and associated videos) for the Open University is a model of lucid and stimulating exposition. A similar level of treatment applied to a much longer period would be highly desirable.

Curl, James Stevens, *A Dictionary of Architecture and Landscape Architecture* (2006) is very good on the definitions of architectural details, particularly of Classical architecture, and has an exceptionally good bibliography for its subject area, available on http://fds.oup.com/www.oup.co.uk/pdf/reference/opr/architecture_bibliography.pdf. However it is quite limited in scope, since it has no entries for countries or building types, and tends to be Eurocentric.

Fleming, J., Honour, H., and Pevsner, N., *The Penguin Dictionary of Architecture and Landscape Architecture* (2004) is generally very well written, but slightly unbalanced in its coverage. It is relatively weak outside western Europe; and within Europe, the authors seem more at home in France and Italy than anywhere else.

Guedes, P. (ed.), *Macmillan Encyclopedia of Architectural and Technological Change* (1979) is outstandingly good on the architectural expression of materials, structures, and services. It is very regrettable that it has not had a successor, since it is now 30 years out of date.

*Mainstone, Rowland J., *Developments in Structural Form* (2nd edn, 1998) is a magisterial account of the development of architectural form in relation to the necessities of structure.

Moffett, Marian, Fazio, Michael, and Wodehouse, Lawrence, *A World History of Architecture* (2003) is shaky in detail and rather Eurocentric (the coverage of China, Japan, and India is not very extensive), but otherwise it is a very good introduction—readable, very well illustrated, and with a good bibliography, in the form of an essay rather than a list.

Nuttgens, Patrick, *The Story of Architecture* (1997) is the best narrative account, which can be read with pleasure from start to finish.

Oxford Art Online (formerly Grove) has an extremely detailed coverage of every aspect of architecture. As its title suggests, its approach is more in line with traditional art history, with an interest in attribution/style/dating, so that it tends to lack explanations of why buildings look as they do, or to give any visual appraisals.

Pearman, Hugh, *Contemporary World Architecture* (1998) does not share the standpoint of this book, being rather uncritical of 'starchitecture', but it is a very perceptive and illuminating survey. The author runs an excellent website, Gabion (www.hughpearman.com), though the same caveat applies.

Placzek, Adolf K., *Macmillan Encyclopedia of Architects* (1982) strikes a very good balance between relevant biographical information and description of architecture.

Sennott, R. Stephen, *Encyclopedia of 20th Century Architecture* (2004) is very comprehensive, apart from its lack of entries on countries or building types; it gives a useful analysis of materials and structures.

*Tadgell, C. His series on world architecture, beginning with *Antiquity: origins, classicism and the new Rome* (2007), is comprehensive and beautifully illustrated. However, the author has a tendency to provide too much context and background, and there is insufficient visual appraisal.

General Surveys

Aalto, Alvar

Weston, R., *Alvar Aalto* (1995) is a thorough and well-illustrated, if slightly uncritical, account.

Acoustics

Beranek, L.L., *Music, Acoustics and Architecture* (1962) examines the interrelationships clearly.

Adam, Robert

Fleming, John, *Robert Adam and his Circle, Edinburgh and Rome* (1962) is a delightful and very well-written account of the architect's milieu, but is weak on architectural history.

Rowan, A., 'Bob the Roman', exhibition catalogue, Sir John Soane's Museum, London (2003), is the most useful recent work on the architecture as a whole.

Afghanistan

Szabo, Albert, *Afghanistan: an atlas of indigenous domestic architecture* (1991) is a model treatment of a country's vernacular architecture. The Timurid architecture of Heart was long neglected by historians until the work of Terry Allen, and *The Timurid Architecture of Iran and Turan*, by Lisa Golombek and Donald Wilber (1988).

Africa

*Elleh, Nnamdi, *African Architecture: Evolution and Transformation* (1997) and Garlake, P., *Early Art and Architecture of Africa* (2002) together give the reader a synoptic survey of a wide-ranging subject.

Airports

Pearman, Hugh, *Airports: a century of architecture* (2004) brings the subject up to date, with a wealth of analysis and perceptive comment.

Almshouses

Godfrey, W. H., *The English Almshouse* (1955) is a model of how to write a book about a building type.

Amsterdam School

De Wit, W., *The Amsterdam School* (1983) sets the architects' work in its local context, thus explaining much about its distinctive appearance.

Arab States

Kultermann, U., *Contemporary Architecture in the Arab States* (1999) is a very balanced survey of an area of the world which has tended to be overlooked by architectural critics.

Armenia

*Maranci, Christian, *Mediaeval Armenian Architecture: constructions of race and nation* (2001) is good on the relationship between architecture and national identity, and the historiography thereof. Otherwise the country's architecture is rather overlooked.

Mathews, T. F., *Art and Architecture in Byzantium and Armenia: liturgical and exegetical approaches* (1995) has some very useful insights into the importance of the relationship between architecture and liturgy.

Asplund

*Blundell Jones, Peter, *Gunnar Asplund* (2005) is the long overdue standard work on the subject.

Austria, Modern

Blau, Eve, *The Architecture of Red Vienna, 1919–1934* (1999) is an excellent example of how to write about the relationship between architecture and politics.

Baker, Laurie

'Laurie Baker', special issue of *A & U* no. 12 (363) December 2000, pp.3–145 is an exemplary survey and analysis of the work of a particular architect.

Baroque

Blunt, A. (ed.), *Baroque and Rococo Architecture Decoration* (1978) is a wide-ranging survey, by far the best of its kind, mainly because it is based upon a very precise use of the terms, previously examined in more detail in Blunt, A., *Some uses and misuses of the terms baroque and rococo applied to architecture* (1973).

Norberg-Schultz, C., *Late Baroque and Rococo Architecture* (1974) is very well illustrated, with useful plans, both literal and analytic, but the text has an unfortunate fondness for phrases such as 'pulsating juxtaposition' (e.g. p.128).

Sitwell, Sacheverell, *Southern Baroque* (1924): though Sitwell was no scholar, and even at the time his work contained inaccuracies in dating and attributions, this is much more than a period piece.

Venturi, R., *Complexity and Contradiction in Architecture* (1977) is very perceptive about the Baroque, and it is a pity that he did not write more about the subject itself, rather than using his analysis of the Baroque merely to attack certain versions of Modernism.

Baroque, Germany, Southern

Bourke, J(ohn), *Baroque Churches of Central Europe* (1962) is by far the best work. Like the architects whose work he describes, he is an 'Augenmensch'; and he has seen all the churches '... in the most varying conditions of weather and lighting and worship' (p.23). How different from H.-R. Hitchcock's *Rococo Architecture in Southern Germany* (1968), an arid discussion of stylistic labels!

Baroque, Italy

Lees-Milne, J., *Baroque in Italy* (1959): like Sacheverell Sitwell (see under **Baroque** above), Lees-Milne shows a strong visual sense.

Varriano, J., *Italian Baroque and Rococo Architecture* (1986) is extensive, thorough, and very perceptive.

Baroque, Naples

Blunt, A., *Neapolitan Baroque and Rococo Architecture* (1975) is a very illuminating work of research, since the great qualities of Neapolitan architecture (in the work of e.g. Fanzago or Sanfelice) have tended to be overlooked.

Baroque, Rome

Blunt, A., *A Guide to Baroque Rome* (1982) is a very modest title for a book which contains a wealth of visual analysis combined with very detailed information about every Baroque building in Rome.

Portoghesi, P., *Roma Barocca* (1966, English translation 1970) has the best collection of photographs of the subject, but the text is quite unintelligible to the English reader.

Baroque, Sicily

Blunt, A., *Sicilian Baroque* (1968). For some places and buildings, the detail is distinctly sketchy and possibly unreliable, because this is rather an under-researched subject. However, Blunt captures the visual essence of one of the most dramatic incarnations of the Baroque, and re-discovers the work of architects such as Rosario Gagliardi. The text is complemented by Tim Benton's outstanding photographs.

Beaux Arts

Drew Egbert, D., *The Beaux-Arts Tradition in French Architecture* (1980) is analytically the best book on the subject, and indeed one of the best works on architecture of any type or period.

Drexler, A. (ed.), *The Architecture of the Ecole des Beaux Arts* (1977) has exhaustive stunning illustrations and a useful supporting text.

Behrens

*Anderson, Stanford, *Peter Behrens and a New Architecture for the Twentieth Century* (2000) gives a much more nuanced picture of Behrens' work than his previous reputation as a pioneer of Modernism.

Belgium, Modern

Though written as a guidebook, and limited to Brussels, Burniat, P. *et al.*, *L'Architecture Moderne à Bruxelles* (2000) is

of wider significance, and has very useful descriptions of particular buildings.

Bernini

His work as an architect has received less critical attention than Borromini, though a useful summary of his work (including sculpture) is given by Hibbard, H., *Bernini* (1965).

In some respects, the most insight is to be gained by reading Fréart de Chantelou, P., *Diary of the Cavaliere Bernini's Visit to France* (1985), one of the most revealing accounts of how any major architect *looked* at (not thought about) architecture.

Borromini

Blunt, A., *Borromini* (1979) is very perceptive, though, surprisingly, like most English-language works on Borromini, it does not make enough use of Borromini's own *profession de foi*, the *Opus Architectonicum* (text by Virgilio Spada, first published 1725; reprint edited and with an introduction by Joseph *Connors, 1998).

In unravelling the complicated history of a particular building, *Connors, J(oseph), *Borromini and the Roman Oratory: Style and Society* (1980) also gives many general insights into the world of the Roman Baroque architect and patron.

Bramante

Bruschi, A., *Bramante* (1977) is a slightly underwhelming work on such an important architect, but competent enough, but with very useful line drawings.

Brazil

Fraser, V., *Building the New World: studies in the modern architecture of Latin America 1930–1960* (2000) analyses the rise of Modernism during this period, illustrating a brilliant, but neglected episode in its history, particularly in Brazil.

Kidder Smith, G. E., *Brazil Builds: Architecture new and old, 1652–1942* (1943) is in a brilliant series which also includes Italy, Sweden, and Switzerland (for detailed references, see under those headings).

Brick

*Campbell, J. W. P., *Brick. A World History* (2003) is a very good balance between striking illustrations and explanatory text. However, because of its universal coverage, it cannot be as detailed as some brick-building countries deserve—for instance Lloyd, Nathaniel, *A History of English Brickwork* (1925, reprinted 2008).

The greatest masters of brickwork, the Saljuqs, also deserve a separate study. Unfortunately, I have not been able to consult the only reference on the subject I have found, 'A study on the use of brickbonds in Anatolian Seljuk architecture', *Journal of the Faculty of Architecture*, Middle East Technical University, Fall 1980, pp.143–81.

Brutalism

Banham, Reyner, *The New Brutalism: Ethic or Aesthetic?* (1966) is by an 'almost participant', so is perceptive, yet somehow inconclusive. How could such an intelligent critic be so blind to the demerits of exposed concrete in the English climate?

Buddhist Architecture

Fisher, Robert, *Buddhist Art and Architecture* (1993): using a wealth of examples, the author not only carefully explains the evolution of Buddhism as a religion, but also shows the implications for art and architecture—a difficult combination, handled with great skill.

Building Types

J.-N.-L. Durand's *Recueil et parallèle des edifices de tout genre* (1799–1801) offers the first wide-ranging analysis of building types, though it consists mainly of the formal characteristics of plans, all drawn to the same scale (see Szambien, W., *Jean-Nicolas-Louis Durand*,1984).

In the Modernist spirit, Talbot Hamlin considered a series of building types from a different standpoint, i.e. that of user requirements (*Forms and Functions of Twentieth Century Architecture*, 4 vols., 1952). Unfortunately he selected too few examples of each type.

With his usual thoroughness, Pevsner tackled the subject in *A History of Building Types* (1976), but unusually the book lacks analysis and is little more than a series of examples and reading lists, a weakness the author admits.

Although it deals with a restricted set of types (such as prisons or schools), all of which cohere around the notion of organized surveillance, Markus, Thomas A., *Buildings and Power* (1993), sets the standard for detailed and thoughtful historical analysis, showing how illuminating the subject can be, both for appreciating architecture and as a guide for practising architects.

Byzantium

The subject of the liturgy of the Eastern church and its relationship to architecture has attracted far greater attention than its Western counterpart. The leading work is Mathews, T. F., *Art and Architecture in Byzantium and Armenia* (1995).

For a general overview, see Mango, C., *Byzantine Architecture* (1975).

Ousterhout, R., *Master Builders of Byzantium* (1999) covers only the period from the 9th century onward, and, as the title implies, deals mainly with construction.

*Mainstone, Rowland J., *Hagia Sophia: Architecture, Structure and Liturgy of Justinian's Great Church* (1988) is the best single work on this great church, concentrating on all aspects of design and liturgy, but particularly distinguished by its structural analysis, based in part on the author's own surveys.

The indispensable guide for those wishing to look further into the subject is *Kleinbauer, W. Eugene, *Early Christian and Byzantine Architecture: an annotated bibliography and historiography* (1992).

Sumner Boyd, H., and Freely, J., *Strolling Through Istanbul* (1973) is a very informative description of the city's Byzantine and Ottoman architecture.

Canada

*Kalman, H., *A History of Canadian Architecture* (2 vols., 1994) is inspiring, particularly since the writer is alert to the wide range of Canadian architecture.

Car Parks

*Henley, S., *The Architecture of Parking* (2007) is a clever example of finding architectural distinction in an initially unpromising, not to say banal, subject.

Cathedrals

Apart from the references given for each country, Smith, Norman A. F., 'Cathedral Studies: Engineering or History?',

Transactions of the Newcomen Society, vol. 73:1 (2001–2) is a polemical review of the literature.

Central America
Given the scarcity of the literature on this subject, the reader should consult Markman, Sidney David, *Architecture and Urbanization of Colonial Central America, Vol.1, Selected primary documentary and literary sources* (c.1993), but it is rather heavy going.

Chapels
The usually comprehensive *Buildings of England* series gives a very sketchy coverage of chapels, as Pevsner himself admitted.

Dolbey, George W., *The Architectural Expression of Methodism* (1964) only covers the first 100 years, but is useful for that period.

Butler, David M., *The Quaker Meeting Houses of Britain* (1999) has an informative gazetteer.

Chateaux
Girardin, M., *Life in the French Country House* (2000) somehow lacks the éclat of his other work, perhaps because the subject itself was not as important as its English counterpart.

Chicago School
Condit, C. W., *The Chicago School of Architecture* (1964) explains the connection between the great advances in structural technology and architectural expression.

China
*Steinhardt, N. (ed.), *Chinese Architecture* (2002) is highly successful in its aim of presenting the best recent scholarship to make this extremely important subject, hitherto dealt with rather unsatisfactorily by Western historians, fully accessible to the non-specialist reader.

Cinemas
Gray, Richard, *Cinemas in Britain* (1996) is good for its subject; a worldwide survey does not appear to be available.

Classicism
Summerson, J., *The Classical Language of Architecture* (1980) is a straightforward presentation of the subject, urbane and informative, but somewhat lacking in the verve

shown in the author's other work, especially the essays collected in *Heavenly Mansions* (1963).

Classicism, Modern
It is difficult to recommend any books which treat the subject on its own considerable merits, rather than using modern Classicism merely as a counter-weight to Modernism, or berating its proponents for their association with undemocratic regimes. Consequently, the subject requires serious research, particularly on Stile Littorio and the other varieties of modern Classicism which flourished under Mussolini.

Cockerell, C. R.
Watkin, D., *The Life and Work of C. R. Cockerell* (1974) is very readable, but a little too enamoured of Cockerell's erudition as an architect, instead of looking more closely at the visual qualities of Cockerell's work.

Colour
Lancaster, M., *Colourscape* (1996): an architect looks with great sensitivity at the use of colour in architecture and landscape architecture.

Nassau, K. (ed.), *Color for Science, Art and Technology* (1998) explains the essential background to understanding colour, before one can understand its application to architecture.

Taverne, E., and Wagenaar, Cor, *The colour of the city* (1992) complements Michael Lancaster's book.

Composition
Robertson, H., *Principles of Architectural Composition* (1924) is a very clear and logical explanation. The author was inspired by the rather eccentric A. Trystan Edwards' *Things Which are Seen* (1921), who later wrote, more specifically on architecture, *Good and Bad Manners in Architecture* (1925—an inconceivable title for the 21st century) about composition applied to buildings in relation to each other.

The reader is advised to avoid Guadet, J., *Elements et Théorie de l'Architecture* at all costs (4 vols., 1901)—a most disappointing book, platitudes stated at great and elaborate length.

Communism
Aman, Amders, *Architecture and Ideology in Eastern Europe during the Stalin Era* (1993) is a useful source book for an

almost completely unresearched subject—one of the most massive public housing projects in history, which has been virtually unanalysed in the West.

Concert Halls
*Forsyth, Michael, *Buildings for Music* (1985) is of equal interest to lovers of music and architecture: a very stimulating account of the relationship between the two disciplines.

Concrete
Collins, Peter, *Concrete* (1959) is in one respect rather an unbalanced book, since the only architect whose work is analysed in detail, though brilliantly, is Auguste Perret. But the understanding of the material and how it can be expressed architecturally is a masterpiece.

Conservation
Jokilehto, J., *A History of Architectural Conservation* (1999) is a thorough summary.

Construction Process
Fitchen, J. F., *Building Construction before Mechanization* (1986) does not quite live up to the promise of its title, since it is not well researched; a disappointingly inferior work to the more narrowly focused *The Construction of Gothic Cathedrals* (1961).
For England only, in one (long) period, there is much useful information in Salzman, L.F., *Building in England down to 1540* (1952).

Coptic Churches
Butler, A. J., *The Ancient Coptic Churches of Egypt* (2 vols., 1884) is the only significant work on the subject.

Country Houses, English
Before about 1970, there was a large literature on this subject, which to a large extent was repetitive and sterile, concentrating on the allocation of stylistic labels. In two path-breaking books, *The Victorian Country House* (1971) and *Life in the English Country House* (1978), Mark Girouard adopted a very different point of view, i.e. how the changes in the patrons' way of life and the structure of English society had a direct impact upon architecture. Both books (but particularly the first) set out an excellent analysis of

plans, not for their merely formal characteristics, but as a means to meeting the requirements of the users.

Cret, Paul
Richard A. Etlin, *Symbolic Space: French Enlightenment Architecture and its Legacy* (1994) has an interesting chapter on Cret. Grossman, E. G., *The Civic Architecture of Paul Cret* (1996) is rather more pedestrian.

Critical Regionalism
Abel, Chris, *Architecture and Identity: responses to cultural and technological change* (2000) provides a very thoughtful introduction to the issues involved.

Croatia
Gross, Vladimir P., *Early Croatian Architecture* (1987) is full of detail, if somewhat lacking in analysis.

Crusader Castles
Fedden, R., and Thomson, J., *Crusader Castles* (1957) is an excellent résumé of military history combined with architectural appreciation.

Cuba
Loomis, John A., *Revolution of Forms: Cuba's Forgotten Art Schools* (1999) is a useful work on this subject, but these buildings were exceptional in the period since the 1959 revolution. I have not been able to find a survey of this period written in English.

Denmark
Donnelly, Marian C., *Architecture in the Scandinavian Countries* (1992) covers the entire period to the 1970s. The chapters on the period less well known in the English-speaking world, i.e. to about 1890, are exemplary; but in the more familiar modern period, the author is a less reliable guide. Sestoft, Jørgen, *Danish Architecture 1000–1960* (1995) is the only English-language survey.

Disabled, Design For
*Goldsmith, Selwyn, *Designing for the Disabled: The New Paradigm* (1997).

Drawing
Robbins, E(dward), *Why Architects Draw* (1994) reveals some of the mysteries of the craft.

Egypt, Ancient

*Baines, J(ohn), *Atlas of Ancient Egypt* (1980) illustrates all aspects of ancient Egyptian culture, but is particularly good on architecture.

For a useful reference work, see Arnold D., *The Encyclopaedia of Ancient Egyptian Architecture* (2003).

Engineering

Saint, A., *Architect and Engineer* (2007) is a highly stimulating account of the relationship between the two professions, though it slightly avoids the crucial question about the difference in their approach to the visual aspects of design.

Engineering Services

The first, very partial discussion of the subject was by James Marston Fitch, *Architecture and the Esthetics of Plenty* (1961). It is surprising that after Reyner Banham's polemical *Architecture of the Well Tempered Environment* (1969), the only substantial work on the subject is *Baird, G., *The Architectural Expression of Environmental Control Systems* (2001), which gets the balance between technical information and architectural appraisal just right.

But in one respect this lack of interest is understandable, since it merely replicates architects' similar unconcern. At the end of the first period of innovation in modern technology applied to architecture (*c.*1900), a contemporary reviewer claimed that not one of the 44 mechanical services required for tall buildings had to any significant extent been provided in response to demand from the architect. In the last decade the situation has changed, but only slowly, as architects have to come to terms with the need for sustainability (Hagan, S., *Taking Shape*, 2001).

England

Betjeman's *Ghastly Good Taste* (1933; rev. edn 1970) is still one of the most stimulating histories of English architecture, with great sensitivity to its visual character, but without the somewhat cloying nostalgia which mars the author's later work. For individual counties, Betjeman's *Shell Guides* (beginning with Cornwall in 1934) are the indispensable complement to Pevsner.

Goodhart-Rendel, H. S., *English Architecture Since the Regency* (1953) is more of an essay, but worth reading for its flashes of insight, particularly into Victorian architecture.

Harwood, E., *England. A guide to post-war listed buildings* (2000) is more than a guide: with Powers, it is an indispensable account of the period, as illustrated by particular buildings. Above all, the author has a fine eye for detail, and gives a clear visual appraisal of each building.

Nairn, Ian, *Nairn's London* (1966). The author modestly states (p.13) that 'This guide is simply my personal list of the best things in London'; and the reader knows (see **France**) what to expect—a brilliant, catholic analysis of buildings from every period of architecture, from the best critic ever.

The magnificent series of the *Buildings of England* (begun 1951), by Nicholas Pevsner, is unmatched anywhere else in the world. The only possible criticism is that the author often tends to be more interested in solving chronological puzzles, than in aesthetic appreciation. Oddly enough for a Modernist, this criticism does not apply to Pevsner's account of (Victorian) Gothic Revival.

*Powers, Alan, *Britain* (2007), in the excellent series *Modern Architectures in History* (Reaktion Books), is mainly about England. It is a first-rate account of the ideas, personalities, and tendencies of a very complex period; its only slight weakness is that the visual analysis of modern architecture in Britain is not quite at the same level.

Summerson, J., *Architecture in Britain, 1530–1830* (1964) is a clearly written and well-balanced survey.

Enlightenment, The French

The title of Richard A. Etlin's *Symbolic Space: French Enlightenment Architecture and its Legacy* (1994) is rather misleading, as the analysis of the Enlightenment's conception of architecture is quite insubstantial.

Likewise, it is arguable that the author's reluctance to engage with the *ideology* of the French Enlightenment is a serious fault with Braham, A., *The Architecture of the French Enlightenment* (1994).

Erskine

Collymore, P., *The Architecture of Ralph Erskine* (1982) is a sympathetic treatment.

Ethiopia

Gerster, G. (ed.), *Churches in Rock. Early Christian Art in Ethiopia* (1970): particular note should be taken of the contribution by David Buxton.

Etruscan Architecture
Dennis, George, *The Cities and Cemeteries of Etruria* (2 vols., 1878) has not been surpassed in its view of the general outlines of the subject.

Factories
Markus, Thomas A., *Buildings and Power* (1993) gives a thoroughly detailed social and architectural history of the factory before and during the Industrial Revolution.

Banham, R., 'The Daylight Factory', chapter 3 of *A Concrete Atlantis* (1986), suggests how interesting the subject of the mechanized factory could be, but, to the best of my knowledge, the book has had no useful successors, except Wilkinson, C(hris), *Supersheds* (1995).

Fascism
Lane, Barbara Miller, *Architecture and Politics in Germany 1918–1945* (1985) unravels with great clarity the complex relationships between the two subjects.

Finland
Donnelly, Marian C., *Architecture in the Scandinavian Countries* (1992) covers the entire period to the 1970s. The chapters on the period less well known in the English-speaking world, to about 1890, are exemplary; but in the more familiar modern period, the author is less reliable.

*Quantrill, M., *Finnish Architecture and the Modernist Tradition* (1995) is stimulating and informative.

Richards, J. M., *800 years of Finnish Architecture* (1978) is a sound general survey.

Follies
Jones, Barbara, *Follies and Grottoes* (1974) remains the standard work, with a useful gazetteer.

Foster, Norman
The work of a contemporary architect is often very difficult to evaluate, but Moore, Rowan: 'Norman's Conquest', *Prospect*, March 2002 (12) is an extremely incisive analysis.

France
Blunt, A., *Art and Architecture in France 1500–1700* (1953, 1970) does not quite escape the limitations of the Pelican series, a certain dryness and lack of gusto, but it is particularly good on François Mansart.

Bonde, S., *Fortress Churches of Languedoc* (1994) shows genuine historical insight, realizing that the separation between the study of castles and churches was a mistake, i.e. an example of seeing a period non-anachronistically.

Bony, J., *French Gothic Architecture of the Twelfth and Thirteenth Centuries* (1983): a detailed formal and structural analysis.

Braham, A., *The Architecture of the French Enlightenment* (1980); the misleading word in the title is 'of': 'parallel to' would be more accurate, as the massively detailed background information (on patrons / documentation of dates and attributions) in effect becomes the foreground.

Erlande-Brandenburg, Alain, *Histoire de l'architecture française. Du Moyen Age à la Renaissance* (1995) is a balanced work.

Johnston, Roy, *Parisian Architecture of the Belle Epoque* (2007) has a very good selection of illustrations, particularly plans, especially relevant to the awkward sites of many of the buildings analysed, and a clear and analytical text.

Loyer, François, *Histoire de l'architecture française de la révolution à nos jours* (1999) is a provocative and stimulating work of wide scope, which considers both the practical and regional, as well as the theoretical and the Parisian.

Monnier, Gérard (ed.), *L'Architecture Moderne en France*, Vols. 1–3 (1997–2000) is a balanced panorama of rather an unbalanced period, in which 1950–95 is given full due.

Nairn, Ian, *Nairn's Paris* (1968) offers his usual combination of caustic judgements on the familiar, a sharp eye for the undeservedly obscure, and an unbeatable talent for striking similes, always as a prelude to a perceptive visual analysis. Witness his comment on the church in Asfeld-la-Ville (1683) 'dozing away in utter obscurity between Rethel and Laon': 'The only analogy I can think of is a man visiting Maxim's in Paris and going through the card, from aperitif to Napoleon brandy' (p.157).

Stoddard, Whitney S., *Art and Architecture in Medieval France* (1972) is the best overview in English, with a careful analysis of particular buildings.

Gabriel, Ange-Jacques
Gabriel's merits as an architect, even compared to his French contemporaries, let alone on the European scale, are not immediately obvious. However, like a clever lawyer making a plausible case for a dubious client, Christopher *Tadgell, *Ange-Jacques Gabriel* (1978) is the very best that can be done.

Georgia

Mepisashvili, R., and Tsintsadze, V., *The Arts of Ancient Georgia* (1979) introduces an undeservedly neglected culture.

Germany

Bourke, John, *Baroque Churches of Central Europe* (1962) is one of the most stimulating books on *any* period, showing how the requirements of the liturgy were given the most beautiful and varied architectural expression.

Nussbaum, N., *German Gothic Church Architecture* (2000) is highly recommended.

Hitchcock, Henry-Russell, *German Renaissance Architecture* (1981) adequate treats an extremely unpromising subject.

Glass

Wigginton, M., *Glass in Architecture* (1990) is quite useful on the development of glass technology and its contribution to architecture in the 20th century.

Gothic

Fitchen, J., *The Construction of Gothic Cathedrals* (1961).

Prior, E. S., *A History of Gothic Art in England* (1900) is one of the very few attempts to examine Gothic cathedrals from a visual rather than an antiquarian or historical view.

Stoddard, Whitney S., *Art and Architecture in Medieval France* (1972) is particularly good on architecture, especially in its examination of particular cathedrals.

Greece, Ancient

There is extensive literature on this subject, but the lack of any statements by the architects, or by contemporaries, has led to much speculation about the notions of proportion or modular systems, or the purpose of the refinements. Although the accepted standard treatments avoid these errors, they have other weaknesses. Dinsmoor, W. B., *The Architecture of Ancient Greece* (1950) and Lawrence, A. W., *Greek Architecture* (1957) paradoxically make very few architectural judgements, and Robertson, D. S., *Greek and Roman Architecture* (2nd edn, 1943) gives an uneven treatment of building types. Two books to select would be:

Barletta, Barbara, *The Origins of the Greek Architectural Orders* (2002) which summarizes earlier approaches and subsequent interpretations, but most significantly uses the archaeological evidence as the central focus, an approach which has been neglected for a long time. Most importantly for the subsequent understanding, and indeed application, of the forms of Greek architecture, Barletta establishes that: 'The orders were not at any stage the frozen, rigid systems that Vitruvius, or his interpreters, imply. For the Greeks, they remained always capable of change and thus a living, rather than an academic tradition' (p.156).

Scully, Vincent, *The Earth, the Temple, and the Gods* (1979) offers highly stimulating but quite unprovable speculations about the relationship between Greek temples and their sites. E. C. Semple, *The Geography of the Mediterranean Region* (1932), ch. xxi 'The Templed Promontories' is more prosaic, but possibly more successful.

However, a fault which may be ineradicable in any work on the subject is that because of the paucity of hard evidence about the ritual use of the temples, this aspect of classical Greek architecture is not yet understood satisfactorily.

Guarini

*Meek, H. A., *Guarino Guarini and his Architecture* (1988) is a very good introduction to a difficult subject. The problem is making him comprehensible to the non-mathematician and unravelling the significance of Guarini's involvement with the Theatine order: both very complex problems.

Robison, Elwin, 'Optics and Mathematics in the Domed Churches of Guarino Guarini', *Journal of the Society of Architectural Historians* (1991), pp.384–401, is worth studying.

Hawksmoor

Downes, K(erry), *Hawksmoor* (1959) remains the touchstone, though, like most English historians, the author is concerned to dispute whether Hawksmoor is a Baroque architect, clearly he isn't. Goodhart-Rendel, H. S., *Nicholas Hawksmoor* (1924) is much slighter, but scintillates.

Heating

Bruegmann, R., 'Central Heating and Forced Ventilation: Origins and Effects on Architectural Design', *The Journal of the Society of Architectural Historians* (1978) pp.143–60, supplements, and indeed corrects, Banham, R., *Architecture of the Well Tempered Environment* (1969) for the 19th century in Britain (though the article is much narrower in scope).

Hindu Temples, Bengal

McCutchion, D., *Brick Temples of Bengal* (1983) is a very detailed survey, which makes a neglected regional architecture accessible to the Western reader. Its main weakness is an over-reliance on a rather too detailed categorization.

Hospitals

Jeremy *Taylor's *Hospital and Asylum Architecture in England 1840–1914* (1991) and *The Architect and the Pavilion Hospital* (1997) offer a fascinating insight into this specialist branch of architecture, clearly explaining the relationship between hospital practice and the architect's response.

Hôtel Particulier

Gallet, M., *Stately Mansions* (1972) sees the *hôtel particulier* not only as an *architectural*, but also a *building* problem, among other strengths in this classic work.

Hotels

Rutes, W. A.,*Penner, R. H., and Adams, L., *Hotel Design, Planning, and Development* (2001) explores this building type in considerable detail.

Wharton, A. J., *Building the Cold War* (2001) is a surprising insight into the design of the Hilton hotels, as instruments of propaganda in the Cold War, spreading the gospel of capitalism.

Houses

*Quiney, A., *Town Houses of Medieval Britain* (2003) is a scholarly and perceptive work. Even on the scale of a particular country and period, to analyse the architecture of the house is such a daunting task that it is not attempted very often or very satisfactorily.

Hungary

Wiebenson, Dora, and *Sisa, József (ed.), *The Architecture of Historic Hungary* (1998) is the standard work on the subject, though rather underplays the importance of the Communist period.

Indian Subcontinent

Bernier, Ronald, *Himalayan Architecture* (1997) is a very good survey of one region in India.

Branfoot, C., *Gods on the Move. Architecture and Ritual in the South Indian Temple* 2007. An illuminating account of a neglected subject (*see* **Ritual**, below), though the writer is

inclined to be too indulgent to the visual weaknesses of south Indian temples.

Brown, P., *Indian Architecture (Buddhist and Hindu; Islamic Period)* (2 vols., 1942) shares some of the qualities of Fergusson (see below), within a briefer compass.

Cooper, Ilay, and Dawson, B(arry), *Traditional Buildings of India* (1998).

Fergusson, James, *A History of Indian and Eastern Architecture* (1876, revised 1891). The dates and attributions may be questionable, and need revision in the light of later scholarship, but Fergusson's great merit was to accept Indian architecture on its own terms, despite his admiration for Greek Classicism as the standard of excellence. But above all, Fergusson makes strong and well-argued visual judgements, highly stimulating and perceptive. In this respect his work has never been bettered, and on any subject this is one of the finest works of architectural criticism.

Hardy, A(lan), *The Temple Architecture of India* (2007) is now the definitive aount offering a very detailed and insightful analysis.

*Tadgell, C., *The History of Architecture in India* (1990) is largely successful in handling a mass of details, but devotes too much attention to explaining the spiritual background, rather than the architectural foreground.

Iran

Pope, Arthur Upham, *Persian Architecture* (1965). Pope was not a great scholar (apparently he did not even speak Persian), and was slightly obsessed with an irrelevant question, the supposed relationship between Persian and Gothic architecture. Nonetheless, his account of the subject shows great visual sensitivity and is very inspiring. In particular, the book drew attention to the brilliant architecture of the Saljuqs, a subject considered at greater length in the monumental work he edited with P. Ackerman, *A Survey of Persian Art from Prehistoric Times to the Present* (6 vols., 1938–9).

Ireland

Craig, M., *The Architecture of Ireland* (1982) is, to date, the best survey.

Hourihane, C., *Gothic Art in Ireland 1169–1550* (2003) is an excellent account of rather an unresearched subject.

Iron

Steiner, Frances H., *French Iron Architecture* (1984) is good on structures.

*Thorne, R(obert) (ed.), *Structural Iron and Steel, 1850–1900* (2000) forms part of a series on civil engineering, but includes several essays on architecture.

Islamic Architecture

The difficulties of, and opportunities for, studying this subject are well explained in Robert Hillenbrand, 'Studying Islamic architecture . . .', *Architectural History* (2003), p.10, pp.1–18.

Creswell, K. A. C., significantly revised with new material by J. W. Allan, *A Short Account of Early Muslim Architecture* (1989) is a classic—based on extremely thorough inspection and measurement of all the elements of buildings, as a basis for rigorous and carefully argued judgements. However, it has to be said that Creswell's method may lead to a certain weakness, a failure to appreciate the formal relations of the parts (see the excellent review by Meyer Schapiro, *Art Bulletin*, March 1935, pp.109–14).

Ettinghausen, R., and Grabar, O., *Art and Architecture of Islam 650–1250* (1987) and Blair, Sheila S., and Bloom, Jonathan, M., *The Art and Architecture of Islam 1250–1800* (1995) have the major merit of seeing architecture in the context of other arts.

Kuban, D., *Muslim Religious Architecture* (2 vols., 1974, 1985), although out of date when published, and containing several errors of detail, not only gives a very good formal analysis of architecture, including a wealth of plans and elevations, but also describes the different patterns of use and their consequences for architecture.

Hillenbrand, Robert, *Islamic Architecture* (1994) is the definitive survey, despite the deficiencies of its organization around building types, rather than chronology.

Michell, G. (ed.), *Architecture of the Islamic world* (1978), though perhaps less scholarly, gives a better sense of what is distinctive about the Islamic world than most works on the subject.

Italy

The series *Storia dell'architettura italiana* (from 2000–4, various editors) easily supersedes earlier works, for its comprehensiveness and the depth of its architectural analysis.

Apart from the Baroque period (see above, **Baroque**), the following works should be mentioned:

Kidder Smith, G. E., *Italy Builds* (1954), an exemplary analysis of Italy's 'modern architecture and its native inheritance.'

Mallory, N(ina), *Roman Rococo Architecture* (1977) is unfortunately rather difficult to find, but despite a wilful use of the term 'rococo', this a very good book on a much neglected period.

Meeks, C. L. V., *Italian Architecture 1750–1914* (1966). For readers with the stamina to trudge through the dreary wastes of neoclassical and post-Risorgimento architecture, Meeks is the only guide.

Pommer, R., *Eighteenth-Century Architecture in Piedmont: The Open Structures of Juvarra, Alfieri, and Vittone* (1967) is a most infuriating book. The documentation and plans have been most painstakingly investigated, a model of research of this kind; but, ultimately, to what purpose? The book does not answer a single question that occurs to the inquisitive observer seeing e.g. the churches of Guarini or Vittone for the first time, but seems to be entirely for the benefit of his fellow art historians. A great opportunity wasted.

Japan

The great strength of the works by *Coaldrake, William H., *The Way of the Carpenter: Tools and Japanese Architecture* (1990) and *Architecture and Authority in Japan* (1996), is their understanding of the relationship between building and architecture in a particular culture, and also of the critical elements of that culture.

Jones, Inigo

Summerson, J., *Inigo Jones* (2000) is an informative survey, but, like all English writers about Jones, Summerson is far too respectful of his subject, as if somehow the honour of English architecture were at stake. A critical analysis of Jones's works, exposing his essential provincialism and marginality in European terms, is badly needed.

*Worsley, G., *Inigo Jones and the European Classicist Tradition* (2006) is a very good answer to the question: What did Inigo Jones receive from European architecture? No European critic seems even to have been interested in, let alone have an answer for, the question: What did Inigo Jones *give* to European architecture?

An interesting aspect of Jones's work, his roof structures, is capably analysed by David Yeomans in 'Inigo Jones's Roof Structures', *Architectural History* (1986), pp.85–101.

Kahn, Albert

*Hildebrand, G., *Designing for Industry—the Architecture of Albert Kahn* (1974): architecture / industrial design / engineering?—a very interesting answer to these inter-related questions.

Kahn, Louis

*Goldhagen, S.W., *Louis Kahn's Situated Modernism* (2001) deals very competently with the tortured relationship between Kahn and Modernism.

Kent, William

Wilson, M. J., *William Kent* (1984) is the only comprehensive account of Kent's work.

Landscape Architecture

Chadwick, G. F., *The Park and the Town* (1966) is a seminal work, analysing the development of landscape architecture in relation to a particular type of commission, the public park.

*Goode, P., Jellicoe, Geoffrey, and Lancaster, M. L., *The Oxford Companion to Gardens* (1986) contains much incidental information about garden buildings and landscape architecture.

Newton, Norman T., *Design on the Land: the development of Landscape Architecture* (1971) is very broadly based, dealing not only with its stated subject, but also its antecedents in garden design.

Treib, Marc (ed.), *Modern Landscape Architecture: A critical review* (1993) and *The architecture of landscape, 1940–1960* (2002) illustrate very clearly the complicated, and in many respects surprising, relationships between Modernism in architecture and landscape. It is to be hoped that further works will bring the story up to date.

Language and Architecture

Forty, A., *Words and Buildings: A Vocabulary of Modern Architecture* (2000) is a very stimulating analysis of the vocabulary of Modernism (e.g. of 'space', 'function')

marred only by its abstract character, i.e. not enough real examples are analysed.

The most succinct critique of the idea that architecture is a form of language is chapter 17 of Collins, Peter, *Changing Ideals in Modern Architecture, 1750–1950* (1965).

Lasdun, Denys

Curtis, W(illiam) J. R., *Denys Lasdun* (1994) is a good analyis, a little too focused on his Classicism.

Latin America

Fraser, V., *Building the New World: studies in the modern architecture of Latin America 1930–1960* (2000) analyses the rise of Modernism during this period, illustrating a brilliant but neglected episode in its history. For various reasons, it became forgotten that Latin America, particularly Brazil, was in the vanguard of the Modern Movement for much of this period. Fraser's exemplary work throws into high relief the paucity of research on earlier periods in the history of the continent.

Lebanon, Historic

Fedden, R., *Syria and Lebanon* (1965) is an excellent account by a traveller and historian.

Le Corbusier

His *Buildings and Projects* were published by the Fondation Le Corbusier, Paris, in a series of volumes (1983, 1984). Of his writings, *Vers une architecture* (1923; the most recent translation (2008), by John Goodman, *Toward an architecture*, is recommended) is essential reading; his sketchbook, *Journey to the* East (2007), recorded his travels in 1910.

The literature on Le Corbusier is unjustifiably immense. However, the following works may be singled out:

Baker, Geoffrey H., *Le Corbusier: An Analysis of Form* (1996) is exactly what the title suggests.

Benton, T., *et al.*, *History of Architecture and Design 1890–1939* (1975). The Open University series of textbooks (and associated videos) is particularly good on the work of Le Corbusier, based particularly on the detailed and extensive research into the 1920s villas by Tim and Charlotte Benton. The most up-to-date findings of this research are published in Benton, T., *The villas of Le Corbusier and Pierre Jeanneret, 1920–1930* (2007).

Jencks, C., *Le Corbusier and the Tragic View of Architecture* (1974). Though out of date in detail, because of the great mass of subsequent research, in general terms this work is stimulating and observant.

Lettering and Architecture

Gray, N(icolete), *Lettering on Buildings* (1960) is preferred over other works on the subject of lettering in the environment, such as Baines, P., and Dixon, C., *Signs: lettering in the environment* (2003), because of Gray's distinguished work on the history of typography, and lettering as an art form.

Lewerentz, Sigurd

His work is fully documented and illustrated in Dymling, C. (ed.), *Architect Sigurd Lewerentz, Vol. 1 Photographs of the Work* (1997) and Dymling, C. et al., *Sigurd Lewerentz: Two Churches* (1997). For a more analytic approach, see Wilson, C. St J., *Architectural Reflections* (2000).

Lighting

No one book deals comprehensively with the subject of lighting and architecture.

Bowers B., *Lengthening the day: A history of lighting technology* (1998) is very good on technology; Banham reveals some of the dispiriting examples of the use of artificial light sources by early Modernist architects.

*Cuttle C., *Lighting by Design* (2003), has the best all-round treatment, but does not include quite enough historical examples.

Lubetkin, Berthold

Allan, J., *Berthold Lubetkin* (2002) conveys a sense of Lubetkin's political commitment, as well as his great gifts as an architect.

Lutyens, Sir Edwin

To get a sense of Lutyens' work, it is best to avoid the polemicists, pro and contra, and read the survey, Butler, A. S. G., *The Architecture of Sir Edwin Lutyens* (1950).

Mackintosh, Charles Rennie

Howarth, T., *Charles Rennie Mackintosh and the Modern Movement* (1952) is slightly dated in its details, but a classic.

Maderno, Carlo

Hibbard, H., *Carlo Maderno and Roman Architecture 1580–1630* (1971) is a very detailed catalogue of his buildings, but unfortunately lacks any visual analysis.

Maintenance

Brand, S., *How Buildings Learn. What Happens After They're Built* (1994); it is perhaps rather telling that this very stimulating book was *not* written by an architect.

Makovecz, Imre

Heathcote, Edwin, *Imre Makovecz. The wings of the soul* (1997) is a sympathetic view of an original architect.

Malta

Hughes, Q(uentin), *Malta* (1978) is the best survey, but needs to be supplemented on prehistory by Trump, D. H., *Malta Prehistory and Temples* (2002).

Mansart, François

Braham, A., and Smith, P., *François Mansart* (1973) is an informative survey, but none of the literature quite does justice to the subtlety of Mansart's work. The analysis in Blunt, A., *Art and Architecture in France 1500–1700* (1953, 1970) is by far the best, though all too brief. Not surprisingly, given the date of publication, Blunt's *François Mansart and the Origins of French Classical Architecture* (1941) is more concerned with the humanist content of French Classicism than with visual analysis.

Materials

A history of materials and architectural expression would be a difficult, but not impossible task, and has so far not been tried very successfully. Weston, R., *Materials, Form and Architecture* (2003) is less ambitious than the title suggests.

For particular countries, Clifton-Taylor, A., *The Pattern of English Building* (1962) is the model work, as it explains the nature of materials and their geographical distribution, as a basis for analysing their use and visual effect in pre-modern vernacular and 'high' architecture.

Robinson, E (ric), *London Illustrated Geological Walks* (2 vols, 1984, 1985) is a model analysis of the relationship between architecture and materials, of all periods.

Watson, J., *British and Foreign Building Stones* (1911) is not primarily about architecture, but has some useful information.

Maya Architecture

Miller, Mary Ellen, *Maya Art and Architecture* (1999) is a clear account of the present state of knowledge, and the historiography of the subject.

McKim, Mead, and White

Roth, L. M., *McKim, Mead, and White, Architects* (1983) is a balanced assessment.

Mendelsohn, Erich

James, K(athleen), *Erich Mendelsohn and the Architecture of German Modernism* (1997) is a good survey, but does not quite come to terms with Mendelsohn's rather formulaic approach during his German period.

Mesopotamia

Lloyd, S(eton), *The art of the ancient Near East* (1961); the final chapter, on architecture, is rather dated, but is probably the most useful survey for the general reader.

Kubba, Shammil A. A., *Mesopotamian Architecture* (1992) is more up to date than Lloyd in terms of archaeological knowledge, but makes rather unjustifiable, anachronistic judgements about architecture.

Michelangelo

*Ackerman, James S., *The Architecture of Michelangelo* (2 vols., 1961) is a comprehensive and penetrating analysis of Michelangelo's work, showing very clearly how many of his supposedly irrational or wilful architectural details serve a structural or visual purpose.

Mies van der Rohe

There is not much space between hagiography and vituperation in the critical writing on Mies van der Rohe. Schultze, F(ranz), *Mies van der Rohe* (1985) almost gets into the gap, but does include a considerable amount of unnecessary biographical information. The catalogue of the exhibition *Mies in Berlin* (2002) is more focused on design, but this was only a short and not particularly noteworthy period in his career (until 1935).

Military Architecture

Hughes, Q(uentin), *Military Architecture* (1991) gives a broad coverage, but often tends to be too specialist or offer a limited range of examples, such as Crusaders' Castles.

Models

Wilton-Ely, J., 'Architectural model' in *Grove Dictionary of Art* is the best article on an under-researched subject.

Modernism

Collins, Peter, *Changing Ideals in Modern Architecture, 1750–1950* (1965), though very uneven in its choice of subjects (some of which tend to the trivial) and in its judgements, is particularly rewarding in its exposure of the discrepancy between theory and practice in the work of modernists and proto-modernists.

Curtis, W. J. R., *Modern Architecture Since 1900* (1982) is readable and thorough, and particularly valuable for its extensive coverage of the post-1945 period. However, it is rather unopinionated for such controversial subject.

Frampton, K., *Modern Architecture* (1992) does not quite live up to its subtitle 'A Critical History'. Its great strength is its resolute, if not always clearly argued, defence of Modernism.

Hamlin, Talbot, *Forms and Functions of Twentieth Century Architecture* (4 vols., 1952) is a valiant attempt to use the traditional language of building types and visual criteria in defence of Modernism. Unfortunately, it can only be accounted a gallant failure, as exposed in the brilliant review by Colin Rowe (*The Art Bulletin*, 1953, pp.169–74)—much more than a review, in that it discusses the relationship between Modernism and its predecessors.

Jencks, C., *Modern Movements in Architecture* (1973) is by far the author's best book, a stimulating analytic classification of the varieties of Modernism.

Nairn, Ian *Modern Buildings in London* (1964) conveys the special excitement of living at the zenith of Modernism, while generous enough to recognise the merits of contemporary classicism (p.51).

Pevsner, *Pioneers of the Modern Movement* (1936, 1975): its weaknesses, in terms of numerous lacunae and some midjudgements, have frequently been catalogued. However, it is much more than a period piece of a pioneer, since it is a clear statement of the principles of a rational Modernism, of enduring value.

*Wilson, C. St J., *The Other Tradition of Modernism* (1995) states the case for a humane, socially just version of Modernism, an alternative to the orthodoxy of CIAM.

All of the above surveys vary between completely ignoring and doing scant justice to the free-form Modernism of Latin America. The reader is referred to the outstanding work by Fraser, V., *Building the New World: studies in the modern architecture of Latin America 1930–1960* (2000), as a starting point.

Monasteries

Braunfels, W., *Monasteries of Western Europe* (1972) is a detailed survey, though it does not pay quite enough attention to the architectural consequences of the different requirements of the various orders.

Mosques

Hillenbrand, R., *Islamic Architecture* (1994) gives an extended analysis of the mosque as a building type.

*Holod, Renata, and Khan, Hasan-Uddin, *The Mosque and the Modern World* (1997) illustrates the freshness of a continuing tradition.

Kuban, D., *Muslim Religious Architecture* (2 vols., 1974, 1985), although out of date when published, and containing several errors of detail, gives not only a very good formal analysis of the mosque, by means of a wealth of plans and elevations, but also considers how different patterns of use and religious requirements have found architectural expression.

Michell, G. (ed.), *Architecture of the Islamic World: Its History and Social Meaning* (1978) is an excellent overview of the subject.

Nash, John

Summerson, J., *The Life and Work of John Nash* (1980) is a sympathetic account, tolerant of Nash's architectural foibles.

National Romanticism

Lane, Barbara Miller, *National Romanticism and Modern Architecture in Germany and the Scandinavian Countries* (2000) is a clever work of cultural history showing how architecture fitted in with politics, nationalism, and cultural expression in other disciplines.

Nature, Inspiration From

*Powers, A., *Nature in Design* (1999). This subject has offered too many temptations to less careful writers, but here they are avoided, and the result is a stimulating but solidly based account of the subject.

Neoclassicism

Honour, H., *Neo-classicism* (1968) is mainly about painting and sculpture; the analysis of architecture is surprisingly weak.

Netherlands

Rosenberg, Jakob, Slive, Seymour, and ter Kuile, E. H., *Dutch Art and Architecture, 1600 to 1800* (1966) is an adequate if slightly pedestrian survey.

Van der Woud, A., *The Art of Building. From Classicism to Modernity: The Dutch Architectural Debate 1840–1900* (2001) does a great service, by revealing to the English reader a most interesting debate about the subject, which has no counterpart in the English-speaking world.

Neumann, J. B.

*Otto, Christian F., *Space into Light: the churches of Balthasar Neumann* (1979) examines with great sensitivity the interplay between construction, space, and light in the work of this important architect.

Neutra, Richard

Hines, T. S., *Richard Neutra and the Search for Modern Architecture* (1982) is much more than a capable work about Neutra's architecture, as it illustrates the fortunes of Modernism in the United States as seen through the prism of one architect's work.

Niemeyer, Oscar

I have not been able to find a useful work in English devoted only to Niemeyer, but for his period see Fraser, V., *Building the new world: studies in the modern architecture of Latin America 1930–1960* (2001).

Norway

Donnelly, Marian C., *Architecture in the Scandinavian Countries* (1992) covers the entire period to the 1970s. The chapters on the period less well known in the English-speaking world, i.e. to about 1890, are exemplary; but in the more familiar modern period, the author is a less reliable guide. Therefore, it should be supplemented by Norberg-Schulz, C., *Modern Norwegian Architecture* (1986).

Offices

Given that so much of modern life is consumed by office work, this subject awaits a fully comprehensive survey.

*Duffy, C., *The New Office* (1997) is an invaluable view from a thoughtful critic as well as an innovative practitioner.

Willis, C., *Form Follows Finance* (1995) is not just a witty title but a detailed investigation, although the examples are mainly from the US.

Opera Houses

*Forsyth, M(ichael), *Buildings for Music* (1985) is of equal interest to lovers of opera and architecture, as it is a very stimulating account of the relationship between the two disciplines.

Robinson, Michael F., *Opera before Mozart* (1966), although this is not a book about architecture *per se*, its incidental remarks about how opera houses were used in this period are quite fascinating.

Worsthorne, S. T., *Venetian Opera in the Seventeenth Century* (1954), a beautifully produced book, which deals in part with the design of the first opera theatres, particularly in relation to stage machinery.

Organic Architecture

*Van Eck, C., *Organicism in Nineteenth-century Architecture* (1994) is a brilliant analysis of a concept which has been so often misunderstood.

Ottoman Empire

*Goodwin, Godfrey, *A history of Ottoman architecture* (1971) is the definitive work; if the Ottoman archives are ever fully explored his conclusions may be revised, but the broad outlines of Goodwin's account will surely remain definitive. It should be read in conjunction with Necipoğlu, G., *The Age of Sinan: architectural culture of the Ottoman Empire* (2005) for a fuller appreciation of the broader context.

Sumner Boyd, H., and Freely, J., *Strolling Through Istanbul* (1973) is a very informative description of the city's Byzantine and Ottoman architecture.

Ottonian Architecture

Louis Grodecki, *L'architecture ottoniene* (1958) is readable.

Palazzi

Waddy, P., *Seventeenth-Century Roman Palaces: Use and the Art of the Plan* (1990) is one of the rare books which analyses this crucial subject, rather than seeing palazzi as storehouses for works of art. All too rare, unfortunately, as I have not been able to find any other book which does the same for Florence, Naples, or Venice.

Palladio

In the extensive secondary literature, the outstanding works are:

*Ackerman, James S., *Palladio* (1966);

*Ackerman, James S., *Palladio's Villas* (1967). Both works tie together the social and economic context, Palladio's biography, and a searching analysis of his architecture.

Holberton, P., *Palladio's villas* (1990) is significantly subtitled *Life in the Renaissance countryside*, a subject about which it is particularly revealing. It is worth consulting for the cross section of the Villa Maser and its landscape alone, a vital though rarely provided type of illustration.

Rybczynski, W., *The perfect house* (2002) takes a novel and highly rewarding approach, by appraising Palladio's villas from the practical and visual point of view, to see if they live up to his title.

But none of the secondary literature is an adequate substitute for consulting the original. The reader will find great pleasure from Palladio's unexpectedly accessible text, *I Quattro Libri dell'Architettura* (1570), of which the best modern edition is by Robert Tavernor (1997). It is to be hoped that a facing pages translation, long needed, will appear in 2009 (published by The Old School Press).

Parish Churches

Betjeman's 'Introduction' to the *Collins Guide to English Parish Churches* (1958) is more erudite and informative than the author's artless manner might suggest.

Jenkins, S., *England's Thousand Best Churches* (1999) draws largely upon Pevsner for the facts, but displays a much more acute visual sense in relation to the earlier periods.

Martin, C(hristopher), *A Glimpse of Heaven* (2006) is a revelation, in terms of the diversity and quality of the Catholic churches of England and Wales.

Pevsner, N., *Buildings of England* series exhaustively chronicles every parish church in England. However, except when dealing with Victorian or modern churches, he is often more concerned with unravelling the archaeological puzzles set by churches dating from the medieval period.

Twentieth Century Society, *The Twentieth Century Church* (1998) is on the perhaps surprising revival of church architecture, particularly in the post-war period.

Paxton

Chadwick, G. F., *The Works of Sir Joseph Paxton 1803–65* (1961) is inclined to give Paxton too much credit for the success of Crystal Palace, underplaying the all-important contribution of Fox and Henderson. Otherwise, it is a thorough account of every aspect of Paxton's work, as an architect and a landscape architect.

Perret

*Britton, K., *Auguste Perret* (2001) occasionally lacks insight into Perret's particular interest in applying traditional architecture principles, but overall this is a fine survey.

Collins, P(eter), *Concrete: The Vision of a New Architecture* (1959): the title does not give any indication that a large portion of the book is about Perret, for whom, one senses, the writer felt a rather irritated admiration. But the visual judgements, and their relation to theory, are, as usual with this author, first class.

Photography

Elwall, R., *Building with light* (2004) examines the fruitful interaction of the two subjects, architecture and photography.

Picturesque

Watkin, D., *The English Vision: The Picturesque in Architecture, Landscape and Garden Design* (1982) is a good survey, but does not quite answer the question as to why the picturesque is a peculiarly English vision.

Plan

The number of works on architectural history which make a detailed and informative analysis of plans, as a basis for understanding design, is, for whatever reason, surprisingly small; the number of such works 'illustrated' by plans (without a north point or scale, let alone a site plan with proper contours) is by contrast the overwhelming majority.

Among the general works on architecture, Sir Banister Fletcher, *A History of Architecture* (1996) is a glorious exception, since it has a wealth of plans from all periods, usually accompanied by a brief but incisive analysis.

The best particular works I can recommend are:

Girouard, M., *The Victorian Country House* (1971).

Lees-Milne. J., *Roman Mornings* (1992) for its analysis of the plan of the Palazzo Massimo alle Colonne.

Waddy, P., *Seventeenth-Century Roman Palaces: Use and the Art of the Plan* (1990).

Plečnik, Jože

Prelovšek, D., *Jože Plečnik (1872–1957)* (1997) begins to make this enigmatic architect's work accessible to the general reader.

Poland

*Knox, B., *The Architecture of Poland* (1971) is very much in sympathy with the subject, and has some marvellous turns of phrase. Admittedly, the coverage of the post-war period is slightly sketchy.

Polychromy

Jackson, N(eil), 'Clarity or Camouflage? The development of Constructional Polychromy in the 1850s and early 1860s', *Architectural History* (2004), pp.201–26 is an essential review of both the architecture and the literature on the subject.

Portugal

Binney, Marcus, and Bowe, Patrick, *Houses and Gardens of Portugal* (1998) is excellent on the delights of the minor architecture of Portugal.

Kubler, G., and Soria, M., *Art and Architecture in Spain and Portugal and their American dominions, 1500 to 1800* (1959) is an informative, but rather dry, work on a subject which has yet to find a really inspiring treatment.

Watson, W. C., *Portugal* (1908) is dated in some respects, but a useful starting-point.

Prefabrication

Davies, C., *The Prefabricated Home* (2005). The subject has attracted architects and theorists on a cyclical basis from the beginning of the 20th century, but this is the most ingenious and thought-provoking work published so far.

Russell, B(arry), *Building systems, industrialization and architecture* (1981) gives a fully comprehensive treatment of the connected subjects of prefabrication and industrialization from both the technical and architectural standpoints.

Prisons

Evans, R., *The Fabrication of Virtue: English Prison Architecture, 1750–1840* (1982) analyses the development of the type in a particular period.

Markus, Thomas A., *Buildings and Power* (1993) analyses the building type in mainly its institutional aspects, though the architectural implications are quite clear.

Profession of Architect

Saint, A., *The Image of the Architect* (1983) Artist? Hero? Social revolutionary? Developer's lackey? This sparkling book canvasses all these possibilities with great relish.

Proportion

Nobbs, P., *Design* (1937) has a sensible and enlightening chapter, unusually approaching the subject from the practical point of view of the working architect.

Scholfield, P. L., *The Theory of Proportion in Architecture* (1958). Despite some weaknesses in the historical sections (in particular, the medieval period), this is the clearest book on a subject which too easily lends itself to empty theorizing. It corrects some of the ideas on Renaissance proportion set out in the much better known Wittkower, R., *Architectural Principles in the Age of Humanism* (1949).

Public Houses

*Brandwood, G., Davison, A., and Slaughter, M., *Licensed to Sell: The History and Heritage of the Public House* (2004) is an entertaining guide as well as an architectural analysis.

Girouard, M., *Victorian Pubs* (1975) concentrates mainly on London pubs, and does his very best to convince the reader that this really is a subject worthy of his talent.

Queen Anne Revival

Girouard, M., *Sweetness and Light: The Queen Anne Movement 1860–1900* (1977) is a delightfully written and beautifully illustrated account of admittedly rather a minor episode in the history of architecture.

Railway Stations

Meeks, C. L. V., *The Railroad Station* (1964) is almost a fully comprehensive account of the subject (understandably, most of the examples are from Europe and the United States), with a keen appreciation of the varieties of railway station architecture.

In my opinion, the new generation of railway stations (from about 1980 onwards) has not yet found its chronicler.

Regency Architecture

Pilcher, D., *The Regency Style* (1947) has some very idiosyncratic insights about the architecture of this period, particularly on the relationship between architecture, landscape, and the picturesque.

Repton, Humphry

*Carter, G, *Goode P., and Laurie, K., *Humphry Repton* (1983) has some useful essays analysing Repton's design principles and his attitude to the picturesque, as well as a gazetteer of his works.

Richardson, H. H.

*O'Gorman, J(ames) F., *H. H. Richardson: Architectural Forms for an American Society* (1987). Of the large literature on the subject, this is the clearest exposition of Richardson's significance.

Romanesque

Although there is a very large literature on this subject, it cannot be said that there is one work which offers a satisfactory overview, although Conant, K. J., *Carolingian and Romanesque Architecture, 800–1200* (1974) approaches closest to this ideal.

The following works which deal with particular countries should be mentioned:

Anon., *Eglises Romanes France-Belgiques* (1998) is an outstandingly good gazetteer, with useful line drawings and (incomplete) plans, but only a basic analysis.

Bodington, Oliver E., *The Romance* [i.e. Romanesque] *Churches of France* (1925) is very good on materials.

Whitehill, W. M., *Spanish Romanesque of the 11th century* (1941) is a good account of an unfamiliar variety of the Romanesque.

Rome, Roman Empire

Wilson Jones, M., *Principles of Roman Architecture* (2000) supersedes all previous books on Roman architecture, mainly because of its detailed analysis and appreciation of structural and visual problems.

Ritual

The subject is hardly dealt with in the literature. The paradigm is Mark S. Weil, 'The Devotion of the Forty Hours and Roman Baroque Illusions', *Journal of the Courtauld and Warburg Institutes* (1974), pp.218–48, which shows what architectural historians should be researching for other periods (cf. **Indian Subcontinent**, sub Branfoot).

Rundbogenstil

Curran, K., *The Romanesque Revival* (2003) is a somewhat misleading title, as it is a good account of Rundbogenstil.

Ruskin, John

Brooks, Michael W., *John Ruskin and Victorian Architecture* (1987) is generally very uneven, its main strength being its analysis of Ruskin's incandescent prose descriptions of architecture.

Garrigan, K. O., *Ruskin on Architecture: His thought and influence* (1973) is very perceptive on how Ruskin saw architecture (as opulent ornament, and as surface, almost oblivious to the importance of the plan), but very weak on Ruskin's influence.

Russia

Brumfield, W., *A History of Russian Architecture* (2nd edn, 2004) and *The Origins of Modernism in Russian Architecture* (1995) are the definitive works which together bring the reader up to the Soviet period. They need to be supplemented only by the excellent Opolovnikov, A.V., *Wooden architecture of Russia* (1989).

Saljuqs

The literature on one of the world's great architectures is very sparse.

For the Iranian Saljuqs, see Pope, A. U., *Persian Architecture* (1965), chapter IV, which includes a good series of photographs of one of the Masjid-i Jami, Isfahan. The chapter seems to rely on Godard, André, 'Les anciennes mosquées

de l'Iran', *Athar-é Iran* (1936), which I have not been able to consult.

For the Anatolian Saljuqs, Talbot Rice, T., *The Seljuks in Asia Minor* (1961), which deals with all the arts, is, to the best of my knowledge, the most recent general survey accessible to the non-specialist.

The most recent works in the English language are by Hillenbrand, R., *The Art of the Saljuqs in Iran and Anatolia* (1994, proceedings of a symposium held in Edinburgh, 1982) and *Studies in Medieval Islamic Architecture. Volume II (Collected Articles)* (2006) which includes a series of studies of Saljuq architecture.

Sanmicheli, Michele

Puppi, L., *Michele Sanmicheli, architetto* (1986), the standard work, strikingly illustrated by black-and-white photographs, is unfortunately not available in English, though it would be a difficult text to translate into another way of thinking about architecture.

Sansovino, Jacopo

Howard, D(eborah), *Jacopo Sansovino: architecture and patronage in Renaissance Venice* (1975) is exceptionally successful in showing the architect's inventiveness, not only in design, but in accommodating different patrons.

Scale

Licklider, H., *Architectural Scale* (1965). If only there were more books of this quality, illustrating and analysing aspects of design.

The book itself is very well designed, and shows that for many purposes line-drawings are preferable to photographs.

Scandinavia

Donnelly, Marian C., *Architecture in the Scandinavian Countries* (1992) covers the entire period to the 1970s. The chapters on the period less well known in the English-speaking world, i.e. to about 1890, are exemplary; but in the more familiar modern period, the author is a less reliable guide.

Scharoun, Hans

*Blundell Jones, P., *Hans Scharoun* (1995) is the definitive work on one of the leading architects of the 'other tradition' of Modernism.

Schindler, Rudolf
* Sheine, J., *R.M. Schindler* (2001) establishes the position of Schindler as a major figure in the history of Modernism.

Schinkel, Karl Friedrich
Bergdoll, B., *Karl Friedrich Schinkel: An Architect for Prussia* (1994) is the first serious work in English on this important architect.

Schools
Saint, A., *Towards a social architecture: the role of school-building in post-war England* (1987) is a brilliant account not only of the particular building type, but also of the political context in which architects worked, and the viewpoint of public authority architects. Written at the height of the Thatcher years, the writer depicts a completely different context and its corresponding mentality—the school architects' belief in a social purpose for their profession, and a corresponding sense of public service, rather than the egomania encouraged by the dominance of 'the market'.

Scotland
*Glendinning, M., and MacKechnie, A., *Scottish Architecture* (2004) is the most up-to-date survey, informative and opinionated.

Scott, Sir George Gilbert
The boundless energy of Scott has daunted later historians, so that there is no overall survey or analysis of his work. But his *Personal and Professional Recollections* (published 1879, re-issued 1995) are a more than adequate substitute.

Semper, Gottfried
*Mallgrave, H. F., *Gottfried Semper* (1996) has single-handedly rescued Semper's reputation and significance from the undeserved neglect into which it had fallen by about 1900. Mallgrave's observations on the relationship between modernism and historicism make this a compelling work.

Shaw, Norman
Saint, A., *Richard Norman Shaw* (1976) is a model biography of an architect, since it deals with the subject from many angles (office organization, patronage, relationship with artists), but all have a bearing on the analysis of architecture.

Shell Structures
Faber, C., *Candela: The Shell Builder* (1963) not only explains the counter-intuitive technology, but charts its development in the hands of a master.

Shops And Stores
*Morrison, Kathryn A., *English Shops and Shopping: An Architectural History* (2003), based on extensive research, has unearthed some very interesting architecture, as well as the more familiar examples.
For the United States, R. W. *Longstreth has written extensively about the forerunners of modern supermarkets and shopping malls, in: *City Center to Regional Mall* (1997).
The Drive-In, the Supermarket, and the Transformation of Commercial Space in Los Angeles, 1914–1941 (1999).

Signal Boxes
Anon., 'The Power Signal Box: A Building of a New Type', *Architectural Review*, 1965, pp.333–7 is an instructive example of the interaction between new technology and architecture.

Sinan
Necipoğlu, G., *The Age of Sinan: architectural culture of the Ottoman Empire* (2005): as the title suggests, a very broad discussion of an architect's work within a very specific context, revealingly different from that of western Europe. A very stimulating book.

Skyscrapers
Goldberger, P., *The Skyscraper* (1981) is rather disappointing. Its focus is on the United States; it considers the skyscraper as a built object in space, without considering the relationship to its surroundings, and the connections between internal planning, structure, technology and architecture, which could have been examined in greater depth.
Landau, S. B., and Condit, C. W., *Rise of the New York Skyscraper* (1996) is an excellent combination of the history of services, structures, and architecture, with an interesting explanation of the differences between skyscrapers in New York and their more 'Modernist' Chicago counterparts.

The reader is left with the impression that this vast subject awaits a (very) diligent and multi-talented author to compile a global overview.

Soane, Sir John

*Darley, G., *John Soane; An Accidental Romantic* (1999) is a well-researched biography, perhaps stronger on biographical detail than the analysis of architecture (a similar criticism applies to Dorothy Stroud's *Sir John Soane, Architect* (1984). For the latter purpose, Ptolemy Dean, *Sir John Soane and the Country Estate* (1998) is a stimulating view of a part of Soane's work (the country house) by a practising architect. For the best overview, see *John Soane, Master of Space and Light*, exhibition catalogue edited by Margaret Richardson and Mary Anne Stevens (1999).

The text of Soane's Royal Academy lectures, delivered at irregular intervals between 1809 and 1836, are re-published, together with an exhaustive analysis by David Watkin (working with the Soane Museum staff, particularly the archivist, Susan Palmer) in *Sir John Soane: Enlightenment Thought and the Royal Academy lecture* (1996).

Soviet Union

Ikonnikov, A., *Russian Architecture of the Soviet Period* (1988) is by far the best book on the subject, despite its unyieldingly grim Soviet-style layout and turgid manner. It treats every period of Soviet architecture objectively, from Constructivism through Socialist Realism to Soviet Modernism.

As a corrective to the usual lack of understanding shown by Western critics, Catherine Cooke's 'Beauty as a Route to the Radiant Future: Responses of Soviet Architecture', *Journal of Design History*, 1997, pp.137–60 is an honest and conscientious attempt to understand, even in some respects to appreciate, the merits of socialist realism.

Spain

Bevan, B., *History of Spanish Architecture* (1938) is rather sketchy in places, but remains a useful introduction.

Cabrero, G. R., *The modern in Spain, architecture after 1948* (2001), the only English-language account of this period, is fairly objective.

Dodds, J., *Architecture and ideology in early medieval Spain* (1990) is useful on the 8th century onwards.

Harvey, J. H., *The Cathedrals of Spain* (1957) deals sympathetically with a subject which is much neglected, compared to their English and French counterparts.

Kubler, G., and Soria, M., *Art and Architecture in Spain and Portugal and their American dominions, 1500 to 1800* (1959) tends to be uncritical, but sets out the tendencies of development quite clearly.

Whitehill, W. M., *Spanish Romanesque of the 11th century* (1941).

Spence, Sir Basil

Campbell, Louise, *Art and Architecture in Post-War Britain* (1996). The central focus lies on Coventry Cathedral, but the author sensitively charts the general change in the architectural climate while the cathedral was being built.

Sports Buildings

*John, G., and Sheard, R., *Stadia* (2000) provides detailed analysis, with an emphasis upon the technical/user requirements.

Stables

*Worsley, G., *The British Stable* (2004). As the author's beautifully illustrated and thoroughly researched account shows, some stables were more architecturally distinguished than the houses to which they were appended. He also re-discovers a forgotten building type, the Riding House.

Stairs

*Templer, J. A., *The Staircase: History and Theories* (1992) is a very detailed account, both technical and architectural.

Steel

It is disappointing that there is no equivalent of Peter Collins' book on concrete (see above) for steel. The history of the use of steel can be traced by assembling the information from the following:

Jackson, N(eil), *The Modern Steel House* (1996) seems slightly more interested in the personalities involved than in the visual possibilities offered by steel.

Ochshorn, J., 'Steel' in Sennott, R. Stephen, *Encyclopedia of 20th century architecture* is very well illustrated, and a good account of the technology.

*Thorne, R(obert) (ed.), *Structural Iron and Steel, 1850–1900* (2000) forms part of a series on civil engineering, but includes several essays on architecture.

Stirling, Sir James

Architects, critics, and historians have adopted a very tolerant attitude to Stirling's designs, overlooking technical failures in several of his works.

Girouard, M., *Big Jim: the life and work of James Stirling* (1998) is an entertaining biography, with much light cast incidentally upon the work. But to date there is no critical assessment of the quality of his architecture.

Street, G. E.

As with Scott, the sheer volume of Street's work seems to have daunted historians. There is only one full-length study, and that on just one building, the Law Courts. Its complicated history was deftly unravelled by Brownlee, David B., *The Law Courts* (1984)—well documented, but not always easy to see the main issues.

Structures

Gordon, J. E., *Structures, or Why Things Don't Fall Down* (1978) is by far the best introduction for the layperson to the mysteries of compression, tension, shear, and torsion in a variety of structures and technologies: not only buildings and bridges, but also, for example, in catapults, Chinese junks, and bias-cut nighties.

To understand how architectural forms are determined by structural necessities, Gordon should be read as a preparation for *Mainstone, Rowland J., *Developments in structural form* (2nd edn, 1998).

Sullivan, Louis

Twombly, R(obert), *Louis Sullivan: The Life and Work* (1986). Was Sullivan a proto-modernist or merely a decorator? Of all the voluminous literature on the subject, Twombly gives one of the most balanced answers.

Weingarden, Lauren S., *Louis H. Sullivan, The Banks* (1987) could have been a very interesting exercise in revisionism, but unfortunately the architectural criticism is rather weak.

Sustainable Architecture

Edwards, B. W., *Green Architecture—An International Comparison* (2001) is an informative, mainly technical, survey.

*Hagan, S., *Taking Shape* (2001) is a path-breaking work, as it initiates the great debate on how architecture should respond to the Green agenda.

Sweden

Donnelly, Marian C., *Architecture in the Scandinavian Countries* (1992) covers the entire period to the 1970s. The chapters on the period less well known in the English-speaking world, i.e. to about 1890, are exemplary; but in the more familiar modern period, the author is a less reliable guide.

Kidder Smith, G. E., *Sweden Builds* (1957). As in his other works, on Brazil, Italy, and Switzerland, the author is very perceptive about the vernacular tradition, the general course of the history of architecture, and the most significant examples of Modernism.

Switzerland

Kidder Smith, G. E., *Switzerland builds* (1950). See entry above.

Synagogues

*Meek, H. A., *The Synagogue* (1995).

Syria

Fedden, R., *Syria and Lebanon* (1965) has some very lyrical but accurate descriptions of architecture in Damascus and Aleppo.

Theories Of Architecture

Of the classical texts, Vitruvius is diffuse, rambling, and not for the non-specialist; Alberti is more rewarding; but, perhaps because of the careful co-ordination of illustrations with text, Palladio is by far the most stimulating for the non-specialist.

Collins, Peter, *Changing Ideals in Modern Architecture, 1750–1950* (1965). Few critics have had such a sharp eye for the discrepancy between theory and practice, or for the sheer impracticability of so much theory.

Kruft, H.-W., *A History of Western Architectural Theory* (1992) is a useful series of comprehensive summaries; but in terms of incisiveness, it is far outmatched by *Mallgrave, H. F., *Modern Architectural Theory: a Historical Survey, 1673–1968* (2005).

Tower Blocks

*Glendinning, M., and *Muthesius, S., *Tower Block* (1994): an unlikely subject, an almost universally derided building type, but unexpectedly rewarding. The authors rather hopefully provide a gazetteer for would-be tower block tourists.

Town Halls

Cunningham, C., *Victorian and Edwardian Town Halls* (1991) is a fine example of architectural analysis, with two invaluable appendices, cataloguing the major town halls and related municipal buildings from 1820 to 1914.

Turkey

*Bozdogan, S., *Modernism and Nation Building* (2001) is a fascinating account of the forms adopted by architectural Modernism when it is tied in with a wider project of modernization, i.e. that of an entire society.

United States

Condit, Neville, *American Building* (1968) is the most concise exposition of the author's definitive account of the materials and structures available to US architects.

*Gelernter, Mark, *A History of American Architecture: Buildings in their Cultural and Technological Context* (1999) is a carefully calculated combination of cultural, technological, and architectural history, so clearly written as to serve as an introduction, but not so basic that it should be overlooked by the knowledgeable reader.

*Maynard, W. Barksdale, *Architecture in the United States, 1800–1850* (2002) to a certain extent over-emphasizes the British influence during this period, but otherwise is an interesting discussion of both architecture and architectural culture.

Nabokov, P., and Easton, R., *Native American Architecture* (1989) is the definitive work on the architecture of the original inhabitants.

*O'Gorman, J(ames) F., *Three American Architects: Richardson, Sullivan, and Wright, 1865–1915* (1991) is a critical appraisal of the three original heroes of US architecture.

Scully, Vincent, *American Architecture and Urbanism* (1969) is far more than a description, because of its stimulating generalizations.

Upton, Dell, *Architecture in the United States* (1998) is an interpretation of the subject which is not so technologically oriented as many histories of US architecture.

Vlach, J. M., *Back of the big house. The architecture of plantation slavery* (1993) is a valuable account of a little-researched subject.

Universities

Muthesius, S., *The Post-War University* (2001) is mainly restricted to the period of the 1950s and 1970s, but captures the utopian spirit of the times, shared by both architects and educators, and the inevitable opposition.

Vanbrugh, John

Vanbrugh's powerful yet slightly eccentric architecture has often seemed to disconcert English critics, so that they often take refuge in 'safer' questions, e.g. who did what in the Hawksmoor–Vanbrugh relationship? What were the main influences on his work—French military architecture, or even, as seems to have been proved recently, Mughal mausoleums?

No book can, therefore, be unequivocally recommended. Downes, K., *Vanbrugh* (1977) has too much biographical information; Whistler, L., *Sir John Vanbrugh* (1938) and *The Imagination of Vanbrugh and his Fellow Artists* (1954) are rather over-imaginative.

Cast, D., 'Seeing Vanbrugh and Hawksmoor', *The Journal of the Society of Architectural Historians*, 1984, pp.310–27 has some very interesting passages, in which he looks at the role of 'effect' in the work of both architects, a concept which is probably the key to *seeing* their architecture.

Venice

*Goy, R., *Venice, the city and its inhabitants* (1997). As a practising architect, the author brings to the subject a fresh eye, particularly alert to colour, materials, and texture. His *Venetian vernacular architecture* (1997) is an original and stimulating work, discovering a previously overlooked aspect of Venetian architecture.

Hopkins, A(ndrew), *Santa Maria della Salute* (2000) is a useful monograph.

Howard, D(eborah), *The Architectural History of Venice* (2002) is a very readable survey, its particular strength (see **Sansovino** above) being the interaction between site, patron, and architecture.

Howard, D(eborah), *Venice and the East: the Impact of the Islamic World on Venetian Architecture 1100–1500* (2000) is a most original approach, but her case must, unfortunately, be regarded as unproven, partly because of the author's slightly precarious understanding of the architecture of the 'Islamic world'.

Ruskin, J., *The Stones of Venice* (3 vols., 1851–3). The leisured reader should read the whole book; every reader should read Ruskin's glittering description of the first view of San Marco : '…a multitude of pillars and white domes, clustered into a long low pyramid of coloured light…' (Book I Chapter IV Section XIV).

Vernacular Architecture

*Oliver, Paul (ed.), *Encylopaedia of Vernacular Architecture of the World* (3 vols., 1997) is the definitive treatment of the materials, structures, and forms of vernacular architecture, showing its amazing variety and ingenuity in responding to every kind of site and climate.

Rudofsky, B., *Architecture without architects* (1969) has some stunning images of what in some cases might be called 'vernacular architecture'. However, unlike Paul Oliver, Rudofsky's main interest is aesthetic.

Wood

Berg, Arne (ed.), *Architecture in wood: A History of Wood Building and its Techniques in Europe and North America* (1971) has rather uneven coverage of some countries (e.g. England); the best essay is by the editor, 'Wood Building in Northern Europe'.

Buxton, D(avid), *Wooden Churches of Eastern Europe* (1981); the author travelled round the region (including the Ukraine and Romania) under difficult circumstances, writing, as the subtitle indicates, 'An introductory survey'.

Opolovnikov, A., *The Wooden Architecture of Russia* (1989) is an exemplary study, with, incidentally, much to say about conservation and restoration.

Pryce, Will, *Architecture in Wood: A World History* (2005) is the only book which is worldwide in scope. It is the definitive assessment of wood as an architectural material.

Wren, Sir Christopher

Since 1950, there have been several books on Wren, and the most authoritative is that by Downes, K., *The Architecture of Wren* (1982).

Wright, Frank Lloyd

From the vast literature, one general work stands out: Levine, N., *The Architecture of Frank Lloyd Wright* (1995) both in terms of the analysis of particular buildings, and situating Wright in relation to Modernism.

Wyatt, James

Dale, A(nthony), *James Wyatt* (1956). It is difficult to write an interesting book about individual English Palladians, but this book succeeds handsomely.

Index of Contributors with Entries

Picture Acknowledgements

The Publishers are grateful to the following for their permission to reproduce the photographs. Although every effort has been made to contact copyright holders, it has not been possible in every case and we apologise for any that have been omitted. Should the copyright holders wish to contact us after publication, we would be happy to include an acknowledgement in subsequent reprints.

2 RIBA Library Photographs Collection
7 Edwin Smith / RIBA Library Photographs Collection
11 Robert Harding Picture Library Ltd / Alamy
13 © Paul Oliver
23 © Yang Shen / Artifice Images
29 © Tadao Ando Architect & Associates
39 John Donat / RIBA Library Photographs Collection
47 photo: John Gollings
48 Jack Sullivan / Alamy
53 RIBA Library Photographs Collection
61 Seema K K
68 John L. Varriano, *Italian Baroque and Rococo Architecture* (Oxford University Press; 1986), p.47
74 Professor David Robson / Aga Khan Trust for Culture
76 RIBA Library Photographs Collection, from *Encyclopédie d'architecture* (1876), p.34
85 Private Collection, from G. B. Falda, *Vedute dir Roma* 1665–69 Book I, plate 3
95 akg-images
96 Bibliotheca Hertziana – Max-Planck-Institut für Kunstgeschichte, Rome
98 Architect: Aleijadinho, photo: Paul M. R. Maeyaert / Bildarchiv-Monheim / www.arcaid.co.uk
106 Eric de Mare / RIBA Library Photographs Collection
110 © Artifice, Inc. / Artifice Images
113 Andy Crawford / Peter Griffiths – modelmaker © Dorling Kindersley
124 © Robert Fisher
126 RIBA Library Photographs Collection
128 Irish Architectural Archive
131 RIBA Library Photographs Collection
141 akg-images
143 dk / Alamy
164 © Peter Jeffree / Architectural Association
167 courtesy of University of Pennsylvania Visual Resources
170 Bernard Cox / RIBA Library Photographs Collection
176 courtesy of University of Pennsylvania Visual Resources
184 akg-images / Erich Lessing
204 RIBA Library Photographs Collection

222 Bibliotheca Hertziana – Max-Planck-Institut für Kunstgeschichte, Rome
226 Axiom Photographic Agency / Irish Image Collection
230 Simmons Aerofilms / Science & Society
245 a+u (Tokyo), Photo: Yoshihiro Asada
250 RIBA Library Photographs Collection, from Serlio, *Il terzio libro di Sebastiano Serlio Bolognese* (Venice; 1544), p.IX
257 akg-images / Bildarchiv Monheim
267 Hirmer Fotoarchiv
269 Hirmer Fotoarchiv
274 Architectural Press Archive / RIBA Library Photographs Collection
280 akg-images / Stefan Drechsel
282 Edwin Smith / RIBA Library Photographs Collection
286 RIBA Library Photographs Collection, from Arthur F. E. Poley, *St. Paul's Cathedral* (1927), plate III
308 Ash Rare Books, London
311 © Christopher Little / Aga Khan Trust for Culture
315 © Rauno Träskelin
319 Kunsthistorisches Museum, Vienna, Austria / The Bridgeman Art Library, from a painting by Bernardo Bellotto, 1759–61
326 © Peter Jeffree / Architectural Association
331 Bernard Cox / RIBA Library Photographs Collection
333 RIBA Library Photographs Collection, engraving by Jean Marot, from an untitled collection of plates known as *Le grand Marot* (Paris; 1686?), plate 111
343 Architectural Press Archive / RIBA Library Photographs Collection
352 © Vanni Archive / Corbis
354 Mary Evans Picture Library / Alamy
358 RIBA Library Photographs Collection
359 The Provost and Fellows of Worcester College, Oxford
373 RIBA Library Photographs Collection
375 akg-images / Jean-Louis Nou
377 Bernard Çox / RIBA Library Photographs Collection
378 RIBA Library Photographs Collection, from E. Viollet-le-Duc, *Dictionnaire raisonné de l'architecture française* (Paris; 1858), volume 1, p.203
386 Stephen Conlin © Dorling Kindersley
391 imagebroker / Alamy
393 RIBA Library Photographs Collection, from Guarini, Guarino, *Architettura Civile* (Turin 1737), volume 1, plate 48
395 John Donat / RIBA Library Photographs Collection
403 Christopher Hope-Fitch / RIBA Library Photographs Collection
418 Architect: Victor Horta, photo: Richard Bryant / www.arcaid.co.uk

422 RIBA Library Photographs Collection, from Henry Saxon Snell, *Charitable and parochial establishments* (1881), after p.15

427 Michelle Gallet, *Stately Mansions* (Praeger; 1972), plate 164

445 ©The British Library Board. All Rights Reserved 2010, Karle, Chaitya Hall Interior by Stanley Leighton

446 akg-images / Jean-Louis Nou

449 ©The British Library Board. All Rights Reserved 2010, Kantaji Temple, Kantanagar, from a steel engraving after a photograph by John Henry Ravenshaw (1873)

458 RIBA Library Drawings Collection, from a drawing by an unknown Indian artist, *c*.1818

466 Sheila S. Blair & Jonathan M. Bloom

470 Talinn Grigor, 1999, Courtesy of the Aga Khan Visual Archive, M.I.T.

472 Sylvia Cordaiy Photo Library Ltd / Alamy

501 Archives of the Tokyo Central Library

502 © Glow Images / Alamy

517 RIBA Library Photographs Collection, after Colen Campbell, *Vitruvius Britannicus* (1717), volume 1, p.13

523 Digital Image © 2008, The Museum of Modern Art / Scala, Florence

537 John Donat / RIBA Library Photographs Collection

543 © Luisa Auletta / Architectural Association

551 RIBA Library Photographs Collection, from A. Gosset, *Les coupoles d'orient et d'occident* (Paris; 1889), plate 24

561 RIBA Library Photographs Collection

565 RIBA Library Photographs Collection

568 Edwin Smith / RIBA Library Photographs Collection

578 Melvyn Longhurst / Alamy

585 Robert Harding Picture Library Ltd / Alamy

586 Steve Allen Travel Photography / Alamy

591 Roland Halbe / RIBA Library Photographs Collection

595 Janet Hall / RIBA Library Photographs Collection

600 akg-images / Erich Lessing, from an engraving by Du Perac, *c*.1546

603 Architectural Press Archive / RIBA Library Photographs Collection

611 akg-images / Bildarchiv Monheim

621 Janet Hall / RIBA Library Photographs Collection

623 Robert Harding Picture Library Ltd / Alamy

629 Gavin Hellier / Alamy

631 Blickwinkel / Alamy

632 photo: John Gollings

633 Janet Hall / RIBA Library Photographs Collection

640 photo: Richard Waite / www.arcaid.co.uk

647 RIBA Library Photographs Collection

650 Bildarchiv Monheim GmbH / Alamy

653 © Bildarchiv Monheim GmbH / Alamy

657 imagebroker / Alamy

659 photo: Achim Bednorz / Bildarchiv-Monheim / www.arcaid.co.uk

665 Alastair Hunter / RIBA Library Photographs Collection

671 © RMN (Musée d'Orsay) / © Hervé Lewandowski

675 Chartwell Illustrators

676 Chartwell Illustrators

677 Chartwell Illustrators

681 Images&Stories / Alamy

683 Goodwin G., *A History of Ottoman Architecture* (Thames & Hudson Ltd, London; 1971), figure 208, p.217

688 courtesy of University of Pennsylvania Visual Resources

699 RIBA Library Photographs Collection, after Andrea Palladio, *I Quattro Libri dell'Architettura* Book II

709 Emmanuel Thirard / RIBA Library Photographs Collection

711 JTB Photo Communications, Inc. / Alamy

715 Alinari Archives-Florence

725 akg-images

735 RIBA Library Photographs Collection

753 RIBA Library Photographs Collection

757 RIBA Library Photographs Collection, from Viollet-le-Duc, E., *Dictionnaire raisonné de l'architecture française* (Paris, 1858), volume 1, p.72

761 © Angelo Hornak / Corbis

769 Architect: Gerrit Rietveld, photo: Richard Bryant / www.arcaid.co.uk

773 Architectural Press Archive / RIBA Library Photographs Collection

774 Werner Otto / Alamy

778 W. J. Anderson & R. Phene Spiers, *The Architecture of Greece and Rome* (1902) p.205, plate 132

780 RIBA Library Photographs Collection, from Serlio, *Il terzo libro di Sebastiano Serlio* (Venice; 1544) plate LXIX

782 Rolf Richardson / Alamy

790 William Brumfield, Tulane University, New Orleans

791 William Brumfield, Tulane University, New Orleans

801 Alinari Archives-Florence

808 RIBA Library Photographs Collection

809 © Reyner Banham / Architectural Association

811 RIBA Library Photographs Collection, from K. F. Schinkel, *Sammlung architektonischer Entwürfe* (Berlin; 1819-40), volume 1, plate 37

817 RIBA Library Photographs Collection

824 photo: John Gollings

831 RIBA Library Photographs Collection
835 photo: Tim Benton
840 FG + SG Architectural Photography, Lisbon
845 RIBA Library Drawings Collection
848 Cosmo Condina / Alamy
852 Bildarchiv Monheim GmbH / Alamy
869 David Robertson / Alamy
873 photo: Richard Einzig / arcaid.co.uk
890 Robert Harding Picture Library Ltd / Alamy
894 Johnny Greig Travel Photography / Alamy
897 RIBA Library Photographs Collection
917 RIBA Library Photographs Collection
920 © Robert Fisher
923 RIBA Library Photographs Collection, from Victor Louis,
    Salle de spectacle de Bordeaux (Paris; 1782), plate 15
937 Alastair Hunter / RIBA Library Photographs Collection

948 RIBA Library Photographs Collection, from Giacomo Lauro,
    Antiquae urbis splendor (Rome; 1637)
957 Architect: Thomas Jefferson, photo: Will Pryce / Thames and
    Hudson / www.arcaid.co.uk
959 © James Stirling / Architectural Association
963 Architect: Gordon Bunshaft (SOM), photo: Mark Fiennes /
    www.arcaid.co.uk
971 RIBA Library Photographs Collection, from Colen Campbell,
    Vitruvius Britannicus (1717), volume 1, p.61
976 © FR Yerbury / Architectural Association
979 © Paul Oliver
1015 Gerhard Stromberg
1026 Edwin Smith / RIBA Library Photographs Collection
1029 © François Guyot / Architectural Association
1030 Collection of Frank Lloyd Wright Preservation Trust
1039 Aflo Co. Ltd / Alamy